PREFACE TO THE SIXTH EDITION OF *HORIZONS*

Dear Colleagues,

Welcome to the sixth edition of *Horizons*!

In creating *Horizons*, we have sought to design an introductory program that engages students, draws them into the francophone world, and helps them acquire the skills they need to communicate their own thoughts in French. In this edition, we have focused on keeping the content current and on appealing to the interests and learning styles of today's students by making the following updates:

- We have revised the vocabulary presentations and dialogues to include more current vocabulary of interest to our students and, while maintaining the use of "standard" French, to reflect the language as it is spoken today. We have also changed some of the proper names used to reflect those in current use.

- The geo-cultural openers, the **Notes culturelles,** and the end-of-chapter **Comparaisons culturelles** have been fully updated to present the very latest cultural information and to focus on aspects of contemporary life of interest to students.

- Many of the exercises have been revised to make them more interesting to students and more visually engaging on the page. Numerous new photos also give the pages a more current and appealing look.

- The **Interlude musical** sections include several new selections and we have interspersed numerous new **Sélection musicale** suggestions throughout the chapters.

We have also added the following new features to the sixth edition:

- An all-new **Chapitre de révision** is composed of five segments, each of which reviews two chapters of the book and revolves around a modern topic, such as "living green." Each of the five review segments opens with a reading selection that sets the theme, allows students to practice reading strategies, and fosters conversation on topics today's students find interesting. This section is followed by a grammar review section practicing the key grammar elements from the related chapters. In both sections, students are given multiple opportunities to personalize and discuss the theme and to develop their communication skills. This review chapter is multi-functional: you may choose to use each segment as a review after completing a pair of chapters, or you can use all or part of the chapter as an end-of-semester or end-of-course review. It may also serve as a "bridging the gap" chapter before beginning the next semester. The former review chapter, **Un drôle de mystère,** remains available on the Instructor's Companion Website and on *iLrn*.

- New **Vocabulaire sans peine!** annotations encourage students to use cognate patterns as an easy way to expand vocabulary.

- The *iLrn*™ Heinle Learning Center has been updated to offer the latest technological features. In addition to the numerous interactive grammar review modules, students will also find pronunciation modules and new supplementary culture videos.

- Two *Share It!* activities per chapter now allow students to interact online by sharing texts and visuals on *iLrn* and commenting on one another's postings.

- New PowerPoint slides have been created to make your class preparation and the presentation of grammar and vocabulary easier.

The most popular features of *Horizons* remain unchanged. As before, *Horizons 6e* continues to have numerous carefully sequenced communicative activities; integrated practice of reading, writing, listening, and speaking with accompanying learning strategies; and an easy-to-follow chapter structure with vocabulary, grammar, and review modules laid out on two-page spreads. The hallmark of *Horizons* remains its focus on building the skills needed for everyday communication and developing cultural understanding and appreciation of the francophone world. We hope you will enjoy teaching from it!

The *Horizons* author team,

Joan Manley

Stuart Smith

John McMinn

Marc Prévost

THE *HORIZONS* PROGRAM

In writing *Horizons,* it has been our goal to create a program to help teachers address the "five C's"—communication, culture, comparisons, connections, community—and to create the kind of book we ourselves wanted to use: a communication-based program with a global francophone focus that provides a clear presentation of vocabulary, grammar, and pronunciation, along with multiple opportunities for students to function in the language.

The *Horizons* textbook contains ten standard chapters plus a preliminary chapter and a review chapter. All chapters except the review chapter are made up of four **Compétences,** each based on a specific language function. The four **Compétences** in the preliminary chapter have two vocabulary presentations each. This chapter is designed to get students speaking in French as soon as possible and covers basic functions such as greeting people, spelling, counting, and getting acquainted in class. The review chapter provides additional reading practice on engaging topics related to chapters in the book, along with communicative review activities and opportunities for open conversation. The four **Compétences** of the ten principal chapters each contain three parts. The first **Compétence** is composed of a vocabulary presentation followed by one structure presentation and a *Lecture/Compréhension auditive* section, which consists of either pre-reading and reading practice or pre-listening and listening practice using reading or listening strategies. Each of the next two **Compétences** consists of a vocabulary presentation followed by two structure presentations. The last **Compétence** is composed of a vocabulary presentation followed by one structure presentation and a *Vidéoreprise* section, in which review activities are integrated with episodes from the *Horizons* video, **Les Stagiaires. Lecture et Composition** and **Comparaisons culturelles** sections wrap up each chapter, and are followed by the **Résumé de grammaire,** which summarizes all of the grammar from the chapter on two facing pages, and then by the end-of-chapter *Vocabulaire,* which contains the active vocabulary from each **Compétence.**

The Features

With our communicative and cultural goals in mind, we have included the following elements in our program:

A modular design. *Horizons* has a clear, easy-to-follow structure. Each new vocabulary and grammar section is laid out across two pages, so that presentation of vocabulary or grammar always appears on the left-hand page and exercises on the right. This format enhances teaching flexibility and enables students to find the new information they need to study more easily. When topics require more practice, a section is expanded to four pages and/or the topic is recycled across several sections or chapters.

A manageable scope and sequence. *Horizons* emphasizes the structures needed for common communication situations. The large number of activities and suggestions in the marginal annotations of the AIE provide instructors flexibility in creating a syllabus for a variety of student needs.

Visual and contextualized presentation of new vocabulary and structures. All new material is presented in context, making learning easier and facilitating true communication. Grammar explanations are concise and clear and students are given self-check questions so they can verify their own comprehension of new rules and forms. Functional dialogues illustrate new structures in context and also supply students with models of how to fulfill communicative functions in specific contexts.

Interesting and realistic exercises that progress from recognition to production and from more structured to increasingly open-ended. In *Horizons,* material is presented so that it helps increase students' confidence as their skills develop. New material is first presented in context, followed by recognition activities to familiarize students with it. After the recognition activities, new structures are explained and students work with them in numerous, varied activities. Production activities build from simple exercises, where students answer with a word or a phrase, to realistic role-plays. Personalized exercises encourage students to express their own thoughts in French. All activities create meaningful communication; even the simplest have been designed so that students think about what they are saying. Students use grammar, vocabulary, and pronunciation as the tools of communication, not as ends in themselves. A unique feature of *Horizons* is its presentation of pronunciation, which is integrated into explanations of structures. For example, the vowel sounds of **le** and **les** are taught with the definite article in the context of distinguishing singular and plural nouns.

Learning strategies with activities. Students develop skills more quickly when taught strategies. In the first **Compétence** of each chapter of *Horizons,* students are explicitly taught reading and listening strategies and are given activities to practice them. These strategies are then recycled and practiced again in the Student Activities Manual. In the **Lecture** part of the **Lecture et Composition** section at the end of chapters, students are asked to reapply and expand the reading strategies they have learned to read a variety of texts (realia, song lyrics, poems, articles, literary texts). In the **Composition** section, students learn and practice writing strategies.

Process-writing activities. In the **Composition** sections, pre-writing activities guide students as they organize their thoughts before writing compositions. Teachers' annotations suggest peer-review activities to guide students as they revise what they have written and finally produce short pieces that can become part of a portfolio or posted on *iLrn*.

A focus on the francophone world and activity-based culture sections. Each regional unit (two chapters) of *Horizons* revolves around a story of visitors to a different part of the francophone world (**Côte d'Azur, Québec, Louisiane, Paris, Normandie, les Antilles**). Each chapter opens with a photo exposé of the region with geographical information and accompanying activities to set the scene and give students a visual representation of the area. As students follow the characters through the region, they learn about its culture: the customs, perspectives, and daily life of the people. Additionally, the ***Bienvenue en Europe francophone*** photo spread that follows ***Chapitre 5*** and the ***Bienvenue en Afrique francophone*** photo spread that follows ***Chapitre 10*** introduce students to additional fascinating francophone cultures. Chapters end with a ***Comparaisons culturelles*** section, which gives students information about various aspects of francophone culture and encourages them to make cross-cultural comparisons. Shorter ***Notes culturelles*** are interspersed in the margin of the text to catch the student's eye and to provide interesting bits of information.

Integrated review sections. At the end of each chapter, the ***Résumé de grammaire*** is a useful study tool that summarizes all of the grammar topics presented in the chapter on a concise two-page spread. Both the ***Résumé de grammaire*** and the review activities that close the fourth ***Compétence*** of each chapter are designed to help students become responsible for their own learning and review for exams.

Plentiful teacher notes. On-page teacher notes make *Horizons* user-friendly for instructors with varying levels of experience. These notes help teachers create lesson plans, suggest additional activities, and provide further cultural and linguistic information to share with students. The additional grammar review activities on the *Instructor's Resource CD-ROM* and the new PowerPoint slides for presenting grammar and vocabulary further ease the instructor's workload.

Video program. The *Horizons* video, ***Les Stagiaires,*** integrates the vocabulary and grammar from each chapter into a series of vignettes about two new interns working in an office. Their daily interactions and adventures with their co-workers depict real-life uses of French in a variety of situations, allowing students to practice listening skills with the vocabulary and structures they have studied up to that point. A short scene with accompanying pre- and post- viewing activities, is integrated with each chapter's review activities in the ***Vidéoreprise*** section of the fourth ***Compétence.***

A book-specific website. The text's Premium Website gives students access to the complete in-text audio program, the complete SAM audio program, and the complete video program.

Language learning through technology. The *iLrn™ Heinle Learning Center* allows you to assign, assess, and track students' progress with a click of the mouse. With the *iLrn™ Heinle Learning Center,* everything students need to master the skills and concepts of the course is built right into the dynamic learning environment. The *iLrn™ Heinle Learning Center* includes an audio and video-enhanced eBook, assignable textbook activities, auto-graded vocabulary and grammar quizzes, partnered voice-recorded activities, an online Student Activities Manual with audio, interactive enrichment activities, and a diagnostic study tool to better prepare students for exams. Students will also find interactive grammar and pronunciation review modules, a new series of cultural videos, cultural Web search activities, chapter-specific Web links, audio-enhanced flashcards, and vocabulary and grammar podcasts.

Components of the *Horizons* Program

Student Textbook

Annotated Instructor's Edition with Text Audio CD Program

Text Audio Program accessible via the Premium Website and iLrn

Student Activities Manual (SAM) (Cahier d'activités écrites et orales)

SAM Audio Program accessible via the Premium Website and iLrn

SAM Answer Key and Audioscript

Testing Audio CD to accompany the Testing Program in the Instructor Resource Materials accessible via the Instructor Companion Site or iLrn

Video *Les Stagiaires* available on DVD, the Premium Website and the iLrn™ Heinle Learning Center

Premium Website Students have complimentary access to the complete in-text audio program. Premium password-protected resources include the complete SAM audio program and the complete video program.

iLrn™ Heinle Learning Center A comprehensive course management system complete with an audio and video-enhanced eBook, eSAM, diagnostic tools for students, . . . and more!

TEACHING SUGGESTIONS

The following suggestions explain how you might teach the chapters and supplemental sections of *Horizons*. The examples in these suggestions are from **Chapitre 1.** We suggest that you assign the *Student Preface* as homework during the first days of class and that you discuss the following sections in class: *Goals and Expectations, Motivation, Learning Techniques.* You may wish to use this section as the foundation for a foreign language study-skills workshop at your university.

TEACHING A CHAPTER
Introducing a New Two-Chapter Set

Each set of two chapters tells a story about someone who visits a francophone region. The first two chapters take place in Nice. Here are some suggestions for introducing them. Subsequent chapters may be introduced in a similar manner.

To introduce the area's geographic features and culture

- Have students look at the map of France at the end of the textbook. Point out Nice and other major cities and some of the better-known regions of France. Have students brainstorm about what they know about any of the regions. Then have them read the text and look at the photos in the textbook in small groups and answer the questions in the activity section.

- Play a trivia game with students, asking questions about the regions, their history, and their cultures. Since students may not know a lot about them, multiple-choice questions are the best format for this activity, because they allow students to make educated guesses. You may wish to assign students to do some online research and write questions to ask one another.

- Assign the Internet activity in the textbook and have groups of students make presentations about different aspects of what they find.

To introduce the chapter, story, and characters

- Before beginning, have students read the list of communicative functions on the opening page of each chapter and say what kinds of expressions they would use in English in such contexts.

- Prepare transparencies or a PowerPoint slide of the main characters for the chapters. Point to the picture of each character and talk about him/her. In **Chapitre 1,** for example, introduce Léa as follows: **C'est Léa. Elle est américaine, mais elle habite à Nice maintenant. Elle étudie le français à l'Université de Nice.** Afterwards ask short-answer questions: **C'est Léa ou Lisa? Elle est américaine ou canadienne?** Finally, have students name the things they have in common with Léa.

The different sections of a chapter may be presented as follows:

Compétence 1

Compétence 1 has a vocabulary section, followed by one structure section and a **Lecture** or **Compréhension auditive** section, consisting of either pre-reading and reading practice (in the first chapter of each set) or pre-listening and listening practice (in the second). Begin the class with the warm-up activities suggested in the margins of the AIE, then present the new vocabulary in the following manner:

- Introduce the new vocabulary via the PowerPoint slides or eBook, flashcards, props, or modeling.
- Follow up with yes/no questions concerning the vocabulary. For example, in **Chapitre 1,** ask questions such as, **Léa est un homme? Oui ou non?** Continue with either/or questions: **Léa est un homme ou une femme?** Then, ask students to describe the characters pictured using the new vocabulary. Finally, ask students to make statements describing themselves. By starting with simple questions, you can familiarize students with the new vocabulary and structures before they are asked to produce them.
- Set the scene for the conversation and, using the appropriate section of the Text Audio, have students listen to it first with books closed. Give them the questions in the margins of the *AIE,* telling them to listen first for that information only. After they have listened twice, ask the questions, then have students read along in the book while listening to the conversation a third time.
- Do the exercises. Since there are several activities, you may wish to do only those most appropriate for your class, if you are pressed for time. Alternate doing whole-class activities with pair or group activities. Also alternate doing book activities with non-book activities. There are numerous supplemental activities in the margins of the *AIE,* and many exercises in the book can be done with books closed.
- Finish the section by having students prepare the ***À vous!*** role-play activity. Remind them to reuse and combine what they are learning rather than to translate. After they have prepared their conversation, tell them to go back and read over their conversation a second time, focusing on pronunciation.

You may present the structure section in the following manner:

- Go over the grammar explanations using the eBook or PowerPoint slides, or assign them as homework. Tell students that they should prepare the self-check questions ***(Pour vérifier)*** in the margins of the *Student Text* next to each grammar explanation. These will allow students to check that they understand the explanations and will spur questions about any points of confusion. Ask students the answers to the ***Pour vérifier*** sections to see if they are ready to continue.
- Proceed to the activities. Periodically remind students to pay attention to any newly presented pronunciation rules as they go from one activity to the next. Since there are numerous activities, you may wish to do only those most appropriate for your class. Alternate doing activities in the *Student Text* with activities suggested in the margin of the *AIE* or your own.

The ***Stratégies et Lecture*** section of the first chapter of each set teaches reading strategies. In **Chapitre 1,** students learn to use cognates and to read for the gist. The strategies are followed by a reading establishing the storyline for the chapter set. The pre-reading activities are designed to guide students through a first reading of the story. These activities may be done together as a class, in student groups, or, for classes with limited meeting times, you may prefer to have students prepare this section at home. Students may also prepare the reading at home, and you can use the comprehension questions to check how well they have understood. In the second chapter of each set, the students apply listening strategies to a listening comprehension passage. Vocabulary presented in these sections is taught for recognition only. The pre-reading and pre-listening activities are essential for student comprehension of the reading or listening passages. Readings and listening comprehension exercises are on the Text Audio. You can present this section in the following manner:

- Explain the purpose of this section and the value of learning strategies. Students may not understand the reason for focusing on learning strategies at the beginning.
- Present reading or listening strategies explicitly, or through examples, use an inductive approach.
- Use the activities provided to practice the strategies.
- Encourage students to read or listen for the main idea, not word for word.
- The readings are designed to be read silently for comprehension, not aloud. You may wish to have students read along as you play the Text Audio, so that they will not try to read word for word.
- Do the comprehension activities.
- End with a quick summary of the story or listening passage. In early chapters, guide students through the summary, having students complete statements such as: **Léa et Lisa sont de… Léa étudie à… Léa et David sont dans le même cours de… David pense que Lisa est Léa parce que ce sont des sœurs…**

Compétences 2, 3, 4

Compétences 2 and ***3*** each have a vocabulary section, followed by two structure sections. ***Compétence 4*** has a vocabulary section, followed by one structure section and a review section ***(Vidéoreprise),*** which gives students a global review of the chapter and also introduces the chapter's episode of the video. Present the vocabulary and structure sections as you did in ***Compétence 1.*** You may have students prepare the ***Vidéoreprise*** section in class (alone, with a partner, or in a group) while you do individual oral testing, or assign all or parts of it for students to prepare at home. You may wish to refer them to the ***Résumé de grammaire*** section to help them prepare. Finally, introduce the video and have students do the pre- and post-viewing activities as you show it.

Lecture et Composition

The end-of-chapter reading may be presented in the following way:

- Remind students that the reading selections in this section are "real" French. The readings are varied, including realia, articles, and short pieces of literature. Explain to students that it is relatively easy to develop reading skills compared to speaking skills. Encourage them to look at French websites related to current events and their personal interests.
- The vocabulary in this section is meant for recognition only and not for active use. It is not included in the Testing Program, and it is important that your students understand this. Initially they could feel intimidated by all the new vocabulary in this section, which could undermine their interest in the text and their openness to developing better reading comprehension. Unless you intend to design a special test that includes this vocabulary, you should let them know at the outset that they will not be responsible for producing it. Ideally,

your students should be less concerned with how they will be tested on this material, and more interested in reading an authentic text related to the chapter theme.

- In **Chapitre 1,** point out the meaning of the word **élève** and that the name of the **élève** in question is Hamlet. Ask students what they associate with the name Hamlet. Have them glance over the reading and say who is having the conversation and where they believe it is taking place.
- Go over the reading strategy and do the accompanying activities.
- Have students quickly recall the reading strategies taught in previous sections and have them scan the reading for cognates.
- Assign the reading as homework or do it together as a class.
- Do the comprehension activities together, or have students write answers to turn in.

You may do the **Composition** section as follows:

- Go over the writing strategy and assign the pre-writing activities and the composition as homework.
- Put students in pairs. Have them read each other's compositions and discuss any mistakes. Circulate among them, helping them with questions. Have some students read their compositions to the class and follow up with questions, or tell students to familiarize themselves with their partner's composition and have others ask one or two questions about each partner's paper. You may wish to allow pairs of students to work together to prepare these questions.
- Do the other activities based on the composition.
- Assign the *Share It!* activity.

Comparaisons culturelles

Comparaisons culturelles presents important cultural information and invites students to make cross-cultural comparisons. In **Chapitre 1,** students are introduced to the French education system. You may present this section as follows:

- Begin by naming the topic you are about to discuss, for example, in **Chapitre 1,** the French education system. Have students write down either something they know about it or an impression they have of it. Then ask them to write down one question they have about it.
- As in the **Lecture et Composition** section, the new vocabulary in this section is meant for recognition only and not for active use. You may wish to mention this to students, unless you intend to make a special test that includes this vocabulary.
- Have students imagine what they would say to describe their own education system to a foreigner.
- Ask students to read the text in the book and answer the **Compréhension** questions. (This may be prepared at home.)
- Discuss the **Compréhension** questions. Have students look back at the questions they originally wrote down about the topic. If the culture section hasn't answered the questions, discuss them as a class or assign them as a research project.
- Assign the *Share It!* activity.

Résumé de grammaire

The **Résumé de grammaire** summarizes the grammar points taught in the chapter. Students can use it as a reference or review tool to prepare for the end-of-chapter test. There are accompanying grammar review sheets on the PowerLecture.

Vocabulaire

The active vocabulary in each chapter's four **Compétences** is listed in the end-of-chapter **Vocabulaire** for easy reference. Audio flashcards accompany the end-of-chapter vocabulary lists. **Vocabulaire supplémentaire** in the margins of each chapter is presented so that students can personalize their conversations and is considered supplementary. It does not appear in the end-of-chapter lists or in the Testing Program. It is left up to your discretion whether or not to require students to learn the **Vocabulaire supplémentaire.**

Using the Supplemental Sections

Interlude musical

The **Interlude musical** sections introduce students to songs of various styles from all over the francophone world. A song corresponding thematically or grammatically to each chapter of *Horizons* has been selected for these sections, which follow every unit of two chapters. The activities on these pages are intended as a preview to the lyrics of the song. You or your students can access the lyrics and videos of each song by searching online.

Bienvenue en Europe francophone / Bienvenue en Afrique francophone

These sections use a photo journal style to introduce students to the fascinating variety of countries and cultures that make up the francophone world. These sections can be covered at home or in class and lend themselves to special projects that you can assign as homework.

SUGGESTIONS FOR PAIR- AND GROUP-WORK IN THE CLASSROOM

Group and pair activities provide communicative oral practice of thematic vocabulary and grammatical points that have been presented to students in class. The following strategies may be used in combination or independently once pairs or groups have been designated:

- *Brainstorming:* A few minutes of brainstorming may be helpful, allowing students the opportunity to look up unknown words, review structures, ask the instructor questions, etc. This can be done either in groups or with the whole class.
- *Unrehearsed role-playing:* In dialogue-based activities, depending on how well students have internalized the material to be practiced, the instructor may ask pairs or groups of students to act out their dialogues with little or no advance preparation time. This technique may be more appropriate once students have reached more advanced stages of the course.
- *Rehearsed role-playing:* In dialogue-based activities, the instructor can ask students to prepare each dialogue for presentation in front of the whole class or a group. In such cases, students may be encouraged to use simple props, such as desks, chairs, and personal belongings as theatrical devices to enliven and dramatize the performance.
- *Expansions:* Student pairs and groups may be asked to expand on the context already provided, using their imagination and common sense. As this is a more challenging activity, it may be used most appropriately when internalization of structures and vocabulary has been achieved or as a follow-up.

Several techniques may be employed for evaluating and correcting pair- and group-work. Among these are the following:

- *Class presentation:* Once students have finished a dialogue or any other pair-/group-work, the instructor can ask them to present it in front of the whole class. Students in the audience may be asked to correct errors and pronunciation or to ask questions.
- *Instructor monitoring:* Especially in smaller classes, the instructor may monitor students' progress by circulating around the classroom, listening to each group as it works on the activity and providing guidance and suggestions.
- *Audio recording:* Depending on the availability of equipment, the instructor may ask each student pair or group to record their presentation. Afterward, students may listen to the audio for self-correction, or it may be corrected by their peers or the instructor.
- *Video recording:* In dialogue-based activities, this may be suitable at the more advanced stages of the course or when students present long dialogues. Presentation of video role-plays to the whole class is an entertaining and highly motivating technique for engaging students in self-correction.

Most importantly of all, encourage students to enjoy communicating their own thoughts in French!

TEACHING FRENCH THROUGH MUSIC

Since all of us grow up singing or hearing songs of various kinds, teaching French through music is one of the most natural ways to complement coursework with authentic materials. This brief overview offers general suggestions for incorporating songs in the language classroom as a means of immersing students in language and culture.

As with any teaching materials, songs work best when integrated relative to long-term objectives. Chosen to specifically complement *Horizons,* the **Interlude musical** sections will provide a basic structure upon which to build. Moreover, your students will already have practiced listening with the *Horizons* audio program and should adapt naturally to exploring the featured songs. Additionally, the **Sélection musicale** margin notes encourage students to enjoy further listening practice.

If you find your class members curious to know even more about particular artists or places, beyond the notes and activities provided, you might also consider looking online. A fair number of stable, well-maintained websites exist for teaching French through songs, especially from France and Canada and from the artists themselves. There, one can find biographical information, audio and video excerpts, and other related materials such as artwork or blogs. You may also wish to explore sites sponsored by cultural organizations, as well as professional journals such as *Le français dans le monde*. One valuable resource for teachers is Tim Murphey's book *Music and Song* (Oxford, 1992).

Where to start? It can be as simple as humming a line to students, reactivating vocabulary and grammar they have just learned, asking who their own favorite artists are, or relating the music and themes to cultural points covered in *Horizons*. Occasionally, it is possible to sing along with a given song. Besides doing one's best to ensure that students are in sync with the lesson expansion, mapping out what can be done before, during and after an **Interlude musical** is a central component of success. The following outline may provide inspiration for those seeking a springboard to further activities at any level.

Pre-Class

- Assign pre-listening as homework.
- Assign a related reading, or information to be gathered or shared online.
- Have students bring in a related object, image, or article.
- Ask musically-inclined students to bring an instrument.
- Show an informational film clip or concert excerpt.
- Share one version of a song, before playing an older or newer version the following day.
- Have students choose the song to be studied in class (from a pre-selected group).
- Have students use the Internet to find various kinds of information over several days, as a longer project.

Pre-Listening

- Ask what words relate to the song's theme; have students write a short text using them.
- Ask about the musical genre into which the song fits.
- Ask what ideas the first listening of the song or viewing of the video suggests.
- Discuss what gestures might accompany the words.
- If singing, first highlight key vocabulary and practice pronunciation singularities.
- Have students predict the song's subject and formulate hypotheses through the title or first line, or through a listening without the text (or with video: based on the first images).

While Listening (First Listen, Second Listen)

- Remove selected words; have students fill in blanks.
- Remove selected words; provide a word list and have students circle what they hear (or, with words cut out and handed to pairs in envelopes, have students place words in the blanks).
- Provide sentences or paragraphs out of order and have students reorganize them.
- Have students circle key sounds.
- Have students raise hands upon hearing key words.
- Place students in groups for analysis or rewriting of selected verses.
- Have students fill in a chart with missing information (e.g., who does what, where, when, why).
- Have students fill in a questionnaire including descriptive vocabulary, analysis prompts, and suggestions for further evaluating the song.

Post-Listening, Follow-Up

- Ask students to describe the place, the people, the themes; gender, social, racial, or ethnic roles.
- Ask students to describe stylistic singularities: words, melody, rhythm, structure.
- Practice the grammatical singularities most relevant to the day's lesson.
- Practice vocabulary. (Build lists of similar words, find definitions, write a summary or new song or story using 5–7 key words.)
- Have students change the song's grammar or vocabulary. (Change present tense to past or future, verbs or pronouns or adjectives into their opposites.)
- Have students summarize each phase of the song's story (each verse or group of verses).
- Have students formulate hypotheses (to practice verb tenses).
- Ask what different titles might be used to sum up the song.
- Have students match the song to a proverb from a list.
- Have students write their own versions, using similar words or structures.
- Have students prepare a storyboard with their own imagined versions of a video.

- Have students sketch a cover and/or insert design for an imagined CD release (in the country of origin, in the country in which your class is taking place).
- Have students create a related comic book **(un roman photo).**
- Have students write a related postcard to a friend or to a person in the song.
- Have students write a main character's story, CV, Dear Abby letter, or personal announcement, in which they play the role of that person.
- Have students create a phone conversation between people mentioned in the song.
- Group songs together; have students create playlists and justify their choices.
- Create a class blog for students to share information about French music.

Aaron Prevots
Associate Professor of French
Southwestern University
Georgetown, Texas

Joan H. Manley
University of Texas—El Paso, Emeritus

Stuart Smith
Austin Community College

John T. McMinn
Austin Community College

Marc A. Prévost
Austin Community College

HORIZONS

Sixth Edition

Australia • Brazil • Japan • Korea • Mexico • Singapore • Spain • United Kingdom • United States

Horizons, Sixth Edition
Manley | Smith | McMinn | Prévost

Product Director: Beth Kramer
Senior Product Manager: Nicole Morinon
Managing Developer: Katie Wade
Content Developers: Isabelle Alouane and Mayanne Wright
Senior Content Project Manager: Esther Marshall
Content Coordinator: Gregory Madan
Managing Media Developer: Morgen Gallo
Market Development Manager: Ben Rivera
Manufacturing Planner: Betsy Donaghey
Production Service: PreMediaGlobal
Senior Art Director: Linda Jurras
Text Designer: Alisa Aronson
Cover Designer: Wing Ngan
Rights Acquisition Specialist: Jessica Elias
Cover Credits: ©Gettyimages/John Seaton Callahan (right); ©Gettyimages/Georges Courreges (desert/middle); ©Gettyimages/Giovanni Bertolissio (bridge/left)
Compositor: PreMediaGlobal

© 2015, 2012, 2009, Cengage Learning

ALL RIGHTS RESERVED. No part of this work covered by the copyright herein may be reproduced, transmitted, stored, or used in any form or by any means graphic, electronic, or mechanical, including but not limited to photocopying, recording, scanning, digitizing, taping, Web distribution, information networks, or information storage and retrieval systems, except as permitted under Section 107 or 108 of the 1976 United States Copyright Act, without the prior written permission of the publisher.

> For product information and technology assistance, contact us at
> **Cengage Learning Customer & Sales Support, 1-800-354-9706**
> For permission to use material from this text or product,
> submit all requests online at **www.cengage.com/permissions**.
> Further permissions questions can be emailed to
> **permissionrequest@cengage.com**.

Library of Congress Control Number: 2013944597

Student Edition:

ISBN-13: 978-1-285-42828-4
ISBN-10: 1-285-42828-5

Loose Leaf Edition:

ISBN-13: 978-1-285-45100-8
ISBN-10: 1-285-45100-7

Annotated Instructor's Edition:
ISBN-13: 978-1-285-45089-6
ISBN-10: 1-285-45089-2

20 Channel Center Street
Boston, MA 02210
USA

Cengage Learning is a leading provider of customized learning solutions with office locations around the globe, including Singapore, the United Kingdom, Australia, Mexico, Brazil and Japan. Locate your local office at: **international.cengage.com/region**

Cengage Learning products are represented in Canada by Nelson Education, Ltd.

For your course and learning solutions, visit **www.cengage.com**.

Purchase any of our products at your local college store or at our preferred online store **www.cengagebrain.com**.

TABLE DES MATIÈRES

Le monde francophone	Themes and Functions	Vocabulary	Culture
CHAPITRE PRÉLIMINAIRE: On commence! • 2			
Regional Focus: Bienvenue dans le monde francophone! • 4			
COMPÉTENCE 1	Greeting people	Les formules de politesse 6 Les salutations familières 8	
COMPÉTENCE 2	Counting and describing your week	Les nombres de zéro à trente 10 Les jours de la semaine 12	
COMPÉTENCE 3	Talking about yourself and your schedule	Un autoportrait 14 L'heure 16	
COMPÉTENCE 4	Communicating in class	En cours 20 Des expressions utiles et l'alphabet 22	
COMPARAISONS CULTURELLES • 24			**L'heure officielle** 24
VOCABULAIRE • 26			

Table des matières **iii**

Sur la Côte d'Azur

	Themes and Functions	Vocabulary
CHAPITRE 1: À l'université • 28		
Regional Focus: La France et ses régions • 30		
COMPÉTENCE 1	**Identifying people and describing appearance**	Les gens à l'université *32*
COMPÉTENCE 2	**Describing personality**	Les personnalités *38*
COMPÉTENCE 3	**Describing the university area**	Le campus et le quartier *44*
COMPÉTENCE 4	**Talking about your studies**	L'université et les cours *50*
LECTURE ET COMPOSITION • 56		
COMPARAISONS CULTURELLES • 58		
RÉSUMÉ DE GRAMMAIRE • 60		
VOCABULAIRE • 62		
CHAPITRE 2: Après les cours • 64		
Regional Focus: Nice • 66		
COMPÉTENCE 1	**Saying what you like to do**	Le temps libre et les loisirs *68*
COMPÉTENCE 2	**Saying how you spend your free time**	Le week-end *74*
COMPÉTENCE 3	**Asking about someone's day**	La journée *82*
COMPÉTENCE 4	**Going to the café**	Au café *88*
LECTURE ET COMPOSITION • 94		
COMPARAISONS CULTURELLES • 96		
RÉSUMÉ DE GRAMMAIRE • 98		
VOCABULAIRE • 100		
Interlude musical • 102		*Je suis* (Amel Bent) *Chantez, chantez* (Amadou Bagayoko and Mariam Doumbia)

Structures	Culture	Learning Strategies, Readings, Listening Passages, Writing Strategies
Les adjectifs et **il est / elle est** + adjectif ou **c'est** + nom *34* Les pronoms sujets, le verbe **être**, la négation et d'autres adjectifs *40* Les questions *42* Le genre, l'article indéfini et l'expression **il y a** *46* **C'est** ou **il est / elle est** et la place de l'adjectif *48* L'article défini *52* **Vidéoreprise:** *Les Stagiaires 54*		**Stratégies et Lecture** *36* **Pour mieux lire:** *Using cognates and familiar words to read for the gist* **Lecture:** *Qui est-ce?*
		Pour mieux lire: *Scanning to preview a text 56* **Lecture:** *L'accent grave* **Pour mieux écrire:** *Using and combining what you know 57* **Composition:** *Un autoportrait*
	Les études *58*	
L'infinitif *70* Les verbes en **-er** et les adverbes *76* Quelques verbes à changements orthographiques *80* Les mots interrogatifs *84* Les questions par inversion *86* Les nombres de trente à cent et l'argent *90* **Vidéoreprise:** *Les Stagiaires 92*		**Stratégies et Compréhension auditive** *72* **Pour mieux comprendre:** *Listening for specific information* **Compréhension auditive:** *On sort ensemble?*
		Pour mieux lire: *Making intelligent guesses 94* **Lecture:** *Aux Trois Obus* **Pour mieux écrire:** *Using logical order and standard phrases 95* **Composition:** *Au café*
	Les cafés en France *96*	

En Amérique	Themes and Functions	Vocabulary
CHAPITRE 3: Un nouvel appartement • 104		
Regional Focus: En Amérique: Le Canada et le Québec • 106		
COMPÉTENCE 1	Talking about where you live	Le logement *108*
COMPÉTENCE 2	Talking about your possessions	Les effets personnels *114*
COMPÉTENCE 3	Describing your room	Les meubles et les couleurs *120*
COMPÉTENCE 4	Giving your address and phone number	Des renseignements *126*
LECTURE ET COMPOSITION • 132		
COMPARAISONS CULTURELLES • 134		
RÉSUMÉ DE GRAMMAIRE • 136		
VOCABULAIRE • 138		
CHAPITRE 4: En famille • 140		
Regional Focus: En Amérique: En Louisiane • 142		
COMPÉTENCE 1	Describing your family	Ma famille *144*
COMPÉTENCE 2	Saying where you go in your free time	Le temps libre *150*
COMPÉTENCE 3	Saying what you are going to do	Le week-end prochain *156*
COMPÉTENCE 4	Planning how to get there	Les moyens de transport *162*
LECTURE ET COMPOSITION • 168		
COMPARAISONS CULTURELLES • 170		
RÉSUMÉ DE GRAMMAIRE • 172		
VOCABULAIRE • 174		
Interlude musical • 176		*Fille de Ville* (Marie-Élaine Thibert) *Nonc Willie* (Bruce Daigrepont)

Structures	Culture	Learning Strategies, Readings, Listening Passages, Writing Strategies
Les nombres au-dessus de 100 et les nombres ordinaux *110* Le verbe **avoir** *116* Quelques prépositions *118* La possession et les adjectifs possessifs **mon, ton** et **son** *122* Les adjectifs possessifs **notre, votre** et **leur** *124* Les adjectifs **ce** et **quel** *128* Vidéoreprise: *Les Stagiaires 130*		**Stratégies et Lecture** *112* **Pour mieux lire:** *Guessing meaning from context* **Lecture:** *Un nouvel appartement*
		Pour mieux lire: *Previewing content 132* **Lecture:** *Les couleurs et leurs effets sur la nature humaine* **Pour mieux écrire:** *Brainstorming 133* **Composition:** *Un mail*
	Le Québec d'aujourd'hui *134*	
Les expressions avec **avoir** *146* Le verbe **aller**, la préposition **à** et le pronom **y** *152* Le pronom sujet **on** et l'impératif *154* Le futur immédiat *158* Les dates *160* Les verbes **prendre** et **venir** et les moyens de transport *164* Vidéoreprise: *Les Stagiaires 166*		**Stratégies et Compréhension auditive** *148* **Pour mieux comprendre:** *Asking for clarification* **Compréhension auditive:** *La famille de Robert*
		Pour mieux lire: *Using your knowledge of the world 168* **Lecture:** *Deux mots* **Pour mieux écrire:** *Visualizing your topic 169* **Composition:** *Ma famille*
	L'histoire des Cadiens *170*	

À Paris	Themes and Functions	Vocabulary
CHAPITRE 5: Les projets • 178		
Regional Focus: La France • 180		
COMPÉTENCE 1	**Saying what you did**	Le week-end dernier *182*
COMPÉTENCE 2	**Telling where you went**	Je suis parti(e) en voyage *188*
COMPÉTENCE 3	**Discussing the weather and your activities**	Le temps et les projets *194*
COMPÉTENCE 4	**Deciding what to wear and buying clothes**	Les vêtements *200*
LECTURE ET COMPOSITION • 208		
COMPARAISONS CULTURELLES • 210		
RÉSUMÉ DE GRAMMAIRE • 212		
VOCABULAIRE • 214		
Bienvenue en Europe francophone • 216		
CHAPITRE 6: Les sorties • 220		
Regional Focus: Paris • 222		
COMPÉTENCE 1	**Inviting someone to go out**	Les invitations *224*
COMPÉTENCE 2	**Talking about how you spend and used to spend your time**	Aujourd'hui et dans le passé *230*
COMPÉTENCE 3	**Talking about the past**	Une sortie *236*
COMPÉTENCE 4	**Narrating in the past**	Les contes *242*
LECTURE ET COMPOSITION • 248		
COMPARAISONS CULTURELLES • 250		
RÉSUMÉ DE GRAMMAIRE • 252		
VOCABULAIRE • 254		
Interlude musical • 256		*La garde-robe d'Élizabeth* (Amélie-les-crayons) *Premier amour* (Tony Parker/Rickwel)

Structures	Culture	Learning Strategies, Readings, Listening Passages, Writing Strategies
		Stratégies et Lecture 186 **Pour mieux lire:** *Using the sequence of events to make logical guesses* **Lecture:** *Qu'est-ce qu'elle a fait?*
Le passé composé avec **avoir** 184 Le passé composé avec **être** 190 Les expressions qui désignent le passé et reprise du passé composé 192 Le verbe **faire**, l'expression **ne... rien** et les expressions pour décrire le temps 196 Les expressions avec **faire** 198 Les pronoms **le, la, l'** et **les** 202 Vidéoreprise: *Les Stagiaires* 206		
		Pour mieux lire: *Using visuals to make guesses* 208 **Lecture:** *Je blogue donc je suis* **Pour mieux écrire:** *Using standard organizing techniques* 209 **Composition:** *Un voyage en France*
	Le sport et le temps libre des Français 210	

Structures	Culture	Learning Strategies, Readings, Listening Passages, Writing Strategies
		Stratégies et Compréhension auditive 228 **Pour mieux comprendre:** *Noting the important information* **Compréhension auditive:** *On va au cinéma?*
Les verbes **vouloir**, **pouvoir** et **devoir** 226 L'imparfait 232 Les verbes **sortir**, **partir** et **dormir** 234 L'imparfait et le passé composé 238 Le passé composé et l'imparfait 240 Le passé composé et l'imparfait (reprise) 244 Vidéoreprise: *Les Stagiaires* 246		
		Pour mieux lire: *Using standard formats* 248 **Lecture:** *Deux films français* **Pour mieux écrire:** *Using standard formats* 249 **Composition:** *Un film à voir*
	Le cinéma: les préférences des Français 250	

La Normandie	Themes and Functions	Vocabulary
CHAPITRE 7: La vie quotidienne • 258		
Regional Focus: La France et sa diversité • 260		
COMPÉTENCE 1	Describing your daily routine	La vie de tous les jours *262*
COMPÉTENCE 2	Talking about relationships	La vie sentimentale *270*
COMPÉTENCE 3	Talking about what you did and used to do	Les activités d'hier *278*
COMPÉTENCE 4	Describing traits and characteristics	Les traits de caractère *284*
LECTURE ET COMPOSITION • 290		
COMPARAISONS CULTURELLES • 294		
RÉSUMÉ DE GRAMMAIRE • 296		
VOCABULAIRE • 298		
CHAPITRE 8: La bonne cuisine • 300		
Regional Focus: La Normandie • 302		
COMPÉTENCE 1	Ordering at a restaurant	Au restaurant *304*
COMPÉTENCE 2	Buying food	Les courses *314*
COMPÉTENCE 3	Talking about meals	Les repas *322*
COMPÉTENCE 4	Choosing a healthy lifestyle	La santé *328*
LECTURE ET COMPOSITION • 336		
COMPARAISONS CULTURELLES • 338		
RÉSUMÉ DE GRAMMAIRE • 340		
VOCABULAIRE • 342		
Interlude musical • 344		*Retomber amoureux* (Chimène Badi) *Pour toi* (Princess Sarah)

Structures	Culture	Learning Strategies, Readings, Listening Passages, Writing Strategies
		Stratégies et Lecture 268 **Pour mieux lire:** *Using word families and watching out for* **faux amis** **Lecture:** *Il n'est jamais trop tard!*
Les verbes réfléchis au présent 264		
Les verbes réciproques au présent et les verbes réfléchis et réciproques au futur immédiat 272		
Les verbes en **-re** 276		
Les verbes réfléchis et réciproques au passé composé 280		
Les verbes réfléchis et réciproques à l'imparfait et reprise de l'usage du passé composé et de l'imparfait 282		
Les pronoms relatifs **qui, que** et **dont** 286 **Vidéoreprise:** *Les Stagiaires* 288		
		Pour mieux lire: *Recognizing conversational style* 290 **Lecture:** *Conte pour enfants de moins de trois ans* **Pour mieux écrire:** *Organizing a paragraph* 293 **Composition:** *Le matin chez moi*
	L'amour et le couple 294	

Structures	Culture	Learning Strategies, Readings, Listening Passages, Writing Strategies
		Stratégies et Compréhension auditive 312 **Pour mieux comprendre:** *Planning and predicting* **Compréhension auditive:** *Au restaurant*
Le partitif 310		
Les expressions de quantité 318		
L'usage des articles 320		
Le pronom **en** et le verbe **boire** 324		
Les verbes en **-ir** 326		
Le conditionnel 330 **Vidéoreprise:** *Les Stagiaires* 334		
		Pour mieux lire: *Reading a poem* 336 **Lecture:** *Déjeuner du matin* **Pour mieux écrire:** *Finding the right word* 337 **Composition:** *Une critique gastronomique*
	À table! 338	

Aux Antilles	Themes and Functions	Vocabulary
CHAPITRE 9: En vacances • 346		
Regional Focus: La France d'outre-mer • 348		
COMPÉTENCE 1	**Talking about vacation**	Les vacances *350*
COMPÉTENCE 2	**Preparing for a trip**	Les préparatifs *356*
COMPÉTENCE 3	**Buying your ticket**	À l'agence de voyages *362*
COMPÉTENCE 4	**Deciding where to go on a trip**	Un voyage *368*
LECTURE ET COMPOSITION • 374		
COMPARAISONS CULTURELLES • 376		
RÉSUMÉ DE GRAMMAIRE • 378		
VOCABULAIRE • 380		
CHAPITRE 10: À l'hotel • 382		
Regional Focus: Les Antilles • 384		
COMPÉTENCE 1	**Deciding where to stay**	Le logement *386*
COMPÉTENCE 2	**Going to the doctor**	Chez le médecin *392*
COMPÉTENCE 3	**Running errands on a trip**	Des courses en voyage *398*
COMPÉTENCE 4	**Giving directions**	Les indications *406*
LECTURE ET COMPOSITION • 412		
COMPARAISONS CULTURELLES • 414		
RÉSUMÉ DE GRAMMAIRE • 416		
VOCABULAIRE • 418		
Interlude musical • 420		*Donne-moi une vie* (Yannick Noah) *Je sais* (Shy'm)
Bienvenue en Afrique francophone • 422		

Structures	Culture	Learning Strategies, Readings, Listening Passages, Writing Strategies
Le futur 352 Les verbes **dire, lire** et **écrire** 358 Les pronoms compléments d'objet indirect **(lui, leur)** et reprise des pronoms compléments d'objet direct **(le, la, l', les)** 360 Les verbes **savoir** et **connaître** 364 Les pronoms **me, te, nous** et **vous** 366 Les expressions géographiques 370 **Vidéoreprise:** *Les Stagiaires* 372		**Stratégies et Lecture** 354 **Pour mieux lire:** *Recognizing compound tenses* **Lecture:** *Quelle aventure!* **Pour mieux lire:** *Understanding words with multiple meanings* 374 **Lecture:** *Ma grand-mère m'a appris à ne pas compter sur les yeux des autres pour dormir* **Pour mieux écrire:** *Revising what you write* 375 **Composition:** *Un itinéraire*
	La culture créole aux Antilles 376	
Les expressions impersonnelles et l'infinitif 388 Les expressions impersonnelles et les verbes réguliers au subjonctif 394 Les verbes irréguliers au subjonctif 396 Les expressions d'émotion et de volonté et le subjonctif 400 Le subjonctif ou l'infinitif? 404 Reprise de l'impératif et les pronoms avec l'impératif 408 **Vidéoreprise:** *Les Stagiaires* 410		**Stratégies et Compréhension auditive** 390 **Pour mieux comprendre:** *Anticipating a response* **Compréhension auditive:** *À la réception* **Pour mieux lire:** *Using word families* 412 **Lecture:** *Avis de l'hôtel* **Pour mieux écrire:** *Making suggestions* 413 **Composition:** *Suggestions de voyage!*
	La musique francophone: les influences africaines et antillaises 414	

Table des matières **xiii**

CHAPITRE DE RÉVISION: La vie moderne • 426

RÉVISION: CHAPITRES 1–2:	**Les profils en ligne** • 428	
RÉVISION: CHAPITRES 3–4:	**Vivre vert** • 432	
RÉVISION: CHAPITRES 5–6:	**Ma vie, c'est une BD!** • 436	
RÉVISION: CHAPITRES 7–8:	**La vie saine** • 440	
RÉVISION: CHAPITRES 9–10:	**L'écotourisme** • 444	

TABLEAUX DES VERBES • 448

VOCABULAIRE
    FRANÇAIS – ANGLAIS • 454

VOCABULAIRE
    ANGLAIS – FRANÇAIS • 473

INDEX • 488

PREFACE

Do you have a gift for languages?

Have you ever heard people say that they know someone who has a gift for languages? What does that mean? Are some people born with a special ability to learn languages? How do you know if you have a gift for languages? If you understood the sentence you just read, then you have a gift for languages. After all, you have already learned to speak and understand at least one language well—English. Everybody is born with a natural ability to learn languages, but some individuals seem to learn languages more quickly than others do. This is because, over time, we develop different learning styles.

The process individuals use to learn languages depends a great deal on their personality. As with any other process, such as learning a new computer program or writing a composition for English class, individuals can attain similar results, although they approach the task differently. Some language learners like to plan each step before beginning. Others prefer to jump in as soon as they know enough to get started, and continue from there using a hit-or-miss method. Some language learners like to understand in detail why a language works the way it does before they try to use it, whereas others are ready to try speaking as soon as they know only the most basic rules, making educated guesses about how to express themselves.

Both methods have advantages and disadvantages. Some people become so bogged down in details that they lose sight of their main purpose—communication. Others pay so little attention to details that what they say is unintelligible. No matter what sort of learner you are, the most important part of the language-learning process is to constantly try to use the language to express yourself. Always alternate study of vocabulary and structures with attempts to communicate.

Since you now know that you have a gift for languages, you might think of the following pages as a user's manual that suggests how to use your language-learning capacity to learn French efficiently. Some of the learning techniques will work for you, others may not fit your learning style. Read through the following three sections before beginning your French studies, and refer to them later to develop the language-learning process that works best for you.

- **Goals and expectations:** How much French should you expect to learn in your first year of study and how much time and effort will be required of you?
- **Motivation:** How do you motivate yourself to study and practice the language?
- **Learning techniques:** What are some study tips that will facilitate learning French?

GOALS AND EXPECTATIONS
Who can learn a language?

Many people believe that, as an adult, you cannot learn a language as well as you might have when you were a child. It is true that children are good language learners, but there is no reason why adults cannot learn to speak a language with near-native fluency. Children learn languages well because they can adapt very easily and they do it willingly. Being able to adapt is very important in language learning. Children are not afraid to try something new, and they are not easily embarrassed if things do not turn out as they expect. Adults, on the other hand, are often afraid of doing something wrong or looking ridiculous. Don't be afraid to experiment, using what you already know to guess at how to express yourself in French. It does no harm if you try to say something and you do not get the expected response. Just try again.

By the time people become adults, they generally learn by analyzing, rather than by doing. They have also grown so accustomed to their own way of doing things that they are reluctant to change. Similarly, adult language learners often feel that the way English works is the natural way. They try to force the language they are learning into the same mold. In fact, languages work in a variety of ways, all equally natural. Learn to accept that the French way of doing things is just as natural and valid as the English way.

Another difference in the way that children and adults learn languages is that children spend a lot more time focused on what they are doing. When children learn languages, they spend almost every hour they are awake for several years doing nothing but learning the language. Learning to communicate is their principal objective in life. Most adults, on the other hand, spend just a few hours a week studying a new language, and during this time they are often distracted by many other aspects of their lives. In a classroom setting where small children have contact with a foreign language for just a few hours per week, children do not learn better than adults. In fact, adults have several advantages over children, such as their ability to organize and their longer attention spans. Your ability to develop fluency in French depends mainly on three things: the amount of time you spend with the language, how focused you are, and how willing you are to try to communicate using it.

How well will you speak after a year?

Those of you who are new to foreign language study probably have a variety of ideas about what you will be doing in this course. People who become frustrated in foreign language study generally do so because they start off with the wrong expectations. Some people begin a foreign language course with a negative attitude, thinking that it is impossible to really learn a language without going to a country where it is spoken. Although it is indeed usually easier to learn French in a French-speaking region, you can learn to speak French very fluently here as well. Once again, it is a question of spending time with the language, while focusing on how to communicate with it.

There are also some students who begin foreign language classes with expectations that are too high, thinking that they will begin speaking French with complete fluency nearly overnight. Learning a language takes time. Even after two years of concentrated study, it is reasonable to have achieved only basic fluency. If you set a goal for yourself to have everyday conversation skills after your second year of study, and if you work hard toward this goal, you will be able to function in most everyday conversation settings; however, you will still frequently have to look for words, you will probably still speak in short simple sentences, and you will often have to use circumlocution to get your meaning across. In *Horizons,* you will learn how to function in the most common situations in which you are likely to find yourself in a francophone region. To illustrate how much you will learn during the first few weeks of study, take out a sheet of paper, and list, in English, the first eight questions you would probably ask in the following situation: Before the first day of class, you sit down next to a student you have never seen before and you begin to chat.

In this situation, students generally ask questions like the following:

- How are you doing?
- What's your name?
- What are you studying?
- Where are you from?
- Where do you live? / Do you live on campus?
- Do you like it there?
- Do you work? Where?
- When are you graduating?

This is the extent of the conversation that you have with many people you will meet, and you will be able to do this in French after only a few weeks.

How much time and effort must you invest to be a successful language learner?

There are three Ps involved in learning a language: patience, practice, and persistence. We have already said that success in learning a foreign language depends on how much time you spend studying and practicing it. You might wonder how time-consuming French class will be. The amount of time required depends on your study skills and attention span. However, nobody can be successful without devoting many hours to studying and using the language. Generally, to make steady progress at the rate that material is presented in most college or university classes, you should expect to spend two to three hours on the language outside of class, for every hour that you are in class.

What is involved in learning to express yourself in another language?

Students studying a foreign language for the first time may have false expectations about what is involved in learning to speak another language. Many people think that you just substitute a French word for the equivalent word in English. Most of the time, you cannot translate word for word from one language to another. For example, if a French speaker substituted the equivalent English word for each French word in the following sentence, it would create a very unusual sentence.

Nous ne l'avons pas encore fait.
*We not it have not still done.

You might be able to figure out that this sentence means, "We haven't done it yet," but sometimes translating word for word can give a completely wrong meaning. For example, if you translate the following sentence word for word, you would think that it has the first meaning that follows it, whereas it really has the second. This is because the indirect object pronoun **vous** *([to] you)* precedes the verb in French.

Je voudrais vous parler demain, s'il vous plaît.
*I would like you to speak tomorrow, if it you pleases.
I would like to speak to you tomorrow, please.

You probably noticed in this last example that one word in English may be translated by several words in French and vice versa (**voudrais** = *would like,* **vous** = *to you,* **parler** = *to speak,* **s'il vous plaît** = *please*).

Differences in languages are not due simply to a lack of one-to-one correspondence between words and structures. Cultural differences also strongly affect how we communicate. Culture and language are so interrelated that it is impossible to learn a language fluently without becoming familiar with the culture(s) where it is spoken. For example, in French, a cultural difference that affects the spoken language is that French society is not as informal as ours. Adults generally do not call each other by their first names, and the words for *sir* and *madam* are used much more frequently than in English. For example, it is normal to say **Bonjour, monsieur** *(Hello, sir),* whereas English speakers say *Hello.*

Cultural differences affect the spoken language and also nonverbal communication. For instance, when the French speak to each other, they generally stand closer than we do. When we are talking to a French-speaker, we may feel that our space is invaded and back away. The French may interpret this as being standoffish. As you can see, learning to communicate in French entails a lot more than substituting French words for English words in a sentence.

Does practice make perfect?

Your goal in learning French should not be to say everything perfectly. If you set this goal for yourself, you will probably be afraid to open your mouth, fearing mistakes. Your goal should be to communicate clearly, but you should expect to make mistakes when speaking. If you make a mistake that impedes communication, those you are speaking to will ask for clarification or repeat what you have said to be sure of what you mean. Listen carefully to how they express themselves, and make adjustments the next time you need to convey a similar message.

Although perfection is not the goal of language learners, practice is vital to success. (Remember the three Ps of language learning: patience, practice, and persistence.) You can learn every vocabulary word and rule in the book, but unless you practice regularly, listening to French and attempting to speak it, you will not learn the language. Practicing a language is just as necessary for success as practicing a sport or a musical instrument. Imagine that you are a football player or pianist. You might know every play in the book, or you might understand music theory completely, but unless you practice, you will never be able to perform. It is important to learn the rules of French, but you must also practice it regularly.

What do you do if foreign languages make you panic?

Most individuals feel nervous when they have to speak to strangers. This is true when you speak your own language, and it's even truer when speaking a foreign language. There is no reason to be nervous, yet fear of looking ridiculous is often difficult to control. It is normal to experience some anxiety in class. If you suffer extreme anxiety in language class—to such a degree that it impedes your ability to concentrate—it is best to recognize that you fear having to perform in class. Go see your instructor and discuss your anxiety. In order to conquer it, you must acknowledge it.

MOTIVATION
How can learning a foreign language help you?

Learning a foreign language should be fun. After all, you will spend a lot of class time chatting with classmates, which most of us find enjoyable. However, learning French takes time and effort. No matter how much you enjoy it, there will be times when you need to motivate yourself to study or practice. You can use motivation techniques for practicing a language similar to those musicians or athletes use to practice an instrument or a sport.

Many musicians and athletes have a personal goal. They imagine themselves playing a great concert at Carnegie Hall or winning a big game, receiving applause and praise. Similarly, each time you start to practice French, imagine yourself speaking French fluently with a beautiful accent. In this mental image, you might be a diplomat, or you might be talking to the waiter at a French restaurant, impressing your friends.

Some people who practice an instrument or a sport do so for personal growth. Many people feel that learning a new language helps them discover a new side of their personality. By learning to appreciate another culture, you learn to understand your own better. You also come to know yourself better and you broaden your horizons.

Of course, a lot of people are motivated to practice an instrument or a sport because they make their living from it. This is good motivation for learning a language too. In today's international economy, the best jobs are going more and more to those who speak more than one language, and who have an understanding of other cultures. Many jobs in the travel industry, in communications, in government, and in companies dealing in international trade and business require proficiency in another language.

How can you learn to enjoy studying?

As with any accomplishment, learning a foreign language requires a lot of work. You will enjoy it more if you think of it as a hobby or a pastime and as an opportunity to develop a skill. Here are some training techniques that can help you learn a new language.

- Get into a routine. Devote a particular time of day to studying French. It is best to find a time when you are fresh and free of distractions, so you can concentrate on what you are doing. If you study at the same time every day, getting started will become habitual, and you will have won half the battle. Once you are settled working and learning, it becomes fun.

- Make sure that the place where you study is inviting and that you enjoy being there.

- Study frequently for short periods of time, rather than having marathon sessions. After about two hours of study, the ability of the brain to retain information is greatly reduced. You tend to remember what you learn at the beginning of each study session and at the end. What you study in the middle tends to become blurred. To illustrate this, read the following words one time, then turn the page and see how many you remember. dog, house, sofa, cat, rooster, room, telephone, mouse, book, pencil, television. Most people can remember the first word and the last. The longer the list, the harder it is to remember the words in the middle. The same is true with studying. Study smaller "chunks" of material more frequently, and set reasonable goals for yourself. Don't try to learn it all at once.

- Study with a classmate or a friend. It is much easier to practice talking with someone else, and it is easier to spend more time working with the language if you are interacting with another person. Also, by studying with classmates, you will feel more comfortable speaking in front of them, which eliminates some of the embarrassment some adults feel when trying to pronounce foreign words in front of the whole class.

- Play games with the language. It is fun to learn how to say things in a new language. For instance, ask yourself how you would say things you hear on the radio or

television in French. If you do know how to say something in French that you hear, your knowledge will become more certain. If you don't know how to say something in French, that's normal if you are a beginner. When you finally learn the word or expression you were wondering about, you will remember it more easily, because you have already thought about it.
- Surround yourself by French. Rent French movies or watch DVDs of American movies in the French-language track, listen to French music, and search the Web for French websites with recent news or topics that interest you. Websites with a lot of pictures are the best, because the pictures give you clues to the meaning of unfamiliar words. You probably will not understand very much at first in movies and songs, but they will motivate you to learn more. They teach you about cultural differences, and they help give you a sense of good pronunciation.
- Don't let yourself get frustrated. If you are frustrated each time you sit down to study, ask yourself why. First of all, make sure that you are not studying when you are too tired or hungry. Also, make sure that you clearly understand your assignment and its purpose. Learn to distinguish a language-learning problem from a problem understanding instructions. If you are confused about what you are to do or why, see your instructor during office hours or contact another student. (This is another reason to study with a classmate!)

LEARNING TECHNIQUES
How can you spend your study time most efficiently?

Individuals organize material differently as they learn it. Some people learn better by seeing something; others learn better by hearing it. The following are some study tips for how to go about learning French. You may find that some of these methods work for you and others do not. Be creative in practicing your French, using a variety of study techniques.

General study tips
- Learn not to translate word for word. Learn to read and listen to whole sentences at a time.
- Keep a log of your study time in a small spiral notebook. This will help you learn to study more efficiently. Each time you sit down to study new material, write down the time you begin. When you finish, write down the time you stop, and two or three sentences summarizing what you studied. Students often feel frustrated that they spend a lot of time studying, but they do not retain much. By keeping a log, you will know exactly how much time you spend on French. Writing one or two sentences summarizing what you studied helps you check your retention.
- Alternate speaking, listening, reading, and writing activities. By changing tasks frequently, you will be able to study longer without losing your concentration.

Vocabulary-learning techniques
- Use your senses. Pronounce words aloud as you study them. Close your eyes as you pronounce the word and picture the thing or activity represented by nouns or verbs.
- Use flashcards. When possible, draw a simple picture instead of the English word. Also, write a sentence using the word on the card, trying to remember it each time you look at the card. Use different colored inks to help you visualize the meaning of words. For example, when studying colors, write them on the flashcard in that color. When learning food items, write the words for red foods, such as strawberries and tomatoes, in red, the words for green foods in green, etc. Write words that can be associated with shapes, such as tall, short, big, small, round, or square, with letters having similar shapes.
- Learn useful common phrases such as "What time is it?" or "How are you?" as a whole.
- Label household items in French on masking tape.
- Tape lists of vocabulary in places where you spend time doing routine tasks.
- Study vocabulary in manageable "chunks." Each morning, write out a list of 20 new words and carry it in your pocket. A few times during the day, spend two minutes trying to remember the words on the list. Take out the list and review the words you forgot for two minutes. By the end of the day, you will have spent just a few minutes and you will have learned the 20 words.
- Learn 10 useful phrases every day.
- Audio of the end-of-chapter vocabulary words is downloadable from the *Horizons* Premium Website. Download it and play it at home, while you jog, or in your car.
- Make tests for yourself. At the end of a study session, write the English words or phrases on a sheet of paper. Put the sheet of paper away for a few hours. Later, take it out and see how many of the French equivalents of these words or phrases you remember.
- Group words in logical categories. For example, learn words for fruits together, words for animals together, sports-related vocabulary together, etc.
- Make flashcards with antonyms on each side, such as hot/cold, near/far, to go to sleep/to wake up, etc.
- Use related English words to help you remember the French. For example, the French word for *to begin* is **commencer.** Associate it with *to commence.* Be creative in finding associations. For example, the word for *open* is **ouvert.** You can associate it with *overture,* which is the opening part of a musical piece, or an *overt* action, which is one that is done in the open. Write related English words on flashcards.
- Learn to say **"Comment dit-on… ?"** *("How do you say . . . ?")* when you do not know a word or phrase.
- Remember that we cannot say everything even in our own language. If you do not know a word, try to think of another way to say what you want. Use circumlocution. For example, if you do not know how to say "to drive," say "to take the car" instead.

Grammar-learning techniques

- Play teacher. Try to guess what your instructor would ask you to do if he or she were giving a quiz the next day.
- Do the ***Pour vérifier*** self-checks in the margins next to explanations of structures.
- Use color coding to help you remember grammatical information. For example, all nouns in French are categorized either as masculine or feminine, and you must memorize in which category each noun belongs. When you make flashcards, write feminine nouns on pink cards or with pink/red ink and use blue for masculine nouns. Use an eye-catching color on flashcards to indicate points you want to remember, such as irregular plurals or verbs that take **être** in the **passé composé.**
- If you like to use lists to study, organize them so that they help you remember information about words. For example, to remember noun gender, write masculine words in a column on the left and feminine words in a column on the right. If you can visualize where the word is on the list, you can remember its gender.
- Learn to accept ambiguity. Sometimes, as soon as you learn a new rule, you find out that it doesn't always work the way you expect it to.

Pronunciation-learning techniques

- Repeat everything you hear in French under your breath or in your head, even if you have no idea what it means. This will not only help your pronunciation, it will help your listening comprehension and your ability to learn vocabulary. For instance, if you keep repeating an unfamiliar word you hear in your head, when you finally find out what it means, you will remember it very easily.
- Read French words aloud as you study.
- Listen to the audio that goes with the book and the Student Activities Manual several times. It is impossible to concentrate both on meaning and pronunciation the first time you listen to them. Listen to them at least once focusing on pronunciation only.
- Make recordings of yourself and compare them to those of native speakers.
- Exaggerate as you practice at home. Any pronunciation that is not English will seem like exaggeration. Psychologically, it is very difficult to listen to yourself speaking another language. Pretend you are a French actor playing a role as you practice pronunciation.
- Listen to French songs on the Internet. Search for the lyrics and sing along.

Using the Text Audio Recordings and the SAM Audio Recordings

There are two distinct sets of audio programs that go with each chapter of the *Horizons* program: the Text Audio and the SAM Audio. The recordings on the Text Audio correspond to the listening sections marked with an audio icon in the textbook. The SAM Audio corresponds to the listening activities in the Student Activities Manual. The audio that accompanies the text is on the *Horizons* Premium Website. It is also accessible via the *iLrn™ Heinle Learning Center*. This audio allows you to review material covered in class on your own, or to prepare for the next day's class. When using the audio, it is important to make sure that you have accessed the right audio for either the textbook activities or the SAM.

In order to get maximum benefit from the recorded listening activities, approach them with the right attitude. It takes time, patience, and practice to understand French spoken at a normal conversational speed. Do not be surprised if you find it difficult at first. Relax and listen to passages more than once. You will understand a little more each time. Remember that you will not understand everything and that, for some exercises, you are only expected to understand enough to answer specific questions. Read through exercises prior to playing the audio, so that you know what to listen for.

If you find you do not have enough time to process and respond to a question before the next one begins, pause the audio to give yourself more time. Most importantly, be patient and remember that you can always listen again.

Be willing to listen to the audio activities several times. It is important to listen to them at least one separate time, focusing solely on pronunciation. Practice, patience, and persistence pay!

We hope that the preceding suggestions on how to go about learning French will serve you well, helping you to become a successful language learner. Good luck with your French studies, and most of all, enjoy yourself!

HORIZONS ILRN™ HEINLE LEARNING CENTER AND PREMIUM WEBSITE

As a student of French, you have access to a multitude of online resources. They can be accessed at www.cengagebrain.com. Here is what you will find on each one.

Horizons iLrn™ Heinle Learning Center:
Audio-enhanced vocabulary flashcards
Grammar tutorials
Grammar and pronunciation podcasts
Concentration games
Crossword puzzles
Glossary
Web links
Basic tutorial quizzes
Google Earth™ coordinates

Horizons Premium Website:
Text Audio
SAM Audio
Video

ACKNOWLEDGMENTS

We are grateful to a great many people for helping us transform our collective classroom experience into this text. Principal among these are Beth Kramer and Nicole Morinon, for the opportunity to work with Cengage Learning and for their support; Esther Marshall, Isabelle Alouane, Mayanne Wright, Greg Madan, Linda Jurras, Morgen Gallo, Peter Schott, John Farrell, Sev Champeny, native reader and proofreader, Julie Low, photo researcher, and Jenna Gray, PreMediaGlobal project manager. Our thanks also go to: Annick Penant who helped with the culture updates, Myriam Arcangeli, who worked on the review chapter, Jessica Sturm, from Purdue University, who updated the Web quizzes and cultural activities, Lara Finklea who updated the sample lesson plans, and our other freelancers.

We would particularly like to thank our reviewers of the current and previous editions.

Ahmed Bouguarche, *California State University—Northridge*
Alexandra Kuzmich, *Rochester Institute of Technology*
Amy Griffin Sawyer, *Clemson University*
Amy Hubbell, *Kansas State University*
Anna Brichko, *Mission College*
Annabelle Dolidon, *Portland State University*
Anne-Hélène Miller, *East Carolina University*
Anne-Marie Obajtek-Kirkwood, *Drexel University*
Antoinette Sol, *University of Texas—Arlington*
Bonnie Sarnoff, *Limestone College*
Caroline Jumel, *Oakland University*
Catherine Webster, *University of Central Oklahoma*
Cheryl Hansen, *Weber State University*
Christy Frembes, *State University of New York—Oneonta*
Claude Fouillade, *New Mexico State University*
Colleen Sandford, *Suffolk County Community College*
Constance Dickey, *Syracuse University*
Daniel E. Rivas, *Irvine Valley College*
Elaine Ancekewicz, *George Mason University*
Elaine Hayashi, *Oregon State University*
Gabriella Baika, *Auburn University*
Gloria Pastorino, *Fairleigh Dickinson University*
Hervé Corbe, *Youngstown State University*
Jaklin Yermian, *Los Angeles Valley College*
Janet Solberg, *Kalamazoo College*
Janette Funaro, *Johnson County Community College*
Jean-Luc Desalvo, *San José State University*
Jessica Sturm, *Purdue University*
Joan Debrah, *University of Hawaii—Manoa*
Jody Ballah, *University of Cincinnati—Raymond Walters College*
Johanna Needham, *Tacoma Community College*
John Moran, *New York University*
Joseph Price, *Texas Tech University*
Karina Rodegra, *University of Central Florida*
Keith Palka, *Central Michigan University*
Kelle Truby, *University of California—Riverside*
Kindra Santamaria, *Texas Christian University*
Kory Olson, *Richard Stockton College*
Lee Slater, *Old Dominion University*
Lisa Blair, *Shaw University*
Maria Melgarejo, *St. Cloud State University*
Marie Glynn, *Washington State University*
Mark Andrew Hall, *Ithaca College*
Martina Wells, *Chatham College*
Martine Howard, *Camden County College*
Meekyoung Yi, *Northern Virginia Community College*
Mercedes Rooney, *State University of New York—New Paltz*
Meredith Josey, *Western Washington University*
Michael Saclolo, *St. Edward's College*
Monique Manopoulos, *California State University—Hayward*
Monique Zibi, *Lone Star College—Kingwood*
Monty Laycox, *University of Central Missouri*
Nathalie Cornelius, *Bloomsburg University of Pennsylvania*
Nedialka Koleva, *Mesa Community College*
Nikki Kaltenbach, *Purdue University—Westville*
Nina Furry, *University of North Carolina at Chapel Hill*
Pamela Mansfield, *Union County College*
Pamela Park, *Idaho State University*
Patricia Cesario, *Suffolk County Community College*
Patricia Scarampi, *Lake Forest College*
Richard Gray, *Carson-Newman College*
Ruth Caldwell, *Luther College*
Shawn Morrison, *College of Charleston*
Stéphane Natan, *Rider University*
Susan Clay, *Clemson University*
Tamara Lindner, *University of Southwestern Louisiana*
Thierry Torea, *Hobart and William Smith Colleges*
Thomas Buresi, *Southern Polytechnic State University*
Vicki Earnest, *Calhoun Community College*
Vikrant Ahuja, *Mott Community College*
Yvon Joseph, *Suffolk County Community College*

A special thanks to both Jims, Laura, Andrew, Annick, Daniel, and Joel.

Last, but obviously not least, we thank each other for the tolerance, mutual encouragement, and strengthened bonds of friendship such an endeavor requires.

Merci mille fois!

THE *HORIZONS* VIDEO PROGRAM, *LES STAGIAIRES*

Les Stagiaires was written by the *Horizons*' authors to offer students more exposure to the text's vocabulary and grammar in a seamlessly integrated manner. The video, comprising ten episodes, provides learners with further listening practice. Students have the opportunity to learn about and experience French culture in the context of a storyline that involves seven characters and their interactions in a French office environment. The activities in each chapter's ***Vidéoreprise*** section are now designed with pre- and post-viewing activities. In addition, these activities simultaneously review the entire chapter's vocabulary and grammar.

In this video, we meet two interns, Amélie Prévot and Rachid Bennani. They are just starting their summer internships at Technovert, a small green-technology company.

Amélie Prévot　　**Rachid Bennani**

Henri Vieilledent is the founder, owner, and leader of this dynamic and fast-growing company. Coffee and croissants are his daily motivators.

Henri Vieilledent　　**Camille Dupont**

His faithful assistant, Camille Dupont, helps him run the business . . . and keeps his coffee-and-croissant supply abundant.

Céline Diop

One of Vieilledent's weapons in his efforts to make the company flourish and remain competitive is Céline Diop. The confident and driven sales manager also becomes an effective and appreciated mentor to the two young interns.

You might not be able to tell right away, but Matthieu Sauvage is a wiz. His area of expertise? Computers. However, interactions with the staff can sometimes be challenging for him. He can be extremely shy and awkward. When Amélie joins the Technovert staff, will Matthieu finally take a risk and break his painful timidity?

Matthieu Sauvage　　**Christophe Vieilledent**

Finally, Christophe Vieilledent is the company's gofer—though he doesn't go for . . . a lot! The mail delivery and other odd jobs he does around the building do not keep him from indulging in his favorite pastime: reading manga. With a father in high places he is able to keep a low profile . . .

Preface **xxi**

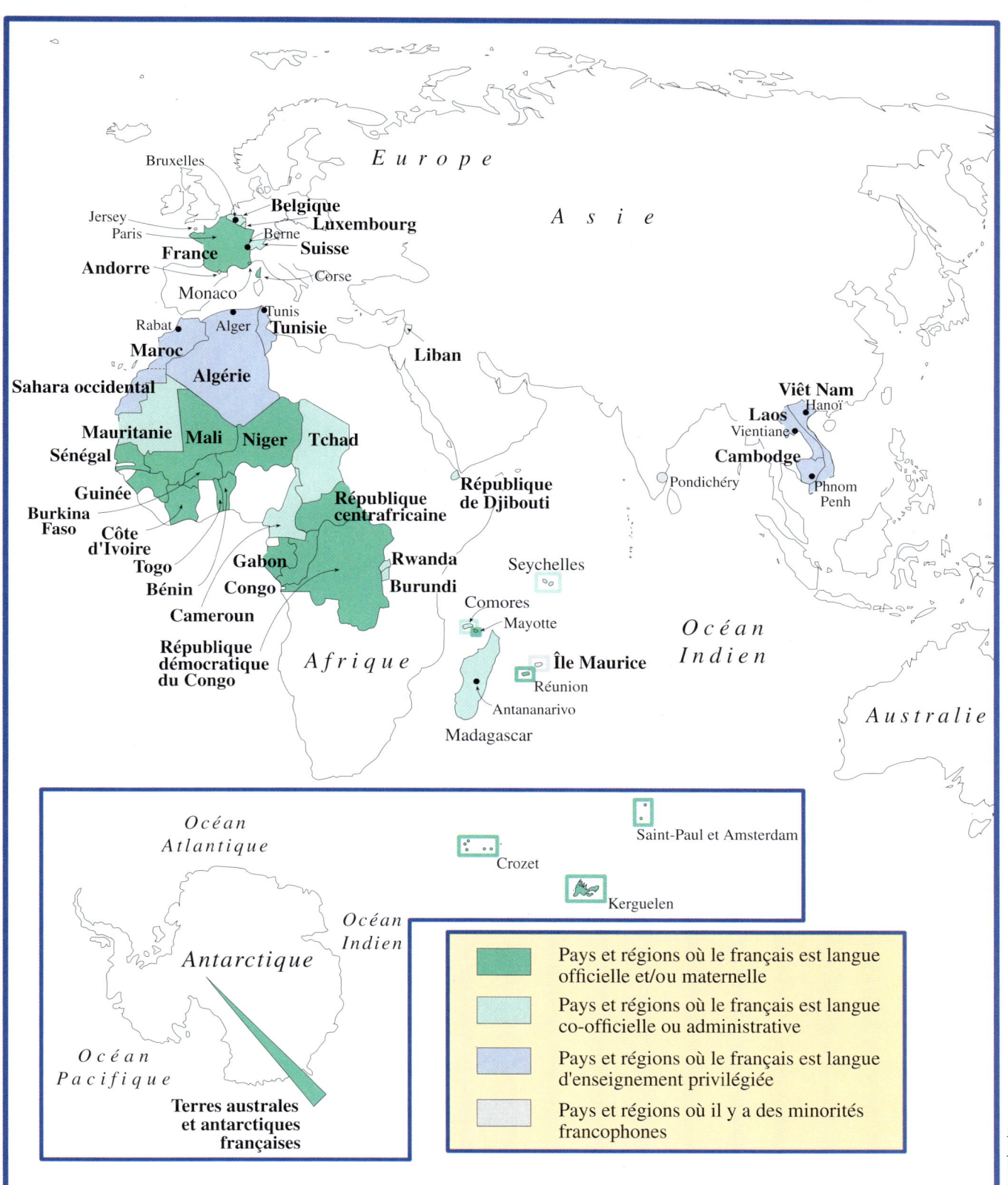

Le monde francophone
On commence!

	iLrn Heinle Learning Center		Internet web search
	www.cengagebrain.com		Pair work
	Audio		Group work

P

COMPÉTENCE

1 Greeting people
Les formules de politesse
Les salutations familières

2 Counting and describing your week
Les nombres de zéro à trente
Les jours de la semaine

3 Talking about yourself and your schedule
Un autoportrait
L'heure

4 Communicating in class
En cours
Des expressions utiles et l'alphabet

Comparaisons culturelles *L'heure officielle*

Vocabulaire

BIENVENUE DANS LE MONDE FRANCOPHONE!

With what do you immediately associate France and French culture – food and wine, film, art, music, literature, fashion…? Did you also know that France is a world leader in agriculture, science, technology, medicine, telecommunications, and aerospace engineering, and is the fifth largest export nation in the world?

 **PowerPoint P-1**

Suggestion. Ask students if they are familiar with these French names and if they can think of any others: Chanel, Vuitton, Alexandre Dumas, Victor Hugo, Bic, Yoplait, Danone, Pasteur, Airbus, Debussy, Vanessa Paradis.

Note. Each chapter of *Horizons* opens with a francophone culture section. Vocabulary used in this section is not treated as active vocabulary.

Le penseur de Rodin

La fusée Ariane 5

Le TGV

Bienvenue dans le monde francophone! *Welcome to the French-speaking world!*

On parle français au Québec...

et à Tahiti!

iLrn In the **Culture Modules** in the video library, see **The Francophone World**.

Look in the front of the book at the map of the countries and regions where French is spoken. Are you surprised that some of these countries and regions are francophone? Pick one of them and research its history on the Web to find out why people speak French there, and if they speak any other languages.

Suggestion for *Le savez-vous?* Divide the class into teams and use the questions for a trivia game. You may wish to add additional questions of your own.

Quick-reference answers.
1. a. about 40 **b.** every continent **c.** the north and west **d.** Quebec **e.** false **f.** true **g.** French Guiana **h.** Haiti, Guadeloupe, Martinique **i.** France, Belgium, Andorra, Switzerland, Monaco, Luxembourg **2.** about 270 million **3.** close to two million **4.** 11 million **5.** English, French **6.** f

Did you know that French is spoken throughout the world? Want to discover the world? Discover French – a language you can use right here in North America . . . and across the continents!

Le savez-vous?

What makes French one of the most important global languages? Take this quiz and find out. If you don't know, guess!

1. Look at the map in the front of the book to answer questions **a–i**.
   a. In how many countries is French spoken: about 5, about 25, about 40, or about 100?
   b. In or near which continents does French have a linguistic or cultural influence: Europe and Africa; Europe, Africa, and the Americas; or every continent?
   c. Are most of the francophone countries in Africa located in the north, the south, the east, or the west?
   d. Which province in Canada has the largest number of French speakers: British Columbia, Newfoundland and Labrador, or Quebec?
   e. True or false? French is not spoken in any areas of the South Pacific.
   f. True or false? There is a francophone influence in the USA, particularly in Louisiana and in the northeast.
   g. Where in South America is French spoken?
   h. In which three of these places in the Caribbean is French an important language: the Dominican Republic, Haiti, Guadeloupe, the Virgin Islands, the Bahamas, Martinique, the Cayman Islands?
   i. In which six of these European countries is French spoken: France, Portugal, Belgium, Italy, Andorra, Switzerland, Monaco, Albania, Luxembourg?
2. About how many people in the world speak French as their primary or secondary language: about 100 million, about 270 million, about 550 million?
3. In the USA, how many people speak French at home: close to one million, close to two million?
4. About how many French speakers are there in Canada: 5 million or 11 million?
5. The top two most frequently studied foreign languages worldwide and the only two global languages are _____ and _____.
6. French is an official language of: **a.** the United Nations, **b.** the International Olympic Committee, **c.** UNESCO, **d.** NATO, **e.** the European Union, **f.** all of these

---

On parle français au *French is spoken in* **et à** *and in*

Bienvenue dans le monde francophone! | cinq **5**

COMPÉTENCE 1

Greeting people

PowerPoint P-2

LES FORMULES DE POLITESSE

To greet adult strangers and those to whom you show respect, say:

Note culturelle

People in France generally shake hands when they meet and they often do not just say *bonjour*. Instead, they include the word *monsieur, madame, mademoiselle,* or the person's name. Traditionally, *madame* was used to address married women and *mademoiselle* for unmarried women. The use of *mademoiselle* was banned in official government documents in 2012 to make the treatment of women and men parallel. However, it is still commonly used by people to address very young women. In English, do you prefer to use *Ms.* or *Mrs.* and *Miss*?

1-2

— Bonjour, madame.
— Bonjour, monsieur. Je suis Hélène Cauvin. Et vous, comment vous appelez-vous?
— Je m'appelle Jean-Luc Bertin.

— Bonsoir, monsieur. **Comment allez-vous?**
— Bonsoir, madame. **Je vais très bien, merci.** Et vous?
— **Assez** bien.

Note de vocabulaire

1-3

1. **Bonjour** can be used to say *hello* at any time of day, but **bonsoir** can only be used to to say *good evening*.
2. Use **je vais** to say *how you are doing*. Use **je suis** to say *who you are* or to describe yourself.

Et vous? Comment allez-vous?
Je vais très bien.   Assez bien. / **Pas mal.** / **Comme ci comme ça.**   Pas très bien.

Notes
1. Boldfaced words are glossed at the bottom of the page. Try to guess their meaning from the context before looking at the glosses.
2. Audio for items accompanied by this symbol are accessed online.

iLrn Prononcez bien! See Modules 5, 6, 12, and 28.

PRONONCIATION

Les consonnes muettes et la liaison   1-4

Suggestion for *Prononciation*. Point out that the liaison mark is used to mark pronunciation and is not part of written French. For additional exercises on the *Prononciation* sections, also see the *Student Activities Manual* and *iLrn*.

In French, consonants at the end of words are often silent and **h** is always silent, as it is in some English words such as *hour* and *honest*. The consonants **c, r, f,** and **l** (CaReFuL) are the only consonants that are generally pronounced at the end of a word. However, do not pronounce the final **r** of **monsieur.**

Mar**c**   bonjou**r**   acti**f**   Chanta**l**

— Bonjou**r**, monsieur. Je m'appelle Pau**l** Richar**d**. Et vous, comment vous appelez-vous?
— Je m'appelle Henri Dula**c**. Comment allez-vous?
— Je vais très bien, merci.

If a consonant at the end of a word is followed by a word beginning with a vowel sound (**a, e, i, o, u, y**) or a mute **h,** the final consonant sound is often pronounced and is linked to the beginning of the next word. This linking is called **liaison.** In liaison, a single **s** is pronounced like a **z.**

Comment vous‿appelez-vous?   Comment‿allez-vous?

Comment allez-vous? *How are you?*   **Je vais très bien, merci.** *I'm doing very well, thank you.*   **Assez** *Fairly, Rather*   **Pas mal.** *Not bad(ly).*
Comme ci comme ça. *So-so.*

A Prononcez bien! Copy these sentences, crossing out the consonants that should not be pronounced and marking where liaison would occur.

EXEMPLE Comment‿allez-vous, monsieur?

1. Je suis Chantal Hubert.
2. Bonjour, madame. Comment allez-vous?
3. Très bien, monsieur. Comment vous appelez-vous?
4. Je m'appelle Henri Dufour. Et vous?

Now go back and reorder the four sentences to create a logical conversation to read aloud with a partner.

B Bonjour, monsieur/madame. Imagine that you are meeting a new French business associate. Read the following conversation with another student, changing the words in italics so that they describe you and your partner.

— Bonjour, *madame*. Comment allez-vous?

— Bonjour, *monsieur*. Je vais *très bien*, merci. Et vous?

— *Assez bien*, merci. Je suis *Jules Alami*. Et vous, comment vous appelez-vous?

— Je m'appelle *Emma Delors*.

C Que dit-on? Complete the conversations and act them out with a partner. Expand them and present them to the class.

1.

2.

3.

D Bonsoir! Imagine that you are at a formal reception. Go around the room and greet at least three people, exchanging names, and finding out how they are doing. Be sure to shake hands.

PowerPoint P-3

LES SALUTATIONS FAMILIÈRES

Note culturelle

When people greet one another in France, they usually shake hands or exchange a brief kiss on each cheek called a *bise*. What do people do when they greet each other in your region?

Suggestions. A. Briefly mention the difference between the uses of **tu** and **vous**. This is explained in detail in *Chapitre 1*. **B.** Point out that **Salut!** can be used to say *Hi!* and *Bye!*

1-5

Vocabulaire supplémentaire

Comment t'appelles-tu? / Comment tu t'appelles? *What's your name?* (familiar)
Comment vas-tu? *How are you?* (familiar)
Ciao! *Bye!* (familiar)
Bon week-end! *Have a good weekend!*
Bonne journée! *Have a good day!*

1-6

Note. The *Vocabulaire supplémentaire* provides options for personalized communication, but it is not tested in the *Testing Program*.

To greet classmates, friends, family members, or children, say:

— **Salut**, Pierre. **Ça va?**
— Salut, Juliette. **Ça va.** Et toi, **comment ça va**?
— Pas mal.

— Bonjour, je m'appelle Pauline. Et toi, tu t'appelles comment?
— Moi, je m'appelle Lucas.

Here are several ways to say good-bye. Use **À plus!** *and* **Salut!** *only in familiar situations. The other expressions may be used in either formal or familiar situations.*

Au revoir! *Good-bye!*
À tout à l'heure! *See you in a little while!*
À bientôt! *See you soon!*

À demain! *See you tomorrow!*
À plus tard! / À plus! *See you later!*
Salut! *Bye!*

PRONONCIATION

Les voyelles a, e, é, i, o et u 1-7

Prononcez bien! See Modules 7–10, 13, 23, and 27.

When you pronounce vowels in English, your tongue or lips move as you say them, so that the position of your mouth is not the same at the end of a vowel as at the beginning. In French, you hold your tongue and mouth firmly in one place while pronouncing vowels. This gives vowels a tenser sound. Practice saying these sounds.

a [a]:	à	ça	va	madame	mal	assez
e [ə]:	je	ne	que	de	demain	devoirs
é [e]:	café	pâté	bébé	été	préféré	répété
i [i]:	quiche	idéal	Paris	machine	six	merci
o [o]:	bientôt	vélo	hôtel	kilo	mots	trop
u [y]:	tu	salut	Luc	super	du	université

The vowel **o** has two pronunciations, [o] or [ɔ], and the vowel **e** has three pronunciations, [ə], [e], or [ɛ]. You will learn more about this in **Chapitre 3**. Final *unaccented* **e** is not generally pronounced, unless it is the only vowel in a word, as in **je**.

Franc*e̶*   madam*e̶*   appell*e̶*   un*e̶*   Ann*e̶*

Compare these words:

Mari**e** / mari**é**   divorc**e** / divorc**é**   fatigu**e** / fatigu**é**

Salut! *Hi!, Bye!*   **Ça va?** *How's it going?*   **Ça va.** *It's going fine.*   **Comment ça va?** *How's it going?*

A 🔊 **Prononcez bien!** Listen as different people give their name and indicate whether it is the first or second name shown.

1. Alisa   Élisa
2. Amélie   Émelie
3. Ali   Éli
4. Éliana   Iliana
5. Élona   Ilona
6. Albert   Hubert
7. Mariel   Muriel
8. Arielle Urielle
9. Abdel   Abdul
10. Éric   Ulrick
11. Nicolas Nicolo
12. Mano   Manu

B **Dans quelle situation?** Read each of these phrases aloud and say whether you would be more likely to hear it in situation **A** or **B**.

A.    B.

1. Bonjour, madame.
2. Salut, Thomas.
3. Très bien, merci. Et vous?
4. Tu t'appelles comment?
5. À plus!
6. Comment allez-vous?
7. Ça va. Et toi?
8. Comment vous appelez-vous?

Now give a logical response to each of the items above.

C **On dit…** What would you say in French . . .

1. to greet your professor during the day? in the evening?
2. to ask your professor's name? to tell him/her your name?
3. to ask your professor how he/she is doing?
4. to say that you are doing very well? fairly well? not badly? not very well?
5. to greet a classmate? to ask a classmate's name?
6. to ask a friend how it's going? to tell him/her that it's going well?
7. to say good-bye to someone? to say that you will see him/her tomorrow? soon? later today?

D **Que disent-ils?** Imagine that you and a classmate are meeting for the first time in class. Prepare a brief conversation with a partner in which you greet each other, exchange names, ask and say how it is going, and say good-bye. Shake hands or exchange **bises**.

Now redo the conversation as strangers meeting at a formal conference.

COMPÉTENCE 2

Counting and describing your week

 PowerPoint P-4

LES NOMBRES DE ZÉRO À TRENTE

Note culturelle

The French manner of counting on one's fingers is with palms facing in and starting with the thumb rather than the index finger. Ask your classmates how they count on their fingers. Are there any variations by nationality or regional origin?

Comptez de zéro à trente, **s'il vous plaît!**

0 zéro		
1 un	11 onze	21 vingt et un
2 deux	12 douze	22 vingt-deux
3 trois	13 treize	23 vingt-trois
4 quatre	14 quatorze	24 vingt-quatre
5 cinq	15 quinze	25 vingt-cinq
6 six	16 seize	26 vingt-six
7 sept	17 dix-sept	27 vingt-sept
8 huit	18 dix-huit	28 vingt-huit
9 neuf	19 dix-neuf	29 vingt-neuf
10 dix	20 vingt	30 trente

2 + 2 = 4   **Combien** font deux et deux?
             Deux et deux font quatre.
10 − 3 = 7   Combien font dix moins trois?
             Dix moins trois font sept.

Note. The teacher notes in each *Compétence* begin with a warm-up activity that reviews material from an earlier *Compétence*.

Warm-up. How would you respond if someone said the following to you? (Some have more than one possibility.) **1.** Bonjour, monsieur/madame. **2.** Salut. **3.** Comment vous appelez-vous? **4.** Tu t'appelles comment? **5.** Ça va? **6.** Comment allez-vous? **7.** À demain. **8.** À tout à l'heure.

Suggestions for *Prononciation*. **A.** Point out that: **1.** the **an / en** sound is similar to the English word *on* without the final *n* **2.** the **in / un / ain** sound is similar to the English word *an* without the final *n* **3.** the [ɔ̃] sound is similar to the English word *own* without pronouncing the final *n* **4.** the **on** in **monsieur** is an exception **5.** some speakers pronounce **un / um** as [œ̃]. **B.** Give students the phrase **C'est un bon vin blanc américain, Henri** to practice all the nasal sounds. **C.** For additional exercises on the *Prononciation* sections, also see the *Student Activities Manual* and *iLrn*.

PRONONCIATION

Les nombres et les voyelles nasales 1-9   **iLrn** *Prononcez bien!* See Modules **11, 32, 35, 36, 37,** and **38.**

Although final consonants are generally silent in French, they are pronounced in the following numbers when counting. In **sept**, the **p** is silent, but the final **t** is pronounced. The final **x** in **six** and **dix** is pronounced like the *s* in *so*.

   cinq   six   sept   huit   neuf   dix

Many numbers also contain nasal vowels. In French, when a vowel is followed by the letter **m** or **n** in the same syllable, the **m** or **n** is silent and the vowel is nasal. Use the words below as models of how to pronounce each of the nasal sounds. The letter combinations that are grouped together are all pronounced alike.

[ɑ̃]:	**an / am**	blanc	anglais	dimanche	chambre
	en / em	trente	comment	ensemble	embêtant
[ɛ̃]:	**in / im**	cinq	quinze	vingt	important
	un / um	un	lundi	brun	parfum
	ain / aim	demain	américain	mexicain	faim
[ɔ̃]:	**on / om**	onze	bonjour	non	nom
[jɛ̃]:	**ien**	bien	combien	canadien	rien
[wɛ̃]:	**oin**	moins	loin	coin	soin

Comptez *Count*   **de** *from*   **à** *to*   **s'il vous plaît** *please*   **Combien** *How much, How many*

10 *dix* | CHAPITRE PRÉLIMINAIRE

A. Prononcez bien!
How are the italicized letters in the following French-English cognates pronounced? Sort the words under the appropriate columns. Then listen and repeat, comparing the pronunciation of these words with their English cognates.

*im*bécile   *em*blème   j*un*gle   *im*pact   *am*bition   b*un*galow   c*om*plice
*in*stitut   *en*semble   refr*ain*   *an*thologie   s*ain*t   *am*phibien   b*om*be
*an*droïde   *con*cert   c*om*bat   bar*on*   *em*ployé   *en*cyclopédie   acti*on*

[ɛ̃] as in **un, cinq:**	[ɑ̃] as in **trente:**	[ɔ̃] as in **onze:**

Script for A. Prononcez bien!
[ɛ̃] as in **un, cinq:** imbécile, institut, jungle, refrain, impact, saint, bungalow

[ɑ̃] as in **trente:** androïde, emblème, ensemble, anthologie, ambition, employé, amphibien, encyclopédie

[ɔ̃] as in **onze:** concert, combat, baron, complice, bombe, action

B. C'est logique!
Complete each list with the logical numbers. Practice reading them aloud with a partner.

1. 1 □ 3 □ 5 □ □ 9 □ 11 □ □ 15 □ 17 □
2. 2 □ 4 □ □ 8 □ 10 □ □ 14 □ □ 18 □ 20
3. 0 □ 5 □ 10 □ □ 20 □ □ 30
4. 20 □ 19 □ 18 □ □ 16 □ 15 □
5. 10 □ 11 □ 12 □ □ 14 □ 15 □
6. 11 □ 13 □ 15 □ □ 19 □ 21 □ 23 □ 25 □

C. Combien font...?

1. 2 + 3 =
2. 1 + 3 =
3. 14 + 16 =
4. 18 + 12 =
5. 15 + 11 =
6. 13 − 5 =
7. 17 − 11 =
8. 30 − 13 =
9. 21 − 6 =

Suggestion for C. Combien font...? Before beginning the exercise, point out the examples of math problems on p. 10.

Suggestion for D. En taxi. Before beginning the activity, have students use the pronunciation rules they have learned to practice pronouncing the street names.

Suggestions for practicing numbers.
A. Have students write the numbers 0–30 in order on a piece of paper. Call out twenty numbers in random order, having students cross them out as you say them. Then have a student read aloud the ten numbers that remain. **B.** Have students write any five numerals between 0 and 30 on a sheet of paper. Randomly call out numbers, having students mark out the numerals if they have them on their paper. The first student with all five numerals marked out wins. **C.** Read pairs of numbers aloud and have students repeat the one that is larger: **2, 12; 9, 5; 6, 7; 11, 1; 20, 15; 3, 9; 4, 14; 18, 15; 19, 17; 20, 30. D.** Have students write a number between 1 and 30 on a sheet of paper. Class members take turns trying to guess a student's number. That student responds **plus que ça** *(more than that)* or **moins que ça** *(less than that)* until the class narrows it down to the correct number.

D. En taxi.
You've taken a taxi in a francophone country. Tell the driver the address of your destination.

EXEMPLE 28, avenue des Champs-Élysées
Vingt-huit avenue des Champs-Élysées, s'il vous plaît.

1. 27, boulevard Diderot
2. 11, rue Petit
3. 16, place Saint-Denis
4. 25, rue Bonaparte
5. 15, rue Sébastopol
6. 12, rue Garibaldi
7. 30, boulevard Gabriel
8. 7, rue du Temple

E. Comparaisons culturelles.
There are about 270 million French speakers in the world, of which 65 million live in France. Here are the ten countries with the largest number of French speakers after France. You will hear the number of speakers. Fill in the missing numbers.

1. la République démocratique du Congo: ___ millions
2. l'Algérie: ___ millions
3. la Côte d'Ivoire: ___ millions
4. le Canada: ___ millions
5. le Maroc: ___ millions
6. le Cameroun: ___ millions
7. la Tunisie: ___ millions
8. la Belgique: ___ millions
9. la Roumanie: ___ millions
10. le Sénégal: ___ millions

Suggestion for E. Comparaisons culturelles. This exercise is intended to familiarize students with the countries of the francophone world. You may wish to have students look at the map in the front of the book and find the countries listed. Populations are rounded to the nearest million, and include those who speak French as a second language.

Script for E. Comparaisons culturelles. 1. la République démocratique du Congo 24 millions **2.** l'Algérie 16 millions **3.** la Côte d'Ivoire 13 millions **4.** le Canada 11 millions **5.** le Maroc 10 millions **6.** le Cameroun 7 millions **7.** la Tunisie 7 millions **8.** la Belgique 6 millions **9.** la Roumanie 6 millions **10.** le Sénégal 4 millions

 PowerPoint P-5

Note *culturelle*

The first day of the week on French calendars is *lundi*, not *dimanche*. Do you think this would make it more convenient for planning your weekend?

Suggestion. You may wish to point out that you can also say: **On est quel jour? / On est...** and **Quel jour sommes-nous? / Nous sommes...**

Vocabulaire supplémentaire

pendant la semaine *during the week*
sauf *except*

Note *de vocabulaire*

1. Days of the week are not capitalized in French.

2. Use **du... au...** to say *from... to...* with days of the week when talking about what one does in general every week, but use **de... à...** instead to talk about what one is doing one particular week. **Je travaille** *du lundi au vendredi.* **Cette** *(This)* **semaine, je travaille** *de lundi à mercredi.*

3. Notice that you use two words, **ne... pas**, to say what someone does *not* do. They are usually placed around the verb in a sentence. You will learn more about this in **Chapitre 1.**

LES JOURS DE LA SEMAINE

To ask and tell the day of the week, say:

— **C'est quel jour, aujourd'hui?**
— C'est lundi.

lundi	mardi	mercredi	jeudi	vendredi	samedi	dimanche
⑰	18	19	20	21	22	23
24	25	26	27	28	29	30

© Cengage Learning

Do not translate the word **on** *to say that you do something* **on** *a certain day. To say that you do something* **every** *Monday (or another day), use* **le** *with the day of the week.*

Je travaille **lundi.**   *I work on Monday. (this coming Monday)*

Je travaille **le lundi.**   *I work on Mondays. (every Monday)*

To say **from** *what day* **to** *what day you do something every week, use* **du... au...** *Use* **tous les jours** *to say you do something* **every day.**

Je travaille **du** lundi **au** vendredi.   *I work Mondays to Fridays. (every week)*

Je travaille **tous les jours.**   *I work every day.*

Use **le matin, l'après-midi,** *or* **le soir** *to say you do something* **in the morning, in the afternoon,** *or* **in the evening,** *and* **le week-end** *to say* **on the weekend.** *Use* **avant** *to say* **before** *and* **après** *to say* **after.**

Le matin, je suis **à la maison** avant **le cours de français.**

L'après-midi, **je ne suis pas** à la maison. Je suis **en cours** de français et après, je suis **dans un autre cours.**

Le soir, **je travaille.**

Le week-end, **je ne travaille pas.** Je suis à la maison.

Line art on this page: © Cengage Learning

Les jours de la semaine *The days of the week*   **C'est quel jour, aujourd'hui?** *What day is it today?*   **à la maison** *at home*   **le cours de français** *French class*   **je ne suis pas** *I am not*   **en cours** *in class*   **dans un autre cours** *in another class*   **je travaille** *I work*   **je ne travaille pas** *I don't work*

Two friends are talking about their schedule this semester.
— **Tu es** en cours quels jours **ce semestre**?
— Je suis en cours le lundi, le mercredi et le vendredi.
— Tu travailles **aussi**?
— **Oui,** je travaille le mardi matin, le jeudi matin et le week-end.

A Salut!
Say good-bye to a friend and say that you'll see him/her on the indicated day.

EXEMPLE Monday   Au revoir! À lundi!

1. Sunday
2. Friday
3. Thursday
4. Tuesday
5. Saturday
6. Wednesday

B C'est quel jour?
Complete the statements that follow.

1. Aujourd'hui, c'est…
2. Demain, c'est…
3. Après-demain, c'est…
4. Les jours du week-end sont…
5. Avant le week-end, c'est…
6. Après le week-end, c'est…
7. Les jours du cours de français sont…
8. Je suis en cours…
9. Je travaille…
10. Je suis souvent *(often)* à la maison…

C Emploi du temps.
A student is talking about her week. Select the option in parentheses that is logical in each sentence.

1. Aujourd'hui, c'est (jeudi, le jeudi) et demain, c'est (vendredi, le vendredi).
2. Ce semestre, je suis en cours tous les jours (du, au) lundi (du, au) jeudi. Je ne suis pas en cours (vendredi, le vendredi).
3. Je suis en cours de français (après-midi, l'après-midi).
4. Ce semestre, je suis à la maison le matin (avant, après) le cours de français et je travaille l'après-midi (avant, après) le cours de français.
5. Ce semestre, je travaille (samedi, le samedi).
6. Ce week-end, je travaille (lundi, dimanche) aussi.

Now go back and change the statements so that each one is true for you. If a statement is already true, read it as it is.

D Et toi?
Complete these statements with the appropriate days of the week to describe yourself. Then, circulate through the classroom to try to find two people who completed at least three of the statements the same way you did. Write down their names.

EXEMPLE Je suis en cours **du lundi au vendredi.**
Je suis en cours du lundi au vendredi. Et toi?
Moi aussi, je suis en cours du lundi au vendredi. /
Moi, je suis en cours le mardi et le jeudi.

1. Ce semestre, je suis en cours…
2. Je ne suis pas en cours…
3. Je travaille… (Je ne travaille pas.)
4. Je suis souvent *(often)* à la maison…

À VOUS!

With a partner, read aloud the conversation at the top of the page, paying particular attention to the pronunciation. Then act it out, adapting it to make it true for you. Switch roles and do it again.

Tu es *You are*   **ce semestre** *this semester*   **aussi** *also, too*   **Oui** *Yes*

COMPÉTENCE 3

Talking about yourself and your schedule

 PowerPoint P-6

UN AUTOPORTRAIT

Note culturelle

In France, all students finishing secondary school have studied several years of a foreign language, and many have studied more than one. How does this compare to the situation in your area?

Note de grammaire

1. The words **je**, **ne**, and **de** change to **j'**, **n'**, and **d'** before vowels or a mute **h**. Similarly, **parce que** *(because)* changes to **parce qu'**. This is called elision.

2. Many adjectives in French add an **e** when describing females.

Warm-ups. A. Ask students simple math problems. **B.** Say various days and have students say whether they are in class, at work, or at home then. **(le lundi matin: Je suis en cours le lundi matin. / Je travaille le lundi matin. / Je suis à la maison le lundi matin.)**

Note. The expressions on this page are presented as lexical items only. Verb forms, negation, elision, and adjective agreement are explained in *Chapitre 1*.

Vocabulaire sans peine!

Vocabulaire sans peine! notes in the margin will help you learn vocabulary quickly by pointing out cognate patterns between English and French. Cognates are words that look similar and have the same meaning in two languages.
Note these patterns of adjectives indicating where people are from:
-ain = *-an*
américain(e) = *American*
africain(e) = *African*
-ien(ne) = *-ian*
canadien(ne) = *Canadian*
australien(ne) = *Australian*
How would you say these in French?
Mexican
Colombian

🔊 1-13

Use these expressions to talk about yourself. Include the ending in parentheses if you are a female.

Je suis... Je ne suis pas...	étudiant(e). professeur. américain(e). canadien(ne). **de** Chicago. **d'ici.**
J'habite... Je n'habite pas...	à Toronto. **seul(e).** avec **un ami / une amie.** avec deux amis / deux amies. avec ma famille. avec **un colocataire / une colocataire.** avec **un camarade de chambre / une camarade de chambre.**
Je travaille... Je ne travaille pas...	**beaucoup.** à l'université. **pour** Apple.
Je parle... Je ne parle pas...	anglais. français. espagnol. beaucoup en cours.
Je pense que le français est...	intéressant. assez **facile.** **un peu** difficile. super! assez cool!

Je suis canadienne, de Montréal, mais j'habite à Paris maintenant. Je parle anglais et français.

In the following conversation, two people meet at a Canadian-American cultural event in Montreal.

— **Vous êtes** canadien?
— Oui, je suis d'ici. Et vous, vous êtes canadienne aussi?
— Non, je suis de Cleveland.
— **Mais** vous parlez très bien français! Vous habitez ici **maintenant**?
— Oui, **parce que** je suis étudiante à l'université. Et vous, vous travaillez ici?
— Non, je suis étudiant aussi.

---

de (d') *from* **d'ici** *from here* **J'habite** *I live* **seul(e)** *alone* **un ami** *a friend* (male) **une amie** *a friend* (female) **un colocataire** *a housemate* (male) **une colocataire** *a housemate* (female) **un camarade de chambre** *a roommate* (male) **une camarade de chambre** *a roommate* (female) **beaucoup** *a lot* **pour** *for* **Je parle** *I speak, I talk* **Je pense que** *I think that* **facile** *easy* **un peu** *a little* **Vous êtes** *You are* (formal) **Mais** *But* **maintenant** *now* **parce que** *because*

14 quatorze | CHAPITRE PRÉLIMINAIRE

A. Moi, je... Choose the words in parentheses to describe yourself.

1. (Je suis / Je ne suis pas) étudiant(e).
2. (Je suis / Je ne suis pas) de Los Angeles.
3. (Je suis / Je ne suis pas) canadien(ne).
4. (J'habite / Je n'habite pas) à Minneapolis.
5. (J'habite / Je n'habite pas) avec ma famille.
6. (Je travaille / Je ne travaille pas) à l'université.
7. (Je parle / Je ne parle pas) très bien français.

B. Descriptions. A Canadian student is talking about himself. Change the words in italics as needed to make the paragraph true for you.

Je m'appelle *Chris Jones*. Je suis *canadien* et je suis de *Toronto*. J'habite *avec un colocataire* à *Chapel Hill*. Je suis *étudiant* à *l'université de Caroline du Nord*. Je parle *un peu* français. Je parle *anglais et espagnol*. Je pense que le français est *très facile*.

C. En rond. Work in groups of three. For each item, say what is true for you and ask the student on your right about himself/herself, using **Et toi?** He/She will complete the item and ask the person to his/her right the same question, who will answer and then ask you. Start each item with a different person.

1. Je m'appelle... Et toi?
2. Je suis... Et toi?
3. Je suis de... Et toi?
4. J'habite à... Et toi?
5. J'habite avec... (J'habite seul[e].) Et toi?
6. Je travaille... (Je ne travaille pas.) Et toi?
7. Je parle... Et toi?
8. Je pense que le français est... Et toi?

D. Et vous? Imagine that you and your partner have just met at an international professional conference in Denver. Take turns asking and answering these questions.

1. Comment vous appelez-vous?
2. Comment allez-vous?
3. Vous êtes étudiant(e)?
4. Vous travaillez aussi?
5. Vous êtes américain(e)?
6. Vous êtes d'ici?
7. Vous habitez à Denver maintenant?
8. Vous parlez espagnol?

À VOUS!

With a partner, read aloud the conversation on the preceding page, paying particular attention to the pronunciation. Then act it out, adapting it to make it true for you. Afterward, switch roles and do it again.

Note for the conversation (on the preceding page). New vocabulary includes all glossed words and **non, vous parlez, vous habitez,** and **vous travaillez.**

Suggestion for the conversation (on the preceding page). Present the conversation using the audio. Set the scene and have students listen with books closed for this information. **1.** What are the nationalities of the people? **2.** What does each person do? Then, have students read along as you play the conversation again.

Warm-up for A. Moi, je... Introduce the expressions **C'est vrai** and **Ce n'est pas vrai.** Make a statement about yourself and have a student say whether or not it is true for you: **1.** Je suis professeur. **2.** Je suis étudiant(e). **3.** J'habite à New York (Seattle, etc.). **4.** Je travaille à *[your school]*. **5.** Je pense que le français est facile. **6.** Je ne suis pas français(e). **7.** Je ne parle pas anglais. **8.** Je parle anglais maintenant. **9.** Je ne travaille pas. **10.** Je travaille à l'université. **11.** Je travaille maintenant. **12.** Je suis en cours de français maintenant.

 PowerPoint P-7

L'HEURE

Note culturelle

Traditionally, the French workday followed a particular pattern: breakfast in the early morning, work, a two-hour break for lunch, then work in the afternoon and into the evening. Most people went home for lunch to eat and be with their family. As France has become more urban, however, *la journée continue,* or a nine-to-five schedule, has become a way of life. There is a shorter lunch break, and people have lunch at work or in a nearby restaurant, fast-food chain, or café. How does this compare to a typical workday in your area?

Note de vocabulaire

1. Some people use **douze heures** for **midi**.
2. One may also tell time by telling the minutes after the hour, instead of using **et quart, et demie,** and **moins le quart.** For example, one hears **Il est trois heures quinze** or **Il est cinq heures trente.**
3. Use **du matin / de l'après-midi / du soir** only for indicating *A.M.* and *P.M.* when telling time. Use **le matin / l'après-midi / le soir** to say *in the morning / afternoon / evening* in all other cases.
4. Although *at* may be dropped in English, **à** cannot be omitted in French. To ask *(At) What time is French class?*, use **À quelle heure est le cours de français?**

Note. The use of the 24-hour clock is introduced in the *Comparaisons culturelles* section of this chapter and taught for active use in *Chapitre 6.*

Suggestions for presenting the time. First present the question **Quelle heure est-il?** and demonstrate telling time on the hour only. Give students paper-plate clocks with moveable hands and, as you say what time it is, have them show the time on their clocks. Next, present telling time between the hour and half-hour only and repeat the same activity. Then, do the same for telling time after the half-hour. Finally, have students tell time in five-minute intervals for one hour.

Quelle heure est-il? *What time is it?*

To tell time **on the hour,** use:

Il est + *number* + **heure(s).**   **Il est trois heures.**   *It's 3:00.*

When telling the time, use **une** *for* **one.** *The word* **heures** *has an* **s** *except in* **une heure.** *Don't use* **heure** *after* **midi** *and* **minuit.**

Il est une heure.   Il est deux heures.   Il est midi.   Il est minuit.

To tell time **after the hour up to the half hour,** use:

Il est + *number of hour* + **heure(s)** + *minutes*.   **Il est trois heures cinq.**   *It's 3:05.*

For **a quarter after,** *use* **et quart** *and for* **half after,** *use* **et demie.** *With* **midi** *and* **minuit,** *use* **et demi** *without the final* **e.** *These are the only times* **et** *is used in telling time.*

Il est une heure dix.   Il est une heure et quart.   Il est une heure et demie.   Il est midi et demi.   Il est minuit et demi.

To tell time **until the next hour,** use:

Il est + *number of next hour* + **heure(s) moins** + *minutes until the hour.*   **Il est six heures moins cinq.**   *It's 5:55.*

For **a quarter until the hour,** *use* **moins le quart.** *This is the only time* **le** *is used in telling time.*

Il est deux heures moins vingt-cinq.   Il est deux heures moins vingt.   Il est deux heures moins le quart.

Line art on this page: © Cengage Learning

The following clock is useful in visualizing how time is expressed. With **moins...**, remember to use the number of the *upcoming* hour.

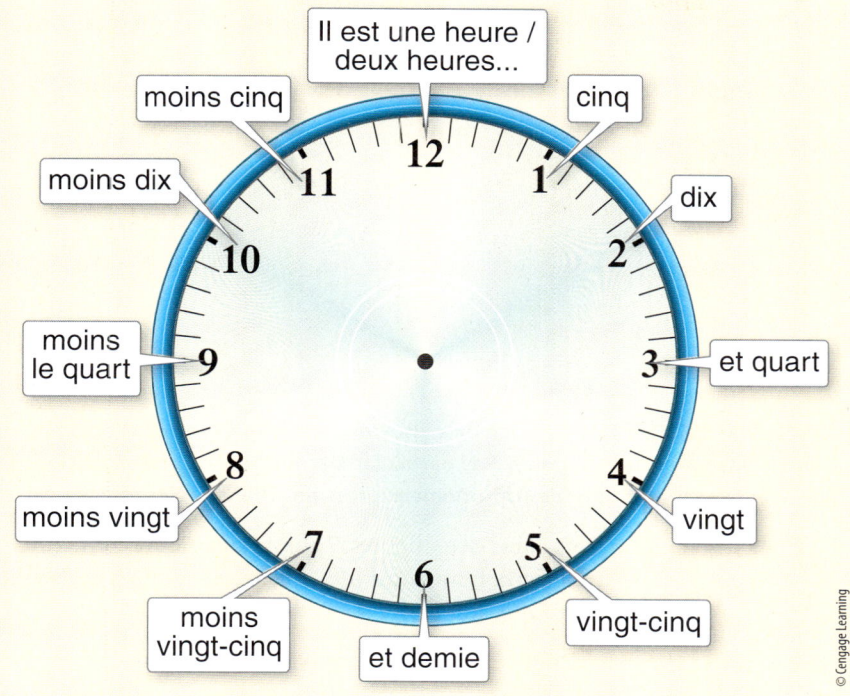

Instead of using **A.M.** and **P.M.**, use the expressions that follow, except with **midi** or **minuit**.

du matin *(after midnight until noon)*	Il est huit heures **du matin.**
de l'après-midi *(after noon until 6 P.M.)*	Il est une heure **de l'après-midi.**
du soir *(6 P.M. until midnight)*	Il est neuf heures **du soir.**

Use **à** to ask or tell **at what time** something takes place.

Le cours de français est **à quelle heure**?

 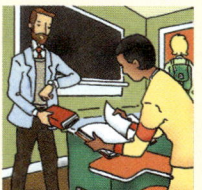

Le cours de français **commence** à une heure.

Le cours de français **finit** à deux heures et quart.

To say that you do something **from** a certain time **to** another, use **de... à.**

Le lundi, je suis en cours **de** neuf heures **à** une heure.

You can find a list of the new words from this *Compétence* on page 27 and access the audio online.

---

commence *begins* **finit** *finishes, ends*

PRONONCIATION

L'heure et la liaison
1-14

Notice that there is liaison before the word **heure(s)** and that the pronunciation of some numbers changes in this liaison. Practice pronouncing these times.

Quelle heure est‿il?

Il est deux‿heures.   Il est sept‿heures.
Il est trois‿heures.   Il est huit‿heures.
Il est cinq‿heures.   Il est neuf‿heures.
Il est six‿heures.   Il est dix‿heures.

Il est dix heures moins le quart.

A Prononcez bien!
For each time shown, ask your partner what time it is, using the two expressions given. Pay particular attention to the pronunciation. Your partner will respond with the appropriate expression. Change roles after each item.

EXEMPLE   2:00   Il est deux heures. / Il est deux heures et demie.
— Il est deux heures ou *(or)* il est deux heures et demie?
— Il est deux heures.

1. *2:10*   Il est deux heures dix. / Il est deux heures et quart.
2. *3:15*   Il est trois heures vingt. / Il est trois heures et quart.
3. *4:20*   Il est quatre heures vingt-cinq. / Il est quatre heures vingt.
4. *5:30*   Il est cinq heures et demie. / Il est cinq heures et quart.
5. *6:45*   Il est six heures moins le quart. / Il est sept heures moins le quart.
6. *8:35*   Il est neuf heures moins vingt-cinq. / Il est huit heures moins vingt-cinq.
7. *9:50*   Il est neuf heures moins dix. / Il est dix heures moins dix.
8. *12:00 A.M.*   Il est midi. / Il est minuit.

B Quelle heure est-il?
Take turns asking and telling the time with a partner.

EXEMPLE
— Quelle heure est-il?
— Il est une heure de l'après-midi.

1.    2.    3.    4.

5.    6.    7.    8.

C Il est quelle heure?
1-15
Write the times you hear. Notice how the word **heure(s)** is abbreviated in French.

EXEMPLE   VOUS ENTENDEZ *(YOU HEAR)*: Il est dix heures et quart.
VOUS ÉCRIVEZ *(YOU WRITE)*: **10h15**

D **Où êtes-vous?** Say whether or not you are usually at the indicated place or with the indicated people at the time given.

EXEMPLE Le lundi à 9h15 du matin, *je suis / je ne suis pas* en cours.
Le lundi à neuf heures et quart du matin, je suis en cours.
Le lundi à neuf heures et quart du matin, je ne suis pas en cours.

1. Le lundi à 7h00 du matin, *je suis / je ne suis pas* à la maison.
2. Le mercredi à 2h30 de l'après-midi, *je suis / je ne suis pas* en cours de français.
3. Le jeudi à 5h20 de l'après-midi, *je suis / je ne suis pas* dans un autre cours.
4. Le vendredi à 10h45 du soir, *je suis / je ne suis pas* avec des amis.
5. Le samedi à minuit, *je suis / je ne suis pas* seul(e).
6. Le dimanche à 7h30 du soir, *je suis / je ne suis pas* avec ma famille.

E **Quand?** Complete these sentences so that they are true for you the first day of the week you have your French class.

EXEMPLE Je suis à la maison **avant sept heures et demie.**
   before   [time]

1. Je suis à la maison _____ _____.
   before   [time]
2. Je suis à l'université _____ _____. (J'habite sur *[on]* le campus.)
   after   [time]
3. Le cours de français commence _____ _____.
   at   [time]
4. Le cours de français finit _____ _____.
   at   [time]
5. Je suis en cours _____ _____ _____ _____.
   from   [time]   to   [time]
6. Je travaille _____ _____ _____ _____. (Je ne travaille pas.)
   from   [time]   to   [time]
7. Je suis à la maison _____ _____.
   after   [time]

F **Mon emploi du temps.** On a sheet of paper, make two copies of this schedule, changing it to describe your schedule on one copy and leaving the other one blank. With a partner, take turns describing your schedules. On the blank schedule, fill in your partner's schedule as he/she describes it to you.

EXEMPLE **Le lundi, je suis en cours de dix heures à une heure. Je travaille de deux heures à quatre heures. Je suis à la maison après cinq heures. Le mardi...**

lundi		mardi	
8:00		8:00	
9:00		9:00	
10:00	en cours	10:00	
11:00		11:00	
12:00		12:00	
1:00		1:00	
2:00	travail	2:00	
3:00		3:00	
4:00		4:00	
5:00	à la maison	5:00	

Suggestion for F. Mon emploi du temps. You may prefer to distribute two photocopies of a blank schedule to each student to save class time.

Supplemental activity. Read these pairs of times and have students repeat the later one: **1.** Il est trois heures. / Il est cinq heures. **2.** Il est quatre heures et demie. / Il est quatre heures et quart. **3.** Il est une heure moins le quart. / Il est une heure moins dix. **4.** Il est deux heures moins vingt. / Il est deux heures moins cinq. **5.** Il est huit heures dix. / Il est huit heures moins dix. **6.** Il est onze heures et demie. / Il est midi moins dix. **7.** Il est une heure et demie. / Il est onze heures. **8.** Il est cinq heures moins dix. / Il est cinq heures moins le quart.

COMPÉTENCE 4

Communicating in class

 PowerPoint P-8

EN COURS

Note culturelle

Generally, homework is less controlled at French universities than in the U.S. and Canada, and course grades are mainly determined by a few tests. Students are responsible for their daily progress. Would you prefer to have this type of system?

Warm-ups. A. Make statements like the following ones about yourself and elicit similar statements from students by saying **Et vous?** at the end of each one. **1.** Je m'appelle *[your name]*. Et vous? **2.** Je suis de *[your hometown]*. Et vous? **3.** Je suis *[your nationality]*. Et vous? **4.** J'habite *[with whom]*. Et vous? **5.** Je travaille à l'université. Et vous? **6.** Je suis professeur. Et vous? **7.** Je travaille *[days]*. Et vous? **8.** Le lundi *[or another day]*, je travaille de *[time]* à *[time]*. Et vous? **9.** Je suis en cours *[days]*. Et vous? **10.** Je parle français, anglais, *[a language]*. Et vous? **B.** Say various times of day and have students say whether they are generally home at that time.

Suggestions. A. Teach these expressions for recognition only. These expressions may be presented and practiced using total physical response activities. **B.** Give one of the classroom commands and either act it out or do something else. Students say **oui,** if you are following the directions, **non,** if not. **C.** Perform an action and give students two statements to choose from to indicate which directions you are following. **D.** Play **Jacques a dit** *(Simon says)*, using classroom commands.

Le professeur **dit aux** étudiants:

EN COURS

Ouvrez votre livre à la page 23.

Fermez votre livre.

Écoutez la question.

Répondez à la question.

Allez au tableau.

Écrivez la réponse avec une phrase complète.

Prenez une feuille de papier et un crayon ou un stylo.

Faites l'exercice A à la page 21.

Donnez-moi votre feuille de papier.

À LA MAISON

Lisez la page 17 et **apprenez** les mots de vocabulaire.

Préparez l'examen pour le **prochain** cours.

Faites **les devoirs** dans **le cahier.**

Line art on this page: © Cengage Learning

dit aux *says to the*   **Écoutez** *Listen to*   **Faites** *Do*   **Donnez-moi** *Give me*   **Lisez** *Read*   **apprenez** *learn*   **prochain(e)** *next*   **les devoirs** *the homework*   **le cahier** *the workbook*

PRONONCIATION

Prononcez bien! See Modules 16 and 31.

Les voyelles groupées

Practice the pronunciation of the following vowel combinations. Notice that the combination **eu** has two different sounds, depending on whether it is followed by a pronounced consonant in the same syllable.

- a + u / e + u / o + u

au, eau [o]:	au	aussi	beaucoup	tableau
eu [ø]:	deux	un peu	jeudi	monsieur
eu [œ]:	heure	neuf	professeur	seul(e)
ou [u]:	vous	douze	jour	pour

- a + i / e + i / o + i / u + i

ai [ɛ]:	français	je vais	je sais	vrai
ei [ɛ]:	treize	seize	beige	neige
oi [wa]:	moi	toi	trois	au revoir
ui [ɥi]:	huit	minuit	aujourd'hui	je suis

A. Prononcez bien!
Listen and repeat the following cognates, paying attention to the pronunciation of the italicized vowel combinations. Then, go back and say whether the words describe you (Je suis… / Je ne suis pas…). Use the form indicated in parentheses if you are a female.

1. *au*stralien(ne)
2. *au*daci*eu*x (*au*daci*eu*se)
3. c*ou*rag*eu*x (c*ou*rag*eu*se)
4. c*ou*rt*oi*s(e)
5. japon*ai*s(e)
6. millionn*ai*re
7. chin*oi*s(e)
8. b*ou*rge*oi*s(e)
9. s*ui*sse

B. Comment dit-on…?
Decide which of the words given could be used to make logical commands. Read all of the possibilities aloud.

1. (Allez / Lisez / Écoutez) la phrase.
2. (Faites / Allez / Écrivez) les devoirs.
3. (Comptez / Fermez / Ouvrez) de 0 à 30.
4. (Fermez / Donnez-moi / Allez) le cahier.
5. (Allez / Fermez / Ouvrez) au tableau.
6. (Répondez / Lisez / Apprenez) les mots de vocabulaire.

C. En cours.
In groups, make up commands your instructor might give you by matching items from the two columns. Which group can come up with the most commands?

Lisez…	… le professeur.
Apprenez…	… l'exercice A.
Comptez…	… de 0 à 30.
Écoutez…	… les devoirs.
Prenez…	… une feuille de papier.
Écrivez…	… la phrase.
Faites…	… les mots de vocabulaire.

Vocabulaire sans peine!

Noticing cognate patterns can help you learn new words more quickly. Many adjectives ending in -*ous* in English are similar in French, but end with -**eux** (-**euse**).

-**eux** (-**euse**) = -*ous*
sérieux (sérieuse) = *serious*
victorieux (victorieuse) = *victorious*

How would you say these in French?
religious
scandalous

Suggestion for *Prononciation*. You may wish to point out that some speakers pronounce **ai** as [e] when it is in an open syllable. For additional exercises on the *Prononciation* sections, see the *Student Activities Manual* and *iLrn*.

Script for A. Prononcez bien!
1. australien, australienne 2. audacieux, audacieuse 3. courageux, courageuse 4. courtois, courtoise 5. japonais, japonaise 6. millionnaire 7. chinois, chinoise 8. bourgeois, bourgeoise 9. suisse

Follow-up for B. *Comment dit-on…?* Have students say whether you are instructing them to do something **en cours** or **à la maison** if you give the following instructions. 1. Fermez votre livre. 2. Apprenez les mots de vocabulaire. 3. Écoutez et répondez, s'il vous plaît. 4. Allez au tableau. 5. Prenez une feuille de papier. 6. Lisez les pages 12, 13 et 14. 7. Faites les devoirs dans le cahier. 8. Ouvrez votre livre à la page 23.

 PowerPoint P-9

DES EXPRESSIONS UTILES ET L'ALPHABET

When you hear new words, it may be helpful to see how they are spelled. You can ask:

Ça s'écrit comment?	How is that written?
Ça s'écrit avec ou sans accent?	Is that written with or without an accent?
Ça s'écrit avec un ou deux **s** en français / en anglais?	Is that written with one or two **s**'s in French / in English?

a	a	**A**nne	**q**	ku	**Q**uentin
b	bé	**B**runo	**r**	erre	**R**omane
c	cé	**C**aroline	**s**	esse	**S**téphane
d	dé	**D**idier	**t**	té	**T**ristan
e	e	**E**mma	**u**	u	**U**rsula
f	effe	**F**rançoise	**v**	vé	**V**alérie
g	gé	**G**abriel/**G**érard	**w**	double vé	**W**ladimir
h	hache	**H**ugo	**x**	iks	**X**avier
i	i	**I**sabelle	**y**	i grec	**Y**ves
j	ji	**J**ules	**z**	zède	**Z**oé
k	ka	**K**arima			
l	elle	**L**ola	é = **e** accent aigu		ç = **c** cédille
m	emme	**M**argot	è = **e** accent grave		' = apostrophe
n	enne	**N**athan	â = **a** accent circonflexe		- = trait d'union
o	o	**O**livier	ï = **i** tréma		ll = deux l
p	pé	**P**ascal			

You may also need to use these expressions.

Comment? Répétez, s'il vous plaît.	*What? Please repeat.*
— Vous comprenez?	*— Do you understand?*
— Oui, je comprends.	*— Yes, I understand.*
Non, je ne comprends pas.	* No, I don't understand.*
— Comment dit-on *a pen* en français?	*— How does one say **a pen** in French?*
— On dit **un stylo**.	*— One says **un stylo**.*
— Qu'est-ce que ça veut dire **votre**?	*— What does **votre** mean?*
— Ça veut dire *your*.	*— It means **your**.*
— Je ne sais pas.	*— I don't know.*
— Merci. / Merci bien.	*— Thank you., Thanks.*
— De rien.	*— You're welcome.*
— Pardon. / Excusez-moi.	*— Excuse me.*

Note d'orthographe

1. The **cédille** occurs only on the letter **c** and causes it to be pronounced /s/ before the vowels **a, o,** and **u**.
2. The accent marks occur only on vowels, and the **accent aigu** only on the vowel **e**.
3. Accents in French do not indicate stress. They are used to indicate a difference in pronunciation (**é** versus **è**), to differentiate two words (**ou** [*or*] versus **où** [*where*]), or for historical reasons.

You will learn about accent marks and the use of the **cédille** in *Chapitre 2*. For now, learn the accents as part of the spelling of a new word.

Note de vocabulaire

1. There are several ways to say *You're welcome*.
De rien.
Il n'y a pas de quoi.
Je vous en prie. (formal)
Je t'en prie. (familiar)
2. **Pardon** and **excusez-moi** are not always interchangeable. Generally, use **pardon** to pass through a crowd or get someone's attention. Use **excusez-moi (excuse-moi** [familiar]) if you want to say you're sorry about something you have done or to get someone's attention.

Prononcez bien! See Modules 2 and 3.

Suggestion for *A. Des animaux*. Have students spell the words back to you as you write them, so that students may check their work.

Script for *A. Des animaux*. EXEMPLE
A-N-I-M-A-L **1.** G-I-R-A-F-E **2.** R-H-I-N-O-C-É-R-O-S **3.** C-H-I-M-P-A-N-Z-É **4.** É-L-É-P-H-A-N-T **5.** C-R-O-C-O-D-I-L-E **6.** S-E-R-P-E-N-T **7.** L-É-Z-A-R-D **8.** O-I-S-E-A-U **9.** C-H-I-E-N **10.** C-H-A-T

Follow-up for *A. Des animaux*. Write each of these words on a separate slip of paper. Have students take turns drawing a slip and spelling out the word they draw for the rest of the class to write down. You may need to add additional words, depending on the size of your class: **bonsoir, monsieur, parlez, travaille, café, après, bientôt, heure, français, américaine, après-midi, plaît, naïve, université, appelle, garage, généreux, joyeux, prestigieux, vertueux.**

A **Des animaux.** Listen as the names of some animals are spelled out and write them down.
1-18

EXEMPLE   VOUS ENTENDEZ: A-N-I-M-A-L
                VOUS ÉCRIVEZ: **animal**

B Comparaisons culturelles.
Working with a group, see how many of the names of these francophone places you can complete within the time limit set by your professor. The team with the most correct names wins. When you are done, take turns spelling out the names of the places.

EXEMPLE _Q_ uébec Q-U-E accent aigu B-E-C

1. _____ rance
2. _____ lgérie
3. _____ ôte d'Ivoire
4. _____ ahiti
5. _____ uadeloupe
6. _____ aroc
7. _____ énégal
8. _____ ouisiane
9. _____ elgique

Quick-reference answers for *B. Comparaisons culturelles.* 1. F 2. A 3. C 4. T 5. G 6. M 7. S 8. L 9. B

Supplemental information. Text messages generally use abbreviations, such as **XLntb** for **excellent,** or letters that are pronounced like the desired sounds, such as **Je c** for **Je sais.** It is also common to drop silent letters, especially at the end of a word. (Source: http://french.about.com/library/writing/bl-texting.htm)

C Les SMS *(text messages).*
Here are some common abbreviations used in French text messages (**les SMS** or **les textos**). First, spell them out, using the French alphabet and numbers. Then, match each one to its equivalent. In some cases, attempting to read the symbols aloud may help you determine the meaning.

| de rien | ciné *(cinema)* | à demain | je sais | excellent | à plus (tard) |
| Tu es OK? | | bonjour | salut | s'il vous plaît | |

1. A+
2. Je c
3. 2 ri 1
4. a2m1
5. 6né
6. XLnt
7. TOK
8. SLT
9. SVP
10. bjr

Quick reference answers for *C. Les SMS*. 1. à plus (tard) 2. je sais 3. de rien 4. à demain 5. ciné 6. excellent 7. Tu es OK? 8. salut 9. s'il vous plaît 10. bonjour

D Qu'est-ce que ça veut dire? Comment dit-on…?
With a partner, take turns asking and telling what each of the following words or phrases means.

EXEMPLE   ouvrez   — Qu'est-ce que ça veut dire *ouvrez*?
— Ça veut dire *open*!

| ouvrez | fermez | le prochain cours | les mots | apprenez |
| faites | un crayon | un stylo | l'examen | lisez |

Now, ask your partner how to say in French each of the following words or phrases. When he/she tells you, ask how it is spelled.

EXEMPLE   *open*   — Comment dit-on *open* en français?
— On dit *ouvrez.*
— Ça s'écrit comment?
— Ça s'écrit O-U-V-R-E-Z.

| open | please | Thanks! | You're welcome. | the workbook |
| I don't know. | Excuse me. | the homework | the next class | |

Supplemental activities. A. Have students indicate whether these expressions would more likely be said by **les étudiants** or **le professeur:** 1. Vous comprenez? 2. Apprenez les mots de vocabulaire pour demain. 3. Je ne comprends pas. Qu'est-ce que ça veut dire en anglais? 4. Je ne sais pas la réponse. 5. Faites les devoirs dans le cahier. 6. Donnez-moi les devoirs, s'il vous plaît. **B.** Have students play Hangman using the names of francophone countries from the map in the front of the book, the French names listed with the alphabet, or other words they know. **C.** Tell students to introduce themselves to a classmate, who will ask them to spell their last name. **EXEMPLE** — Bonjour, je suis Paul Wyndel. / — Wyndel? Ça s'écrit comment? / W-Y-N-D-E-L. Et toi, tu t'appelles comment? / — Je m'appelle Lynn Phan. / — Phan? Ça s'écrit comment? / — P-H-A-N.

E Réponses.
Look back at the expressions above and below the alphabet on the preceding page. What would you say in the following situations?

1. You understood the question, but you don't know the answer.
2. You want to know how to say *giraffe* in French.
3. You want to know if *giraffe* is written with one *f* or two in French.
4. You want to know what the word **fou** means in English.
5. You need to pass through a group of students.
6. You stepped on someone's foot.

You can find a list of the new words from this ***Compétence*** on page 27 and access the audio online.

COMPARAISONS CULTURELLES

L'HEURE OFFICIELLE

Note. The vocabulary in this section does not appear in the end-of-chapter vocabulary lists, and is meant for recognition only. You may wish to let students know in advance whether you intend to test them on this vocabulary. The use of the 24-hour clock is practiced for active use in *Chapitre 6*.

Suggestions for *A. Horaire de train*.
A. Elicit from students the pronunciation of the words **train** and **arrive**. **B.** Have students also state times in conversational time. Point out that they would generally hear them stated in official time. **C.** Tell students that the **TGV (train à grande vitesse)** travels at around 186 miles per hour.

In all schedules and sometimes in conversations, the French use the 24-hour clock rather than the conversational manner of telling time that you have already learned. With the 24-hour clock, you continue counting 13 to 24, instead of beginning with 1 to 12 o'clock again during the P.M. hours. For example, 2:00 A.M. is **deux heures** and 2:00 P.M. is **quatorze heures.** The expressions **du matin, de l'après-midi,** and **du soir** are not used with the 24-hour clock.

When using the 24-hour clock, state the hour and the number of minutes after the hour with a number, instead of using **midi, minuit, et quart, et demie,** or **moins le quart.** You will need the numbers **quarante** *(forty)* and **cinquante** *(fifty)*.

How would you express each of these times in conversational time? In official time?

| 12:30 A.M. | 3:45 A.M. | 1:20 P.M. |
| 10:40 A.M. | 12:15 P.M. | 11:55 P.M. |

Il est quatorze heures six.

A **Horaire de train.** You are flying into Paris to study for a month at a French language institute in the town of **Le Creusot**. The institute's website lists the following **TGV** trains you can take daily from the **Gare de Lyon** station in Paris to **Le Creusot**. Say what time each train arrives, using official time. The first one has been done as an example.

Paris - Le Creusot TGV	
Départ Paris Gare de Lyon	Arrivée Le Creusot TGV
6h10	7h32
7h30	8h54
13h00	14h27
16h00	17h22
18h00	19h25
20h00	21h22

EXEMPLE 6h10
Le train de six heures dix arrive à sept heures trente-deux.

B À la télé. A friend wants to watch these shows on TV5, the international French TV station. Tell him what time each one is on. First use official time, then convert it to conversational time.

EXEMPLE *Monsieur Dictionnaire*
Monsieur Dictionnaire est à treize heures vingt-huit, c'est-à-dire *(that is to say)* à une heure vingt-huit de l'après-midi.

1. *Des chiffres et des lettres*
2. *Objectif nature*
3. *Chaplin*
4. *Le journal de France 2*
5. *Un livre un jour*
6. *Pauline et François*

Suggestions for B. À la télé. A. Model the pronunciation of the names of the shows. **B.** Have students visit the website TV5.org. **C.** Tell students that a **journal** is a newscast. **D.** Have students go back and redo various activities from pages 18–19, giving the time in official time.

Grille des programmes

Mercredi 25 avril

Matin
- 04:01 UN PRINTEMPS EN MÉDITERRANÉE
- 04:54 COURTS SÉJOURS
- 05:00 FLASH INFO
- 05:02 LE JOURNAL DE RADIO-CANADA
- 05:29 TV5MONDE LE JOURNAL AFRIQUE
- 05:42 TÉLÉMATIN
- 06:30 LE JOURNAL DE LA RTBF
- 07:00 TV5MONDE LE JOURNAL
- 07:23 PORTRAITS
- 07:30 TV5MONDE LE JOURNAL
- 07:53 ET DIEU CRÉA... LAFLAQUE
- 08:00 TÉLÉMATIN
- 08:48 KAAMELOTT
- 09:00 TV5MONDE LE JOURNAL
- 09:24 CHACUN SA TERRE
- 09:30 TV5MONDE LE JOURNAL
- 09:53 DES HOMMES ET DES BÊTES
- 10:01 COQUELICOT & CANAPÉ
- 10:28 UN LIVRE UN JOUR
- 10:31 L'ÉPICERIE
- 10:55 UN OBJET, UNE HISTOIRE
- 11:00 TV5MONDE LE JOURNAL
- 11:23 L'INVITÉ
- 11:32 «10»
- 11:55 FLASH INFO

Après-midi
- 12:01 VU SUR TERRE
- 12:54 COURTS SÉJOURS
- 13:00 LE JOURNAL DE LA RTS
- → 13:28 MONSIEUR DICTIONNAIRE
- 13:30 FLASH INFO
- 13:33 TOUT LE MONDE VEUT PRENDRE SA PLACE
- → 14:19 DES CHIFFRES ET DES LETTRES
- 14:49 PLUS BELLE LA VIE
- 15:15 TV5MONDE LE JOURNAL
- → 15:25 OBJECTIF NATURE
- 15:30 T'CHOUPI ET DOUDOU
- 15:35 PETIT LAPIN BLANC
- 15:39 PETIT LAPIN BLANC
- → 15:44 CHAPLIN
- 15:51 LOU!
- 16:04 STELLINA
- 16:29 «10»
- 16:56 MERCI PROFESSEUR!
- → 17:00 LE JOURNAL DE FRANCE 2
- → 17:26 UN LIVRE UN JOUR
- 17:28 LE POINT
- 18:29 QUESTIONS POUR UN CHAMPION
- 19:00 TV5MONDE LE JOURNAL
- 19:24 LE JOURNAL DE L'ÉCONOMIE
- 19:30 DES RACINES & DES AILES

Soir
- 21:30 TV5MONDE LE JOURNAL
- → 22:00 PAULINE ET FRANÇOIS
- 23:37 HURLEMENT D'UN POISSON
- 00:00 TV5MONDE LE JOURNAL
- 00:22 KAAMELOTT
- 00:35 LA GRANDE LIBRAIRIE
- 01:36 NEC PLUS ULTRA
- 02:02 ACOUSTIC
- 02:30 FLASH INFO
- 02:34 LE MARQUIS

C À discuter

1. Is the 24-hour clock used in your country? In what circumstances?
2. Does using the 24-hour clock make things clearer or less clear to you? Why?

Visit www.cengagebrain.com for additional cultural information and activities.

VOCABULAIRE

Audio Flashcards

COMPÉTENCE 1

Greeting people

GREETING PEOPLE
Bonjour. — Hello., Good morning.
Bonsoir. — Good evening.
monsieur (M.) — Mr., sir
madame (Mme) — Mrs., madam
mademoiselle (Mlle) — Miss
Comment allez-vous? — How are you? (formal)
   Je vais très bien. — I'm doing very well.
   Assez bien. — Fairly well.
   Comme ci comme ça. — So-so.
   Pas mal. — Not bad(ly).
   Pas très bien. — Not very well.
Salut! — Hi!, Bye!
Comment ça va? / Ça va? — How's it going? (familiar)
   Ça va. — It's going fine.
et — and
Et vous? — And you? (formal)
Et toi? — And you? (familiar)
moi — me
merci — thank you, thanks

EXCHANGING NAMES
Comment vous appelez-vous? — What's your name? (formal)
Tu t'appelles comment? — What's your name? (familiar)
   Je m'appelle... — My name is...
   Je suis... — I am, I'm...

SAYING GOOD-BYE
À bientôt. — See you soon.
À demain. — See you tomorrow.
À plus tard. / À plus. — See you later.
À tout à l'heure. — See you in a little while.
Au revoir. — Good-bye.

COMPÉTENCE 2

Counting and describing your week

COUNTING TO 30
Comptez de... à... — Count from... to...
   s'il vous plaît — please (formal)
   un, deux, trois, quatre, — one, two, three, four,
   cinq, six, sept, huit, — five, six, seven, eight,
   neuf, dix, onze, douze, — nine, ten, eleven, twelve,
   treize, quatorze, quinze, — thirteen, fourteen, fifteen,
   seize, dix-sept, — sixteen, seventeen,
   dix-huit, dix-neuf, — eighteen, nineteen,
   vingt, vingt et un, — twenty, twenty-one,
   vingt-deux, vingt-trois, — twenty-two, twenty-three,
   vingt-quatre, vingt-cinq, — twenty-four, twenty-five,
   vingt-six, vingt-sept, — twenty-six, twenty-seven,
   vingt-huit, vingt-neuf, — twenty-eight, twenty-nine,
   trente — thirty
Combien font deux et deux? — How much is two plus two?
   Deux et deux font quatre. — Two plus two equals four.
Combien font cinq moins deux? — How much is five minus two?
   Cinq moins deux font trois. — Five minus two equals three.
un nombre — a number

TELLING THE DAY OF THE WEEK
les jours de la semaine — the days of the week
aujourd'hui — today
C'est quel jour, aujourd'hui? — What day is today?
   C'est... — It's...
      lundi — Monday
      mardi — Tuesday
      mercredi — Wednesday
      jeudi — Thursday
      vendredi — Friday
      samedi — Saturday
      dimanche — Sunday

DESCRIBING YOUR SCHEDULE
Tu es...? — Are you...?
   Je suis / Je ne suis pas... — I'm / I'm not...
      en cours — in class
      à la maison — at home
      dans un autre cours — in another class
le cours de français — French class
Tu travailles? — Do you work?
   Je travaille... — I work...
   Je ne travaille pas... — I don't work...
Quels jours...? — What days...?
   le lundi — on Mondays
   le lundi matin — (on) Monday mornings
   du lundi au vendredi — from Monday to Friday (every week)

le matin, l'après-midi, le soir — in the morning, in the afternoon, in the evening
la semaine — the week
tous les jours — every day
le week-end — weekends / on the weekend
ce semestre — this semester
avant — before
après — after
aussi — also, too

COMPÉTENCE 3

Talking about yourself and your schedule

TALKING ABOUT YOURSELF

un autoportrait	a self-portrait
Vous êtes…?	Are you…?
Je suis / Je ne suis pas…	I am / I am not…
américain(e)	American
canadien(ne)	Canadian
de (d')… (+ city)	from… (+ city)
d'ici	from here
étudiant(e)	a student
professeur	a professor
Vous habitez…?	Do you live…?
J'habite / Je n'habite pas…	I live / I do not live…
à… (+ city)	in… (+ city)
avec ma famille	with my family
avec un(e) ami(e)	with a friend
avec un(e) camarade de chambre	with a roommate
avec un(e) colocataire	with a housemate
seul(e)	alone
Vous parlez…?	Do you speak…?
Je parle / Je ne parle pas…	I speak / I do not speak…
anglais	English
espagnol	Spanish
français	French
beaucoup en cours	a lot in class
Je pense que le français est…	I think that French is…
un peu difficile	a little difficult / hard
assez facile	fairly easy
intéressant	interesting
super	great
assez cool	pretty cool
Vous travaillez…?	Do you work…?
Je travaille…	I work…
Je ne travaille pas…	I do not work…
pour…	for…
à l'université	at the university
ici	here
maintenant	now
mais	but
non	no
oui	yes
parce que	because

TELLING TIME

l'heure	the time
une heure	an hour
Quelle heure est-il?	What time is it?
Il est une heure /	It's one o'clock /
deux heures	two o'clock
midi / minuit	noon / midnight
et quart / et demi(e)	a quarter past / half past
moins le quart	a quarter till
À quelle heure?	At what time?
à… heure(s)	at… o'clock
du matin	A.M., in the morning [when telling time]
de l'après-midi	P.M., in the afternoon [when telling time]
du soir	P.M., in the evening [when telling time]
Le cours de français est… de… à…	French class is… from… to…
Le cours de français commence à… / finit à…	French class starts at… / finishes at…

COMPÉTENCE 4

Communicating in class

Comment? Répétez, s'il vous plaît.	What? Please repeat.
Vous comprenez?	Do you understand?
Oui, je comprends. / Non, je ne comprends pas.	Yes, I understand. / No, I don't understand.
Comment dit-on… en français / en anglais?	How does one say… in French / in English?
On dit…	One says…
Je ne sais pas.	I don't know.
Qu'est-ce que ça veut dire?	What does that mean?
Ça veut dire…	That means…
Ça s'écrit comment?	How is that written?
Ça s'écrit avec ou sans accent?	That's written with or without an accent?
Ça s'écrit…	That's written…
Merci (bien).	Thank you., Thanks.
De rien.	You're welcome.
Pardon. / Excusez-moi.	Excuse me.
Le professeur dit aux étudiants…	The professor says to the students…
Ouvrez votre livre à la page 23.	Open your book to page 23.
Fermez votre livre.	Close your book.
Écoutez la question.	Listen to the question.
Répondez à la question.	Answer the question.
Allez au tableau.	Go to the board.
Écrivez la réponse avec une phrase complète.	Write the answer with a complete sentence.
Prenez une feuille de papier et un crayon ou un stylo.	Take out a piece of paper and a pencil or a pen.
Faites l'exercice A à la page 21.	Do exercise A on page 21.
Donnez-moi votre feuille de papier.	Give me your piece of paper.
Lisez la page 17.	Read page 17.
Apprenez les mots de vocabulaire.	Learn the vocabulary words.
Préparez l'examen pour le prochain cours.	Prepare for the exam for the next class.
Faites les devoirs dans le cahier.	Do the homework in the workbook.

Pour l'alphabet, voir la page 22.

Sur la Côte d'Azur
À l'université

 Internet web search
 iLrn Heinle Learning Center
 www.cengagebrain.com
 Pair work
 Horizons Video: Les Stagiaires
 Group work
 Audio

1

COMPÉTENCE

1 Identifying people and describing appearance
Les gens à l'université

Identifying and describing people
Les adjectifs et **il est / elle est** + *adjectif ou* **c'est** + *nom*

Stratégies et Lecture
- **Pour mieux lire:** *Using cognates and familiar words to read for the gist*
- **Lecture:** *Qui est-ce?*

2 Describing personality
Les personnalités

Describing people
Les pronoms sujets, le verbe **être**, *la négation et d'autres adjectifs*

Asking what someone is like
Les questions

3 Describing the university area
Le campus et le quartier

Saying what there is
Le genre, l'article indéfini et l'expression **il y a**

Identifying and describing people and things
C'est *ou* **il est / elle est** *et la place de l'adjectif*

4 Talking about your studies
L'université et les cours

Identifying people and things
L'article défini

Vidéoreprise   *Les Stagiaires*

Lecture et Composition
- **Pour mieux lire:** *Scanning to preview a text*
- **Lecture:** *L'accent grave*
- **Pour mieux écrire:** *Using and combining what you know*
- **Composition:** *Un autoportrait*

Comparaisons culturelles   *Les études*

Résumé de grammaire

Vocabulaire

vingt-neuf | 29

LA FRANCE ET SES RÉGIONS

 PowerPoint 1-1

Quelles régions françaises **connaissez-vous**? La Normandie? La Provence? La Champagne? **Voici** des photos de quatre régions pittoresques. **Laquelle voudriez-vous visiter?**

La Vallée de la Loire

La Côte d'Azur

---

connaissez-vous *do you know*   **Voici** *Here are*   **Laquelle voudriez-vous visiter?** *Which one would you like to visit?*
La Vallée de la Loire *The Loire Valley*   **La Côte d'Azur** *The French Riviera*

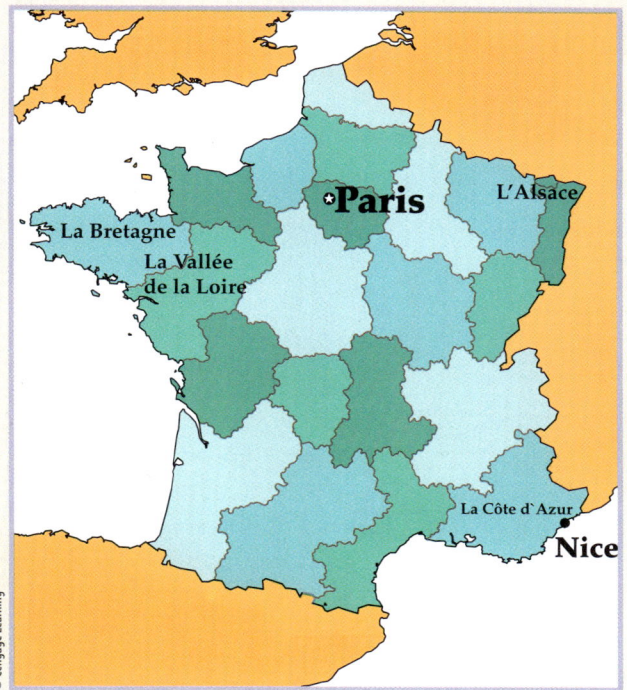

La France (la République française)

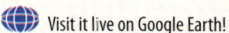 Visit it live on Google Earth!

NOMBRE D'HABITANTS:
65 350 000 (les Français)

CAPITALE: Paris

Le savez-vous?

Look at the map and photos and guess which province each sentence below describes. Which would you most like to visit?

| la Côte d'Azur | la Vallée de la Loire |
| la Bretagne | l'Alsace |

1. This region shows both French and German influences in its architecture and culture because it was formerly part of Germany.

2. This area is known for its numerous castles and excellent wine.

3. Named for the color of the sky and water, this region is located along the Mediterranean sea.

4. The stone megaliths and tables reflect the traditions of the ancient people who inhabited this region from 3 000 to 5 000 years before our era.

La Bretagne

Which are the most famous castles along the Loire? Who set up the megaliths in Carnac (**Bretagne**)? Why is Alsace a mix of French and German culture? Search for information on the Web on any of these topics and share it with the class.

Quick-reference answers for
Le savez-vous? **1.** l'Alsace **2.** la Vallée de la Loire **3.** la Côte d'Azur **4.** la Bretagne

Suggestion. Point out that the castle of Azay-le-Rideau (seen in the second photo on the preceding page) is said to have been the inspiration for Sleeping Beauty's castle.

L'Alsace

La France et ses régions | *trente et un* **31**

COMPÉTENCE 1

Identifying people and describing appearance

 PowerPoint 1-2

LES GENS À L'UNIVERSITÉ

> **Note culturelle**
>
> Les études universitaires *(university studies)* sont très importantes en France. La majorité des universités sont des universités publiques. Généralement, il y a une université publique dans toutes *(all)* les grandes villes *(cities)* de France. La majorité des étudiants vont *(go)* à l'université dans la ville la plus proche de chez eux *(in the closest city to their home)*. La situation est-elle semblable *(Is the situation similar)* dans votre région?

Ce sont mes amis David et Léa. Ils sont étudiants à l'Université de Nice.

C'est David, **un jeune homme** français.
Il est étudiant.
Il est de Nice.

C'est Léa, **une jeune femme** américaine.
Elle est étudiante.
Elle est de Los Angeles.

C'est Jean, **le frère de** David.
Il n'est pas étudiant.
Il travaille.

C'est Lisa, **la sœur jumelle de** Léa.
Elle n'est pas étudiante.
Elle travaille.

Lisa et Léa ne sont pas françaises. Elles sont américaines. Léa est à Nice **pour étudier.** Lisa est en France **pour voir sa** sœur et pour visiter la France.

Comment est David?

grand?   petit?   gros?   mince?   jeune?   vieux?   beau?   laid?

David est petit, mince et beau!

> **Note de vocabulaire**
>
> Use **c'est** or **ce sont** to identify people and things and **il est, elle est, ils sont,** or **elles sont** to describe them. Also notice that adjectives have a different form depending on whether a man or a woman is being described.

Comment est Léa?

grande?   petite?   grosse?   mince?   jeune?   vieille?   belle?   laide?

Léa est petite, mince et belle!

David et Léa sont **célibataires.** Et vous? Êtes-vous célibataire, **comme** David et Léa, ou **alors** êtes-vous fiancé(e), marié(e) ou divorcé(e)?

Line art on this page: © Cengage Learning

> **Note.** Each chapter of *Horizons* is divided into four *Compétences.* The first *Compétence* of each chapter consists of a vocabulary presentation followed by a structure explanation section and either a reading or listening comprehension section with learning strategies. The next two *Compétences* consist of a vocabulary presentation followed by two structure explanation sections. The final *Compétence* is composed of a vocabulary presentation followed by a structure explanation section and a review revolving around the *Horizons* video *Les Stagiaires.* New structures used in the opening sections of each *Compétence* are presented lexically, and students are asked to use them only as such. Relevant grammatical structures are explained in the structure sections that follow, in which students are given the opportunity to manipulate them. If you wish, you may proceed at any time to a grammar explanation when presenting vocabulary.

Les gens *People*   **Ce sont...** *They are / These are / Those are . . .*   **mes amis** *my friends*   **C'est...** *He is / She is / It is / This is / That is . . .*   **un jeune homme** *a young man*   **une jeune femme** *a young woman*   **le frère de** *the brother of*   **la sœur de** *the sister of*   **jumeau (jumelle)** *twin*   **pour étudier** *in order to study*   **pour voir** *in order to see*   **sa (son, ses)** *his/her/its*   **Comment est... ?** *What is . . . like?*   **célibataire** *single*   **comme** *like, as*   **alors** *so, then, therefore*

David **rencontre** Léa **pendant la première semaine des cours.**

DAVID: Salut! Je suis David Cauvin. **Nous sommes** dans le **même** cours de littérature, non?

LÉA: Oui, c'est ça. Bonjour! Je m'appelle Léa Clark. Tu es d'ici?

DAVID: Oui, je suis de Nice. Et toi, **tu es d'où**?

LÉA: Moi, je suis de Los Angeles, mais j'habite ici maintenant parce que je suis étudiante à l'université.

Warm-up. Questions orales: **1.** Vous êtes américain(e)? **2.** Vous habitez à *[city]*? **3.** Vous parlez anglais? **4.** Vous parlez français aussi? **5.** Vous êtes étudiant(e)? **6.** Vous travaillez aussi? **7.** C'est quel jour, aujourd'hui? **8.** Vous êtes en cours quels jours?

Note for the conversation. New vocabulary presented in the conversation includes all glossed words, and **littérature.**

A Mes amis.
Relisez les descriptions de David, Léa, Jean et Lisa à la page précédente et complétez chaque phrase avec le choix *(choice)* correct en italique.

1. David est *un jeune homme / une jeune femme.*
2. Il est *américain / français / canadien.* Il est *de Paris / de Nice.*
3. Léa est *professeur / étudiante* à l'Université de Nice.
4. C'est *la sœur jumelle / le frère jumeau* de Lisa.
5. Jean est le frère *de David / de Léa et Lisa.*
6. *Léa / Lisa* est à Nice pour étudier.
7. *Léa / Lisa* est à Nice pour voir sa sœur et pour visiter la France.
8. David et Léa sont *mariés / célibataires* et moi, je suis *célibataire / fiancé(e) / marié(e) / divorcé(e) / veuf (veuve* [widowed]).

B Et votre ami(e)?
Faites des phrases pour parler de votre meilleur(e) ami(e) *(your best friend).*

1. C'est *un homme / une femme.*
2. Il/Elle *est / n'est pas* jeune.
3. Il/Elle *est / n'est pas* d'ici.
4. Il/Elle *est / n'est pas* étudiant(e).
5. Il/Elle *travaille / ne travaille pas.*
6. Il/Elle est *grand(e) / petit(e) / de taille moyenne* (medium-sized).
7. Il/Elle est *célibataire / fiancé(e) / marié(e) / séparé(e) / divorcé(e) / veuf (veuve* [widowed]).

Suggestion for the conversation. Set the scene and have students listen to the conversation twice with books closed. Display these partial statements and have students listen for how to complete them. **1.** Léa est de… **2.** David est de… **3.** David et Léa sont dans le même *(same)* cours de… Afterward, have students listen again while reading along.

Warm-up for *A. Mes amis.* C'est Léa ou David? **1.** C'est un jeune homme. **2.** C'est une jeune femme. **3.** Elle est étudiante. **4.** Elle est américaine. **5.** Il est français. **6.** Il est étudiant. **7.** Elle est belle. **8.** Il est petit. **9.** Il est beau aussi.

Follow-up for *B. Et votre ami(e)?* Décrivez David et Léa avec un antonyme. **EXEMPLE** David n'est pas marié. **Il est célibataire. 1.** David n'est pas gros. **2.** David n'est pas vieux. **3.** David n'est pas laid. **4.** Léa n'est pas mariée. **5.** Léa n'est pas laide. **6.** Léa n'est pas vieille.

 ### À VOUS!

Avec un(e) partenaire, relisez à haute voix *(aloud)* la conversation entre David et Léa. Ensuite, adaptez la conversation pour décrire *(to describe)* votre situation.

You can find a list of the new words from this **Compétence** on page 62 and access the audio online.

---

rencontre (rencontrer *to meet* [for the first time or by chance], *to run into* [someone]) **pendant** *during* **la première semaine des cours** *the first week of classes* **Nous sommes** *We are* **même** *same* **tu es d'où?** *where are you from?*

Compétence 1 | trente-trois **33**

 **PowerPoint 1-3**

IDENTIFYING AND DESCRIBING PEOPLE

✓ Pour vérifier

These self-check questions are provided throughout the book. Read the entire explanation before trying to answer the questions.

1. What is the base form of an adjective? What do you usually do to make it feminine if it ends in **e**? in **é**? another vowel? a consonant?

2. What is the feminine form of **gros**? **canadien**? **beau**? **vieux**?

3. What do you usually do to make an adjective plural? What if it ends in **x** or **s**?

4. What two expressions are used to *identify* who someone is with a *noun*? What are the negative forms of these expressions?

5. When *describing* someone with an *adjective,* how do you say *he is? she is? they are* for a group of all females? *they are* for a group of all males or for a mixed group? What are the negative forms of these expressions?

6. Is there a difference in pronunciation between **espagnol** and **espagnole**? between **petit** and **petite**? Is the final **s** of the plural form of an adjective pronounced?

iLrn Grammar Tutorials

Note *de grammaire*

Also use **il est, elle est, ils sont,** and **elles sont** to state someone's profession (including **étudiant[e]**), nationality, or religion. However, unlike in English, do not include the French equivalent of the word *a*.

Elle est étudiante. *She's a student.*
Il est américain. *He's (an) American.*
Ils sont catholiques. *They're Catholic(s).*

You will learn more about this later in this chapter.

Note. Here students are introduced to the use of **c'est / ce sont** and **il/elle est** and **ils/elles sont** to identify and describe people. More information about their use, the concept of grammatical gender, and the use of **il/elle est** and **ils/elles sont** to represent things is presented later in this chapter.

Suggestion. Point out that the feminine form of adjectives such as **canadienne** and **américaine** loses its nasality.

Les adjectifs et **il est / elle est** *+ adjectif ou* **c'est** *+ nom*

Adjective forms vary depending on whether they describe a male or a female and whether they describe one person or more than one. The masculine singular form of the adjective is the base form. Add an **e** to change this form to feminine, unless it already ends in an *unaccented* **e**. If it ends in an *accented* **é**, add another **e** to form the feminine. Add an **s** to make an adjective plural, unless it ends in **s** or **x**.

MASCULINE		FEMININE	
SINGULAR	PLURAL	SINGULAR	PLURAL
petit	petit**s**	petit**e**	petit**es**
jeune	jeune**s**	jeune	jeune**s**
marié	marié**s**	marié**e**	marié**es**
français	français	français**e**	français**es**

Gros doubles its final consonant before adding the **e** for the feminine form, as do adjectives ending in **-en,** like canadi**en.**

MASCULINE		FEMININE	
SINGULAR	PLURAL	SINGULAR	PLURAL
gros	gros	gros**se**	gros**ses**
canadien	canadien**s**	canadien**ne**	canadien**nes**

The adjectives **beau, jumeau,** and **vieux** are irregular.

MASCULINE		FEMININE	
SINGULAR	PLURAL	SINGULAR	PLURAL
beau	beaux	belle	belles
jumeau	jumeaux	jumelle	jumelles
vieux	vieux	vieille	vieilles

Notice how to say *he/she/it/this/that is* and *these/those/they are.* When *identifying* people with *nouns,* use **c'est** and **ce sont.** When *describing* people with *adjectives,* use **il est, elle est, ils sont,** and **elles sont.** Use **ils** for a group of males or a mixed group and **elles** for a group of all females.

To *identify* people with *nouns,* use:	To *describe* people with *adjectives,* use:
c'est / **ce sont** + noun	**il/elle est** / **ils/elles sont** + adjective
C'est Jean. *It/This/He is Jean.*	**Il est célibataire.** *He is single.*
Ce sont mes amis. *They are my friends.*	**Ils sont français.** *They are French.*

To negate the verb, place **ne (n')** *before* it and **pas** *after* it. **Ne** becomes **n'** before vowel sounds.

Ce n'est pas ma sœur.	**Elles ne sont pas américaines.**
She/This isn't my sister.	*They aren't American.*

PRONONCIATION

*i*Lrn Prononcez bien! See Module 22.

 Il est + *adjectif* / **Elle est** + *adjectif*

Since most final consonants are silent in French, you will not hear or say the final consonant of masculine adjective forms, unless they end in **c, r, f,** or **l**. When the **e** is added to make the feminine form, the consonant is no longer final and is pronounced.

  petit / petite   français / française

When a masculine adjective form ends in a pronounced final consonant, or in **e** or **é**, however, you will hear no difference between the masculine and feminine forms.

  espagnol / espagnole   jeune / jeune   marié / mariée

The final **s** of plurals is not pronounced, nor is a consonant that immediately precedes it, unless it is **c, r, f,** or **l**. The masculine plural forms sound like the masculine singular forms and the feminine plural forms sound like the feminine singular forms. You must pick up the plurality from the context.

  Il est petit. / Ils sont petits.   Elle est petite. / Elles sont petites.

 A **Prononcez bien!** Écoutez les phrases. C'est la phrase **a** pour Gabriel Bellon ou la phrase **b** pour Gabrielle Lacoste?

1. **a.** Gabriel est grand.
   b. Gabrielle est grande.
2. **a.** Gabriel n'est pas petit.
   b. Gabrielle n'est pas petite.
3. **a.** Gabriel est français.
   b. Gabrielle est française.
4. **a.** Gabriel n'est pas canadien.
   b. Gabrielle n'est pas canadienne.
5. **a.** Gabriel n'est pas gros.
   b. Gabrielle n'est pas grosse.

a. Gabriel Bellon

b. Gabrielle Lacoste

Maintenant, lisez une seule *(a single)* phrase de chaque paire. Votre partenaire va dire si *(is going to say if)* vous dites la phrase **a** ou la phrase **b**.

B **Qui est-ce? Comment sont-ils?** D'abord *(First)*, utilisez **c'est** ou **ce sont** pour identifier chaque personne. Ensuite *(Then)*, dites si chaque adjectif décrit la personne. Utilisez **il est / il n'est pas, elle est / elle n'est pas, ils sont / ils ne sont pas** ou **elles sont / elles ne sont pas** et la forme correcte de l'adjectif.

EXEMPLE   C'est David. Il n'est pas grand. Il est petit…

David (grand/petit/ mince/gros/ beau/laid)

1. Léa (grand/petit/ mince/gros/ beau/laid)

2. David et Jean (français/ américain/jumeau/ vieux/jeune)

3. Léa et Lisa (français/ américain/jumeau/ vieux/jeune)

Suggestion. Point out the pronunciation of **il, ils, elle,** and **elles,** then do this activity: Écoutez les phrases et dites si elles décrivent *(describe)* **David, Léa** ou **les deux. 1.** Il est petit. **2.** Il est beau. **3.** Elle n'est pas grande. **4.** Ils sont étudiants. **5.** Il n'est pas américain. **6.** Elle est américaine. **7.** Elle est petite.

Script for A. Prononcez bien! 1. Gabrielle est grande. **2.** Gabriel n'est pas petit. **3.** Gabrielle est française. **4.** Gabrielle n'est pas canadienne. **5.** Gabriel n'est pas gros.

Follow-ups for A. Prononcez bien! A. Have students write sentences to describe Gabriel Bellon and Gabrielle Lacoste. Ask them to read one choice from each pair and have the class say which one is being described. **B.** Léa and David are alike. Describe Léa according to the description of David. **EXAMPLE** David est petit. **Léa est petite.** David est jeune (mince, étudiant, beau, célibataire).

Follow-up for B. Qui est-ce? Comment sont-ils? EXAMPLE David est américain ou français? **Il est français. Il n'est pas américain. 1.** David est grand ou petit? **2.** Jean et David sont français ou américains? **3.** Léa est laide ou belle? **4.** David et Léa sont dans le même cours d'espagnol ou de littérature? **5.** Lisa est à Nice pour étudier ou pour voir sa sœur? **6.** David et Léa sont étudiants ou professeurs? **7.** Léa et Lisa sont américaines ou françaises? **8.** Léa et Lisa sont de New York ou de Los Angeles?

STRATÉGIES ET LECTURE

It may seem overwhelming to read a lengthier text in French at first. However, there are strategies you can use to learn to read more easily. This section is designed to help you learn to apply these strategies.

> **POUR MIEUX LIRE:** Using cognates and familiar words to read for the gist
>
> Cognates are words that look the same or similar in two languages and have the same meaning. Take advantage of cognates to help you read French more easily. There are some patterns in cognates. What three patterns do you see here? What do the last two words in each column mean?
>
> soudainement *suddenly*   obligé *obliged*   hôpital *hospital*
> décidément *decidedly*   sauvé *saved*   île *isle, island*
> complètement *?*   compliqué *?*   honnête *?*
> généralement *?*   décidé *?*   forêt *?*
>
> Recognizing words you have already learned in different forms will also help you read. Use the two familiar phrases on the left to guess the meanings of those on the right.
>
> Comment dit-on *pen* en français? → Qu'est-ce que tu dis?
> Je ne sais pas la réponse. → Lisa ne sait pas quoi répondre.

A **Avant de lire.** Can you state the general idea of the following sentences? Do not try to read them word by word; rather, focus on the words that you can understand.

Lisa hésite un moment avant de répondre.
C'est juste à ce moment que Léa arrive.
Léa sauve la pauvre Lisa.
David voit Léa et Lisa et s'exclame: «Je vois double!»

B **Mots apparentés.** Before reading the following text, *Qui est-ce?*, skim through it and list the cognates you see. You should find about twenty.

Lecture: *Qui est-ce?*

Lisa Clark is visiting her twin sister, Léa, a student at the University of Nice. As she waits for her sister in front of the **musée des Beaux-Arts,** a young man approaches. Since she does not speak French very well, Lisa is unsure what to say when he speaks to her.

— Salut, Léa! Ça va?

Lisa hésite un moment avant de répondre.

— Non, non... euh, ça va, mais... euh... je regrette... je ne suis pas Léa. Je suis Lisa.

— Qu'est-ce que tu dis, Léa?

Lisa pense: «*He thinks I'm Léa. How do I tell him . . . ?*»

— Non, non, répond Lisa. Vous ne comprenez pas. Je ne suis pas Léa.

— Comment ça, tu n'es pas Léa?

Décidément, ce jeune homme ne comprend rien! Lisa insiste.

— Je ne suis pas Léa. Vous ne comprenez pas! Écoutez! Je ne suis pas Léa! Je ne suis pas étudiante.

— Mais qu'est-ce que tu dis? demande David. Tu es malade? C'est moi, David. Nous sommes dans le même cours de littérature.

Lisa pense: «*I'm never going to get this guy to understand. He's so sure I'm Léa.*»

C'est juste à ce moment que Léa arrive. La pauvre Lisa est sauvée.

— Salut, Lisa! Bonjour, David!

David, très surpris de voir les sœurs jumelles, s'exclame:

— Mais, ce n'est pas possible! Je vois double! Maintenant, je comprends. C'est ta sœur jumelle, Léa.

— Mon pauvre David! Voilà, je te présente ma sœur, Lisa.

— Bonjour, Lisa. Désolé pour la confusion, mais quelle ressemblance!

A Avez-vous compris? Qui parle: **David, Lisa** ou **Léa**?

1. Vous ne comprenez pas. Je ne suis pas Léa.
2. Mais nous sommes dans le même cours de littérature.
3. Je ne suis pas étudiante à l'Université de Nice.
4. Je ne parle pas très bien français.
5. Je te présente ma sœur.

B D'abord... Which happens first, **a** or **b**?

1. a. David dit bonjour à Lisa.
   b. Lisa arrive au musée des Beaux-Arts.
2. a. David dit: «Bonjour, Léa.»
   b. Lisa pense: «Il ne comprend pas.»
3. a. Lisa hésite à répondre parce qu'elle ne parle pas très bien français.
   b. Lisa répond: «Non, non, vous ne comprenez pas.»
4. a. David comprend que Léa et Lisa sont sœurs jumelles.
   b. Léa arrive.
5. a. David dit: «Désolé *(Sorry)* pour la confusion.»
   b. David comprend la situation.

COMPÉTENCE 2

Describing personality

 PowerPoint 1-4

Note culturelle

Où habitent la majorité des étudiants en France?
35 % chez leurs parents *(with their parents)*
33 % seuls ou en couple
12 % en résidence collective *(group housing [such as dorms])*
10 % en colocation *(shared rentals)*
Remarquez que les résidences *(dormitories)* universitaires ne sont pas souvent *(often)* sur le «campus» de l'université. Elles sont groupées dans un endroit à part *(grouped in a separate place)* appelé la «Cité universitaire».

Note de vocabulaire

1. With the abbreviated form **sympa**, do not add an **e** to make it feminine, but do add an **s** in the plural.
2. Use **le foot(ball)** for *soccer* and **le foot(ball) américain** for *football*.
3. There are three ways to say *my* (**mon, ma, mes**) and *your* [singular familiar] (**ton, ta, tes**), depending on whether the possession you are identifying is masculine or feminine, singular or plural. You will learn about this later.

Warm-up. Votre meilleur(e) ami(e) *(Your best friend)* **1.** C'est un homme ou une femme? **2.** Il/Elle est jeune? **3.** Il/Elle est marié(e)? **4.** Il/Elle est d'ici? **5.** Il/Elle est grand(e) ou petit(e)? **6.** Il/Elle est étudiant(e)?

Vocabulaire sans peine!

Noticing cognate patterns can help you learn new words more quickly.
-if(-ive) = *-ive*
agressif = *aggressive*
-iste = *-ist(ic)*
matérialiste = *materialistic*

How would you say these words in French?
*impulsive   imaginative
conformist   perfectionist*

LES PERSONNALITÉS

Je suis très…   Je suis **plutôt**…   Je suis assez…   Je suis un peu…
Je **ne** suis **pas (du tout)**…

optimiste / pessimiste
idéaliste / réaliste

intelligent(e) / **bête**
intellectuel(le)

timide / extraverti(e)

dynamique / paresseux (paresseuse)
sportif (sportive)

intéressant(e) / ennuyeux (ennuyeuse)
amusant(e) / **marrant(e)**

agréable / désagréable
**gentil (gentille) / méchant(e)
sympathique (sympa) / antipathique**

What are you like, compared to your best friend?

Je suis **plus** dynamique **que** mon meilleur ami (ma meilleure amie).
Je suis **aussi** sportif (sportive) **que** mon meilleur ami (ma meilleure amie).
Je suis **moins** timide **que** mon meilleur ami (ma meilleure amie).

Une **nouvelle** amie, Nadia, parle avec David.

NADIA: **Tes amis** et toi, vous êtes étudiants, non?
DAVID: Oui, nous sommes étudiants à l'Université de Nice.
NADIA: Vous êtes plutôt intellectuels, alors?
DAVID: Mes amis sont assez intellectuels, mais moi, **pas tellement.** Et toi? Tu es étudiante aussi?
NADIA: Non, **les études, ce n'est pas mon truc.**
DAVID: Et le sport? **Tu aimes** le sport?
NADIA: Oui, j'aime bien le tennis, mais je n'aime pas beaucoup **le football.**

Line art on this page: © Cengage Learning

---

plutôt *rather*   **ne… pas (du tout)** *not (at all)*   **bête** *stupid, dumb*   **dynamique** *active*   **paresseux (paresseuse)** *lazy*
ennuyeux (ennuyeuse) *boring*   **marrant(e)** *funny*   **gentil(le)** *nice*   **méchant(e)** *mean*   **sympathique / sympa** *nice*
antipathique *disagreeable, unpleasant*   **plus… que** *more … than*   **mon meilleur ami (ma meilleure amie)** *my best friend*
aussi… que *as … as*   **moins… que** *less … than*   **nouveau (nouvelle)** *new*   **Tes amis** *Your friends*   **pas tellement** *not so much*
les études *studies, going to school*   **ce n'est pas mon truc** *it's not my thing*   **Tu aimes** *You like*   **le foot(ball)** *soccer*

A. Ils sont comment? Complétez les phrases.

EXEMPLE Danny DeVito est (plus, moins, aussi) grand que Tom Cruise.
Danny DeVito est moins grand que Tom Cruise.

1. Johnny Depp est (plus, moins, aussi) beau que Jack Black.
2. Jim Carrey est (plus, moins, aussi) marrant que Will Ferrell.
3. Serena Williams est (plus, moins, aussi) sportive que Venus Williams.
4. Scarlett Johansson est (plus, moins, aussi) belle que Jennifer Aniston.
5. Ellen DeGeneres est (plus, moins, aussi) intéressante qu'Oprah Winfrey.
6. Donald Trump est (plus, moins, aussi) désagréable que Kim Kardashian.

B. Comment sont-ils? Complétez les phrases suivantes pour parler de vous, vos amis et vos professeurs.

MOI

1. *J'aime / Je n'aime pas* le sport.
2. *Je suis / Je ne suis pas* sportif (sportive).
3. Je suis *plutôt extraverti(e) / un peu timide*.
4. *Je parle / Je ne parle pas* beaucoup.

MON MEILLEUR AMI / MA MEILLEURE AMIE

7. *Il/Elle aime / Il/Elle n'aime pas* les études.
8. *Il/Elle est / Il/Elle n'est pas* intellectuel(le).
9. *Il/Elle est / Il/Elle n'est pas* très intelligent(e).
10. Il/Elle est *agréable / désagréable*.

MES AMIS ET MOI

5. Nous sommes *dynamiques / paresseux*.
6. *Nous sommes / Nous ne sommes pas* très sympas.

MES PROFS

11. Ils sont *sympas / antipathiques*.
12. *Ils sont / Ils ne sont pas* intelligents.

C. Et vous? Comment êtes-vous?

très   plutôt   assez   un peu   ne... pas du tout

EXEMPLE optimistic
Je suis très / plutôt / assez / un peu optimiste.
Je ne suis pas (du tout) optimiste.

1. idealistic
2. mean
3. lazy
4. intellectual
5. shy
6. boring
7. athletic
8. married

À VOUS!

Avec un(e) partenaire, relisez à haute voix *(aloud)* la conversation entre Nadia et David. Ensuite, adaptez la conversation pour décrire *(to describe)* votre situation.

PowerPoint 1-5

DESCRIBING PEOPLE

Les pronoms sujets, le verbe **être,** *la négation et d'autres adjectifs*

Below are the subject pronouns *(I, you, he . . .)* and the forms of the verb **être** *(to be)*.

Use **tu** to say *you* when speaking to a friend, family member, classmate, child, or animal. Use **vous** to say *you* when speaking to any unknown adult, someone to whom you should show respect, or when talking to more than one person.

For **je** and other one-syllable words ending in **e** (**ne, que, me, le...**), replace the **e** with an apostrophe before a vowel or mute **h**. This is called *elision*.

The word **être** is the infinitive, the verb form you find in the dictionary. This chart shows the conjugation, the forms to use with different subject pronouns.

✓ Pour vérifier

1. Would you use **tu** or **vous** to address a child? two children? a salesclerk? an adult you've just met?

2. How do you say *I* in French? When do words like **je, ne,** and **que** replace the final **e** with an apostrophe (**j', n', qu'**)? What is this called?

3. How do you say *he* in French? *she*? *they* for a group of all females? *they* for a group of all males? *they* for a mixed group?

4. What is an infinitive? How do you say *to be*? What form of **être** do you use with each subject pronoun?

5. What do you place before a conjugated verb to negate it? What do you place after it? What happens to **ne** when it is followed by a vowel sound?

6. What are five irregular patterns of adjective agreement?

7. What is the feminine form of **gentil**? of **beau**? of **nouveau**? of **vieux**?

iLrn Prononcez bien! See Module 20.
iLrn Grammar Tutorials

ÊTRE *(to be)*					
je	suis	*I am*	nous	sommes	*we are*
tu	es	*you are*	vous	êtes	*you are*
il	est	*he is, it is*	ils	sont	*they are*
elle	est	*she is, it is*	elles	sont	*they are*

To negate a conjugated verb, place **ne... pas** around it. Remember to use **n'** before a vowel sound or mute **h**.

ne (n') + verbe + pas		
je **ne** travaille **pas**	je **n'**habite **pas**	je **n'**aime **pas**
je **ne** suis **pas**	tu **n'**es **pas**	il/elle **n'**est **pas**
nous **ne** sommes **pas**	vous **n'**êtes **pas**	ils/elles **ne** sont **pas**

Note *de grammaire*

With noun subjects or compound subjects, use the verb form that goes with the corresponding subject pronoun.

David is = *he is* (**il est**) = **David est**
David and I are = *we are* (**nous sommes**) = **David et moi sommes**
your friends and you = *you (plural) are* (**vous êtes**) = **tes ami(e)s et toi, vous êtes**
my friends are = *they are* (**ils/elles sont**) = **mes ami(e)s sont**

Note the patterns of these common adjective endings.

MASCULINE	FEMININE	MASCULINE		FEMININE	
		SINGULAR	PLURAL	SINGULAR	PLURAL
-eux	-euse(s)	paress**eux**	paress**eux**	paress**euse**	paress**euses**
-en(s)	-enne(s)	canadi**en**	canadi**ens**	canadi**enne**	canadi**ennes**
-if(s)	-ive(s)	sport**if**	sport**ifs**	sport**ive**	sport**ives**
-el(s)	-elle(s)	intellectu**el**	intellectu**els**	intellectu**elle**	intellectu**elles**
-er(s)	-ère(s)	premi**er**	premi**ers**	premi**ère**	premi**ères**

Gentil doubles the final consonant before adding the **e** for the feminine form (**gentil → gentille**).

The adjectives **beau, nouveau, jumeau,** and **vieux** are irregular, but follow a similar pattern.

Note. The subject pronoun **on** is introduced in *Chapitre 4*. The rules for adjective placement are taught in the next *Compétence*.

MASCULINE		FEMININE	
SINGULAR	PLURAL	SINGULAR	PLURAL
beau	beaux	belle	belles
nouveau	nouveaux	nouvelle	nouvelles
jumeau	jumeaux	jumelle	jumelles
vieux	vieux	vieille	vieilles

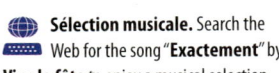 **Sélection musicale.** Search the Web for the song "**Exactement**" by **Vive la fête** to enjoy a musical selection containing these structures.

A Tu ou vous? Demandez à ces personnes d'où elles sont *(where they are from)*.

EXEMPLES your classmate: **Tu es d'où?**
your boss: **Vous êtes d'où?**

1. your roommate
2. your teacher
3. a salesclerk
4. two friends
5. your parents
6. a new elderly neighbor

B Quel pronom? Complétez les phrases avec le bon pronom sujet personnel *(correct subject pronoun)*: **je, tu, il, elle, nous, vous, ils, elles**.

1. David est étudiant à l'université, mais _____ n'est pas très intellectuel. Nadia n'est pas intellectuelle non plus *(either)*. _____ est plutôt sportive!
2. Léa et Lisa ne sont pas paresseuses. _____ sont dynamiques. David et Jean sont dynamiques aussi, mais _____ sont moins dynamiques que Léa et Lisa. Mes amis et moi, _____ sommes assez dynamiques aussi. Et tes amis et toi, _____ êtes dynamiques?
3. David et Léa ne sont pas mariés. _____ sont célibataires. Moi, _____ suis célibataire aussi. Et toi, _____ es célibataire ou marié(e)?

C Comment sont-ils? Dites si ces adjectifs décrivent *(describe)* bien ces personnes. Changez la forme de l'adjectif si nécessaire.

EXEMPLE Léa... beau, laid   **Léa est belle. Elle n'est pas laide.**

Léa...
intellectuel, gros, paresseux, dynamique

Léa et Lisa...
américain, français, gentil, antipathique, beau

David et Jean...
laid, beau, vieux, jeune

Moi, je...
dynamique, paresseux, ennuyeux, sportif

D Descriptions. Décrivez ces personnes avec une phrase à l'affirmatif et une autre phrase au négatif.

EXEMPLE **Moi, je suis (très) optimiste. Je ne suis pas (du tout) pessimiste.**

- moi, je
- le professeur de français
- les étudiants du cours de français
- ma famille et moi
- mes parents
- mes amis et moi

très	plutôt	assez	un peu	ne... pas (du tout)
dynamique	sportif	paresseux	intellectuel	
optimiste	pessimiste	réaliste	idéaliste	
gentil	antipathique	sympa	intéressant	
intelligent	intéressant	ennuyeux	marrant	

Follow-up for A. Tu ou vous? Tell students that Jean is asking Léa questions. Display his questions for students to complete with **tu es** or **vous êtes**. Students may do this activity in pairs, with stronger students answering the questions as if they were Léa and making up any information they don't know about her. **1.** Léa, _____ étudiante? **2.** Lisa et toi, _____ intellectuelles? **3.** _____ américaine? **4.** Ta famille et toi, _____ de Los Angeles? **5.** David et toi, _____ dans le même cours de littérature? **6.** _____ sportive? **7.** Tes amis et toi, _____ sportifs?

Warm-up for B. Quel pronom? Tell students that David is talking about his friends and himself. Students make three columns on a sheet of paper: **David / David et ses** *(his)* **amis / Ses amis**. Tell them to write the number of each sentence they hear under the column that indicates about whom David is speaking. Do the first sentence as an example. **1.** Ils ne sont pas très sportifs. **2.** Je ne suis pas très intellectuel. **3.** Ils sont très intelligents. **4.** Nous sommes étudiants à l'Université de Nice. **5.** Je suis célibataire. **6.** Ils sont plutôt extravertis. **7.** Nous sommes très dynamiques.

Supplemental activity. Have students say whether these adjectives now describe them more or less than five years ago (**Je suis plus/aussi/moins... maintenant.**): sportif (sportive), optimiste, idéaliste, intellectuel(le), grand(e), paresseux (paresseuse), timide.

 **PowerPoint 1-6**

ASKING WHAT SOMEONE IS LIKE

✓ **Pour vérifier**

1. What are three ways of asking a question that can be answered with **oui** or **non**? What happens to your intonation in each case?
2. What happens to **que** before a vowel sound?

iLrn Prononcez bien! See **Module 21.**

Note. Inversion is presented in **Chapitre 2.**

Suggestion. You may wish to point out that the more traditional **n'est-ce pas?** is largely being replaced by **non?** in conversation.

Supplemental activity. Tell students that you are going to make some statements and ask some questions about their class. If you make a statement, they are to write nothing on their paper. If you ask a question, they are to answer it by writing **oui** or **non** on their paper. **1.** Nous sommes dans le même cours de français, n'est-ce pas? **2.** Le cours de français est facile? **3.** Est-ce que les étudiants sont intelligents? **4.** Ils ne sont pas paresseux. **5.** Vous parlez très bien français. **6.** Est-ce que vous comprenez bien en cours? **7.** Vous étudiez à l'université, non?

Les questions

There are several ways to ask a question that will be answered *yes* or *no*.

- You can ask a question with rising intonation. A statement normally has falling intonation.

  Tu es extravertie? Tu es sportive?

- You can ask a question by placing **est-ce que** before the subject and the verb and using rising intonation. Note that **que** becomes **qu'** before vowel sounds.

  Est-ce que tes amis sont étudiants? Est-ce qu'ils sont intellectuels?

  Est-ce que tu es marié? Est-ce qu'elle est étudiante?

- If you are presuming that someone will probably answer *yes,* you can use either **n'est-ce pas?** *(right?)* or **non?** at the end of a question with rising intonation.

  Il est marié, n'est-ce pas? Il est marié, non?

A Personnalités. Recopiez le tableau qui suit *(the chart that follows)* sur une feuille de papier. Posez des questions à d'autres étudiants pour trouver une personne qui correspond à chaque *(each)* adjectif.

EXEMPLES — Mario, est-ce que tu es sportif?
— Non, je ne suis pas sportif.

— Brianna, est-ce que tu es sportive?
— Oui, je suis sportive.

sportif (sportive) Brianna	plutôt extraverti(e)	un peu timide
très optimiste	un peu paresseux (paresseuse)	assez intellectuel(le)
marié(e)	idéaliste	très dynamique

Maintenant, présentez un(e) des étudiant(e)s à la classe.

EXEMPLE C'est Brianna. Elle est sportive.

B Encore des questions! Formez des questions logiques avec le verbe **être** et posez-les à votre partenaire.

EXEMPLE — Est-ce que tu es marié(e)?
— Oui, je suis marié(e). / Non, je ne suis pas marié(e).

Est-ce que	tu... nous... tes amis... ton meilleur ami / ta meilleure amie...	marié(e)(s) assez intellectuel(le)(s) d'ici en cours à une heure plus extraverti(e)(s) que toi très sportif(s) (sportive[s]) aussi intelligent(e)(s) que toi

Supplemental activity. Write sets of the same three personality traits on two slips of paper of different colors. Have students place themselves in two rows facing one another. Distribute the slips of paper of one color to one row and the matching slips of the other color to the other row, mixing up the order. Tell students that they have a clone on the other side, and going down the row, have them ask somebody on the other side a yes/no question. Have them take turns asking questions until they figure out who their clones are. Make several of the sets vary only by one trait and tell students that many of them are out of the same gene pool, but that they are not clones.

C Et Léa? Léa répond aux questions d'une nouvelle amie. Utilisez ses réponses pour déterminer quelles questions son amie lui a posées *(her friend asked her)*.

EXEMPLE — Est-ce que tu es professeur?
— Non, je ne suis pas professeur.

1. — _____?
   — Oui, je suis étudiante.
2. — _____?
   — Oui, je suis plutôt intellectuelle.
3. — _____?
   — Oui, les cours sont faciles.
4. — _____?
   — Oui, les professeurs sont gentils.
5. — _____?
   — Non, Lisa n'est pas étudiante.
6. — _____?
   — Oui, elle est sportive.
7. — Et ta sœur et toi? _____?
   — Non, nous ne sommes pas canadiennes.
8. — _____?
   — Oui, nous sommes américaines.

D Entretien. Interviewez votre partenaire.

1. Est-ce que tu es américain(e)? Ta famille et toi, vous êtes d'ici?
2. Est-ce que tu es dans un autre cours après le cours de français? Est-ce que les études sont faciles ou difficiles pour toi? Tes amis et toi, est-ce que vous êtes intellectuels? Est-ce que ton meilleur ami (ta meilleure amie) est plus intellectuel(le) ou moins intellectuel(le) que toi? Est-ce qu'il/elle est étudiant(e) aussi?
3. Est-ce que tu aimes le sport? Tu es plutôt sportif (sportive)? Est-ce que tu es très dynamique ou plutôt paresseux (paresseuse)?

COMPÉTENCE 3

Describing the university area

 PowerPoint 1-7

LE CAMPUS ET LE QUARTIER

Note culturelle

La vie *(The life)* d'un étudiant universitaire en France est différente comparée à celle *(to that)* d'un étudiant universitaire aux USA. En France, les activités extrascolaires (culturelles ou sportives) sont bien moins développées. Est-ce que la vie sur le campus est importante pour vous?

Note de vocabulaire

The word **universitaire** is an adjective and must be paired with a noun that it is describing; for example, *university dorms* (**des résidences universitaires**). The word **université** is a noun: **J'habite près de l'université.**

Warm-up activities. A. Do these statements describe **David** or **Léa**?
1. Elle est américaine. **2.** Il est étudiant à l'Université de Nice. **3.** Il est français.
4. Elle est étudiante à l'Université de Nice.
5. Elle n'est pas française. **6.** Il est de Nice.
B. Complete these sentences logically:
1. Je suis… **2.** Ma famille et moi, nous sommes… **3.** Mes amis sont… **4.** Mon (Ma) meilleur(e) ami(e) est… **5.** *[to a classmate]* Toi, tu es… **6.** *[to your professor]* Vous êtes très…

Suggestions. A. Point out **il y a** and **un, une,** and **des.** Ask students why there might be two different forms for the word *a*. The concept of grammatical gender and the use of the indefinite article are explained and practiced in the next section, but you may wish to point them out now. **B.** Explain the difference between **un cinéma** and **un théâtre,** between **une bibliothèque** and **une librairie,** and between the noun **l'université** and the adjective **universitaire.**

Qu'est-ce qu'il y a **sur** votre campus?

Sur le campus, **il y a…**

des salles *(f)* de cours | **des bureaux** *(m)* pour les professeurs (profs) | **un amphithéâtre** | une bibliothèque avec Wi-Fi

des résidences *(f)* | un stade des matchs *(m)* de foot(ball) américain | une librairie | un parking

Dans le quartier universitaire, près de l'université, il y a…

des bâtiments *(m)* modernes | des maisons *(f)* | un parc des arbres *(m)* | des concerts *(m)* de rock *(m)* de jazz *(m)* de musique *(f)* pop(ulaire) de musique classique

Line art on this page: © Cengage Learning

Qu'est-ce qu'il y a…? *What is there…?*   **sur** *on*   **il y a** *there is, there are*   **un bureau** *an office*   **un amphithéâtre** *a lecture hall*   **une résidence** *a dormitory*   **Dans le quartier universitaire** *In the university neighborhood*   **près de** *near*   **un bâtiment** *a building*

une boîte de nuit   un théâtre   un cinéma   une salle de gym
des films *(m)*
étrangers /
américains

 Léa parle avec un ami.

RÉMI: Comment est **ton** université, **là-bas** en Californie? Tu aimes le campus?

LÉA: Oui, il est très agréable. Les vieux bâtiments sont très **jolis.**

RÉMI: Qu'est-ce qu'il y a sur le campus?

LÉA: Il y a une grande bibliothèque et beaucoup d'arbres, mais **il n'y a pas assez de** parkings.

RÉMI: Qu'est-ce qu'il y a dans le quartier?

LÉA: Il y a de jolies maisons, des cafés, deux ou trois **bons** restaurants et beaucoup de **mauvais** fast-foods.

Vocabulaire supplémentaire

un arrêt de bus *a bus stop*
une association d'étudiants *a student association*
un centre médical *a health center*
un court de tennis *a tennis court*
une fontaine *a fountain*
un gymnase *a gym*
un labo(ratoire) *a lab*
une piscine *a pool*
un service administratif *an administrative office*
une statue
un terrain de sport *a sports field*

Chez nous. Décrivez votre université.

1. Sur le campus, il y a *plus de nouveaux bâtiments / plus de vieux bâtiments.*
2. *Il y a / Il n'y a pas* le Wi-Fi dans tous les *(all the)* bâtiments.
3. *Il y a / Il n'y a pas* assez de résidences sur le campus.
4. *Il y a / Il n'y a pas* beaucoup d'arbres sur le campus.
5. Le restaurant universitaire est un *bon / mauvais* restaurant. *(Il n'y a pas de restaurant sur le campus.)*
6. *Il y a / Il n'y a pas* assez de parkings.
7. Le week-end, il y a souvent *(often) des matchs de football américain / des concerts / des films étrangers / des films américains / ???.*
8. Dans le quartier près de l'université, il y a *des cafés / un joli parc / ???.*
9. *BookPeople / Monster Books / ???* est une bonne librairie dans le quartier.

À VOUS!

Avec un(e) partenaire, relisez à haute voix la conversation entre Rémi et Léa. Ensuite, adaptez la conversation pour décrire votre université.

étranger (étrangère) *foreign*   **ton (ta, tes)** *your*   **là(-bas)** *(over) there*   **joli(e)** *pretty*   **il n'y a pas** *there isn't, there aren't*
assez de *enough*   **bon(ne)** *good*   **mauvais(e)** *bad*

 **PowerPoint 1-8**

✓ Pour vérifier

1. What are the two forms of the word for *a*? When do you use each? How do you say *some*?

2. How do you say *there is*? *there are*? *there isn't*? *there aren't*?

3. In what three circumstances do you use **de (d')** instead of **un, une,** or **des**? What is an exception to replacing **un, une,** or **des** with **de (d')** in a negative sentence?

iLrn Grammar Tutorials

Vocabulaire sans peine!

Nouns ending in **-tion** and **-té** are usually feminine. Notice these cognate patterns.

-tion = *-tion*
une nation = *a nation*
-té = *-ty*
une activité = *an activity*

How would you say these nouns in French?

a conversation   an administration
a minority   a majority

Suggestions. A. Have students look up words whose gender seems illogical according to their meaning, for example *beard, blouse, mustache,* or *purse.* **B.** Point out the use of the *(m)* and *(f)* to indicate gender when needed. **C.** Suggest that students use flashcards of different colors, putting feminine words on one color of card and masculine words on another, or that they write the words using different colors of ink.

Suggestions. Tell students to position their lips as if to whistle when pronouncing the letter **u** /y/. Contrast the pronunciation of **des** and **de** as well as that of **un** and **une.** Remind students that the final consonants of **un** and **des** are only pronounced in liaison.

SAYING WHAT THERE IS

Le genre, l'article indéfini et l'expression **il y a**

To say *there is* or *there are* in French, use the expression **il y a (un, une, des…).** To say *there isn't* or *there aren't*, use **il n'y a pas (de…).**

All nouns in French have a gender (masculine or feminine). The categorization of most nouns as masculine or feminine cannot be guessed, unless they represent people.

The short word **un** *(a, an),* **une** *(a, an),* or **des** *(some)* before a noun is called the *indefinite article*. Use **un** with masculine singular nouns, **une** with feminine singular nouns, and **des** with all plural nouns.

Always learn a new noun as a unit with the article **(un, une)** in order to remember its gender!

	MASCULINE	FEMININE
SINGULAR	un théâtre	une bibliothèque
PLURAL	des théâtres	des bibliothèques

To make a noun plural, add an **s** to the end of it, unless it ends in **s, x,** or **z**. Nouns that end in **-eau (bureau)** form their plural with an **x (bureaux).**

Un, une, and **des** change to **de (d')** in the following cases.

- After most negated verbs.
  Il y a **un** stade. → Il **n'y** a **pas de** stade.
  Il y a **une** résidence. → Il **n'y** a **pas de** résidence.
  Écrivez **des** phrases complètes. → N'écrivez **pas de** phrases complètes.
  Il y a **des** étudiants dans la classe. → Il **n'y** a **pas d'**étudiants dans la classe.

  But not after the verb **être:**
  C'est **un** bon restaurant. → Ce **n'est pas un** bon restaurant.

- After expressions of quantity, such as **assez, beaucoup,** and **combien.**
  Il y a **un** parking. → Il y a **assez de** parkings.
  Il y a **une** bibliothèque? → Il y a **beaucoup de** bibliothèques.
  Il y a **des** cinémas. → Il y a **combien de** cinémas?

- Directly before a plural adjective.
  Il y a **des** bâtiments modernes. → Il y a **de jolis** bâtiments.

PRONONCIATION

L'article indéfini 1-25

Be careful to pronounce **un** and **une** differently. Use the very tight sound **u** with lips pursed, as in **tu,** to say **une.** To pronounce the **u** sound, position your mouth to pronounce a French **i** with your tongue held high in your mouth. Then, purse your lips. The vowel sound of **un** is nasal. Pronounce the **n** in **un** only when there is **liaison** with a following noun beginning with a vowel sound.

une résidence   un bâtiment   une amie   un‿ami

A. Prononcez bien!
Complétez les questions suivantes sur cette photo avec **un, une** ou **des**. Après, posez les questions à votre partenaire. Faites attention à la prononciation.

1. C'est _____ bibliothèque, _____ petite salle de cours ou _____ grand amphithéâtre?
2. Il y a _____ professeur?
3. Les autres *(others)*, ce sont _____ étudiants ou _____ professeurs?
4. Il y a _____ tableau dans l'amphithéâtre?

© Lisa Klumpp/Getty Images

B. Comparaisons culturelles.
Relisez les **Notes culturelles** aux pages 38 et 44. Sur le campus d'une université française, est-ce qu'il est probable qu'on trouve ces choses *(one finds these things)*?

EXEMPLES un restaurant universitaire
Oui, il y a un restaurant universitaire.

des matchs de football
Non, il n'y a pas de matchs de football.

> des amphithéâtres   un stade   des bureaux de profs
> une bibliothèque   des résidences   des salles de cours
> une boîte de nuit   des matchs de football américain

Maintenant, dites s'il y a ces choses *(these things)* sur votre *(your)* campus.

C. Chez nous.
Complétez chaque phrase avec **un, une, des,** ou **de (d')**. Ensuite *(Then)*, dites si les deux dernières phrases *(the last two sentences)* de chaque groupe sont vraies ou fausses.

1. C'est _____ restaurant.
   Il y a _____ bon restaurant sur notre *(our)* campus.
   Il y a _____ bons restaurants dans le quartier.

2. C'est _____ bibliothèque.
   Il n'y a pas _____ bibliothèque sur notre campus.
   Il y a _____ bibliothèque municipale près d'ici.

3. C'est _____ parking.
   Il y a assez _____ parkings sur notre campus.
   Il y a _____ parkings payants *(pay)* près d'ici.

4. Ce sont _____ arbres.
   Il y a beaucoup _____ arbres sur notre campus.
   Il y a _____ parc avec _____ beaux arbres dans le quartier.

© Cengage Learning

Follow-up for A. Prononcez bien! First, read these sentences and have the students write only the article they hear. After correcting their work, repeat the sentences and have students say whether they are true or false for your campus and have them correct the statements that are false. Follow up by reading similar sentences as dictation. Have students explain the reasons for the use of **de** in numbers 2, 6, 7, and 9. **1.** Sur le campus de l'université, il y a une librairie. **2.** Il n'y a pas de résidences. **3.** Il y a un stade. **4.** Il y a des amphithéâtres. **5.** Il y a une bibliothèque. **6.** Il y a de grands bâtiments. **7.** Il n'y a pas de café. **8.** Il y a un grand parking. **9.** Il y a assez de parkings.

Suggestion for B. Comparaisons culturelles. Remind students of the pronunciation of **un, une, des,** and **de**, and to use **de (d')** rather than **un, une,** or **des** in a negative sentence.

Follow-up for B. Comparaisons culturelles. Est-ce qu'il y a les choses *(things)* indiquées dans chaque endroit *(each place)*? **EXEMPLE** à l'université (une bibliothèque, une boîte de nuit) **À l'université, il y a une bibliothèque. Il n'y a pas de boîte de nuit. 1.** dans la salle de cours (un professeur, des matchs de football, des arbres, un tableau) **2.** dans le quartier universitaire (des maisons, un cinéma, des films étrangers, un théâtre)

Suggestion for C. Chez nous. Remind students of when to use **de (d')** rather than **un, une,** or **des**.

Follow-ups for C. Chez nous. A. Have students correct the false statements. **B.** Complétez ces phrases. **1.** À l'université, il y a... **2.** Il y a beaucoup de... **3.** Il n'y a pas assez de... **4.** Il n'y a pas de... (Repeat the same items with **Dans le quartier universitaire...** and with **Dans mon quartier...**)

 **PowerPoint 1-9**

IDENTIFYING AND DESCRIBING PEOPLE AND THINGS

C'est ou *il est / elle est* et la place de l'adjectif

All nouns in French are masculine or feminine. There is no neuter. Generally, use **il** or **elle** to say *it* and **ils** or **elles** to say *they* when talking about things, depending on the gender of the noun being referred to.

Le campus? **Il** est beau.   Les parkings? **Ils** sont petits!
La bibliothèque? **Elle** est jolie.   Les résidences? **Elles** sont très vieilles!

Note that **c'est,** as well as **il est / elle est,** can mean *he is / she is / it is,* and **ce sont,** as well as **ils sont / elles sont,** can mean *they are.* These expressions are not interchangeable.

Use **c'est** and **ce sont**:

- with *nouns* to identify or describe.
  C'est David.
  C'est un jeune homme sympathique.
  C'est mon ami.
  C'est le frère de Jean.

Use **il est / elle est** and **ils sont / elles sont**:

- with *adjectives* to describe.
  Il est petit et sympathique.
- with *prepositional phrases* to say such things as where someone or something is or is from.
  Il est de Nice.
  Il est en cours.
- with *nationalities, professions* (including **étudiant[e]**), *and religions* without the indefinite article.
  Il est français.
  Il est étudiant.
  Il est catholique.

In French, most descriptive adjectives are placed *after* the noun they describe.

un campus moderne   une boîte de nuit populaire   des amis sympas

However, these 15 very common adjectives are placed *before* the noun.

beau (belle)	jeune	bon (bonne)	grand(e)	autre
joli(e)	vieux (vieille)	mauvais(e)	petit(e)	même
	nouveau (nouvelle)	gentil(le)	gros(se)	seul(e) *(only)*
				premier (première)

un joli campus   une grande boîte de nuit   de bons amis

The adjectives **beau, nouveau,** and **vieux** have alternate masculine singular forms, **bel, nouvel,** and **vieil,** that are used before nouns beginning with a vowel sound.

MASCULINE SINGULAR (PLUS CONSONANT SOUND)	MASCULINE SINGULAR (PLUS VOWEL SOUND)	FEMININE SINGULAR
un beau quartier	un bel ami	une belle amie
un nouveau quartier	un nouvel ami	une nouvelle amie
un vieux quartier	un vieil ami	une vieille amie

✓ **Pour vérifier**

1. Do you use **c'est** and **ce sont** or **il est / elle est** and **ils sont / elles sont** with a noun to identify or describe someone or something? with an adjective to describe? with a prepositional phrase to say such things as where someone or something is or is from? with nationalities, professions, and religions without the indefinite article?

2. Are most adjectives placed before or after the noun they describe? Which 15 adjectives are placed before the noun they describe?

3. What are the alternate masculine singular forms of **beau, nouveau,** and **vieux**? When are they used?

Note *de grammaire*

Remember to use **il y a** to say *there is / there are.* Use **c'est / ce sont** and **il est / elle est / ils sont / elles sont** to say *this/that/he/she/it is* and *these/those/they are.*
Sur le campus, **il y a** beaucoup de nouveaux bâtiments. **Ils sont** beaux!
On the campus, ***there are*** *a lot of new buildings.* ***They are*** *beautiful!*

Suggestion. Remind students to use **elles sont** for groups of all feminine nouns and **ils sont** for groups of all masculine nouns or for mixed groups.

Suggestions. A. Point out the feminine form of **bon (bonne). B.** Give students the mnemonic device BAGS (beauty, age, goodness, and size) to help remember which adjectives precede the noun. **C.** To help students remember how to spell the alternate forms **bel, nouvel,** and **vieil,** point out that they are truncated versions of the feminine forms.

🌐 **Sélection musicale.** Search the Web for the song "**Je suis un homme**" by Zazie to enjoy a musical selection containing these structures.

A Qu'est-ce que c'est? Identifiez ces personnes et ces choses. Après, décrivez-les avec l'adjectif le plus logique de chaque paire.

EXEMPLES

café
(grand / petit)
(agréable / désagréable)
C'est un café.
Il est petit.
Il est agréable.

étudiantes
(sympa / antipathique)
(intéressant / ennuyeux)
Ce sont des étudiantes.
Elles sont sympas.
Elles sont intéressantes.

1.
homme
(paresseux / dynamique)
(intéressant / ennuyeux)
(beau / laid)
(grand / petit)

2.
étudiants
(gros / mince)
(beau / laid)
(intellectuel / paresseux)
(jeune / vieux)

3.
femme
(paresseux / sportif)
(gros / mince)
(jeune / vieux)
(grand / petit)

4.
maisons
(moderne / vieux)
(joli / laid)
(grand / petit)
(agréable / désagréable)

B C'est un(e)... / Ce sont des... Maintenant, identifiez et décrivez chaque personne ou chose de l'exercice précédent. Utilisez le nom et un adjectif logique.

EXEMPLES

café
(grand / petit)
(agréable / désagréable)
C'est un petit café.
C'est un café agréable.

étudiantes
(sympa / antipathique)
(intéressant / ennuyeux)
Ce sont des étudiantes sympas.
Ce sont des étudiantes intéressantes.

C Léa. Léa parle de ses études. Complétez chaque phrase par **c'est, ce sont, il est, elle est, ils sont** ou **elles sont**.

1. Le cours de littérature, _____ mon cours préféré. _____ plutôt facile. _____ à huit heures du matin. _____ dans un grand amphithéâtre.
2. Mes profs? _____ intéressants. _____ de bons profs. _____ à l'université tous les jours. _____ intelligents. _____ sympas.
3. Mon meilleur ami, _____ David. _____ d'ici. _____ un bon ami. _____ très marrant. _____ français. _____ le frère de Jean.

D Compliments. Écrivez la forme correcte de l'adjectif le plus logique au bon endroit *(in the right position)* dans la phrase pour faire un *compliment*.

EXEMPLE C'est une _____ femme **dynamique**. (paresseux / dynamique)

1. C'est un _____ restaurant _____. (bon / mauvais)
2. Ce sont de/des _____ chiens *(dogs [m])* _____. (méchant / sympathique)
3. C'est un _____ campus _____. (beau / laid)
4. C'est une _____ femme _____. (ennuyeux / intéressant)
5. C'est un _____ homme _____. (laid / beau)
6. C'est une _____ résidence _____. (nouveau / vieux)
7. C'est un _____ amphithéâtre _____ (nouveau / vieux)

Follow-up for *B. C'est un(e)... / Ce sont des...* Have students say the opposite of each sentence they created using **Ce n'est pas... / Ce ne sont pas...** Remind them that **un, une,** and **des** are not replaced by **de** in a negative sentence when the verb in the sentence is a form of **être**. EXEMPLES Ce n'est pas un grand café. Ce n'est pas un café désagréable. Ce ne sont pas des étudiantes antipathiques. Ce ne sont pas des étudiantes ennuyeuses.

Follow-up for *C. Léa.* Have students use **C'est/Ce sont** or **Il est/Elle est/Ils sont/Elles sont** in the affirmative or negative to create sentences with these cues. EXEMPLE le professeur de français (un homme) **C'est un homme. / Ce n'est pas un homme.** **1.** le professeur de français (un homme, une femme, de Paris, français, sympa, à la maison maintenant, dans son *(his / her)* bureau après le cours, professeur d'histoire aussi, une personne paresseuse, le meilleur ami / la meilleure amie de mes parents) **2.** *[use the names of two students in the class and change the gender of the cues as needed, i.e., Joel and Chris]* (mes amis, gentils, en cours maintenant, américains, intelligents, étudiants, des jeunes gens sympathiques)

Follow-up for *D. Compliments.* Have students go back and say the opposite for each item. EXEMPLE C'est une _____ femme **paresseuse.** (paresseux / dynamique)

COMPÉTENCE 4

Talking about your studies

 PowerPoint 1-10

L'UNIVERSITÉ ET LES COURS

Est-ce que vous aimez l'université?

J'aime beaucoup...   J'aime assez...   Je n'aime pas (du tout)...   Je préfère...

les professeurs	la bibliothèque	les devoirs	**les fêtes**
les étudiants	le labo(ratoire) de langues	les examens	le sport
le campus		la salle d'informatique	les matchs de basket
les cours en ligne			

Qu'est-ce que vous étudiez?

J'étudie la philo(sophie).   Je n'étudie pas la littérature.

LES LANGUES (f)
l'allemand (m)
l'anglais (m)
l'espagnol (m)
le français

LES SCIENCES HUMAINES (f)
l'histoire (f)
la psycho(logie)
les sciences po(litiques) (f)

LES ARTS (m)
le théâtre
la musique
la peinture

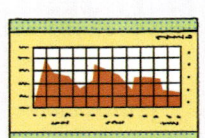

LE COMMERCE
la compta(bilité)
le marketing

LES TECHNOLOGIES
l'informatique (f)
les mathématiques
(les maths) (f)

LES SCIENCES (f)
la bio(logie)
la chimie
la physique

J'aime beaucoup le cours de... Il est facile / difficile / intéressant.

David et Léa parlent de **leurs** études.

DAVID: Qu'est-ce que tu étudies ce semestre?
LÉA: J'étudie le français et la littérature classique. Et toi?
DAVID: J'étudie la philosophie et la littérature classique, comme toi.
LÉA: Comment sont tes cours?
DAVID: J'aime beaucoup le cours de philosophie. Il est très intéressant. Je n'aime pas du tout le cours de littérature, parce que le prof est ennuyeux.

---

une fête a party   **l'allemand** German   **les sciences politiques** government, political science   **la peinture** painting
la comptabilité accounting   **l'informatique** computer science   **la chimie** chemistry   **leur(s)** their

---

Note culturelle

Les universités françaises sont divisées en facultés *(schools or divisions)* telles que *(such as)* la faculté des lettres, la faculté des sciences et la faculté de médecine. Les étudiants universitaires de première année *(first-year college students)* entrent directement dans les cours de leur spécialité. À votre université, est-ce que les étudiants entrent directement dans les cours de leur spécialité ou est-ce que tous les étudiants doivent *(all students must)* commencer par les cours requis *(required)*, tels que *(such as)* les maths et les langues?

Vocabulaire sans peine!

Like nouns ending in **-tion** and **-té**, those ending in **-ique** and **-ie** are usually feminine. Notice these cognate patterns.

-ique = *ic(s)*
l'électronique = *electronics*
-ie = *-y*
l'archéologie = *archeology*

How would you say these nouns in French?

statistics   robotics
anthropology   sociology

Warm-ups. A. Have students use **il y a** to name as many things as they can that are found **1.** on campus, **2.** in the neighborhood. Then have them name one or more thing(s) that is (are) not found in each of these places. You may wish to do this as a chain activity where each student repeats the items named and adds a new one. **B.** Have students introduce a classmate (**C'est...**) and say two things to describe him/her (**Il/Elle est...**). **C.** Tell students that they can also use **une soirée** to talk about a party in the evening (except for a child's party) and that the slang expression **une teuf** is also used by young people to say *a party*.

Note for the conversation. New vocabulary presented in the conversation includes **leurs** and **classique**.

🔊 1-26

A Préférences. Interviewez votre partenaire sur ses préférences.

EXEMPLE   le français / les mathématiques
— Est-ce que tu préfères le français ou les mathématiques?
— Je préfère le français.

1. les langues étrangères / les arts
2. le français / l'espagnol / l'allemand
3. la musique / le théâtre / la peinture
4. les sciences naturelles / les sciences sociales
5. la chimie / la physique / la biologie
6. l'histoire / les sciences politiques / la psychologie
7. le commerce / les technologies
8. l'informatique / la comptabilité / les mathématiques
9. les cours dans les grands amphithéâtres / dans les petites salles / dans le laboratoire de langues / dans la salle d'informatique / en ligne
10. les examens / les devoirs / les fêtes

B Opinions. Faites des comparaisons.

EXEMPLES   Les maths sont plus/moins/aussi faciles que la psychologie.
La chimie est plus/moins/aussi utile que la biologie.

les maths	facile	la psychologie
la chimie	utile *(useful)*	la biologie
la comptabilité	difficile	le marketing
la philosophie	intéressant	la littérature
les étudiants	sympa	les profs
les matchs de basket	amusant	les matchs de foot

La cour de la Sorbonne

C Entretien. Interviewez votre partenaire.

1. Qu'est-ce que tu étudies ce semestre? Comment sont tes cours ce semestre? Comment sont tes profs? Quels cours est-ce que tu préfères? Pourquoi *(Why)*?
2. Tu aimes être en cours le matin, l'après-midi ou le soir? Tu aimes les cours en ligne?
3. Qu'est-ce que tu aimes à l'université? Qu'est-ce que tu n'aimes pas?

À VOUS!

Avec un(e) partenaire, relisez à haute voix la conversation entre David et Léa. Ensuite, adaptez la conversation pour décrire vos cours ce semestre.

 PowerPoint 1-11

IDENTIFYING PEOPLE AND THINGS

L'article défini

The words **le, la, l', les** *(the)* before nouns are called the *definite article*. The form you use depends on the noun's gender and number and whether it starts with a consonant or vowel sound.

	SINGULAR BEFORE CONSONANT SOUND	SINGULAR BEFORE VOWEL SOUND	PLURAL
MASCULINE	**le** livre	**l'**homme	**les** livres, **les** hommes
FEMININE	**la** librairie	**l'**étudiante	**les** librairies, **les** étudiantes

Use the definite article before nouns:

- To specify items, as when using *the* in English.
  Apprenez **les** mots de vocabulaire.   Learn **the** vocabulary words.
- To say what you like, dislike, or prefer.
  Je n'aime pas **les** devoirs.   I don't like homework.
- To talk about something as a general category or an abstract noun.
  Les langues sont faciles pour moi.   Languages are easy for me.

In the last two cases, note that there is no article in English.

✓ **Pour vérifier**

1. What are the four forms of the word for *the* in French? When do you use each one?
2. Besides meaning *the*, what are two other uses of the definite article in French?
3. When is the **s** of the plural form **les** pronounced?

Suggestions. A Remind students to learn new nouns with their articles to remember the gender. **B.** You may wish to point out that the sciences given in this chapter are feminine; that, while the word **langue** is feminine, the names of all the languages are masculine; that words ending in **-té, -tion, -ique,** and **-ie** are usually feminine and those derived from English (**le marketing**) are nearly always masculine.

 Sélection musicale. Search the Web for the song **"Salut à toi"** by Kiemsa to enjoy a musical selection containing these structures.

PRONONCIATION

La voyelle **e** et l'article défini   1-27

As you know, a *final* unaccented **e** is usually not pronounced, unless it is the only vowel, as in **le.**
  grand**e**   histoir**e**   langu**e**   bibliothèqu**e**   j'aim**e**

Otherwise, an unaccented **e** has three different pronunciations, depending on what follows it.

- In short words like **le** or **je,** or when **e** is followed by a single consonant within a word, pronounce it as in:
  j**e**   n**e**   l**e**   r**e**garde   d**e**voirs

- When, as in **les, e** is followed by an unpronounced consonant at the end of a word, pronounce it as in:
  l**es**   m**es**   parl**ez**   aim**ez**   étudi**ez**

- In words like **elle,** where **e** is followed by two consonants within a word, or by a single pronounced consonant at the end of a word, pronounce it as in:
  int**e**llectuel   b**e**lle   qu**e**l   **e**spagnol   bask**e**t

Since the final **s** of plural nouns is not pronounced, you must pronounce the article correctly to differentiate singular and plural nouns. Listen carefully as you repeat each of the following nouns. Notice the **z** sound of final **s** in liaison.

  le livre   la science   l'étudiant   l'étudiante
  les livres   les sciences   les‿étudiants les‿étudiantes

A Prononcez bien!
Listen as David talks about university life. In each sentence, you will hear the singular or plural form of one of the following nouns. Indicate which form you hear by writing the article on your paper.

1. le professeur – les professeurs
2. le cours – les cours
3. l'étudiant – les étudiants
4. le devoir – les devoirs
5. le livre – les livres
6. l'exercice – les exercices
7. le campus – les campus
8. la bibliothèque – les bibliothèques

B Vos cours.
Est-ce que vous étudiez les matières suivantes *(following subjects)*?

EXEMPLE Oui, j'étudie la chimie.
Non, je n'étudie pas la chimie.

1. 2. 3. 4.
5. 6. 7. 8.

C Et vous?
Complétez les phrases pour parler de vos cours et de votre université.

1. J'étudie…
2. J'aime beaucoup…
3. Je n'aime pas beaucoup…
4. Je comprends bien…
5. Je ne comprends pas bien…
6. Je pense que le cours de… est…

D Entretien.
Complétez les questions suivantes avec l'article défini (**le, la, l', les**), l'article indéfini (**un, une, des**) ou **de (d')**. Après, posez ces questions à votre partenaire.

1. Tu aimes _____ sport? Est-ce qu'il y a _____ grand stade sur _____ campus de cette *(this)* université? Est-ce qu'il y a souvent *(often)* _____ matchs de football américain le week-end? Tu préfères _____ foot, _____ football américain ou _____ basket?

2. _____ campus ici est agréable? Il y a _____ vieux bâtiments sur le campus? Il y a _____ bâtiments modernes? Est-ce qu'il y a beaucoup _____ arbres? Il y a assez _____ parkings? Est-ce qu'il y a _____ grande bibliothèque? Est-ce que _____ bibliothèque est moderne?

3. Tu comprends bien _____ français? _____ langues sont faciles ou difficiles pour toi? Tu aimes _____ cours de français? Combien _____ étudiants est-ce qu'il y a dans le cours? Est-ce qu'il y a _____ étudiants étrangers dans _____ cours? _____ cours est difficile? Est-ce qu'il y a _____ examen aujourd'hui?

VIDÉOREPRISE

Les Stagiaires (The Interns)

The entire **Vidéoreprise** section is designed to be a pre-viewing series for the video, as well as a chapter review that can be used independently from the video. There are also additional grammar review exercises on the Instructor's Companion Website and on iLrn.

See the **Résumé de grammaire** section at the end of each chapter for a review of all the grammar of the chapter.

The fourth **Compétence** of each chapter of **Horizons** ends with a **Vidéoreprise** section that reviews the grammar presented in the chapter through activities that revolve around a segment of the **Horizons** video, *Les Stagiaires*. In the video, two students, Rachid Bennani and Amélie Prévot, have just begun an internship at the company Technovert. Before you watch the first episode, do these exercises to review what you have learned in **Chapitre 1** and learn more about the characters that you will see in the video.

A Qui est-ce? Voici des descriptions des deux stagiaires de la vidéo, Rachid et Amélie. Complétez chaque phrase avec **c'est, il est** ou **elle est**.

____1____ Rachid Bennani.
Sur cette photo, ____2____ au *(at the)* bureau de Technovert.
____3____ un jeune homme sympa.
____4____ intéressant.
____5____ étudiant à l'École de Commerce Extérieur.
____6____ du Maroc *(from Morocco)*.

____7____ Amélie Prévot.
____8____ une femme intelligente.
____9____ française.
____10____ très belle.
____11____ stagiaire à Technovert.
____12____ aussi étudiante.

Maintenant, identifiez un(e) des étudiant(e)s de votre classe et parlez un peu de lui *(him)* ou d'elle.

B Rachid. Rachid parle de ses *(his)* études. Complétez les phrases avec la forme correcte du verbe **être**.

EXEMPLE Je <u>suis</u> étudiant à l'École de Commerce Extérieur.

1. Je _____ en cours tous les jours.
2. Les cours _____ faciles pour moi.
3. Mes profs _____ gentils.
4. Mon meilleur ami _____ étudiant.
5. Mes amis et moi, nous _____ assez intellectuels.

 Maintenant, changez les phrases précédentes pour décrire votre situation et posez des questions à votre partenaire basées sur ces phrases.

EXEMPLE — Je suis étudiant(e) à... Et toi? Est-ce que tu es aussi étudiant(e) à...?
— Oui, je suis aussi étudiant(e) à...

C Descriptions. Amélie parle de ses nouveaux collègues à Technovert. Traduisez *(Translate)* les adjectifs pour compléter les phrases. Faites attention à la forme et à la position de l'adjectif.

EXEMPLE Rachid est un ami *(good)*. **Rachid est un bon ami.**

1.

   M. Vieilledent, c'est mon chef *[boss]* *(new)*.
   C'est un homme *(smart)*.
   Ce n'est pas un homme *(young)*.

2.

   Son fils *(His son)*, Christophe, est un jeune homme *(lazy)*.
   Ce n'est pas un homme *(active)*.
   Ce n'est pas un homme *(very smart)*.

3.

   Matthieu, l'informaticien *(computer specialist)*, est un homme *(shy)*.
   C'est un homme *(handsome)*.
   Matthieu et Rachid sont des collègues *(nice)*.

4.

   Céline, la directrice du marketing, est une femme *(pretty)*.
   Camille, l'assistante de M. Vieilledent, est une femme *(smart)*.
   Camille est une amie de Céline *(good)*.

D Mes études. Amélie parle de ses études. Complétez ce qu'elle dit avec **un, une, des, le, la, l', les** ou **de (d')**. Ensuite, adaptez le paragraphe pour décrire vos cours, votre université et le quartier universitaire.

Ce semestre, j'étudie __1__ marketing et __2__ comptabilité. J'aime __3__ université parce qu'il y a __4__ salle d'informatique moderne et il y a aussi __5__ nouveaux laboratoires de langues. __6__ quartier est beau et il y a beaucoup __7__ arbres. Dans le quartier, il y a __8__ cinéma où on passe *(they show)* __9__ films étrangers. J'aime beaucoup __10__ films étrangers.

Suggestion for the video. Tell students not to worry about understanding every word, but to use what they do know and the context to guess what is being said. The video is available on DVD and on *iLrn*. The videoscript is available on the Instructor's Companion Website, **www.cengage.com/french/horizons6e,** and on iLrn.

Access the Video *Les Stagiaires* on iLrn.

 Épisode 1: Comment sont-ils?

AVANT LA VIDÉO

Dans ce clip, Amélie, Rachid et Camille parlent de certains de leurs *(about some of their)* collègues. Avant de regarder le clip, choisissez *(choose)* les adjectifs à connotation positive: **intelligent, paresseux, nerveux, timide, dynamique.**

APRÈS LA VIDÉO

Regardez le clip et dites *(say)* comment Camille décrit *(describes)*:
- Céline
- Christophe
- Matthieu

LECTURE ET COMPOSITION

LECTURE

POUR MIEUX LIRE:
Scanning to preview a text

You are going to read a work by Jacques Prévert (1900–1977), one of France's most popular writers of the last century, from his collection **Paroles** (1949). You have learned to use cognates to make reading easier. It can also help you read if you scan a text before reading it in order to anticipate its content.

On peut deviner! Scan the reading *L'accent grave* and answer these questions to prepare yourself for understanding the text.

1. This is clearly a conversation. Who is it between? Where do you think it takes place?
2. What is the student's name? Where have you heard this name before? What was that character famous for saying?

Note. In the *Lecture et Composition* section, students practice reading and writing strategies. The vocabulary in this section is presented for recognition only and is not considered active. It is not included on the end-of-chapter vocabulary lists or on the tests in the *Testing Program*.

Suggestion. Ask students the significance of the title *L'accent grave*.

L'accent grave

Le professeur Élève Hamlet!

L'élève Hamlet *(sursautant)* … Hein… Quoi… Pardon… **Qu'est-ce qui se passe…** Qu'est-ce qu'il y a… Qu'est-ce que c'est?…

Le professeur *(mécontent)* **Vous ne pouvez pas répondre** «présent» **comme tout le monde?** Pas possible, vous êtes **encore dans les nuages.**

L'élève Hamlet Être ou ne pas être dans les nuages!

Le professeur **Suffit. Pas tant de manières.** Et conjuguez-moi le verbe être, comme tout le monde, **c'est tout ce que je vous demande.**

L'élève Hamlet To be. . .

Le professeur En Français, s'il vous plaît, comme tout le monde.

L'élève Hamlet Bien, monsieur. *(Il conjugue:)*
Je suis ou je ne suis pas, tu es ou tu n'es pas, il est ou il n'est pas, nous sommes ou nous ne sommes pas…

Le professeur *(excessivement mécontent)* Mais **c'est vous qui n'y êtes pas,** mon pauvre ami!

L'élève Hamlet C'est exact, monsieur le professeur, Je suis «où» je ne suis pas. Et, **dans le fond,** hein, à la réflexion, être «où» ne pas être, c'est **peut-être** aussi la question.

Jacques Prévert, "L'accent grave" in *Paroles* © Éditions GALLIMARD.
© Fatras / succession Jacques Prévert pour les droits électroniques réservés

---

un élève *a student, a pupil*   **sursautant** *looking up startled*   **Hein** *Huh*   **Quoi** *What*   **Qu'est-ce qui se passe?** *What's going on?*   **mécontent** *displeased*   **Vous ne pouvez pas répondre…?** *Can't you answer…?*   **comme tout le monde** *like everyone*   **encore dans les nuages** *still in the clouds*   **Suffit.** *Enough.*   **Pas tant de manières.** *Don't make such a fuss.*   **c'est tout ce que je vous demande** *that's all I'm asking of you*   **c'est vous qui n'y êtes pas** *you're the one that's not all there*   **dans le fond** *really, basically*   **peut-être** *perhaps*

Process-writing follow-ups for *Un autoportrait*. A. Have student pairs exchange papers and read each other's composition, then have them go around the room and introduce their partner to several classmates, telling the classmates a few things they learned about their partner from the composition. Supply the following verb forms: **il/elle s'appelle, il/elle étudie, il/elle aime, il/elle habite. B.** Have student pairs work together to prepare at least five sentences comparing themselves to each other. Then, have them take turns reading their sentences to the class. **EXEMPLE Alex: Rebecca est plus sportive que moi. Rebecca: Alex est moins dynamique que moi.**

COMPOSITION

POUR MIEUX ÉCRIRE: Using and combining what you know

Certain strategies can help you learn to write better in a foreign language. When you write, avoid translating. It is very difficult to translate correctly. Use and combine what you already know in French instead. Link sentences with words like **et, mais, alors,** or **parce que** to make your writing flow better.

Organisez-vous. You will be writing a short description of yourself and your studies. First, organize your thoughts by completing these sentences in French.

1. Je m'appelle…
2. Je suis de (d')… et/mais j'habite à…
3. Du point de vue *(view)* physique, je suis…
4. Du point de vue personnalité, je suis…
5. Je suis étudiant(e) à… où j'étudie…
6. Sur le campus, il y a…, mais il n'y a pas…
7. Dans le quartier universitaire, il y a…, mais il n'y a pas…
8. En général, j'aime / je n'aime pas l'université parce que…

Compréhension

1. Dans quel cours sont-ils? À votre avis *(In your opinion)*, les élèves sont très jeunes, assez jeunes ou pas jeunes? Pourquoi *(Why)*?
2. Qu'est-ce que ça veut dire, **ou**? et **où**? Qu'est-ce que ça veut dire **être ou ne pas être**? et **être où ne pas être**?
3. Comment est l'élève Hamlet? attentif ou inattentif? conformiste ou rebelle? bon ou mauvais? intelligent? intellectuel?
4. Comment est le professeur? patient ou impatient? intéressant ou ennuyeux? sympathique ou antipathique?

Un autoportrait

Write a short paragraph introducing yourself. Use the sentences you completed in **Organisez-vous** above to guide you. Remember to use words like **et, mais,** or **parce que** to make your paragraph flow better.

EXEMPLE Je m'appelle Daniel Reyna. Je suis de San Antonio, mais maintenant j'habite à Austin…

iLrn Share It!

COMPARAISONS CULTURELLES

iLrn In the **Culture Modules** in the video library, see **Universities**.

LES ÉTUDES

How similar **(semblable)** is the French education system to the education system in your area? Read these descriptions of secondary schools and universities in France and compare them to schools in your region, by saying one of the following:

> *C'est très semblable ici. / C'est assez semblable ici. / C'est très différent ici.*

1. The French equivalent of the high school diploma is called **le baccalauréat** or **le bac.** There are three types of **baccalauréat** degrees. The **baccalauréat technologique (bac techno)** mixes general and vocational education and prepares students to continue their professional education at the post-secondary level. The **baccalauréat professionnel (bac pro)** is designed to prepare students to enter directly into the workplace. The **baccalauréat général (bac général)** prepares students to continue on to higher education. Students who pursue the **baccalauréat général** do so in a chosen category (called **série**), **la série littéraire (L), la série scientifique (S),** or **la série économique et sociale (ES).**

2. At the end of their secondary studies, French students must pass a series of difficult national exams, also called **le baccalauréat** or **le bac,** covering all the material they have studied, in order to receive the **baccalauréat** degree. Students who do not pass may retest the two subjects in which they did the least well a few weeks later or may retake the last year at the **lycée** and retest all exams.

3. Every student who has received the **bac** is eligible for a nearly free university education. Students only pay the equivalent of a few hundred dollars per year to attend French universities, because the government finances higher education.

4. Students have a large range of choices for continuing their education after the **bac,** as listed in the chart on the next page. However, students are only accepted into certain specialized schools or fields by competitive exams. To be accepted at the most competitive French universities, the **grandes écoles,** which prepare students for high-level positions in the public and private sectors, students generally take two years of preparatory courses and must pass a highly competitive exam.

Note. The vocabulary in this section does not appear in the end-of-chapter vocabulary lists, and is meant for recognition only. You may wish to let students know whether you intend to test them on this vocabulary.

Suggestions. A. Although students are reacting to these descriptions in French, you may wish to let them discuss the items in English. **B.** You may wish to discuss the feeling among some French people that the French education system perpetuates an elitist system, the financial difficulties of the system, the use and importance of **concours,** and the difficulty of changing areas of specialization past a certain level.

Dans une université:	**Dans un lycée:**
THREE-YEAR DEGREE: une licence	**TWO-YEAR CERTIFICATE:** un BTS (brevet de technicien supérieur)
FIVE-YEAR DEGREE: un master	**TWO YEARS OF PREPARATORY SCHOOL:** les classes préparatoires aux grandes écoles (CPGE)
EIGHT-YEAR DEGREE: un doctorat	
FIVE- TO ELEVEN-YEAR DEGREES: un diplôme de médecine, de chirurgie dentaire ou de pharmacie	**Dans une grande école (GE):**
	THREE- TO FIVE-YEAR DEGREES: un diplôme d'ingénieur, de sciences, d'économie, de commerce, de lettres...
Dans un institut universitaire de technologie (IUT):	**Dans une école spécialisée:**
TWO-YEAR DEGREE: un DUT (diplôme universitaire de technologie)	**TWO- TO FIVE-YEAR DEGREE:** un diplôme d'art
	THREE- TO FIVE-YEAR DEGREES: un diplôme de travail social ou de commerce
TWO-YEAR DEGREE: un DEUST (diplôme d'études universitaires scientifiques et techniques)	**SIX-YEAR DEGREE:** un diplôme d'architecte

5. In France, most older universities do not have campuses. Each **faculté** *(division or school)* has buildings, often older ones, where classes meet, and often each **faculté** is centered in a different area of town. Many of the more modern universities, however, do have a campus that is more similar to universities in the United States and Canada.

Compréhension

1. What is the French equivalent of a "high school diploma"? What do students have to do to earn it? What do you think are the advantages and disadvantages of a system in which students must pass a rigorous cumulative exam in order to receive a secondary education diploma?

2. What are the three types of **baccalauréats?** For students preparing the **baccalauréat général,** in what general fields can they earn their diploma? Would you have liked to pick your "major" while still in high school? What might be the advantages and disadvantages?

3. What options do French students have for continuing their studies after the **lycée**? How do these compare to the options in your area?

4. Who is entitled to a college education? Is it expensive? What are the advantages and disadvantages of making higher education almost free?

5. What are the older French universities like? What is a division, or school, called within a French university?

6. Reread the four ***Notes culturelles*** from earlier in this chapter. How much of a role do extracurricular activities and sports play in university life? Can students enter directly into courses of their field of study? Where do most students live? How does this compare to your university?

Supplemental information.
1. Recent government focus for primary and secondary education has been on providing new programs, more personalized assistance, economic aid for lower-income families, and increased opportunities for internships to improve subject mastery; on providing equal learning opportunities to students with disabilities; on improving the nutritional qualities of the food served in schools; and on encouraging students and faculty to interact online, using social networks such as Twitter. **2.** The **grandes écoles** have been consistently ranked very highly in the *Financial Times'* survey of the best European universities. Recent focus in these schools has been on improving quality of education, preparing graduates for global leadership, and increasing the number of students from impoverished areas.

iLrn Share It!

Visit www.cengagebrain.com for additional cultural information and activities.

RÉSUMÉ DE GRAMMAIRE

SUBJECT PRONOUNS, THE VERB *ÊTRE* AND *IL Y A*

Conjugate verbs by changing their forms to correspond to each of the subject pronouns. Here is the conjugation of **être**.

ÊTRE *(to be)*					
je	**suis**	*I am*	nous	**sommes**	*we are*
tu	**es**	*you are*	vous	**êtes**	*you are*
il/elle	**est**	*he/she/it is*	ils/elles	**sont**	*they are*

Je **suis** timide.
Tu **es** étudiant?
Le professeur **est** sympa.
Nous **sommes** d'ici.
Vous **êtes** français?
Ils **sont** en cours.

To negate a verb, place **ne** before it and **pas** after. **Ne** becomes **n'** before vowels or a silent **h**.

Je **ne** suis **pas** optimiste.
Tu **n'**es **pas** d'ici!

Use **il est / elle est** and **ils sont / elles sont** with *adjectives*, to describe people or things, or with *prepositional phrases* to say such things as where someone or something is or is from. Also use them, without the indefinite article, to state professions, nationalities, or religions.

Il est sympathique.
Il est en cours.
Il est catholique.
Elle est française.
Ils sont étudiants.

Use **c'est** and **ce sont** instead of **il est / elle est** and **ils sont / elles sont** to say *he/she/it/this/that is* or *they/these/those are* when identifying or describing someone with *a noun*.

C'est un bon ami.
Ce sont mes amis.

Use **il y a** instead of **être** to say *there is* or *there are*. Its negated form is **il n'y a pas**.

— **Il y a** un examen demain?
— Non, **il n'y a pas** d'examen.

NOUNS AND ARTICLES

Nouns in French are classified as either masculine or feminine. The form of the definite and indefinite articles depends on a noun's gender and whether it is singular or plural.

INDEFINITE ARTICLE *(a, an, some)*		
	SINGULAR	PLURAL
MASCULINE	**un** cours, **un** examen	**des** cours, **des** examens
FEMININE	**une** salle, **une** étudiante	**des** salles, **des** étudiantes

Il y a **des** restaurants près d'ici?
Chez Pierre est **un** bon restaurant.
Tu as *(have)* **une** amie américaine?

The indefinite article changes to **de** (**d'** before vowel sounds) . . .

- after negated verbs (except after **être**).
- after expressions of quantity like **beaucoup, assez**, or **combien**.
- directly before plural adjectives.

Il **n'y** a **pas de** librairie ici.
(Ce **n'est pas une** librairie.)
Il y a **beaucoup de** devoirs et **d'**examens.
Ce sont **de bons** amis.

DEFINITE ARTICLE *(the)*		
	SINGULAR	PLURAL
MASCULINE	**le** cours, **l'**examen	**les** cours, **les** examens
FEMININE	**la** salle, **l'**étudiante	**les** salles, **les** étudiantes

Où sont **les** étudiants?
Ils sont à **la** bibliothèque.

Le and **la** elide to **l'** before vowel sounds.

Use the definite article to say *the* and . . .

- to say what you like or prefer.
- to make generalized statements.

J'aime **la** musique classique.
Les concerts de rock sont amusants.
Je n'aime pas **le** jazz.

The definite article *never* changes to **de** (**d'**).

ADJECTIVES

Adjectives have masculine and feminine, singular and plural forms, which correspond to the nouns they describe. Add an **e** to the masculine form of most adjectives to form the feminine, unless it already ends in an *unaccented* **e**. Add an **s** to make an adjective plural, unless it already ends in **s**, **x**, or **z**.

MASCULINE		FEMININE	
SINGULAR	**PLURAL**	**SINGULAR**	**PLURAL**
joli	jolis	jolie	jolies
divorcé	divorcés	divorcée	divorcées
français	français	française	françaises
jeune	jeunes	jeune	jeunes

The following adjective endings have other changes before adding the **e** for the feminine form.

	MASCULINE		FEMININE	
	SINGULAR	**PLURAL**	**SINGULAR**	**PLURAL**
-eux / -euse:	ennuyeux	ennuyeux	ennuyeuse	ennuyeuses
-en / -enne:	canadien	canadiens	canadienne	canadiennes
-if / -ive:	sportif	sportifs	sportive	sportives
-el / -elle:	intellectuel	intellectuels	intellectuelle	intellectuelles
-er / -ère:	étranger	étrangers	étrangère	étrangères

The adjectives **bon (bonne)**, **gros (grosse)**, and **gentil (gentille)** double their final consonants.

Adjectives generally are placed *after* nouns they describe. However, the following adjectives go *before* nouns.

beau (belle)	jeune	bon (bonne)	grand(e)	autre
joli(e)	vieux (vieille)	mauvais(e)	petit(e)	même
	nouveau	gentil(le)	gros(se)	seul(e)
	(nouvelle)			premier (première)

The adjectives **beau**, **nouveau**, and **vieux** have irregular forms. The alternate singular forms **bel**, **nouvel**, and **vieil** are used before masculine singular nouns beginning with a vowel sound.

MASCULINE		FEMININE	
SINGULAR	**PLURAL**	**SINGULAR**	**PLURAL**
beau (bel)	beaux	belle	belles
nouveau (nouvel)	nouveaux	nouvelle	nouvelles
vieux (vieil)	vieux	vieille	vieilles

QUESTIONS

Questions that are answered with **oui** or **non** have rising intonation. You may just use rising intonation or you may begin the question with **est-ce que**, which elides to **est-ce qu'** before vowel sounds.

If you expect the answer to a question to be **oui**, use **n'est-ce pas?** or **non?** to translate tag questions like *right?, isn't he?, can't you?,* or *won't they?* in English.

Le parc est **joli.** / La maison est **jolie.**

Il est **divorcé.** / Elle est **divorcée.**

Mes amis sont **français.** / Mes amies sont **françaises.**

Il n'est pas **jeune.** / Elle n'est pas **jeune.**

Le film est **ennuyeux.** / La fête est **ennuyeuse.**

Paul est **canadien.** / Marie est **canadienne.**

David est **sportif.** / Lisa est **sportive.**

Ils sont **intellectuels.** / Elles sont **intellectuelles.**

Il est **étranger.** / Elle est **étrangère.**

Il est **bon.** / Elle est **bonne.**

Il est **gros.** / Elle est **grosse.**

Il est **gentil.** / Elle est **gentille.**

C'est un **cours intéressant**, mais il y a beaucoup d'**examens difficiles.**

Sur le campus, il y a beaucoup de **nouveaux bâtiments** et une **grande bibliothèque.**

un **beau** parc / un **bel** homme / une **belle** femme

un **nouveau** film / un **nouvel** ami / une **nouvelle** amie

un **vieux** bâtiment / un **vieil** homme / une **vieille** femme

Le professeur est bon?

Est-ce qu'il est sympa?

Tu étudies le français, **n'est-ce pas?**

Nous sommes dans le même cours, **non?**

VOCABULAIRE

 Audio Flashcards

COMPÉTENCE 1

Identifying people and describing appearance

NOMS MASCULINS

mes amis	my friends
un cours de littérature	a literature class
un frère	a brother
les gens	people
un (jeune) homme	a (young) man

NOMS FÉMININS

mes amies	my friends
une (jeune) femme	a (young) woman
la France	France
une semaine	a week
une sœur	a sister
l'université	the university

ADJECTIFS

américain(e)	American
beau (belle)	handsome, beautiful
célibataire	single
divorcé(e)	divorced
fiancé(e)	engaged
français(e)	French
grand(e)	tall, big
gros(se)	fat
jeune	young
jumeau (jumelle)	twin
laid(e)	ugly
marié(e)	married
même	same
mince	thin
petit(e)	short, small
premier (première)	first
vieux (vieille)	old

EXPRESSIONS VERBALES

C'est...	He is / She is / It is / This is / That is ...
Ce sont...	They are / These are / Those are ...
Ce n'est pas...	He is not / She is not / It is not / This is not / That is not ...
Ce ne sont pas...	They are not / These are not / Those are not ...
Comment est...?	What is ... like?
Il est / Elle est...	He is / She is / It is ...
Ils sont / Elles sont...	They are ...
Il n'est pas / Elle n'est pas...	He is not / She is not / It is not ...
Ils ne sont pas / Elles ne sont pas...	They are not ...
Nous sommes...	We are ...
(pour) étudier	(in order) to study
(pour) visiter	(in order) to visit
(pour) voir	(in order) to see
rencontrer	to meet (for the first time or by chance), to run into
Tu es...	You are ...

DIVERS

à	to, at, in
alors	so, then, therefore
c'est ça	that's right
comme	like, as, for
de	of, from, about
d'où	from where
non?	right?
pendant	during
son / sa / ses	his, her, its

COMPÉTENCE 2

Describing personality

NOMS MASCULINS

tes amis	your friends
le foot(ball)	soccer
mon meilleur ami	my best friend
le sport	sports
le tennis	tennis

NOMS FÉMININS

tes amies	your friends
les études	studies, going to school
ma meilleure amie	my best friend
la personnalité	personality

ADJECTIFS

agréable	pleasant
amusant(e)	fun, amusing
antipathique	disagreeable, unpleasant
bête	stupid, dumb
désagréable	unpleasant
dynamique	active
ennuyeux (ennuyeuse)	boring
extraverti(e)	extroverted, outgoing
gentil (gentille)	nice
idéaliste	idealistic
intellectuel(le)	intellectual
intelligent(e)	intelligent
intéressant(e)	interesting
marrant(e)	funny
méchant(e)	mean
nouveau (nouvelle)	new
optimiste	optimistic
paresseux (paresseuse)	lazy
pessimiste	pessimistic
réaliste	realistic
sportif (sportive)	athletic
sympathique / sympa	nice
timide	timid, shy

EXPRESSIONS VERBALES

être	to be
je suis...	I am ...
tu es...	you are ...
il est...	he is / it is ...
elle est...	she is / it is ...
nous sommes...	we are ...
vous êtes...	you are ...
ils sont...	they are ...
elles sont...	they are ...
j'aime... / je n'aime pas...	I like ... / I don't like ...
tu aimes...	you like ...

DIVERS

assez	rather
aussi... que	as ... as
Ce n'est pas mon truc.	That's not my thing.
Est-ce que...	(particle used in questions)
moins... que	less ... than
ne... pas	not
ne... pas du tout	not at all
n'est-ce pas?	right?
pas tellement	not so much
plus... que	more ... than
plutôt	rather
un peu	a little

COMPÉTENCE 3

Describing the university area

NOMS MASCULINS

un amphithéâtre	a lecture hall
un arbre	a tree
un bâtiment	a building
un bureau (*pl* des bureaux)	an office
un café	a café
un campus	a campus
un cinéma	a movie theater
un concert (de jazz, de rock, de musique pop[ulaire], de musique classique)	a (jazz, rock, pop music, classical music) concert
un fast-food	a fast-food restaurant
un film	a movie, a film
un match de foot(ball) américain	a football game
un parc	a park
un parking	a parking lot
un quartier (universitaire)	a (university) neighborhood
un restaurant	a restaurant
un stade	a stadium
un théâtre	a theater (for live performances)
le Wi-Fi	Wi-Fi

NOMS FÉMININS

une bibliothèque	a library
une boîte de nuit	a nightclub
une librairie	a bookstore
une maison	a house
une résidence	a dormitory
une salle de cours	a classroom
une salle de gym	a gym, a fitness club

ADJECTIFS

bon(ne)	good
catholique	Catholic
étranger (étrangère)	foreign
joli(e)	pretty
mauvais(e)	bad
moderne	modern
populaire	popular
seul(e)	only
universitaire	university

EXPRESSIONS VERBALES

Comment est...?	What is... like?
Il y a...	There is, There are...
Il n'y a pas (de)...	There isn't, There aren't...
Qu'est-ce qu'il y a...?	What is there...?

DIVERS

assez (de)	enough (of)
avec Wi-Fi	with Wi-Fi
beaucoup (de)	a lot (of)
combien (de)	how much (of), how many (of)
dans	in
des	some
là(-bas)	(over) there
près de	near
sur	on
ton, ta, tes	your
un(e)	a, an

COMPÉTENCE 4

Talking about your studies

NOMS MASCULINS

l'allemand	German
l'anglais	English
les arts	the arts
le basket	basketball
le commerce	business
un cours en ligne	an online course
les devoirs	homework
l'espagnol	Spanish
un examen	an exam
le français	French
un labo(ratoire) de langues	a language lab
le marketing	marketing
le théâtre	theater, drama

NOMS FÉMININS

la bio(logie)	biology
la chimie	chemistry
la compta(bilité)	accounting
une fête	a party
l'histoire	history
l'informatique	computer science
une langue	a language
la littérature classique	classical literature
les mathématiques (les maths)	mathematics (math)
la musique	music
la peinture	painting
la philo(sophie)	philosophy
la physique	physics
la psycho(logie)	psychology
une salle d'informatique	a computer lab
les sciences (humaines)	the (social) sciences
les sciences po(litiques)	political science, government
les technologies	technical courses, technologies

EXPRESSIONS VERBALES

Comment sont...?	What are... like?
Est-ce que vous aimez...?	Do you like...?
J'aime beaucoup / assez...	I like a lot / somewhat...
Je n'aime pas (du tout)...	I don't like... (at all).
Je préfère...	I prefer...
Qu'est-ce que vous étudiez / tu étudies?	What are you studying?, What do you study?
J'étudie...	I'm studying, I study...
Je n'étudie pas...	I'm not studying, I don't study...

DIVERS

en ligne	online
le, la, l', les	the
leur(s)	their

Vocabulaire | soixante-trois 63

Sur la Côte d'Azur

Après les cours

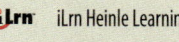	iLrn Heinle Learning Center		Internet web search
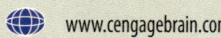	www.cengagebrain.com		Pair work
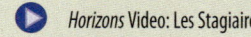	*Horizons* Video: Les Stagiaires		Group work
	Audio		

2

COMPÉTENCE

1 Saying what you like to do
Le temps libre et les loisirs

Saying what you like to do
  L'infinitif

Stratégies et Compréhension auditive
- **Pour mieux comprendre:** *Listening for specific information*
- **Compréhension auditive:** *On sort ensemble?*

2 Saying how you spend your free time
Le week-end

Telling what you do, how often, and how well
  *Les verbes en **-er** et les adverbes*

Telling what you do
  Quelques verbes à changements orthographiques

3 Asking about someone's day
La journée

Asking for information
  Les mots interrogatifs

Asking questions
  Les questions par inversion

4 Going to the café
Au café

Paying the bill
  Les nombres de trente à cent et l'argent

Vidéoreprise *Les Stagiaires*

Lecture et Composition
- **Pour mieux lire:** *Making intelligent guesses*
- **Lecture:** *Aux Trois Obus*
- **Pour mieux écrire:** *Using logical order and standard phrases*
- **Composition:** *Au café*

Comparaisons culturelles *Les cafés en France*

Résumé de grammaire

Vocabulaire

soixante-cinq | 65

NICE

Quand vous visitez une nouvelle **ville,** qu'est-ce que vous préférez **faire**? Visiter les sites historiques et les musées? faire du shopping? dîner au restaurant? profiter des festivals? **sortir** en boîte de nuit? **faire une promenade**? admirer la vue panoramique?
À Nice, il est difficile de **choisir**!

La Promenade des Anglais

Le Carnaval de Nice

Le quartier médiéval du Vieux Nice

Quand *When* **ville** *city* **faire** *to do* **sortir** *to go out* **faire une promenade** *to take a walk* **choisir** *to choose*

Le marché Saleya

Les ruines romaines du quartier Cimiez

Nice

🌐 Visit it live on Google Earth!

NOMBRE D'HABITANTS: **345 000 (et son agglomération** *[metropolitan region]*: **950 000) (les Niçois)**

DÉPARTEMENT: **Alpes-Maritimes**

RÉGION: **Provence-Alpes-Côte d'Azur**

Le savez-vous?

Voudriez-vous visiter ou étudier à Nice? Quel endroit *(place)* ou événement *(event)* à Nice de la liste ci-dessous *(below)* correspond à chaque description?

la Promenade des Anglais	**le marché Saleya**
le Carnaval de Nice	**le quartier Cimiez**
le Vieux Nice	

1. Dans ce quartier chic, il y a des ruines romaines, le musée Matisse et un monastère franciscain du XVIe siècle *(from the XVIth century)*. Les jardins *(gardens)* du monastère offrent une vue magnifique de Nice et de la mer Méditerranée.

2. Les touristes et les Niçois visitent cet endroit pour faire des promenades ou du roller *(rollerblading)* ou pour contempler la Baie des Anges dans une des célèbres chaises bleues *(famous blue chairs)*.

3. Cette célébration date de 1294. Aujourd'hui, plus d'un million de personnes participent à cet événement durant deux semaines en février ou mars.

4. Il y a toujours beaucoup d'étudiants dans les restaurants et les boîtes de nuit des rues étroites *(narrow streets)* de ce vieux quartier animé.

5. Les couleurs et le parfum des roses et des autres fleurs de ce marché enchantent les touristes et les Niçois.

🌐 France is divided into regions and departments. Nice is in the region **Provence-Alpes-Côte d'Azur** and in the department **Alpes-Maritimes.** On the Web, find out what the ten largest cities in France are, and which region and department they are in. Then pick the city you would most like to visit besides Paris and find five interesting facts about it to share with the class.

Le marché *The market*

Les jardins du monastère franciscain de Cimiez

COMPÉTENCE 1

Saying what you like to do

 PowerPoint 2-1

LE TEMPS LIBRE ET LES LOISIRS

— Qu'est-ce que vous aimez **faire** après les cours?
— J'aime...   — Je n'aime pas...   — Je préfère...

— Qu'est-ce que **vous voudriez** faire aujourd'hui après les cours?
— **Je voudrais**...

SORTIR AVEC DES AMIS

aller au cinéma
(aller) voir un film

aller au café
(aller) **prendre un verre**

aller en boîte (de nuit)
(aller) danser

dîner au restaurant

faire du sport
jouer au tennis / au basket /
au football / au volley

faire de l'exercice
faire du vélo
faire du jogging

RESTER À LA MAISON

lire

bricoler

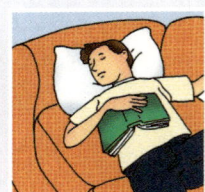
dormir

inviter des amis à la maison

parler au téléphone
envoyer des textos (m)

jouer de la guitare / **de la batterie** / du piano

Line art on this page: © Cengage Learning

le temps libre free time   **un loisir** a leisure activity, a pastime   **faire** to do   **vous voudriez** you would like   **Je voudrais** I would like   **sortir** to go out   **aller** to go   **prendre un verre** to have a drink   **faire du vélo** to ride a bike   **rester** to stay, to remain   **bricoler** to do handiwork   **envoyer un texto** to send a text message   **de la batterie** drums

---

Note culturelle

Les cinq loisirs préférés des Français sont faire du sport (24 %), lire (12 %), jardiner *(to garden)* (8 %), aller au cinéma (6 %) et bricoler (6 %). Mais les pratiques ne correspondent pas toujours aux préférences. Les cinq loisirs les plus souvent pratiqués par les Français sont regarder la télé (78 %), lire (77 %), écouter de la musique (76 %), faire du sport (62 %) et aller au cinéma (60 %). Comment est-ce que vous passez votre temps libre en général? Est-ce que vous préférez faire autre chose?

Note de vocabulaire

1. To say what you *like*, use **j'aime**. To say what you *would like* use **je voudrais**.
2. There are many ways to say *an e-mail*: **un mail, un e-mail, un email, un mel, un mèl, un mél, un courriel, un courrier électronique**.
3. For *to send a text message*, one also says **envoyer un SMS**.

Warm-up activity. Provide these choices: **J'aime beaucoup... J'aime assez... Je n'aime pas...** Ask students how they feel about various aspects of university life (**les professeurs, les étudiants, le laboratoire de langues...**) and how they feel about various courses (**la biologie, la comptabilité...**).

Suggestion. Point out the false cognate **rester**, and that **surfer** is used for Internet surfing. Water surfing is **faire du surf**.

Supplemental activity. Which is better exercise? jouer au tennis ou dîner au restaurant, faire de l'exercice ou regarder la télévision, dormir ou faire du jogging, prendre un verre ou jouer au basket, écouter la radio ou jouer au tennis, faire du vélo ou rester à la maison, écrire des mails ou jouer au basket?

68 soixante-huit | CHAPITRE 2

Vocabulaire supplémentaire

courir to run
cuisiner to cook
dessiner to draw
faire de la muscu(lation) to do bodybuilding
faire de l'aérobic / de la gym(nastique)
jardiner to garden
marcher to walk
nager to swim
peindre to paint
promener le chien to walk the dog
voyager to travel

écouter la radio / de la musique

regarder la télé(vision) / une vidéo / un DVD
jouer à des jeux vidéo *(m)*

travailler sur l'ordinateur
surfer sur Internet
écrire des mails *(m)*

1-29

David invite Léa à sortir.

DAVID: Tu es **libre ce soir**? Tu voudrais faire **quelque chose**?
LÉA: **D'accord.** Où est-ce que tu voudrais aller?
DAVID: Je ne sais pas. **Ça te dit d'**aller en boîte?
LÉA: Non, **pas vraiment.** Je préfère aller au cinéma.
DAVID: Bon, alors **allons** au cinéma! **On va** prendre un verre avant?
LÉA: **Pourquoi pas? Vers** quelle heure?
DAVID: Vers sept heures, sept heures et demie... au café La Martinique?
LÉA: D'accord. Alors, à plus tard.
DAVID: Salut, Léa. À ce soir!

Note for the conversation. New vocabulary includes all glossed words.

Suggestion for the conversation. Set the scene and have students listen with books closed to determine what two things David and Léa decide to do. Then have students read along as you play the conversation again.

A Qu'est-ce que vous aimez faire? Complétez les phrases.

1. Après les cours, j'aime... Aujourd'hui, après les cours, je voudrais...
2. Le samedi matin, j'aime... Ce samedi matin, je voudrais...
3. Le samedi soir, j'aime... Ce samedi soir, je voudrais...
4. Le dimanche, je préfère... Ce dimanche, je voudrais...
5. À la maison, j'aime... Je n'aime pas du tout...

B Invitations. Invitez votre partenaire à faire une des choses suivantes. Ensuite, changez de rôles et faites des projets pour un autre jour.

EXEMPLE demain: jouer au tennis
— **Tu es libre demain? Tu voudrais jouer au tennis avec moi?**
— **Oui, d'accord. / Pas vraiment. Je préfère aller au cinéma.**
— **À quelle heure?**
— **Vers deux heures.**
— **À deux heures? Alors, à demain.**
— **Salut, à demain.**

cet après-midi	jouer au tennis
ce soir	dîner au restaurant
demain après-midi	aller voir un film
demain soir	faire du jogging
vendredi soir	aller prendre un verre
???	???

À VOUS!

Avec un(e) partenaire, relisez à haute voix la conversation entre David et Léa. Ensuite, choisissez une activité et invitez votre partenaire à la faire *(to do it)*.

You can find a list of the new words from this *Compétence* on page 100 and access the audio online.

écrire un mail to write an e-mail   **libre** free   **ce soir** tonight, this evening   **quelque chose** something   **D'accord** Okay
Ça te / vous dit de...? Do you feel like . . . ?   **pas vraiment** not really   **allons** let's go   **On va...?** How about we go . . . ?, Shall we go . . . ?   **Pourquoi pas?** Why not?   **Vers** About, Around, Toward

 **PowerPoint 2-2**

✓ **Pour vérifier**

1. What do you call the basic form of the verb that you find listed in the dictionary?
2. What are the four possible endings for infinitives in French?
3. When you have a sequence of more than one verb in a clause, which one is conjugated? Which ones are in the infinitive?

Suggestions. A. Have students scan a page of the glossary and pick out infinitives. **B.** Have students look up words for other sports and musical instruments they want to know.

SAYING WHAT YOU LIKE TO DO

L'infinitif

To name an activity in French, use the verb in the infinitive. The infinitive is the basic form of the verb that you find listed in the dictionary. French infinitives are single words ending in **-er, -ir, -oir,** or **-re,** like **jouer** *(to play),* **dormir** *(to sleep),* **voir** *(to see),* or **être** *(to be).* In French, whenever there are two or more verbs together in a clause, the first verb is conjugated, but verbs that immediately follow are in the infinitive.

— Qu'est-ce que tu **aimes faire**? — Est-ce que tu **voudrais sortir**?
— J'**aime jouer** au football américain. — Non, je **préfère rester** à la maison.

Use **jouer** *au* to talk about playing most sports using balls or pucks. Many other sports use **faire** *du / de la / de l' / des.*

jouer **au** baseball   jouer **au** golf   faire **du** ski   faire **de l'**exercice

Use **jouer** *du / de la / de l' / des* to talk about playing most musical instruments.

jouer **du** piano   jouer **de la** guitare

As with **un, une,** and **des; du, de la,** and **de l'** change to **de (d')** after a negative expression.

— Tu joues **de la** guitare?   — Tu fais **du** jogging le week-end?
— Non, je ne joue pas **de** guitare.   — Non, je ne fais pas **de** jogging.

Prononcez bien! See Module 17.

PRONONCIATION

La consonne **r** et l'infinitif 1-30

The consonant **r** is one of the few (CaReFuL) consonants that are often pronounced at the end of words. The final **r** of infinitives ending in **-er,** however, is not pronounced. The **-er** ending is pronounced [e], like the **é** in **café.**

parler   inviter   danser   aller
regarder jouer   écouter   dîner

The **r** in infinitives ending in **-ir, -oir,** or **-re** is pronounced. To pronounce a French **r,** hold the back of your tongue firmly arched upward in the back of your mouth and pronounce a vocalized English *h* sound in your throat.
Pronounce the **-ir** verb ending as [iR], unless the verb ends in **-oir** [waR].

sortir   dormir   voir

The **e** in the infinitive ending of **-re** verbs is pronounced when this ending is preceded by a consonant, but not when it is preceded by a vowel.

faire   lire   être   prendre

70 *soixante-dix* | CHAPITRE 2

A Prononcez bien! Demandez à votre partenaire quelle activité il/elle préfère. Faites attention à la prononciation de l'infinitif.

EXEMPLE lire / surfer sur Internet
— **Tu préfères lire ou surfer sur Internet?**
— **Je préfère lire.**

1. faire de l'exercice / dormir
2. sortir avec des amis / rester à la maison
3. prendre un verre au café / dîner au restaurant
4. jouer au tennis / regarder un match de tennis à la télé
5. regarder la télé / aller au cinéma
6. être à la maison / être en cours
7. parler à un ami au téléphone / inviter un ami à la maison
8. écrire des mails / envoyer un texto à un ami
9. faire du jogging / faire du vélo

Note *de vocabulaire*

To say you don't like either activity, use **ne... ni... ni...** *(neither . . . nor . . .)*: **Je n'aime ni lire ni surfer sur Internet.** To say that you like *both* activities, use **J'aime les deux.**

B Chacun ses goûts. Est-ce que vous aimez ces activités?

J'aime beaucoup...   Je n'aime pas beaucoup...
J'aime assez...   Je n'aime pas du tout...

EXEMPLE J'aime assez bricoler.

1.
2.
3. 
4.
5.
6.
7.

C Entretien. Interviewez votre partenaire.

1. Qu'est-ce que tu aimes faire après les cours? Qu'est-ce que tu voudrais faire aujourd'hui après les cours?
2. Est-ce que tu aimes rester à la maison le week-end? Qu'est-ce que tu aimes faire le week-end? Qu'est-ce que tu voudrais faire ce week-end?
3. Est-ce que tu aimes travailler sur l'ordinateur? Tu aimes surfer sur Internet? Tu préfères téléphoner, écrire des mails ou envoyer des textos à des amis?
4. Est-ce que tu voudrais aller au cinéma ce week-end? Quel film est-ce que tu voudrais voir? Tu préfères aller voir un film au cinéma ou regarder un film à la maison?

STRATÉGIES ET COMPRÉHENSION AUDITIVE

Note. Odd-numbered chapters introduce a storyline in a reading. Even-numbered chapters present listening strategies and a recorded passage. To do this section in class, use the Text Audio CD or iLrn. You may prefer to go over the strategies and have students do the pre-listening and listening exercises at home. Remind them to use the In-text Audio instead of the SAM Audio. You can use the post-listening exercises as a comprehension check the following day. New vocabulary in this section is not considered active.

POUR MIEUX COMPRENDRE: *Listening for specific information*

It takes time and practice to understand a foreign language when you hear it. However, using listening strategies can help you learn to understand spoken French more quickly.

Often, you do not need to comprehend everything you hear. Practice listening for specific details, such as times, places, or prices. Do not worry about understanding every word.

🔊 **A** **Quand?** Écoutez ces trois scènes. Indiquez le jour et l'heure choisis *(chosen)*.
1-31

SCÈNE A: LE JOUR _____
           L'HEURE _____

SCÈNE B: LE JOUR _____
           L'HEURE _____

SCÈNE C: LE JOUR _____
           L'HEURE _____

Script for *A. Quand?*

SCÈNE A
— Émilie, tu veux aller au cinéma avec moi ce soir? Il y a un bon film au ciné-club.
— Je suis désolée, mais je ne suis pas libre ce soir. Tu ne veux pas plutôt y aller lundi?
— Bon, d'accord. Lundi à six heures?
— Ça marche!

SCÈNE B
— Je voudrais t'inviter au restaurant ce soir.
— Ce n'est pas possible ce soir. J'ai un examen demain et je dois travailler.
— Et jeudi soir?
— Oui, jeudi, ça va. À quelle heure?
— À huit heures et demie?
— Très bien.

SCÈNE C
— Mélanie veut sortir ce soir, mais je ne suis pas libre.
— Alors, pourquoi ne pas l'inviter à venir avec nous au cinéma mercredi?
— Bonne idée. Le film est à quelle heure?
— À neuf heures et quart.

Script for *B. Qu'est-ce qu'elles font?*

SCÈNE A
— Qu'est-ce qu'on fait ce soir? Tu veux sortir?
— Oui, pourquoi pas. Allons danser avec David.
— Moi, je préfère aller au cinéma.

SCÈNE B
— David m'a invitée au restaurant. Tu veux nous accompagner?
— Non merci, je préfère rester à la maison ce soir.

SCÈNE C
— Tu veux aller prendre un verre maintenant? J'ai un peu soif.
— Merci, mais je vais à la gym.

🔊 **B** **Qu'est-ce qu'elles font?** Léa invite Lisa à sortir. Pour les trois scènes,
1-32 indiquez ce que Lisa préfère faire.

SCÈNE A: _____   SCÈNE B: _____   SCÈNE C: _____

Compréhension auditive: *On sort ensemble?*

🔊 David, Lisa, and Léa run into two of David's friends. Listen to their conversation.
1-33 Do not try to understand every word. The first time, listen only for the leisure activities they mention. Each time you hear one mentioned, write it down.

A Vous comprenez?
Écoutez une seconde fois *(time)* la conversation entre David et ses amis et répondez à ces questions.

1. Est-ce que Thomas et Elsa sont des amis de Léa?
2. Faites une liste de trois choses que Thomas et Elsa découvrent *(discover)* au sujet de Léa et de Lisa *(about Léa and Lisa)*.
3. Qu'est-ce que les cinq jeunes gens décident de faire ensemble *(together)*? Qu'est-ce que David, Léa et Lisa voudraient faire après?

B Tu voudrais sortir?
Invitez votre partenaire à faire les choses suivantes. Utilisez *B. Invitations* à la page 69 comme modèle.

Script for *On sort ensemble?*
THOMAS: Regarde, Elsa... voilà David. Eh, salut, David!
ELSA: Salut, David. Ça va?
DAVID: Salut. Oui, ça va bien. Et vous?
ELSA: Pas mal.
THOMAS: Moi, ça va assez bien.
DAVID: Thomas, Elsa, je voudrais vous présenter mes amies américaines, Léa et Lisa Clark. Léa, Lisa, voici mes amis Thomas Dutoit et Elsa Hardy.
THOMAS: Bonjour.
ELSA: Bonjour, Lisa. Bonjour, Léa.
LÉA ET LISA: Bonjour.
ELSA: Alors, vous êtes d'où?
LÉA: Nous sommes de Los Angeles. Mais moi, j'habite ici maintenant parce que je suis étudiante à l'université.
THOMAS: Et toi, Lisa, tu n'habites pas ici, alors?
LISA: Non, j'habite à Los Angeles. Je suis ici pour voir ma sœur.
THOMAS: Écoutez... justement nous allons voir le nouveau film de Steven Spielberg à L'Étoile. Vous voulez venir avec nous?
DAVID: Je suis désolé, mais j'ai déjà vu ce film. Léa, Lisa et moi pensions aller prendre un verre au café et ensuite aller à la bibliothèque. Venez donc prendre un verre avec nous avant d'aller voir le film!
ELSA: Quelle heure est-il?
LÉA: Cinq heures moins le quart.
ELSA: Bon, d'accord. Je veux bien.
THOMAS: Moi aussi!

Suggestion for *B. Tu voudrais sortir?*
Have students find out from their partners which activities they like (— Tu aimes...? — Moi aussi, j'aime... / Moi, je n'aime pas beaucoup...). When they find one they both enjoy, have them make plans to do it together.

voir un film

jouer au foot

faire du vélo

COMPÉTENCE 2

Saying how you spend your free time

 PowerPoint 2-3

LE WEEK-END

Comment est-ce que vous aimez **passer** le week-end? Qu'est-ce que **vous faites d'habitude** le samedi? Est-ce que vous passez **la matinée** à la maison?

(presque) toujours	**souvent**	**quelquefois**	**rarement**	**ne... jamais**
(almost) always	often	sometimes	rarely	never

Je reste souvent au lit **jusqu'à** 10 heures. | Le samedi matin, je mange **d'abord** quelque chose. | Quelquefois l'après-midi, je **révise** mes cours (j'étudie). | Le soir, je ne reste presque jamais **chez moi. Je vais** souvent au cinéma.

Est-ce que vous aimez faire du sport? Vous jouez bien au foot? Est-ce que vous aimez faire de la musique? Est-ce que vous jouez bien du piano?

très bien	**assez bien**	**assez mal**	**très mal**
very well	fairly well	fairly badly	very badly

Je nage assez mal. | **Je gagne** souvent **quand** je joue au hockey. Je joue **mieux** au hockey **qu'**au foot. | Je joue assez bien du piano. | Je chante très bien.

Line art on this page: © Cengage Learning

---

passer *to pass, to spend* (time) **vous faites** (**faire** *to do, to make*) **d'habitude** *usually, generally* **la matinée** *the morning* **jusqu'à** *until* **d'abord** *first* **réviser** *to review* **chez moi** *at home, at my house* (**chez...** = *to / at / in / by the house of...*) **Je vais** (**aller** *to go*) **Je gagne** (**gagner** *to win*) **quand** *when* **mieux (que)** *better (than)*

Note culturelle

En général, les Français pratiquent le sport dans des clubs sportifs au lieu de faire partie d'une équipe à l'école (*instead of being part of a team at school*) ou à l'université. Le football est de loin (*by far*) le sport le plus populaire. Les dix sports avec le plus grand nombre de pratiquants (*the largest number of participants*) dans l'ordre d'importance sont: 1. le football 2. le tennis 3. l'équitation (*horseback-riding*) 4. le judo 5. le basket 6. le handball 7. le rugby 8. le golf 9. le canoë / le kayak 10. la pétanque (*bocce ball*). Quelles sont les activités sportives les plus populaires dans votre région?

Léa et David parlent de leurs activités (f) du week-end.

LÉA: Qu'est-ce que **tu fais** d'habitude le week-end?

DAVID: Le samedi matin, je reste au lit, le samedi après-midi, je joue au tennis et le soir, j'aime sortir. Et toi?

LÉA: Le matin, je révise mes cours, l'après-midi, j'aime **faire du shopping** et le soir, moi aussi, j'aime sortir.

DAVID: Alors, tu es libre samedi soir? Tu voudrais sortir? Il y a un bon film au ciné-club **à la fac.** C'est un classique de Truffaut.

LÉA: Oui, oui, j'aime bien les vieux films de Truffaut.

DAVID: Le film commence à huit heures. Je **passe** chez toi vers sept heures?

LÉA: D'accord! À samedi, alors.

Le temps libre.
Complétez ces phrases pour parler de vous.

1. Le samedi matin, je passe *presque toujours / souvent / rarement* la matinée à la maison. *(Je ne passe jamais la matinée à la maison.)*
2. Le samedi matin, je reste au lit jusqu'à *sept heures / dix heures / ???*.
3. D'habitude, le samedi matin, je mange quelque chose *à la maison / dans un fast-food / au café / ???*. *(Je ne mange pas le samedi matin.)*
4. Comme *(As)* exercice, je préfère *faire du sport / faire du jogging / nager / ???*. *(Je n'aime pas faire d'exercice.)*
5. Quand je joue *au tennis / au basket / ???*, je gagne *toujours / souvent / rarement*. *(Je n'aime pas faire de sport.)*
6. Je joue *mieux / aussi bien / moins bien* au basket qu'au hockey.
7. Je vais plus souvent au cinéma *seul(e) / avec des amis / avec mon meilleur ami / avec ma meilleure amie / avec ma famille / ???*.
8. Je chante *très bien / assez bien / ???*.
9. Je joue *du piano / de la guitare / de la batterie / ???*. *(Je ne joue pas d'instrument de musique.)*

Vous dansez bien?

À VOUS!

Avec un(e) partenaire, relisez à haute voix la conversation entre David et Léa. Ensuite, adaptez la conversation pour décrire vos activités du week-end et pour inviter votre partenaire à faire quelque chose que vous voudriez faire.

---

tu fais (faire *to do, to make)* **faire du shopping** *to go shopping* **à la fac** *at the university* **passer** *to pass (by)*

TELLING WHAT YOU DO, HOW OFTEN, AND HOW WELL

✓ Pour vérifier

1. How do you determine the stem of an **-er** verb? What endings do you add to it?
2. When do you drop the final **e** of words like **je, ne,** and **le**?
3. Where do you generally place adverbs such as **bien**?
4. Which **-er** verb endings are silent? Which ones are pronounced?

iLrn Grammar Tutorials

Note de grammaire

Verbs whose infinitives do not end in **-er,** and a few irregular verbs whose infinitives do, such as **aller,** do not follow the pattern of conjugation shown here. You will learn how to conjugate such verbs later. You may want to use these forms now to talk about yourself.

I go	je vais
I sleep	je dors
I do, I make	je fais
I read	je lis
I write	j'écris
I take	je prends
I go out	je sors

Vocabulaire sans peine!

Most English verbs ending with **-ate** were French **-er** verbs that were borrowed into English.

imiter to imitate
décorer to decorate

Also notice these cognate patterns among **-er** verbs.

-iser = **-ize**
utiliser to utilize
économiser to economize
-fier = **-fy**
défier to defy
identifier to identify

How would you say the following verbs in French?

to manipulate, to calculate
to digitalize, to hypnotize
to notify, to justify

🌐 **Sélection musicale.** Search the Web for the song **"Elle chante pour moi"** by Faudel to enjoy a musical selection using this vocabulary.

Les verbes en -er et les adverbes

Regular verbs are groups of verbs that follow a predictable pattern of conjugation. The largest group of regular verbs have infinitives ending in **-er.** Most verbs ending in **-er** that you have learned, *except* **aller,** are conjugated in the present tense by dropping the **-er** and adding the following endings: **-e, -es, -e, -ons, -ez, -ent.**

PARLER (to speak, to talk)	
je parl**e**	nous parl**ons**
tu parl**es**	vous parl**ez**
il/elle parl**e**	ils/elles parl**ent**

The present tense can be expressed in three ways in English. Express all three of the following English structures by a single verb in French.

I work.
I am working. } Je travaille.
I do work.

We study.
We are studying. } Nous étudions.
We do study.

Here are the regular **-er** verbs that you have seen so far.

aimer	to like, to love	jouer	to play
bricoler	to do handiwork	manger	to eat
chanter	to sing	nager	to swim
commencer	to begin, to start	parler	to speak, to talk
compter	to count	passer	to pass (by), to spend (time)
danser	to dance	penser	to think
dîner	to have dinner	préférer	to prefer
donner	to give	regarder	to look (at), to watch
écouter	to listen (to)	répéter	to repeat
envoyer	to send	rester	to stay, to remain
étudier	to study	réviser	to review
fermer	to close	surfer	to surf (the Internet)
habiter	to live	travailler	to work
inviter	to invite		

Remember that words such as **je, le, que,** and **ne** make elision before a vowel sound.

j'aime / je **n**'aime pas   **j**'habite / je **n**'habite pas

Adverbs such as **bien, souvent, rarement,** and **beaucoup** tell how well, how often, or how much you do something. In French, these adverbs are generally placed *directly after the conjugated verb*. **D'abord, quelquefois,** and **d'habitude** may also be placed at the beginning or end of the clause.

Thomas regarde **souvent** la télé.   Thomas **often** watches T.V.
Quelquefois, je joue **bien** au tennis.   **Sometimes,** I play tennis **well.**
D'habitude, je travaille le week-end.   **Usually,** I work weekends.

Notice that **ne... jamais** (*never*) follows the same placement rule as **ne... pas.**

Je **ne** joue **jamais** au golf.   I **never** play golf.

PRONONCIATION

 Les verbes en -er

All the present tense endings of **-er** verbs, except for the **nous (-ons)** and **vous (-ez)** forms, are silent.

je rest~~e~~	il rest~~e~~	ils rest~~ent~~
tu rest~~es~~	elle rest~~e~~	elles rest~~ent~~

Rely on context to distinguish between **il** and **ils,** or **elle** and **elles.** You will hear a difference only with verbs beginning with a vowel sound.

il travaill~~e~~ — il~~s~~ travaill~~ent~~   il aim~~e~~ — ils‿aim~~ent~~

The **-ons** ending of the **nous** form rhymes with **maison** and the **-ez** of the **vous** form rhymes with **café** and sounds like the **-er** ending of the infinitive. There is liaison between the **s** of **nous** and **vous** and verbs beginning with vowel sounds.

nou~~s~~ parlons   nous‿étudions
vou~~s~~ parlez   vous‿étudiez

A Prononcez bien!
Écrivez ces phrases sur une feuille de papier. D'abord, complétez chacun des verbes avec la terminaison appropriée. Ensuite, barrez *(cross out)* chaque terminaison qui n'est pas prononcée. Finalement, lisez chaque phrase à haute voix *(aloud)* et dites si elle est vraie en disant **c'est vrai** ou **ce n'est pas vrai.**

EXEMPLE Le samedi soir, j'aim~~e~~ rester à la maison.
            C'est vrai. / Ce n'est pas vrai.

1. Le samedi soir, j'aim___ sortir avec des amis.
2. *[to a classmate]* Et toi, tu aim___ beaucoup sortir, non?
3. *[to a classmate]* Tes amis et toi, vous invit___ souvent des amis à la maison, non?
4. Mes amis et moi, nous préfér___ aller danser.
5. Mais mon meilleur ami préfèr___ rester à la maison.
6. Les étudiants aim___ mieux sortir que de travailler.

Note. Students learn about spelling change verbs, and have further opportunities for practice with **-er** verbs in the next section.

B Opinions.
Comment est le/la colocataire idéal(e)?

EXEMPLE travailler beaucoup
            Il/Elle travaille beaucoup.
            Il/Elle ne travaille pas beaucoup.

1. aimer beaucoup aller en boîte
2. parler souvent au téléphone
3. bricoler bien
4. passer toujours le week-end à la maison
5. inviter souvent des amis à la maison
6. regarder toujours la télé le week-end
7. écouter toujours du hip-hop

Suggestion for *B. Opinions* and *C. Et toi?* Remind students that the **-er** verb endings for **je, tu,** and **il(s)/elle(s)** are silent.

Follow-up for *B. Opinions*. As a composition topic, have students write a short paragraph describing the ideal housemate or roommate.

Comment est le/la colocataire idéal(e)?

C Et toi?
Interviewez un(e) partenaire en formant des questions avec les verbes de l'exercice précédent.

EXEMPLE — Est-ce que tu travailles beaucoup?
            — Oui, je travaille beaucoup.
              Non, je ne travaille pas beaucoup.

Après, parlez de votre partenaire à la classe.

EXEMPLE Il/Elle travaille beaucoup et...

D Le samedi.
Est-ce que vous faites toujours, souvent ou rarement ces choses le week-end? N'oubliez pas *(Don't forget)* de conjuguer le verbe!

(presque) toujours   souvent   quelquefois   rarement   ne... jamais

EXEMPLE   le samedi matin: passer la matinée à la maison
Le samedi matin, je passe toujours (souvent...) la matinée à la maison.
Je ne passe jamais la matinée à la maison.

Un restaurant dans le Vieux Nice

1. le samedi matin:
   rester au lit jusqu'à midi
   manger à la maison
   jouer au tennis
2. le samedi après-midi:
   nager
   bricoler
   surfer sur Internet
3. le samedi soir:
   dîner au restaurant
   danser en boîte
   chanter dans un karaoké
4. le dimanche
   passer la matinée avec la famille
   jouer du piano
   manger dans un fast-food

Maintenant, demandez à votre professeur s'il/si elle fait souvent les choses indiquées.

EXEMPLE   le samedi matin: passer la matinée à la maison
Le samedi matin, est-ce que vous passez souvent la matinée à la maison?

E C'est vrai?
Formez des phrases pour décrire *(to describe)* votre classe.

EXEMPLE   nous / parler beaucoup en cours
Nous parlons beaucoup en cours.
Nous ne parlons pas beaucoup en cours.

1. le professeur / parler quelquefois anglais en cours
2. les étudiants / commencer à très bien parler français
3. nous / travailler beaucoup en cours
4. je / aimer dormir en cours
5. les étudiants / travailler quelquefois ensemble *(together)*
6. nous / regarder des vidéoclips en cours
7. je / écouter toujours le prof en cours
8. les étudiants / manger quelquefois en cours

F Talents.
Dites si ces personnes font bien ou mal ces choses.

très bien   assez bien   assez mal   très mal

EXEMPLE   Ma sœur **joue très bien (assez mal) de la guitare.**
Ma sœur **ne joue pas de guitare.**
Je n'ai pas de sœur. *(I don't have a sister.)*

1. Mon meilleur ami (Ma meilleure amie)...
Mon frère...

2. Mes parents...
Moi, je...

3. Moi, je...
Mon ami _____ [name a friend]...

4. Mes ami(e)s _____ et _____
[name two friends]...
Mes amis et moi, nous...

G Entretien. Interviewez votre partenaire.

1. Tu es musicien(ne)? Est-ce que tu danses bien ou mal? Est-ce que tu chantes bien? Tu préfères écouter la radio ou regarder la télé? Est-ce que tu regardes souvent la télé quand tu manges? Tu écoutes de la musique quand tu étudies?

2. Est-ce que tu es sportif (sportive)? Est-ce que tu aimes le sport? Quel sport est-ce que tu préfères, le football américain, le basket, le golf ou le baseball? Est-ce que tu joues au tennis? au golf? au volley? (Est-ce que tu gagnes souvent?)

3. Est-ce que tu restes souvent à la maison le week-end? Est-ce que tu bricoles quelquefois le week-end? Est-ce que tu étudies? Est-ce que tu préfères bricoler ou étudier?

H Qu'est-ce qui se passe? Décrivez la scène chez la famille Li ce week-end. Donnez au moins cinq détails.

 **PowerPoint 2-5**

✓ **Pour vérifier**

1. In verbs like **préférer**, which forms have a spelling change in the stem in the present tense? What is the change? Which forms have stems like the infinitive?

2. In verbs that end in **-yer**, like **envoyer**, which forms have a spelling change in the stem in the present tense? What is the change? Which forms have stems like the infinitive?

3. What is special about the **nous** form of a verb with an infinitive ending in **-ger**? in **-cer**?

4. What is the difference in pronunciation between **é** and **è**?

Vocabulaire sans peine!

Note the following cognate patterns with these verbs with spelling changes.

-nounce = **-noncer**
to pronounce **prononcer**
to denounce **dénoncer**

-erate = **-érer**
to accelerate **accélérer**
to cooperate **coopérer**

How would you say:
to announce, to renounce
to tolerate, to exasperate

Suggestion. Point out the new verb **voyager.**

TELLING WHAT YOU DO

Quelques verbes à changements orthographiques

A few **-er** verbs have spelling changes in their stems in the present tense.

- When the next-to-last syllable of an infinitive has an **e** or **é,** this letter often changes to **è** in all forms except **nous** and **vous.** The stem for the **nous** and **vous** forms is like the infinitive.

PRÉFÉRER (to prefer)		RÉPÉTER (to repeat)	
je préf**è**re	nous préférons	je rép**è**te	nous répétons
tu préf**è**res	vous préférez	tu rép**è**tes	vous répétez
il/elle préf**è**re	ils/elles préf**è**rent	il/elle rép**è**te	ils/elles rép**è**tent

- In verbs with infinitives ending in **-yer,** the **y** changes to **i** in all forms except **nous** and **vous.**

ENVOYER (to send)	
j'envo**i**e	nous envo**y**ons
tu envo**i**es	vous envo**y**ez
il/elle envo**i**e	ils/elles envo**i**ent

- Verbs ending in **-cer** and **-ger** also have spelling changes. With verbs ending in **-ger,** like **manger, nager,** and **voyager,** an **e** is inserted before the **-ons** ending in the **nous** form. With verbs ending in **-cer,** like **commencer,** the **c** changes to a **ç** before the **-ons** ending in the **nous** form.

VOYAGER (to travel)		COMMENCER (to start, to begin)	
je voyage	nous voyag**e**ons	je commence	nous commen**ç**ons
tu voyages	vous voyagez	tu commences	vous commencez
il/elle voyage	ils/elles voyagent	il/elle commence	ils/elles commencent

iLrn **Prononcez bien!** See Modules 18, 29, and 34.

PRONONCIATION

Les verbes à changements orthographiques 1-36

Spelling changes occur in verbs to reflect pronunciation. The letter **é (e accent aigu)** sounds like the vowel of **les.**

— Vous pr**é**f**é**rez passer la matin**é**e à la maison?
— Non, nous pr**é**f**é**rons passer la matin**é**e au caf**é**.

The letter **è (e accent grave)** often occurs in the final syllable of words ending in a silent **e (Michèle),** and sounds similar to the *e* in the English word *let.*

Je préf**è**re aller à la biblioth**è**que avec Mich**è**le.

In French, **c** and **g** are pronounced soft (the **c** like an **s** and the **g** like a French **j**) before an **e, i,** or **y.** They are pronounced hard (the **c** like **k** and the **g** similar to the *g* in the English word *go*) before an **a, o, u,** or a consonant.

Soft **g: Ge**orges, **Gé**rard, **Gi**lbert   Hard **g: Ga**brielle, Hu**go, Gu**illaume
Soft **c: Cé**cile, Mauri**ce**   Hard **c: Ca**therine, **Co**lette

The letter **ç** is used to indicate that a **c** is soft before **a, o,** or **u.** In verb endings, use **ç** to keep **c** soft before **o,** and introduce an **e** to keep **g** soft before **o.**

commen**ç**ons   man**ge**ons   voya**ge**ons   na**ge**ons

A. Prononcez bien!
Dans les mots suivants, la lettre **c** est prononcée [s]. Lesquels de ces mots requièrent *(require)* une cédille?

1. mena**c**e / mena**c**ant
2. fa**c**ade / fa**c**ile
3. Ni**c**e / ni**c**ois
4. Fran**c**e / fran**c**ais
5. proven**c**al / Proven**c**e
6. pronon**c**iation / pronon**c**ons

Maintenant, dites si vous aimez les gens avec les traits de caractère suivants. Faites attention à la prononciation des lettres **c** et **g**.

J'aime bien les gens... / Je n'aime pas les gens...

> créatifs cultivés arrogants vulgaires
> menaçants superficiels imaginatifs généreux
> calmes courageux égoïstes gentils

B. Préférences.
Complétez ces questions avec le verbe indiqué et interviewez votre partenaire.

1. Avec qui *(With whom)* est-ce que tu _____ (préférer) sortir?
2. Est-ce que tu _____ (envoyer) souvent des textos à des amis?
3. Quel jour est-ce que tes amis _____ (préférer) sortir?
4. Vous _____ (manger) souvent ensemble *(together)*?
5. Est-ce que vous _____ (préférer) dîner ensemble à la maison ou au restaurant?
6. En général, est-ce que les étudiants _____ (préférer) dîner au restaurant ou étudier à la bibliothèque?
7. Tu _____ (aimer) voyager? Tu _____ (voyager) souvent?
8. Tes amis et toi, vous _____ (voyager) souvent ensemble?

C. Posez vos stylos!
Par équipes *(In teams)*, utilisez des verbes en **-er** de la liste à la page 76 pour compléter chaque phrase que votre professeur vous donnera *(will give you)*. Arrêtez d'écrire quand le professeur dira **Posez vos stylos!** *(Stop writing when the professor says Put down your pens!)* Chaque groupe gagnera *(will earn)* un point pour chaque phrase correcte et logique.

EXEMPLE En cours de français, le professeur...

En cours de français, le professeur préfère parler français.
Il écoute les étudiants.
Il répète souvent.
Il envoie beaucoup de mails...

Tes amis et toi, est-ce que vous passez beaucoup de temps au café?

COMPÉTENCE 3

Asking about someone's day

 PowerPoint 2-6

LA JOURNÉE

Note culturelle

D'après une étude *(According to a study)* de l'Institut national de la statistique et des études économiques (Insee) en France, le Français moyen *(average)* consacre *(dedicates)* 11 heures 45 de sa journée aux besoins *(needs)* physiologiques (dormir, manger, faire sa toilette [*to wash up*]); 4 heures 07 au travail, aux études et au transport; 3 heures 10 aux tâches *(tasks)* domestiques et 4 heures 58 aux loisirs ou aux amis. Combien de temps consacrez-vous à ces activités tous les jours?

—Quand est-ce que vous êtes à l'université?
—Je suis à l'université...   le lundi, le mardi... de dix heures à quatre heures.
　　　　　　　　　　　　　le matin, l'après-midi, le soir.
　　　　　　　　　　　　　tous les jours, **sauf** le week-end.
　　　　　　　　　　　　　toute la journée.

—Où est-ce que vous **déjeunez** d'habitude?
—Je déjeune...   chez moi / chez des amis / chez...
　　　　　　　　au restaurant universitaire.
　　　　　　　　au café Trianon / dans un fast-food...

—Qu'est-ce que vous aimez faire après les cours?
—J'aime...   aller au parc / aller à la bibliothèque / aller chez un(e) ami(e).
　　　　　　rentrer à la maison.
　　　　　　dormir...

—**Avec qui** est-ce que vous **aimez mieux** sortir?
—J'aime mieux sortir...   avec mon ami(e)...
　　　　　　　　　　　　avec **mon copain (ma copine).**
　　　　　　　　　　　　avec **mon mari (ma femme).**

—Pourquoi est-ce que vous préférez sortir **avec lui / avec elle**?
—Parce qu'il/elle est...   amusant(e), riche, intéressant(e), beau (belle)...

—Quand est-ce que vous préférez sortir **ensemble**?
—Nous préférons sortir...   le vendredi soir.
　　　　　　　　　　　　　le samedi après-midi...

Note de vocabulaire

1. The adjective **tout** is placed before a noun's article. It means *the whole* or *all* before singular nouns (**toute la journée**) and *all* or *every* before plural nouns (**tous les jours**). It has four forms: **tout** *(masc. sing.)*, **toute** *(fem. sing.)*, **tous** *(masc. plur.)*, and **toutes** *(fem. plur.)*.

2. Use the following pronouns after prepositions such as **avec** or **chez**.

avec moi *with me*
avec toi *with you*
avec lui *with him*
avec elle *with her*
avec nous *with us*
avec vous *with you*
avec eux *with them (m)*
avec elles *with them (f)*

🔊 1-37

Jean **demande** à Léa comment elle passe une journée typique.

JEAN: Quand est-ce que tu es en cours ce semestre?

LÉA: Je suis en cours tous les jours, sauf le week-end. Le lundi, par exemple, je suis en cours de midi à trois heures. Je passe la matinée à la bibliothèque.

JEAN: Et après les cours, qu'est-ce que tu fais en général?

LÉA: **Après,** je rentre à la maison. Je travaille ou **je dors** un peu.

JEAN: Et le soir?

LÉA: Le soir, je reste à la maison et je révise mes cours ou je surfe sur Internet.

Warm-up activity. 1. C'est quel jour, aujourd'hui? **2.** Nous sommes en cours quels jours? **3.** Quelle heure est-il maintenant? **4.** Le cours de français commence à quelle heure? **5.** Il finit à quelle heure? **6.** Après quelle heure est-ce que vous êtes à la maison le *[day of the week]* soir? **7.** Quels jours de la semaine est-ce que vous aimez sortir avec des amis?

Note for the conversation. New vocabulary includes all glossed words and **par exemple** and **en général.**

Suggestion for the conversation. Set the scene. Have the students listen with books closed and pick out all the activities Léa mentions. Then, have them listen again while reading along.

---

sauf *except*　**toute la journée** *all day*　**déjeuner** *to eat lunch*　**rentrer** *to return, to go back (home)*　**Avec qui** *With whom*　**aimer mieux** *to like better, to prefer*　**mon copain (ma copine)** *my boyfriend (my girlfriend)*　**mon mari (ma femme)** *my husband (my wife)*　**avec lui (avec elle)** *with him (with her)*　**ensemble** *together*　**demander** *to ask (for)*　**Après** *Afterwards, After*　**je dors (dormir** *to sleep)*

A　Précisions. Demain, David déjeune avec des amis au café Chez Marie. Quelle est la réponse logique pour chaque question?

1. Quel jour est-ce que nous déjeunons ensemble?
2. À quelle heure?
3. Qui déjeune avec nous?
4. Pourquoi est-ce que tu n'invites pas Thomas?
5. Où est-ce que nous déjeunons?
6. Qu'est-ce que tu voudrais faire après?

a. Au café Chez Marie.
b. Elsa et Cyril.
c. Vendredi.
d. Aller au cinéma.
e. Parce qu'il travaille.
f. À midi et demi.

Chez Marie
Pizzas – Snack – Bar
27, rue de Rennes

euros

Calzone: 6,00
Tomate, champignons, œuf, crème fraîche

Marguerite: 5,00
Tomate, fromage

Poivrons: 5,80
Tomate, fromage, champignons, poivrons

Reine: 5,80
Tomate, fromage, olives, champignons, jambon

Service continu de midi à 2h du matin.

B　C'est vrai? Lisez chaque phrase et dites si **c'est vrai** ou si **ce n'est pas vrai**.

1. Je suis à l'université tous les jours, sauf le dimanche.
2. Nous sommes en cours de français le matin, tous les jours sauf le week-end.
3. Le cours de français est de dix heures à onze heures.
4. Les autres étudiants et moi passons beaucoup de temps ensemble après les cours.
5. Nous déjeunons souvent ensemble.
6. Le samedi, j'étudie le français toute la journée.
7. J'aime mieux aller en cours de français que de sortir avec des amis.

Maintenant, corrigez les phrases qui ne sont pas vraies.

C　Entretien. Interviewez votre partenaire.

1. Quels jours est-ce que tu es à l'université? De quelle heure à quelle heure est-ce que tu es en cours? Est-ce que tu restes à l'université toute la journée? À quelle heure est-ce que tu rentres à la maison?
2. Quand est-ce que tu étudies? Où est-ce que tu aimes mieux étudier: chez toi ou à la bibliothèque? Avec qui est-ce que tu préfères étudier?
3. Où est-ce que tu aimes mieux déjeuner? À quelle heure? Est-ce que tu déjeunes souvent chez toi? Où est-ce que tu préfères manger le soir? Est-ce que tu dînes plus souvent chez toi ou au restaurant? Est-ce que tu manges souvent dans un fast-food? Qu'est-ce que tu préfères: les hamburgers, la pizza ou les tacos?
4. Qu'est-ce que tu aimes faire le week-end? Où est-ce que tu aimes mieux aller avec des amis: au cinéma, au café ou en boîte? Avec qui est-ce que tu préfères sortir? Pourquoi est-ce que tu aimes sortir avec lui (elle)? Quand est-ce que vous aimez mieux sortir?

À VOUS!

Avec un(e) partenaire, relisez à haute voix la conversation entre Jean et Léa. Ensuite, adaptez la conversation pour décrire votre situation. Changez de rôles.

 **PowerPoint 2-7**

ASKING FOR INFORMATION

Pour vérifier

1. How do you form an information question?
2. Does **qui** or **que** become **qu'** before a vowel?
3. When are three times you do not use **est-ce que**?
4. How do you say *Who is this? What is this?*

Grammar Tutorials

Suggestions. A. Remind students to use **parce que** to say *because* and that it elides before a vowel sound. **B.** You may also wish to supply the questions **De quelle heure à quelle heure...?** and **Jusqu'à quelle heure...?**

Les mots interrogatifs

You have learned to ask questions with **est-ce que**. To ask for information such as *what, when,* or *why,* add the appropriate question word before **est-ce que**.

où *where*	**Où est-ce que** vous étudiez?
que (qu') *what*	**Qu'est-ce que** vous étudiez?
pourquoi *why*	**Pourquoi est-ce que** vous étudiez le français?
quand *when*	**Quand est-ce que** vous étudiez?
qui / avec qui *who(m) / with whom*	**Avec qui est-ce que** vous étudiez?
comment *how*	**Comment est-ce que** vous passez la journée?
quel(s) jour(s) *(on) what / which day(s)*	**Quels jours est-ce que** vous êtes en cours?
à quelle heure *at what time*	**À quelle heure est-ce que** vous êtes en cours?

Note that **que** makes elision before a vowel sound, but **qui** does not.

Qu'est-ce que vous aimez faire le soir?   Avec **qui** est-ce que vous aimez sortir?

Do not use **est-ce que** with **qui** when it is the subject of the verb, or with **où** or **comment** when they are followed directly by **être**.

qui *who*	**Qui** travaille avec toi?
où *where*	**Où est** la bibliothèque?
comment *how*	**Comment est** l'université?

Use **Qui est-ce?** to ask *who* someone is. Use **Qu'est-ce que c'est?** to ask *what* something is.

— Qui est-ce?
— C'est Jean.

— Qu'est-ce que c'est?
— C'est un livre.

Suggestion for *Prononciation*. Point out that words borrowed from Latin at a later time are pronounced with the [w] (**aquarium, quartet, quartz, quantum**).

PRONONCIATION

Les lettres **qu** *et la prononciation du mot* **quand** *en liaison* 1-38

In French, **qu** is usually pronounced as in the word **quiche**. It is generally only pronounced with the *w* sound heard in the English word *quite* when it is followed by **oi**, as in **pourquoi**.

    qui   que   quand   quelle heure   pourquoi

Note that **d** in liaison is pronounced as a **t**.

    Quand‿est-ce que tu travailles?

A Prononcez bien! Des amis décident de déjeuner ensemble. D'abord, lisez la liste des mots donnés en faisant attention à la prononciation de la combinaison **qu**. Ensuite, complétez les questions avec le mot qui convient et lisez à haute voix la conversation avec votre partenaire.

> Qui   Que (Qu')   Quand   Où
> Pourquoi   À quelle heure

— Tu voudrais déjeuner avec nous?
— __1__ ?
— Aujourd'hui.
— Oui, d'accord. __2__ ?
— Vers midi.
— __3__ est-ce que tu voudrais manger?
— Chez moi.
— __4__ est-ce que tu prépares?
— Une pizza.
— __5__ est-ce que tu invites?
— Quentin et toi.
— __6__ est-ce que tu voudrais faire après?
— Aller au cinéma.
— __7__ ?
— Parce que je voudrais voir le nouveau film avec Marion Cotillard.

B Beaucoup de questions. Formez des questions en utilisant l'équivalent français des mots interrogatifs donnés. Ensuite, posez-les à un(e) autre étudiant(e).

1. _____ est-ce que tu étudies? *(What? Where? With whom? When?)*
2. _____ est-ce que tu aimes mieux déjeuner? *(At what time? With whom? Where?)*
3. _____ est-ce que tu dînes d'habitude le samedi soir? *(Where? With whom? At what time?)*

C Un jeu. Par équipes *(In teams)*, pensez à une question appropriée pour obtenir chaque réponse, en utilisant un mot interrogatif **(qui, que…)** basé sur les mots en gras *(boldfaced)*. Les équipes sélectionnent tour à tour *(take turns)* un élément. Les équipes gagnent les points indiqués pour chaque bonne réponse.

	A	B	C	D
5 points	Ça va **bien**, merci.	Je m'appelle **Léa Clark**.	Il est **5 heures**.	Aujourd'hui, c'est **lundi**.
10 points	C'est **Lisa**.	C'est **un parc**.	David est **sympa**.	Léa est **à la maison**.
15 points	Lisa aime **la musique**.	Thomas travaille **toute la journée**.	David aime sortir **avec Léa**.	Je rentre **à une heure**.
20 points	**Léa et David** étudient les maths.	Nous aimons mieux **aller au cinéma**.	**Parce que le prof est très intéressant**.	Léa parle **bien** français.

Suggestions for A. Prononcez bien!
A. Point out to students that they need to read the answers to know how to complete the questions. **B.** Have them prepare the items working alone, then correct the answers by having a pair of students act out the conversation.

Follow-up for A. Prononcez bien! Have students create a conversation in which they invite their partners to go out. The person invited should ask at least four logical questions about the outing. Tell students to use **A. Prononcez bien!** as a model.

Warm-up for C. Un jeu. Provide these statements and ask students what questions elicit them. Tell them to base the questions on the underlined part of the responses. First, remind them of the difference between yes/no and information questions and of when not to use **est-ce que**. EXEMPLE J'aime déjeuner au restaurant *[name a restaurant near the university]*. Où est-ce que vous aimez déjeuner? **1.** Je déjeune au restaurant *[name a restaurant]* le lundi, le mercredi et le vendredi. **2.** Je déjeune avec mon ami(e) *[name a friend]*. **3.** J'aime déjeuner au restaurant *[name restaurant]* parce qu'il est près de l'université. **4.** Je déjeune à midi. **5.** Je mange un sandwich. **6.** Après les cours, j'aime rentrer chez moi. **7.** Je rentre à la maison en bus.

PowerPoint 2-8

✓ *Pour vérifier*

1. How would you invert the question: **Il est ici?**
2. Do you ever use **est-ce que** and inversion in the same question?
3. When do you insert a **-t-** between a verb and an inverted subject pronoun?
4. Generally, can you invert nouns, or only pronouns? What do you do if the subject of the question is a noun? How would you invert the question: **Marie déjeune à midi?**
5. What is the inverted form of **il y a?** of **c'est?**
6. How would you invert: **Où est-ce que vous déjeunez?**

iLrn Grammar Tutorials

Suggestion. Point out that **qu'est-ce que (qu')** becomes **que (qu')** in inversion questions and that inversions with noun subjects are not common in conversation. Also tell students that they have been using inversion since the first day of class, then give them these answers and have them ask the logical questions. **1.** Je m'appelle Maxime Dubœuf. **2.** Très bien, merci. Et vous? **3.** Il est six heures. **4.** On dit «un stylo».

ASKING QUESTIONS

Les questions par inversion

You can ask a question using rising intonation or **est-ce que.** You can also use inversion; that is, you can invert the subject pronoun and the verb. Add a hyphen when the subject and verb are inverted.

Est-ce que tu travailles le lundi? = **Travailles-tu le lundi?**

- Invert the *conjugated* verb and the *subject pronoun*. Do not invert a following infinitive.

  Aimes-tu aller au cinéma?   **Voudriez-vous** aller danser?

- Never use both **est-ce que** and inversion in the same question.

  Joues-tu de la guitare?   OR   **Est-ce que tu joues** de la guitare?

- Inversion is not normally used with **je.**

- When the subject is **il** or **elle** and *the verb ends in a vowel*, place a **-t-** between the verb and the pronoun. Do not add **-t-** if the verb ends in a consonant.

  Parle-**t**-il anglais?   Est-il d'ici?
  Travaille-**t**-elle ici?   Est-elle d'ici?

- If the subject of the question is a *noun*, rather than a *pronoun*, state the noun first, then supply a matching pronoun for inversion.

  Le prof est-**il** français?   **Marie** parle-t-**elle** français?
  Les cours sont-**ils** difficiles?   **Ophélie et Juliette** étudient-**elles** ici?

- The inverted form of **il y a** is **y a-t-il. C'est** becomes **est-ce.**

  Y a-t-il un café dans le quartier?   **Est-ce** un bon café?

- To ask information questions, place the question word before the inverted verb. **Qu'est-ce que** becomes **que (qu')** when using inversion.

  Où voudrais-tu aller?   **Que** voudrais-tu faire?   **Qu'**aimes-tu faire?

PRONONCIATION

L'inversion et la liaison 1-39

When the subject is **il, elle, ils,** or **elles,** there is liaison between the verb and its pronoun in inversion.

Lisa est‿elle américaine?
David et Thomas parlent‿ils anglais?

 1-40  **A** **Prononcez bien!** D'abord, écoutez et répétez ces questions. Ensuite, posez-les à un(e) autre étudiant(e). Faites attention à la prononciation!

Gisèle, où est-elle ce soir? Est-elle seule? Étudie-t-elle? Thomas et Gisèle aiment-ils la musique? Dansent-ils bien? Et toi? Aimes-tu danser? Dansons-nous en cours quelquefois? Tes amis et toi, aimez-vous aller en boîte ensemble? Aimez-vous mieux aller au cinéma? Y a-t-il un bon cinéma dans le quartier universitaire?

Script for A. Prononcez bien! Gisèle, où est-elle ce soir? Est-elle seule? Étudie-t-elle? Thomas et Gisèle aiment-ils la musique? Dansent-ils bien? Et toi? Aimes-tu danser? Dansons-nous en cours quelquefois? Tes amis et toi, aimez-vous aller en boîte ensemble? Aimez-vous mieux aller au cinéma? Y a-t-il un bon cinéma dans le quartier universitaire?

Thomas   Gisèle

B Entretien. Changez ces phrases pour parler de vous. Après, posez une question logique à un(e) autre étudiant(e). Utilisez l'inversion.

EXEMPLE Je travaille *le matin.* Et toi?...
Je travaille le soir. Et toi? Quand travailles-tu?

1. Je suis en cours *le lundi, le mercredi et le jeudi.* Et toi?...
2. J'étudie *chez moi.* Et toi?...
3. J'étudie *avec des amis.* Et toi?...
4. Je préfère étudier *le français.* Et toi?...
5. Je préfère étudier *le français parce que le cours est intéressant.* Et toi?...

C Jouons au tennis! David parle avec Lisa. Posez les mêmes questions à un(e) partenaire en utilisant *l'inversion.*

EXEMPLE Tu es sportive?
Es-tu sportive?

1. Tu aimes jouer au tennis?
2. Tu gagnes souvent?
3. Est-ce que tu voudrais jouer au tennis ce week-end?
4. Quand est-ce que tu préfères jouer?
5. À quelle heure est-ce que tu voudrais commencer?
6. Qu'est-ce que tu voudrais faire après?
7. Tes amis sont sportifs?
8. Est-ce qu'ils jouent au tennis?
9. Ton meilleur ami est sportif aussi?
10. Est-ce qu'il joue bien au tennis?

D Le samedi. Voici un samedi typique pour Adrien, l'ami de David. Posez cinq questions à un(e) autre étudiant(e) sur ce qu'Adrien fait *(on what Adrien does)* le samedi. Utilisez un mot interrogatif dans chaque question. Dites **il fait** pour *he does,* si nécessaire.

qui   que   où   quand   pourquoi   comment

Étienne   Adrien   Dominique

ses copains *(his friends)*

Warm-up for A. Prononcez bien! *(on the preceding page).* Have students look over the exercise to find the inverted verb forms and determine where liaison would occur.

Follow-up for A. Prononcez bien! *(on the preceding page).* Give students this dictation: **Gisèle, où est-elle ce soir? Reste-t-elle à la maison? Gisèle et Thomas, sont-ils ensemble? Dansent-ils bien? Et toi, qu'aimes-tu faire le soir? Voudrais-tu aller au cinéma ce soir? Y a-t-il un cinéma dans le quartier?**

Suggestion for B. Entretien and C. Jouons au tennis! Give students time to prepare. Correct their prepared work together before having students interview each other.

Warm-up for B. Entretien. To review the question words, provide this conversation and have students complete it with the correct interrogative words. **Un ami invite David à jouer au tennis et David pose des questions à cet ami. Complétez leur conversation. 1. — _____ joues-tu? — Avec Florence et Marie. 2. — _____ aimes-tu jouer avec elles? — Parce qu'elles ne gagnent pas souvent. 3. — _____ jouent-elles? — Assez bien. 4. — _____ commencez-vous le match? — À trois heures. 5. — _____ jouez-vous? — Au parc. 6. — _____ voudrais-tu faire après? — Allons prendre un verre.**

Suggestion for D. Le samedi. Allow students to work in groups to prepare their questions before asking them of their partners. You may need to guide students with these cues. Create questions to find out: **1.** where Adrien studies in the morning. **2.** with whom he reviews for class. **3.** at what time he eats lunch. **4.** where he eats lunch. **5.** with whom he eats lunch. **6.** what he does in the afternoon. (Point out the expression **il fait** given in the direction line, and its pronunciation.) **7.** with whom he plays soccer. **8.** where they play. **9.** what he does in the evening. **10.** with whom he spends Saturday evenings.

COMPÉTENCE 4

Going to the café

 PowerPoint 2-9

Note culturelle

Au café et au restaurant en France, le service est compris *(included)* dans les prix. Beaucoup de Français ne laissent pas de pourboire *(tip)* supplémentaire, d'autres laissent entre 5 % et 10 %. Est-ce que le service est compris dans les prix des cafés et restaurants de votre région? Laissez-vous toujours *(Do you always leave)* un pourboire ou uniquement si *(if)* c'est mérité?

Note de vocabulaire

To say *I'm hungry / I'm not hungry*, say **J'ai faim / Je n'ai pas faim.** (Literally *I have hunger / I don't have hunger.*) To say *I'm thirsty / I'm not thirsty*, say **J'ai soif / Je n'ai pas soif.** (Literally *I have thirst / I don't have thirst.*) **J'ai** rhymes with the **ais** of **anglais** and **faim** rhymes with **vin**.

Warm-up. Review the numbers from 0 to 30 and explain the use of the euro. Dictate the following prices for students to write down in numerals (30 €, 21 €, 17 €, 5 €, 15 €, 4 €, 9 €, 14 €, 18 €, 16 €, 26 €, 23 €).

Suggestion. Point out that: **1.** one says **un express, un expresso,** or **un café. 2.** an **Orangina** is a carbonated orange drink. **3.** the **c** in **blanc** is not pronounced. **4.** the name **un demi** comes from **un demi-litre,** because it used to refer to *a half-liter* of draft beer. (It is now only a quarter of a liter.) **5.** a French sandwich is traditionally served on half of a **baguette** with butter or Dijon-style mustard as the only condiment. **6.** (in the *Note culturelle*) the word for *tip* (**pourboire**) means *(in order) to drink.*

🌐 **Sélection musicale.** Search the Web for the song *"L'eau et le vin"* by Vanessa Paradis to enjoy a musical selection containing this vocabulary.

AU CAFÉ

Vous êtes au café. Qu'est-ce que vous allez prendre?

Je voudrais…   Pour moi…   Je vais prendre…

un expresso   un café au lait   un thé au citron

une eau minérale   un jus de fruit ou un jus d'orange   **un coca (light)**   un Orangina

un verre de vin rouge ou un verre de vin blanc   **un demi**   une bière

un sandwich au jambon   un sandwich au fromage   des frites

 1-41

David et Léa **commandent une boisson** au café.

DAVID: **Je n'ai pas très faim,** mais **j'ai soif.** Je vais prendre un demi. Et toi?
LÉA: Moi, je voudrais bien un chocolat **chaud.**
DAVID: Monsieur, s'il vous plaît.
LE SERVEUR: Bonjour. Vous désirez?
DAVID: Pour moi, un demi. Et pour mon amie, un chocolat chaud.
LE SERVEUR: Très bien.

Line art on this page: © Cengage Learning

---

un coca (light) *a (diet) Coke, a (diet) cola*   **un demi** *a draft beer*   **commander** *to order*   **une boisson** *a drink, a beverage*
Je n'ai pas très faim (J'ai faim) *I'm not very hungry (I'm hungry)*   **j'ai soif** *I'm thirsty*   **chaud(e)** *hot*
le serveur (la serveuse) *the server*

88 *quatre-vingt-huit* | CHAPITRE 2

Après, David et Léa **paient.**

DAVID:	Ça fait combien, monsieur?
LE SERVEUR:	Ça fait sept euros cinquante.
DAVID:	**Voilà** dix euros.
LE SERVEUR:	Et **voici** votre **monnaie**. Merci bien.

Note culturelle

La monnaie d'usage en France est l'euro, comme dans tous les pays membres de l'Union monétaire européenne (UME). L'euro, représenté par le symbole €, est divisé en 100 centimes. Le mot *argent* veut dire *money* en français, mais on entend *(one hears)* aussi des termes d'argot *(slang)* tels que *le fric, un radis (a radish)* ou *une balle (a bullet)* pour parler de l'argent. En anglais, est-ce qu'il y a une expression en argot pour dire *money* ou *a dollar*?

A Préférences. Proposez les choses suivantes à un(e) autre étudiant(e).

EXEMPLE  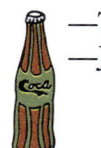 —Tu voudrais une eau minérale ou un coca?
—Je voudrais une eau minérale / un coca.

1.

2.  3.

4.   5.

Note for the conversation. New vocabulary includes all glossed words and **Vous désirez?, Ça fait combien?,** and **un euro.** Point out the expression **Je voudrais bien...**

Suggestion for the conversation. Point out **j'ai faim** and **j'ai soif,** which are taught here as lexical items. Have students listen with books closed and pick out the two drinks ordered and the total price. Then, have them listen and read along.

B J'aime... Est-ce que vous aimez les choses indiquées dans l'exercice précédent? Utilisez **le, la, l'** ou **les** pour indiquer ce que vous aimez ou ce que vous n'aimez pas.

EXEMPLE J'aime bien l'eau minérale. Je n'aime pas du tout le coca.

Suggestion for B. J'aime... Point out that in number three, you use the plural, **J'aime les sandwichs...** as in English, *I like sandwiches...* Remind students that **le, la, l',** and **les** do not change to **de** in the negative.

À VOUS!

Avec deux autres étudiants, relisez à haute voix la conversation au café. Ensuite, adaptez la conversation pour commander ce que *(what)* vous voudriez. La troisième personne va jouer le rôle du serveur/de la serveuse. N'oubliez pas *(Don't forget)* de payer. Changez de rôles.

 You can find a list of the new words from this **Compétence** on page 101 and access the audio online.

---

ils paient (payer *to pay)*   **Voilà** *There is, There are*   **voici** *here is, here are*   **la monnaie** *change*

 **PowerPoint 2-10**

PAYING THE BILL

✓ *Pour vérifier*

1. How do you say **30**? **40**? **50**? **60**? **70**? **80**? **90**?
2. When do you use **et** with numbers? Do you use **et** with 81 and 91?
3. How do you say *one hundred*? Do you translate the word *one*?

Les nombres de trente à cent et l'argent

— Un thé au citron, c'est combien?
— 3,50 € (trois euros cinquante).

30	trente	70	soixante-dix
31	trente et un	71	soixante et onze
32	trente-deux	72	soixante-douze
33	trente-trois…	73	soixante-treize…
40	quarante	80	quatre-vingts
41	quarante et un	81	quatre-vingt-un
42	quarante-deux	82	quatre-vingt-deux
43	quarante-trois…	83	quatre-vingt-trois…
50	cinquante	90	quatre-vingt-dix
51	cinquante et un	91	quatre-vingt-onze
52	cinquante-deux	92	quatre-vingt-douze
53	cinquante-trois…	93	quatre-vingt-treize…
60	soixante	100	cent
61	soixante et un		
62	soixante-deux		
63	soixante-trois…		

Suggestions. A. Point out that: **1. et** is used in 21, 31, 41, 51, 61, and 71, but not with 81 and 91. **2.** the **e** in **quatre-vingts** is pronounced, making **quatre** two syllables. **3.** in the word **quatre-vingts, vingts** ends in **s**, but in the other numbers in the eighties and nineties, it does not. **4. cent** means *one hundred*, and you do not use **un** before it. **B.** Explain the euro system, how prices are abbreviated, the use of the comma in prices, and how prices are read. Have students check the Internet to find out the current value of the euro.

Supplemental activities. A. Tell students they are at an auction and whatever you bid, they must bid 5 € higher: **5 €, 25 €, 40 €, 55 €, 10 €, 30 €, 15 €, 65 €, 85 €, 45 €.** **B.** Say these pairs of numbers and have students repeat the larger one: **2/12, 30/20, 14/40, 50/60, 34/38, 16/6, 21/41, 69/67, 52/32, 11/59. C.** Have a lottery in class. Each student writes ten numbers on a sheet of paper. Randomly call out numbers. The winner is the person who has the most numbers called out. To verify, he/she should read his/her winning numbers back to the class. **D.** Have students secretly write down a number between 1 and 100. As classmates try to guess a student's number, he/she responds **plus que ça** or **moins que ça** to indicate whether his/her number is greater or less than the one guessed until the class determines what it is.

© Oliver Hoffmann/Shutterstock.com

iLrn Prononcez bien! See Module 4.

PRONONCIATION

Les nombres 1-42

Suggestion. You may wish to explain to students that the final **q** of **cinq** is traditionally considered silent before nouns beginning with consonants, but is often pronounced in conversational French.

Some French numbers are pronounced differently, depending on what follows them.

deux̸	deux̸ cafés	deux ^{z} euros
trois̸	trois̸ cafés	trois ^{z} euros
six ^{s}	six̸ cafés	six ^{z} euros
huit ^{t}	huit̸ cafés	huit ^{t} euros
dix ^{s}	dix̸ cafés	dix ^{z} euros

90 quatre-vingt-dix | CHAPITRE 2

A **Prononcez bien!** Commandez ces boissons. Faites attention à la prononciation des nombres.

EXEMPLES trois demis   **Trois demis, s'il vous plaît.**
trois expressos **Trois expressos, s'il vous plaît.**

| deux demis | trois demis | six demis | huit demis | dix demis |
| deux expressos | trois expressos | six expressos | huit expressos | dix expressos |

Maintenant, lisez ces prix *(prices)*. N'oubliez pas *(Don't forget)* de faire la liaison avec le mot **euro** si *(if)* nécessaire.

1 €   11 €   2 €   12 €   3 €   13 €   6 €   16 €   10 €   20 €
61 €   71 €   82 €   92 €   63 €   73 €   86 €   96 €   100 €   80 €

B **Prix indicatifs.** Combien coûte chaque chose?

EXEMPLE une baguette   **C'est 90 centimes.**

1. un journal
2. un expresso
3. un croissant
4. un litre de lait
5. un billet de cinéma
6. un litre d'essence *(gasoline)*

C **Votre monnaie.** Vous êtes au café et vous payez pour vos amis et vous. Suivez l'exemple.

EXEMPLE 6,85 € (10 €)
— **C'est combien, monsieur?**
— **Six euros quatre-vingt-cinq, madame.**
— **Voilà dix euros.**
— **Et voici votre monnaie.**

1. 12,98 € (15 €)
2. 32,45 € (40 €)
3. 23,68 € (30 €)
4. 14,88 € (15 €)
5. 36,75 € (40 €)
6. 7,95 € (10 €)
7. 2,50 € (5 €)
8. 16,80 € (20 €)
9. 13,25 € (20 €)

D **Ça fait combien?** Écrivez les prix *(prices)* que vous entendez.

EXEMPLE VOUS ENTENDEZ: C'est dix euros cinquante.
VOUS ÉCRIVEZ: **10,50 €**

VIDÉOREPRISE

Les Stagiaires

Rappel!
So far in the video, Amélie and Rachid, two new interns at the Technovert company, have met and found out a little about their new colleagues, M. Vieilledent (the boss), Camille (M. Vieilledent's assistant), Céline (the sales manager), Matthieu (the company's shy techie), and Christophe (M. Vieilledent's son and the company's gofer).

See the *Résumé de grammaire* section at the end of each chapter for a review of all the grammar presented in the chapter.

The entire **Vidéoreprise** section is designed to be a pre-viewing series for the video, as well as a chapter review that can be used independently from the video. There are also additional grammar review exercises on the Instructor's Companion Website and on iLrn.

Follow-up for A. Loisirs préférés.
Have students make a list of five things they could invite a classmate to do. Then, have them take turns asking a classmate to do one of them. The classmate must respond by suggesting another activity. **EXEMPLE** — Tu voudrais aller au cinéma ce soir? — Non, je préfère aller danser.

Warm-up for B. Qu'est-ce qu'ils font?
Provide these sentences and have students complete them with the correct form of the verb **aimer** and the name of an activity. **EXEMPLE** Moi, j'... après les cours. Moi, j'aime rentrer à la maison après les cours. **1.** Et toi, *[insert the name of another student]*, est-ce que tu... après les cours? **2.** Le samedi matin, j'... **3.** Le week-end, j'... avec des amis. **4.** Mes amis... le samedi soir. **5.** Mon meilleur ami (Ma meilleure amie)... le week-end. **6.** Mes amis et moi... ensemble. **7.** Mes parents... le samedi. **8.** Et vous, *[insert the professor's name]*, est-ce que vous... le samedi?

In **Épisode 2,** Camille realizes that Matthieu, the company's computer specialist, is interested in Amélie, as he tries to find out from her what kinds of things Amélie likes to do. Before you watch the episode, do these exercises to review what you have learned in **Chapitre 2.**

A Loisirs préférés.
Camille parle des loisirs préférés des employés de Technovert. Complétez chaque phrase avec l'expression indiquée.

EXEMPLE Christophe aime **lire** *(to read)* des mangas.

1. Matthieu aime _____ *(to play)* à des jeux vidéo et _____ *(to work)* sur l'ordinateur.
2. M. Vieilledent aime _____ *(to go)* au café où il aime prendre un café et _____ *(to eat)* des croissants.
3. Rachid aime _____ *(to see)* un film ou _____ *(to dance)* avec ses *(his)* amis.
4. J'aime _____ *(to exercise)*. J'aime surtout *(most of all)* _____ *(to swim)*.
5. Amélie aime _____ *(to go out)* avec des amis. Elle aime _____ *(to have lunch)* au restaurant.
6. Céline aime _____ *(to talk)* au téléphone et _____ *(to write)* des mails.

Maintenant, demandez à votre partenaire s'il/si elle aime faire les choses mentionnées par Camille.

EXEMPLE — Est-ce que tu aimes lire des mangas?
— J'aime lire, mais je n'aime pas les mangas.

B Qu'est-ce qu'ils font?
Rachid et Amélie parlent ensemble. Imaginez comment ils complètent les phrases suivantes. Complétez chacune logiquement avec un verbe conjugué et un adverbe.

EXEMPLE mon meilleur ami / jouer au tennis
Mon meilleur ami joue assez bien au tennis.
Mon meilleur ami ne joue jamais au tennis.

toujours	souvent	quelquefois	rarement	ne... jamais
beaucoup	assez	(un) peu	ne... pas du tout	
très bien	assez bien	assez mal	très mal	

1. moi, je / nager
2. ma meilleure amie / aimer le sport
3. mes amis / jouer au golf
4. je / manger à la maison
5. ma famille et moi / dîner ensemble
6. nous / manger au restaurant
7. ma famille et moi / aimer voyager
8. nous / voyager ensemble

Maintenant, utilisez les mêmes éléments pour former des phrases pour parler de vous et de vos connaissances *(acquaintances)*.

C   C'est combien? Voilà le menu du café en face de *(across from)* Technovert. Demandez à votre partenaire le prix de cinq ou six choses.

EXEMPLE   — Un expresso, c'est combien?
— C'est deux euros quarante-cinq.

L'heure du thé
Prix Service Compris (15 %)

Expresso	2,45	Thé (avec lait ou citron)	3,50
Double expresso	4,10	Thé à la menthe	3,50
Café au lait	3,40	Thé au fruit de la passion	3,50
Infusion	3,50	Thé à la framboise	3,50
(Tilleul, verveine, menthe, tilleul-menthe, verveine-menthe, camomille)		Cappuccino	4,30
		Croissants	1,60
Lait chaud	2,90	Confiture pot	1,40
Café décaféiné	2,60	Tartines beurrées	2,80
Double expresso avec pot de lait	3,60	Grog au rhum	6,10
Chocolat	3,50	Vin chaud	3,75
Café ou chocolat viennois	4,30	Irish Coffee	7,80

Source: L'heure du thé

Maintenant, dites ce que vous aimez prendre aux moments donnés.

1. Quand j'ai très soif, j'aime prendre...
2. Le matin, j'aime bien prendre...
3. Maintenant, je voudrais...
4. Avec un hamburger, j'aime prendre...
5. Quand je dîne au restaurant, j'aime prendre... comme *(as a)* boisson.

D   Questions. Céline et Amélie décident de sortir ensemble. Complétez leur conversation comme indiqué ci-dessous. Utilisez **est-ce que** pour poser les questions.

— Je voudrais sortir ce soir.
— _____?
   What would you like to do?
— Je voudrais aller voir le film *Star Time*.
— _____?
   Why would you like to see Star Time?
— Parce que c'est un film d'action. Et toi? _____?
   Would you like to see Star Time too?
— Oui, bien sûr!
— _____? _____?
   Are you free this evening?   *Would you like to go to the movies with me?*
— D'accord. _____?
   What time does the movie start?
— À 8h30. Je passe chez toi vers 8 heures?
— D'accord. À ce soir, alors.

Maintenant, recommencez la conversation. Utilisez l'inversion pour poser les mêmes questions.

Suggestion for the video. Tell students not to worry about understanding every word, but to use what they do know and the context to guess what is being said. The video is available on DVD and on *iLrn*. The videoscript is available on the Instructor's Companion Website, **www.cengage.com/french/horizons6e,** and on iLrn.

Access the Video *Les Stagiaires* on iLrn.

 Épisode 2: Elle est belle, non?

AVANT LA VIDÉO

Dans ce clip, Matthieu pose beaucoup de questions à Camille au sujet d'Amélie. Quand Céline et Camille se rendent compte *(realize)* qu'il s'intéresse à Amélie, elles font un pari *(bet)* de dix euros: Aura-t-il *(Will he have)* le courage d'inviter Amélie à sortir ou non? Avant de regarder le clip, imaginez une des questions que Matthieu pose à Camille au sujet d'Amélie.

APRÈS LA VIDÉO

Regardez le clip et notez les questions posées par *(asked by)* Matthieu.

LECTURE ET COMPOSITION

LECTURE

POUR MIEUX LIRE:
Making intelligent guesses

By using cognates and what you already know about cafés, you should be able to make intelligent guesses about what is offered on this Parisian café menu. The following exercise will guide you.

Vous savez déjà... What you already know about cafés and restaurants will help you determine the following information.

1. Under **Buffet chaud,** what would **une omelette jambon** be? **une omelette fromage**? **une omelette nature**?
2. What you see at the bottom of the menu indicates that checks are accepted under one condition. What is the condition?
3. At the bottom of the menu, you see that the management claims it is not responsible for something. For what does management claim not to be responsible?

Note. The vocabulary in this section does not appear in the end-of-chapter vocabulary lists and is meant for recognition only. You may wish to let students know in advance whether you intend to test them on this vocabulary.

AUX TROIS OBUS
120, rue Michel-Ange
Paris

NOS SALADES

SALADE VERTE	2,60			
SALADE NIÇOISE	7,00			
(Tomate, œuf, thon, olives, salade, anchois, riz, poivron)				
SALADE 3 OBUS	7,00	SALADE MIXTE	5,00	
(Salade, choux-fleur, foies de volaille, jambon, œuf dur)		*(Tomates, œuf dur, salade)*		
		SALADE CHEF	7,00	
SALADE POULET	7,00	*(Tomates, pommes à l'huile, jambon, gruyère, salade, œuf dur)*		
(Émincé de poulet, maïs, riz, tomates, poivron, salade)		SALADE DE CRUDITÉS	6,00	
		(Concombres, tomates, carottes, choux)		

BUFFET CHAUD

ŒUFS AU PLAT NATURE (3 œufs)	4,00	CROQUE-MONSIEUR	4,00
ŒUFS PLAT JAMBON (3 œufs)	4,50	CROQUE-MADAME	4,80
OMELETTE NATURE	4,00	HOT-DOG	4,00
OMELETTE JAMBON	4,50	FRANCFORTS FRITES	5,00
OMELETTE FROMAGE	4,50	ASSIETTE DE FRITES	2,60
OMELETTE MIXTE *(jambon, fromage)*	6,50		
OMELETTE PARMENTIER	4,50		

```
MOULES MARINIERES      7,00 €
FRISEE AUX LARDONS     7,00 €
ROTI DE BOEUF PUREE    7,50 €
CASSOULET AU CONFIT   11,00 €
ST JACQUES PROVENCALE 14,00 €
```

NOS SANDWICHES

		JAMBON DE PAYS	4,00
		PÂTÉ	2,20
JAMBON DE PARIS	2,20	TERRINE DU CHEF	4,00
SAUCISSON SEC	2,20	CLUB SANDWICH	6,00
SAUCISSON A L'AIL	2,20	*(Pain de mie, poulet, jambon, tomates, œuf, laitue, mayonnaise)*	
RILLETTES	2,20		
MIXTE *(jambon, gruyère)*	3,50	JAMBON A L'OS	4,00
SANDWICH CRUDITÉS	3,50	GRUYÈRE, CAMEMBERT	2,20

Suppl. Pain mie 0,50   Campagne 0,80

FROMAGES

Camembert	2,60		
Roquefort	3,00		
Brie	3,00		
Cantal	3,00	Gruyère	3,00
Chèvre	3,00	Assiette de fromages	5,00

PRIX SERVICE COMPRIS (15%)   La direction n'est pas responsable des objets oubliés dans l'établissement.
Les chèques sont acceptés sur présentation d'une pièce d'identité.

Process-writing follow-up for *Au café*. Have students compare their conversation with those of two classmates and prepare a scene together to act out for the class. Bring props for a café and film the scenes. Also ask the other students follow-up questions after each performance: **Qu'est-ce qu'ils aiment faire? Qu'est-ce qu'ils voudraient faire aujourd'hui? À quelle heure?**, etc.

Follow-up for A. Mots apparentés. Have students practice saying prices with **euros**, using the menu items. Ask them about the price of various items **(Une omelette nature, c'est combien?).** Give them the current exchange rate and have them convert the prices to dollars.

Compréhension

A Mots apparentés. Read the menu and use cognates to identify:

1. Two kinds of sandwiches.
2. Three or four items used in the salads.
3. Two or three items you could order from the **buffet chaud.**

B Lisez bien. Read the menu and answer these questions.

1. C'est combien, une salade verte? une salade niçoise? une salade de crudités? une omelette jambon?
2. Le service est-il compris? À quel pourcentage?

C Bon appétit! Make a list of everything you can identify on this menu, then order something in French.

COMPOSITION

POUR MIEUX ÉCRIRE:
Using logical order and standard phrases

When writing about an activity that you have done often, such as ordering at a café or restaurant, it is useful to start by jotting down the usual sequence of events and typical phrases that are used at each step. This will provide you with a basic framework that you can flesh out with details.

Organisez-vous. You are going to prepare a scene in which two friends meet, talk, and order at a café. Before you begin, make sure you remember how to do these things in French.

- How do you greet a friend?
- How do you call the server over and order a drink?
- How do you talk about what you do on the weekend?
- How do you ask what your companion likes to do and say what you like or do not like to do?
- How do you invite a friend to do something?
- How do you pay the bill?
- How do you say good-bye?

Au café

Using your answers from the preceding activity, write a conversation in which you meet another student at a café. You greet each other, order a drink, and start to chat about what you have in common. Remember to add details, such as when you like to do some things or why you do not like to do other things. You finally make plans to do something later, you get the bill, and you pay.

iLrn Share It!

Lecture et Composition | *quatre-vingt-quinze* **95**

COMPARAISONS CULTURELLES

LES CAFÉS EN FRANCE

Note. The vocabulary in this section does not appear in the end-of-chapter vocabulary lists and is meant for recognition only. You may wish to let students know in advance whether you intend to test them on this vocabulary.

En France, il existe **toute une vie autour des** cafés. **On y va** pour passer du temps avec des amis, discuter, **s'amuser,** prendre un verre ou regarder **les passants**! On ne va pas au café seulement pour boire quelque chose, mais aussi pour le contact social.

Café Le Procope

Fréquenté dans le passé par des **hommes de lettres**, des artistes et des politiciens, comme Voltaire, Victor Hugo, Benjamin Franklin, Napoléon et bien d'autres, Le Procope, créé en 1686, est le café le plus ancien de Paris. Aujourd'hui, c'est un endroit élégant où intellectuels jeunes et moins jeunes **se retrouvent.**

Le café du coin est un centre social traditionnel pour les populations rurales et il **apporte une âme** à son quartier dans les grandes villes. Les cafés ont aussi une importance touristique en France. Aux cafés, les touristes ont l'impression de voir la France de l'intérieur et de **faire partie de la vie quotidienne** française.

Aller au café du coin est un rituel quotidien pour certains Français.

L'accès à Internet est commun dans les cafés fréquentés par les étudiants.

Dans les grandes villes, la connexion Wi-Fi est de plus en plus considérée comme un service de base dans les quartiers d'étudiants et **d'affaires. Cependant,** en France, il est moins commun qu'**aux États-Unis** de voir des gens utiliser un ordinateur ou un téléphone portable en ignorant d'autres personnes **assises** à la même table.

---

toute une vie autour de *a whole lifestyle around*   **On y va** *People go there*   **s'amuser** *to have fun*   **les passants** *the passers-by*   **hommes de lettres** *literary figures*   **se retrouvent** *get together*   **Le café du coin** *The corner café*   **apporte une âme** *gives a soul*   **faire partie de la vie quotidienne** *to be part of daily life*   **d'affaires** *business*   **Cependant** *However*   **aux États-Unis** *in the United States*   **assises** *seated*

Dans les cafés, **les prix** sont généralement **moins élevés** au bar. Si vous préférez être en terrasse, les prix sont souvent **plus élevés**.

Les chaises font face à la rue, parce qu'un des plaisirs du café est de **pouvoir** regarder les passants.

Malgré leur renommée, il y a de moins en moins de cafés traditionnels en France et de plus en plus de fast-foods comme McDonald's (Macdo) et Quick ou de chaînes de *coffee shops* comme Starbucks. Aujourd'hui, avec **des trajets** de plus en plus longs pour aller au travail le matin et des pauses pour déjeuner à midi de plus en plus **courtes,** les établissements qui offrent des boissons et sandwichs **à emporter** sont de plus en plus **nombreux. En outre,** les téléphones portables et les réseaux sociaux sur Internet comme Facebook ou Twitter remplacent les cafés pour certains jeunes Français comme **lieux de rencontre.**

Suggestion. Point out that it is more common for the French to sit side by side at a sidewalk café than face to face so they can talk while looking out towards the street.

Compréhension

1. Pourquoi les Français aiment-ils aller au café?
2. Quel est le café le plus ancien de Paris? Nommez des hommes célèbres qui ont fréquenté ce café.
3. Dans quels cafés le Wi-Fi est-il commun? Citez une différence entre les habitudes des Français et des Américains dans les cafés avec accès à Internet.
4. Pourquoi y a-t-il de moins en moins de cafés traditionnels en France? Donnez deux raisons.
5. Quels sont deux renseignements utiles pour les touristes dans les cafés en France?
6. À votre avis *(In your opinion)*, le café est-il plus populaire en France qu'ici? Qu'est-ce que vous aimez faire au café?

iLrn Share It!

Visit www.cengagebrain.com for additional cultural information and activities.

les prix *prices*   **moins élevés** *lower*   **plus élevés** *higher*   **pouvoir** *to be able to*   **Malgré leur renommée** *Despite their fame*   **des trajets** *routes*   **courtes** *short*   **à emporter** *to go*   **nombreux** *numerous*   **En outre** *Moreover*   **lieux de rencontre** *meeting places*

RÉSUMÉ DE GRAMMAIRE

THE INFINITIVE, -ER VERBS, AND ADVERBS

Qu'est-ce que tu aimes **faire** le soir?
J'aime **rester** à la maison et **lire** ou **sortir** pour **aller voir** un film.
Mes amis **aiment** sortir, mais moi j'**aime** rester à la maison.

The first verb in a clause is conjugated. Verbs after the first verb are in the infinitive (the base form of the verb). French infinitives end in **-er, -ir, -oir,** or **-re.**

Here is the pattern of conjugation for verbs ending in **-er**, except **aller.**

PARLER (to speak)	
je parl**e**	nous parl**ons**
tu parl**es**	vous parl**ez**
il/elle parl**e**	ils/elles parl**ent**

Nous voyag**e**ons souvent ensemble.
Nous commen**ç**ons l'examen.

With verbs ending in **-ger,** insert an **e** before the **-ons** ending in the **nous** form.

With verbs ending in **-cer,** the **c** changes to a **ç** before the **-ons** ending in the **nous** form.

If the next-to-last syllable of an **-er** infinitive has an **e** or an **é**, this letter often changes to an **è** in all forms except **nous** and **vous.**

Après les cours, je **préfère** rentrer à la maison. Mais le vendredi après-midi, mes amis et moi **préférons** aller prendre un verre.

PRÉFÉRER (to prefer)	
je préf**è**re	nous préférons
tu préf**è**res	vous préférez
il/elle préf**è**re	ils/elles préf**è**rent

With verbs ending in **-yer,** the **y** changes to an **i** in all forms, except **nous** and **vous.**

J'**envoie** souvent des textos.
Vous **envoyez** rarement des textos.

ENVOYER (to send)	
j'envoie	nous envoyons
tu envoies	vous envoyez
il/elle envoie	ils/elles envoient

The present tense in French is the equivalent of three present tenses in English.

Je parle français. { *I speak French.*
I am speaking French.
I do speak French. }

Je danse **souvent** le week-end.
Je joue **bien** au tennis.
Je vais **quelquefois** au cinéma.
D'abord, je révise mes cours.
Je travaille le soir, **d'habitude.**
Je **ne** travaille **jamais** le samedi.

Adverbs that tell how much, how often, or how well you do something are generally placed immediately after the verb. **D'abord, quelquefois,** and **d'habitude** are also placed at the beginning or end of the clause and **ne... jamais** surrounds the conjugated verb.

98 *quatre-vingt-dix-huit* | CHAPITRE 2

INFORMATION QUESTIONS AND INVERSION

To ask information questions, place the appropriate question word (**où, qui,** etc.) before **est-ce que**.

Où est-ce que tu travailles?	*(Where . . . ?)*
Qui est-ce que tu voudrais inviter?	*(Who . . . ?)*
Avec qui est-ce que tu déjeunes?	*(With whom . . . ?)*
Pourquoi est-ce que tu es ici?	*(Why . . . ?)*
Qu'est-ce que tu voudrais?	*(What . . . ?)*
Quand est-ce que tu déjeunes?	*(When . . . ?)*
À quelle heure est-ce que tu dînes?	*(At what time . . . ?)*
Quels jours est-ce que tu es en cours?	*(What / Which days . . . ?)*
Comment est-ce que tu aimes passer la matinée?	*(How . . . ?)*

Do not use **est-ce que** with **qui** when it is the subject of the verb, or with **où** or **comment** when they are followed by **être**.

You can also form questions by inverting the verb and its subject pronoun. Remember that:

- You do not normally use inversion with **je**.
- If the subject of the verb is a noun, state the noun, then insert the corresponding pronoun to invert with the verb.
- When the inverted subject is **il** or **elle** and the verb ends *in a vowel*, place a **-t-** between the verb and the pronoun.
- The inverted forms of **il y a** and **c'est** are **y a-t-il** and **est-ce**.

Je suis en cours le mardi et le jeudi. Et toi? **Quand est-ce que** tu es en cours?

Qui travaille ici?
Où est la salle de gym?
Comment sont tes cours?

Où travaillez-vous?
À quelle heure **êtes-vous** en cours?
(Est-ce que) je comprends bien?
Les cours **sont-ils** difficiles?
Marie **parle-t-elle** français?
Marie **est-elle** d'ici?
Y a-t-il un café dans le quartier?
Est-ce un bon café?

THE NUMBERS FROM 30 TO 100 AND MONEY

The **euro** is the official currency of France. A euro is composed of 100 **centimes.** Read prices as:

10,10 € = dix euros dix
84,35 € = quatre-vingt-quatre euros trente-cinq
65,75 € = soixante-cinq euros soixante-quinze
100,50 € = cent euros cinquante

The numbers from 30 to 100 are based on:

30 trente
40 quarante
50 cinquante
60 soixante
70 soixante-dix
80 quatre-vingts
90 quatre-vingt-dix
100 cent

— C'est combien, un expresso?
— C'est **deux euros quarante.**

VOCABULAIRE

  Audio Flashcards

COMPÉTENCE 1

Saying what you like to do

EXPRESSIONS VERBALES

Allons au cinéma / au café… !	Let's go to the movies / to the café … !
J'aime…	I like …
Je préfère…	I prefer …
Je voudrais…	I would like …
aller en boîte (de nuit) / au café / au cinéma	to go to a (night)club / to the café / to the movies
bricoler	to do handiwork
danser	to dance
dîner au restaurant	to have dinner at a restaurant
dormir	to sleep
écouter la radio / de la musique	to listen to the radio / music
écrire un mail	to write an e-mail
envoyer un texto	to send a text message
faire	to do, to make
faire de l'exercice	to exercise
faire du jogging	to jog, to go jogging
faire du ski	to ski, to go skiing
faire du sport	to play sports
faire du vélo	to ride a bike
faire quelque chose	to do something
inviter des amis à la maison	to invite friends to the house
jouer à des jeux vidéo	to play video games
jouer au baseball / au basket / au football / au football américain / au golf / au tennis / au volley	to play baseball / basketball / soccer / football / golf / tennis / volleyball
jouer du piano / de la batterie / de la guitare	to play piano / drums / guitar
lire	to read
parler au téléphone	to talk on the phone
prendre un verre	to have a drink
regarder la télé(vision)	to watch TV
regarder une vidéo / un DVD	to watch a video / a DVD
rester à la maison	to stay home
sortir avec des ami(e)s	to go out with friends
surfer sur Internet	to surf the Net
travailler sur l'ordinateur	to work on the computer
voir un film	to see a movie
On va…?	How about we go … ?, Shall we go … ?
Qu'est-ce que vous aimez faire?	What do you like to do?
Qu'est-ce que vous voudriez faire?	What would you like to do?
Tu voudrais…?	Would you like … ?

DIVERS

À ce soir!	See you tonight!, See you this evening!
après les cours	after class
Ça te dit de… ? / Ça vous dit de… ?	Would you feel like … ?
D'accord!	Okay!
un loisir	a leisure activity, a pastime
Pourquoi pas?	Why not?
quelque chose	something
le temps libre	free time
Tu es libre ce soir?	Are you free this evening / tonight?
vers	about, around, toward
(pas) vraiment	(not) really, truly

COMPÉTENCE 2

Saying how you spend your free time

NOMS MASCULINS

le ciné-club	the cinema club
un classique	a classic

NOMS FÉMININS

une activité	an activity
la fac	the university, the campus

EXPRESSIONS VERBALES

Qu'est-ce que vous faites?	What are you doing?, What do you do?
Qu'est-ce que tu fais?	What are you doing?, What do you do?
chanter	to sing
commencer	to begin, to start
faire de la musique	to play music
faire du shopping	to go shopping
gagner	to win
jouer au hockey	to play hockey
manger	to eat
nager	to swim
passer chez…	to go by … 's house
passer le week-end / la matinée	to spend the weekend / the morning
préférer	to prefer
répéter	to repeat
rester au lit	to stay in bed
réviser les cours	to review (for) classes
je vais	I am going, I go
voyager	to travel

ADVERBES

(très / assez) bien	(very / fairly) well
d'abord	first
d'habitude	usually
jusqu'à	until
(très / assez) mal	(very / fairly) badly
mieux (que)	better (than)
ne… jamais	never
presque	almost
quand	when
quelquefois	sometimes
rarement	rarely
souvent	often
toujours	always

DIVERS

chez…	to / at / in / by … 's house
le samedi matin / après-midi / soir	(on) Saturday mornings / afternoons / evenings
le week-end	the weekend, weekends, on the weekend

COMPÉTENCE 3

Asking about someone's day

NOMS MASCULINS

l'après-midi	the afternoon
mon copain	my boyfriend
un fast-food	a fast-food restaurant
un jour	a day
mon mari	my husband
le matin	the morning
un parc	a park
le soir	the evening

NOMS FÉMININS

ma copine	my girlfriend
ma femme	my wife
la journée	the day

EXPRESSIONS VERBALES

aimer mieux	to like better, to prefer
aller au parc	to go to the park
déjeuner	to have lunch, to eat lunch
demander	to ask (for)
je dors	I am sleeping, I sleep
manger dans un fast-food	to eat in a fast-food restaurant
rentrer	to return, to go back (home)

EXPRESSIONS ADVERBIALES

après	afterwards
l'après-midi	in the afternoon, afternoons
de... heures à... heures	from . . . o'clock to . . . o'clock
ensemble	together
le matin	in the morning, mornings
le soir	in the evening, evenings
tous les jours	every day
toute la journée	all day

EXPRESSIONS INTERROGATIVES

à quelle heure	at what time
avec qui	with whom
comment	how
où	where
pourquoi (parce que)	why (because)
quand	when
quel(s) jour(s)	(on) what / which day(s)
que (qu'est-ce que)	what
Qu'est-ce que c'est?	What is this/that/it?, What are these/those/they?
qui	who(m)
Qui est-ce?	Who is he/she/it/this/that?, Who are they?

DIVERS

avec elle/elles	with her/them (f)
avec lui/eux	with him/them (m or mixed)
en général	in general
par exemple	for example
riche	rich
sauf	except
tout/toute/tous/toutes	all, whole
typique	typical

COMPÉTENCE 4

Going to the café

NOMS MASCULINS

l'argent	money, silver
un café (au lait)	a coffee (with milk)
un centime	a cent
un chocolat (chaud)	a (hot) chocolate
un coca (light)	a (diet) Coke, a (diet) cola
un demi	a draft beer
un euro	a euro
un expresso	an espresso
un jus de fruit / d'orange	a fruit / an orange juice
un Orangina	an Orangina
un sandwich au fromage / au jambon	a cheese / ham sandwich
un serveur	a server
un thé (au citron)	a tea (with lemon)
un verre de vin blanc / rouge	a glass of white / red wine

NOMS FÉMININS

une bière	a beer
une boisson	a drink, a beverage
une eau minérale	a mineral water
des frites	(some) fries
la monnaie	change
une serveuse	a server

NOMBRES

quarante, quarante et un...	forty, forty-one...
cinquante, cinquante et un...	fifty, fifty-one...
soixante, soixante et un...	sixty, sixty-one...
soixante-dix, soixante et onze...	seventy, seventy-one...
quatre-vingts, quatre-vingt-un...	eighty, eighty-one...
quatre-vingt-dix, quatre-vingt-onze...	ninety, ninety-one...
cent	one hundred

DIVERS

Ça fait combien?	How much is it?
Ça fait... euros.	That makes... euros.
C'est combien?	How much is it?
chaud(e)	hot
commander	to order (food and drink)
J'ai faim. / Je n'ai pas faim.	I'm hungry. / I'm not hungry.
J'ai soif. / Je n'ai pas soif.	I'm thirsty. / I'm not thirsty.
payer	to pay
Qu'est-ce que vous allez prendre?	What are you going to have?
Vous désirez?	What would you like?
Je vais prendre...	I'm going to have...
Je voudrais...	I would like...
Pour moi... s'il vous plaît.	For me... please.
voici	here is, here are
voilà	there is, there are
votre (vos)	your

INTERLUDE MUSICAL

JE SUIS

AMEL BENT

You can find these songs on iTunes. You can also search the Internet for videos to hear them performed and to find the lyrics.

Preview all songs for appropriateness of content for your students.

Amel Bent Bachir, known as Amel Bent, is a dancer and singer of popular French music and RnB. Born in France of an Algerian father and Moroccan mother, Amel originally intended to study psychology. In the song *Je suis,* Amel's theme is the universality of the human experience, as she compares herself and her experiences to those of everyone else. The following activities will help you better understand the song.

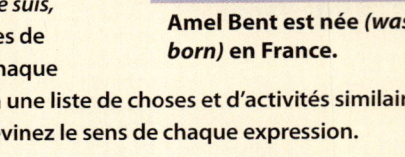

Amel Bent est née *(was born)* en France.

A Je suis. Dans la chanson *(song) Je suis,* la chanteuse compare ses expériences de jeunesse *(childhood)* avec celles de chaque *(those of every)* jeune personne. Voilà une liste de choses et d'activités similaires à celles *(those)* qu'elle mentionne. Devinez le sens de chaque expression.

1. chaque fille ou garçon
2. chaque rue et quartier
3. les jeux d'enfants
4. des heures de colle
5. les cœurs et les vœux des enfants
6. faire des bêtises
7. plonger dans un rêve
8. jouer au ballon
9. sauter à la corde
10. sécher les cours
11. jouer sur le palier
12. grandir dans le même quartier

a. *every street and neighborhood*
b. *every girl or boy*
c. *to do dumb things*
d. *hours of detention*
e. *to cut class*
f. *to play ball*
g. *to jump rope*
h. *to plunge into a dream*
i. *the hearts and wishes of children*
j. *children's games*
k. *to grow up in the same neighborhood*
l. *to play in the corridor*

B Je suis toi! Lisez la deuxième partie de la *Note de vocabulaire* à la page 82. Comment dit-on les choses suivantes? Utilisez les pronoms **moi, toi, lui, elle, nous, vous, eux** ou **elles.**

1. *I am you.*
2. *I am him and her.*
3. *I am them.*
4. *I am you and us.*

CHANTEZ, CHANTEZ

AMADOU ET MARIAM

Amadou Bagayoko and Mariam Doumbia met at Mali's *Institute for the Young Blind* and married in 1980. In 1986, they moved from Mali to Côte d'Ivoire to advance their career. Mixing rock guitar with traditional Malian sounds, their music is known as Afro-blues. Like many francophone Africans, they speak both French and an African language. The song **Chantez, chantez** is mainly in French, with a few lines in Bambara, another language spoken in Mali. The following activity will help you better understand the song.

Amadou et Mariam sont du Mali.

Chérie (Sweetheart). Dans la chanson *Chantez, chantez,* Amadou parle de son amour *(love)* pour Mariam et de sa bonne volonté envers tout le monde *(goodwill toward everyone).* Choisissez *(Choose)* un mot logique pour compléter chaque phrase. Il y a plus d'une possibilité pour certaines phrases.

aime	donne	parle
voix *(voice)*	tiens *(hold)*	jure *(swear)*
adore	guitare	
préfère	chante	

1. Écoutez cette *(this)* _____.
2. _____ -moi ta main *(your hand)* / ton cœur *(your heart)*.
3. _____ -moi dans tes bras *(your arms)*.
4. C'est toi que je (j') _____.
5. Je ne _____ que pour toi. *(I only _____ for you.)*
6. Je ne _____ qu'avec toi. *(I only _____ with you.)*
7. Je ne _____ que par toi. *(I only _____ by you.)*

belle	du bonheur *(happiness)*	perdre *(to lose)*
reste	liberté	jolie
abandonner	jouer	de l'amour *(love)*
sauter *(to jump)*	gentille	
danser	chanter	

8. _____ à côté de *(beside)* moi.
9. Tu es la plus _____.
10. Je ne veux pas te (t') _____. *(I don't want to _____ you.)*
11. Nous allons *(We are going to)* _____ ensemble.
12. _____ pour tout le monde.

En Amérique: Au Québec
Un nouvel appartement

	iLrn Heinle Learning Center		Internet web search
	www.cengagebrain.com		Pair work
	Horizons Video: Les Stagiaires		Group work
	Audio		

3

COMPÉTENCE

1 Talking about where you live
Le logement

Giving prices and other numerical information
Les nombres au-dessus de 100 et les nombres ordinaux

Stratégies et Lecture
- **Pour mieux lire:** *Guessing meaning from context*
- **Lecture:** *Un nouvel appartement*

2 Talking about your possessions
Les effets personnels

Saying what you have
Le verbe **avoir**

Saying where something is
Quelques prépositions

3 Describing your room
Les meubles et les couleurs

Identifying your belongings
La possession et les adjectifs possessifs **mon, ton** *et* **son**

Indicating to whom something belongs
Les adjectifs possessifs **notre, votre** *et* **leur**

4 Giving your address and phone number
Des renseignements

Telling which one
Les adjectifs **ce** *et* **quel**

Vidéoreprise *Les Stagiaires*

Lecture et Composition
- **Pour mieux lire:** *Previewing content*
- **Lecture:** *Les couleurs et leurs effets sur la nature humaine*
- **Pour mieux écrire:** *Brainstorming*
- **Composition:** *Un mail*

Comparaisons culturelles *Le Québec d'aujourd'hui*

Résumé de grammaire

Vocabulaire

cent cinq | 105

EN AMÉRIQUE: LE CANADA ET LE QUÉBEC

 PowerPoint 3-1

Dans quelle province canadienne y a-t-il le plus de francophones? Voudriez-vous visiter cette province?

Plus vaste que l'Alaska, le Québec est la plus grande des provinces canadiennes et plus de 25 % de la population canadienne habite dans cette province.

Suggestions. A Have students look at the map of the francophone world in the front of the book and answer these questions. **1.** In which states of the USA is there a strong francophone influence? **2.** On which Caribbean islands is French widely spoken? **3.** Where in South America is French spoken? **B.** Point out that the word **Québec** (no article) refers to the city of Quebec and **le Québec** refers to the province.

la plus grande *the largest*

106 cent six | CHAPITRE 3

Montréal, grand centre culturel et commercial, est la plus grande ville du Québec.

Le Québec

Visit it live on Google Earth!

NOMBRE D'HABITANTS: 7 886 100

CAPITALE: **Québec**

Le savez-vous?

Lisez le texte qui accompagne les photos. Ensuite, complétez ces phrases. Aimeriez-vous mieux *(Would you prefer)* visiter la ville de Québec ou de Montréal?

1. Le _____ est la plus grande province du Canada et plus de _____ % de la population canadienne y habite *(lives there)*. C'est la province francophone la plus importante du Canada!

2. _____ est la plus grande ville de la province de Québec, mais _____ est sa capitale. Québec est la plus _____ ville du Canada.

La ville de Québec est la capitale de la province de Québec. Fondée en 1608, c'est la plus vieille ville du Canada.

Do you know why there are so many francophones in Quebec? How would you characterize the linguistic situation in Canada today? Research online the history of French in Canada and the current linguistic situation there and report your findings.

En Amérique: Le Canada et le Québec | *cent sept* **107**

COMPÉTENCE 1

Talking about where you live

PowerPoint 3-2

 In the **Culture Modules** in the video library, see **Housing**.

Sélection musicale. Search the Web for the song **"Le temps de partir"** by Brigitte Boisjoli to enjoy a musical selection related to this vocabulary.

Warm-ups. A. Thomas, un étudiant de l'Université Laval au Québec, est très extraverti et sportif, mais pas du tout intellectuel. Aime-t-il ces activités? Répondez **oui** ou **non**: **1.** lire **2.** travailler sur l'ordinateur **3.** danser **4.** jouer au tennis **5.** inviter des amis à la maison **6.** réviser les cours **7.** sortir **8.** faire du vélo **9.** faire du ski **B.** Have students call out adjectives they associate with an ideal roommate. **C.** Have students prepare four or five questions to ask each other as potential roommates, or tell them they are meeting a new roommate for the first time and they need to greet each other, exchange names, and share information about themselves.

Suggestion. Point out the use of **mon, ma, mes** and elicit from students why there are three forms. The possessive adjectives are explained in the next **Compétence**.

Vocabulaire supplémentaire

une caravane *a travel trailer*
une cave *a cellar*
un duplex *a split-level apartment*
un prêt immobilier *a home loan*
un garage *a garage*
un grenier *an attic*
un jardin *a yard, a garden*
un loft
un mobil-home *a mobile home*
une buanderie *a laundry room*
une salle de jeux *a game room*
une salle de séjour *a family room, a den*
un studio *a studio apartment, an efficiency*
des W.-C. *(m) a restroom*

Note. You may wish to point out that in Canada one says **une salle d'eau** rather than **des toilettes** and **une salle de lavage** for *a laundry room*.

Supplemental activity. Quelles pièces de la maison associez-vous à ces activités? (manger, parler avec des amis, dormir, déjeuner, jouer à des jeux vidéo, préparer un sandwich, danser, lire, parler au téléphone)

LE LOGEMENT

J'habite…	dans une maison
	dans un appartement
	dans un grand **immeuble**
	dans une résidence universitaire
	chez mes parents
Ma maison est…	grand(e) / petit(e)
Mon appartement est…	moderne / vieux (vieille)
Ma chambre est…	joli(e) / laid(e)
	(trop) cher (chère)
	confortable

J'habite…	sur le campus	**en centre-ville**
	tout près de l'université	**en ville**
	(assez) loin de l'université	**en banlieue**
		à la campagne

Le loyer est de… 550 $ (cinq cent cinquante dollars) **par mois**
600 $ (six cents dollars)
1 200 $ (mille deux cents dollars)

Je n'ai pas de loyer!

Chez moi, il y a six **pièces** (f).

une chambre   une salle de bains
une cuisine   une salle à manger   un salon   des toilettes (f)

Le logement *Lodging, Housing* **un immeuble** *an apartment building* **trop** *too* **cher (chère)** *expensive* **(tout) près (de)** *(very) near* **(assez) loin (de)** *(rather) far (from)* **en centre-ville** *downtown* **en ville** *in town* **(une ville** *a city / town)* **en banlieue** *in the suburbs* **à la campagne** *in the country(side)* **Le loyer** *The rent* **par mois** *per month* **Je n'ai pas** *I don't have* **une pièce** *a room*

Robert, un jeune Américain, **va** étudier à l'Université Laval, au Québec. Il téléphone à son ami Thomas, avec qui il pense habiter.

une fenêtre — l'ascenseur *(m)* — l'appartement de Thomas
au troisième étage (3ᵉ)
au deuxième étage (2ᵉ)
au premier étage (1ᵉʳ) *on the second floor*
au rez-de-chaussée (R.d.C.) *on the first/ground floor*
au sous-sol *in the basement*
l'escalier *(m)*
la porte

ROBERT: Où est-ce que tu habites?
THOMAS: J'habite dans un immeuble en centre-ville.
ROBERT: **À quel étage?**
THOMAS: Mon appartement est au deuxième étage.
ROBERT: Tu habites seul?
THOMAS: Non, j'habite avec mon ami Gabriel.
ROBERT: L'université est loin de chez toi?
THOMAS: Non, pas très loin. Et il y a **un arrêt de bus** tout près. C'est très **pratique**.
ROBERT: Et l'appartement est agréable?
THOMAS: Oui, j'aime beaucoup mon appartement. Il est assez grand et pas trop cher.

A Et vous?
Complétez les phrases avec les mots en italique qui correspondent le mieux à votre situation.

1. J'habite dans *un appartement / une maison / une chambre*.
2. *Mon appartement / Ma chambre / Ma maison* est *sur le campus / (tout) près de l'université / (très / assez) loin de l'université*.
3. Il/Elle est *en centre-ville / en ville / en banlieue / à la campagne*.
4. Il/Elle est *joli(e) / grand(e) / moderne / confortable / ???*.
5. Il/Elle *est / n'est pas* trop cher (chère).
6. Le loyer est de *plus / moins* de cinq cents dollars par mois.
7. Chez moi, il y a *une / deux / trois / quatre / ???* chambre(s).
8. Je passe beaucoup de temps dans *la cuisine / le salon / ma chambre / ???*.
9. Ma chambre est *au rez-de-chaussée / au premier étage / ???*.
10. *Il y a un ascenseur / Il n'y a pas d'ascenseur* chez moi.

B Entretien.
Interviewez votre partenaire.

1. Est-ce que tu habites chez tes parents? Est-ce que tu habites dans une maison, dans un appartement ou dans une résidence universitaire?
2. Tu habites près de l'université, loin de l'université ou sur le campus? Est-ce que c'est pratique? Est-ce qu'il y a un arrêt de bus tout près?
3. Préfères-tu habiter en centre-ville, en ville, en banlieue ou à la campagne? Préfères-tu habiter au rez-de-chaussée ou au premier étage?
4. Quelles pièces est-ce qu'il y a chez toi? Dans quelle pièce aimes-tu passer beaucoup de temps?

À VOUS!

Avec un(e) partenaire, relisez à haute voix la conversation entre Robert et Thomas. Ensuite, adaptez la conversation pour décrire votre propre situation.

Note culturelle

Dans les immeubles au Québec et en France, faites attention: Le premier étage est l'étage au-dessus du *(above the)* rez-de-chaussée. C'est-à-dire *(That is to say)* que le rez-de-chaussée correspond à *the first floor / ground floor* aux USA et le premier étage correspond à *the second floor*. À quel étage est votre chambre/votre appartement?

Note for the conversation. New words presented in the conversation include all of the boldfaced/glossed words, the expresssion **téléphoner à**, and the words with the accompanying illustration.

Suggestion for the conversation. Go over the *Note culturelle* and point out the floors and other vocabulary on the illustration of Thomas's building. Set the scene and have students listen with books closed for three facts about Thomas's apartment as you play the conversation. Check their comprehension; then have them read along as you play the conversation again.

Suggestion for A. Et vous? Remind students to use **il** to say *it* for an apartment and **elle** to say *it* for a room or house.

 You can find a list of the new words from this *Compétence* on page 138 and access the audio online.

---

va (aller *to go*) **À quel étage?** *On what floor?* (**un étage** *a floor* [of a building]) **un arrêt de bus** *a bus stop*
pratique *practical, convenient*

 PowerPoint 3-3

GIVING PRICES AND OTHER NUMERICAL INFORMATION

✓ Pour vérifier

1. How do you say 100? 1,000? 1,000,000? Before which two of these numbers do you never put **un**?

2. How do you say 1,503? 12,612?

3. In the numbers 200, 2,000, and 2,000,000, which two words would have an **s**, **cent**, **mille**, or **million**? Which one of those words would drop the **s** if another number followed it?

4. Do you use a period or a comma to express decimals in French?

5. How do you say *first*? *fifth*? How do you say *on the* with a floor?

Suggestion. Review the numbers from 0 to 100 before presenting the larger numbers. Have students count by fives from 0 to 100.

Vocabulaire supplémentaire

un milliard *one billion*
deux milliards *two billion*

Supplemental activities. A. Quel étage est plus haut *(higher)*? **1.** le rez-de-chaussée ou le premier **2.** le deuxième ou le quatrième **3.** le neuvième ou le cinquième **4.** le dixième ou le vingtième **5.** le deuxième ou le douzième **B.** Questions orales. **1.** À quel étage est-ce que vous habitez? À quel étage est-ce que vous préférez habiter? **2.** Est-ce que nous sommes dans un grand immeuble? Nous sommes à quel étage maintenant? **3.** Le restaurant universitaire est à quel étage? Et le laboratoire de langues? Et la bibliothèque?

Note. The **de** is not written between the numeral **1 000 000** and a noun, but it is said. For example, one reads **un million d'habitants** for **1 000 000 habitants**.

Les nombres au-dessus de 100 et les nombres ordinaux

Here is how to say numbers over 100.

100 cent		**1 000** mille	
101 cent un		**1 001** mille un	
102 cent deux		**1 352** mille trois cent cinquante-deux	
199 cent quatre-vingt-dix-neuf		**2 000** deux mille	
200 deux cents		**1 000 000** un million	
201 deux cent un		**2 234 692** deux millions deux cent trente-quatre mille six cent quatre-vingt-douze	
999 neuf cent quatre-vingt-dix-neuf			

Note the following about numbers:

- **Cent** means *one hundred*, never say **un cent**. **Mille** means *one thousand*, never say **un mille**. On the other hand, do say **un million**. Use **de (d')** after the word **million(s)** whenever a noun follows it directly.

    cent habitants   **mille habitants**   **un million d'habitants**

- **Million** takes an **s** in the plural. **Cent** generally only takes an **s** when plural if not followed by another number. Never add an **s** to **mille**.

    deux **cents** habitants   deux **cent** cinquante habitants
    trois **millions** d'habitants   trois **millions** six **mille** habitants

- There is no hyphen between **cent, mille,** or **un million** and another number.

    un million deux cent cinquante-quatre mille habitants

- In France and in Quebec, commas are used to denote decimals, and a space (or a period) is used after thousands, millions, etc. Read a decimal as **virgule (1,5 = un virgule cinq)**.

USA	FRANCE / QUÉBEC
1.5	1,5
1,000	1 000 or 1.000

Use **À quel étage?** to ask *On what floor?* To say *on the* with a floor, use **au**. When counting floors, use the ordinal numbers and remember that in a French-speaking country, the first floor (**le premier étage**) is the floor above the ground floor (**le rez-de-chaussée**).

—À quel étage habitez-vous? — *What floor do you live on?*
—J'habite au troisième étage. — *I live on the third* (= American *fourth*) *floor.*

In French, to convert cardinal numbers *(two, three, four . . .)* to ordinal numbers *(second, third, fourth . . .)*, add the suffix **-ième**. Drop a final **e** from cardinal numbers before adding **-ième**.

deux → deuxième   **quatre → quatrième**   **mille → millième**

These ordinal numbers are irregular: **premier (première), cinqu*i*ème, neu*v*ième.**

A C'est combien? De combien est le loyer?

EXEMPLE 900 $ Le loyer est de neuf cents dollars par mois.

1. 865 $
2. 490 $
3. 1 545 $
4. 3 110 $
5. 670 $
6. 750 $
7. 1 385 $
8. 2 235 $

B Maisons à vendre. Lisez ces prix.

1. 150 279 $
2. 999 999 $
3. 399 459 $
4. 679 825 $
5. 15 999 500 $
6. 1 950 500 $
7. 885 700 $
8. 248 500 $

C Ça coûte combien? Choisissez un prix pour chaque article sur ce prospectus publicitaire *(flyer)*. Ensuite, comparez vos choix à ceux de votre partenaire.

EXEMPLE — Moi, je pense que le téléviseur de 40 pouces coûte… Et toi?
— Moi…

| 331,88$ | 349,50$ | 650,65$ |
| 999,99$ | 1 799,00$ | 2 499,99$ |

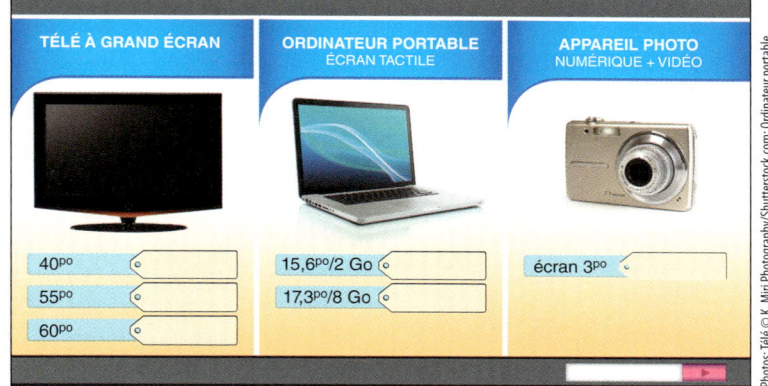

Note de vocabulaire

1. Use **un téléviseur** when talking about a *TV set*.
2. In Québec, the size of such things as TV screens is indicated in **pouces** *(inches)*, shown as **po**.
3. **Go** is short for **giga-octet** *(gigabyte)*. You can find the words for the latest electronic devices at http://www.fnac.com/.

D Chez Thomas. Posez les questions suivantes à un(e) partenaire, qui répondra d'après *(will respond according to)* l'illustration.

1. Il y a un ascenseur dans l'immeuble où habite Thomas? Il y a un escalier?
2. À quel étage est le vieux monsieur? Qu'est-ce qu'il fait *(What is he doing)*?
3. À quel étage habitent Thomas et son *(his)* colocataire? Qu'est-ce qu'ils font *(What are they doing)*?
4. À quel étage habite la jeune femme? Elle regarde la télé ou elle écoute de la musique?
5. Où habitent les enfants? Qu'est-ce qu'ils font?

l'appartement de Thomas

Follow-ups for A. C'est combien? A. Have students find the exchange rate for the U.S. / Canadian dollar. Discuss how to convert Canadian dollars to U.S. dollars and have them convert the prices in *A. C'est combien?*, which are in Canadian dollars, to U.S. dollars. You might also have them convert them into euros. **B.** Dictate rent prices and have students write them. Use house purchase prices to practice larger numbers. **C.** Show Internet advertisements of homes for sale in Quebec or France and have students describe them, giving prices and addresses.

Follow-ups for C. Ça coûte combien? A. Have students work in teams to guess the correct price of each item. Answers: téléviseur de 40po **999,99$**, téléviseur de 55po **1 799,00$**, téléviseur de 60po **2 499,99$**, appareil photo numérique **349,50$**, ordinateur portable 15,6po/2 Go **331,88$**, ordinateur portable 17,3po/8 Go **650,65$ B.** To have students practice writing the numbers, tell them that the items pictured are 10% off today. Have them write out the amount of the checks.

STRATÉGIES ET LECTURE

POUR MIEUX LIRE: Guessing meaning from context

You can often guess the meaning of unknown words from context. Read this passage in its entirety, then guess the meaning of the boldfaced words.

L'immeuble de Thomas **se trouve** en centre-ville. Arrivé **devant** l'immeuble, Robert **entre**, il **monte** l'escalier et il **sonne** à la porte de l'appartement de son ami. Une jeune femme **ouvre** la porte. Après un instant, elle **referme** la porte.

Some words may have different meanings in different contexts. For example, the word **bien** can mean *well* or it can be used for emphasis, meaning *indeed*. It may also be used in place of **très,** to mean *very*. Read the following sentences and use the context to decide if **bien** means *well, indeed,* or *very*.

—Tu comprends bien?
—Oui, mais c'est bien compliqué!

—C'est bien ici que Thomas habite?
—Oui, c'est bien ça.

The word **même** has several meanings, including both *self* and *same*. Read the following sentences and use the context to determine whether **même** means *self* or *same*.

Les prénoms Gabriel et Gabrielle se prononcent de la même manière.

Je travaille pour moi-même.

A **Selon le contexte.** The boldfaced word in each of the following sentences can have a different meaning, depending on the context. Can you guess the different meanings?

Bravo! **Encore! Encore!**
Ça, c'est **encore** plus compliqué.
Je suis au premier étage, alors je monte **encore** un étage pour aller au deuxième?

B **Vous savez déjà...** You already know the boldfaced words in sentence **a.** Guess the meaning of the boldfaced words in sentence **b,** using the context.

1. a. **Ouvrez** votre livre, **lisez** le paragraphe et **fermez** le livre.
   b. Robert **ouvre** la lettre de Thomas, **lit** les instructions et **referme** la lettre.
2. a. **Prenez** une feuille de papier.
   b. Elle **prend** la lettre.
3. a. **Donnez**-moi un café, s'il vous plaît.
   b. Thomas **donne** l'adresse de l'appartement à Robert.

Lecture: *Un nouvel appartement*

1-45

Robert, un jeune Américain de Louisiane, arrive devant l'immeuble où habitent Thomas et son colocataire, Gabriel.

Robert ouvre la lettre de Thomas, consulte les instructions et vérifie l'adresse. Il lit: «Mon appartement se trouve au 38, rue Dauphine. C'est un grand immeuble avec une porte bleue. J'habite au deuxième étage.» «Oui, c'est bien ça», pense-t-il. Il descend de la voiture, entre dans l'immeuble et monte l'escalier.

Il sonne à la porte de l'appartement. Quelques instants après, une jolie jeune femme lui ouvre la porte.
—Euh... Bonjour, je suis Robert. C'est bien ici que Gabriel et Thomas habitent?
—Gabrielle, c'est moi, Mais...

Robert, très surpris, l'interrompt:
—Gabriel, c'est vous? Euh... Mais vous êtes une femme.
—Eh oui, monsieur, comme vous le voyez, je suis une femme!
—Euh, je veux dire... Euh, excusez-moi. Maintenant, je comprends! C'est que je pensais rencontrer Gabriel, un homme et non pas Gabrielle, une femme. Excusez-moi. Alors, vous êtes Gabrielle. Et moi, je suis Robert, Robert Martin. Thomas est ici?
—Thomas? Dit-elle d'un air surpris.
—Eh oui, Thomas, mon ami. Il habite ici avec vous, non?
—Mais certainement pas! dit-elle d'un ton un peu énervé.

Quand elle essaie de fermer la porte, Robert s'exclame:
—Un instant, s'il vous plaît. Regardez! Voici l'adresse que mon ami m'a donnée.
Elle prend la lettre, lit les instructions et commence à comprendre.
—En fait oui, c'est bien ici le 38, rue Dauphine, mais vous êtes au *premier* étage et votre ami habite au *deuxième* étage.
—Au premier étage? Ah! Oui, je comprends maintenant. *First floor,* c'est le rez-de-chaussée et *second floor,* c'est le premier étage. Alors, je monte encore un étage pour trouver l'appartement de mon ami?
—Oui, c'est bien ça. Au revoir, et bienvenue au Québec, Robert!
—Au revoir, Gabrielle, et merci.

A Vrai ou faux?

1. Robert arrive au 38, rue Dauphine, l'adresse de son ami Thomas.
2. Il monte directement au deuxième étage.
3. Il sonne et Gabrielle, la jeune femme qui habite avec Thomas, ouvre la porte.
4. Gabriel est un prénom masculin et Gabrielle est son *(its)* équivalent féminin en français.
5. En France et au Québec, le *first floor* est le rez-de-chaussée et le *second floor* est le premier étage.

B Voilà pourquoi. Complétez le paragraphe pour expliquer la confusion de Robert.

> homme   premier   premier   deuxième   deuxième   Thomas   Thomas

Robert entre dans l'immeuble pour trouver l'appartement de __1__. Thomas habite au __2__ étage avec Gabriel, un ami. Robert monte au __3__ étage et sonne. Une jeune femme ouvre la porte. C'est Gabrielle, mais elle n'habite pas avec Thomas. Robert ne comprend pas; il pense que la jeune femme habite avec __4__. Voilà le problème: Robert est au __5__ étage et Thomas et son ami Gabriel habitent au __6__ étage. C'est un autre Gabriel, un jeune __7__, pas une jeune femme, qui habite avec Thomas.

COMPÉTENCE 2

Talking about your possessions

 PowerPoint 3-4

LES EFFETS PERSONNELS

iLrn In the **Culture Modules** in the video library, see **Technology**.

Note culturelle

L'accent du français canadien est plus nasal qu'en France. Il y a aussi certaines différences de vocabulaire. Au Canada, on entend *(one hears)*, par exemple, **un copain/une copine de chambre** pour **un(e) camarade de chambre** et **un vivoir** ou **un living** pour **un salon**. Y a-t-il des différences régionales en anglais?

Vocabulaire supplémentaire

une cuisinière *a stove*
un (four à) micro-ondes *a microwave (oven)*
un lave-vaisselle *a dishwasher*
un lave-linge *a washer*
un lecteur MP3 *an MP3 player*
une moto *a motorcycle*
un réfrigérateur (un frigo)
un sèche-linge *a dryer*
une table basse *a coffee table*

Warm-up. Quelle est la réponse logique? **1.** J'habite dans une grande maison. J'habite dans un grand immeuble en ville ou j'habite en banlieue? **2.** J'habite au huitième étage. J'habite dans un immeuble ou dans une maison? **3.** J'habite dans une résidence universitaire. J'habite avec un(e) camarade de chambre ou avec ma famille? **4.** Il y a un arrêt de bus tout près de mon appartement. J'habite en ville ou à la campagne? **5.** J'aime beaucoup mon appartement. Il est grand et confortable ou petit et laid? **6.** J'habite tout près d'ici. J'habite en ville ou dans une maison à la campagne?

Suggestions. A. Point out the difference between **une chaise** and **un fauteuil** and the difference in pronunciation between **un tableau** and **une table**. Tell students that one also says **un sofa** or **un divan** for *a couch*. In Quebec, one more commonly says **un divan**. Point out the liaison in **tout_est_en_ordre**. **B.** Point out that the locations are described from the point of view of someone looking at the room, facing the couch.

Avez-vous beaucoup de **choses**? Moi, **j'ai...**

une lampe
un tableau
un canapé
un fauteuil
un chat
une plante
un chien   un tapis   une table   une chaise
un lecteur DVD/Blu-ray et des DVD *(m)*
un lecteur CD et des CD *(m)*
une chaîne hi-fi
une télé

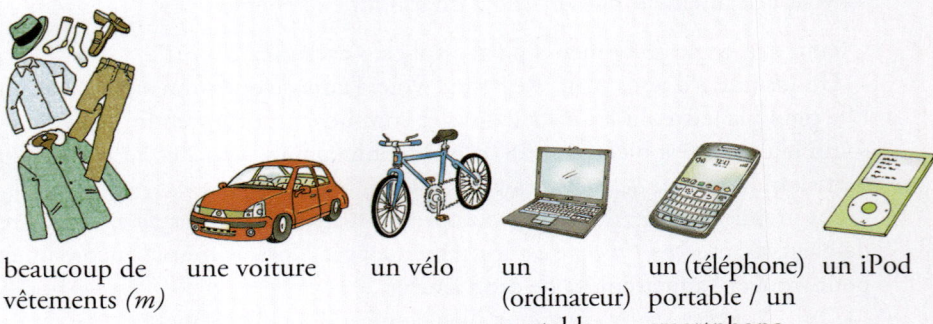

beaucoup de vêtements *(m)*   une voiture   un vélo   un (ordinateur) portable   un (téléphone) portable / un smartphone   un iPod

Chez Thomas, **tout est en ordre** et **bien rangé**. Qu'est-ce qu'il y a...?

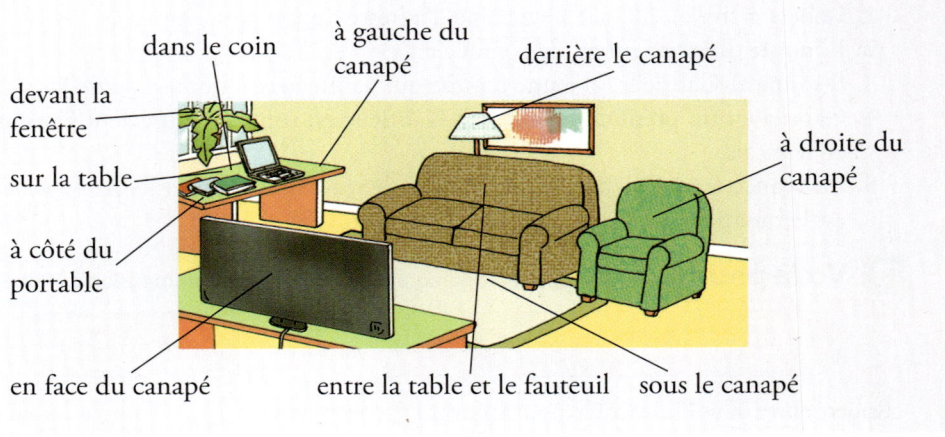

dans le coin
à gauche du canapé
derrière le canapé
devant la fenêtre
sur la table
à droite du canapé
à côté du portable
en face du canapé   entre la table et le fauteuil   sous le canapé

Line art on this page: © Cengage Learning

Avez-vous (avoir *to have*)   **une chose** *a thing*   **j'ai (avoir** *to have*)   **tout est en ordre** *everything is in order*
bien rangé(e) *neat, put away, straightened up*

114 cent quatorze | CHAPITRE 3

Avant d'arriver au Québec, Robert **cherche** un appartement. Il téléphone à Thomas.

THOMAS: Tu cherches un appartement ici à Québec? Écoute, tu sais, moi, je **partage** un appartement avec mon ami Gabriel. **Nous avons** trois chambres; tu voudrais habiter avec nous?
ROBERT: **Peut-être.** Comment est **ton** appartement?
THOMAS: Il est assez grand et confortable, mais pas trop cher. Tu aimes les animaux?
ROBERT: Oui, pourquoi? **Tu as** des animaux?
THOMAS: Gabriel **a** un chien et un chat. Ils sont quelquefois **embêtants** et ils aiment dormir **partout.**
ROBERT: Pas de problème. J'aime bien les animaux. Vous **fumez**?
THOMAS: Non, je ne fume pas et Gabriel **non plus.**
ROBERT: Bon, moi non plus. Alors, ça va.

A Cherchez l'intrus! Quel objet de chaque liste ne va pas logiquement à l'endroit *(place)* indiqué?

EXEMPLE sur la table: un portable / un iPod / un vélo / des livres
Sur la table, il y a un portable, un iPod et des livres, mais il n'y a pas de vélo!

1. sur la table: un lecteur DVD / un portable / un fauteuil / un chat / une lampe
2. devant la fenêtre: une table / un tableau / une chaise / une plante
3. dans le salon: un canapé / un lit / un lecteur CD / une chaîne hi-fi / une lampe
4. dans la chambre: des vêtements / un chien / un lecteur DVD / une voiture / une télé

B Qu'est-ce que c'est? Regardez l'illustration du salon de Thomas en bas de *(at the bottom of)* la page précédente. Qu'est-ce qu'il y a à chaque endroit *(place)*?

EXEMPLE sur la table
Il y a des livres et un portable sur la table.

1. devant la fenêtre
2. en face du canapé
3. derrière le canapé
4. à droite des livres
5. à côté du portable
6. dans le coin
7. à gauche du portable
8. entre le fauteuil et la table
9. sous le canapé

C Entretien. Interviewez votre partenaire.

1. Tu as beaucoup de choses chez toi? Qu'est-ce qu'il y a dans le salon? En général, est-ce que tout est en ordre et bien rangé dans ta chambre ou est-ce que ta chambre est souvent en désordre?
2. Est-ce que tu aimes les animaux? Tu as des animaux? Tu préfères les chiens ou les chats?
3. Est-ce que tu fumes?

À VOUS!

Avec un(e) partenaire, relisez à haute voix la conversation entre Thomas et Robert. Ensuite, imaginez que votre partenaire veuille *(wants)* habiter chez vous. Adaptez la conversation pour décrire votre situation.

---

chercher to look for   **partager** to share   **Nous avons** (avoir to have)   **Peut-être** Maybe, Perhaps   **ton/ta/tes** your (singular familiar)
Tu as (avoir to have)   **a** (avoir to have)   **embêtant(e)** annoying   **partout** everywhere   **fumer** to smoke   **non plus** neither

 **PowerPoint 3-5**

SAYING WHAT YOU HAVE

Le verbe **avoir**

To say what someone has, use the verb **avoir**. Its conjugation is irregular.

AVOIR (to have)	
j'**ai**	nous **avons**
tu **as**	vous **avez**
il/elle **a**	ils/elles **ont**

✓ *Pour vérifier*

1. What does **avoir** mean? What are its forms? Why might one confuse the **tu** and **ils/elles** forms of **avoir** (to have) with those of **être** (to be)?

2. What does the indefinite article (**un, une, des**) change to after expressions of quantity such as **combien** or **beaucoup**? When else does this change occur?

3. Which of these nouns would have a plural ending with **-x** instead of **-s**: **un hôpital, un animal, un tableau, un bureau, une table, un canapé**?

Remember to use **de (d')** rather than **des** after **combien** (*how much, how many*), as you do after quantity expressions like **beaucoup** and **assez**. Also remember to use **de (d')** instead of **un, une,** or **des** after most negated verbs other than **être**.

AFFIRMATIVE	NEGATIVE	AFTER A QUANTITY EXPRESSION
J'ai **des** chats.	Je n'ai pas **de** chats.	Combien **de** chats as-tu?
BUT:		
C'est **un** chat.	Ce n'est pas **un** chat.	C'est beaucoup **de** chats.

Grammar Tutorials

Vocabulaire sans peine!

Many adjectives ending in *-al* in English have French cognates with masculine plural forms ending in **-aux**.

régional → régionaux

How would you say these words in French? What would their masculine plural forms be?

normal
horizontal
vertical

Although the plural of most nouns and adjectives is formed by adding **-s**, words ending in **-eau, -au,** or **-eu** usually form their plural with **-x**. Words ending in **-al** often change this ending to **-aux** in the plural. Acronyms like **DVD** and **CD** do not add **-s** in the plural.

| un tableau | un bureau | un animal | un CD | un DVD |
| des tableau**x** | des bureau**x** | des anim**aux** | des CD | des DVD |

PRONONCIATION

Avoir et Être 1-47

Be careful to pronounce the forms of the verbs **avoir** and **être** distinctly. Open your mouth wide to pronounce the **a** in **tu as** and **il/elle a**. Contrast this with the vowel sound in **es** and **est**. Pronounce **ils sont** with an **s** sound, and the liaison in **ils ont** with a **z** sound.

être: Tu es professeur.   avoir: Tu as beaucoup de cours.
Elle est professeur.   Elle a beaucoup de cours.
Ils sont professeurs.   Ils ont beaucoup de cours.

 A **Prononcez bien!** Posez ces questions à votre partenaire. Faites attention à la prononciation des verbes **avoir** et **être**.

EXEMPLE a. — Tu es plutôt extraverti(e)?
— Oui, je suis plutôt extraverti(e).
Non, je ne suis pas très extraverti(e).
b. — Tu as beaucoup d'amis?
— Oui, j'ai beaucoup d'amis.
Non, je n'ai pas beaucoup d'amis.

1. a. Tu es d'ici?   b. Tu as beaucoup de choses chez toi?
2. a. Ton meilleur ami est sympa?   b. Il a beaucoup d'amis?
3. a. Tes parents, ils sont sportifs?   b. Ils ont un vélo?
4. a. Ils sont plutôt intellectuels?   b. Ils ont beaucoup de livres?

B Qu'est-ce qu'ils ont? Dites si ces personnes ont ou n'ont pas les choses suivantes.

EXEMPLE Moi, je (j')... un chat
un chien
Moi, j'ai un chat. Je n'ai pas de chien.

1. Chez moi, je (j')...   une chaîne hi-fi
                                  des CD de hip-hop
2. Mon meilleur ami (Ma meilleure amie)...   une voiture
                                  beaucoup de vêtements
3. En cours de français, nous...   beaucoup de devoirs
                                  un examen aujourd'hui
4. Généralement, les étudiants à l'université...   beaucoup de temps libre
                                  beaucoup de devoirs

C Combien? Circulez parmi les étudiants. Demandez à au moins trois étudiants combien ils ont de chaque *(each)* chose illustrée.

EXEMPLE — Combien de chiens est-ce que tu as?
— J'ai un (deux, trois...) chien(s). / J'ai beaucoup de chiens. / Je n'ai pas de chiens.

EXEMPLE   1.   2.   3.   4.

D Oui ou non? Vous cherchez un nouveau logement. Lisez ces textos d'autres étudiants qui voudraient partager leur *(their)* appartement / maison. Complétez leurs phrases avec la forme correcte du verbe **avoir**. Ensuite, dites si vous voudriez habiter avec ces personnes. Répondez **oui**, **non** ou **peut-être**.

Nous _____ un très bel appartement et le loyer n'est pas trop élevé *(high)*. Les chambres _____ beaucoup de fenêtres et une belle vue.

Tu aimes les animaux? J'_____ trois colocataires et ils _____ neuf chats.

Mon colocataire _____ beaucoup d'amis qui fument dans l'appartement.

Tu _____ une voiture? Mon immeuble n'_____ pas de parking.

J'_____ un appartement. Il est au cinquième étage, mais nous _____ deux nouveaux ascenseurs.

L'immeuble n'_____ pas assez d'eau chaude *(hot water)*, mais le loyer est de seulement *(only)* deux cents dollars par mois et j'_____ un très joli appartement.

 **PowerPoint 3-6**

SAYING WHERE SOMETHING IS

✓ **Pour vérifier**

1. How do you say *on? under? facing? next to?*

2. What does the preposition **de** mean? With which two forms of the definite article does it combine to form **du** and **des**?

Grammar Tutorials

Note. The contractions with the preposition **de** are recycled in the next **Compétence**, where they are used to indicate possession.

Supplemental activity. Say sentences such as these and have students write only the form of the preposition **de** that they hear. 1. L'université est loin de chez moi. 2. Il y a un parc en face de mon appartement. 3. Le campus est près du centre-ville. 4. La bibliothèque est en face des résidences. 5. Le restaurant est près de la bibliothèque. 6. Il y a un parking en face du restaurant. 7. Il y a aussi un restaurant en face de chez moi. 8. J'habite loin de l'université. 9. Il y a un parking près des résidences. 10. Il y a une librairie à côté de la bibliothèque.

Quelques prépositions

You can use the following prepositions to tell where something or someone is.

sur *on*	**près (de)** *near*
sous *under*	**loin (de)** *far (from)*
entre *between*	**à côté (de)** *next to, beside*
dans *in*	**à droite (de)** *to the right (of)*
devant *in front of*	**à gauche (de)** *to the left (of)*
derrière *behind*	**en face (de)** *across (from), facing*
	dans le coin (de) *in the corner (of)*

The preposition **de** *(of, from, about)*, which is used as part of some of the prepositions above, contracts with the forms of the definite article **le** and **les**, to become **du** and **des**. It does not change when followed by **la** or **l'**.

CONTRACTIONS WITH *DE*

de + le	→	du	J'habite près **du** centre-ville.
de + la	→	de la	La salle de cours est près **de la** bibliothèque.
de + l'	→	de l'	Mon appartement est près **de l'**université.
de + les	→	des	Il n'y a pas de parking près **des** résidences.

PRONONCIATION

De, du, des 1-48

Be careful to pronounce **de, du,** and **des** distinctly.

- As you know, the **e** in words like **de, le,** and **ne** is pronounced with the lips slightly puckered. The tongue is held firm in the lower part of the mouth.
- The **u** in **du**, as in **tu**, is pronounced with the tongue arched firmly near the roof of the mouth, like the French vowel **i** in **il**, but with the lips puckered.
- The vowel in **des** is a sharp sound like the **é** in **café**, pronounced with the corners of the lips spread.

Warm-up for A. Prononcez bien! Mettez veut dire *put*. Prenez un stylo. Maintenant, mettez le stylo... devant vous / derrière vous / sur votre livre / sous le livre / dans le livre / entre le livre et vous. (You may want to repeat variations on these phrases at a faster and faster speed while students try to keep up.)

A **Prononcez bien!** D'abord, complétez ces phrases avec la forme correcte de la préposition **de (de, d', du, de la, de l', des)**. Ensuite, lisez les phases à haute voix *(aloud)* en faisant attention à la prononciation et dites si chaque phrase est vraie ou fausse.

1. La salle de cours est près _____ ascenseur.
2. Je suis assis(e) *(am seated)* à côté _____ porte.
3. La porte est à gauche _____ moi.
4. Le professeur est en face _____ un ordinateur.
5. Il y a un tableau en face _____ étudiants.
6. Le professeur est près _____ tableau.
7. Il y a un ordinateur dans le coin _____ salle de cours.
8. Il y a des fenêtres à droite _____ étudiants.

B **Descriptions.** Faites des phrases pour décrire ce salon.

EXEMPLE les livres / la table
Les livres sont sur la table.

1. le chat / la table
2. la télé / le fauteuil
3. les plantes / la télé
4. le chien / le fauteuil et la télé
5. le chien / le fauteuil
6. la table / le salon
7. la porte / le fauteuil
8. les livres / l'ordinateur
9. l'ordinateur / la table
10. l'escalier / les tableaux

C **Qui est-ce?** Utilisez trois prépositions pour indiquer où un(e) des étudiant(e)s de votre cours est assis(e) *(is seated)* et les autres étudiants devineront *(will guess)* qui est la personne décrite.

EXEMPLE — Elle est assise près de la fenêtre. Elle est à droite de Brent et elle est derrière Catherine.
— C'est Julie?
— Oui.

D **À vendre.** Avec un(e) partenaire, préparez au moins huit phrases décrivant cette maison.

EXEMPLE Quand vous entrez *(enter)* dans la maison, les toilettes sont à gauche de la porte et le bureau est à droite. Derrière les toilettes, il y a…

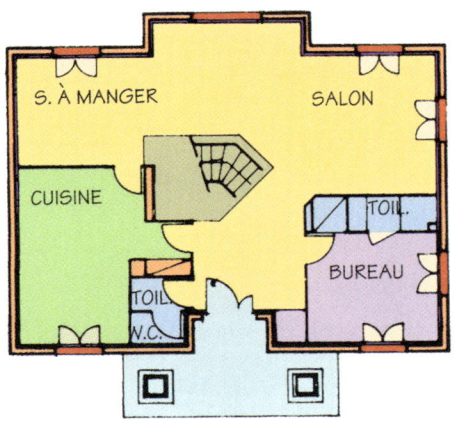

au rez-de-chaussée

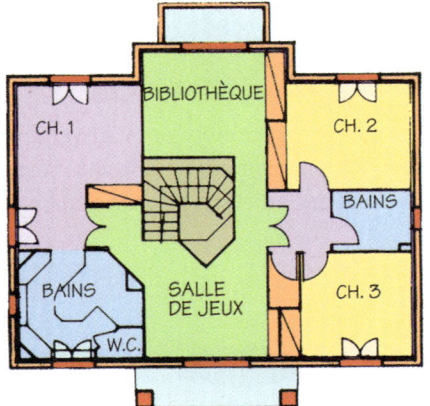

au premier étage

Maintenant, dessinez *(draw)* votre maison idéale. Décrivez cette maison à votre partenaire qui va la dessiner selon votre description *(who will draw it from your description)*.

COMPÉTENCE 3

Describing your room

 PowerPoint 3-7

LES MEUBLES ET LES COULEURS

Thomas **montre** les chambres à Robert.

Voici **ma** chambre. **Les murs** sont beiges et le tapis et les rideaux sont bleus. **La couverture** est bleue, rouge et verte.
Ma chambre est toujours **propre** et en ordre. Tout est **à sa place**.

Voici la chambre de Gabriel. **Sa** chambre est souvent un peu **sale** et en désordre. Il **laisse** tout **par terre**.

Et vous? Comment est votre chambre, en ordre ou en désordre?
De quelle couleur (f) est votre tapis? De quelle couleur sont vos murs?
Voici des adjectifs pour indiquer la couleur de quelque chose.

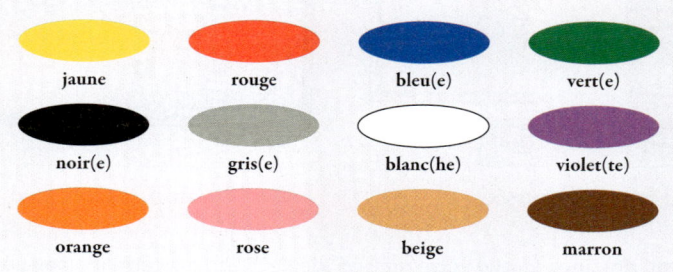

Line art on this page: © Cengage Learning

Les meubles Furniture, Furnishings   **montrer** to show   **mon/ma/mes** my   **un mur** a wall   **une couverture** a (bed)cover, a blanket   **propre** clean   **à sa place** in its place   **son/sa/ses** his/her/its   **sale** dirty   **laisser** to leave   **par terre** on the floor, on the ground

---

Note culturelle

Thomas montre l'appartement à Robert parce que Robert va habiter avec lui. Si *(If)* vous êtes invité(e) chez un(e) Québécois(e) ou un(e) Français(e), ne vous attendez pas à *(don't expect to)* faire le tour de sa maison ou de son appartement. En général, dans les cultures francophones, on *(one)* reste dans le salon et la salle à manger. Est-ce qu'on montre souvent sa maison aux invités dans votre région? Pourquoi ou pourquoi pas?

Note de vocabulaire

Laisser means *to leave* in the sense of leaving something somewhere, but not in the sense of leaving a place.

Warm-up. Questions orales. 1. Est-ce que vous avez un appartement? **2.** Est-ce que vous avez une maison? **3.** Est-ce que vous préférez partager un appartement / une maison ou habiter seul(e)? **4.** Est-ce que vous aimez les animaux? **5.** Est-ce que vous avez des animaux (une voiture, un vélo, un lecteur CD, beaucoup de CD, des plantes)? Combien de… avez-vous?

Note de grammaire

As adjectives, the words for colors follow the noun they describe and must agree with it in gender and number: **des chaises bleues**. **Orange** and **marron** are exceptions. They are invariable and never change form. All colors are invariable when followed by adjectives such as **clair** *(light)*, **foncé** *(dark)*, or **vif** *(bright)*: **Ma voiture est bleu clair.**

Vocabulaire supplémentaire

bleu ciel sky blue
bleu clair light blue
bleu foncé dark blue
bleu vif bright blue
de toutes les couleurs with all colors
multicolore multicolored
à fleurs floral
écossais(e) plaid
imprimé(e) print
rayé(e) striped
uni(e) solid-colored

🔊 Thomas montre les chambres à Robert.

THOMAS: Voici la chambre de Gabriel à côté de la cuisine. Sa chambre est toujours en désordre. Il laisse ses vêtements partout. **Quel bazar!**

ROBERT: C'est ta chambre en face de la chambre de Gabriel?

THOMAS: Oui, **comme tu vois,** je préfère avoir tout bien rangé et **chaque chose** à sa place.

ROBERT: Et ça, c'est ma chambre **au bout du couloir**?

THOMAS: Oui, **viens voir…** Tu as un lit, un bureau et une grande fenêtre avec **une** belle **vue.** J'**espère** que **ça te plaît.**

ROBERT: Oui, merci, **ça a l'air bien**!

THOMAS: Les murs sont blancs. Tu préfères une autre couleur?

ROBERT: Non, **justement,** le blanc, c'est ma couleur **préférée.**

THOMAS: Moi, je préfère le vert.

A Chez vous?
Décrivez votre chambre en choisissant l'adverbe qui convient.

(presque) toujours   souvent   quelquefois
rarement   ne… (presque) jamais

EXEMPLE Ma chambre est en ordre.
Ma chambre est presque toujours en ordre.
Ma chambre n'est presque jamais en ordre.

1. Ma chambre est propre.
2. Ma chambre est en désordre.
3. Mes livres sont sur l'étagère.
4. Ma chambre est sale.
5. Mes vêtements sont par terre.
6. Mes livres sont sur le lit.
7. Je laisse mes vêtements partout.
8. Mes vêtements sont dans le placard ou dans la commode.

B Les couleurs.
Complétez les phases suivantes avec le nom d'une couleur.

1. Ma couleur préférée, c'est le…
2. J'ai beaucoup de vêtements…
3. Les murs de ma chambre sont…
4. La couverture de mon lit est…
5. Les rideaux de ma chambre sont…
6. Ma voiture est…
7. Chez moi, le canapé est…
8. Le tapis de la salle de bains est…

À VOUS!

Avec un(e) partenaire, relisez à haute voix la conversation entre Thomas et Robert. Ensuite, imaginez que votre partenaire va habiter *(is going to live)* chez vous et adaptez la conversation pour décrire votre propre maison / appartement.

Quel bazar! *What a mess!*   **comme tu vois** *as you see*   **chaque chose** *each thing*   **au bout de** *at the end of*   **le couloir** *the hallway, the corridor*   **viens voir** *come see*   **une vue** *a view*   **espérer** *to hope*   **ça te plaît** *you like it*   **ça a l'air bien** *it seems nice*   **justement** *as a matter of fact, precisely, exactly*   **préféré(e)** *favorite*

🌐 **Sélection musicale.** Search the Web for the song **"Y a une fille qui habite chez moi"** by Bénabar to enjoy a musical selection containing related vocabulary.

Note *de vocabulaire*

1. The formal/plural version of **ça te plaît** is **ça vous plaît.** Use **ça me plaît** to say *I like it.*
2. **Espérer** is a spelling-change verb and is conjugated like **préférer.**
3. **Préféré** *(favorite)* is an adjective and must match the noun it describes in gender and number: **Ce sont mes vêtements préférés.**

Note for the conversation. New words presented in the conversation include all boldfaced/glossed words.

Suggestion for the conversation. Play the conversation and have students listen with books closed for three things about Robert's new room.

Follow-ups for *A. Chez vous?* A. Thomas range sa chambre. Où est-ce qu'il met *(put)* ces choses? Complétez les phrases suivantes. **1.** Il met ses vêtements dans… ou dans… **2.** Il met sa couverture sur… **3.** Il met ses livres sur… **4.** Il met son ordinateur sur… **5.** Il met son poster au… **B.** Répondez aux questions en vous basant sur l'illustration de la chambre de Gabriel à la page précédente. **1.** Qu'est-ce qu'il y a dans la chambre? **2.** Est-ce qu'il y a une étagère? des livres? des plantes? **3.** Qu'est-ce qu'il y a sur le lit? sous le lit? par terre? sur le bureau? **4.** Où est le chien? le vélo? Où sont les vêtements? les livres? **5.** De quelles couleurs est la couverture? le vélo? De quelle couleur sont les rideaux?

Warm-up for *B. Les couleurs.* Ask students **Quelle couleur associez-vous aux choses suivantes: une feuille de papier? le café? un citron? une carotte? un dollar? un taxi? le jambon? les arbres? une banane? un verre de vin? un stylo? le stylo du professeur? une plante? une plante morte *(dead)*? les chaises de la salle de cours? le tableau de la salle de cours? les murs de la salle de cours? le livre de français? le cahier? notre** *(our)* **université? l'université de…?** (You can also use the colors of local sports teams.)

🌐 **iLrn** You can find a list of the new words from this *Compétence* on page 139 and access the audio online.

 PowerPoint 3-8

IDENTIFYING YOUR BELONGINGS

✓ Pour vérifier

1. How do you say *John's friend* and *Mary's car* in French?

2. With which two forms of the definite article does **de** combine to form the contractions **du** and **des**?

3. How do you say *my*? How do you say *your* (singular familiar)? What are the forms of each word?

4. When do you use **mon, ton,** and **son,** instead of **ma, ta,** and **sa** before a feminine noun?

5. Does French have different words for *his, her,* and *its*? How do you say *his house* and *her house* in French? How do you say *his dog* and *her dog*?

La possession et les adjectifs possessifs **mon, ton** *et* **son**

In French, use a phrase with **de,** rather than *'s* to indicate possession or relationship.

| *There is Thomas's room.* | Voilà la chambre **de** Thomas. |
| *That's Gabriel's dog.* | C'est le chien **de** Gabriel. |

Remember that **de** contracts with the articles **le** and **les** to form **du** and **des.** It does not change when followed by **la** or **l'.**

| le livre **du** professeur | les livres **des** étudiants |
| la porte **de l'**appartement | la porte **de la** cuisine |

The possessive adjectives **mon/ma/mes** *(my)*, **ton/ta/tes** *(your* [singular familiar]*)*, and **son/sa/ses** *(his, her, its)* agree in gender and number with the noun that follows them. However, before feminine singular nouns that begin with a vowel sound, use **mon/ton/son.**

	MASCULINE SINGULAR	**FEMININE SINGULAR** (plus consonant sound)	**FEMININE SINGULAR** (plus vowel sound)	**PLURAL**
my	**mon** lit	**ma** commode	**mon** étagère	**mes** rideaux
your	**ton** lit	**ta** commode	**ton** étagère	**tes** rideaux
his/her/its	**son** lit	**sa** commode	**son** étagère	**ses** rideaux

—C'est **la couverture de Thomas**?
—Non, ce n'est pas **sa** couverture. C'est **ma** couverture. Et ce sont **mes** rideaux, aussi.

The use of the forms **son/sa/ses** depends on the gender and number of the object possessed, not the person who owns it. **Son/sa/ses** can all mean *his, her,* or *its*.

Suggestion. Point out that the [e] sound indicates plurality. **Singulier ou pluriel?** mon lit, mes murs, ma voiture, tes rideaux, ton poster, ta commode, ses CD, son appartement, sa cuisine, sa chambre.

C'est **son** fauteuil.

C'est **son** fauteuil.

Et c'est aussi **son** fauteuil.

Warm-up for A. Compliments. Show the illustration of Thomas's room from p. 120. Point to items and have students identify them as Thomas would. **EXEMPLE** C'est mon lit.

Follow-ups for A. Compliments. A. Tell students that they were only making these compliments to be polite. Later, they tell another friend the truth and describe them with the opposite adjective. **EXEMPLE** Sa maison est laide. **B.** Have students use the same items to describe their things. **EXEMPLE** Ma maison est jolie. / Je n'ai pas de maison.

A **Compliments.** Une amie vous montre *(is showing you)* sa maison. Formez la phrase la plus logique pour faire des compliments.

EXEMPLE maison (jolie, laide)
Ta maison est jolie.

1. bureau (en désordre, en ordre)
2. tapis (beau, laid)
3. chambre (désagréable, agréable)
4. maison (grande, petite)
5. plantes (jolies, laides)
6. placards (trop petits, immenses)
7. étagère (en désordre, bien rangée)
8. chien (beau, laid)

B **De quelle couleur?** Demandez à votre partenaire de quelle couleur sont ces choses. Utilisez **ton**, **ta** ou **tes**.

EXEMPLE voiture
—De quelle couleur est ta voiture?
—Ma voiture est grise. / Je n'ai pas de voiture.

| chambre | canapé | couverture | tapis | rideaux | vêtements préférés |

Maintenant, décrivez les affaires *(belongings)* de votre partenaire à la classe.

EXEMPLE Sa voiture est grise. / Il/Elle n'a pas de voiture.

C **C'est à moi!** Un locataire change d'appartement et il voudrait tout prendre avec lui *(him)*, mais l'autre locataire n'est pas d'accord. Jouez les rôles avec un(e) partenaire.

EXEMPLE la plante
—Bon, je prends *(I'm taking)* ma plante.
—Ah non, ce n'est pas ta plante. C'est ma plante!

1. le bureau
2. les rideaux
3. le poster
4. la commode
5. l'étagère
6. les chiens

D **La chambre de qui?** Complétez chaque phrase avec **son**, **sa** ou **ses** pour dire *his*. Après, lisez chaque phrase et choisissez *(choose)* un(e) autre étudiant(e) pour dire si la phrase décrit la chambre de Robert ou la chambre de Gabriel.

EXEMPLE **Sa** chambre est en ordre. **C'est la chambre de Robert.**

1. _____ tapis est jaune.
2. _____ rideaux sont gris.
3. _____ vélo est rouge.
4. _____ couverture est verte.
5. _____ murs sont blancs.
6. Il n'y a pas de posters dans _____ chambre.
7. Beaucoup de _____ affaires *(belongings)* sont par terre.
8. Il y a un livre rouge sous _____ bureau.
9. _____ chambre est propre.
10. _____ chambre est sale.

la chambre de Robert

la chambre de Gabriel

E **Comparaisons.** Regardez bien les illustrations de l'activité **D. La chambre de qui?** Fermez votre livre et travaillez en groupe pour comparer de mémoire les chambres de Robert et de Gabriel. Le groupe qui trouve le plus grand nombre de comparaisons correctes gagne.

EXEMPLE Les murs de Robert sont blancs, mais les murs de Gabriel sont gris. Le bureau de Robert est devant sa fenêtre et…

Compétence 3 | *cent vingt-trois* **123**

PowerPoint 3-9

✓ **Pour vérifier**

1. How do you say *our*, *your* (formal, plural), and *their* in French?
2. Do these words have separate forms for masculine and feminine?

Grammar Tutorials

Prononcez bien! See Module 13.

Note. The distinction between /ɔ/ and /o/ is often neutralized except in final syllables.

INDICATING TO WHOM SOMETHING BELONGS

Les adjectifs possessifs **notre**, **votre** *et* **leur**

The possessive adjectives for *our*, *your* (formal or plural), and *their* have only two forms, singular and plural.

	MASCULINE SINGULAR	FEMININE SINGULAR (plus consonant sound)	FEMININE SINGULAR (plus vowel sound)	PLURAL
my	**mon** lit	**ma** chambre	**mon** amie	**mes** livres
your (sing. fam.)	**ton** lit	**ta** chambre	**ton** amie	**tes** livres
his, her, its	**son** lit	**sa** chambre	**son** amie	**ses** livres
our	**notre** lit	**notre** chambre	**notre** amie	**nos** livres
your (pl./form.)	**votre** lit	**votre** chambre	**votre** amie	**vos** livres
their	**leur** lit	**leur** chambre	**leur** amie	**leurs** livres

PRONONCIATION

La voyelle **o** *de* **notre** / **votre** *et de* **nos** / **vos**   1-50

Compare the **o** sounds in **notre** / **votre** and **nos** / **vos**. The lips are puckered to make both of these sounds and the tongue is held firm, but the **o** in **nos** / **vos** is pronounced with the back of the tongue arched higher in the mouth than for the **o** in **notre** and **votre**. The letter **o** is pronounced with the sound of **nos** when it is the last sound in a syllable, when it is followed by an **s**, or when it is written **ô**. Otherwise, it is pronounced with the more open sound of **notre**.

notre chien / nos chiens   votre chat / vos chats

Follow-ups for A. Prononcez bien!
A. Redo activity **B. De quelle couleur?** on page 123 and have students ask you about the color of your belongings, using **votre** or **vos**. **B.** Give students nouns such as the following and have them work in pairs to prepare questions for you. EXEMPLE mes cours ce semestre **Aimez-vous vos cours ce semestre? / À quelle heure sont vos cours ce semestre?...** (mes étudiants, mon bureau, mon étagère, la vue de mon bureau, ma maison / mon appartement, ma voiture, etc.)

A Prononcez bien! Complétez les questions suivantes avec **votre** ou **vos**, puis lisez chacune d'elles. Faites attention à la prononciation de la voyelle **o**.

EXEMPLE <u>Votre</u> quartier est joli?

1. _____ appartement est très cher?
2. _____ chiens sont méchants?
3. _____ cuisine est grande?
4. _____ parents passent beaucoup de temps dans l'appartement?
5. _____ appartement a beaucoup de fenêtres?

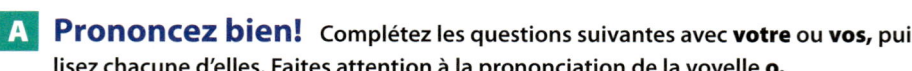

Maintenant, imaginez que deux amis veuillent *(want)* persuader un troisième ami de partager leur appartement. Comment répondent-ils aux questions? Utilisez **notre** ou **nos** dans les réponses.

EXEMPLE —<u>Votre</u> quartier est joli?
—**Oui, notre quartier est très joli.**

B Tu ou vous? Robert passe le week-end chez les parents de ses amis Patrick et Antoine Dupont et il veut savoir à qui chaque chose appartient *(wants to know to whom everything belongs)*. Complétez ce qu'il dit avec **ton/ta/tes** ou **votre/vos**.

EXEMPLES Patrick, c'est ____ vélo?   Mme Dupont, c'est ____ voiture?
Patrick, c'est ton vélo?   Mme Dupont, c'est votre voiture?

1. Patrick et Antoine, c'est _____ maison? Ce sont _____ parents?
2. M. Dupont, c'est _____ garage? Ce sont _____ voitures?
3. M. et Mme Dupont, j'aime bien _____ quartier. Ce sont _____ voisins *(neighbors)*?
4. Patrick, c'est _____ chambre? Tu laisses souvent _____ vêtements par terre ou ils sont toujours dans _____ placard ou dans _____ commode?
5. M. et Mme Dupont, c'est _____ bureau? J'aime bien _____ étagère. Il y a de la place pour tous _____ livres.
6. Patrick et Antoine, c'est _____ salle de jeux? Où sont _____ jeux vidéo? Ah, voilà… ça, Antoine, c'est _____ jeu préféré, non?

C Je préfère notre université. Comparez votre université avec une autre université dans votre région ou avec une université connue *(well-known)*. Formez des phrases avec **notre/nos** ou **leur/leurs**.

EXEMPLE campus / beau
Leur campus est plus beau que notre campus.
Notre campus est plus beau que leur campus.
Leur campus est aussi beau que notre campus.

1. campus / grand
2. cours / difficiles
3. étudiants / sympas
4. professeurs / intéressants
5. bâtiments / modernes

L'Université Laval

D Préférences. Dites si vous aimez ces choses et demandez à un(e) partenaire s'il/si elle aime ces choses aussi. Utilisez **son/sa/ses** ou **leur/leurs**.

EXEMPLES la musique de Jennifer Lopez
— **Moi, j'aime bien la musique de Jennifer Lopez. Et toi, est-ce que tu aimes sa musique?**
— **Oui, j'aime bien sa musique.**
   Je ne connais pas sa musique *(I don't know her music)*.

la musique du groupe Coldplay
— **Moi, j'aime bien la musique du groupe Coldplay. Et toi, est-ce que tu aimes leur musique?**
— **Oui, j'aime bien leur musique.**
   Je ne connais pas leur musique.

la musique des Black Eyed Peas	les vidéos de Lady Gaga	la musique de Beyoncé
les chansons *(songs)* des Beatles	les livres de J. K. Rowling	les films avec Jim Carrey

COMPÉTENCE 4

Giving your address and phone number

 PowerPoint 3-10

DES RENSEIGNEMENTS

Pour **s'inscrire** à l'université, Robert **doit** donner les **renseignements suivants.**

Quel est votre nom de famille?	Martin.
Quel est votre prénom?	Robert.
Quelle est votre adresse?	C'est le 215, Ursline St.
Quelle est votre (adresse) mail?	RobMart@airmail.net
Quel est votre numéro de téléphone?	C'est le (337) 988–1284.
Dans quel pays habitez-vous?	Les États-Unis.
Quel État? (Quelle province?)	La Louisiane.
Quelle ville?	Lafayette.
Quelle est votre nationalité?	Américaine.

Note culturelle

Le RÉSO est le nom de la ville souterraine *(underground)* **de Montréal. Il comprend 30 kilomètres de tunnels et galeries où on trouve bureaux, résidences de luxe, centres commerciaux, boutiques, restaurants et hôtels. Il y a sept stations de métro et deux gares** *(train stations)***! Chaque jour** *(Each day)***, plus de 500 000 personnes utilisent le RÉSO. C'est super en hiver** *(winter)***! Est-ce que vous connaissez** *(Do you know)* **d'autres villes souterraines?**

Note de vocabulaire

1. Most states ending in **-e** are feminine and most other states are masculine (**la Louisiane, le Texas**).
2. Although a male French-speaker such as Robert would identify himself as **américain**, since the word **nationalité** is feminine, it is correct to complete the form with the feminine **américaine**.
3. In an e-mail address, say **arobase** for *@*, **soulignement** for *underscore*, **tiret** for *dash*, **point** for *dot*, and **barre oblique** or **slash** for *slash*.
4. You generally use **demander** to say *to ask*, but use **poser une question** for *to ask a question*.
5. Canadian zip codes are composed of alternating letters and numbers with a space in the middle. The first set indicates the region and the second the city. **Le père Noël** *(Santa Claus)* has his own zip code: Père Noël, Pôle Nord H0H 0H0, CANADA.

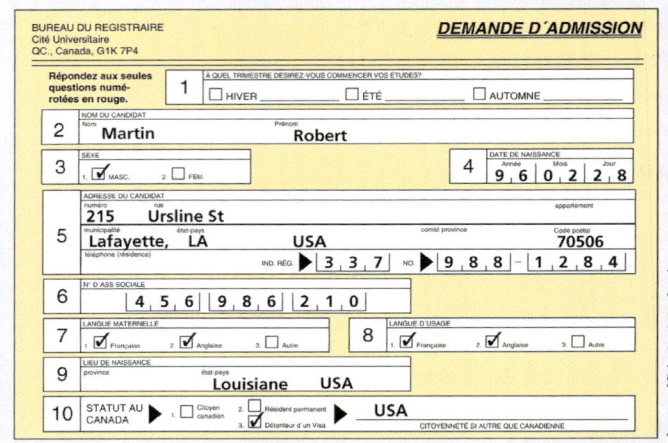

1-51

Robert parle de son appartement et son ami Alex lui **pose des questions.**

ALEX: Quelle est ton adresse?
ROBERT: C'est le 38, **rue** Dauphine.
ALEX: Et c'est quel appartement?
ROBERT: C'est le numéro 231.
ALEX: Et le code postal?
ROBERT: G1K 7X2.
ALEX: Quel est ton numéro de téléphone?
ROBERT: C'est le 692-2691.
ALEX: Et il est comment, le quartier?
ROBERT: Il est agréable et près de tout.
ALEX: L'appartement n'est pas trop cher? C'est combien, le loyer?
ROBERT: Je partage mon appartement avec deux amis, Thomas et Gabriel. C'est 825 dollars par mois, partagés entre nous trois. Alors pour moi, ça fait 275 dollars.

Suggestion for the conversation. Point out the use and value of Canadian dollars. Have students listen to the conversation with books closed for three questions Robert's friend asks.

Warm-up. Voici les adresses de quelques sites touristiques au Québec. Écrivez les nombres. (Teacher note: The sites located at these addresses are indicated in parentheses for your information.)
1. 170, rue Dalhousie (Musée naval de Québec)
2. 100, rue St-Louis (Fortifications de Québec, Québec)
3. 7450, boulevard Ste-Anne (Cuivres d'art Albert Gilles, Château-Richer)
4. 7960, boulevard Henri-Bourassa (Moulin des Jésuites de Charlesbourg)
5. 8862, boulevard Ste-Anne (Musée de l'abeille, Château-Richer)
6. 1045, rue des Parlementaires (Hôtel du Parlement de Québec)

---

s'inscrire *to register* **doit (devoir** *must, to have to***) les renseignements** *(m) information* **suivant(e)** *following*
poser une question *to ask a question* **une rue** *a street*

A Et Thomas? Quels renseignements est-ce que Thomas donne?

nom de famille   loyer   numéro de téléphone   province
prénom   ville   adresse mail   adresse
code postal   pays   nationalité

EXEMPLE Bertrand
C'est son nom de famille.

1. Thomas
2. Québec
3. le Québec
4. le Canada
5. le 38, rue Dauphine
6. G1K 7X2
7. le 692-2691
8. Thomas1@homemail.com
9. 825$ par mois
10. canadienne

Note de vocabulaire

In French, the province is **le Québec** and the city, **Québec.** When people say **J'habite au Québec,** they are talking about the *province*. When they say **J'habite à Québec,** they are talking about the *city*.

Note for the conversation *(on the preceding page).* New words presented in the conversation include **poser une question, une rue, le code postal,** and **partagé(e).**

Suggestion for B. Un abonnement and **À vous!** Have students create new identities so that they do not give out personal information.

B Un abonnement.
Vous vendez des abonnements *(are selling subscriptions)* pour les magazines *Ben* et *Brune*. Demandez les renseignements nécessaires à plusieurs étudiants pour compléter le formulaire d'abonnement.

EXEMPLE — Quel est votre nom de famille?
— C'est Sodji.

BULLETIN D'ABONNEMENT

Je désire m'abonner pour un an (6 numéros)
à _____ BEN _____ BRUNE.

Découper et retourner ce formulaire d'abonnement accompagné de votre règlement à:

BEN / BRUNE - SERVICE ABONNEMENTS

NOM ....
PRÉNOM ....
ADRESSE MAIL ....
ADRESSE ....
....
CODE POSTAL ....
VILLE .... PAYS ....
NUMÉRO DE TÉLÉPHONE ....
NUMÉRO DE PORTABLE ....

À VOUS!

Avec un(e) partenaire, relisez à haute voix la conversation entre Alex et Robert. Ensuite, adaptez la conversation pour décrire votre propre situation.

You can find a list of the new words from this *Compétence* on page 139 and access the audio online.

 **PowerPoint 3-11**

TELLING WHICH ONE

Les adjectifs *ce* et *quel*

To say *this/that* and *these/those*, use **ce (cet, cette, ces)**. Notice that the masculine singular **ce** changes to **cet** before a vowel sound.

	MASCULINE	MASCULINE	FEMININE
	(plus consonant sound)	(plus vowel sound)	(plus consonant or vowel sound)
SINGULAR	**ce** canapé	**cet** appartement	**cette** rue
PLURAL	**ces** canapés	**ces** appartements	**ces** rues

To say *which* and *what*, use **quel (quels, quelle, quelles)**. The form you use depends on the gender and number of the noun it modifies.

	MASCULINE	FEMININE
SINGULAR	**quel** appartement	**quelle** rue
PLURAL	**quels** appartements	**quelles** rues

Quel est ton **nom**?
Quels meubles as-tu?

Quelle est ton **adresse**?
Quelles couleurs préfères-tu?

Quel and **qu'est-ce que** both mean *what*, but they are not interchangeable. Use:

QUEL	QU'EST-CE QUE (QU')
• directly before a noun Tu es de **quel pays**? • before **est** or **sont** followed by a noun **Quel est** ton nom? **Quels sont** tes loisirs préférés?	• before a subject and verb **Qu'est-ce que** tu as chez toi? **Qu'est-ce qu'**il y a dans ton quartier?

✓ **Pour vérifier**

1. How do you say *this, that, these,* and *those*? When do you use the alternate masculine form **cet**?

2. When do you use **quel** to say *what*? When do you use **qu'est-ce que**? What are the four forms of **quel**?

Note de vocabulaire

1. If you need to distinguish *this* from *that,* you can add the suffixes **-ci** and **-là** to the noun.

ce livre-ci ou **ce livre-là** *this book or that book*

ces maisons-ci ou **ces maisons-là** *these houses or those houses*

2. **Quel** followed by a noun is also used as an exclamation. It is most often the equivalent of *What . . . !* or *What a . . . !* in English.

Quels chiens embêtants! *What annoying dogs!*

Quelle chance! *What luck!*

Quelle belle maison! *What a pretty house!*

🌐 **Sélection musicale.** Search the Web for the song "**Je suis**" by Florent Pagny to enjoy a musical selection illustrating the use and pronunciation of the demonstrative adjective.

PRONONCIATION

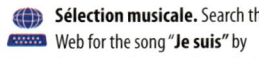 **Prononcez bien!** See Modules 9–10.

La voyelle *e* de *ce/cet/cette/ces* 1-52

You already know that a final **e** is usually not pronounced in French, except in short words like **je**. As you notice in **ce/cet/cette/ces,** unaccented **e** has three different pronunciations, depending on what follows it.

In short words like **ce** and **que,** or when **e** is followed by a single consonant within a word, pronounce it as in:

j**e**   n**e**   l**e**   r**e**garde   v**e**ndredi

When, as in **ces,** **e** is followed by an unpronounced consonant at the end of a word, pronounce it as in:

l**e**s   m**e**s   parl**e**z   mang**e**r   premi**e**r

In words like **cette** and **cet,** where **e** is followed by two consonants within a word, or a single pronounced consonant at the end of a word, pronounce it as in:

qu**e**l   ch**e**r   b**e**lle   **e**lle   ch**e**rche

A Prononcez bien!
Demandez à votre partenaire s'il/si elle aime ces choses. Faites attention à la prononciation de **ce (cet)/cette/ces**.

EXEMPLE — Tu aimes ce tableau?
— Oui, j'aime bien ce tableau. / Non, je n'aime pas ce tableau.

EXEMPLE tableau   1. canapé   2. escalier   3. lampe

4. tableaux   5. étagère   6. rideaux   7. commode

Line art on this page: © Cengage Learning

B Entretien.
Complétez les questions suivantes avec la forme correcte de **quel** ou avec **qu'est-ce que (qu'est-ce qu')**. Ensuite, posez les questions à votre partenaire.

1. ___ il y a dans ta chambre?
2. Dans ___ pièce est-ce que tu passes le plus de temps?
3. ___ meubles est-ce que tu voudrais acheter *(to buy)* pour ton salon?
4. ___ tu voudrais acheter pour ta chambre?
5. Ta chambre est à ___ étage?
6. De ___ couleurs sont les murs de ta chambre?
7. ___ tu voudrais changer chez toi?

C Au Canada.
Travaillez en équipes *(teams)*. Complétez les questions suivantes avec la forme correcte de **quel/quelle/quels/quelles** et **ce (cet)/cette/ces** comme dans l'exemple. Ensuite, répondez aux questions. La première équipe qui complète tout correctement et qui répond correctement aux questions gagne.

EXEMPLE **Quelle** est la province canadienne avec le plus de francophones?
Cette province est plus grande que l'Alaska.
C'est le Québec.

1. _____ est la plus grande ville du Québec?
   _____ ville n'est pas la capitale de la province.
2. _____ est la plus vieille ville du Canada?
   Fondée en 1608, _____ ville est la capitale de la province de Québec.
3. _____ pourcentage *(m)* de la population canadienne habite au Québec?
   _____ pourcentage est entre 20 et 30 %.
4. _____ explorateur est le premier Français à explorer le Canada?
   _____ explorateur arrive au Canada en 1534.
5. De _____ couleurs est le drapeau *(flag)* canadien?
   _____ couleurs sont deux des couleurs du drapeau des États-Unis.

Follow-up for A. Prononcez bien! Point out the use of **Quel...!** as an exclamation, as explained in the *Note de vocabulaire* on the preceding page. Provide the following list of adjectives and have students make an exclamation about each of the items pictured. Remind them to use the correct form and position of each adjective: **beau / joli / laid / bizarre / intéressant / moderne / vieux.**

Suggestion for C. Au Canada. Tell students that they can find the answer to item 4 in the *Comparaisons culturelles* section at the end of the chapter.

Answers for C. Au Canada. 1. Montréal 2. Québec 3. 25 % 4. Jacques Cartier 5. rouge et blanc

Supplemental activity. Have students ask classmates about their favorite people and things using the following cues. Have them react to the person or place named using a form of the demonstrative adjective, as in the example. Tell them to use **Je ne connais pas...** to say that they aren't familiar with something or someone. **EXEMPLE** son restaurant préféré —**Quel est ton restaurant préféré?** —**J'aime beaucoup Pizza Nizza.** —**Moi aussi, j'aime beaucoup ce restaurant. / Moi, je n'aime pas ce restaurant. / Je ne connais pas ce restaurant.** 1. sa librairie préférée 2. son livre préféré 3. son acteur préféré 4. son actrice préférée 5. ses films préférés 6. sa voiture préférée

VIDÉOREPRISE

Les Stagiaires

See the **Résumé de grammaire** section at the end of each chapter for a review of all the grammar presented in the chapter.

Rappel!
So far in the video, Amélie and Rachid, two new interns at the Technovert company, have become better acquainted with their new colleagues. Matthieu, the company's shy techie, revealed to Camille a secret interest in Amélie, which led to a bet between Camille and Céline as to whether Matthieu would ever have the courage to ask Amélie out.

The entire **Vidéoreprise** section is designed to be a pre-viewing series for the video, as well as a chapter review that can be used independently from the video. There are also additional grammar review exercises on the Instructor's Companion Website and on iLrn.

In *Épisode 3* of *Les Stagiaires*, Amélie considers rooming with Céline, the Technovert marketing director, who has been looking for someone to share her apartment for a while. Before you watch the episode, review what you learned in *Chapitre 3* by doing these exercises in which Céline discusses her apartment with other prospective apartment mates.

A Quelques questions.
Une amie pose des questions à Céline parce qu'elle pense peut-être habiter chez elle. Complétez les questions avec **de, d', du, de la, de l'** ou **des**.

1. Est-ce que tu habites près ou loin _____ centre-ville?
2. Tu habites près _____ université?
3. Y a-t-il un arrêt de bus près _____ appartement?
4. Qu'est-ce qu'il y a en face _____ chez toi, de l'autre côté _____ rue?
5. Est-ce qu'il y a une salle de bains à côté _____ chambres?

 Maintenant, posez ces questions à un(e) partenaire pour parler de sa maison, de son appartement ou de sa résidence.

B L'appartement de Céline.
Céline décrit son appartement. Complétez le paragraphe suivant avec les expressions indiquées.

Quand on entre dans mon appartement, la cuisine et le salon sont __1__ *(to the right)* et les deux chambres et la salle de bains sont __2__ *(to the left)*. La porte du salon est __3__ *(facing the)* porte d'entrée. Il faut *(One must)* passer par le salon pour aller à la cuisine et il y a une petite salle à manger __4__ *(between)* les deux pièces. La salle de bains est __5__ *(at the end of the)* couloir, __6__ *(next to the)* deuxième chambre.

C Quelques questions.
Une amie voudrait passer chez Céline pour voir son appartement. Quelle question avec **quel/quelle/quels/quelles** est-ce qu'elle pose à Céline pour obtenir les réponses suivantes?

EXEMPLE Le nom de la rue, c'est *rue du Stade*.
Quel est le nom de la rue?

1. L'adresse exacte de l'immeuble, *c'est le 125 rue du Stade*.
2. C'est l'appartement *numéro 12*.
3. Mon numéro de téléphone, c'est *le 06 35 42 89 95*.
4. Je rentre chez moi *vers six heures et demie* ce soir.

D Qu'est-ce que vous avez? Céline parle à une amie. Complétez les phrases suivantes avec le verbe **avoir** dans le premier espace et le bon adjectif possessif dans le deuxième.

EXEMPLE J'**ai** un portable. **Mon** numéro de téléphone, c'est le 06 35 42 89 95.

1. J' _____ un appartement en centre-ville. _____ adresse, c'est le 125 rue du Stade, appartement 12.
2. Le quartier _____ beaucoup de restaurants et de cafés. C'est un quartier très agréable et j'aime beaucoup _____ ambiance.
3. Quelquefois, je passe le week-end chez mes parents. Ils _____ une maison en banlieue. _____ jardin *(yard)* est très joli.
4. Chez moi, j' _____ un petit chien. _____ chien est sympa, mais il aboie *(barks)* toujours quand quelqu'un s'approche de *(someone approaches)* la porte.
5. Le seul inconvénient de mon appartement, c'est que dans le parking de mon immeuble, nous n' _____ pas assez de places pour _____ voitures.

Maintenant, changez les phrases pour décrire votre situation.

E C'est combien? Céline cherche du mobilier *(furnishings)* pour son appartement sur *Craigslist*. Donnez le prix de chaque objet comme dans l'exemple. Utilisez **ce, cet, cette** ou **ces**.

EXEMPLE

TABLE, 6 CHAISES 450 €
Tél: 06 96 78 26 65

Cette table et ces chaises coûtent *(cost)* quatre cent cinquante euros.

1. TABLE, 6 CHAISES
laquées noires, très propres
1 150 €
Tél: 06 53 44 94 95

2. FAUTEUIL, CANAPÉ
fleuris 550 €
Tél: 06 31 42 51 15

3. TÉLÉ Sony,
état neuf 700 €
Tél: 06 12 21 49 14

4. LIT «king» complet:
base, lit en pin, matelas,
le tout en très bon état 150 €
Tél: 06 11 09 07 67

5. TABLE D'ORDINATEUR
blanche, 3 tiroirs, en bon
état 115 €
Tél: 06 89 85 10 11

6. ORDINATEUR Toshiba,
excellente condition 495 €
Tél: 06 55 64 69 94

Suggestions for E. C'est combien?
A. Remind students that they do not have to understand every word to be able to do this activity. Have the class guess unfamiliar words from context.
B. Remind students of how French phone numbers are read and have them take turns asking and answering the question **Quel est le numéro de téléphone?** for each of the items.

Suggestion for the video. Tell students not to worry about understanding every word, but to use what they do know and the context to guess what is being said. **B.** The video is available on DVD and on *iLrn*. The videoscript is available on the Instructor's Companion Website, www.cengage.com/french/horizons6e, and on iLrn.

Access the Video *Les Stagiaires* on iLrn.

▶ Épisode 3: Un nouvel appartement

AVANT LA VIDÉO

Dans cet épisode, Céline demande à Amélie si elle voudrait être sa colocataire. Avant de regarder l'épisode, pensez à trois questions qu'on pose souvent à un(e) colocataire potentiel(le).

APRÈS LA VIDÉO

Regardez le clip et notez trois questions qu'Amélie pose à Céline à propos de l'appartement et de ses habitudes.

LECTURE ET COMPOSITION

LECTURE

POUR MIEUX LIRE:
Previewing content

Looking at the title of an article and thinking about the topic can help you anticipate its content and read it more easily. You are going to read an article by an interior decorator in Quebec about how colors can change your moods. Before you begin to read, look at the title of the article. What is it about? What feelings do you associate with the following colors?

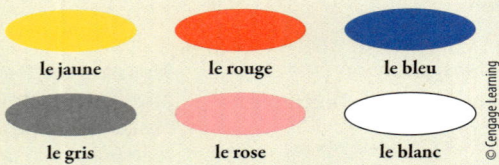

le jaune   le rouge   le bleu
le gris   le rose   le blanc

Associations. Quelle(s) couleur(s) associez-vous le plus aux choses suivantes?

1. la passion
2. la dépression
3. la concentration
4. l'énergie
5. la relaxation
6. la pureté
7. l'appétit
8. l'irritation

Suggestion for Associations. After students read the article, ask them what colors the article says are associated with each noun and if it matches what they wrote.

Les couleurs et leurs effets sur la nature humaine

Les couleurs changent nos **humeurs** et reflètent notre personnalité. **Pour mieux vous faire connaître** les effets qu'ont les couleurs sur la nature humaine, nous avons préparé un guide qui va vous aider à choisir les couleurs pour votre maison ou appartement.

Les couleurs chaudes: le rouge et le jaune

Le rouge stimule le métabolisme, le rythme cardiaque et la température **corporelle.** Le rouge est une couleur agressive, vitale et passionnante. **Puisque** c'est une couleur qui stimule l'appétit, le rouge est souvent utilisé pour les salles à manger et les restaurants.

Le jaune stimule la mémoire, le mouvement, la coordination et le système digestif. Le jaune et le rouge sont considérés comme «énergiques». Mais **faites attention,** le jaune dans une chambre de bébé **peut rendre** l'enfant irritable.

Les couleurs froides: le bleu et le vert

Le bleu encourage la concentration, **fait ralentir** le rythme cardiaque et la respiration et **fait baisser** la température du **corps.** Cette couleur est très recommandée dans un bureau.

Le vert augmente la relaxation. Le corps et **l'esprit se détendent** dans une atmosphère verte. Il est **donc parfait** pour une chambre à coucher.

---

humeurs *moods*   **Pour mieux vous faire connaître** *To inform you better about*
corporelle *body*   **Puisque** *Since*   **faites attention** *be careful*   **peut rendre** *can make*   **froides** *cold*   **fait ralentir** *slows down*   **fait baisser** *lowers*
corps *body*   **l'esprit** *the mind*   **se détendent** *relax*   **donc** *therefore*
parfait *perfect*

Les couleurs neutres: le blanc, le gris et le noir

Le blanc stimule les fonctions vitales, par conséquent **le sommeil** n'est pas aussi **bénéfique** dans une chambre blanche. Le blanc est aussi associé à la pureté et à l'honnêteté.

Le gris incite à la dépression et à l'indifférence. Il est préférable de l'utiliser comme accent plutôt que couleur dominante dans votre décor.

Le noir est une couleur distincte, audacieuse et classique. Le noir est un fond idéal **pour faire ressortir** les autres couleurs, mais il peut être **étouffant** en trop grande quantité.

© Kate Macrae

---

le sommeil sleep   **bénéfique** beneficial   **pour faire ressortir** to make stand out   **étouffant** stifling

Note. The vocabulary in this section does not appear in the end-of-chapter vocabulary lists and is meant for recognition only. You may wish to let students know in advance whether you intend to test them on this vocabulary.

Process-writing follow-up for *Un mail*. Have students exchange e-mails, and then imagine that they and their partners have decided to become housemates. Tell them to choose one of their places and prepare a conversation in which the new housemate asks for information, such as the address, telephone number, rent, etc.

Compréhension

Quelles couleurs? Complétez les phrases suivantes en indiquant les couleurs appropriées d'après la lecture du texte.

1. Si vous désirez manger moins, évitez *(avoid)* le _____ pour décorer votre salle à manger.
2. Pour mieux vous concentrer, étudiez dans une pièce _____.
3. Si votre bébé pleure *(cries)* beaucoup, utilisez le _____ dans sa chambre et évitez le _____.
4. Si vous souffrez de dépression, évitez le _____ dans votre décor.
5. Si vous avez souvent froid *(feel cold)* chez vous, utilisez le _____ et évitez le _____.

Quick-reference answers for *Compréhension*. 1. rouge 2. bleue 3. vert, jaune 4. gris 5. rouge, bleu

COMPOSITION

POUR MIEUX ÉCRIRE: Brainstorming

Brainstorming on a topic before writing about it can help you organize your thoughts. To brainstorm, first think about what general sections you will want to include in your writing, then jot down as many notes for each section as you can. Finally, use these sections to organize your writing.

Organisez-vous. Imagine that you are responding to a roommate ad in Quebec. What would you want to know about the apartment and its occupant? Jot down as many words and phrases in French as you can under each heading in this chart, using a separate piece of paper.

location	rooms and furnishings	roommate's personality/ habits

Un mail

You are moving to Quebec and respond to an ad for a roommate. Write an e-mail in which you introduce yourself and tell the sort of place you are looking for. Then, write three paragraphs asking about the apartment's location, the rooms and furnishings, and what the roommate is like. Begin with **Cher monsieur / Chère madame** and end the e-mail with **En attendant votre réponse.** Don't forget to sign your name.

iLrn Share It!

COMPARAISONS CULTURELLES

LE QUÉBEC D'AUJOURD'HUI

Grâce à son histoire, à sa langue et à **ses coutumes,** le Québec est, **à bien des égards,** une société distincte à l'intérieur du Canada. Dans cette province, la seule où le français est **l'unique** langue officielle, 80 % de la population parle français à la maison, 8 % parle anglais et 12 % parle d'autres langues.

En 1534, Jacques Cartier **découvre** un pays où habitent les Amérindiens et les Inuits. Il **établit** une colonie qu'il appelle la Nouvelle France. Cette colonie se développe rapidement: en 1608, Samuel de Champlain **fonde** la ville de Québec et, en 1642, Paul de Maisonneuve **crée** Montréal.

Malheureusement, les Français et les Anglais **se battent** pour le contrôle du Canada. L'armée anglaise est plus nombreuse, et les Anglais gagnent **la guerre.** En 1763, la France cède ses territoires canadiens aux Anglais et pendant 200 **ans,** les Québécois **vivent** sous la domination anglophone.

Grâce à *Thanks to* **ses coutumes** *its customs* **à bien des égards** *in many regards* **l'unique** *the only* **découvre** *discovers* **établit** *establishes* **fonde** *founds* **crée** *creates* **Malheureusement** *Unfortunately* **se battent** *battle* **la guerre** *the war* **ans** *years* **vivent** *live*

Dans les années 1960, les Québécois prennent conscience de leur identité et de leur culture francophone et un mouvement pour un Québec francophone se développe. **On appelle ce mouvement** la Révolution tranquille. En 1976, **une loi** pour la défense du français est votée et oblige **les immigrés à apprendre** le français. Aujourd'hui, les immigrés qui arrivent **de partout dans le monde** représentent 11,5 % de la population du Québec.

Le Québec d'aujourd'hui est une société multi-ethnique **qui** s'inspire des contributions **que lui apportent ces immigrés** et ses peuples **indigènes** (les Inuits et les Amérindiens), **aussi bien que de ses racines** françaises et anglaises. **Pourtant,** le Québec **maintient surtout** un attachement profond à son héritage français.

Source: www.gouv.qc.ca

Compréhension

1. Au Québec, 80 % de la population parle _____, 8 % parle _____ et 12 % parle d'_____. Quelle est la situation linguistique dans votre région?

2. Au cours du 17e et du 18e siècles, les _____ et les _____ se battent pour le contrôle du Canada. En 1763, les _____ gagnent la guerre. Comment est-ce que l'histoire de votre région influence sa situation linguistique?

3. Le Québec d'aujourd'hui est une société francophone qui est aussi une société multi-ethnique. Il s'ouvre aux contributions que lui apportent ses peuples _____ et ses _____ venant de toutes les parties du monde. Quelles cultures ont influencé votre société?

Dans les années 1960 *In the sixties* **On appelle ce mouvement** *This movement is called* **une loi** *a law* **les immigrés à apprendre** *immigrants to learn* **de partout dans le monde** *from throughout the world* **qui** *that* **que lui apportent ces immigrés** *that these immigrants bring to it* **indigènes** *indigenous* **aussi bien que de ses racines** *as well as by its roots* **Pourtant** *However* **maintient surtout** *maintains especially*

iLrn Share It!

Visit www.cengagebrain.com for additional cultural information and activities.

RÉSUMÉ DE GRAMMAIRE

cent	= *one hundred*
mille	= *one thousand*
un million	= *one million*
un million d'habitants	
300	trois cents
301	trois cent un
3 000	trois mille
3 100 000	trois millions cent mille

Ma rue, c'est la première (deuxième, troisième, quatrième, cinquième, sixième, septième, huitième, neuvième, dixième, onzième...) rue à droite.

—J'**ai** un appartement. Et toi? Tu **as** une maison?
—Ma famille **a** une petite maison. J'habite chez mes parents.

—Tu as **des** chats, non?
—Non, ce ne sont pas **des** chats. J'ai **des** chiens.
—Combien **de** chiens as-tu?
—Quatre.
—Tu n'as pas **de** problèmes avec tes colocataires?
—Non, je n'ai pas **de** colocataire.

un tableau → des tableaux
un bureau → des bureaux
un animal → des animaux

Je rentre **de** l'université à cinq heures.

Ma résidence est **près d'**ici, **derrière** la bibliothèque et **à côté de** la librairie.

NUMBERS ABOVE 100

- Use **un** in **un million,** but not before the words **cent** and **mille.** The word **million(s)** is followed by **de (d')** when followed directly by a noun.
- **Million** takes an **s** when plural. **Cent** generally only takes an **s** when plural if not followed by another number. Never add an **s** to **mille.**
- There is no hyphen between the words **cent, mille,** or **million** and another number.
- Use commas to denote decimals, and spaces or periods to set off numbers in the thousands, millions, etc.

ORDINAL NUMBERS

Use **premier (première)** to say *first*. To form the other ordinal numbers *(second, third, fourth . . .),* add the suffix **-ième** to the cardinal numbers (**deux, trois, quatre...**). Drop a final **e** of cardinal numbers before adding **-ième.** Note the spelling changes in **cinquième** *(fifth)* and **neuvième** *(ninth).*

AVOIR

The verb **avoir** *(to have)* is irregular.

j' **ai**	nous **avons**
tu **as**	vous **avez**
il/elle **a**	ils/elles **ont**

UN, UNE, DES → DE (D')

Use **de (d')** rather than **un, une,** or **des** after . . .

- most verbs in the negative form, except **être.**
- quantity expressions like **combien, beaucoup,** and **assez.**

PLURALS ENDING WITH -X

In the plural, most words ending in **-eau, -au,** or **-eu** end in **-x** rather than **-s,** and the ending **-al** becomes **-aux.**

PREPOSITIONS

When used alone, the preposition **de** means *of, from,* or *about*. **De** is also used in some of the following prepositions.

sur	on	près (de)	near
sous	under	loin (de)	far (from)
entre	between	à côté (de)	next to, beside
dans	in	à droite / gauche (de)	to the right / left (of)
devant	in front of	en face (de)	across (from), facing
derrière	behind	dans le coin (de)	in the corner (of)

De contracts with the articles **le** and **les**, but not with **la** or **l'**.

CONTRACTION:			NO CONTRACTION:		
de + le	→	du	de + la	→	de la
de + les	→	des	de + l'	→	de l'

POSSESSION

De is used instead of *'s* to indicate possession. Remember the contractions **de** + **le** → **du** and **de** + **les** → **des.**

le bureau du professeur	*the professor's office*
la voiture de mon frère	*my brother's car*

The possessive adjectives also indicate possession.

	MASCULINE SINGULAR	FEMININE SINGULAR (+ consonant sound)	FEMININE SINGULAR (+ vowel sound)	PLURAL
my	**mon** vélo	**ma** voiture	**mon** adresse	**mes** meubles
your (sing. fam.)	**ton** vélo	**ta** voiture	**ton** adresse	**tes** meubles
his/her/its	**son** vélo	**sa** voiture	**son** adresse	**ses** meubles
our	**notre** vélo	**notre** voiture	**notre** adresse	**nos** meubles
your (form./pl.)	**votre** vélo	**votre** voiture	**votre** adresse	**vos** meubles
their	**leur** vélo	**leur** voiture	**leur** adresse	**leurs** meubles

Use the forms **mon, ton,** and **son** rather than **ma, ta,** and **sa** before feminine nouns beginning with vowel sounds.

The use of the forms **son/sa/ses** *(his, her, its)* depends on the gender and number of the object possessed, not the person who owns it. **Son/sa/ses** can all mean *his, her,* or *its*.

CE (CET)/CETTE/CES AND QUEL/QUELLE/QUELS/QUELLES

Use the demonstrative adjective **ce (cet)/cette/ces** to say both *this/these* and *that/those*. The masculine **ce** becomes **cet** before masculine singular nouns beginning with a vowel sound.

	SINGULAR	PLURAL
MASCULINE (+ *consonant sound*)	ce chien	ces chiens
MASCULINE (+ *vowel sound*)	cet animal	ces animaux
FEMININE	cette étagère	ces étagères

Use **quel/quelle/quels/quelles** to say *which* or *what* directly before a noun or the verbs **est** and **sont.** It agrees with the gender and number of the noun it modifies.

	MASCULINE	FEMININE
SINGULAR	quel état	quelle ville
PLURAL	quels états	quelles villes

Je n'aime pas habiter dans la résidence parce qu'elle est loin **du** parking et ma chambre est en face **des** ascenseurs, à côté **de l'**escalier et loin **de la** salle de bains!

—C'est ta voiture?
—Non, c'est la voiture **de** mon amie.

—C'est la porte **de la** salle de bains?
—Non, c'est la porte **du** placard.

—Tu habites encore chez **tes** parents?
—Non, j'habite chez **mon** frère.
—Où est **sa** maison?
—Pas loin de chez **nos** parents.
—Dans quelle rue est la maison de **vos** parents?
—**Leur** adresse est le 435, rue Martin.

Mon amie s'appelle Marion.

son quartier = *his/her/its neighborhood*
sa porte = *his/her/its door*
ses murs = *his/her/its walls*

—Tu habites dans **cette** rue?
—Oui, j'aime beaucoup **ce** quartier. Mon appartement est dans **cet** immeuble.
—Mon appartement est derrière **ces** arbres.

—Dans **quelle** ville habites-tu?
—J'habite à Sherbrooke.
—**Quelle** est ton adresse?
—C'est le 1202, rue Galt.
—**Quel** est ton numéro de téléphone?
—C'est le (819) 569-1208.

VOCABULAIRE

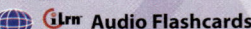 Audio Flashcards

COMPÉTENCE 1

Talking about where you live

NOMS MASCULINS

un appartement	an apartment
un arrêt de bus	a bus stop
un ascenseur	an elevator
le centre-ville	downtown
un dollar	a dollar
un escalier	stairs, a staircase
un étage	a floor
un immeuble	an apartment building
le logement	lodging, housing
le loyer	the rent
le rez-de-chaussée	the ground floor
un salon	a living room
un sous-sol	a basement

NOMS FÉMININS

la banlieue	the suburbs
la campagne	the country(side)
une chambre	a bedroom
une cuisine	a kitchen
une fenêtre	a window
une maison	a house
une pièce	a room
une porte	a door
une salle à manger	a dining room
une salle de bains	a bathroom
des toilettes	a restroom, a toilet
une ville	a city

ADJECTIFS

cher (chère)	expensive
confortable	comfortable
pratique	practical, convenient

DIVERS

à la campagne	in the country(side)
À quel étage?	On what floor?
au sous-sol	in the basement
au rez-de-chaussée	on the ground/first floor
au premier (deuxième...) étage	on the second (third...) floor
cent	a/one hundred
dans une résidence universitaire	in a university dorm
en banlieue	in the suburbs
en centre-ville	downtown
en ville	in town
Je n'ai pas de...	I don't have...
loin (de)	far (from)
mille	a/one thousand
un million (de)	a/one million
par mois	per month
(tout) près (de)	(very) near
téléphoner (à)	to phone
trop	too (much/many)
il/elle va	he/she is going, he/she goes

Pour les nombres ordinaux, voir la page 110.

COMPÉTENCE 2

Talking about your possessions

NOMS MASCULINS

un animal (*pl* des animaux)	an animal
un canapé	a couch
un CD	a CD
un chat	a cat
un chien	a dog
un DVD	a DVD
des effets personnels	personal belongings
un fauteuil	an armchair
un iPod	an iPod
un lecteur CD/DVD/Blu-ray	a CD/DVD/Blu-ray player
un ordinateur	a computer
un (ordinateur) portable	a laptop
un (téléphone) portable	a cell phone
un smartphone	a smartphone
un tableau (*pl* des tableaux)	a painting
un tapis	a rug
un vélo	a bicycle
des vêtements	clothes

NOMS FÉMININS

une chaîne hi-fi	an audio system
une chaise	a chair
une chose	a thing
une lampe	a lamp
une plante	a plant
une table	a table
une télé	a TV
une voiture	a car

PRÉPOSITIONS

à côté (de)	next to, beside
à droite (de)	to the right (of)
à gauche (de)	to the left (of)
dans	in
dans le coin (de)	in the corner (of)
de	of, from, about
derrière	behind
devant	in front of
en face (de)	across from, facing
entre	between
sous	under
sur	on

VERBES

arriver	to arrive
avoir	to have
chercher	to look for
fumer	to smoke
partager	to share

DIVERS

combien (de)	how many, how much
embêtant(e)	annoying
en ordre	in order, orderly
non plus	neither
partout	everywhere
Pas de problème.	No problem.
peut-être	maybe, perhaps
(bien) rangé(e)	neat, put away, straightened up
ton/ta/tes	your (sing. fam.)
tout	everything, all

COMPÉTENCE 3

Describing your room

NOMS MASCULINS

un adjectif	an adjective
un bureau (*pl* des bureaux)	a desk
un couloir	a hall, a corridor
un lit	a bed
des meubles	furniture, furnishings
un mur	a wall
un placard	a closet
un poster	a poster
un rideau (*pl* des rideaux)	a curtain

NOMS FÉMININS

une commode	a dresser, a chest of drawers
une couleur	a color
une couverture	a (bed)cover, a blanket
une étagère	a bookcase, a shelf
une vue	a view

ADJECTIFS POSSESSIFS

mon/ma/mes	my
ton/ta/tes	your
son/sa/ses	his, her, its
notre/nos	our
votre/vos	your
leur/leurs	their

EXPRESSIONS VERBALES

Ça a l'air bien.	It seems nice.
Ça te plaît.	You like it.
comme tu vois	as you see
espérer	to hope
indiquer	to indicate
laisser	to leave
montrer	to show
Viens voir!	Come see!

LES COULEURS

De quelle couleur est…?	What color is…?
De quelle couleur sont…?	What color are…?
beige	beige
blanc(he)	white
bleu(e)	blue
gris(e)	gray
jaune	yellow
marron	brown
noir(e)	black
orange	orange
rose	pink
rouge	red
vert(e)	green
violet(te)	purple

DIVERS

à sa place	in its place
au bout (de)	at the end (of)
chaque	each
en désordre	in disorder, disorderly
justement	as a matter of fact, precisely, exactly
par terre	on the floor, on the ground
préféré(e)	favorite
propre	clean
Quel bazar!	What a mess!
sale	dirty

COMPÉTENCE 4

Giving your address and phone number

NOMS MASCULINS

un code postal	a zip code
un État	a state
les États-Unis	the United States
un nom (de famille)	a (sur/last)name, a noun
un numéro de téléphone	a telephone number
un pays	a country
un prénom	a first name
des renseignements	information

NOMS FÉMININS

une adresse (mail)	an (e-mail) address
la Louisiane	Louisiana
une nationalité	a nationality
une province	a province
une rue	a street

DIVERS

ce (cet)/cette	this, that
ces	these, those
il/elle doit…	he/she must…
partagé(e)	shared, divided
poser une question	to ask a question
quel/quelle/quels/quelles	which, what
s'inscrire	to register
suivant(e)	following

En Amérique: En Louisiane
En famille

- iLrn Heinle Learning Center
- www.cengagebrain.com
- *Horizons* Video: Les Stagiaires
- Audio
- Internet web search
- Pair work
- Group work

4

COMPÉTENCE

1 Describing your family
Ma famille

Describing feelings and appearance
  Les expressions avec **avoir**

Stratégies et Compréhension auditive
- **Pour mieux comprendre:** *Asking for clarification*
- **Compréhension auditive:** *La famille de Robert*

2 Saying where you go in your free time
Le temps libre

Saying where you are going
  Le verbe **aller**, *la préposition* **à** *et le pronom* **y**

Suggesting activities and telling people what to do
  Le pronom sujet **on** *et l'impératif*

3 Saying what you are going to do
Le week-end prochain

Saying what you are going to do
  Le futur immédiat

Saying when you are going to do something
  Les dates

4 Planning how to get there
Les moyens de transport

Deciding how to get there and come back
  Les verbes **prendre** *et* **venir** *et les moyens de transport*

Vidéoreprise *Les Stagiaires*

Lecture et Composition
- **Pour mieux lire:** *Using your knowledge of the world*
- **Lecture:** *Deux mots*
- **Pour mieux écrire:** *Visualizing your topic*
- **Composition:** *Ma famille*

Comparaisons culturelles *L'histoire des Cadiens*

Résumé de grammaire

Vocabulaire

cent quarante et un | **141**

EN AMÉRIQUE: EN LOUISIANE

PowerPoint 4-1

Que savez-vous de la Louisiane francophone et de ses traditions? **Connaissez-vous** la cuisine ou la musique de cette région?

Il y a deux traditions francophones en Louisiane, **les Cadiens** et les Créoles. Les Cadiens sont les descendants des Acadiens déportés du Canada par les Anglais après 1755. Les Créoles sont les descendants des premiers **colons** français et européens, d'**immigrés** des îles caraïbes **ou encore** d'**esclaves échappés** de cette région.

La ville de Lafayette est au cœur de la région cadienne, l'Acadiane, 22 paroisses dans la partie sud de la Louisiane. La Nouvelle-Orléans est au cœur de la région créole.

Les Cadiens et les Créoles aiment bien manger et ils sont **fiers** de leurs cuisines. La cuisine cadienne est une cuisine **campagnarde** des bayous. La cuisine créole **tire ses racines** des familles aristocrates européennes de La Nouvelle-Orléans. Les deux cuisines sont similaires et beaucoup de **plats** sont à base d'une sauce appelée «un roux» (composée de **beurre** et de **farine**), de **riz** et de «la sainte trinité»: l'oignon, **le poivron vert** et le céleri. En général, les plats sont très **épicés** comme **les écrevisses** ou **les crevettes étouffées,** le jambalaya, le gumbo, **l'andouille** et **le boudin.**

Les Cadiens et les Créoles sont fiers de leur cuisine.

Que savez-vous de *What do you know about* **Connaissez-vous** *Are you familiar with* **les Cadiens** *the Cajuns* **colons** *settlers, colonists* **immigrés** *immigrants* **ou encore** *as well as* **esclaves échappés** *escaped slaves* **au cœur de** *in the heart of* **paroisses** *parishes* **la partie sud** *the southern part* **fiers** *proud* **campagnarde** *country style* **tire ses racines** *gets its roots* **plats** *dishes* **beurre** *butter* **farine** *flour* **riz** *rice* **le poivron vert** *green bell pepper* **épicés** *spicy* **les écrevisses** *crawfish* **les crevettes** *shrimp* **étouffées** *stewed* **l'andouille** *andouille (a smoked pork sausage with garlic)* **le boudin** *blood sausage*

142 cent quarante-deux | CHAPITRE 4

Les Cadiens et les Créoles aiment aussi la musique et la danse. Le zydeco et le swamp pop sont deux genres de musique originaires de la Louisiane. Dérivé du blues, de la musique country et du swing, les instruments traditionnels du zydeco sont le violon, l'accordéon, la guitare, l'harmonica et **le frottoir.** Le swamp pop est **un mélange** de zydeco, de rock et de boogie.

Le frottoir et l'accordéon sont deux instruments traditionnels du zydeco.

Un «fais dodo» est une soirée dansante cadienne. Le nom «**fais dodo**» **vient de la berceuse:** *Fais dodo Colas mon p'tit frère.* **On chantait cette chanson pour que les enfants dorment pendant que** les parents dansaient et chantaient **aux bals** avec leurs amis.

Un fais dodo est une soirée dansante cadienne.

La Louisiane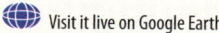

NOMBRE D'HABITANTS: **4 600 000** (les Louisianais)
(Un peu moins de 195 000 parlent français, cadien *[cajun]* ou créole et parmi eux *[among them]* 180 000 parlent ces langues à la maison.)

CAPITALE: **Bâton-Rouge**

Le savez-vous?

Que savez-vous de la Louisiane francophone? Avez-vous visité la Louisiane? Quel mot de la liste va avec chaque définition?

> le zydeco   la sainte trinité   les Créoles
> les Cadiens   Lafayette   La Nouvelle-Orléans
> un fais dodo   un roux   le frottoir   l'Acadiane

1. les descendants des habitants de la Louisiane avant son annexion par les États-Unis, principalement d'origines européennes et africaines
2. les descendants des Francophones expulsés du Canada par les Anglais au dix-huitième siècle *(century)*
3. la ville au cœur de la région créole
4. la ville au cœur de la région cadienne
5. les 22 paroisses de la région cadienne au sud de la Louisiane
6. un genre de musique influencé par le blues, la musique country et le swing et le plus souvent joué à l'accordéon
7. un instrument du zydeco
8. une sauce qui est la base des cuisines cadienne et créole
9. trois ingrédients de nombreux *(numerous)* plats cadiens et créoles: l'oignon, le poivron vert et le céleri
10. une soirée dansante cadienne

Quick-reference answers for *Le savez-vous?*
1. les Créoles **2.** les Cadiens **3.** La Nouvelle-Orléans
4. Lafayette **5.** l'Acadiane **6.** le zydeco **7.** le frottoir
8. un roux **9.** la sainte trinité **10.** un fais dodo

Search for a video and lyrics of a Zydeco song in French that you like. Also search for Cajun or Creole recipes from Louisiana. Share what you find with the class.

Laissez les bons temps rouler!

Suggestion. Search for a video of the lullaby *Fais dodo Colas mon p'tit frère* on the Internet and play it for the class.

le frottoir *the rubboard* **un mélange** *a mix* **fais dodo** *go to sleep* **vient de la berceuse** *comes from the lullaby* **On chantait cette chanson pour que les enfants dorment pendant que** *People used to sing this song so the children would sleep while* **aux bals** *at dances* **Laissez les bons temps rouler!** *Let the good times roll!* (regional)

COMPÉTENCE 1

Describing your family

PowerPoint 4-2

 In the **Culture Modules** in the video library, see *The Modern Family*.

Note culturelle

En 1916, l'État de Louisiane exige que la scolarité se fasse *(requires that education be done)* en anglais. L'anglais commence alors à être la langue prédominante chez les jeunes. Plus de 90 % de la population née *(born)* en Acadiane avant cette époque est bilingue français-anglais, mais moins de 10 % de leurs petits-enfants *(grandchildren)* parlent français. Certains Américains voudraient faire de l'anglais la seule langue officielle aux États-Unis. Que pensez-vous de cette idée?

Vocabulaire supplémentaire

adopté(e) *adopted*
un beau-frère *a brother-in-law*
une belle-sœur *a sister-in-law*
l'aîné (l'aînée) *the oldest child*
le cadet (la cadette) *the middle child, the younger child*
le benjamin (la benjamine) *the youngest child (of more than two)*
un demi-frère (une demi-sœur) *a stepbrother, a half-brother (a stepsister, a half-sister)*
un ex-mari (une ex-femme) *an ex-husband (an ex-wife)*
un fils unique (une fille unique) *an only child*
des petits-enfants (un petit-fils, une petite-fille) *grandchildren (a grandson, a granddaughter)*
porter des lentilles *(f)* *to wear contact lenses*

Note de vocabulaire

Use **avoir l'air** (+ adjective) to say someone *looks young, happy …* **Il a l'air sympa.** *(He looks nice.)*. Use **ressembler à** to say a person *looks like* someone: **Je ressemble à ma mère.** *(I look like my mother.)*

MA FAMILLE

Robert et ses amis **ont l'intention de** passer une semaine de **vacances** *(f)* chez **le père** de Robert à Lafayette. Robert parle de sa famille.

Voici ma famille. Mes parents sont divorcés maintenant. Ils ont quatre **enfants,** trois **garçons** et **une fille.**

(mes grands-parents)

mon grand-père (Il est **décédé** maintenant.)   ma grand-mère

(mes parents)

mon père   ma mère   mon oncle   ma tante

moi   mes frères   ma sœur   son mari   mon cousin   ma cousine

le **fils** et la fille de ma sœur (mon neveu et ma nièce)

Mon père s'appelle Luke.
Il **a (environ) 50 ans** *(m)*.
Il est **encore** jeune, mais il **a l'air** plus âgé.
Il est **de taille moyenne.**
Il **a les cheveux courts** et gris.

Il **a les yeux** *(m)* marron.
Il **a une barbe** grise et une moustache.
Il **porte des lunettes** *(f)*.

Et vous? Comment êtes-vous?

J'ai les yeux **noirs** / marron / **noisette** / verts / bleus / gris.
J'ai les cheveux courts / **mi-longs** / longs et noirs / **bruns** / **châtains** / auburn / blonds / gris / blancs / **roux.**

Line art on this page: © Cengage Learning

---

avoir l'intention de *to intend to*   **les vacances** *vacation*   **le père** *the father*   **des enfants** *children*   **un garçon** *a boy*   **une fille** *a girl, a daughter*   **décédé(e)** *deceased*   **un fils** *a son*   **avoir… ans** *to be … years old*   **environ** *about*   **encore** *still*   **avoir l'air…** *to look, to seem …*   **de taille moyenne** *of medium height*   **avoir les cheveux…** *to have … hair*   **court(e)** *short*   **avoir les yeux…** *to have … eyes*   **une barbe** *a beard*   **porter** *to wear*   **des lunettes** *glasses*   **noirs** *(with eyes) very dark brown, almost black*   **noisette** *(inv) hazel*   **mi-longs** *(with hair) shoulder-length*   **bruns** *(with hair) medium to dark brown*   **châtains** *(with hair) light to medium brown*   **roux** *(with hair) red*

Warm-up. Questions orales. Habitez-vous avec votre famille? Habitez-vous dans une maison, dans un appartement ou dans une chambre en résidence universitaire? Avez-vous un(e) camarade de chambre ou un(e) colocataire? Quel est son prénom? Comment est-il/elle? Comment est le/la colocataire idéal(e)?

Robert parle de sa famille avec Thomas.

THOMAS: Vous êtes combien dans ta famille?
ROBERT: Nous sommes sept: mon père, **ma belle-mère,** ma mère, mes deux frères, ma sœur et moi. Ma sœur est mariée et elle habite à La Nouvelle-Orléans.
THOMAS: Elle est plus jeune ou **plus âgée que** toi? Quel âge a-t-elle?
ROBERT: Elle a 28 ans.
THOMAS: Comment s'appelle-t-elle?
ROBERT: Elle s'appelle Sarah.

A La famille. Donnez l'équivalent féminin.

EXEMPLE le frère   la sœur

1. le père
2. l'oncle
3. le garçon
4. le neveu
5. le beau-père
6. le cousin
7. le fils
8. le grand-père

B Généalogie. Complétez les phrases.

EXEMPLE Les parents de mon père, ce sont **mes grands-parents.**

1. Le père de mon père, c'est _____. Sa femme, c'est _____.
2. La sœur de ma mère, c'est _____. Son mari, c'est _____. Leurs enfants sont _____. Leur fils, c'est _____ et leur fille, c'est _____.
3. Le fils de ma sœur, c'est _____. Sa fille, c'est _____.

C Mon meilleur ami. Changez les mots en italique pour décrire votre meilleur ami.

1. Il s'appelle *Emmitt / Chuong / ???* et il a *18 / 25 / 38 / 45 / ???* ans.
2. Il est *grand / petit / de taille moyenne.*
3. Il a les cheveux *longs / mi-longs / courts* et *blonds / noirs / ???.*
4. Il a les yeux *marron / gris / ???.*
5. Il a l'air *intellectuel / sportif / jeune / ???.*

D Entretien. Posez ces questions à votre partenaire. Ensuite, changez de rôles.

1. Vous êtes combien dans ta famille? Tu as des frères et sœurs? (Ils sont plus âgés ou moins âgés que toi?)
2. Avec quel membre de la famille préfères-tu passer du temps? Comment s'appelle-t-il/elle? Quel âge a-t-il/elle? Il/Elle est grand(e), petit(e) ou de taille moyenne? Il/Elle a les yeux de quelle couleur? Il/Elle a les cheveux longs, mi-longs ou courts? Il/Elle a les cheveux de quelle couleur? Il/Elle a l'air plutôt sportif (sportive) ou plutôt intellectuel(le)? Il/Elle porte des lunettes?

À VOUS!

Avec un(e) partenaire, relisez à haute voix la conversation entre Thomas et Robert. Ensuite, adaptez la conversation pour parler d'un membre de votre famille.

---

une belle-mère (un beau-père, des beaux-parents) *a stepmother / a mother-in-law (a stepfather / a father-in-law, stepparents / in-laws)*   **plus âgé(e) que** *older than*

Compétence 1 | *cent quarante-cinq* **145**

 **PowerPoint 4-3**

DESCRIBING FEELINGS AND APPEARANCE

Les expressions avec avoir

Use these expressions with **avoir** to describe people or say how they feel.

avoir (environ)... ans	to be (around)... years old	avoir faim	to be hungry
avoir l'air...	to look..., to seem...	avoir soif	to be thirsty
avoir une barbe / une moustache / des lunettes	to have a beard / a mustache / glasses	avoir froid	to be cold
		avoir chaud	to be hot
		avoir raison	to be right
		avoir tort	to be wrong
avoir les yeux bleus / verts...	to have blue / green... eyes	avoir peur (de)	to be afraid (of)
		avoir sommeil	to be sleepy
avoir les cheveux longs / roux...	to have long / red... hair		

— Mon fils **a peur** des chiens.
— Quel **âge** a-t-il? Il **a l'air** très jeune.
— Tu **as raison.** Il **a quatre ans.**

— *My son is afraid of dogs.*
— *How old is he? He looks very young.*
— *You're right. He's four.*

Notice these three expressions that also use **avoir** in French.

avoir besoin de (d') + noun or infinitive	*to need* + noun or infinitive
avoir envie de (d') + noun or infinitive	*to feel like* + noun or verb
avoir l'intention de (d') + infinitive	*to intend* + infinitive

J'**ai besoin de** la voiture. — *I need the car.*
J'**ai envie de** sortir. — *I feel like going out.*
J'**ai l'intention de** rentrer à midi. — *I intend to return at noon.*
Tu **as besoin de** manger? — *Do you need to eat?*
Tu **as envie de manger** un sandwich? — *You feel like eating a sandwich?*

Pour vérifier

1. How do you say *I'm hungry? I'm thirsty? I'm hot? I'm cold? I'm sleepy? I'm afraid? I'm right? I'm never wrong? I need to stay home? I feel like staying home? I intend to stay home?*

2. How do you say *How old is he? He's 24? He has short black hair and brown eyes? He seems nice? He has a black beard, a mustache, and glasses?*

Note de vocabulaire

1. Use **les** when talking about someone's hair and eyes. **Les cheveux** and **les yeux** are both masculine plural, so follow them with an adjective in the masculine plural form. **Ma sœur a les cheveux bruns et les yeux verts.** *Auburn*, **marron**, and **noisette**, however, are invariable.

2. Brown eyes can be **noirs** (*almost black or dark brown*) or **marron** (*light to medium brown*). Brown hair can be **bruns** (*dark or medium brown*) or **châtains** (*light to medium brown*). The words **brun, roux, auburn,** and **châtain** are mainly used to describe someone's hair.

3. You can say that someone is *blond* or *a blond, brunette* or *a brunette,* or *red-headed* or *a red-head,* using **blond(e), brun(e),** or **roux (rousse). Elle est rousse, mais sa sœur est blonde.** *She's a red-head, but her sister's a blonde.*

4. To say you are *very hot / cold / hungry*... use **très. J'ai très chaud.**

Vocabulaire supplémentaire

avoir un tatouage / un piercing
avoir un bouc *to have a goatee*
avoir des pattes (f) *to have sideburns*
être chauve *to be bald*
avoir la tête rasée *to have a shaved head*

🌐 **Sélection musicale.** Search the Web for the song "**J'ai besoin d'un chum**" by Céline Dion to enjoy a musical selection containing structures and vocabulary from this *Compétence*.

Suggestions. A. Emphasize the liaison in **les yeux,** that **cheveux** and **yeux** both rhyme with **deux,** and that **faim** rhymes with **vingt. B.** Remind students that **marron** is invariable and point out that **noisette** and **auburn** are also invariable.

🟢 **A Comment est-il?** Répondez aux questions pour faire une description du meilleur ami de Robert.

1. Comment s'appelle-t-il? Quel âge a-t-il?
2. Il a les cheveux de quelle couleur? Il a les cheveux longs ou courts? Il a les yeux de quelle couleur?
3. Il a une barbe? Il porte des lunettes? Il a l'air sympa?

Maintenant, changez la description précédente d'Antoine pour parler de vous.

EXEMPLE Je m'appelle Pat. J'ai 25 ans. J'ai les cheveux...

Antoine, 20 ans

146 cent quarante-six | CHAPITRE 4

B **Les activités de Robert.** Quelles sont les activités que Robert a probablement envie de faire? Quelles sont les activités qu'il a probablement besoin de faire?

EXEMPLES faire ses devoirs   **Il a besoin de faire ses devoirs.**
regarder la télé   **Il a envie de regarder la télé.**

1. aller au cinéma
2. aller prendre un verre
3. aller travailler
4. étudier
5. sortir avec des amis
6. faire la lessive *(the laundry)*

Maintenant, circulez dans la classe et trouvez quelqu'un qui a l'intention de faire les activités mentionnées ce week-end.

EXEMPLE faire tes devoirs
— As-tu l'intention de faire tes devoirs ce week-end?
— Oui, j'ai l'intention de faire mes devoirs dimanche soir.

C **Moi, j'ai…** Utilisez une expression avec **avoir** de la liste à la page précédente. Faites attention au contexte.

EXEMPLE Je voudrais aller prendre un verre.   **J'ai soif.**

1. Brrrr… Fermez la fenêtre.
2. Ah! C'est un serpent!
3. Voilà. Ma réponse est correcte.
4. J'ai envie de manger quelque chose.
5. Je voudrais un coca.
6. J'ai besoin de dormir.

D **Qu'est-ce qu'ils ont?** Aujourd'hui, la fille d'une amie fête ses cinq ans *(is celebrating her fifth birthday)*. Que dit sa mère? Utilisez une expression avec **avoir**.

1. Ma fille… aujourd'hui.
2. Ses amis…
3. Mon frère…
4. Mes cousins…

5. Mon mari et moi, nous…
6. Moi, j'…
7. Le chien de mon fils…
8. Tu… de faire ça au chien!

E **Entretien.** Interviewez votre partenaire.

1. Qu'est-ce que tu as envie de faire ce week-end? Qu'est-ce que tu as besoin de faire? Qu'est-ce que tu as l'intention de faire dimanche soir?
2. Tu as faim maintenant? Tu as soif? Est-ce que tu as l'intention de manger quelque chose après le cours? As-tu sommeil maintenant? As-tu l'intention de dormir après le cours?

STRATÉGIES ET COMPRÉHENSION AUDITIVE

Script for A. Je ne comprends pas.
SCÈNE A
— Je suis Philippe Dewailly.
— Bonjour, Monsieur De... euh, Dega... Excusez-moi, ça s'écrit comment?
— Dewailly. D-E-W-A-I-L-L-Y.
— Ah! Eh bien, bonjour, Monsieur Dewailly.

SCÈNE B
— Alors, vous êtes étudiante, non?
— Oui. Et vous, vous êtes étudiante aussi?
— Non, moi, je suis médecin ici à Lafayette.
— Vous êtes...? Je ne comprends pas. Qu'est-ce que ça veut dire **médecin**?
— Oh, vous savez, je m'occupe des malades dans un hôpital.

SCÈNE C
— Et vous, vous êtes médecin aussi?
— Non, moi, je suis pharmacien.
— Comment?
— Pharmacien. Je travaille dans une pharmacie.
— Ah oui, je comprends maintenant.

POUR MIEUX COMPRENDRE: Asking for clarification

When you do not understand something, it is useful to be able to ask for clarification. You already know three ways to do this: by asking for something to be repeated, by asking what a word means, or by asking how a word is spelled.

Comment? Répétez, s'il vous plaît.
Je ne comprends pas. Qu'est-ce que ça veut dire, **belle-sœur**?
Ça s'écrit comment?

A Je ne comprends pas.
Listen to three conversations. In each, which method is used to ask for clarification: **a**, **b**, or **c**?

a. asking for something to be repeated (**Comment? Répétez, s'il vous plaît.**)
b. asking the meaning of a word (**Qu'est-ce que ça veut dire...?**)
c. asking the spelling of a word (**Ça s'écrit comment?**)

Line art on this page: © Cengage Learning

Warm-up for B. Comment? How would you ask for clarification in these situations? **1.** You didn't quite hear what someone said. **2.** You can't quite recognize someone's last name and would like to know how it is spelled. **3.** You aren't certain whether a friend said he works at the university or is a student there. **4.** Someone recommends the **sandwich au jambon,** but you don't know what **jambon** means.

Script for B. Comment?
SCÈNE A
— Bon, un expresso, 1 dollar 50, un coca, 1 dollar et une bière ** *(cough)* dollars... Alors, ça fait ** *(cough)* dollars.
— Euh...

SCÈNE B
— Tu voudrais venir manger avec nous?
— Ça dépend. Il est loin d'ici, le restaurant?
— Non, il est tout près... sur le boulevard Arnould.
— Le boulevard Ar... Arn... euh...

SCÈNE C
— Je vous recommande le jus de pamplemousse. Il est très bon.
— Le jus de... pam... ple... mousse? Mais...?

B Comment?
Listen to these three other scenes, in which one of the speakers is having difficulty understanding. In each case, what could he or she say to ask for clarification?

Compréhension auditive: *La famille de Robert*

Robert is describing his family to a friend who is studying French. Use what you know and your ability to guess logically to help you understand what he says. The first time, listen only for the number of times his friend asks for clarification.

A La famille de Robert.
Écoutez encore une fois *(again)* la description de la famille de Robert et complétez l'arbre généalogique *(family tree)* avec les prénoms des membres de sa famille.

Suggestion for A. La famille de Robert.
Before beginning, have students look over the illustration and determine the relationships shown. Point out that not all family members are mentioned.

Script for A. La famille de Robert.
— J'ai une sœur qui s'appelle Sarah et deux frères, Paul et Yves.
— Yves? Ça s'écrit comment?
— Y-V-E-S.
— Ah, je comprends.
— Mes parents n'habitent plus ensemble. Mon père s'appelle Luke. Il habite ici à Lafayette et ma mère habite à Atlanta. Elle s'appelle Julie.
— Tes parents sont divorcés?
— Oui, depuis longtemps. Ma mère et mes deux frères habitent avec ma grand-mère à Atlanta. Ma sœur, Sarah, est mariée et elle habite à La Nouvelle-Orléans. Mon père habite ici à Lafayette. Il travaille à l'université.
— Il est professeur?
— Oui, c'est ça. Et ma mère est pédiatre.
— Pédiatre? Qu'est-ce que ça veut dire?
— Ça veut dire *pediatrician*.

B C'est qui?
Écoutez encore une fois la description de la famille de Robert et répondez aux questions.

1. Qui habite à Lafayette?
2. Qui habite à Atlanta?
3. Qui habite à La Nouvelle-Orléans?
4. Qui est marié?
5. Qui est divorcé?
6. Comment dit-on **pédiatre** en anglais?
7. Dans la famille de Robert, qui est pédiatre?
8. Quelle est la profession du père de Robert?

COMPÉTENCE 2

Saying where you go in your free time

 PowerPoint 4-4

LE TEMPS LIBRE

Chez vous, où est-ce qu'**on va** pour passer **son temps libre**?

On aime beaucoup les activités culturelles et **de temps en temps,** on va…

au musée pour voir **une exposition**

au théâtre pour voir **une pièce**

à un concert ou à un festival de musique

On aime aussi **les activités de plein air** et on va souvent…

au parc pour faire du jogging

à la piscine pour nager

à la plage pour **prendre un bain de soleil**

Pour **retrouver des amis,** on va…

à un match de basket

en boîte

à l'église

Pour faire du shopping, on va… Et pour **acheter** des livres, on va…

au centre commercial

dans les petits magasins

à la librairie

Line art on this page: © Cengage Learning

Note culturelle

Pour connaître la culture cadienne, visitez l'Acadiane où beaucoup de villes sont nommées en souvenir de villes françaises (Abbeville), de saints (Saint Martinville), d'Acadiens réfugiés (Thibodaux) ou de héros (Lafayette). Pour connaître la culture créole, visitez plutôt La Nouvelle-Orléans. Aimeriez-vous *(Would you like)* mieux visiter l'Acadiane ou La Nouvelle-Orléans? Pourquoi?

Vocabulaire supplémentaire

à la synagogue
à la mosquée
au temple *to church* (Protestant), *to temple*
au lac *to the lake*
au bar

Note de grammaire

1. Use **pour** before infinitives to say *in order to*. In English, *in order to* may be shortened to just *to*: *One goes to the bookstore (in order) to buy books.* **On va à la librairie *pour* acheter des livres.**
2. With the verb **retrouver**, say whom you are meeting: **Je retrouve mes amis au café.** To say *We meet (each other) at the café,* use **On *se* retrouve au café.**
3. Notice the accent spelling change in the conjugation of **acheter** *(to buy).*

j'achète	nous achetons
tu achètes	vous achetez
il/elle achète	ils/elles achètent

4. The name of a place generally follows the type of place. For example, for *Tinseltown Cinema,* say **le cinéma Tinseltown.**

Warm-up. Dans votre famille, qui aime faire ces choses? (Dites **Personne n'aime…** pour dire *No one likes…*) aller au cinéma, lire, danser, jouer au volley, déjeuner au restaurant, prendre un verre, faire du jogging, travailler sur l'ordinateur, parler au téléphone, aller au parc, manger dans un fast-food, bricoler, envoyer des textos à des amis

---

on va *one goes* **son temps libre** *one's free time* **de temps en temps** *from time to time* **une exposition** *an exhibit* **une pièce** *a play* **les activités de plein air** *outdoor activities* **prendre un bain de soleil** *to sunbathe* **retrouver des amis** *to meet friends* **acheter** *to buy*

Robert et Gabriel parlent de leurs projets *(m)* pour ce soir.

GABRIEL: **On sort** ce soir?
ROBERT: D'accord. On va au cinéma?
GABRIEL: Ah, non, je préfère **connaître** un peu la région. **On dit que** la cuisine **cadienne** est **extra**! Allons **plutôt** au restaurant.
ROBERT: D'accord. Allons dîner au restaurant Préjean. C'est un très bon restaurant où **on sert** les spécialités de la région, et il y a un orchestre cadien. Ça te dit?
GABRIEL: Oui, bonne idée. Allons au restaurant et après, allons écouter de la musique zydeco.
ROBERT: Pas de problème. **On peut** toujours **trouver** des concerts ici!

Note for the conversation. New vocabulary includes all glossed words and also **un projet, la région, la cuisine, une spécialité, un orchestre, bonne idée.**

Suggestions for the conversation. Before beginning, explain that **on** can mean *one*, but that, when used in questions such as **On danse?,** it functions as a suggestion (*Shall we dance? / How about dancing?*). (Students will learn more about **on** later.) Have students listen to the conversation with books closed to answer this question: **Qu'est-ce que Gabriel et Robert ont l'intention de faire ce soir?**

 **A Où va-t-on pour...** Demandez à un(e) partenaire où on va pour faire les choses suivantes.

EXEMPLE lire
— Où est-ce qu'on va pour lire?
— On va à la bibliothèque.

1. dîner
2. voir une pièce
3. retrouver des amis
4. prendre un verre
5. faire du shopping
6. nager
7. voir une exposition
8. prendre un bain de soleil
9. acheter des livres
10. faire du jogging

au restaurant
au musée
à la piscine
au café
au centre commercial
à l'église
au parc
au théâtre
à la plage
à la librairie
à la bibliothèque

Follow-up for A. Où va-t-on pour... Quels verbes associez-vous à ces choses? *(Possible answers are given in parentheses.)* **1.** une plage (nager, prendre un bain de soleil, jouer au volley) **2.** un restaurant (manger, dîner, déjeuner) **3.** une exposition (regarder, voir) **4.** un café (prendre un verre, parler, manger, retrouver des amis) **5.** un film (regarder, voir) **6.** un concert (écouter, aller) **7.** un centre commercial (acheter)

 **B Entretien.** Interviewez votre partenaire.

1. Où aimes-tu passer ton temps libre? Qu'est-ce que tu aimes faire après les cours? le week-end?
2. Où aimes-tu retrouver tes amis? Où aimez-vous aller ensemble? Aimez-vous les activités de plein air? Préférez-vous aller à la plage, à la piscine ou au parc? Aimes-tu nager? prendre un bain de soleil?
3. Aimes-tu faire du shopping? Préfères-tu acheter des vêtements, des livres, des DVD ou des CD? Dans quel magasin aimes-tu faire du shopping? Ce magasin est au centre commercial? C'est un magasin cher? Aimes-tu faire des achats en ligne *(buy things online)*?
4. Aimes-tu les activités culturelles? Préfères-tu aller au musée, au théâtre ou à un concert? Préfères-tu aller voir une pièce, une exposition ou un film?

À VOUS!

Avec un(e) partenaire, relisez à haute voix la conversation entre Gabriel et Robert. Ensuite, imaginez que vous êtes chez un(e) ami(e) dans une autre ville et que vous parlez de vos projets pour ce soir. Décidez ensemble d'un type de cuisine (mexicaine, italienne, française, japonaise, chinoise...) et d'un genre de musique (du rock, du jazz, du hip-hop...) populaire dans votre région et refaites la conversation pour parler de vos projets.

You can find a list of the new words from this **Compétence** on page 174 and access the audio online.

On sort...? *How about going out...?*   **connaître** *to know, to get to know*   **On dit que** *They say that*   **cadien(ne)** *Cajun*   **extra(ordinaire)** *great*   **plutôt** *instead, rather*   **on sert** *they serve* (**servir** *to serve*)   **On peut** *One can* (**pouvoir** *can, may, to be able*)   **trouver** *to find*

 **PowerPoint 4-5**

SAYING WHERE YOU ARE GOING

✓ Pour vérifier

1. What are the forms of **aller**?

2. With which forms of the definite article does **à** contract? What are the contracted forms? With which forms does it not contract? How do you say *to the café? to the library? to the university? to the students?*

3. What does the word **y** mean and how do you pronounce it? What happens to words like **je** and **ne** before **y**?

4. Where do you place **y** in a sentence where there is a verb followed by an infinitive? Where do you place it otherwise?

iLrn Grammar Tutorials

*Le verbe **aller**, la préposition **à** et le pronom **y***

To talk about going places, use the irregular verb **aller** *(to go)*.

ALLER *(to go)*	
je **vais**	nous‿**allons**
tu **vas**	vous‿**allez**
il/elle **va**	ils/elles **vont**

Use the preposition **à** *(to, at, in)* to say where you are going. When **à** falls before **le** or **les**, the two words contract to **au** and **aux**.

PREPOSITION À + LE, LA, L', LES	
à + le → au	Je vais **au** cinéma.
à + la → à la	Je vais **à la** librairie.
à + l' → à l'	Gabriel va **à l'**université.
à + les → aux	Robert va **aux** festivals de musique de la région.

The pronoun **y** *(there)* is used to avoid repeating the name of the place where one is going. Pronounce it like the letter **i**. Treat **y** as a vowel sound and use elision and liaison before it.

Je vais **au parc**. J'**y** vais avec mes cousins. Nous‿**y** allons à trois heures.

Y is generally placed *immediately* before the verb. It goes before the infinitive if there is one. If not, it goes before the conjugated verb.

— Il voudrait aller **au cinéma**?   — Ils vont **au musée**?
— Oui, il voudrait **y** aller.   — Oui, ils **y** vont.

In the negative, **y** remains *immediately* before the infinitive or the conjugated verb.

— Tu voudrais aller **au parc**?   — Tu **y** vas aujourd'hui?
— Non, je n'ai pas envie d'**y aller**.   — Non, je n'**y vais** pas aujourd'hui.

Whenever you use **aller** to talk about going somewhere and don't name the place you are going, use **y** even when the word *there* would not be stated in English.

On **y** va? *Shall we go (there)?*   J'**y** vais. *I'm going (there).*

PRONONCIATION

iLrn *Prononcez bien!* See Modules 23 and 16.

Les lettres **a, au** et **ai** 2-7

- Pronounce **a** or **à** with the mouth wide open as in the word *father*, but with the tongue slightly higher and closer to the front of the mouth.

  Ton *a*mi v*a* *à* P*a*ris.   Tu v*a*s *à* P*a*ris *a*vec t*a* c*a*m*a*ra*de*?

- Pronounce **au** like the **o** in **nos**.

  Ton beau-père va *au* rest*au*rant?   Les *au*tres y vont *au*ssi?

- Pronounce the **ai** of **je vais** like the **ais** of **français**. Be sure to distinguish this sound from the **a** of **tu vas** or **il va**.

  Je v*ais* au café.   Tu n'y vas jam*ais*?

A Prononcez bien! D'abord, pratiquez la prononciation des formes de la préposition **à** dans la troisième colonne. Ensuite, formez des phrases logiques en vous servant d'un élément de chaque colonne.

EXEMPLE Mon ami a envie de voir un film. Il va au cinéma.

Mon ami a envie de voir un film. Il…		piscine
Toi, tu as envie de nager. Tu…		arrêt de bus
Nous avons soif. Nous…	allez	librairie
Mes amis vont en cours. Ils…	vais	au	café
Vous voudriez acheter un livre. Vous…	va	à la	université
Mon frère aime écouter de la musique. Il…	allons	à l'	cinéma
Je prends *(am taking)* le bus ce matin. Je…	vas	aux	concerts de ses artistes préférés
	vont		

B On sort. Robert parle avec Thomas de ses amis et de sa famille. Complétez ses phrases. Utilisez la forme convenable du verbe **aller** et de la préposition **à** (au, à la, à l', aux).

EXEMPLE Je **vais à la** piscine.

la piscine

la piscine
1. Toi et moi, nous…

l'église
2. Mes cousins…

la bibliothèque
3. Toi, tu…

l'université
4. Ma sœur…

le musée
5. Gabriel et son frère…

la librairie
6. Mon père…

le parc
7. Notre chien…

les matchs de basket de l'université
8. Le week-end, mes amis…

Line art on this page: © Cengage Learning

C Où aiment-ils aller? Demandez à votre partenaire si ces personnes aiment aller aux endroits indiqués. Il/Elle va utiliser le pronom **y** dans ses réponses et va aussi dire si les personnes y vont souvent, rarement…

EXEMPLE tu: au musée
— **Tu aimes aller au musée?**
— **Oui, j'aime y aller. J'y vais souvent / quelquefois…**
  Non, je n'aime pas y aller. Je n'y vais jamais.

1. tu: à l'opéra, à un match de basket
2. tes amis et toi: en boîte, au centre commercial
3. ton meilleur ami (ta meilleure amie): au parc, à l'église
4. tes parents: à la piscine, à un concert de musique hip-hop

 PowerPoint 4-6

SUGGESTING ACTIVITIES AND TELLING PEOPLE WHAT TO DO

✓ Pour vérifier

1. What are the three possible uses of the pronoun **on**? What form of the verb do you always use with **on**?
2. How do you form the imperative (commands)? With which verbs do you drop the final **s** in the **tu** form of the imperative?
3. What are the command forms of **avoir** and **être**? How do you tell a friend: *Be on time! Be good! Let's be calm! Have confidence! Let's have patience!*

 Grammar Tutorials

Sélection musicale. Search the Web for the song "**Toi plus moi**" by Grégoire to enjoy a musical selection containing these structures.

Suggestion. Point out the expressions **avoir de la patience, avoir confiance, être à l'heure, être calme,** and **être sage.** Point out that parents use **Sois sage** to tell a child to behave.

Note. The imperative is recycled in *Compétence 3* with **prendre** and **venir** and in *Chapitre 5* with **faire** to provide additional practice with verbs that do not end in -**er**.

Supplemental activity. Play **Jacques a dit** *(Simon Says).* **1.** Jacques a dit: «Allez à la fenêtre.» **2.** Jacques a dit: «Regardez-moi.» **3.** Jacques a dit: «Prenez votre livre.» **4.** Ouvrez votre livre à la page 210. **5.** Jacques a dit: «Ouvrez votre livre à la page 210.» **6.** Fermez votre livre. **7.** Jacques a dit: «Fermez votre livre.» **8.** Allez au tableau. **9.** Jacques a dit: «Allez au tableau.» **10.** Jacques a dit: «Dansez le twist.»

Suggestion. Activities **A, B,** and **C** each demonstrate a different use of the pronoun **on.** Point out how **on** is used in each case and that the verb form is always the same.

Suggestions for A. Endroits logiques. **A.** Point out in the example that with **on,** you use the possessive adjectives **son, sa, ses** to say *one's.* **B.** Do each item separately with a time limit and check the answers before going on to the next one. The group with the most logical places wins one point for each place named.

Follow-up for A. Endroits logiques. Faites une liste de 5 choses qu'on fait souvent ici dans notre région. EXEMPLE **On nage souvent ici.**

Le pronom sujet **on** *et l'impératif*

Use **on** as the subject of a sentence when you are referring to people in general *(one, people, they)*. Consider the difference between these sentences.

À Paris, **on** parle français.   *In Paris, **they** speak French. (general group)*
Tes amis? **Ils** parlent français?   *Your friends? Do **they** speak French? (specific people)*

The pronoun **on** is also often used instead of **nous** to say *we.* **On** takes the same form of the verb as **il** and **elle,** regardless of its translation in English.

Gabriel et moi, **on** aime sortir.   *Gabriel and I, we like to go out.*

You can propose doing something with someone *(How about . . . ? Shall we . . . ?)* by asking a question with **on.**

On va au cinéma?   *How about going to the movies?*
Qu'est-ce qu'**on** fait ce soir?   *What shall we do this evening?*

The imperative (command form) can also be used to make suggestions, as well as to tell someone else to do something. Use the imperative as follows.

- To make suggestions with *Let's . . . ,* use the **nous** form of the verb, without the pronoun **nous.**

  Allons au cinéma!   *Let's go to the movies!*
  Ne **restons** pas à la maison!   *Let's not stay home!*

- To give instructions, or to tell someone to do something, use either the **tu** form of the verb or the **vous** form of the verb, as appropriate, without the pronoun. In **tu** form commands, drop the final **s** of -**er** verbs and of **aller.** However, as you learn other verbs that do not end in -**er,** do not drop the **s** in the commands.

  Va à la bibliothèque! / **Allez** à la bibliothèque!   *Go to the library!*
  Ne **mange** pas ça! / Ne **mangez** pas ça!   *Don't eat that!*

The verbs **être** and **avoir** have irregular command forms.

ÊTRE (be . . .)		AVOIR (have . . .)	
Sois sage!	*Be good!*	**Aie** confiance!	*Have confidence!*
Soyons calmes!	*Let's be calm!*	**Ayons** de la patience!	*Let's have patience!*
Soyez à l'heure!	*Be on time!*	**Ayez** confiance!	*Have confidence!*

A Endroits logiques. En groupes, pensez à des endroits *(places)* où on fait les choses suivantes. Le groupe qui pense au plus grand nombre d'endroits logiques gagne.

EXEMPLE   On y écoute de la musique.
   On écoute de la musique à un concert, à un festival de musique, dans sa voiture, sur son iPod, à la radio...

1. On y étudie.
2. On y va pour faire de l'exercice.
3. On y retrouve ses amis.
4. On y achète des livres.
5. On y regarde un film.
6. On y mange.

B Tes amis et toi?
Posez ces questions à votre partenaire. Il/Elle va répondre en utilisant le pronom **on**.

EXEMPLE —Tes amis et toi, vous préférez aller à quel restaurant?
— **On préfère aller au restaurant Vermilionville.**

1. Tes amis et toi, quand est-ce que vous aimez sortir ensemble?
2. Est-ce que vous allez souvent au cinéma ensemble?
3. Est-ce que vous regardez souvent des DVD ensemble?
4. Dans quel restaurant est-ce que vous mangez le plus souvent?
5. Est-ce que vous parlez beaucoup au téléphone?

C On... ?
Un(e) ami(e) vous invite *(invites you)* à faire ces choses. Répondez à ses suggestions selon vos goûts *(according to your tastes)*.

EXEMPLE —On joue à des jeux vidéo?
— **D'accord. Jouons à des jeux vidéo.**
  Non, ne jouons pas à des jeux vidéo.
  Regardons plutôt un DVD.

1.
2.
3.
4.

Line art on this page: © Cengage Learning

D Pour réussir.
Donnez des conseils à un groupe de nouveaux étudiants. Utilisez l'impératif.

EXEMPLE préparer les examens avec d'autres étudiants
  Préparez les examens avec d'autres étudiants.
  Ne préparez pas les examens avec d'autres étudiants.

1. aller à tous les cours
2. être à l'heure
3. avoir confiance
4. copier sur un autre étudiant
5. aller en boîte tous les soirs
6. avoir peur de parler au prof

Maintenant, avec un(e) partenaire, préparez cinq autres conseils pour un groupe de nouveaux étudiants.

E Des parents difficiles.
Des parents disent à leur fils adolescent qu'il doit faire *(must do)* l'une des choses indiquées et qu'il ne doit pas faire l'autre. Qu'est-ce qu'ils lui disent? Utilisez l'impératif et soyez logique!

EXEMPLE arrêter *(to stop)* de fumer / fumer dans la maison
  Arrête de fumer. Ne fume pas dans la maison.

1. être plus propre / laisser tes vêtements partout
2. rester au lit tout le temps / être plus dynamique
3. jouer à des jeux vidéo tout le temps / avoir un peu d'ambition
4. aller au café tous les jours / réviser tes cours
5. manger toujours la même chose / avoir un peu d'imagination

Follow-up for C. On... ? Have students list the following for your area: 1. a good place to eat 2. an interesting place to visit 3. an activity they like and a place to do it. Then, have them use this information to invite a classmate to do something. EXEMPLE —On mange à Pizza Nizza? —D'accord. Mangeons à Pizza Nizza.

Supplemental activities. A. Provide these cues and tell students to give you logical suggestions of what to do based on what you say: aller au café, manger quelque chose, aller voir l'exposition au musée des beaux-arts, rester au lit, aller à la plage, nager à la piscine, aller au cinéma, jouer au basket, aller à la librairie, aller au centre commercial. EXEMPLE J'ai soif. **Allez au café.** 1. J'ai faim. 2. J'ai envie de voir un film. 3. J'ai l'intention de prendre un bain de soleil. 4. J'aime beaucoup l'art impressionniste. 5. J'ai besoin d'acheter de nouveaux vêtements. 6. J'ai envie d'acheter des livres. 7. J'ai sommeil. 8. J'ai besoin de faire de l'exercice. **B.** Have students work in groups to list things a guardian angel (**un ange gardien**) and the devil (**le diable**) would tell a student to do. Half of each group plays the guardian angel and the other half plays the devil. See which group can think of the most creative sets of commands. EXEMPLE Travaille beaucoup. / Non, passe la journée au lit.

Follow-up for E. Des parents difficiles. Have students give logical commands to a child to do or not to do the following things. 1. jouer dans la rue 2. demander la permission avant de sortir 3. rester près de la maison 4. manger beaucoup de pizza 5. rentrer tard à la maison 6. nager seul à la piscine 7. aller au lit avant minuit 8. avoir peur 9. avoir de la patience 10. être calme 11. être méchant avec le chien 12. être gentil avec le chien

COMPÉTENCE 3

Saying what you are going to do

 PowerPoint 4-7

LE WEEK-END PROCHAIN

Robert va passer le week-end prochain à La Nouvelle-Orléans. Et vous? Qu'est-ce que vous allez faire?

Je vais… / Je ne vais pas…

quitter la maison **tôt**

partir pour le week-end

visiter une autre ville

faire un tour de la ville

aller **boire** quelque chose au café

rentrer **tard**

Note culturelle

The French Quarter de La Nouvelle-Orléans s'appelle **le Vieux Carré**. Les maisons anciennes ornées de jolis balcons rappellent *(recall)* les villes du sud de la France. Le Vieux Carré est connu *(known)* pour sa célébration de Mardi gras. Les Français ont introduit cette fête d'origine religieuse en Louisiane en 1699! Voudriez-vous fêter Mardi gras à La Nouvelle-Orléans? Pourquoi (pas)?

Note de vocabulaire

1. **Quitter** *(to leave)* must be followed by the place or person you are leaving. (Je quitte l'université à 3 heures.) Use **partir** *(to leave)* in the sense of *to depart*. (Je vais bientôt partir.)
2. Use **visiter** to say that you visit a *place*. Use **aller voir** to say that you visit a *person*.

Robert et Thomas **font des projets** *(m)* pour le week-end prochain.

THOMAS: Qu'est-ce qu'on fait ce week-end?

ROBERT: J'ai beaucoup de projets pour ce week-end. Jeudi matin, on va partir très tôt pour La Nouvelle-Orléans. **D'abord,** on va visiter la ville. **Ensuite,** on va **aller voir** ma sœur. On va **passer la soirée** chez elle. Vendredi, on va faire un tour du **Vieux Carré.** On va rentrer à Lafayette assez tard.

THOMAS: Et samedi?

ROBERT: À midi, on va déjeuner au restaurant Prudhomme. C'est un restaurant célèbre pour sa cuisine régionale. **Et puis,** le soir, on va aller à Eunice, une petite ville pas loin de Lafayette. Il y a une soirée de musique et de folklore cadiens tous les samedis.

THOMAS: **Génial!**

Line art on this page: © Cengage Learning

Le week-end prochain Next weekend   **quitter** to leave   **tôt** early   **partir** to leave   **boire** to drink   **tard** late   **faire des projets** to make plans   **D'abord** First   **Ensuite** Then, Afterwards   **aller voir** to go see, to visit (a person)   **passer la soirée** to spend the evening   **le Vieux Carré** the French Quarter   **Et puis** And then   **Génial!** Great!

A Le week-end prochain. Est-ce que vous allez faire les choses suivantes samedi prochain?

EXEMPLE rester à la maison
Je vais rester à la maison. / Je ne vais pas rester à la maison.

1. quitter la maison tôt
2. partir pour la journée
3. faire un tour de la ville
4. visiter une autre ville
5. aller voir des amis
6. retrouver des amis en ville
7. aller boire quelque chose
8. dîner au restaurant
9. rentrer tard
10. passer la soirée à la maison
11. inviter des amis à la maison
12. regarder des DVD

B Entretien. Interviewez votre partenaire.

1. Quel(s) jour(s) est-ce que tu quittes la maison tôt? D'habitude, à quelle heure est-ce que tu quittes la maison le lundi? le mardi? Est-ce que tu rentres tard quelquefois? Quels jours est-ce que tu rentres tard? À quelle heure est-ce que tu rentres?
2. Est-ce que tu aimes partir quelquefois pour le week-end? Est-ce que tu aimes aller voir des amis qui habitent dans une autre ville? Quelle ville aimes-tu visiter? Qu'est-ce que tu aimes faire dans cette ville?
3. Vas-tu souvent au café? Qu'est-ce que tu aimes boire le matin? Et quand tu as très soif? Et quand tu as froid? Et quand tu as chaud?
4. En général, quel(s) jour(s) est-ce que tu passes la journée à la maison? et la soirée? Est-ce que tu passes toute la journée chez toi de temps en temps?

Warm-up for *B. Entretien*. Gabriel est très dynamique. Il n'aime pas rester à la maison. Est-ce qu'il aime faire les choses suivantes? Répondez par **oui** ou par **non**: 1. faire un tour de la ville 2. rester au lit 3. partir pour le week-end 4. regarder des DVD toute la journée 5. rester à la maison 6. jouer au tennis 7. regarder la télé tout le temps

Suggestion for *B. Entretien*. Point out that these questions are in the present tense.

Supplemental activity. Have students refer to the dialogue and the illustrations on the preceding page and answer these questions. Have them answer with short answers, since they do not know yet how to form the immediate future. 1. À quelle heure est-ce que Robert va quitter la maison? 2. Est-ce que Robert a une grande ou une petite voiture? 3. Comment est Robert? Il a une moustache (une barbe, des lunettes)? 4. Quelle ville est-ce que Robert, Gabriel et Thomas vont visiter? Quel membre de la famille de Robert est-ce qu'ils vont aller voir? 5. Où vont-ils aller pour boire quelque chose? 6. Est-ce qu'ils vont rentrer tôt ou tard?

À VOUS!

Avec un(e) partenaire, relisez à haute voix la conversation entre Thomas et Robert. Ensuite, imaginez qu'un(e) ami(e) passe le week-end chez vous et que vous parlez de vos projets pour vendredi, samedi et dimanche.

You can find a list of the new words from this ***Compétence*** on page 175 and access the audio online.

 **PowerPoint 4-8**

SAYING WHAT YOU ARE GOING TO DO

✓ Pour vérifier

1. How do you say what you are going to do? How do you say what you are not going to do? How would you say *I'm going to stay home*? *I'm not going to study*? *I'm going to go to the mall*?

2. Where do you place the pronoun **y** in the immediate future?

3. What is the immediate future form of **il y a**? How do you negate it?

4. How do you say *today*? *tomorrow*? *this morning*? *tomorrow morning*? *this month*? *next month*? *this year*? *next year*?

iLrn Grammar Tutorials

Sélection musicale. Search the Web for the song "**Je vais changer le monde**" by Jean-François Bastien to enjoy a musical selection containing this structure.

Suggestion. Point out that the verb **aller** may occur twice in a sentence in the immediate future, as does the verb *to go* in English. **Je vais aller au cinéma.** *I'm going to go to the movies.*

Le futur immédiat

To say what you *are going to do,* use a form of **aller** followed by an infinitive.

je vais étudier	nous allons rentrer
tu vas travailler	vous allez sortir
il/elle/on va lire	ils/elles vont nager

—Qu'est-ce que tu **vas faire** demain?   —*What **are** you **going to do** tomorrow?*
—Je **vais sortir**.   —*I'm going to go out.*

In the negative, put the **ne... pas** around the conjugated form of **aller.**

Je **ne vais pas** sortir ce soir.   *I'm not going to go out tonight.*

Place the pronoun **y,** when needed, *immediately before* the infinitive.

Ma sœur va aller en boîte, mais moi, je **ne vais pas y aller.**

Il y a becomes **il va y avoir** when saying *there is/are going to be.*

Il va y avoir un concert demain. **Il ne va pas y avoir** de film.

Use these expressions to tell when you are going to do something.

maintenant *now*	**plus tard** *later*
aujourd'hui *today*	**demain** *tomorrow*
ce matin *this morning*	**demain matin** *tomorrow morning*
cet après-midi *this afternoon*	**demain après-midi** *tomorrow afternoon*
ce soir *tonight / this evening*	**demain soir** *tomorrow night / evening*
lundi *Monday*	**lundi prochain** *next Monday*
ce week-end *this weekend*	**le week-end prochain** *next weekend*
cette semaine *this week*	**la semaine prochaine** *next week*
ce mois-ci *this month*	**le mois prochain** *next month*
cette année *this year*	**l'année prochaine** *next year*

Warm-ups for A. Que vont-ils faire?
A. Read the following pairs of adverbs of time and have students repeat the one that is later: **1.** maintenant ou plus tard **2.** demain ou aujourd'hui **3.** le week-end prochain ou ce week-end **4.** ce soir ou demain matin **5.** vendredi ou lundi **6.** vendredi matin ou vendredi après-midi **7.** cet après-midi ou ce soir **8.** cette année ou l'année prochaine **9.** cette semaine ou lundi prochain **10.** le mois prochain ou ce mois-ci **B.** Donnez l'équivalent au présent. **EXEMPLE** le mois prochain: **ce mois-ci** (la semaine prochaine, demain, plus tard, demain soir, demain après-midi, demain matin, l'année prochaine) **C.** Donnez l'équivalent au futur. **EXEMPLE** ce mois-ci: **le mois prochain** (cette semaine, aujourd'hui, maintenant, ce soir, cet après-midi, ce matin, cette année).

A **Que vont-ils faire?** Dites ou demandez si ces personnes vont faire les choses indiquées aux moments donnés.

EXEMPLE Ce soir, moi, je **vais** travailler.
Ce soir, moi, je **ne vais pas** travailler.

1. Ce soir, je _____ rentrer tard.
2. Demain matin, je _____ quitter la maison tôt.
3. Samedi prochain, mes amis et moi _____ passer la soirée ensemble.
4. Le week-end prochain, mon meilleur ami (ma meilleure amie) _____ aller voir sa famille.
5. La semaine prochaine, en cours de français, nous _____ avoir un (d')examen.
6. Les cours universitaires _____ se terminer *(to end)* le mois prochain.
7. *[au professeur]* L'année prochaine, vous _____ continuer à travailler ici?
8. *[à un(e) autre étudiant(e)]* L'année prochaine, tu _____ étudier ici?

158 cent cinquante-huit | **CHAPITRE 4**

B Et ensuite? Qu'est-ce que ces personnes vont faire **d'abord** et qu'est-ce qu'elles vont faire **ensuite**?

EXEMPLE moi, je: manger / préparer le dîner
D'abord, moi, je vais préparer le dîner et ensuite, je vais manger.

1. nous: travailler tout l'après-midi / aller prendre un verre
2. moi, je: dormir / rentrer à la maison
3. mon frère: retrouver sa copine en ville / dîner au restaurant avec elle
4. vous: dîner au restaurant / sortir danser
5. mes amis: préparer le dîner / aller au supermarché (*supermarket*)
6. toi, tu: faire cet exercice / commencer l'exercice suivant

C Projets. Demandez à votre partenaire si ces personnes vont faire les choses indiquées aux moments donnés.

EXEMPLE tes amis et toi / jouer à des jeux vidéo ce soir
— **Tes amis et toi, vous allez jouer à des jeux vidéo ce soir?**
— **Oui, nous allons jouer à des jeux vidéo ce soir.**
Non, nous n'allons pas jouer à des jeux vidéo ce soir.

1. tu / rester au lit demain matin
2. tu / retrouver des amis au café ce week-end
3. tes amis et toi / aller en boîte samedi prochain
4. nous / avoir des devoirs de français ce soir

Line art on this page: © Cengage Learning

D Pourquoi y vont-ils? Robert dit où ces personnes vont aller ce week-end et ce qu'elles vont y faire. Complétez ce qu'il dit.

EXEMPLE moi, je / musée
Moi, je vais aller au musée ce week-end. Je vais y voir une exposition.

1. moi, je / au centre commercial
2. mes amis / à la piscine
3. nous / au cinéma
4. Gabriel / à la salle de gym
5. mes amis et moi / à la librairie
6. mon père et ma belle-mère / au théâtre

E Entretien. Interviewez un(e) partenaire avec les questions suivantes.

1. Avec qui est-ce que tu vas passer l'après-midi, samedi? (Qu'est-ce que vous allez faire ensemble?)
2. Est-ce que tu vas retrouver des amis en ville samedi soir? (Où? Qu'est-ce que vous allez faire ensemble?)
3. Où est-ce que tu vas passer la journée, dimanche? Qu'est-ce que tu vas faire l'après-midi et le soir?
4. Quand est-ce que tu vas réviser tes cours ce week-end? Avec qui est-ce que tu vas étudier?

 PowerPoint 4-9

SAYING WHEN YOU ARE GOING TO DO SOMETHING

✓ Pour vérifier

1. Do you generally use cardinal or ordinal numbers to give dates in French? What is the exception?
2. In what two ways can the year 1789 be expressed in French? How do you say the year 2016?
3. How do you say *in* with months and years? How do you say *in January*? *in 2017*?
4. What are these dates in French: 15/3/1951 and 11/1/2022?

In the **Culture Modules** in the video library, see **Celebrations**.

Vocabulaire supplémentaire
LES FÊTES ET LES OBSERVANCES RELIGIEUSES

un anniversaire de mariage *a wedding anniversary*
la fête des Mères / la fête des Pères
la fête nationale *the national holiday*
Hanoukka *(f)*
le (réveillon du) jour de l'An *New Year's (Eve)*
Noël *(m) Christmas*
Pâques *(f) Easter*
la pâque juive *Passover*
le ramadan
la Saint-Valentin
Yom Kippour
Bon anniversaire! *Happy Birthday!*
Bonne année! *Happy New Year!*
Joyeux Noël! *Merry Christmas!*

Vocabulaire sans peine!

The word **anniversaire** means both *birthday* and *anniversary* in French. Note the cognate pattern *-ary* = **-aire**.

le contraire = *the contrary*
révolutionnaire = *revolutionary*
nécessaire = *necessary*

How would you say the following in French?
commentary
imaginary
ordinary

Suggestion for *A. Quel mois?*
Point out to students that the French say **Thanksgiving** to talk about the American / Canadian holiday, but in Quebec they say **le jour d'Action de Grâce.**

Les dates

To express the date in French, use **le** and the cardinal numbers (**deux, trois…**), except for *the first* of the month. For *the first,* use the ordinal number: **le premier (1ᵉʳ).**

—Quelle est la date aujourd'hui? / C'est quelle date aujourd'hui?
—C'est **le premier… le deux… le trois… le quatre…**

janvier	avril	juillet	octobre
février	mai	août	novembre
mars	juin	septembre	décembre

—Quelle est la date de la fête *(holiday)* nationale française?
—C'est le 14 (quatorze) juillet.

You can express the years 1100–1999 in French in either of two ways. Years starting at 2000 are only expressed using the word **mille.**

1945: mille neuf cent quarante-cinq / dix-neuf cent quarante-cinq
2015: deux mille quinze

Note that the day goes before the month in French.

14/7/1789 = le quatorze juillet dix-sept cent quatre-vingt-neuf

Use **en** to say *in* what month or year. Use **le** when saying *on* a certain date.

—Ton anniversaire *(birthday)*, c'est quand?
—C'est **en** novembre. C'est **le** 18 novembre *([on] November 18ᵗʰ).* Je vais faire une fête **le** 16 novembre *(I am going to have a party [on] November 16ᵗʰ).*

—**En** quelle année vas-tu finir tes études?
—**En** 2019.

A. Quel mois?
Regardez la liste de fêtes dans la marge de cette page et complétez ces phrases avec le nom du mois correspondant.

EXEMPLE Le jour de l'An, c'est en **janvier.**

1. Le réveillon du jour de l'An, c'est en…
2. L'année scolaire commence en…   Elle finit en…
3. La fête nationale française, c'est en…   Notre fête nationale, c'est en…
4. La fête des Mères, c'est en…   La fête des Pères, c'est en…
5. Thanksgiving, c'est en…

B. Encore des dates.
Demandez à votre partenaire la date des jours indiqués.

aujourd'hui	demain	de lundi	de ton anniversaire
de notre fête nationale		de Noël	de *Halloween*
du jour de l'An *(New Year's Day)*		de la Saint-Valentin
	de ta fête préférée	

160 cent soixante | CHAPITRE 4

C Votre anniversaire. Les autres étudiants vont essayer de deviner *(will try to guess)* la date de votre anniversaire. Répondez **avant** ou **après** jusqu'à ce qu'ils devinent juste *(guess right)*.

EXEMPLE —Ton anniversaire, c'est en mars?
—Après.
—C'est en mai?
—Oui.
—C'est le quinze mai?
—Avant...

D Comparaisons culturelles. Lisez à haute voix ces dates importantes.

EXEMPLE 4/7/1776 (le début de la Révolution américaine)
le quatre juillet mille sept cent soixante-seize
(le quatre juillet dix-sept cent soixante-seize)

1. 1/11/1718 (Bienville fonde La Nouvelle-Orléans.)
2. 14/7/1789 (la prise de la Bastille)
3. 30/4/1812 (La Louisiane devient *[becomes]* un État des États-Unis.)
4. 11/11/1918 (le jour de l'Armistice de la Première Guerre mondiale)
5. 6/6/1944 (le jour du débarquement en Normandie)

E À quelle date? Dites si ces personnes vont faire les choses indiquées aux dates données.

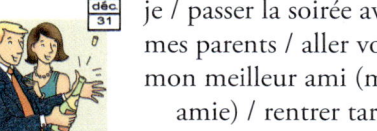

EXEMPLE 25/12 je / aller voir mes parents
Le 25 décembre, je vais aller voir mes parents.
Le 25 décembre, je ne vais pas aller voir mes parents.

beaucoup de mes amis / faire un pique-nique
ma famille / aller voir des feux d'artifice *(fireworks)*
mes amis et moi / aller à la plage

1. 4/7

beaucoup de mes amis / dîner au restaurant
je / sortir avec un(e) ami(e) (des amis)
je / acheter des chocolats pour mes amis

2. 14/2

je / passer la soirée avec des amis
mes parents / aller voir des amis
mon meilleur ami (ma meilleure amie) / rentrer tard

3. 31/12

je / inviter des amis chez moi
mes amis et moi / faire une fête
je / avoir ?? ans

4. la date de votre anniversaire

F Entretien. Interviewez votre partenaire.

1. Quelle est la date aujourd'hui? Quelle est la date de ton anniversaire? Qu'est-ce que tu vas probablement faire ce jour-là *(that day)*? Quelle est la date de ta fête préférée? Qu'est-ce que tu aimes faire ce jour-là?
2. Quelle est la date du dernier *(last)* jour du cours de français? Qu'est-ce que tu vas faire après ton dernier cours ce semestre / trimestre? Est-ce que tu vas continuer à étudier ici l'année prochaine?

COMPÉTENCE 4

Planning how to get there

 PowerPoint 4-10

LES MOYENS DE TRANSPORT

Note culturelle

Le sud *(south)* de la Louisiane est recouvert *(covered)* d'eau. Les Acadiens arrivant du Canada en 1764 apprennent vite *(quickly learn)* à s'adapter à cette région de bayous et de marais *(swamps)*. En raison de *(Because of)* l'inaccessibilité de leur région, les Acadiens restent isolés et conservent largement leur héritage français. Toutefois *(However)*, depuis le 19ᵉ siècle *(century)*, la culture cadienne se trouve envahie par le monde anglophone *(finds itself invaded by the English-speaking world)*. Que savez-vous de *(What do you know about)* l'histoire des groupes ethniques et culturels de votre région?

Note de vocabulaire

1. **Un bus** runs within cities and **un car** runs between cities. *A tour bus* is also called **un car**. *A school bus* is **un car scolaire**.
2. Use **à moto(cyclette)** (f) to say *by motorcycle*, and **à scooter** to say *by scooter*. Although it is considered correct to say **à vélo / à moto / à scooter**, many people say **en vélo / en moto / en scooter**.

🔊 2-9

In the **Culture Modules** in the video library, see **Transportation**.

Warm-up. Où vont-ils aller? EXEMPLE Robert va voir une exposition. **Il va aller au musée. 1.** Demain matin, il va déjeuner avec une amie en ville. **2.** Ils vont faire du shopping. **3.** Après, ils vont voir un film. **4.** Thomas va nager. **5.** Gabriel va jouer au volley avec des amis. **6.** Après, il va dormir.

Note for the conversation. New vocabulary includes all glossed words and **un voyage**.

Suggestion for the conversation. Introduce the word **revenir (on revient)**. Have students listen with books closed for this information. **Où est-ce que Robert et ses amis vont aller? Comment vont-ils y aller? Quand vont-ils revenir?**

Robert et ses amis vont aller à La Nouvelle-Orléans en voiture. Et vous? Comment préférez-vous voyager?

Pour visiter une autre ville, je préfère y aller...

en avion *(m)*   en train *(m)*   en bateau *(m)*   en car / en autocar *(m)*

Il y a d'autres possibilités pour aller en ville. Comment **venez-vous** en cours?

Je viens en cours...

à pied *(m)*   à vélo *(m)*   en taxi *(m)*

en voiture *(f)*   en métro *(m)*   en bus / en autobus *(m)*

Robert parle à Thomas du voyage à La Nouvelle-Orléans.

ROBERT: Bon, demain matin, on va à La Nouvelle-Orléans. Tout est **prêt**?

THOMAS: Oui. On y va en car?

ROBERT: Non, on va **louer** une voiture, c'est plus pratique.

THOMAS: C'est loin? **Ça prend combien de temps pour y aller?**

ROBERT: Ça prend environ deux heures et demie en voiture, **pas plus**.

THOMAS: Et **on revient** quand?

ROBERT: On revient **après-demain.**

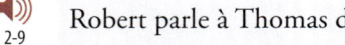

Line art on this page: © Cengage Learning

les moyens *(m)* **de transport** means of transportation   **vous venez / Je viens (venir** to come**)**   **prêt(e)** ready   **louer** to rent   **Ça prend combien de temps pour y aller?** How long does it take to go there?   **pas plus** no more   **on revient (revenir** to come back**)**   **après-demain** the day after tomorrow

162 cent soixante-deux | **CHAPITRE 4**

A Moyens de transport. Complétez les phrases pour parler de vous.

> en avion   en train   en car   en bateau   en voiture
> à pied   à vélo   en taxi en métro   en bus

1. Pour faire un long voyage, je préfère voyager…
2. Je n'aime pas beaucoup voyager…
3. Je ne voyage presque jamais…
4. Je préfère aller en ville…
5. D'habitude, je viens en cours…
6. Je ne viens presque jamais en cours…

B On y va comment? Dites où chacun va et comment.

EXEMPLE Ils **vont à La Nouvelle-Orléans en voiture.**

1. Je…   2. Ils…

3. Vous…   4. Nous…   5. Elle…

Line art on this page: © Cengage Learning

C Entretien. Interviewez votre partenaire.

1. Quelle ville est-ce que tu visites souvent? Comment est-ce que tu préfères y aller? (en voiture? en train? en avion?) Ça prend combien de temps pour y aller?
2. Tu voyages souvent en avion? Tu as peur de voyager en avion? Pour aller de chez toi à l'aéroport, ça prend combien de temps? Qu'est-ce que tu aimes faire pendant *(during)* les longs voyages en avion? (dormir? lire? parler?…)
3. Quels jours est-ce que tu viens en cours? Comment préfères-tu venir en cours? Comment viens-tu en cours, d'habitude? Comment est-ce que tu rentres chez toi?

À VOUS!

Avec un(e) partenaire, relisez à haute voix la conversation entre Robert et Thomas. Ensuite, adaptez la conversation pour parler d'un voyage que vous allez faire ensemble pour visiter une autre ville. Parlez de comment vous allez voyager et de combien de temps ça va prendre pour y aller.

 **PowerPoint 4-11**

DECIDING HOW TO GET THERE AND COME BACK

✓ **Pour vérifier**

1. What are the forms of **venir**? of **prendre**? What two verbs are conjugated like **venir**? like **prendre**? What verb do you use to say you are *having* something to eat or drink? When is **apprendre** followed by **à**?

2. In what forms of the verbs **venir** and **prendre** are the vowels nasal? **Je viens / tu viens / il vient** rhyme with what word? **Je prends / tu prends / il prend** rhyme with what word? How do you pronounce the **ils/elles viennent** form? the **ils/elles prennent** form?

Note *de vocabulaire*

1. Use **en** with **aller, venir,** or **voyager** to say you are traveling *by* a means of transportation. **Je viens *en* bus, *en* taxi, *en* train…**

2. Use **prendre** to say what means of transportation you are *taking*. In this case, you can generally use the same article with the noun that you would in English: *I take the bus, a cab, the train…* **Je prends *le* bus, *un* taxi, *le* train…**

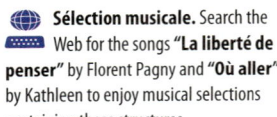 Grammar Tutorials

🌐 **Sélection musicale.** Search the Web for the songs "**La liberté de penser**" by Florent Pagny and "**Où aller**" by Kathleen to enjoy musical selections containing these structures.

Les verbes **prendre** *et* **venir** *et les moyens de transport*

The conjugations of **prendre** *(to take)* and **venir** *(to come)* are irregular.

PRENDRE *(to take)*		**VENIR** *(to come)*	
je **prends**	nous **prenons**	je **viens**	nous **venons**
tu **prends**	vous **prenez**	tu **viens**	vous **venez**
il/elle/on **prend**	ils/elles **prennent**	il/elle/on **vient**	ils/elles **viennent**

Prendre means *to take*.

    Je **prends** des notes en cours.   **Prenez** votre livre.

Use **prendre** to say that you are *taking* a means of transportation. Remember that you can also use **aller, venir,** or **voyager** and the preposition **en** (or **à** with **vélo**) to say that you are *going, coming,* or *traveling by* a particular means of transportation. To say *on foot,* use **à pied**.

    Je **prends** mon vélo.   Je **prends** l'avion.
    J'y **vais à vélo.**   Je **voyage en avion.**   Je **viens** en cours **à pied.**

Use **prendre** as *to have* when talking about *having* something to eat or drink.

    Je vais **prendre** un sandwich et une eau minérale.

Comprendre *(to understand)* and **apprendre** *(to learn)* are conjugated like **prendre**. When **apprendre** is followed by an infinitive, the infinitive is preceded by **à**.

    J'**apprends à** parler français. Ma sœur **apprend** le français aussi.
    Tu **comprends**?

Use **venir** to say *to come*. **Revenir** *(to come back)* and **devenir** *(to become)* are conjugated like **venir**.

    Vous **revenez** tard et il **devient** impatient.

Suggestion. Point out to students that one says **suivre un cours** and **passer un examen**, instead of using **prendre**. The conjugation of the verb **suivre** is in the *Appendix*.

PRONONCIATION

Les verbes **prendre** *et* **venir** 2-10

In the **je, tu,** and **il/elle/on** forms of the verb **venir**, the vowel combination **ie** has the nasal sound [jɛ̃]. The consonants after **ie** are all silent. All three forms rhyme with the word **bien**. In the **ils/elles viennent** form, however, the **ie** is not nasal and the **nn** is pronounced.

    je viens   tu viens   il vient   ils viennent   elles viennent

Similarly, the **e** in the **je, tu,** and **il/elle/on** forms of the verb **prendre** is nasal and the consonants after the vowel are silent. All three forms rhyme with the word **quand**. In the **ils/elles prennent** form, however, the **e** is not nasal. It is pronounced like the **è** in **mère** and the **nn** is pronounced.

    je prends   tu prends   il prend   ils prennent   elles prennent

The **e** in the **nous** and **vous** forms of both verbs is pronounced like the **e** in **je**.

    nous venons   vous venez   nous prenons   vous prenez

A. Prononcez bien! D'abord, écoutez les phrases et indiquez pour chacune si on parle d'**une personne** ou de **plus d'une personne**. Après, écrivez deux phrases avec le verbe **prendre** et deux phrases avec le verbe **venir**. Lisez-les à un(e) partenaire qui va dire si vous parlez **d'une personne** ou **de plus d'une personne**.

B. Qu'est-ce qu'on fait? Conjuguez les verbes entre parenthèses et posez les questions à votre partenaire.

1. Quels jours est-ce que tu *(venir)* en cours? Est-ce que tu *(prendre)* le bus pour venir en cours? Est-ce que tu *(venir)* en cours à pied ou à vélo quelquefois?
2. Est-ce que les autres étudiants du cours de français *(venir)* toujours en cours? Est-ce qu'ils *(comprendre)* bien le français? Est-ce que nous *(apprendre)* beaucoup en cours?
3. Est-ce que le cours de français *(devenir)* plus difficile? Est-ce que le (la) prof *(devenir)* impatient(e) quand les étudiants *(ne pas apprendre)* le vocabulaire?
4. Est-ce que tu *(avoir)* l'intention de revenir à cette université l'année prochaine? Est-ce que tu *(avoir)* l'intention de devenir prof après tes études?

C. Que font-ils? Faites une phrase logique à partir de chaque sujet donné pour parler de votre cours de français.

EXEMPLE Moi, je ne viens pas en cours en bus.

moi, je le (la) prof nous les étudiants	(ne/n')	prendre apprendre comprendre venir revenir devenir	(pas)	des/de notes en cours bien le professeur beaucoup de verbes beaucoup de vocabulaire à l'université le week-end impatient(e)(s) paresseux (paresseuse[s]) le bus pour venir en cours en cours à pied en cours en bus

D. La santé. Votre ami voudrait être en meilleure santé *(health)*. Donnez-lui des conseils. Utilisez l'impératif.

EXEMPLE Je prends un coca ou un jus d'orange?
Prends un jus d'orange! Ne prends pas de coca!

1. Je prends une bière ou une eau minérale?
2. Je viens en cours en voiture ou à vélo?
3. Je prends une salade ou des frites?
4. Je vais au parc ou je reste à la maison?
5. Je vais au parc en voiture ou à pied?
6. Je prends un bain de soleil ou je nage?

Prenons les vélos!

Suggestion for A. Prononcez bien. Provide an example before beginning.

Script for A. Prononcez bien! 1. Ils prennent le métro pour aller à l'université. 2. Ils ne comprennent pas toujours. 3. Elle n'apprend pas beaucoup. 4. Il ne prend jamais de notes. 5. Elles apprennent à bien prononcer. 6. Il prend le bus tous les jours. 7. Est-ce qu'ils comprennent? 8. Il vient à l'université tous les jours. 9. Ils viennent ici ensemble. 10. Elle revient sur le campus le week-end. 11. Il devient impatient. 12. Elles reviennent demain.

Follow-up for C. Que font-ils? Est-ce que ces personnes de notre cours font les choses suivantes? **EXEMPLE** Moi, je... (prendre le bus pour venir en cours) Moi, je ne prends pas le bus pour venir en cours. 1. Moi, je... (venir en cours en voiture, prendre un café avant le cours de français, comprendre toujours en cours) 2. Nous... (venir en cours de français tous les jours, apprendre l'espagnol, comprendre mieux le français tous les jours) 3. Le professeur... (comprendre bien les étudiants, apprendre une autre langue, revenir à l'université le week-end) 4. En général, ici, les étudiants... (venir en cours en bus, comprendre une deuxième langue, apprendre beaucoup)

Suggestions for D. La santé. A. Before doing this exercise, review the imperative, reminding students to drop the final **s** from **tu** form commands of verbs that end in **-er,** but not from those of verbs like **prendre** and **venir.** Elicit the command forms of **prendre** and **venir** from students. **B.** Have students redo the exercise using **vous** and **nous** form commands.

VIDÉOREPRISE

Les Stagiaires

Rappel!
Dans le dernier *(last)* épisode de la vidéo, Amélie et Céline ont décidé d'être colocataires et d'habiter ensemble dans l'appartement de Céline.

See the *Résumé de grammaire* section at the end of each chapter for a review of all the grammar presented in the chapter.

The entire **Vidéoreprise** section is designed to be a pre-viewing series for the video, as well as a chapter review that can be used independently from the video. There are also additional grammar review exercises on the Instructor's Companion Website and on iLrn.

Dans l'*Épisode 4,* Céline et Amélie parlent de la famille d'Amélie et de celle de *(that of)* Christophe. Avant de regarder l'épisode, faites ces exercices pour réviser ce que vous avez appris dans le *Chapitre 4.*

A La famille de Christophe.
Rachid parle à Christophe de sa famille. Complétez leur conversation avec les mots logiques.

RACHID: Alors, Christophe, c'est vrai que M. Vieilledent est ton 1 ?
CHRISTOPHE: Oui, c'est vrai.
RACHID: Tu as une grande 2 ? Tu as des 3 et sœurs?
CHRISTOPHE: Moi, je suis le seul 4 , mais j'ai deux 5 , Léa et Emma.
RACHID: Elles sont plus 6 ou plus jeunes que toi?
CHRISTOPHE: Je suis le plus jeune. Elles 7 vingt-six et vingt-quatre 8 .
RACHID: Et ta 9 , elle s'appelle comment?
CHRISTOPHE: Elle s'appelle Pauline, mais mes parents ne sont plus ensemble. Ils sont 10 .

Maintenant, préparez une conversation avec un(e) partenaire dans laquelle *(in which)* vous parlez de vos familles.

B Aujourd'hui.
Utilisez des expressions avec **avoir** pour dire comment l'équipe *(team)* de Technovert se sent *(feels)* aujourd'hui.

EXEMPLE M. Vieilledent voudrait des croissants parce qu'il **a faim.**

1. Camille voudrait boire quelque chose parce qu'elle _____.
2. Matthieu voudrait enlever son pull *(to take off his sweater)* parce qu'il _____.
3. Amélie a besoin d'un pull parce qu'elle _____.
4. Christophe voudrait faire la sieste *(to take a nap)* parce qu'il _____.
5. Rachid _____ d'étudier parce qu'il a un examen demain.

C Les anniversaires.
Les résultats du trimestre sont tellement bons que M. Vieilledent pense donner un bonus à chaque employé(e) pour son anniversaire. Donnez la date de l'anniversaire de chacun.

EXEMPLE Camille: 25/1
L'anniversaire de Camille, c'est le vingt-cinq janvier.

1. Céline: 30/3
2. Christophe: 16/5
3. Matthieu: 21/8
4. Rachid: 1/6
5. Amélie: 14/2

D Pauvre Matthieu.
Matthieu voudrait sortir avec Amélie, mais il n'a pas le courage de lui parler *(to talk to her)* parce qu'il est trop timide. Est-ce que Camille dit *(tells)* à Matthieu de faire ou de ne pas faire les choses suivantes pour l'encourager *(to encourage him)*? Utilisez l'impératif des verbes suivants à la forme affirmative ou négative pour former des phrases logiques.

EXEMPLE être timide
Ne sois pas timide!

1. avoir un peu de courage
2. être ridicule
3. avoir peur de parler à Amélie
4. aller à son bureau sans rien dire *(without saying anything)*
5. regarder Amélie tout le temps sans parler
6. parler avec elle de temps en temps
7. prendre l'initiative de parler à Amélie
8. inviter Amélie au nouveau restaurant du quartier

E Parlons ensemble. M. Vieilledent parle aux stagiaires de leur travail. Complétez les phrases suivantes avec l'impératif des verbes entre parenthèses. Mettez l'un des verbes à la forme de **vous** et l'autre à la forme de **nous** pour faire des phrases logiques.

EXEMPLE Rachid et Amélie, **venez** (venir) avec moi, s'il vous plaît.
Allons (aller) dans mon bureau.

1. S'il vous plaît, _____ (entrer) dans mon bureau, tous les deux, et asseyez-vous *(have a seat)*, je vous en prie. Si vous voulez bien, _____ (prendre) un peu de temps pour parler de votre travail à Technovert.
2. _____ (commencer) par vos responsabilités. _____ (ne pas hésiter) à poser des questions si vous ne comprenez pas quelque chose.
3. _____ (venir) me voir *(to see me)* s'il y a un problème et _____ (trouver) une solution ensemble.
4. _____ (partager) vos idées et vos opinions avec moi. _____ (être) toujours ouverts et francs les uns avec les autres.
5. _____ (travailler) tous ensemble! _____ (ne pas avoir) peur de faire des suggestions. Ma porte est toujours ouverte.

F Le week-end. Rachid pose des questions à Amélie. Complétez chaque question avec la forme correcte du verbe logique entre parenthèses.

1. (aller, venir) Le week-end, est-ce que tu _____ plus souvent chez tes amis ou est-ce que tes amis _____ plutôt chez toi?
2. (aller, prendre) Qui _____ sa voiture généralement quand tes amis et toi _____ en ville le week-end?
3. (aller, avoir) Est-ce que tu _____ envie de sortir samedi soir ou est-ce que tu _____ rester chez toi?
4. (aller, avoir) Et dimanche, qu'est-ce que tu _____ l'intention de faire? Tu _____ étudier?
5. (avoir, devenir) Est-ce que tu _____ une page sur Facebook? On _____ amis sur Facebook?

Maintenant, utilisez ces questions pour interviewer un(e) partenaire.

Suggestion for the video. Tell students not to worry about understanding every word, but to use what they do know and the context to guess what is being said. The video is available on DVD and on iLrn. The videoscript is available on the Instructor's Companion Website, **www.cengage.com/french/horizons6e**, and on iLrn.

Access the Video **Les Stagiaires** on iLrn.

 Épisode 4: Vive la famille!

AVANT LA VIDÉO

Dans cet épisode, Céline parle de la famille de Christophe et pose des questions à Amélie au sujet de sa famille. Avant de regarder l'épisode, imaginez une des questions que Céline pose à Amélie.

APRÈS LA VIDÉO

Regardez l'épisode et notez une chose au sujet de la famille de Christophe et une chose au sujet de la famille d'Amélie.

LECTURE ET COMPOSITION

LECTURE

POUR MIEUX LIRE:
Using your knowledge of the world

You are going to read the poem *Deux mots* by Jean Gentil that appeared in 1878 in *Le Louisianais,* a newspaper published in the town of Convent in the Saint James Parish of Louisiana. In this poem, Jean Gentil expresses the importance of the freedom of religion. Using what you already know about different religions of the world will help you understand as you read. Before reading it, do this activity to make your reading easier.

Associations. À quelle religion de la liste associez-vous les choses ou les personnes suivantes?

le catholicisme **le protestantisme**
le judaïsme **l'islamisme**

1. Rome et le pape
2. le Pater noster
3. Martin Luther
4. un rabbin
5. le Talmud
6. le Coran

Deux mots

Homme, sois catholique,
Si ça te fait plaisir;
Sois **aristotélique**,
Si c'est là ton désir;
Jure par le pape et Rome,
En disant ton Pater,
Ou bien proteste comme
A protesté Luther;
Suis le Talmud **lui-même**,
En rabbin révérend,
Ou bien, si ton **cœur** l'aime,
Obéis au Coran;
Bien plus, si tu préfères
Les Kings et **le Chou-King**,
Ce sont là **tes affaires**,
Et j'aime assez Péking.
Chacun de nous est libre,
Et **croit comme il l'entend:**
Je prends mon équilibre;
Tu peux en faire autant.
Aussi, petits bonhommes
De trois ou quatre jours,
Étant ce que nous sommes,
Respectons-nous toujours.
Mais si **l'apostasie**
Est une indignité,
Certes, l'hypocrisie
Est **une lâcheté.**

Source: Jean Gentil, "Deux mots" in *Le Louisianais,* June 1878

Si ça te fait plaisir *If that makes you happy* **aristotélique** *(someone who follows the philosophy of Aristotle)* **Jure par** *Swear by* **En disant** *By saying* **Suis** *Follow* **lui-même** *itself* **cœur** *heart* **Obéis** *Obey* **le Chou-King** *(a Chinese dynasty)* **tes affaires** *your business* **Chacun** *Each one* **croit comme il l'entend** *believes as he thinks best* **Tu peux en faire autant** *You can do the same* **Étant ce que** *Being what* **l'apostasie** *apostasy (abandoning your beliefs)* **Certes** *Certainly* **une lâcheté** *a cowardly act*

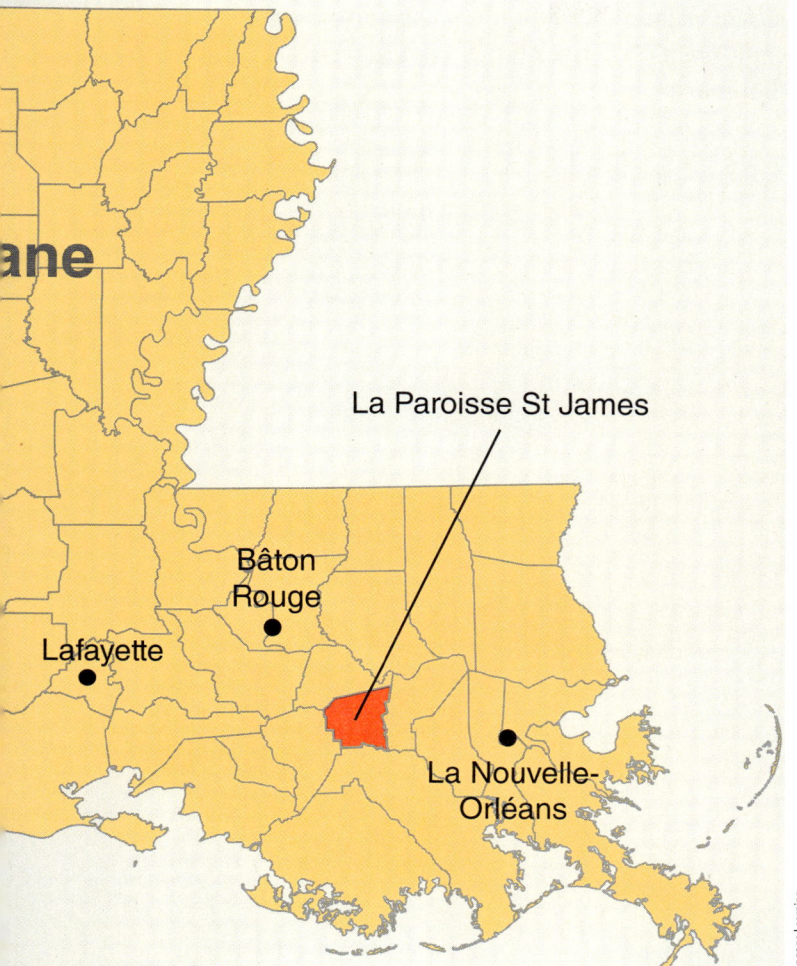

COMPOSITION

POUR MIEUX ÉCRIRE:
Visualizing your topic

Sometimes it is easier to write a description of people or things if you visualize or look at images of them. An image such as a family tree provides a logical order to a description.

Organisez-vous. Vous allez écrire une description de votre famille. D'abord, dessinez *(draw)* un arbre généalogique de votre famille. À côté de chaque membre de votre famille sur l'arbre généalogique, écrivez tous les mots que vous associez à cette personne: son âge, sa profession, son apparence physique, son caractère et ses activités.

Process-writing follow-up for *Ma famille*. Have students do the following after they have completed their compositions. Échangez votre rédaction avec un(e) autre étudiant(e). Lisez sa composition et décrivez la famille de votre partenaire à la classe.
EXEMPLE Dans sa famille, ils sont sept: sa mère et ses deux frères... Ses frères habitent avec sa mère. Sa mère s'appelle...

Compréhension

Deux mots. Lisez le poème et répondez aux questions suivantes.

1. De quelles religions ou philosophies est-ce que Jean Gentil parle dans le poème?
2. Dans le poème, il dit «Je prends mon équilibre, Tu peux en faire autant.» Qu'est-ce que ça veut dire?
3. Que pense-t-il de l'hypocrisie?
4. Est-ce que vous trouvez le message de ce poème publié en 1878 tout aussi valable *(just as pertinent)* aujourd'hui?

Ma famille

Faites une description écrite détaillée de votre famille. Basez votre description sur l'arbre généalogique que vous venez de créer *(that you just created)*.

iLrn Share It!

Lecture et Composition | *cent soixante-neuf* **169**

COMPARAISONS CULTURELLES

L'HISTOIRE DES CADIENS

Suggestion. Tell students that in 2004, the State of Louisiana established July 28 as **Une Journée de Commémoration du Grand Dérangement** to recognize the genocide of the Acadians in the 18th century.

La majorité des Cadiens en Louisiane aujourd'hui sont les descendants des Acadiens **venus** du Canada. Le mot *cajun* est dérivé du mot *acadien*. Pourquoi ces Acadiens **sont-ils venus** en Louisiane?

En 1604, les Français **fondent** une colonie dans **la partie est** du Canada qu'ils appellent l'Acadie.

L'Acadie

En 1713, les Anglais prennent possession de l'Acadie. Les Acadiens prospèrent et, en 1755, ils sont au nombre de 15 000. Cela **inquiète** les autorités anglaises, qui commencent alors à déporter les Français. Cette expulsion des Acadiens est **appelée** «le Grand Dérangement».

---

venus *who came*   **sont-ils venus** *did they come*   **fondent** *found*   **la partie est** *the eastern part*   **inquiète** *worries*   **appelée** *called*

Après une période noire **pendant laquelle** beaucoup d'Acadiens **meurent,** certains groupes d'Acadiens viennent **s'établir dans la partie sud** de la Louisiane. **En raison de** l'inaccessibilité de la région, ces Francophones restent **isolés pendant** plus de 200 ans, et leur culture et leur langue restent dominantes dans le sud de la Louisiane.

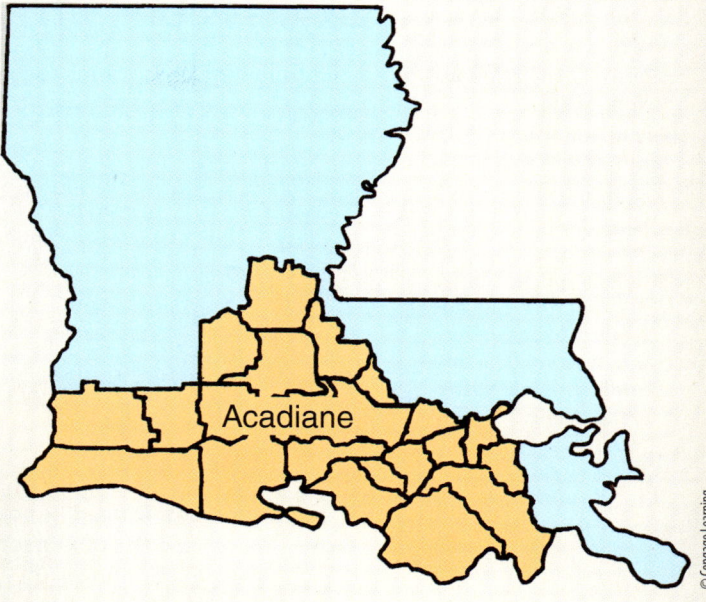

Vers la fin du 19ᵉ siècle, des vagues d'Anglophones commencent à arriver dans la région. En 1916, l'État de Louisiane **exige que la scolarité se fasse** en anglais et l'anglais devient de ce **fait** la langue prédominante chez les jeunes. L'usage du français en Louisiane **diminue.**

En 1968, la Louisiane **met** en place le CODOFIL, le Conseil pour le Développement du Français en Louisiane, pour **protéger** la langue et la culture françaises. Et en 1971, l'État crée la région d'Acadiane, **comprenant 22 paroisses** francophones dans la partie sud de l'État.

Compréhension

1. La majorité des Cadiens en Louisiane sont les descendants de quel groupe?
2. Qu'est-ce que «le Grand Dérangement»?
3. Pourquoi est-ce que l'anglais devient la langue prédominante après 1916?
4. Quel est le but *(goal)* du CODOFIL? Que pensez-vous de cette idée de créer une agence pour la défense de la langue et de la culture d'une minorité? Est-ce qu'il y a des organisations publiques dans votre région qui protègent la langue ou la culture d'une minorité?

Suggestion. Search the Web for the extract of Jean Arceneaux's work **"Je suis cadien"**, *"I will not speak French on school grounds."*

Share It!

Visit **www.cengagebrain.com** for additional cultural information and activities.

---

pendant laquelle *during which* **meurent** *die* **s'établir dans la partie sud** *establish themselves in the southern part* **En raison de** *Because of* **isolés pendant** *isolated for* **Vers la fin du 19ᵉ siècle, des vagues** *Towards the end of the 19th century, waves* **exige que la scolarité se fasse** *requires that education be done* **fait** *act, deed, fact* **diminue** *diminishes* **met** *puts* **protéger** *to protect* **comprenant 22 paroisses** *including 22 parishes (equivalent of counties)*

RÉSUMÉ DE GRAMMAIRE

J'**ai faim** et **soif.** On va au café?

Fermons la fenêtre! Nous **avons froid.**

Tu **as raison.** Tu comprends bien!

J'**ai sommeil**! Je vais au lit.

Il **a peur des** chiens.

Ma tante s'appelle Sonia. Elle **a 34 ans.** Elle **a les cheveux longs** et **les yeux noirs.** Elle **a des lunettes.** Elle **a l'air** intellectuelle.

—Qu'est-ce que tu **as l'intention de** faire?

—Je ne sais pas. J'**ai besoin de** travailler, mais j'**ai envie de** sortir.

—Où **vas**-tu cet après-midi?

—Je **vais au** cinéma. Mes parents **vont aux** nouvelles expositions de deux artistes de la ville et ma sœur **va à la** bibliothèque. Et vous deux, où **allez**-vous?

—Nous **allons à l**'église.

—Je vais à l'université. Tu voudrais **y** aller avec moi?

—Non, je n'**y** vais pas aujourd'hui.

On parle français en Louisiane.

Nous, **on aime** sortir le week-end.

—**On sort** ce soir?

—D'accord. **Allons** au cinéma.

—Non, **n'allons pas** au cinéma. **Dînons** plutôt au restaurant.

EXPRESSIONS WITH *AVOIR*

The following expressions use **avoir**. Note the use of the definite article with **avoir les yeux / les cheveux.**

avoir faim	to be hungry	avoir... ans	to be... years old
avoir soif	to be thirsty	avoir les cheveux longs	to have long hair
avoir chaud	to be hot	avoir les yeux marron	to have brown eyes
avoir froid	to be cold	avoir l'air	to look..., to seem...
avoir raison	to be right	avoir une barbe /	to have a beard /
avoir tort	to be wrong	une moustache /	a mustache /
avoir sommeil	to be sleepy	des lunettes	glasses
avoir peur (de)	to be afraid (of)		

avoir besoin de (d') + noun or infinitive	*to need* + noun or infinitive
avoir envie de (d') + noun or infinitive	*to feel like* + noun or verb
avoir l'intention de (d') + infinitive	*to intend* + infinitive

THE VERB *ALLER*, THE PREPOSITION *À*, AND THE PRONOUN *Y*

Use the verb **aller** and the preposition **à** *(to, at, in)* to say where someone is going. When **à** falls before **le** or **les,** the two words contract to **au** and **aux.**

ALLER (to go)	
je **vais**	nous **allons**
tu **vas**	vous **allez**
il/elle/on **va**	ils/elles **vont**

Use the pronoun **y** to mean *there*, even when *there* is only implied in English. Place it *immediately before* the infinitive if there is one. Otherwise, place it *immediately before* the conjugated verb. Treat **y** as a vowel for purposes of elision and liaison.

THE SUBJECT PRONOUN *ON* AND COMMAND FORMS *(L'IMPÉRATIF)*

Use **on** as the subject of a sentence to refer to people in general *(one, people, they)*, or instead of **nous** to say *we*. **On** takes the same verb form as **il/elle,** no matter what the translation is in English.

You can invite someone to do something with you by asking a question with **on** *(Shall we . . . ? / How about . . . ?)*. To say *Let's . . .* , use the **nous** form of the appropriate verb without the pronoun **nous.**

To tell someone to do something, use the **tu** or **vous** form of the verb, as appropriate, without the pronoun **tu** or **vous**. In **tu** form commands, drop the final **s** of **-er** verbs and **aller**.

Avoir and **être** have irregular command forms.

ÊTRE (be...)	AVOIR (have...)
sois	aie
soyons	ayons
soyez	ayez

THE IMMEDIATE FUTURE (LE FUTUR IMMÉDIAT)

To talk about what someone *is going to do*, use a conjugated form of the verb **aller** followed by an infinitive. To say what someone is *not* going to do, place **ne... pas** around the conjugated form of **aller**. **Il y a** becomes **il va y avoir**.

DATES

To tell the date, use **le** and the cardinal numbers (**deux, trois, quatre...**), except for *the first* (**le premier**). The day goes *before* the month: **30/9/2015**.

You can express the years 1100–1999 in two ways. Years from 2000 on are only expressed using the word **mille**. Use **en** to say *in* what year or month. Do not use a word to say *on* with a date.

THE VERBS *PRENDRE* AND *VENIR* AND MEANS OF TRANSPORTATION

Prendre *(to take)* and **venir** *(to come)* are irregular.

PRENDRE (to take)		VENIR (to come)	
je **prends**	nous **prenons**	je **viens**	nous **venons**
tu **prends**	vous **prenez**	tu **viens**	vous **venez**
il/elle/on **prend**	ils/elles **prennent**	il/elle/on **vient**	ils/elles **viennent**

Prendre means *to take*. You can also use it as *to have* when talking about having something to eat or drink. **Comprendre** *(to understand)* and **apprendre** *(to learn)* are conjugated like **prendre**.

Revenir *(to come back)* and **devenir** *(to become)* are conjugated like **venir**.

Use the preposition **en** (or **à** with **vélo**) to say *by* what means you are traveling with verbs like **aller, venir,** and **voyager**. When using **prendre** to say what means of transportation you are taking, you can often use the same article with the noun that you would in English.

Va au restaurant Préjean et **mange** les spécialités de la maison.
Mangez bien. **Ne mangez pas** de dessert.

Sois à l'heure pour tes cours.
N'aie pas peur! **Aie** confiance!
N'ayons pas peur! **Soyons** calmes!
Ayez de la patience! **Ne soyez pas** impatient!

—Qu'est-ce que tu **vas faire** ce soir? Tu **vas sortir**?
—Non, je **ne vais pas sortir**. Je **vais rester** à la maison. **Il va y avoir** un match de foot à la télé.

—Quelle est la date, aujourd'hui? C'est **le trente septembre**?
—Non, c'est **le premier octobre**.

1910 **mille neuf cent dix / dix-neuf cent dix**

Mon anniversaire, c'est **en mars**. Je vais faire une fête le 15 mars.

Je vais finir mes études **en 2019 (deux mille dix-neuf)**.

—**Venez**-vous à l'université en voiture?
—Non, je ne **viens** pas en cours en voiture. Je **prends** mon vélo. **Prenez**-vous votre voiture?

Le matin, il **prend** un café et un croissant.
Tu **comprends**?
Nous **apprenons** beaucoup dans ce cours.

Ses fils **reviennent** de plus en plus tard à la maison et le père **devient** impatient.

D'habitude, ils **voyagent en avion**, mais aujourd'hui ils **prennent le train**.

Résumé de grammaire | cent soixante-treize

VOCABULAIRE

  Audio Flashcards

COMPÉTENCE 1

Describing your family

LA FAMILLE
des beaux-parents / un beau-père / une belle-mère	stepparents, in-laws / a stepfather, a father-in-law / a stepmother, a mother-in-law
un(e) cousin(e)	a cousin
un(e) enfant	a child
un fils / une fille	a son / a daughter
un frère / une sœur	a brother / a sister
un garçon / une fille	a boy / a girl
des grands-parents / un grand-père / une grand-mère	grandparents / a grandfather / a grandmother
un neveu (pl des neveux) / une nièce	a nephew / a niece
un oncle / une tante	an uncle / an aunt
des parents / un père / une mère	parents / a father / a mother

NOMS FÉMININS
une barbe	a beard
des lunettes	glasses
une moustache	a mustache
des vacances	vacation

ADJECTIFS
âgé(e)	old
auburn (inv)	auburn
blond(e)	blond(e)
brun(e)	medium / dark brown (with hair)
châtain	light / medium brown (with hair)
court(e)	short
décédé(e)	deceased
long(ue)	long
mi-longs	shoulder-length (with hair)
noir(e)	black, very dark brown (with eyes)
noisette (inv)	hazel (with eyes)
roux (rousse)	red (with hair)

EXPRESSIONS VERBALES
avoir besoin de	to need
avoir chaud / froid	to be hot / cold
avoir envie de	to feel like, to want
avoir faim / soif	to be hungry / thirsty
avoir l'air...	to look..., to seem...
avoir les cheveux / les yeux...	to have... hair / eyes
avoir l'intention de	to intend to
avoir peur (de)	to be afraid (of)
avoir raison / tort	to be right / wrong
avoir sommeil	to be sleepy
Comment s'appelle-t-il/elle? Il/Elle s'appelle...	What is his/her name? His/Her name is...
porter	to wear, to carry
Quel âge a...? avoir (environ)... ans	How old is...? to be (about)... years old
Vous êtes combien dans votre (ta) famille? Nous sommes...	How many people are there in your family? There are... of us.

DIVERS
de taille moyenne	of medium height
encore	still
environ	about
La Nouvelle-Orléans	New Orleans

COMPÉTENCE 2

Saying where you go in your free time

NOMS MASCULINS
un centre commercial	a shopping mall
un concert	a concert
un festival	a festival
un magasin	a store
un musée	a museum
un orchestre	an orchestra, a band
un parc	a park
des projets	plans
le temps libre	free time
un théâtre	a theater

NOMS FÉMININS
une activité (de plein air)	an (outdoor) activity
la cuisine	cooking, cuisine
une église	a church
une exposition	an exhibit
une librairie	a bookstore
la musique zydeco	Zydeco music
une pièce (de théâtre)	a play
une piscine	a swimming pool
une plage	a beach
une région	a region
une spécialité	a specialty

EXPRESSIONS VERBALES
acheter	to buy
aie, ayons, ayez	have, let's have, have
aller (à)	to go (to)
avoir confiance	to have confidence
avoir de la patience	to have patience
connaître	to know, to get to know, to be acquainted / familiar with
prendre un bain de soleil	to sunbathe
retrouver	to meet
servir	to serve
sois, soyons, soyez	be, let's be, be
trouver	to find

DIVERS
à l'heure	on time
bonne idée	good idea
cadien(ne)	Cajun
calme	calm
culturel(le)	cultural
de temps en temps	from time to time
extra(ordinaire)	great
on	one, people, they, we
On...?	Shall we...?, How about...?
on dit que	they say that
on peut	one can
plutôt	rather, instead
pour	in order to
sage	good, well-behaved
y	there

COMPÉTENCE 3

Saying what you are going to do

NOMS MASCULINS

un anniversaire	a birthday
le folklore	folklore

NOMS FÉMININS

une fête	a holiday, a party
la soirée	the evening

EXPRESSIONS VERBALES

aller voir	to go see, to visit (a person)
boire	to drink
faire une fête	to have a party
faire des projets	to make plans
faire un tour	to take a tour, to go for a ride
il va y avoir	there is / are going to be
partir (pour le week-end)	to go away, to leave (for the weekend)
quitter	to leave
visiter	to visit (a place)

LES DATES

En quelle année?	In what year?
Quelle est la date?	What is the date?
C'est quelle date?	What is the date?
C'est le premier (deux, trois...)	It's the first (second, third...) of
janvier / février / mars / avril / mai / juin / juillet / août / septembre / octobre / novembre / décembre	January / February / March / April / May / June / July / August / September / October / November / December

EXPRESSIONS ADVERBIALES

ce matin	this morning
ce mois-ci	this month
ce soir	tonight, this evening
ce week-end	this weekend
cet après-midi	this afternoon
cette année	this year
cette semaine	this week
d'abord	first
demain matin / après-midi / soir	tomorrow morning / afternoon / evening
ensuite	then, afterwards
l'année prochaine	next year
la semaine prochaine	next week
le mois prochain	next month
le week-end prochain	next weekend
lundi (mardi...) prochain	next Monday (Tuesday...)
plus tard	later
(et) puis	(and) then
tard	late
tôt	early

DIVERS

célèbre	famous
génial(e) (*m pl* géniaux)	great
national(e) (*m pl* nationaux)	national
prochain(e)	next
régional(e) (*m pl* régionaux)	regional
le Vieux Carré	the French Quarter

COMPÉTENCE 4

Planning how to get there

NOMS MASCULINS

un (auto)bus	a bus (in a city)
un (auto)car	a bus (between cities)
un avion	a plane
un bateau	a boat
le métro	the subway
un moyen de transport	a means of transportation
un taxi	a cab, a taxi
un train	a train
un voyage	a trip

NOMS FÉMININS

une possibilité	a possibility
des notes	notes

EXPRESSIONS VERBALES

aller à pied	to go on foot
à vélo	by bike
en (auto)bus	by bus
en (auto)car	by bus
en avion	by plane
en bateau	by boat
en métro	by subway
en taxi	by taxi
en train	by train
en voiture	by car
apprendre	to learn
comprendre	to understand
devenir	to become
louer	to rent
prendre	to take
revenir	to come back
venir	to come

DIVERS

après-demain	the day after tomorrow
Ça prend combien de temps?	How long does it take?
Ça prend...	It takes...
impatient(e)	impatient
pas plus	no more
prêt(e)	ready

INTERLUDE MUSICAL

FILLE DE VILLE

MARIE-ÉLAINE THIBERT

Marie-Élaine Thibert has always had a passion for music and dreamed of singing on stage. To fulfill her dream, she had to work hard and overcome her shyness. Her dream finally became a reality when she was selected to sing on *Star Académie* (the Francophone Canadian equivalent of *American Idol*), which made her a star. The following activity will help you better understand her song *Fille de ville*.

Marie-Élaine Thibert est née *(born)* à La Salle, un arrondissement *(district)* de Montréal.

Fille de ville. Dans cette chanson *(this song)*, Marie-Élaine Thibert explique qu'elle n'a rien contre *(has nothing against)* la campagne, mais elle se considère *(considers herself)* clairement une fille de ville. Associez-vous ces choses mentionnées dans la chanson à la campagne ou à la ville?

les champs *(fields)*	l'espace *(space)*
les lumières *(lights)*	les montagnes
le bruit *(noise)*	l'énergie
les bois *(woods)*	les plaines
gronder *(to rumble)*	les odeurs
les lacs et les rivières	les millions de choses à faire
le béton *(concrete)* et la circulation *(traffic)*	les oiseaux *(birds)* et les fleurs

NONC WILLIE

BRUCE DAIGREPONT

Bruce Daigrepont, true to his Cajun heritage, focuses his music around the traditional Cajun instruments, the accordion and fiddle, backed by drums, bass, rubboard, and triangle. His sets are comprised of Cajun waltzes and two-steps, fiddle reels, deep blues, swamp pop, zydeco, and R&B. The following activities will help you better understand his song *Nonc Willie*.

Bruce Daigrepont donne des concerts de musique cadienne partout dans le monde *(world)*.

A **Chez Nonc Willie.** Dans la chanson *(song) Nonc Willie (Uncle Willie)*, le chanteur invite des amis à aller chez Nonc Willie pour s'amuser *(to have fun)*. Voilà les choses à faire chez Nonc Willie. Devinez le sens des mots que vous ne connaissez pas. *(Guess the meaning of the words you don't know.)*

gagner de l'argent	s'amuser	boire de la bière
jouer à des jeux de cartes	acheter des bonbons	se rassembler

Suggestion. Point out that the expression **jouer bourré**, derived from **bourrer** *(to stuff)*, is a reference to a Cajun card game in which the loser has to "stuff" the pot with chips. **Une bourrée** is also an old country dance from the region of Auvergne. It was named **bourrée** because it was originally danced around a fire of **bourrées** *(small wooden branches)*.

B **Dans le passé.** Le chanteur dit «je me souviens» *(I remember)* pour parler de quand il était *(was)* petit. Dans les phrases suivantes, tous les verbes sont au passé. Utilisez le contexte pour deviner leur sens.

Nonc Willie *était* le frère de mon grand-père. Il n'*avait* pas beaucoup d'argent, mais il *s'amusait* bien. Tous ses amis *se rassemblaient* le samedi soir pour jouer aux cartes ensemble. Le gagnant *donnait* un peu d'argent aux enfants qui *observaient* le jeu.

À Paris
Les projets

	iLrn Heinle Learning Center		Internet web search
	www.cengagebrain.com		Pair work
	Horizons Video: Les Stagiaires		Group work
	Audio		

5

COMPÉTENCE

1 Saying what you did
Le week-end dernier

Saying what you did
  Le passé composé avec **avoir**

Stratégies et Lecture
- **Pour mieux lire:** Using the sequence of events to make logical guesses
- **Lecture:** *Qu'est-ce qu'elle a fait?*

2 Telling where you went
Je suis parti(e) en voyage

Telling where you went
  Le passé composé avec **être**

Telling when you did something
  Les expressions qui désignent le passé et reprise du passé composé

3 Discussing the weather and your activities
Le temps et les projets

Talking about the weather and what you do
  Le verbe **faire**, *l'expression* **ne… rien** *et les expressions pour décrire le temps*

Talking about activities
  Les expressions avec **faire**

4 Deciding what to wear and buying clothes
Les vêtements

Avoiding repetition
  Les pronoms **le, la, l'** *et* **les**

Vidéoreprise *Les Stagiaires*

Lecture et Composition
- **Pour mieux lire:** *Using visuals to make guesses*
- **Lecture:** *Je blogue donc je suis*
- **Pour mieux écrire:** *Using standard organizing techniques*
- **Composition:** *Un voyage en France*

Comparaisons culturelles *Le sport et le temps libre des Français*

Résumé de grammaire

Vocabulaire

cent soixante-dix-neuf | **179**

LA FRANCE

PowerPoint 5-1  Voudriez-vous visiter la France? La France vous offre une grande variété de **paysages.** Il y a...

de grandes villes

des plaines

de petits villages **ruraux**

---

paysages *(m) landscapes*   **ruraux** *rural*

des plages de sable

La France (La République française)

Visit it live on Google Earth!

NOMBRE D'HABITANTS:
65 350 000 (les Français)

CAPITALE: **Paris**

Le savez-vous?

Est-ce que vous connaissez *(know)* un peu la France? Regardez la carte *(map)* de la France à la fin du *(at the end of the)* livre. Ensuite, répondez à ces questions. Si vous ne savez pas, devinez! *(If you don't know, guess!)*

1. La France a à peu près la même superficie *(about the same area)* que…
   a. l'Alaska   b. le Texas   c. la Louisiane
2. Regardez la carte de la France. À cause de *(Because of)* sa forme, on appelle la France…
   a. le Pentagone   b. l'Octogone   c. l'Hexagone
3. Il y a huit pays qui bordent la France. Lequel *(Which one)* des pays suivants est au nord *(north)* de la France?
   a. la Suisse   b. la Belgique   c. l'Espagne
4. Quel massif montagneux *(mountain range)* forme une frontière entre la France et l'Espagne?
   a. les Alpes   b. les Pyrénées   c. le Massif Central
5. Quel fleuve *(river)* français traverse *(crosses)* Paris?
   a. la Seine   b. la Loire   c. le Rhône
6. Lyon et Marseille sont les deuxième et troisième villes de la France. Où se trouvent-elles?
   a. dans le nord du pays
   b. dans le centre et dans le sud *(south)* du pays

des fleuves

Quick-reference answers for *Le savez-vous?* 1. b 2. c 3. b 4. b 5. a 6. b

What part of France would you like to visit? Would you like to do a special kind of trip like a bicycle tour or a cooking or wine-tasting tour? Do an online search for various trips to France. Find a trip you would like to take and describe where you are going to go and what you are going to do.

des montagnes

des fleuves *rivers*

La France | cent quatre-vingt-un **181**

COMPÉTENCE 1

Saying what you did

 PowerPoint 5-2

Note culturelle

Quelle activité de loisir est-ce que vous trouvez la plus satisfaisante? Voilà les réponses des Français selon une enquête récente *(according to a recent survey).*
57 % être avec des amis
42 % faire du sport
38 % lire des livres
Comparez votre réponse à celles des Français.

Suggestion for the *Note culturelle.* Refer students back to the *Note culturelle* on page 68 and have them discuss how the most popular pastimes, those most frequently practiced, and those that are considered the most satisfying differ and discuss the possible reasons why.

Vocabulaire sans peine!

Remember that the French ending **-é** is often the equivalent of the English past participle ending *-ed* or of other English past participles such as *spoken, sung,* etc. As in English, such words can be used as part of the past tense and also as adjectives.
-é = *-ed*
continué = *continued*
How would you complete the second expression in French?
they divorced **ils ont divorcé**
a divorced man **un homme...**

Warm-up. Have students describe their best friend (physical appearance, hair and eye color, personality traits) and say where he/she likes to go and what he/she likes to do on the weekend.

Note. The **passé composé** with **avoir** is taught in this ***Compétence,*** and the **passé composé** with **être** in ***Compétence 2.*** The expressions **je suis allé(e) / sorti(e) / resté(e) / rentré(e)** are taught here as lexical items and as a preview for the next ***Compétence,*** although a brief explanation is given on p. 184.

Suggestion. Point out that the sentences on this page are in the past tense and ask students what they notice about the verbs. As a preview for the next ***Compétence,*** point out that the statements on the left have to do with going, coming, and staying, and that those on the right side tell what you did. Ask students what they notice about the structures used in the two categories. You may prefer to present the grammar on page 184 at this time.

LE WEEK-END DERNIER

Alice Pérez, **femme d'affaires** américaine **travaillant** à Paris, parle de ses activités de **samedi dernier.** Et vous?

Où est-ce que vous êtes allé(e)? Qu'est-ce que vous avez fait?

Samedi matin,...

je ne suis pas sortie,
je suis restée chez moi.

J'ai dormi jusqu'à 10 heures.

J'ai **pris** mon **petit déjeuner.**

Samedi après-midi,...

je suis allée en ville.

Je n'ai pas travaillé.

J'ai déjeuné avec une amie et j'ai bien mangé.

Samedi soir,...

je suis sortie.

J'ai vu un film étranger.

J'ai retrouvé un ami au café.

je suis rentrée chez moi.

J'ai lu le journal.

Je **n'**ai **rien** fait.

Line art on this page: © Cengage Learning

Le week-end dernier *Last weekend* **une femme d'affaires (un homme d'affaires)** *a businesswoman (a businessman)* **travaillant** *working* **samedi dernier** *last Saturday* **Où est-ce que vous êtes allé(e)?** *Where did you go?* **Qu'est-ce que vous avez fait?** *What did you do?* **prendre son petit déjeuner** *to have one's breakfast* **ne... rien** *nothing*

C'est lundi et Cathy, la fille d'Alice, parle avec un ami des activités du week-end dernier.

CATHY: Tu as passé un bon week-end?
JÉRÉMY: Oui, pas mal. Samedi matin, j'ai révisé mes cours et samedi après-midi, j'ai joué au foot avec des amis.
CATHY: Qu'est-ce que tu as fait samedi soir?
JÉRÉMY: Je suis sorti. Je suis allé en boîte et j'ai beaucoup dansé.
CATHY: Et **hier**?
JÉRÉMY: Hier matin, **j'ai fait une promenade** sur les Champs-Élysées où j'ai fait du shopping. Et **hier soir,** j'ai regardé la télé.

Sélection musicale. Search the Web for the song **"Champs-Élysées"** by Joe Dassin and sung by Soma Riba to enjoy a musical selection related to this theme.

Note for the conversation. The glossed words are the only new words presented.

Suggestion for the conversation. Set the scene and introduce the word **hier.** Have students listen with books closed for the answers to these questions. **Vrai ou faux?**
1. Jérémy a passé un bon week-end.
2. Samedi, il est resté à la maison.
3. Dimanche, il a révisé les cours.
4. Dimanche soir, il a regardé la télé.
Afterward, have students follow along in the book as you play the conversation again.

A **Activités logiques.** Formez des phrases logiques. Complétez chaque début de phrase à gauche avec la fin de phrase logique à droite.

Je suis resté(e) au lit et...	j'ai pris un verre.
J'ai retrouvé des amis au café où...	j'ai dormi.
J'ai dîné au restaurant où...	j'ai beaucoup dansé.
Je suis allé(e) au cinéma où...	je n'ai pas gagné.
Je suis allé(e) en boîte où...	j'ai vu un film étranger.
J'ai joué au tennis avec une amie, mais...	j'ai très bien mangé.
Je suis allé(e) au parc où...	j'ai fait une promenade.

B **Et vous?** Complétez les phrases pour indiquer comment vous avez passé la journée d'hier.

1. J'ai dormi jusqu'à *8 heures / 10 heures / ???.*
2. J'ai pris le petit déjeuner *chez moi / au café / chez une amie / ???. (Je n'ai pas pris de petit déjeuner.)*
3. J'ai lu *le journal / un livre / un blog / un article sur Internet / ???. (Je n'ai rien lu.)*
4. J'ai déjeuné *chez moi / chez des amis / au restaurant / ???. (Je n'ai pas déjeuné.)*
5. *J'ai travaillé. / Je n'ai pas travaillé.*
6. J'ai dîné *chez moi / chez mes parents / ???. (Je n'ai pas dîné.)*
7. J'ai *beaucoup / peu* mangé. *(Je n'ai pas mangé.)*
8. Le soir, *je suis resté(e) chez moi / je suis sorti(e).*

Hier, j'ai fait une promenade au jardin des Tuileries.

 À VOUS!

Avec un(e) partenaire, relisez à haute voix la conversation entre Cathy et Jérémy. Ensuite, adaptez la conversation pour parler de votre week-end passé. *Note: You may not know how to say everything you did. Pick two or three things that you know how to say or ask your instructor for help.*

You can find a list of the new words from this **Compétence** on page 214 and access the audio online.

hier *yesterday*   **faire une promenade** *to take a walk*   **hier soir** *last night, yesterday evening*

Compétence 1 | *cent quatre-vingt-trois* **183**

PowerPoint 5-3

SAYING WHAT YOU DID

Le passé composé avec *avoir*

To say what happened in the past, put the verb in the **passé composé.** It is composed of two parts, the auxiliary verb and the past participle. The auxiliary verb, usually **avoir,** is conjugated in the present tense. The past participle of all **-er** verbs ends in **-é,** and that of most **-ir** verbs ends in **-i.**

PARLER		DORMIR	
j'**ai parlé**	nous **avons parlé**	j'**ai dormi**	nous **avons dormi**
tu **as parlé**	vous **avez parlé**	tu **as dormi**	vous **avez dormi**
il/elle/on **a parlé**	ils/elles **ont parlé**	il/elle/on **a dormi**	ils/elles **ont dormi**

Many irregular verbs have irregular past participles that must be memorized.

avoir	j'ai **eu**, tu as **eu**...	être	j'ai **été**, tu as **été**...
il y a	il y a **eu**	faire	j'ai **fait**, tu as **fait**...
boire	j'ai **bu**, tu as **bu**...	écrire	j'ai **écrit**, tu as **écrit**...
lire	j'ai **lu**, tu as **lu**...	prendre	j'ai **pris**, tu as **pris**...
voir	j'ai **vu**, tu as **vu**...	apprendre	j'ai **appris**...
		comprendre	j'ai **compris**...

Adverbs indicating *how often* (**toujours, souvent...**) and *how well* (**bien, mal...**) are usually placed between the two parts of the verb. To put a verb in the negative form, place **ne** directly after the subject, and place **pas, jamais,** or **rien** just after the auxiliary verb.

J'ai **beaucoup** travaillé hier matin. Après, je **n'**ai **rien** fait.

The **passé composé** can be translated in a variety of ways in English.

I took the bus.
I have taken the bus. } J'ai pris le bus.
I did take the bus.

✓ Pour vérifier

1. The **passé composé** always has two parts. What are they called?
2. What verb is usually used as the auxiliary verb? Do you conjugate it?
3. How do you form the past participle of all **-er** and most **-ir** verbs? Which verbs that you know have irregular past participles? What are their past participles?
4. How is the negative of verbs formed in the **passé composé**? How do you say *I did nothing / I didn't do anything*?
5. In the **passé composé,** where do you place adverbs like **souvent** or **bien**?
6. What are the three possible English translations of **j'ai mangé**?

iLrn Grammar Tutorials

Note *de grammaire*

Some verbs expressing *going, coming,* and *staying,* such as **aller, sortir, rentrer,** and **rester,** have **être,** not **avoir,** as their auxiliary verb. You will learn about them in the next **Compétence.** For now, remember to use **je suis allé(e), je suis sorti(e), je suis resté(e),** and **je suis rentré(e)** if you want to say *I went, I went out, I stayed,* and *I returned.* (If you are a female, add the extra **e** to the past participle of these verbs, just as you do with adjectives. Do not add this feminine **e** to the verbs you are learning to conjugate with the auxiliary **avoir** in this **Compétence.**)

A **La journée de Cathy.** Voici les activités de Cathy hier. Est-ce qu'elle a fait les choses suivantes?

EXEMPLE Hier matin, Cathy... quitter la maison tôt
Hier matin, Cathy n'a pas quitté la maison tôt.

Hier matin, Cathy...
1. dormir
2. passer la matinée chez elle
3. faire une promenade
4. travailler tôt

Hier soir, Cathy et ses amis...
5. voir un film
6. prendre un café
7. beaucoup parler
8. faire du sport

Warm-up for A. La journée de Cathy.
Regardez les illustrations à la page 182. Est-ce qu'Alice a fait ces choses? Répondez par **oui** ou par **non. 1.** Elle a passé la matinée chez elle. **2.** Elle a pris son petit déjeuner au café. **3.** Elle a quitté la maison samedi après-midi. **4.** Elle a déjeuné seule. **5.** Samedi soir, elle a regardé la télé. **6.** Elle a beaucoup travaillé.

B Qu'avez-vous fait? Dites si ces personnes ont fait les choses suivantes la dernière fois que *(the last time)* vous êtes allé(e) en cours de français.

EXEMPLE Moi, je (j') / dormir jusqu'à 10 heures
Moi, j'ai dormi jusqu'à 10 heures.
Moi, je n'ai pas dormi jusqu'à 10 heures.

AVANT LE COURS

Moi, je (j')…
1. être dans un autre cours
2. passer la matinée chez moi
3. lire le journal

Mon (Ma) meilleur(e) ami(e)…
4. boire un café avec moi
5. manger avec moi
6. passer la matinée avec moi

EN COURS

Les étudiants…
7. dormir en cours
8. bien comprendre la leçon
9. beaucoup apprendre

Nous…
10. avoir un examen
11. écrire beaucoup d'exercices
12. voir un film français

C Entretien. Posez ces questions à votre partenaire sur ce qu'il/elle a fait hier.

EXEMPLE — À quelle heure est-ce que tu as quitté la maison hier?
— J'ai quitté la maison vers 9 heures.
Je n'ai pas quitté la maison hier.

1. Jusqu'à quelle heure est-ce que tu as dormi?
2. Quand est-ce que tu as quitté la maison?
3. Où est-ce que tu as pris ton petit déjeuner?
4. Avec qui est-ce que tu as déjeuné?
5. Qu'est-ce que tu as étudié?
6. Qu'est-ce que tu as fait hier soir?

Après, décrivez la journée de votre partenaire à la classe.

EXEMPLE Rachel a dormi jusqu'à sept heures. Elle a quitté la maison…

D Devinez! Dites à votre partenaire combien des choses suivantes vous avez faites récemment *(recently)* avec des ami(e)s. Votre partenaire va deviner lesquelles *(guess which ones)*.

> boire un café   parler sur Skype   voir un bon film
> visiter une autre ville   faire une promenade
> prendre un verre   déjeuner
> prendre le petit déjeuner   faire du vélo

EXEMPLE — Mes amis et moi, on a fait cinq choses de la liste récemment.
— Vous avez bu un café ensemble?
— Oui, on a bu un café. / Non, on n'a pas bu de café.
— Vous avez parlé sur Skype?…

On a joué au frisbee à la plage.

STRATÉGIES ET LECTURE

> **POUR MIEUX LIRE:** Using the sequence of events to make logical guesses
>
> You can often guess the meaning of unfamiliar verbs in a narrative by thinking about what actions would occur together and in what order. For example, when taking the bus, you wait for the bus first, get on the bus, then get off at your destination. Learn to read a whole sentence or paragraph, rather than one word at a time.
>
> Notice that the prefix **re-** means that an action in a sequence is done again, as in English (*do* and *redo*, *read* and *reread*).
>
> You will also notice that prepositions can indicate relationships between actions. **Pour** means *in order to* when it is followed by a verb. **Sans,** meaning *without*, can also be followed by an infinitive.

A Devinez!
Use the sequence of events in this passage to guess the meaning of the boldfaced words.

Cathy **a ouvert** une enveloppe et elle **a sorti** une feuille de papier. Elle **a lu** les instructions sur la feuille, mais elle n'a pas compris. Alors, elle **a relu** les instructions et elle **a remis** la feuille de papier dans l'enveloppe.

Cathy **a attendu** le bus devant son appartement. Quand il est arrivé, elle **est montée** dedans, et elle **est descendue** quand elle est arrivée à sa destination. Elle **est entrée** dans un café et a commandé un coca. Elle a bu son coca, elle **a payé l'addition** et elle **est repartie.**

Elle est entrée dans une station de métro où elle a acheté un ticket **au guichet,** mais elle n'a pas pris le métro. Elle **a mis** le ticket dans son enveloppe et elle a quitté la station.

Devant un magasin de vélos, Cathy a admiré un vélo rouge dans **la vitrine.** Elle est entrée dans le magasin et a demandé **le prix** du vélo.

B Dans l'ordre logique.
Mettez les activités suivantes de Cathy dans l'ordre logique. La première et la dernière *(last)* sont indiquées.

_____ Elle est allée vers la porte.
_____ Elle a lu les instructions sur la feuille de papier.
___1___ Cathy a vu une enveloppe sur la table.
_____ Elle a sorti une feuille de papier de l'enveloppe.
_____ Elle a ouvert l'enveloppe.
___7___ Elle a ouvert la porte et elle est sortie.
_____ Elle a remis la feuille dans l'enveloppe.

C Quel verbe?
Complétez ces phrases logiquement. N'oubliez pas *(Don't forget)* que **pour** veut dire *in order to* et **sans** veut dire *without*.

1. Cathy a quitté l'appartement sans… (boire son café, ouvrir la porte).
2. Elle a pris le bus pour… (rester à la maison, aller en ville).
3. Elle a retrouvé des amis pour… (passer le week-end seule, aller au cinéma).
4. Elle est allée au guichet pour… (acheter des tickets, boire un coca).
5. Elle est rentrée à la maison sans… (quitter le café, prendre le bus).

Lecture: *Qu'est-ce qu'elle a fait?*

Seule dans son appartement, Cathy Pérez avait l'air un peu agitée. Elle a pris une enveloppe qui était sur la table et en a sorti une feuille de papier. Elle a lu les instructions et a remis la feuille dans l'enveloppe. Elle a pris l'enveloppe et a quitté son appartement.

Cathy est entrée dans un café où elle a commandé un coca et ensuite, elle a demandé l'addition. Quand l'addition est arrivée, elle a payé. Elle a ouvert l'enveloppe, a relu les instructions, a mis l'addition dans l'enveloppe et a quitté le café sans boire son coca. C'est bien bizarre! Pourquoi avait-elle l'air si agitée?

Ensuite, Cathy est allée à la station de métro. Elle est entrée dans la station et sans regarder le plan, est allée au guichet et a demandé un ticket. Quand on lui a donné son ticket, elle l'a mis dans l'enveloppe, a remonté l'escalier et a quitté la station de métro. Pourquoi a-t-elle acheté un ticket sans prendre le métro? Tout cela est fort bizarre!

Cathy a continué sa route jusqu'à un magasin de vélos. Elle a regardé un vélo rouge qui était dans la vitrine. Elle est entrée dans le magasin et elle a demandé le prix du vélo. Elle a écrit le prix du vélo sur une feuille de papier et elle a mis la feuille de papier dans l'enveloppe. Ensuite, elle est sortie du magasin.

Cathy est allée au coin de la rue pour attendre l'autobus. Quand l'autobus est arrivé, elle l'a pris, et puis elle est descendue à l'université. Elle avait l'air un peu plus calme. Pourquoi a-t-elle fait tout ça? Pourquoi a-t-elle mis ces choses dans l'enveloppe? Pourquoi est-elle plus calme maintenant?

A. Comprenez-vous?
Dites ce que Cathy a fait d'abord et ce qu'elle a fait ensuite.

1. Elle a sorti une feuille de papier de l'enveloppe. / Elle a lu les instructions.
2. Elle a quitté son appartement. / Elle est allée au café.
3. Elle a commandé un coca. / Elle est partie sans boire son coca.
4. Elle a payé le serveur. / Elle a demandé l'addition.
5. Elle a demandé un ticket de métro. / Elle est allée au guichet.

B. Maintenant... c'est à vous!
Est-ce que vous trouvez les actions de Cathy plutôt bizarres? Pourquoi est-ce qu'elle a fait tout ça? Imaginez une explication.

Est-ce qu'elle... est agent de police ou détective privé? souffre d'amnésie? travaille pour la CIA? est espionne comme James Bond? collectionne des souvenirs de Paris? fait un exercice pour son cours de français?

Réponse:
Il y a une explication simple et logique! Cathy suit *(is taking)* un cours de français pour étrangers à Paris. Ses devoirs, dans l'enveloppe, consistent à prouver au professeur qu'elle est capable de commander quelque chose à boire au café, de demander le prix d'un vélo et d'acheter un ticket de métro. Elle doit rapporter *(needs to bring back)* l'addition, le prix du vélo et le ticket de métro à son professeur.

COMPÉTENCE 2

Telling where you went

 PowerPoint 5-4

JE SUIS PARTI(E) EN VOYAGE

Note culturelle

En France, les salariés *(employees)* ont entre 30 et 38 jours de vacances par an *(per year)* et aussi environ *(approximately)* 11 jours fériés *(paid holidays)*. Combien de jours fériés avez-vous?

La dernière fois que vous êtes parti(e) en voyage, où est-ce que vous êtes allé(e)? Qu'est-ce que vous avez fait?

Je suis allé(e)	à Denver.	**J'y suis allé(e)**	en avion.
	à New York.		en train.
	???		en autocar.
			en voiture **(de location)**.
Je suis parti(e)	en mars.	Je suis arrivé(e)	le même jour.
	le matin.		trois heures plus tard.
	vers trois heures.		**le lendemain**.
	???		???
Je suis descendu(e)	à l'hôtel.	Je suis resté(e)	**une nuit**.
			le week-end.
			trois jours.
Je suis allé(e)	dans un camping.		
Je suis resté(e)	chez des amis.		
	chez **des parents**.		
Je suis allé(e)	à la plage.	Je suis rentré(e)	trois jours après.
	à un concert.		la semaine suivante.
	en boîte.		deux semaines plus tard.

Note de vocabulaire

1. It is common to say either **je suis descendu(e)** or **je suis resté(e)** with **à l'hôtel**. It is more common to say **rester chez** for *to stay with* (a person). Also use **rester** to say how long you stayed. Say **je suis allé(e) dans un camping**.
2. Use **des parents** to say *relatives* and **mes parents** to say *my parents*.

Warm-up. 1. Avez-vous fait ces choses pendant *(during)* le dernier cours? Avez-vous...? beaucoup parlé, bien écouté, lu quelque chose, mangé, dormi, bu quelque chose, écrit au tableau, été absent(e), posé des questions **2.** Est-ce que nous avons fait les choses suivantes pendant le dernier cours? Avons-nous... (regardé un film, commencé un nouveau chapitre, fait beaucoup d'exercices oraux, écouté des CD, eu un examen)?

🔊 2-14

Alice est partie en week-end. Le mardi suivant, elle parle avec son amie Claire du voyage qu'elle a fait le week-end passé.

CLAIRE: Qu'est-ce que tu as fait le week-end dernier?
ALICE: J'ai pris le train pour aller à Deauville.
CLAIRE: Quand est-ce que tu es partie?
ALICE: Je suis partie samedi matin et je suis rentrée hier soir.
CLAIRE: Tu as trouvé un bon hôtel?
ALICE: Je suis descendue dans un petit hôtel confortable, pas trop loin de la plage.
CLAIRE: **Quelle chance!** Moi aussi, j'ai envie de visiter Deauville.

Note for the conversation. Quelle chance! is the only new vocabulary presented.

Suggestion for the conversation. Tell students that Deauville is a popular vacation destination and point it out on the map. Have students listen to the conversation with books closed for the answers to these questions: **1.** Où est-ce qu'Alice a passé le week-end? **2.** Quand est-ce qu'elle est rentrée?

A En week-end. Décrivez la dernière fois que vous êtes parti(e) en voyage.

1. Je suis allé(e) à (Chicago, Houston, ???).
2. J'y suis allé(e) (en avion, en train, ???).
3. Je suis parti(e) (le soir, vers cinq heures, ???).
4. Je suis arrivé(e) (une heure, trois jours, ???) plus tard.
5. Je suis resté(e) (à l'hôtel, chez des amis, ???).
6. Je suis resté(e) (deux jours, une semaine, ???).

La dernière fois *The last time* **J'y suis allé(e)** *I went there* **de location** *rental* **le lendemain** *the next day, the following day* **Je suis descendu(e) (descendre [dans / à / de])** *I stayed (to stay [at]; to descend, to come down, to get off / out [of] [a vehicle])* **une nuit** *one night* **des parents** *some relatives* **Quelle chance!** *What luck!*

B **Un tour de Paris.** Alice et sa famille adorent visiter Paris et la région parisienne. Regardez les photos et complétez les phrases avec une expression de la colonne de droite.

1. Son mari, Vincent, est allé à la Sainte-Chapelle pour…
2. Ses enfants sont allés à Versailles pour…
3. Ils sont allés à Notre-Dame pour…
4. Ils sont allés au musée d'Orsay pour…
5. Ils sont allés au café sur les Champs-Élysées pour…

voir une nouvelle exposition.
prendre un café.
voir son architecture gothique.
admirer les vitraux *(stained-glass windows)*.
visiter le château.

les Champs-Élysées

la Sainte-Chapelle

le château de Versailles

Notre-Dame

le musée d'Orsay

À VOUS!

Avec un(e) partenaire, relisez à haute voix la conversation entre Claire et Alice. Ensuite, adaptez la conversation pour parler de la dernière fois que vous êtes parti(e) en week-end.

iLrn: You can find a list of the new words from this *Compétence* on page 214 and access the audio online.

 **PowerPoint 5-5**

TELLING WHERE YOU WENT

✓ Pour vérifier

1. Which verbs have **être** as the auxiliary in the **passé composé**? What do you have to remember to do with the past participle of these verbs that you don't do with verbs that have **avoir** as their auxiliary?

2. How do you say *to enter*? What preposition do you use with it? How do you say *to go out*? *to go out of*?

3. What preposition do you use with **partir** to say *to leave from*? What is the difference between **partir** and **quitter**? between **rentrer** and **retourner**?

4. How do you say *to go/come down, to descend*? *to get out of/down from/ off of*? *to stay at*? How do you say *to go up*? *to get on/in*?

iLrn Grammar Tutorials

Note *de grammaire*

1. When **on** means *we*, its past participle may either be left in the masculine singular form (**On est sorti.**) or it may agree (**On est sorti[e]s**). Either is correct.

2. **Passer** takes **être** in the **passé composé** when it means *to pass by*. **Je suis passé(e) chez toi.** It takes **avoir** when it means *to spend time*. **J'ai passé la soirée avec mes amis.**

3. **Rentrer** means *to return/go back home* (or to the place you are staying). Use **retourner** for *to return* in most other cases.

4. **Partir** and **quitter** both mean *to leave*. **Partir** has **être** as its auxiliary, but **quitter** takes **avoir** and *must* have a direct object: **Elle *est partie* tôt. Elle *a quitté la maison* à 6h.**

Le passé composé avec **être**

The following verbs, many of which have to do with coming and going, have **être** as their auxiliary verb in the **passé composé**. The past participle of these verbs agrees with the subject in number and gender. Do not make this agreement when **avoir** is the auxiliary.

Elle est *partie* hier.   Elle a *pris* le train.

ALLER → ALLÉ		SORTIR → SORTI	
je **suis allé(e)**	nous **sommes allé(e)s**	je **suis sorti(e)**	nous **sommes sorti(e)s**
tu **es allé(e)**	vous **êtes allé(e)(s)**	tu **es sorti(e)**	vous **êtes sorti(e)(s)**
il **est allé**	ils **sont allés**	il **est sorti**	ils **sont sortis**
elle **est allée**	elles **sont allées**	elle **est sortie**	elles **sont sorties**
on **est allé(e)(s)**		on **est sorti(e)(s)**	

aller	je suis allé(e)	*I went*
venir / devenir / revenir	je suis venu(e) / devenu(e) / revenu(e)	*I came / became / came back*
arriver	je suis arrivé(e)	*I arrived*
rester	je suis resté(e)	*I stayed, I remained*
entrer (dans)	je suis entré(e) (dans)	*I entered, I went in*
sortir (de)	je suis sorti(e) (de)	*I went out / came out (of)*
partir (de)	je suis parti(e) (de)	*I left*
passer (par/chez/devant)	je suis passé(e) (par/chez/devant)	*I passed (by [. . .'s house])*
rentrer	je suis rentré(e)	*I came home, I returned*
retourner	je suis retourné(e)	*I returned, I went back*
monter (dans)	je suis monté(e) (dans)	*I went up, I got on/in*
descendre (de/dans/à)	je suis descendu(e) (de/dans/à)	*I came down, I got out (of) / off (of) (a vehicle), I stayed (at)*
tomber	je suis tombé(e)	*I fell (down)*
naître	je suis né(e)	*I was born*
mourir	il/elle est mort(e)	*he/she died*

In the **passé composé**, place **y** *(there)* immediately before the auxiliary verb.

J'**y** suis allé(e).   Je n'**y** suis pas allé(e).

Suggestions. A. Point out the verbs with irregular past participles. **B.** Point out: **1.** the new verbs **entrer, retourner, monter, descendre, naître, mourir,** and **tomber 2.** the use of **dans** with **entrer 3. monter dans** as *to get on/in* **4. descendre dans/à** as *to stay at*, **descendre de** as *to get out of/off of/down from* (a vehicle), and the past participle **descendu 5.** the use of **de** with **partir** and **sortir 6.** the difference between **rentrer** and **retourner 7.** the use of **avoir** and **être** with **passer**

PRONONCIATION

Les verbes auxiliaires **avoir** *et* **être**   2-15

As you practice when to use **avoir** and when to use **être** to form the **passé composé**, be careful to pronounce the forms of these auxiliary verbs distinctly.

tu as parlé / tu es parti(e)   il a parlé / il est parti   ils‿ont parlé / ils sont partis

A Prononcez bien! Écoutez les questions suivantes et écrivez les verbes auxiliaires que vous entendez (hear). Ensuite, posez les questions à un(e) partenaire.

1. Est-ce que tes parents _____ allés à l'université? Est-ce qu'ils _____ étudié le français? Est-ce qu'ils _____ fait du sport?
2. Où est-ce que ta mère _____ née? Où est-ce qu'elle _____ passé sa jeunesse (youth)? Dans quelles villes est-ce qu'elle _____ habité?

B Tu es parti(e) en week-end? Pensez à la dernière fois que vous êtes parti(e) en week-end. Votre partenaire va vous poser des questions au sujet de ce week-end.

EXEMPLE où / aller
— Où est-ce que tu es allé(e)?
— Je suis allé(e) à Deauville.

1. quand / partir
2. comment / y aller
3. quand / arriver
4. où / descendre
5. combien de temps / rester
6. quand / rentrer

Maintenant, posez ces mêmes questions au professeur.

EXEMPLE — Où est-ce que vous êtes allé(e)?
— Je suis allé(e) à Rome.

C Qu'est-ce que tu as fait? Posez ces questions à votre partenaire au sujet de la dernière fois qu'il/qu'elle a mangé au restaurant avec un(e) ami(e) ou avec des amis.

EXEMPLE — Avec qui est-ce que tu es sorti(e)?
— Je suis sorti(e) avec Thomas et Karima.

1. Avec qui est-ce que tu es sorti(e)?
2. Vous êtes allé(e)s à quel restaurant?
3. Vers quelle heure est-ce que vous êtes arrivé(e)s au restaurant?
4. Combien de temps est-ce que vous êtes resté(e)s au restaurant?
5. Vers quelle heure est-ce que tu es rentré(e)?

D Le week-end dernier. Regardez les illustrations et formez des phrases pour dire qui a fait chacune des choses indiquées: **Cathy, Evan** ou **Vincent et Alice.** *Attention!* Certains verbes sont conjugués avec **avoir,** mais d'autres prennent **être.**

EXEMPLE aller à Nice   **Cathy est allée à Nice.**
voir des amis   **Vincent et Alice ont vu des amis.**

Cathy

Evan

Vincent et Alice

1. sortir en couple
2. aller ensemble chez des amis
3. arriver à l'hôtel du Vieux Nice en taxi
4. faire du ski
5. descendre à l'hôtel du Vieux Nice
6. avoir un accident de ski
7. tomber en faisant du ski (while skiing)
8. aller à l'hôpital
9. prendre un verre chez des amis
10. rentrer la jambe cassée (with a broken leg)

Script for A. Prononcez bien! 1. Est-ce que tes parents sont allés à l'université? Est-ce qu'ils ont étudié le français? Est-ce qu'ils ont fait du sport? 2. Où est-ce que ta mère est née? Où est-ce qu'elle a passé sa jeunesse? Dans quelles villes est-ce qu'elle a habité?

Follow-ups for A. Prononcez bien!
A. Hand out index cards with three or four sentences in the **passé composé** on each. Make sure to create sentences with verbs that use both **avoir** and **être** as the auxiliary. Have each student read his/her set aloud. The other students will write down the verb they hear each time. **B.** Give the following sentences about Alice's day as dictation. After correcting them together, have students look back at the illustrations on page 182 and correct the information given, first negating the sentence and then supplying the correct information. EXEMPLE Samedi matin, Alice est restée au lit jusqu'à midi. **Non, Alice n'est pas restée au lit jusqu'à midi. Elle est restée au lit jusqu'à 10 heures.** 1. Elle a pris son petit déjeuner au café. 2. Samedi après-midi, elle est restée à la maison. 3. Elle a déjeuné chez elle. 4. Elle a travaillé. 5. Samedi soir, elle est allée chez un ami. 6. Elle a vu une pièce au théâtre. 7. Samedi soir, elle est allée en ville. 8. Elle a fait beaucoup de choses samedi soir.

Follow-ups for D. Le week-end dernier.
A. Have students think of one question to ask another student for each illustration. **B.** Have students recount Robert's, Thomas's, and Gabriel's trip to New Orleans as depicted on page 156 in the **passé composé**. Ask follow-up questions such as: 1. À quelle heure est-ce que Robert a quitté la maison? 2. Comment est-ce que les trois amis ont voyagé? 3. Quelle ville est-ce qu'ils ont visitée? 4. Quel quartier est-ce qu'ils ont visité? 5. À quelle heure est-ce qu'ils sont rentrés?

Sélection musicale. Search the Web for the song **"Le picbois"** by Boom Desjardins to enjoy a musical selection illustrating the use of this structure.

 PowerPoint 5-6

TELLING WHEN YOU DID SOMETHING

Pour vérifier

1. How do you say *last month*? *last week*? *last year*? *the last time*? How do you say *last*? What is the feminine form? Does it go before or after the noun in most of these expressions? What is the exception? Most of the expressions with **dernier (dernière)** are preceded by **le** or **la**. Which one is not?

2. How do you say that you did something *yesterday*? *yesterday morning*? *yesterday evening / last night*?

3. How would you say *for two hours*? How do you say *for* when talking about time in the past?

4. How do you say *ago*? How do you say *a year ago*? *a long time ago*?

5. What do **déjà** and **ne... pas encore** mean? Where do you place them?

Les expressions qui désignent le passé et reprise du passé composé

The following expressions are useful when talking about the past.

hier (matin, après-midi)	yesterday (morning, afternoon)
hier soir	last night, yesterday evening
lundi (mardi...) dernier	last Monday (Tuesday . . .)
le week-end dernier	last weekend
la semaine dernière	last week
le mois dernier	last month
l'année dernière	last year
la dernière fois	the last time
récemment	recently
Pendant combien de temps?	For how long?
pendant deux heures (longtemps)	for two hours (a long time)
Il y a combien de temps?	How long ago?
il y a trois jours (cinq ans, quelques semaines, deux minutes, trois secondes...)	three days (five years, a few weeks, two minutes, three seconds . . .) ago
déjà	already, ever
ne... pas encore	not yet

Most of these time expressions go at the beginning or end of a clause or sentence. However, **déjà** is placed between the two parts of the verb in the **passé composé**. When using **ne... pas encore,** place **ne** immediately after the subject and **pas encore** between the two parts of the verb.

— Tu as **déjà** fait tes devoirs?   — Have you **already** done your homework?

— Non, je **n'ai pas encore** fait mes devoirs.   — No, I **haven't** done my homework **yet**.

— Moi, j'ai fait mes devoirs **il y a trois heures.**   — I did my homework **three hours ago.**

Note *de vocabulaire*

1. Use **an** (m) instead of **année** (f) after a number: **il y a trois ans.**

2. To say *a week ago*, people in France often use **il y a huit jours**; and to say *two weeks ago,* **il y a quinze jours.**

Suggestion. Tell students to always keep **pas encore** together and that it is most often pronounced with liaison between **pas** and **encore**.

Warm-ups for A. Quand? A. Est-ce que ces expressions évoquent **le passé** ou **le présent**? aujourd'hui, hier, hier soir, maintenant, la semaine dernière, l'année dernière, il y a cinq ans, cette semaine, récemment, cette année, ce mois-ci
B. Write expressions from the list on slips of paper. Pass them out in mixed order. Have one student stand in front of the class and read his/her slip of paper. Form a timeline by having students read the expressions they have, one at a time, and place themselves to the left or right of the students already standing in front of the class, according to whether their expression is before or after the others'.

Suggestion for A. Quand? Allow students time to prepare this exercise.

A **Quand?** Voici le calendrier de Cathy. Quand est-ce qu'elle a fait les choses indiquées? Aujourd'hui, c'est le 14 novembre.

EXEMPLE   beaucoup travailler (la semaine dernière, le mois dernier)
    Cathy a beaucoup travaillé le mois dernier.

1. dîner chez une amie (il y a trois jours, le mois dernier)
2. aller au Louvre (il y a un mois, il y a deux semaines)
3. préparer un examen (la semaine dernière, hier)
4. passer *(to take)* l'examen (la semaine dernière, hier)
5. faire du shopping (il y a une semaine, le week-end dernier)
6. passer le week-end à Deauville (il y a une semaine, le week-end dernier)

B Déjà? Demandez à un(e) partenaire s'il/si elle a déjà fait ces choses. Utilisez **ne... pas encore** pour les réponses négatives.

EXEMPLE faire ses devoirs aujourd'hui
— Tu as déjà fait tes devoirs aujourd'hui?
— Oui, j'ai déjà fait mes devoirs.
   Non, je n'ai pas encore fait mes devoirs.

1. aller au bureau du prof ce semestre/trimestre
2. apprendre tout le vocabulaire de ce chapitre
3. être absent(e) ce mois
4. travailler en groupes avec tous les autres étudiants

C Et toi? Circulez parmi vos camarades de classe et posez des questions pour trouver quelqu'un qui a fait chacune des choses suivantes récemment. Après, dites à la classe qui a fait chaque chose et quand il/elle l'a faite.

EXEMPLE voir un bon film
— Sam, tu as vu un bon film récemment?
— Non, je n'ai pas vu de bon film récemment.
— Lisa, tu as vu un bon film récemment?
— Oui, j'ai vu un bon film hier soir.

Après, à la classe: Lisa a vu un bon film hier soir...

> voir un bon film   faire de l'exercice   partir en week-end   être malade *(sick)*
> aller au café avec des amis   sortir avec des amis
> arriver en cours en retard *(late)*   rentrer à la maison après minuit

D Entretien. Posez ces paires de questions à votre partenaire.

EXEMPLE tu / aller au café ce matin
tu / prendre un café ce matin
— Tu es allé(e) au café ce matin?
— Non, je ne suis pas allé(e) au café.
— Tu as pris un café?
— Oui, j'ai pris un café chez moi.

1. tu / aller au cinéma récemment
   tu / voir un bon film récemment
2. tu / venir en cours la semaine dernière
   tu / bien comprendre la leçon sur le passé composé
3. tes amis et toi, vous / sortir ensemble le week-end dernier
   vous / prendre un verre ensemble récemment
4. tu / étudier ici l'année dernière
   tu / venir étudier ici à l'université il y a combien de temps
5. tu / dormir jusqu'à quelle heure ce matin
   tu / partir de chez toi à quelle heure ce matin
6. tu / rester chez toi samedi dernier
   tu / réviser tes cours pendant combien de temps samedi dernier

---

Warm-ups for C. Et toi? A. Vrai ou faux? (Note: You may need to revise some of these sentences depending on your class in order to have a good mix of true and false answers.) **1.** Nous avons eu un examen hier après-midi. **2.** Le cours a commencé il y a dix minutes. **3.** Hier, nous avons été en cours pendant une heure. **4.** Aujourd'hui, on a parlé français ensemble pour la première fois. **5.** Le semestre / trimestre a commencé il y a trois mois. **6.** Nous avons écouté de la musique en cours la semaine dernière. **7.** Nous avons regardé un film le mois dernier. **B.** Give the preceding sentences as dictation.

Supplemental activities. A. Have students write a paragraph telling what they did yesterday. Ask them to mention at least five things. To get them started, you may want to give them this sentence: **Hier, j'ai quitté la maison à... heures et je suis allé(e)... B. Questions personnelles.** Est-ce que vous êtes parti(e) en week-end récemment? La dernière fois que vous êtes parti(e) en week-end, où est-ce que vous êtes allé(e)? Quand est-ce que vous êtes parti(e)? Est-ce que vous avez pris votre voiture? Où est-ce que vous êtes resté(e)? Combien de temps est-ce que vous êtes resté(e)? Qu'est-ce que vous avez fait? Quand est-ce que vous êtes rentré(e)? **C.** Have students work in pairs to prepare the following conversation: **C'est lundi matin et vous parlez de ce que** *(what)* **vous avez fait le week-end dernier. Pour chaque activité que votre partenaire mentionne, demandez plus de renseignements.**

COMPÉTENCE 3

Discussing the weather and your activities

 PowerPoint 5-7

LE TEMPS ET LES PROJETS

Note culturelle

En France, la température est indiquée en degrés Celsius. Pour calculer l'équivalent en degrés Fahrenheit, utilisez la formule suivante: (°C × 1,8) + 32.

La météo *(weather forecast)* est omniprésente à la télé, dans les journaux et les magazines. C'est aussi le sujet de conversation le plus utilisé en France. **Parler de la pluie et du beau temps** est une expression populaire qui signifie parler de tout et de rien, dire des banalités. Est-ce qu'on parle souvent de la météo chez vous?

Vocabulaire supplémentaire

Il fait bon. *The weather's nice.*
Il fait humide. *It's humid.*
Il y a des nuages. / C'est nuageux. *It's cloudy.*
Il y a du brouillard. *It's foggy.*
Il y a du verglas. *It's icy.*
Il grêle. *It's hailing.*
Il y a un orage. *There's a storm.*
C'est orageux. *It's stormy.*
Le ciel est couvert. *The sky is overcast.*

Warm-up. Avez-vous fait ces choses récemment? Quand? aller en ville, jouer au tennis, réviser vos cours, retrouver des amis au café, aller au théâtre, sortir en boîte, louer un DVD, faire une promenade, aller à la salle de gym, rentrer tard, visiter une autre ville, arriver en cours en retard *(late)*, prendre le petit déjeuner au café, rester à la maison toute la journée

Sélection musicale. Search the Web for the song **"Nuages"** by Grégoire to enjoy a musical selection related to this vocabulary.

Quel temps fait-il aujourd'hui?

Il fait froid.

Il fait **frais.**

Il fait chaud.

Il fait beau.

Il fait mauvais.

Il fait (du) soleil.

Il fait/Il y a du vent.

Il pleut.

Il neige.

Quelle **saison** préférez-vous? Qu'est-ce que vous faites **pendant** cette saison? Est-ce que vos projets **dépendent du temps qu'il fait**?

J'adore **l'été** *(m)*. En été,...

je vais à la plage.
je fais du bateau et du ski nautique.

J'aime l'automne *(m)*. En automne,...

je fais du camping.
je **fais du VTT.**

J'aime beaucoup **l'hiver** *(m)*. En hiver,...

je vais à la montagne.
je fais du ski.

J'adore **le printemps.** Au printemps,...

je vais au parc.
je fais des randonnées.

Line art on this page: © Cengage Learning

Quel temps fait-il? *What is the weather like?*   **frais** *cool*   **la saison** *the season*   **pendant** *during, for*   **dépendre de** *to depend on*   **le temps qu'il fait** *what the weather is like*   **l'été** *summer*   **faire du VTT (vélo tout terrain)** *to go all-terrain biking*   **l'hiver** *winter*   **le printemps** *spring*   **faire une randonnée (faire des randonnées)** *to go for a hike (to go hiking, to hike)*

C'est vendredi après-midi et Alice et Cathy parlent de leurs projets pour le week-end.

ALICE: S'il fait beau demain, je vais faire une promenade au jardin du Luxembourg. J'ai besoin de faire de l'exercice. Et toi, qu'est-ce que tu as l'intention de faire?
CATHY: S'il fait beau, j'ai envie de faire du jogging.
ALICE: Et s'il fait mauvais?
CATHY: S'il fait mauvais, je ne vais rien faire de spécial.

Note de grammaire

The use of **si** (*if*) clauses is as common in French as it is in English. As in English, when the verb in the *if* clause is in the present tense, the verb in the second clause is in the present tense, the immediate future, or the imperative.
S'il pleut, j'aime rester chez moi.
S'il pleut demain, je vais rester chez moi.
S'il pleut demain, je reste chez toi.

Note for the conversation. New vocabulary presented in the conversation includes **si**, **jardin**, and **rien de spécial**.

A Et chez vous?
Chez vous, en quelle saison fait-il le temps indiqué?

EXEMPLE Il neige.
Ici, il neige souvent (rarement, quelquefois) en hiver.
Ici, il ne neige jamais.

1. Il fait frais.
2. Il fait du vent.
3. Il fait mauvais.
4. Il fait très beau.
5. Il fait froid.
6. Il fait chaud.
7. Il fait du soleil.
8. Il pleut.
9. Il neige.

B Et vous?
Complétez les phrases.

1. Quand il fait beau, j'aime...
2. S'il fait beau ce week-end, j'ai l'intention de...
3. Quand il pleut, je préfère...
4. S'il fait mauvais ce week-end, je vais...
5. À la montagne, j'aime...
6. À la plage, j'aime...

Quel temps fait-il aujourd'hui?

C Quel temps fait-il?
Demandez à un(e) partenaire quel temps il fait aux moments indiqués. Il/Elle doit répondre en utilisant au moins *deux* expressions pour décrire le temps.

EXEMPLE en automne
— Quel temps fait-il en automne?
— Il fait beau et il fait frais.

1. en hiver
2. en été
3. en automne
4. au printemps
5. aujourd'hui

Suggestion for the conversation. Set the scene and explain that the **jardin du Luxembourg** is a park in the center of Paris. Point out that **si** means *if* and that it only elides before **il(s)**. Have students listen to the conversation with books closed for the answers to these questions. 1. Qu'est-ce qu'Alice voudrait faire demain s'il fait beau? Pourquoi? 2. Qu'est-ce que Cathy voudrait faire s'il fait beau? Et s'il fait mauvais?

D Entretien.
Posez ces questions à votre partenaire.

1. Aimes-tu l'été? Aimes-tu aller à la plage? Aimes-tu nager? Préfères-tu faire du bateau ou faire du ski nautique?
2. Aimes-tu l'hiver? Aimes-tu aller à la montagne? Préfères-tu faire des randonnées ou faire du ski? Aimes-tu faire du camping? du VTT?
3. Qu'est-ce que tu aimes faire quand il fait chaud? Et quand il fait froid? Et quand il neige?
4. Quelle saison préfères-tu? Quel temps fait-il d'habitude? Qu'est-ce que tu aimes faire pendant cette saison?

Follow-up for A. Et chez vous? Quelle description du temps n'est pas logique par rapport aux autres? (You may wish to show students the statements.) 1. Il fait chaud, il fait du soleil et il neige. 2. Il neige, il fait chaud et il fait froid. 3. Il fait du soleil, il pleut et il fait mauvais. 4. Il fait mauvais, il fait beau et il fait du soleil. 5. Il pleut, il fait du soleil et il fait beau.

À VOUS!

Avec un(e) partenaire, relisez à haute voix la conversation entre Alice et Cathy. Ensuite, adaptez la conversation pour parler de vos projets pour le week-end.

You can find a list of the new words from this **Compétence** on page 215 and access the audio online.

S'il *If it* (**si** *if*)

 **PowerPoint 5-8**

TALKING ABOUT THE WEATHER AND WHAT YOU DO

✓ Pour vérifier

1. What is the present tense of **faire**? How is the **vous** form of this verb different from the usual **vous** form of a verb? What does the verb mean?

2. How do you say that you are doing *nothing*?

3. How do you say *What is the weather like? The weather is nice! It is raining? It is snowing?* How do you say *What is the weather going to be like? It is going to be nice? It is going to rain? It is going to snow?* How do you say *What was the weather like? It was nice? It rained? It snowed?*

4. How do you say *I like snow? I like rain?*

Note de prononciation

The **ai** in **fais** and **fait** rhymes with the **ai** in **français**. The **ai** in **faites** rhymes with the **ai** in **française**, but the **ai** in **faisons** rhymes with the **e** in **je**.

iLrn Grammar Tutorials

Le verbe **faire**, *l'expression* **ne... rien** *et les expressions pour décrire le temps*

To say *to make* or *to do*, use the irregular verb **faire**.

FAIRE (to make, to do)	
je **fais**	nous **faisons**
tu **fais**	vous **faites**
il/elle/on **fait**	ils/elles **font**
PASSÉ COMPOSÉ: **j'ai fait**	

— Qu'est-ce que tu fais ce soir?
— Je reste à la maison. Je fais mes devoirs.

— Qu'est-ce que papa fait dans la cuisine?
— Il fait des sandwichs.

To say that you do *nothing* or you do *not* do *anything*, use **ne... rien**. This expression can be the subject or object of the verb, or the object of a preposition.

Rien n'est prêt.   Je **n'**achète **rien**.   Je **n'**ai besoin de **rien**.

When negating an infinitive, place both parts of the negative expression before it.

Je préfère **ne pas** sortir ce soir.   Je voudrais **ne rien** faire demain soir.

The verb **faire** is used in many, but not all, weather expressions. You will also need the infinitives and past participles **pleuvoir** *(to rain)* → **plu** and **neiger** *(to snow)* → **neigé**. Use **la pluie** to say *(the) rain* and **la neige** to say *(the) snow*.

AUJOURD'HUI	DEMAIN	HIER
Quel temps fait-il?	Quel temps va-t-il faire?	Quel temps a-t-il fait?
Il fait beau / du vent...	Il va faire beau / du vent...	Il a fait beau / du vent...
Il pleut.	Il va pleuvoir.	Il a plu.
Il neige.	Il va neiger.	Il a neigé.

Aimez-vous faire du camping?

A **Que faites-vous?** Dites ou demandez si ces personnes font les choses indiquées.

1. Moi, je...
   faire beaucoup de choses seul(e)
   faire beaucoup de choses le soir

2. Mon meilleur ami (Ma meilleure amie)...
   faire beaucoup de choses pour moi
   faire souvent du VTT

3. En cours, nous...
   faire beaucoup d'exercices ensemble
   faire les devoirs en ligne

4. Mes parents...
   faire beaucoup de choses ensemble
   faire souvent du sport

5. *[au professeur]* Est-ce que vous...?
   faire souvent du camping
   faire souvent du bateau

196 cent quatre-vingt-seize | CHAPITRE 5

B Quel temps va-t-il faire? Voilà la météo *(weather forecast)* pour certaines régions de France pour demain. Pour chaque région, dites quel temps il va faire. Utilisez deux expressions pour chaque région.

EXEMPLE Demain, en Bretagne, il va faire frais et….

1. Demain, en Bretagne…
2. Demain, dans les Alpes…
3. Demain, sur la Côte d'Azur…

Maintenant, imaginez qu'hier dans ces régions, il a fait le même temps qu'il va faire demain. Dites quel temps il a fait dans chaque région.

EXEMPLE Hier, en Bretagne, il a fait frais et…

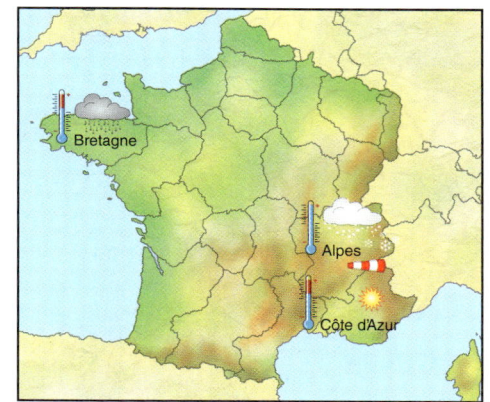
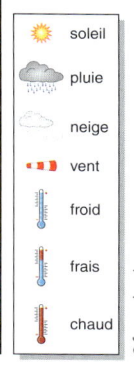

C Qu'est-ce qu'ils ont fait? Alice parle des activités récentes de sa famille et du temps qu'il a fait ce jour-là. Complétez ses phrases. Utilisez deux expressions pour décrire le temps.

EXEMPLE Hier, j'**ai lu un livre**. Il **a fait mauvais et il a plu** toute la journée.

EXEMPLE Hier, j'…
Il… toute la journée.

1. À Deauville, nous…
Il…

2. Vendredi dernier, Vincent et moi…
Il…

3. À Chamonix, les enfants… Il…

4. Hier, Vincent…
Il…

5. Ce matin, Vincent et notre fils… Il…

Warm-up for B. Quel temps va-t-il faire? C'est logique? **1.** Je voudrais faire une randonnée parce qu'il pleut. **2.** Mes parents font du bateau quand il neige. **3.** Je préfère jouer au tennis quand il ne fait pas très chaud. **4.** Je fais toujours du ski quand il pleut. **5.** Quand il fait mauvais, je reste à la maison et je ne fais rien. **6.** Mon ami(e) va aller au parc après les cours parce qu'il fait beau.

D Entretien. Interviewez votre partenaire.

1. Qu'est-ce que tu aimes faire le vendredi soir? le samedi soir? Qu'est-ce que tu fais d'habitude le dimanche matin?
2. Quel temps va-t-il faire ce week-end? Qu'est-ce que tu as envie de faire s'il fait beau? Qu'est-ce que tu as l'intention de faire s'il fait mauvais? Qu'est-ce que tu vas faire samedi soir? Est-ce que tu préfères ne rien faire quelquefois?

Note *de grammaire*

Questions asked with **faire** are often answered with a different verb.
— Qu'est-ce que tu fais le samedi matin?
— Je regarde la télé.

PowerPoint 5-9

✓ **Pour vérifier**

1. How do you say *to go camping? to take a trip? to do housework? to do laundry?*

2. In the expressions with **faire**, which articles change to **de (d')** in a negative sentence? Which do not?

iLrn Grammar Tutorials

Vocabulaire supplémentaire

aller à la chasse/chasser *to go hunting / to hunt*
aller à la pêche/pêcher *to go fishing / to fish*
faire de la muscu(lation) *to do body building*
faire de la varappe / de l'escalade *to go rock climbing*
faire du cheval / de l'équitation *to go horseback riding*
faire du patin (à glace) *to go (ice-)skating*
faire du roller *to go rollerblading*
faire du snowboard *to go snowboarding*
faire la fête *to party*
faire de la marche *to go walking*

Note. Remind students of expressions with **faire** from previous chapters or earlier in this chapter: **faire de la musique, faire des projets, faire un tour, faire du jogging, faire du sport,** and **faire les devoirs.**

Warm-up for A. Un besoin ou une envie? C'est amusant ou ennuyeux? faire une promenade, faire le ménage, faire les devoirs, faire du shopping, faire la cuisine, faire du bateau, faire du camping, faire des courses

Warm-ups for B. Préférences. A. Quelle activité préférez-vous? (You may wish to supply the expressions **J'aime faire les deux. / Je n'aime ni l'un ni l'autre.**) **EXEMPLE** faire une promenade / faire du shopping : **Je préfère faire une promenade. / Je préfère faire du shopping. / J'aime faire les deux. 1.** faire du jogging / faire des promenades **2.** faire la cuisine / faire la vaisselle **3.** faire du bateau / faire du camping **4.** faire du sport / faire du jardinage **5.** faire le ménage / faire la lessive **6.** faire du ski / faire du ski nautique **B.** Have students say how often they do each of the preceding activities. **EXEMPLE** Je fais une promenade tous les jours. / Je fais une promenade deux ou trois fois par semaine. / Je ne fais jamais de promenade.

TALKING ABOUT ACTIVITIES

Les expressions avec faire

The verb **faire** can have a variety of meanings in idiomatic expressions.

LE SPORT ET LES DISTRACTIONS	LE MÉNAGE ET LES COURSES
faire de l'exercice	faire des courses *(to run errands)*
faire du bateau	faire les courses *(to buy groceries)*
faire du camping	faire du jardinage *(to garden)*
faire du jogging	faire la cuisine *(to cook)*
faire du shopping	faire la lessive *(to do laundry)*
faire du ski (nautique)	faire la vaisselle *(to do the dishes)*
faire du sport (du tennis, du hockey,...)	faire le ménage *(to do housework)*
faire du vélo	
faire du VTT	
faire une promenade	
faire une randonnée	
faire un voyage *(to take a trip)*	

The **un, une, des, du, de la,** and **de l'** in the expressions with **faire** become **de (d')** when the verb is negated. The definite article (**le, la, l', les**) does not change.

Je ne fais pas **de** jogging en hiver.   Nous ne faisons pas **la** cuisine le matin.

A **Un besoin ou une envie?** Commencez ces phrases logiquement avec **J'ai envie de...** ou **J'ai besoin de...**

EXEMPLE   faire des devoirs   J'ai besoin de faire des devoirs.
             faire du ski   J'ai envie de faire du ski.

1. faire des courses
2. faire du bateau
3. faire la lessive
4. faire du vélo
5. faire le ménage
6. faire la cuisine
7. faire la vaisselle
8. rester à la maison et ne rien faire

Aimez-vous faire du snowboard?

B **Préférences.** Écrivez les activités suivantes dans l'ordre de vos préférences. Votre partenaire va vous poser des questions pour déterminer l'ordre des activités sur votre feuille de papier.

| faire du jogging | faire des randonnées | faire du jardinage |
| faire la cuisine | faire du vélo | ne rien faire |

EXEMPLE   —Préfères-tu faire du jogging ou ne rien faire?
             —Je préfère ne rien faire.
             —Préfères-tu ne rien faire ou faire la cuisine?...

198 cent quatre-vingt-dix-huit | CHAPITRE 5

C **Que font-ils?** Éric parle des projets de la famille pour aujourd'hui. Complétez ses phrases avec une expression avec **faire**.

1. Maman… ce matin.
2. Maman et Michel…
3. Papa… cet après-midi.

4. Papa et maman…
5. Cathy et moi, nous…
6. Moi, je…

D **Activités.** Complétez les phrases avec une expression avec **faire**. Ensuite, dites si c'est vrai pour vos amis et vous. Corrigez les phrases fausses.

1. Je _____ au centre commercial le samedi.
2. Mes amis et moi aimons jouer au tennis et au basket. Nous _____ ensemble tous les week-ends.
3. Mes parents ont un joli jardin. Ils aiment _____.
4. Chez moi, tout est toujours propre parce que je _____ tous les week-ends.
5. Je vais _____ aujourd'hui après les cours. J'ai besoin d'aller au bureau de poste et à la banque.

| faire la cuisine |
| faire du sport |
| faire du jardinage |
| faire la lessive |
| faire du shopping |
| faire des courses |
| faire une promenade |
| faire le ménage |
| faire la vaisselle |
| faire du vélo |
| faire les courses |

E **Conseils.** Donnez des conseils à un ami. Utilisez une expression avec **faire** et mettez le verbe à l'impératif.

EXEMPLE — La vaisselle est sale.
— Eh bien, fais la vaisselle!

1. J'ai faim.
2. Tous mes vêtements sont sales.
3. J'ai envie de faire de l'exercice.
4. J'ai besoin d'acheter de nouveaux vêtements.
5. Mon appartement est très sale.
6. Il n'y a pas de café, de fromage ou de lait à la maison!

COMPÉTENCE 4

Deciding what to wear and buying clothes

 PowerPoint 5-10

iLrn In the **Culture Modules** in the video library, see **Fashion**.

Vocabulaire supplémentaire

un blouson *a windbreaker, a jacket*
une casquette *a cap*
une ceinture *a belt*
un chapeau *a hat*
des chaussettes *(f) socks*
un col roulé *a turtleneck*
un débardeur *a tank top*
un legging *leggings*
un pyjama *pajamas*
des sous-vêtements *(m) underwear*
un sweat-shirt *a sweatshirt*
un tailleur *a woman's suit*
des hauts talons *(m) high heels*
une tunique *a tunic*
une veste *a sports coat*

LES VÊTEMENTS

Warm-up activity. Questions orales. Quel temps fait-il aujourd'hui? Qu'est-ce que vous aimez faire quand il fait...? Quel temps va-t-il faire ce week-end? Qu'est-ce que vous allez faire? Quel temps a-t-il fait le week-end dernier? Qu'est-ce que vous avez fait?

Qu'est-ce que vous **mettez** pour aller en cours? pour sortir le soir?
Qu'est-ce que vous **avez mis** ce matin? hier soir?

Je mets souvent...   Je mets **parfois**...   Ce matin, j'ai mis...

un jean   un short   un pantalon   une jupe

un pull   un polo ou un tee-shirt   une chemise et une cravate   un chemisier

Note *de vocabulaire*

Porter means *to carry* or *to wear* and **mettre** *to put, to put on,* or *to wear*. They can both be used to say what one wears in general, although **mettre** is more commonly used in this case and in the **passé composé**.
Il porte/met souvent un jean. Il a mis un jean hier. Use **porter** to say what someone is wearing at a particular moment. **Aujourd'hui, il porte un pantalon blanc.**

The forms of **mettre** are:

je mets	nous mettons
tu mets	vous mettez
il/elle/on met	ils/elles mettent

PASSÉ COMPOSÉ: **j'ai mis**

The verb **essayer** means both *to try* and *to try on*. It is a -yer spelling-change verb, like **envoyer**.

The forms of **essayer** are:

j' essaie	nous essayons
tu essaies	vous essayez
il/elle/on essaie	ils/elles essaient

PASSÉ COMPOSÉ: **j'ai essayé**

un survêtement   une robe   un costume   des chaussures (f), des baskets (f), des bottes (f), des sandales (f) ou des tongs (f)

un anorak   un imperméable   un manteau   un maillot de bain ou un bikini

J'emporte...   Je porte...

un parapluie   un sac ou un portefeuille   une montre   des lunettes de soleil

Sélection musicale. Search the Web for the song **"Je vends des robes"** by Nino Ferrer to enjoy a musical selection related to this vocabulary.

Line art on this page: © Cengage Learning

mettez (mettre *to put, to put on*)   **avez mis (mettre** past participle: **mis**)   **parfois** *sometimes*   **emporter** *to take (along), to carry (away)*

200 *deux cents* | CHAPITRE 5

Alice Pérez cherche un nouveau maillot de bain. Elle entre dans un magasin.

LA VENDEUSE: Bonjour, madame. **Je peux vous aider?**
ALICE: Je cherche un maillot de bain.
LA VENDEUSE: **Quelle taille faites-vous?**
ALICE: **Je fais du** 42.
LA VENDEUSE: Nous avons **ces** maillots**-ci.** Ils sont très jolis et ils sont **en solde.**
ALICE: J'aime bien ce maillot noir. **Je peux l'essayer?**
LA VENDEUSE: **Bien sûr,** madame. **La cabine d'essayage** est **par ici.**

Alice sort de la cabine d'essayage.

LA VENDEUSE: Alors, **qu'en pensez-vous**?
ALICE: **Il me plaît** beaucoup. Il **coûte** combien?
LA VENDEUSE: **Voyons,** c'est 65 euros.
ALICE: C'est bien. Alors, je **le** prends.

Note culturelle

Notez que les tailles en France ne sont pas les mêmes qu'aux USA.

Robes et chemisiers		Chemises hommes	
USA	FRANCE	USA	FRANCE
8	38	15	38
10	40	15 ½	39
12	42	16	40
14	44	16 ½	41
16	46	17	42

Chaussures femmes		Chaussures hommes	
USA	FRANCE	USA	FRANCE
5	35	7	39
6	36	8	41
7	37 ½	9	43
8	38 ½	10	44
8 ½	39	11	45
9	40	12	46
9 ½	41	13	47
10	42	14	48

Avez-vous déjà acheté des vêtements avec la taille française sur l'étiquette *(tag)* ou des chaussures avec la pointure *(shoe size)* française?

A **Préférences.** Complétez ces phrases pour parler de vos préférences.

1. Quand il fait froid, je préfère mettre *un pantalon et un pull / un survêtement / un manteau ou un anorak.*
2. Quand il fait chaud, je préfère mettre *un jean / un pantalon / un short / un maillot de bain* et *un polo / un tee-shirt / une chemise / un chemisier.*
3. Pour aller à la plage, je mets le plus souvent *un bikini / un maillot de bain / un short.*
4. Quand il fait du soleil, *je mets / je ne mets pas* souvent *des/de* lunettes de soleil.
5. Quand il pleut, je préfère *emporter un parapluie / mettre un imperméable.*
6. Je porte *souvent / rarement* une montre. *(Je préfère regarder l'heure sur mon téléphone portable.)*
7. Comme chaussures, je préfère mettre *des baskets / des bottes / des sandales / des tongs.*
8. Normalement, je mets mon argent dans *un sac / un portefeuille / ma poche* (pocket).

B **Entretien.** Interviewez votre partenaire.

1. Tu aimes faire du shopping? Tu préfères acheter des vêtements, des CD, des DVD, des jeux vidéo ou des livres?
2. Tu préfères acheter tes vêtements au centre commercial, dans les petits magasins, dans un magasin d'occasion *(second-hand store)* ou sur Internet?
3. Pour aller à un mariage ou à un entretien *(interview)*, qu'est-ce que tu préfères mettre?

À VOUS!

Avec un(e) partenaire, relisez à haute voix la conversation entre la vendeuse et Alice. Après, adaptez la conversation pour acheter un jean, un anorak ou un manteau. Jouez le rôle d'Alice et votre partenaire va jouer le rôle du vendeur (de la vendeuse). Ensuite, échangez les rôles.

---

une vendeuse (un vendeur) *a salesclerk* **Je peux vous aider?** *Can I help you?* **Quelle taille faites-vous?** *What size do you wear?* **Je fais du...** *I wear size...* **ces... -ci / là** *these / those... over here / over there* **en solde** *on sale* **Je peux l'essayer? (essayer)** *Can I try it on? (to try, to try on)* **Bien sûr** *Of course* **La cabine d'essayage** *The fitting room* **par ici** *this way* **qu'en pensez-vous?** *what do you think about it?* **Il me plaît. (plaire)** *I like it. / It pleases me. (to please)* **coûter** *to cost* **Voyons** *Let's see* **le (l')** *it, him* **(la, l')** *it, her*

 **PowerPoint 5-11**

✓ Pour vérifier

1. How do you say the direct object pronouns *him, her, it,* and *them* in French?

2. Where do you place the direct object pronouns and **y** when there is an infinitive? in the **passé composé**? Where do you place them otherwise? Where do you place them in a negative sentence?

Grammar Tutorials

Suggestion. Review the pronoun **y** and point out to students that it follows the same placement rules as the direct object pronouns.

Suggestion. You may wish to present the forms and use of the direct object pronouns and briefly point out their position before the verb, then proceed to *A. Au magasin de vêtements, B. À Paris,* and *C. Le samedi.* You can then present their position with an infinitive and do *D. Intentions,* and then the position and agreement in the **passé composé** and do *E. Et vous?* and *F. Le week-end des Pérez.* Finally, review all the position rules and finish the rest of the activities.

Follow-up for A. Au magasin de vêtements. Avez-vous ces choses avec vous aujourd'hui? **EXEMPLE** *Est-ce que vous avez votre livre de français?* **Oui, je l'ai. / Non, je ne l'ai pas.** *Est-ce que vous avez vos devoirs (votre cahier, vos livres pour vos autres cours, votre vélo, votre voiture, les questions du prochain examen)?*

AVOIDING REPETITION

Les pronoms **le, la, l'** *et* **les**

Use the direct object pronouns **le, la, l',** and **les** to replace a person, animal, or thing that is the direct object of the verb. Use **le** *(him, it)* to replace masculine singular nouns, **la** *(her, it)* to replace feminine singular nouns, and **les** *(them)* to replace all plural nouns. **Le** and **la** become **l'** when the following word begins with a vowel or silent **h.**

— Tu prends ce maillot? — Tu prends cette robe aussi?
— Oui, je **le** prends. — Oui, je **la** prends.
— Tu achètes cette chemise? — Tu achètes ces bottes?
— Oui, je **l'**achète. — Oui, je **les** achète.

	BEFORE A CONSONANT SOUND	BEFORE A VOWEL OR SILENT *H*
him, it (masculine)	le	l'
her, it (feminine)	la	l'
them	les	les

- Like **y**, these pronouns are generally placed *immediately before* the verb, even in the negative.

  — Tu aimes **cette chemise**? — Tu vas **au centre commercial**?
  — Oui, je **l'**aime bien. — Oui, j'**y** vais.
  Non, je ne **l'**aime pas. Non, je n'**y** vais pas.

- Place them *immediately before* an infinitive, if there is one in the clause.

  — Tu vas acheter **cette chemise**?
  — Oui, je vais **l'**acheter. / Non, je ne vais pas **l'**acheter.

- In the **passé composé,** direct object pronouns and **y** are placed *immediately before* the auxiliary verb (the conjugated form of **avoir** or **être**).

  Je **l'**ai fait. J'**y** suis allé(e).
  Je ne **l'**ai pas fait. Je n'**y** suis pas allé(e).

Generally, in the **passé composé,** the past participle agrees in gender and number with the subject when the auxiliary verb is **être,** but not when it is **avoir.** However, the past participle used with **avoir** will agree with *direct objects,* but only if they *precede* the verb, as with direct object pronouns.

Éric a acheté **cette chemise.** Il **l'**a acheté**e** hier.

Cathy a acheté **ces pulls.** Elle **les** a acheté**s** ce matin.

A **Au magasin de vêtements.** Alice et Vincent sont au magasin de vêtements. Complétez ce que chacun dit avec le pronom qui convient (**le, la, l', les**).

1. J'aime ce maillot de bain. Je peux _____ essayer?
2. J'aime ces bottes. Je _____ prends.
3. Je n'aime pas ce bikini. Je ne _____ prends pas.
4. Comment trouves-tu cette robe? Voudrais-tu _____ essayer?
5. Je n'aime pas cet anorak. Je ne vais pas _____ prendre.
6. Regarde cette belle cravate! Je _____ trouve super!

B **À Paris.** Dites si vous reconnaissez *(recognize)* ces sites parisiens. Utilisez **Je reconnais...** *(I recognize . . .)* et le pronom qui convient **(le, la, l', les)**.

Quick-reference answers for B. À Paris.
1. la cathédrale Notre-Dame 2. le Louvre
3. la tour Eiffel 4. la place de la Concorde
5. la Seine

EXEMPLE Cette avenue?
 Oui, je la reconnais. C'est les Champs-Élysées.
 Non, je ne la reconnais pas.

EXEMPLE Cette avenue? 1. Cette cathédrale? 2. Ce musée?

3. Cette tour? 4. Cette place? 5. Ce fleuve *(river)*?

C **Le samedi.** Dites si vous faites ou ne faites pas souvent ces choses. Remplacez les mots en italique avec **le, la, l'** ou **les**.

EXEMPLE écouter souvent *la radio* dans la voiture
 Oui, je l'écoute souvent dans la voiture.

1. faire souvent *le ménage* le samedi
2. passer souvent *le samedi soir* à la maison
3. regarder souvent *la télé* le matin
4. inviter souvent *mon meilleur ami (ma meilleure amie)* chez moi
5. faire souvent *les courses* le week-end
6. prendre souvent *le petit déjeuner* dans un café
7. réviser souvent *mes cours* le samedi soir

Follow-up for B. À Paris. Have students use **y** to answer the following questions. **1.** On va aux Champs-Élysées pour jouer au football ou pour faire du shopping? **2.** On va au Louvre pour voir une exposition ou pour voir un film? **3.** On va à la cathédrale Notre-Dame pour acheter des vêtements ou pour voir une belle église? **4.** On va aux Champs-Élysées pour passer l'après-midi au café ou pour nager? **5.** On va à la place de la Concorde pour voir des bâtiments intéressants ou pour faire du jogging? **6.** On va à Paris pour visiter une belle ville intéressante ou pour faire du ski?

D **Intentions.** Un(e) ami(e) voudrait savoir ce que vous allez faire avec les choses suivantes. Répondez en utilisant un pronom **(le, la, l', les)** et un verbe logique. Jouez les deux rôles avec un(e) partenaire.

EXEMPLE ces frites
 — Qu'est-ce que tu vas faire avec ces frites?
 — Je vais les manger!

1. ces vêtements   4. cette chemise   7. ce journal
2. ce DVD   5. ces bottes   8. ce CD
3. ce jus de fruit 6. cette eau minérale 9. ce sandwich

Compétence 4 | *deux cent trois* 203

Warm-up for E. Et vous? Give students these sentences. Tell them: Remplacez les mots en italique par le pronom qui convient. Faites attention à l'accord du participe passé. **EXEMPLE** Hier, j'ai pris *mon café* au lit. **Je l'ai pris au lit. 1.** Hier matin, j'ai pris *mon petit déjeuner* à la maison. **2.** J'ai fait *mes devoirs de chimie.* **3.** Je n'ai pas lu *le journal.* **4.** L'après-midi, j'ai retrouvé *mes amies Karima et Louise* au café. **5.** Après, nous avons regardé *le nouveau film avec Marion Cotillard* chez Karima. **6.** Hier soir, j'ai regardé *la télé.* **7.** Hier, je n'ai pas fait *la lessive.*

Follow-up for E. Et vous? Have students redo *C. Le samedi* and *D. Intentions* in the passé composé.

Suggestion for F. Le week-end des Pérez. Have a student, or students, read each paragraph with the photos aloud before beginning the items of each section of the activity.

E **Et vous?** Avez-vous fait ces choses le week-end dernier? Répondez en employant le pronom qui convient: **y, le, la, l'** ou **les**.

EXEMPLE Vous avez regardé *la télé* le week-end dernier?
 Oui, je l'ai regardée.
 Non, je ne l'ai pas regardée.

1. Vous êtes resté(e) *chez vous* tout le week-end?
2. Vous avez fait *le ménage*?
3. Vous avez fait *la lessive*?
4. Vous avez lu *le livre de français*?
5. Vous avez fait *vos devoirs*?
6. Vous avez dîné *au restaurant*?
7. Vous êtes allé(e) *au cinéma*?

F **Le week-end des Pérez.** Regardez les explications de ce que les Pérez ont fait le week-end dernier et complétez les réponses. Utilisez **y, le, la, l'** ou **les**.

EXEMPLE Qui est allé *au Quartier latin*?
 Éric et Michèle **y sont allés.**

1. Quand est-ce qu'ils sont allés *au Quartier latin*?
 Ils _____ vendredi après-midi.
2. Qui a commandé *les spaghettis à la carbonara*?
 Éric _____.
3. Qui a acheté *le nouveau livre de Jérôme Ferrari*?
 Michèle _____.
4. Où est-ce qu'ils ont retrouvé *leurs amis*?
 Ils _____ dans un café du quartier.
5. Avec qui est-ce qu'ils ont pris *leur café*?
 Ils _____ avec des amis.
6. Où est-ce qu'Éric et Michèle ont vu *le film avec Jean Reno*?
 Ils _____ au cinéma du Panthéon.

Vendredi après-midi, Éric et sa copine Michèle sont allés au Quartier latin, où ils ont mangé dans un restaurant italien. Michèle a mangé des raviolis et Éric a commandé des spaghettis à la carbonara. Après le repas, ils sont allés dans une librairie où Michèle a acheté un livre de Jérôme Ferrari. Après ça, ils ont retrouvé des amis dans un café du quartier et ils ont pris un café ensemble en terrasse. Plus tard, Éric et Michèle sont allés au cinéma du Panthéon pour voir le nouveau film avec Jean Reno.

7. Quand est-ce qu'Alice est allée *au musée d'Orsay*?

   Elle _____ samedi matin.

8. Où est-ce qu'elle a vu *la nouvelle exposition sur Cézanne*?

   Elle _____ au musée d'Orsay.

9. Elle a vu *les autres expositions du musée*?

   Non, elle _____.

10. Elle est allée *au cinéma* après le musée?

    Non, elle _____.

11. Où est-ce qu'elle a retrouvé *Vincent*?

    Elle _____ dans un restaurant du quartier.

Samedi matin, Alice est allée au musée d'Orsay, où elle a vu la nouvelle exposition de Cézanne. Elle n'a pas eu le temps de voir les autres expositions parce qu'elle est allée acheter une jupe dans un magasin de vêtements. Vers une heure et demie, elle a retrouvé Vincent dans un restaurant du quartier.

G Préférences. Répondez aux questions de votre ami(e) en remplaçant les mots en italique par le pronom qui convient. Jouez les rôles avec un(e) partenaire.

EXEMPLE — Je révise *mes leçons* tous les jours. Et toi?
— Moi aussi, je les révise tous les jours.
  Moi non, je ne les révise pas tous les jours.

1. Je regarde souvent *la télé* le week-end. Et toi?
2. J'ai envie de regarder *la télé* ce soir. Et toi?
3. J'invite souvent *mes parents* à la maison. Et toi?
4. Ce week-end, j'ai l'intention de voir *mes parents*. Et toi?
5. Je trouve *mes cours* plutôt difficiles. Et toi?
6. Ce soir, je vais préparer *le prochain examen de français*. Et toi?
7. Samedi soir, je vais faire *mes devoirs*. Et toi?
8. Samedi dernier, je suis allé(e) *au cinéma*. Et toi?
9. Dimanche dernier, j'ai fait *mes devoirs*. Et toi?
10. Hier soir, j'ai regardé *la télé*. Et toi?

H Entretien. Interviewez votre partenaire. Utilisez **y** ou un pronom complément d'objet direct pour remplacer les mots en italique dans vos réponses.

1. Est-ce que tu achètes *tes vêtements* au centre commercial? Dans quel magasin est-ce que tu achètes *tes vêtements* le plus souvent? Où est-ce que tu as acheté *les vêtements que tu portes maintenant*?
2. Chez toi, dans quelle pièce préfères-tu regarder *la télé*? Aimes-tu faire tes devoirs *dans cette pièce* aussi? Vas-tu passer beaucoup de temps *dans cette pièce* ce soir?
3. Invites-tu souvent *tes amis* chez toi? Où préfères-tu retrouver *tes amis*? La dernière fois que tu es sorti(e) avec des amis, où est-ce que tu as retrouvé *tes amis*?
4. Où aimes-tu passer *ton temps libre*? Où est-ce que tu as passé *la soirée* hier? Est-ce que tu vas passer la soirée *chez toi* ce soir?

VIDÉOREPRISE

Les Stagiaires

Rappel!
Matthieu, l'informaticien timide à Technovert, est amoureux fou d'Amélie *(crazy about Amélie)* mais trop timide pour le lui dire *(to tell her)*. Il parle aux autres pour découvrir tout ce qu'il peut *(to discover all that he can)* à son sujet.

See the **Résumé de grammaire** section at the end of each chapter for a review of all the grammar presented in the chapter.

The entire **Vidéoreprise** section is designed to be a pre-viewing series for the video, as well as a chapter review that can be used independently from the video. There are also additional grammar review exercises on the Instructor's Companion Website and on iLrn.

Dans l'*Épisode 5,* Matthieu parle à Christophe d'une soirée que Christophe, Rachid et Amélie ont passée ensemble. Avant de regarder l'épisode, faites ces exercices pour réviser ce que vous avez appris dans le **Chapitre 5**.

A **Samedi dernier.** Un ami pose des questions à Christophe sur ce qu'il a fait samedi dernier. Complétez ses questions en mettant les verbes au passé composé.

EXEMPLE Tu **es sorti** (sortir) avec des amis ou ils **sont venus** (venir) chez toi?

1. Avec qui est-ce que tu _____ (sortir)?
2. Tu _____ (retrouver) les autres en ville ou vous y _____ (aller) tous ensemble?
3. Tu _____ (prendre) ta voiture?
4. Quel temps est-ce qu'il _____ (faire)? Il _____ (pleuvoir)?
5. Quels vêtements est-ce que tu _____ (mettre) pour sortir?
6. Qu'est-ce que vous _____ (faire)? Vous _____ (dîner) ensemble? Vous _____ (aller) danser? Vous _____ (voir) un film au cinéma?
7. De quoi *(About what)* est-ce que vous _____ (parler)?
8. Tu _____ (rentrer) vers quelle heure?
9. Vous _____ (partir) tous en même temps ou les autres _____ (rester) plus longtemps?

Maintenant, utilisez les questions précédentes pour interviewer un(e) partenaire sur la dernière fois qu'il/elle est sorti(e) avec des amis.

Follow-up for *B. Je veux tout savoir.* Have students answer the following questions using either a direct object pronoun or y. 1. Est-ce que vous prenez *votre petit déjeuner* à la maison, d'habitude? Est-ce que vous avez pris *le petit déjeuner* chez vous hier? Préférez-vous prendre *le petit déjeuner* chez vous, au restaurant, au café ou dans un fast-food? Allez-vous dîner *chez vous* ce soir? 2. Est-ce que vous invitez souvent *vos amis* chez vous? Est-ce que vous aimez regarder *la télé* ensemble? Est-ce que vous avez regardé *la télé* ensemble hier soir? Est-ce que vous allez regarder *la télé* ensemble ce soir? Est-ce que vous êtes allés *au cinéma* ensemble récemment? Avez-vous l'intention d'aller *au cinéma* ce week-end?

B **Je veux tout savoir.** Céline pose des questions à Amélie sur une soirée qu'elle a passée avec Christophe et Rachid. Complétez les réponses d'Amélie en remplaçant les mots en italique par le pronom qui convient: **le, la, l', les** ou **y**. Utilisez le verbe de la question dans la réponse.

EXEMPLE — Alors, Christophe et toi avez passé *la soirée* ensemble l'autre jour?
— Oui, on **l'a passée** ensemble samedi dernier.

1. — Est-ce que tu as retrouvé *Christophe* en ville ou vous y êtes allés ensemble?
   — Je _____ en ville.
2. — Vous êtes allés *en ville* seuls tous les deux?
   — Non, Rachid _____ avec nous.
3. — Comment est-ce que tu trouves *Rachid*?
   — Je _____ très sympa.
4. — Comment est-ce que tu as trouvé *le restaurant* où vous avez dîné?
   — On a dîné dans le restaurant marocain *(Moroccan)* de la sœur de Rachid et moi, je _____ excellent.
5. — Vous êtes allés *en boîte* aussi?
   — Oui, on _____ après le dîner.
6. — Tu vas voir *Christophe et Rachid* le week-end prochain, aussi?
   — Pour l'instant, je n'ai pas l'intention de _____ le week-end prochain, mais on ne sait jamais *(you never know)*.

C. Qui fait quoi? Amélie dîne avec Rachid et Christophe dans le restaurant de la sœur de Rachid. Complétez ses phrases avec une expression logique de la liste. Mettez la forme correcte du verbe **faire** dans le premier espace et le reste de l'expression dans le deuxième espace.

> faire les courses   faire le ménage   faire la vaisselle
> faire la cuisine   faire une promenade

EXEMPLE Ta sœur et toi, vous **faites** toujours **les courses** pour le restaurant très tôt tous les matins, non? Où est-ce que vous trouvez tous les produits pour ces plats marocains *(Moroccan)*?

1. Ta sœur _____ très bien _____. Mon plat *(dish)* est excellent.
2. Céline et moi _____ toujours _____ immédiatement après le dîner parce qu'elle a peur d'avoir des insectes dans la cuisine.
3. Notre appartement est toujours très propre. Céline _____ souvent _____.
4. Je _____ souvent _____ après le dîner si je mange beaucoup pour faciliter la digestion.

D. Quel temps fait-il? Au dîner, Rachid parle du temps qu'il fait au Maroc au cours de l'année. Complétez ses phrases.

1.   2.   3.

1. En été, il fait du _____ et il fait souvent très _____.
2. Quelquefois en hiver, il fait _____, mais il ne _____ presque jamais.
3. Il fait souvent du _____, mais il ne _____ pas beaucoup.

Access the Video *Les Stagiaires* on iLrn.

▶ **Épisode 5: Qu'est-ce que vous avez fait?**

AVANT LA VIDÉO
Dans cet épisode, Matthieu parle à Christophe d'une soirée que Christophe et Rachid ont passée avec Amélie. Avant de regarder l'épisode, pensez à des activités qu'on fait quand on passe une soirée en ville avec des amis.

APRÈS LA VIDÉO
Regardez l'épisode et répondez aux questions suivantes.
- Où est-ce que Christophe, Rachid et Amélie sont allés?
- Qu'est-ce qu'ils ont fait?
- De quoi *(About what)* ont-ils parlé?

LECTURE ET COMPOSITION

LECTURE

POUR MIEUX LIRE:
Using visuals to make guesses

Before reading a text, scan it and use the title and any accompanying visuals (photos, charts, etc.) to help you anticipate content and read more easily.

Un blog. Regardez le texte et les photos. Quel genre de blog est-ce? Quelle sorte de renseignements est-ce que vous pensez y trouver?

Je blogue donc je suis

Les blogs **font** de plus en plus **partie des** loisirs des Français, et la France est devenue championne du **monde** du nombre de blogs par **internaute**. Bloguer est surtout populaire chez les jeunes, surtout les jeunes politiquement engagés, mais **chacun** a sa **propre** raison de bloguer. Pour certains, c'est le désir de faire partie d'une communauté. Pour d'autres, c'est le besoin de mettre en mots ses sentiments, **promouvoir** ses idées ou **décrire** ses expériences. Les blogs de voyage sont **parmi** les plus populaires. Lisez le blog de voyage **qui suit**.

Mon week-end à Paris

Je suis allé passer un week-end à Paris avec des amis. Arrivés le vendredi vers 18h, on a profité de la première soirée pour visiter Montmartre. J'ai trouvé la vue de Paris de là-haut inoubliable.

Le lendemain, on a fait une promenade le long des Champs-Élysées et ensuite, on a longé les quais de la Seine. Après, on a visité Notre-Dame. J'ai admiré la façade avec toutes ses statues et j'ai pris beaucoup de photos.

Le dimanche matin, on a vu une exposition d'art moderne au Centre Pompidou avant de quitter Paris.

Paris, c'est sans doute la plus belle ville du monde!

font partie de *are part of*   **le monde** *the world*   **internaute** *Internet user*
chacun *each one*   **propre** *own*   **promouvoir** *to promote*   **décrire** *to describe*
parmi *among*   **qui suit** *that follows*

COMPOSITION

POUR MIEUX ÉCRIRE:
Using standard organizing techniques

To write well, you first need to organize your ideas. You can sometimes base your organization on a document you already have or can easily create. For example, to describe a book you have read, you can use the table of contents to organize your thoughts. To talk about a trip you have taken, you can use your itinerary, and when writing a blog, you can look at how other blogs are organized.

Organisez-vous. Vous allez écrire un blog sur une semaine imaginaire en France. D'abord, sur une feuille de papier, créez votre itinéraire.

1.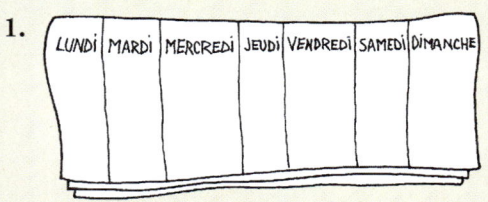

2. Sous chaque jour, écrivez des phrases pour décrire *(describe)* une progression logique de votre séjour *(your stay)*. Dites:
   - quand vous êtes parti(e), et avec qui et comment vous avez voyagé
   - où et à quelle heure vous êtes arrivé(e) en France et dans quelle sorte d'hôtel(s) vous êtes descendu(e)
   - ce que *(what)* vous avez fait chaque jour
   - quand vous avez quitté la France

Process-writing follow-up for *Un voyage en France*. Have students exchange papers with a classmate and ask them to compare their trips to France.

Compréhension

1. Est-ce que les Français aiment bloguer? Quel groupe blogue le plus?
2. Pourquoi est-ce qu'on blogue?
3. Dans ce blog de voyage, quels endroits à Paris est-ce que le blogueur mentionne?

Un voyage en France

En vous basant sur votre itinéraire, écrivez un blog sur votre voyage imaginaire.

EXEMPLE L'été dernier, je suis allé(e) en France avec…

iLrn Share It!

Lecture et Composition | *deux cent neuf* 209

COMPARAISONS CULTURELLES

In the Culture Modules in the video library, see Leisure activities.

LE SPORT ET LE TEMPS LIBRE DES FRANÇAIS

Les Français passent souvent leur temps libre chez eux où ils aiment regarder la télé, écouter de la musique, passer du temps sur Internet et lire.

Les Français aiment beaucoup les activités culturelles aussi et ils consacrent beaucoup de temps à ces activités, **allant** souvent au cinéma, à des expositions d'art, au théâtre, à des concerts… De nombreux festivals et fêtes qui permettent d'avoir accès à l'art, à la musique, **au monde du septième art** et à leur **patrimoine** montrent **l'engouement** des Français pour la culture.

Pourtant, selon une enquête récente **auprès des Français,** l'activité **dite** la plus satisfaisante (après passer du temps entre amis), est faire du sport, et beaucoup d'entre eux pratiquent une activité sportive **plusieurs** fois par mois.

À l'école, le sport est obligatoire et il est **enseigné** comme les autres **matières.** Pourtant, **les élèves ne peuvent pas** pratiquer de sports à l'école après les cours. Ils **doivent** s'inscrire dans un club. Les clubs de football, de tennis et d'**équitation** sont les plus souvent choisis.

allant going **au monde du septième art** to the world of the seventh art (cinema) **patrimoine** heritage **l'engouement** (m) enthusiasm **Pourtant, selon une enquête** However, according to a survey **auprès des Français** with the French **dite** said **plusieurs** several **À l'école** At school **enseigné** taught **matières** subjects **les élèves** the students **ne peuvent pas** can't **doivent** have to **équitation** (f) horseback riding

Beaucoup de Français **ne font pas partie de** clubs, mais ils pratiquent une activité sportive seuls. Ils font du jogging, **de la marche, de la natation** ou du cyclisme. À Paris, tous les week-ends, **les berges** de la Seine sont fermées pour permettre aux cyclistes de se promener; et le vendredi soir, **grâce à** l'association sportive «Pari roller», les Parisiens **peuvent traverser la ville en roller** sur un circuit **interdit à la circulation automobile.**

Les sports d'hiver (**le patin à glace**, le ski, le snowboard), les sports d'été (la natation, **la voile, la planche à voile**) aussi bien que les sports «d'aventure» (**l'escalade, le parapente**, le canoë-kayak) sont aussi très appréciés!

Et chez vous, quels sont les sports les plus populaires dans votre région?

Compréhension

1. Qu'est-ce que les Français aiment faire chez eux pendant leur temps libre? Est-ce que ce sont les mêmes activités que celles *(those)* qui sont populaires chez vous?
2. Quelles sont les activités culturelles les plus populaires en France? Et chez vous?
3. Est-ce que le sport fait partie du cursus scolaire *(school curriculum)* d'un(e) élève français(e)? Et des élèves dans votre région? Qu'est-ce que les jeunes doivent faire *(have to do)* pour participer à des activités sportives après les cours? Est-ce que c'est similaire ou différent dans votre région?
4. Quelles activités sportives sont populaires chez les Français? Et chez vous?

---

ne font pas partie de *don't belong to* · **de la marche** *walking* · **de la natation** *swimming* · **les berges** *the banks* (of a river) · **grâce à** *thanks to* · **peuvent traverser la ville en roller** *can skate across the city* · **interdit à la circulation automobile** *closed to traffic* · **le patin à glace** *ice-skating* · **la voile** *sailing* · **la planche à voile** *windsurfing* · **l'escalade** *rock climbing* · **le parapente** *paragliding*

Visit www.cengagebrain.com for additional cultural information and activities.

RÉSUMÉ DE GRAMMAIRE

PASSÉ COMPOSÉ

J'ai mangé.
I ate.
I have eaten.
I did eat.

Ils n'ont pas beaucoup dormi.
They didn't sleep much.
They haven't slept much.

To say what happened in the past, put the verb in the **passé composé.** It may be translated in a variety of ways. The **passé composé** is composed of an auxiliary verb and a past participle. For most verbs the auxiliary verb is **avoir,** but for a few verbs it is **être.** All **-er** verbs have past participles with **-é** (**parler: j'ai parlé**) and most **-ir** verbs with **-i** (**dormir: j'ai dormi**).

PARLER → PARLÉ	
j'**ai** parlé	nous **avons** parlé
tu **as** parlé	vous **avez** parlé
il/elle/on **a** parlé	ils/elles **ont** parlé

These verbs conjugated with **avoir** have irregular past participles.

— Qu'est-ce que tu **as fait** hier soir?
— J'**ai vu** un film avec des amis et après, on **a pris** un verre au café.

avoir:	j'ai eu	mettre:	j'ai mis	être:	j'ai été
il y a:	il y a eu	prendre:	j'ai pris	faire:	j'ai fait
boire:	j'ai bu	apprendre:	j'ai appris	écrire:	j'ai écrit
lire:	j'ai lu	comprendre:	j'ai compris		
pleuvoir:	il a plu				
voir:	j'ai vu				

A few verbs have **être** as their auxiliary. With these verbs, the past participle agrees with the subject for gender and plurality.

— Est-ce que ta mère et ta tante **sont allées** à Paris avec toi?
— Oui, elles ont fait le voyage avec moi, mais je **suis restée** plus longtemps. Elles **sont rentrées** une semaine avant moi.

ALLER → ALLÉ	
je **suis** allé(e)	nous **sommes** allé(e)s
tu **es** allé(e)	vous **êtes** allé(e)(s)
il **est** allé	ils **sont** allés
elle **est** allée	elles **sont** allées
on **est** allé(e)(s)	

Here are some verbs that have **être** as their auxiliary verb. Use **être** with **passer** only when it means *to pass by* and not when it means *to spend time.*

aller:	je suis allé(e)	monter:	je suis monté(e)
arriver:	je suis arrivé(e)	descendre:	je suis descendu(e)
rester:	je suis resté(e)	venir:	je suis venu(e)
entrer:	je suis entré(e)	revenir:	je suis revenu(e)
sortir:	je suis sorti(e)	devenir:	je suis devenu(e)
partir:	je suis parti(e)	naître:	je suis né(e)
passer:	je suis passé(e)	mourir:	il/elle est mort(e)
rentrer:	je suis rentré(e)	tomber:	je suis tombé(e)
retourner:	je suis retourné(e)		

— Tu as **déjà** dîné?
— Non, je **n'**ai **pas encore** mangé.

— Qu'est-ce que ton mari et toi avez fait l'année dernière pour les vacances?
— On **n'**a **rien** fait.

To negate a verb in the **passé composé**, place **ne** immediately after the subject and **pas, rien** (*nothing*), or **jamais** after the auxiliary verb. Use **ne... pas encore** to say *not yet* and **déjà** to say *already* or *ever*. **Déjà** and adverbs indicating *how often* (**toujours, souvent...**) and *how well* (**bien, mal...**) are usually placed between the auxiliary verb and the past participle.

The following adverbs indicate when something happened in the past. They may be placed at the beginning or end of a clause.

hier (matin, après-midi, soir)	récemment
le week-end (le mois) dernier	pendant deux heures (longtemps)
la semaine (l'année) dernière	il y a quelques secondes (cinq minutes, cinq ans...)
la dernière fois	

FAIRE

The verb **faire** *(to do, to make)* is irregular.

FAIRE *(to do, to make)*	
je **fais**	nous **faisons**
tu **fais**	vous **faites**
il/elle/on **fait**	ils/elles **font**
PASSÉ COMPOSÉ: **j'ai fait**	

Faire is also used in many weather expressions, as well as the expressions listed on page 198.

The **un, une, des, du, de la,** and **de l'** in the expressions with **faire** become **de (d')** when the verb is negated. The definite article (**le, la, l', les**) does not change.

NE... RIEN

Ne... rien means *nothing* or *not anything*. This expression can be the subject or object of the verb, or the object of a preposition.

When negating an infinitive, place both parts of the negative expression before it.

DIRECT OBJECT PRONOUNS

The direct object pronouns are **le, la, l',** and **les.** Use **le** *(him, it)* to replace masculine singular nouns and **la** *(her, it)* to replace feminine singular nouns. **Les** *(Them)* replaces all plural nouns. **Le** and **la** become **l'** when the following word begins with a vowel or silent **h.**

	BEFORE A CONSONANT	BEFORE A VOWEL OR SILENT *H*
him, it (masculine)	le	l'
her, it (feminine)	la	l'
them	les	les

These pronouns are generally placed *immediately before* the verb. They go before the infinitive if there is one. If not, they go before the conjugated verb. In the negative, the pronoun remains *immediately before* the conjugated verb or the infinitive.

In the **passé composé,** direct object pronouns are placed just before the auxiliary verb (the conjugated form of **avoir**), and the past participle agrees with them for gender and plurality by adding **-e, -s,** or **-es.**

— Tu es parti en vacances **pendant combien de temps**?
— **Pendant** quinze jours.
— Tu es rentré **il y a combien de temps**?
— Je suis rentré **mardi dernier.**

Je ne **fais** rien ce week-end.
Qu'est-ce que tu **fais**?
On **fait** quelque chose ensemble?
Faisons quelque chose avec mes amis.
Que **faites**-vous généralement?
Mes amis **font** beaucoup de sport.

— Quel temps **fait**-il?
— Il **fait** beau (mauvais, froid, chaud, frais, [du] soleil, du vent).
Ils **font** la cuisine et nous **faisons** la vaisselle.

Je ne fais jamais **d'**exercice.
Mon colocataire ne fait jamais **le** ménage.

Rien n'est en solde?
Tu **n'**achètes **rien**?
Je **n'**ai besoin de **rien.**
Je préfère **ne rien** acheter.

— Tu prends ce sac?
— Oui, je **le** prends.
— Tu aimes cette robe aussi?
— Oui, je **l'**aime bien.
— Tu achètes tes vêtements ici?
— Oui, je **les** achète souvent ici.

Je **les** achète.
Je ne **les** achète pas.
Je vais **les** acheter.
Je ne vais pas **les** acheter.

— A-t-il acheté les chaussures?
— Oui, il **les** a acheté**es**.
Non, il ne **les** a pas acheté**es**.

VOCABULAIRE

 Audio Flashcards

COMPÉTENCE 1

Saying what you did

NOMS MASCULINS
un homme d'affaires	a businessman
le journal	the newspaper
le petit déjeuner	breakfast

NOM FÉMININ
une femme d'affaires	a businesswoman

EXPRESSIONS ADVERBIALES
hier	yesterday
hier soir	last night, yesterday evening
samedi dernier	last Saturday
le week-end dernier	last weekend

DIVERS
dernier (dernière)	last
faire une promenade	to take a walk
ne... rien	nothing, not anything
prendre son petit déjeuner	to have one's breakfast
travaillant	working

COMPÉTENCE 2

Telling where you went

NOMS MASCULINS
un an	a year
un camping	a campground
un hôtel	a hotel
le lendemain	the next day, the following day
des parents	relatives

NOMS FÉMININS
la chance	luck
une heure	an hour
une minute	a minute
une nuit	a night
une seconde	a second (in time)
une voiture de location	a rental car

EXPRESSIONS VERBALES
descendre (de/à/dans)	to descend, to come down, to get off/out (of) (a vehicle), to stay (at)
entrer (dans)	to enter
faire un voyage	to take a trip
monter (dans)	to go up, to get on/in
mourir (mort[e])	to die (dead)
naître (né[e])	to be born (born)
partir en voyage	to leave on a trip
partir en week-end	to go away for the weekend
passer (chez/devant/par)	to pass (by [...'s house])
retourner	to return, to go back
tomber	to fall

EXPRESSIONS ADVERBIALES
l'année dernière	last year
déjà	already, ever
la dernière fois	the last time
hier (matin, après-midi)	yesterday (morning, afternoon)
hier soir	last night, yesterday evening
Il y a combien de temps?	How long ago?
il y a quelques secondes	a few seconds ago
longtemps	a long time
lundi (mardi...) dernier	last Monday (Tuesday...)
le mois dernier	last month
ne... pas encore	not yet
Pendant combien de temps?	For how long?
pendant deux heures	for two hours
récemment	recently
la semaine dernière	last week
le week-end dernier	last weekend
le week-end passé	the past weekend

DIVERS
Quelle chance!	What luck!
quelques	some, a few

COMPÉTENCE 3

Discussing the weather and your activities

NOMS MASCULINS

l'automne (en automne)	autumn/fall (in autumn/in the fall)
l'été (en été)	summer (in summer)
l'hiver (en hiver)	winter (in winter)
un jardin	a garden
le printemps (au printemps)	spring (in spring)
le temps	the weather, time

NOMS FÉMININS

des distractions	entertainment
la neige	snow
la pluie	rain
une saison	a season

EXPRESSIONS VERBALES

adorer	to love, to adore
aller à la montagne	to go to the mountains
dépendre (de)	to depend (on)
faire de l'exercice	to exercise
faire des courses	to run errands
faire du bateau	to go boating
faire du camping	to go camping
faire du jardinage	to garden
faire du jogging	to go jogging
faire du shopping	to go shopping
faire du ski (nautique)	to (water)ski
faire du sport (du tennis, du hockey...)	to play sports (tennis, hockey...)
faire du vélo	to go bike-riding
faire du VTT	to go all-terrain biking
faire la cuisine	to cook
faire la lessive	to do laundry
faire la vaisselle	to do the dishes
faire le ménage	to do housework
faire les courses	to buy groceries
faire une promenade	to take a walk
faire une randonnée (faire des randonnées)	to take a hike, to hike (to go hiking, to hike)
faire un voyage	to take a trip
neiger	to snow
pleuvoir (Il a plu.)	to rain (It rained.)

DIVERS

ne... rien (de spécial)	nothing, not anything (special)
pendant	during, for
Quel temps fait-il?	What's the weather like?
Il fait beau / chaud / frais / froid / mauvais / (du) soleil / du vent.	It's nice / hot / cool / cold / bad / sunny / windy.
Il y a du vent.	It's windy.
Il pleut.	It is raining., It rains.
Il neige.	It is snowing., It snows.
Quel temps va-t-il faire?	What's the weather going to be like?
Il va faire...	It's going to be...
Il va pleuvoir / neiger.	It's going to rain / to snow.
si	if

COMPÉTENCE 4

Deciding what to wear and buying clothes

NOMS MASCULINS

un anorak	a ski jacket
un bikini	a bikini
un chemisier	a blouse
un costume	a suit (for a man)
un imperméable	a raincoat
un jean	jeans
un maillot de bain	a swimsuit
un manteau	an (over)coat
un pantalon	pants
un parapluie	an umbrella
un polo	a knit shirt
un portefeuille	a wallet
un pull	a pullover sweater
un sac	a purse, a sack, a bag
un short	shorts
un survêtement	a jogging suit
un tee-shirt	a T-shirt
un vendeur	a salesclerk

NOMS FÉMININS

des baskets	tennis shoes, sneakers
des bottes	boots
une cabine d'essayage	a fitting room
des chaussures	shoes
une chemise	a shirt
une cravate	a tie
une jupe	a skirt
des lunettes (de soleil)	(sun)glasses
une montre	a watch
une robe	a dress
des sandales	sandals
des tongs	flip-flops
une vendeuse	a salesclerk

EXPRESSIONS VERBALES

coûter	to cost
emporter	to take (along), to carry (away)
essayer	to try, to try on
Il/Elle me plaît.	I like it.
mettre (je mets, vous mettez) (j'ai mis)	to wear, to put, to put on (I wore, put, put on)
porter	to wear

DIVERS

Bien sûr!	Of course!
ce (cet, cette, ces)...-ci/-là	this/that/these/those... over here/ over there
en solde	on sale
Je peux vous aider?	May I help you?
le (l') / la (l')	him, it / her, it
les	them
parfois	sometimes
par ici	this way
Quelle taille faites-vous?	What size do you wear?
Je fais du...	I wear size...
Qu'en pensez-vous?	What do you think about it?
voyons	let's see

BIENVENUE EN EUROPE FRANCOPHONE

 **PowerPoint BV-1**

En Europe, le français est une langue officielle dans quatre pays et **une principauté:** la France, la Belgique, la Suisse, le Luxembourg et Monaco. **Lesquels aimeriez-vous** visiter?

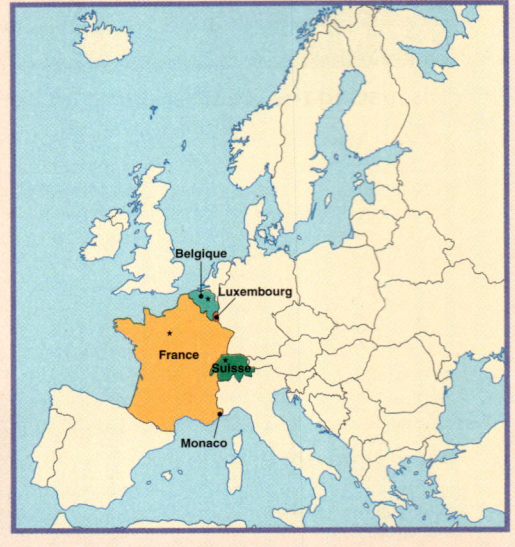

Le **Grand-Duché** du Luxembourg est un des plus petits États d'Europe. Il y a trois langues **officielles** au Luxembourg: le français, le luxembourgeois et l'allemand.

Fondée en 963, la ville de Luxembourg offre la possibilité de voir plus de mille ans d'histoire.

Grâce à sa forte immigration, surtout venant des pays de l'Union européenne, le Luxembourg est devenu un microcosme de l'Europe moderne.

Bienvenue Welcome   **une principauté** a principality   **Lesquels aimeriez-vous** Which ones would you like
Grand-Duché Grand Duchy   **officielles** official   **Grâce à** Thanks to   **surtout venant** especially coming

La Suisse a quatre langues officielles: l'allemand, le français, l'italien et le romanche, et **chacun de** ces groupes linguistiques a **ses propres coutumes** et traditions. Les Suisses sont très **fiers de** leur culture et de leur diversité multiculturelle.

La Suisse offre de très belles vues.

Qu'aimeriez-vous faire en Suisse: du ski, des randonnées en montagne ou de l'alpinisme?

---

chacun de *each of* **ses propres coutumes** *its own customs* **fiers de** *proud of* **Qu'aimeriez-vous** *What would you like*
de l'alpinisme *mountain climbing*

Bienvenue en Europe francophone | *deux cent dix-sept* **217**

Les trois régions qui forment la Belgique, la Région **flamande,** la Région **wallonne** et la Région de Bruxelles (la capitale) donnent à la Belgique une riche diversité culturelle. Les Flamands (58 % [pour cent] de la population) parlent **néerlandais.** Les Wallons (32 % de la population) parlent français. **Quant au reste,** 9 % sont bilingues et 1 % parle allemand.

La Belgique est connue pour la variété de son architecture, pour la beauté de ses **paysages** et pour ses **nombreux châteaux.**

On peut aller sur la Grand-Place à Bruxelles pour admirer son architecture baroque et gothique, prendre un café et faire du shopping.

Monaco est **une principauté** et une monarchie constitutionnelle. Le français y est la langue officielle, mais on y parle aussi l'anglais et l'italien. Près de 5 000 personnes parlent **monégasque,** un dialecte dérivé de l'italien.

Monaco est célèbre pour le tourisme, le luxe et pour ses casinos, **ainsi que** pour son fameux Grand Prix de Formule 1.

flamande Flemish	**wallonne** French-speaking, Walloon	**néerlandais** Dutch	**Quant au reste** As for the rest
paysages landscapes, countryside	**nombreux** numerous	**une principauté** a principality	**monégasque** Monegasque (language native to Monaco)
	ainsi que as well as		

218 *deux cent dix-huit* | Bienvenue en Europe francophone

La France **comprend la France métropolitaine** et **plusieurs** départements, régions et collectivités **d'outre-mer, tels que** la Guadeloupe (dans la mer des Caraïbes, près de l'Amérique centrale), Mayotte (près de l'Afrique) et la Polynésie française (dans le Pacifique). Regardez la carte du monde francophone **au début du** livre. Quelle partie de la France **aimeriez-vous** visiter?

Dans les villes françaises, comme ici à Strasbourg, on peut visiter les parties historiques de la ville.

En sortant des grandes villes, on trouve de beaux paysages et de petits villages fascinants.

Dans le sud de la France, on peut voir des ruines romaines, comme **celles-ci** à Aix-en-Provence.

Aimeriez-vous mieux visiter un des départements ou territoires d'outre-mer, comme Mayotte?

---

comprend *includes*   **la France métropolitaine** *metropolitan France (the part of France in Europe)*   **plusieurs** *several*
d'outre-mer *overseas*   **tels que** *such as*   **au début du** *at the beginning of the*   **aimeriez-vous** *would you like*   **on peut** *one can*
En sortant des *By leaving the*   **celles-ci** *these*

Bienvenue en Europe francophone

À Paris

Les sorties

	iLrn Heinle Learning Center		Internet web search
	www.cengagebrain.com		Pair work
	Horizons Video: Les Stagiaires		Group work
	Audio		

6

COMPÉTENCE

1 Inviting someone to go out
Les invitations

Issuing and accepting invitations
Les verbes **vouloir**, **pouvoir** *et* **devoir**

Stratégies et Compréhension auditive
- **Pour mieux comprendre:** *Noting the important information*
- **Compréhension auditive:** *On va au cinéma?*

2 Talking about how you spend and used to spend your time
Aujourd'hui et dans le passé

Saying how things used to be
L'imparfait

Talking about activities
Les verbes **sortir**, **partir** *et* **dormir**

3 Talking about the past
Une sortie

Telling what was going on when something else happened
L'imparfait et le passé composé

Telling what happened and describing the circumstances
Le passé composé et l'imparfait

4 Narrating in the past
Les contes

Narrating what happened
Le passé composé et l'imparfait (reprise)

Vidéoreprise   *Les Stagiaires*

Lecture et Composition
- **Pour mieux lire:** *Using standard formats*
- **Lecture:** *Deux films français*
- **Pour mieux écrire:** *Using standard formats*
- **Composition:** *Un film à voir*

Comparaisons culturelles   *Le cinéma: les préférences des Français*

Résumé de grammaire

Vocabulaire

deux cent vingt et un | 221

PARIS

 PowerPoints 6-1, 6-2

In the **Culture Modules** in the video library, see **Architecture**.

Paris, la capitale de la France, est une des plus belles villes **du monde.**

La Seine sépare la ville en deux parties, **la rive** gauche et la rive droite. Les deux îles situées **au milieu de** la Seine sont l'île de la Cité et l'île Saint-Louis. C'est sur l'île de la Cité que la ville de Paris est née il y a plus de 2 000 ans.

La célèbre avenue des Champs-Élysées s'étend de la place de la Concorde à l'arc de Triomphe.

Le Louvre, l'un des plus grands musées d'art du monde, fait presque un kilomètre de long.

---

du monde *in the world*   **la rive** *the bank (of a river)*   **au milieu de** *in the middle of*   **s'étend** *extends*

Pour avoir une vue panoramique de la ville, on peut monter en haut de la tour Eiffel.

Paris

🌐 Visit it live on Google Earth!

NOMBRE D'HABITANTS: **2 235 000 (avec la région parisienne: plus de 12 089 000) (les Parisiens)**

DÉPARTEMENT: **Paris**

RÉGION: **Île-de-France**

Le savez-vous?

Devinez quel site touristique représenté ici correspond à chaque description.

| les Champs-Élysées | le Louvre | la tour Eiffel |
| Montmartre | le Quartier latin | |

1. Cet ancien palais royal est devenu un musée en 1791. C'est aujourd'hui un des musées les plus visités du monde.

2. Dans ce quartier, Robert de Sorbon a établi la Sorbonne en 1253, ce qui est aujourd'hui l'Université de Paris. Le latin était la langue officielle dans le quartier jusqu'en 1793.

3. Cette célèbre avenue est longue de presque deux kilomètres et s'étend *(extends)* de l'arc de Triomphe jusqu'à la place de la Concorde.

4. En 1860, la ville de Paris a annexé ce quartier situé sur une colline *(hill)* avec une vue panoramique de la ville. La basilique du Sacré-Cœur, construite entre 1875 et 1914, est le point le plus haut *(highest)* de Paris.

5. L'ingénieur qui a construit ce monument pour l'Exposition universelle de 1889 a aussi travaillé sur la statue de la Liberté à New York. C'est le site touristique le plus visité de France.

Si vous aimez la vie de bohème, visitez le quartier de Montmartre.

Le Quartier latin est un des quartiers les plus sympathiques de Paris.

🌐 Sur ces pages, vous voyez quelques-uns des 180 musées et monuments de Paris. Cherchez des visites virtuelles de la ville de Paris sur Internet. Faites des recherches sur un des sites parisiens que vous aimeriez *(would like)* visiter. Découvrez au moins cinq choses au sujet de ce site.

la vie life

COMPÉTENCE 1

Inviting someone to go out

 PowerPoint 6-3

LES INVITATIONS

Note culturelle

En France, quand on sort entre amis, il est commun que chacun *(each one)* paie sa part. Mais attention! En français, l'expression **je t'invite / je vous invite** indique que vous allez payer. Quand vous sortez avec des amis, est-ce que quelqu'un paie pour tout le groupe ou est-ce qu'il est plus commun que chacun paie sa part?

Warm-ups. A. Have students suggest a place for the following activities: **EXEMPLE**
—**J'ai envie de jouer au tennis.**
—**Alors, on va au parc? 1.** J'ai envie d'aller nager. **2.** J'ai envie de voir la nouvelle exposition d'art. **3.** J'ai envie d'aller faire du shopping. **4.** J'ai envie d'aller prendre un verre. **5.** J'ai envie de voir un film. **6.** J'ai envie de manger quelque chose.
B. Have students use **Tu voudrais…?** or suggestions with **on** and **nous** to invite each other to go see a movie or do something else together.

Suggestion. Refer students back to the *Comparaisons culturelles* section of the *Chapitre préliminaire,* pages 24–25, for additional explanations and activities with the twenty-four hour clock.

Pour inviter **quelqu'un** à sortir, **vous pouvez dire**…

À UN(E) AMI(E)	À UNE AUTRE PERSONNE OU À UN GROUPE DE PERSONNES
Tu veux…?	**Vous voulez…?**
Tu voudrais…?	Vous voudriez…?
Je t'invite à…	Je voudrais vous inviter à…

Si **quelqu'un vous invite,** vous pouvez répondre…

POUR DIRE OUI	POUR DIRE NON
Oui, je veux bien…	Je regrette mais…
Quelle bonne idée!	je ne suis pas libre.
Avec plaisir!	**je ne peux** vraiment **pas.**
D'accord!	**je dois** travailler.

POUR SUGGÉRER UNE AUTRE ACTIVITÉ
Je préfère…
J'aime mieux…
Allons plutôt à…

Les Français **utilisent** l'heure officielle pour tous **les horaires** (le train, le cinéma, **les heures d'ouverture**…). Pour lire l'heure officielle, on utilise uniquement des nombres. Aux États-Unis, on **appelle** cette **façon** de lire l'heure *military time.*

L'HEURE OFFICIELLE		L'HEURE FAMILIÈRE
0h05	zéro heure cinq	minuit cinq
1h15	une heure quinze	une heure et quart (du matin)
12h20	douze heures vingt	midi vingt
13h30	treize heures trente	une heure et demie (de l'après-midi)
20h40	vingt heures quarante	neuf heures moins vingt (du soir)
20h45	vingt heures quarante-cinq	neuf heures moins le quart (du soir)

Séances: du lundi au samedi à 20h30 | mardi à 17h00 | samedi à 16h00.

quelqu'un *someone* **vous pouvez (pouvoir** *can, may, to be able)* **dire** *to say* **Tu veux/Vous voulez (vouloir** *to want)* **quelqu'un vous invite** *someone invites you* **je ne peux pas (pouvoir** *can, may, to be able)* **je dois (devoir** *must, to have to)* **utiliser** *to use, to utilize* **un horaire** *a schedule* **les heures d'ouverture** *opening times* **appeler** *to call* **une façon** *a way*

Éric téléphone à sa copine Michèle.

MICHÈLE: Allô?
ÉRIC: Salut, Michèle. C'est moi, Éric. Ça va?
MICHÈLE: Oui, très bien. Et toi?
ÉRIC: Moi, ça va. Écoute, tu es libre ce soir? Tu voudrais sortir?
MICHÈLE: Oui, je veux bien. Qu'est-ce que tu as envie de faire?
ÉRIC: **Je pensais** aller voir la nouvelle comédie qu'on **passe** au cinéma Gaumont.
MICHÈLE: Tu sais, moi, je n'aime pas **tellement** les comédies. Je préfère les films d'**amour.** Allons plutôt voir le nouveau film d'amour au cinéma Rex.
ÉRIC: Bon, je veux bien. À quelle heure?
MICHÈLE: Il y a **une séance** à vingt heures quarante-cinq.
ÉRIC: Alors, je passe chez toi vers huit heures?
MICHÈLE: D'accord. Alors, au revoir.
ÉRIC: À tout à l'heure, Michèle.

A Invitations.
Circulez dans la classe et utilisez différentes expressions pour inviter d'autres étudiants à faire les choses suivantes. Ils vont accepter ou refuser chaque invitation ou proposer une autre activité.

INVITEZ UN(E) AMI(E) À...
1. aller danser samedi soir
2. dîner au restaurant ce soir
3. aller voir une exposition demain
4. aller prendre un verre aujourd'hui après les cours

INVITEZ UN GROUPE D'AMIS À...
5. aller voir un film d'amour demain
6. réviser ensemble ce soir
7. faire du vélo au parc ce week-end
8. aller au match de football américain / de basket ce week-end

B Je regrette, mais...
Préparez la conversation suivante avec un(e) partenaire.

Un ami téléphone à Éric pour l'inviter à sortir, mais Éric préfère ne rien faire et il refuse. L'ami insiste. Éric est très imaginatif dans ses excuses. Jouez les deux rôles avec un(e) partenaire.

C À quelle heure?
Regardez la liste des séances de la pièce de théâtre *Le Tartuffe* à la page précédente. Exprimez l'heure de chaque séance de deux façons. Ensuite, préparez une conversation avec un(e) partenaire dans laquelle vous l'invitez à voir la pièce et vous choisissez une séance.

EXEMPLE 20h30
Du lundi au samedi, il y a une séance à vingt heures trente; c'est-à-dire *(that is to say)* à huit heures et demie du soir.

À VOUS!

Avec un(e) partenaire, relisez à haute voix la conversation entre Michèle et Éric. Ensuite, adaptez la conversation pour faire des projets pour aller au cinéma ensemble. Servez-vous du *Vocabulaire supplémentaire* et parlez de quel(s) genre(s) de film vous aimez, de quel film vous voudriez voir et de comment et où vous allez vous retrouver *(you are going to meet up)*.

Vocabulaire supplémentaire
LES FILMS

un dessin animé *a cartoon*
un drame
un film d'aventure
un film d'horreur
un film de science-fiction
un film fantastique
un film policier
un film d'animation
une comédie romantique

POUR SE RETROUVER

Je passe chez toi / chez vous. *I'll come by your place.*
Passe / Passez chez moi. *Come by my place.*
Rendez-vous à... *Let's meet at...*

Je pensais *I was thinking*   **passer (un film)** *to show (a movie)*   **tellement** *so much*   **l'amour** *(m) love*   **une séance** *a showing*

PowerPoint 6-4

ISSUING AND ACCEPTING INVITATIONS

✓ Pour vérifier

1. What does **vouloir** mean? What are three meanings of **pouvoir**? What are the meanings of **devoir**? What are the conjugations of these three verbs?

2. The **nous** and **vous** forms have the same vowels in the stem as the infinitive. What vowels do the other forms have?

3. What auxiliary verb do you use to form the **passé composé** of these three verbs? What are their past participles?

Sélection musicale. Search the Web for the songs "**Tu peux compter sur moi**" by Bénabar and "**Je ne veux pas travailler**" by Pink Martini to enjoy musical selections with these verbs.

iLrn Grammar Tutorials

Suggestions. A. Point out that the difference between third person singular and plural forms is audible in **vouloir, pouvoir,** and **devoir.** For practice, read these sentences aloud and have students indicate whether Alice is talking about just **Éric** or both **Éric et Cathy. 1.** Ils doivent travailler ce soir. **2.** Il veut aller au cinéma avec nous, mais il ne peut pas. **3.** Ils veulent rester à la maison. **4.** Il doit rentrer tôt. **5.** Ils ne peuvent pas sortir. You can also use these sentences for dictation. **B.** Point out the proverbs **Vouloir, c'est pouvoir; Ce que femme veut, Dieu le veut;** and **Quand on veut, on peut.**

Follow-ups for A. En cours. A. Dites si on peut faire les choses suivantes en cours de français en général. Ensuite, dites si vous voulez les faire. **EXEMPLE fumer → On ne peut pas fumer en cours. Moi, je ne veux pas fumer.** (utiliser le livre pendant les examens, dormir, parler anglais, sortir pour aller aux toilettes, parler aux autres étudiants, faire les devoirs en cours, répondre au téléphone, envoyer des textos, surfer sur Internet, beaucoup apprendre) **B.** Vous êtes le père ou la mère d'une fille de 14 ans et d'un garçon de 15 ans. Est-ce qu'ils peuvent…? **1.** regarder la télévision jusqu'à une heure du matin tous les jours **2.** dormir jusqu'à midi **3.** boire des boissons alcoolisées **4.** aller danser le samedi soir **5.** rentrer après minuit le samedi **6.** sortir après dix heures le lundi soir **7.** inviter des amis à la maison **8.** fumer

Les verbes vouloir, pouvoir et devoir

The verbs **vouloir** *(to want)* and **pouvoir** *(can, may, to be able)* are useful when inviting someone to do something. They have similar conjugations.

VOULOIR (to want)		POUVOIR (can, may, to be able)	
je **veux**	nous **voulons**	je **peux**	nous **pouvons**
tu **veux**	vous **voulez**	tu **peux**	vous **pouvez**
il/elle/on **veut**	ils/elles **veulent**	il/elle/on **peut**	ils/elles **peuvent**
PASSÉ COMPOSÉ: **j'ai voulu**		PASSÉ COMPOSÉ: **j'ai pu**	

Je **veux** sortir, mais je **ne peux pas**.   *I **want** to go out, but I **can't**.*

Use **devoir** followed by an infinitive to say what you *must* or *have to* do. **Devoir** also means *to owe*.

DEVOIR (must, to have to, to owe)	
je **dois**	nous **devons**
tu **dois**	vous **devez**
il/elle/on **doit**	ils/elles **doivent**
PASSÉ COMPOSÉ: **j'ai dû**	

Je **dois** travailler demain.   *I **have to** work tomorrow.*
Je **dois** 100 dollars à mon frère.   *I **owe** my brother 100 dollars.*

In the **passé composé**, **devoir** can mean that someone *had to* do something or *must have* done something. Context will clarify the meaning.

Michèle n'est pas chez elle. Elle **a dû** partir.
*Michèle isn't home. She **had to** leave. / She **must have** left.*

Il n'a pas pu sortir parce qu'il **a dû** travailler.
*He wasn't able to go out because he **had to** work.*

A **En cours.** Dites si ces personnes veulent faire chaque chose indiquée en cours de français.

EXEMPLE   Je… manger   **Je ne veux pas manger en cours.**

1. Je…
   boire du café
   beaucoup parler

2. Nous…
   souvent travailler en groupes
   souvent partir en avance *(early)*

3. Le prof…
   parler français tout le temps
   toujours comprendre les étudiants

4. Les étudiants…
   toujours comprendre le prof
   souvent poser des questions

Maintenant, dites s'ils peuvent faire chaque chose indiquée en cours de français.

EXEMPLE   Je… manger   **Je ne peux pas manger en cours.**

226 deux cent vingt-six | **CHAPITRE 6**

B Qu'est-ce qu'on doit faire? Pour chaque paire d'activités proposées, indiquez ce que chacun doit et ne doit pas faire en cours de français.

EXEMPLE le prof (être patient / être impatient)
Le prof doit être patient. Il ne doit pas être impatient.

1. le prof (insulter les étudiants / aider les étudiants)
   (toujours parler anglais en cours / parler français en cours)
2. les étudiants (dormir en cours / écouter le prof)
   (faire leurs devoirs / sortir tous les soirs)
3. moi, je (apprendre le vocabulaire et les verbes / toujours sortir avec des amis)
   (dormir en cours / écouter en cours)

C On veut... Aujourd'hui, les Pérez ne peuvent pas faire ce qu'ils veulent. Jouez le rôle d'Alice et expliquez ce que chacun veut et doit faire.

EXEMPLE Moi, je veux dormir, mais je dois sortir le chien.

Moi...

1. Éric...

2. Éric et Cathy...

3. Vincent...

4. Nos amis...

5. Michel...

Line art on this page: © Cengage Learning

Plus tard, Alice dit que chacun n'a pas pu faire ce qu'il voulait *(wanted)* et elle explique ce qu'ils ont dû faire. Qu'est-ce qu'elle dit? Utilisez le passé composé.

EXEMPLE Moi, je n'ai pas pu dormir. J'ai dû sortir le chien.

D Comparaisons culturelles. Un lycéen *(high school student)* parle de la vie des jeunes en France. Complétez ce qu'il dit avec la forme correcte des verbes entre parenthèses. Ensuite, comparez la situation en France avec la situation ici.

EXEMPLE Je **peux** (pouvoir) faire ce que *(what)* je **veux** (vouloir) le mercredi après-midi, parce que je n'ai pas cours. Mais, je **dois** (devoir) assister aux *(attend)* cours le samedi matin.

Ici, on doit assister aux cours toute la journée le mercredi, mais on peut faire ce qu'on veut le samedi matin.

1. Je ne _____ (pouvoir) pas faire de sport après les cours au lycée *(high school)*, parce qu'il n'y a pas beaucoup d'activités extrascolaires. Si on _____ (vouloir) faire du sport, on _____ (devoir) aller à un club de sport.
2. Mes amis et moi _____ (devoir) prendre le bus pour aller en ville, parce qu'on ne _____ (pouvoir) pas avoir de permis de conduire *(driver's license)* avant l'âge de 18 ans.
3. Les jeunes qui _____ (vouloir) apprendre à conduire *(to drive)* _____ (devoir) payer pour aller à une auto-école *(driving school)*. Les lycéens ne _____ (pouvoir) pas suivre de cours de conduite *(take driver's ed)* au lycée.
4. Quand je _____ (vouloir) aller au centre-ville, je _____ (pouvoir) y aller facilement en bus. Les transports publics sont excellents ici.

STRATÉGIES ET COMPRÉHENSION AUDITIVE

POUR MIEUX COMPRENDRE: Noting the important information

When making plans, we often jot down important information for later reference. If a friend invited you to do something, what sort of information would you want to remember? Look at the following invitation and think about what information is given.

Suggestion. Review the twenty-four hour clock before doing the exercises in this section.

Script for A. Prenez des notes.

INVITATION A
— Allô, Éric? C'est Marc. Tu es libre demain? Tu veux jouer au tennis avec moi?
— Oui, je veux bien. Quand?
— Vers 14 heures. On se retrouve au parc?
— Oui, très bien.
— D'accord. À demain, alors.
— À demain.

INVITATION B
— Allô? C'est toi, Éric? C'est Marie.
— Salut, Marie.
— Écoute, j'ai envie d'aller au musée cet après-midi. Tu m'accompagnes?
— Oui, je veux bien. On se retrouve devant le musée?
— Non, passe plutôt chez moi vers midi et demi.
— D'accord.

INVITATION C
— Allô, Éric? C'est Jean-Luc. Michèle et toi, vous êtes libres samedi soir? Je voudrais vous inviter à dîner chez moi.
— Oui, oui, bonne idée. Vers quelle heure?
— Vers 19 heures 30.
— Très bien.

A Prenez des notes. Trois amis invitent Éric à faire quelque chose. Écoutez chaque invitation et prenez des notes en français. Qu'est-ce qu'ils vont faire? Où? Quel jour? À quelle heure?

B À vous. Éric demande à Michèle de l'accompagner. Utilisez vos notes de l'exercice précédent pour jouer les rôles d'Éric et de Michèle avec un(e) partenaire.

EXEMPLE — Je vais jouer au tennis avec Marc demain à... Est-ce que tu voudrais jouer avec nous?
— Oui, je veux bien!

🔊 Compréhension auditive: *On va au cinéma?*

Vincent demande à Alice si elle voudrait aller au cinéma. Lisez les questions de l'exercice suivant. Ensuite, écoutez la conversation et notez les détails importants sur une feuille de papier.

A Quel film? Répondez aux questions suivantes d'après la conversation entre Alice et son mari.

1. Comment est-ce qu'Alice trouve les films de science-fiction?
2. Quel genre *(type)* de film est-ce qu'ils décident d'aller voir?
3. À quelle séance est-ce qu'ils vont aller?

B Vos notes. Utilisez vos notes pour recréer *(to recreate)* la conversation entre Alice et Vincent avec un(e) partenaire.

C Tu veux sortir? Invitez votre partenaire à aller voir un film avec vous. Choisissez une séance et décidez à quelle heure vous allez passer chez votre ami(e).

Script for *On va au cinéma?*
— On va au cinéma ce soir?
— Oui, je veux bien. Quel film est-ce que tu voudrais aller voir?
— Je ne sais pas. Il y a une comédie d'Alain Chabat au cinéma Gaumont Parnasse. Qu'est-ce que tu en penses?
— Allons voir quelque chose d'autre. Je n'ai pas tellement envie de voir une comédie.
— Il y a le nouveau film américain de science-fiction au cinéma Rex. On dit que c'est un très bon film.
— Tu sais bien que je n'aime pas les films de science-fiction. Ils sont souvent bêtes ou très violents.
— Alors, qu'est-ce que tu veux aller voir?
— Allons voir le nouveau film d'amour au cinéma Rex.
— Bon, si tu préfères. C'est à quelle heure?
— Il y a trois séances: une à 18h20, une à 20h45 et la dernière à 23h15.
— Allons à la séance de 18h20 et allons manger après.
— D'accord.

Follow-up for *B. Vos notes.* After students have recreated the conversation, play the audio again so students can see how well they acted it out.

10:35 | 13:20 | 16:05 | 19:00 | 21:45

11:50 | 14:40 | 17:25 | 20:05

12:10 | 13:30 | 15:55 | 18:45 | 21:20

COMPÉTENCE 2

Talking about how you spend and used to spend your time

PowerPoint 6-5

AUJOURD'HUI ET DANS LE PASSÉ

Michèle compare sa **vie** quand **elle était** au **lycée** avec sa vie d'aujourd'hui.

Quand j'étais au lycée…   Aujourd'hui…

J'avais 15 ans.	J'ai 21 ans.
J'étais **lycéenne.**	Je suis étudiante à l'université.
J'habitais avec ma famille.	J'habite avec ma famille.
J'avais cours du lundi au vendredi et aussi le samedi matin.	J'ai cours du lundi au vendredi.
Je n'aimais pas beaucoup **l'école** (f).	J'aime l'université.
Je rentrais souvent à la maison pour déjeuner.	En général, je déjeune au **resto U.**
Le week-end, j'étais toujours **fatiguée** et **je dormais** beaucoup.	Le week-end, je suis souvent fatiguée et je dors beaucoup.
Le vendredi soir, je passais du temps avec ma famille ou **je sortais** avec **des copains.** On allait au cinéma, au café ou à une fête.	Le vendredi soir, **je sors** souvent avec des copains. On va au cinéma, en boîte ou à **une soirée.**
Le samedi, je faisais du sport avec des amis: on jouait au foot ou **on faisait du roller.**	Tous les samedis, je joue au tennis avec des amis et je fais aussi souvent du roller.

---

dans le passé *in the past*   **la vie** *life*   **elle était** *she was*   **le lycée** *high school*   **J'avais 15 ans.** *I was fifteen.*   **un(e) lycéen(ne)** *a high school student*   **J'habitais** *I lived, I used to live*   **J'avais cours** *I had class, I used to have class*   **l'école** *school*   **le resto U** *the university cafeteria*   **fatigué(e)** *tired*   **je dormais** *I slept, I used to sleep*   **je sortais** *I went out, I used to go out*   **un copain (une copine)** *a (boy/girl)friend, a pal*   **je sors (sortir)** *I go out (to go out)*   **une soirée** *a party*   **on faisait du roller** *we went in-line skating, we used to go in-line skating*

Note culturelle

En France, avec Internet et la télé, les blogs et les réseaux sociaux *(social networks)*, les lycéens passent beaucoup de temps dans leur chambre. Mais, retrouver des amis est leur première activité. La plupart des ados *(teenagers)* pratiquent aussi une activité culturelle, artistique ou sportive le mercredi, jour où ils sortent plus tôt de l'école.

Les étudiants universitaires adorent sortir! La majorité va régulièrement au cinéma, au restaurant, au café, en soirée et occasionnellement en boîte. Plus d'un tiers *(third)* choisit régulièrement des sorties culturelles: concert, théâtre, musée.

Quels sont vos loisirs préférés? Êtes-vous différents des Français?

Michèle demande à Éric **ce qu'**il faisait quand il était au lycée aux États-Unis.

MICHÈLE: Qu'est-ce que tu aimais faire quand tu étais au lycée?
ÉRIC: J'aimais passer mon temps avec des copains. Le vendredi soir, on allait aux matchs de football américain ou de basket au lycée.
MICHÈLE: Et le samedi?
ÉRIC: Le samedi matin, je travaillais. Le samedi après-midi, on faisait du skateboard. Le samedi soir, je sortais avec ma copine. On allait au cinéma.
MICHÈLE: Et qu'est-ce que tu faisais le dimanche?
ÉRIC: Le dimanche, je ne faisais rien de spécial. Je restais à la maison. Je regardais la télé ou une vidéo.

A Maintenant ou dans le passé?
Est-ce que Michèle parle de sa vie maintenant ou de sa vie quand elle avait 15 ans? Commencez chaque phrase avec **Quand j'avais 15 ans…** ou **Maintenant…**

1. J'étais lycéenne.
2. J'ai cours du lundi au vendredi.
3. Je n'aimais pas beaucoup l'école.
4. Je déjeune souvent au resto U.
5. Je sors beaucoup le week-end.
6. Mes copains et moi, on aimait aller au café.
7. On faisait souvent du sport ensemble.

B Et vous?
Dites si vous faites ces choses maintenant et si vous faisiez ces choses quand vous aviez 10 ans.

EXEMPLES
Maintenant, j'habite avec ma famille.
Maintenant, j'habite avec ma famille.
Maintenant, je n'habite pas avec ma famille.

Quand j'avais 10 ans, j'habitais avec ma famille.
Quand j'avais 10 ans, j'habitais avec ma famille.
Quand j'avais 10 ans, je n'habitais pas avec ma famille.

1. Maintenant, j'ai cours tous les jours.
   Quand j'avais 10 ans, j'avais cours tous les jours.
2. Maintenant, j'aime mes études.
   Quand j'avais 10 ans, j'aimais l'école.
3. Maintenant, mes copains (copines) et moi, on fait souvent du sport ensemble.
   Quand j'avais 10 ans, on faisait souvent du sport ensemble.
4. Maintenant, je sors souvent le samedi soir.
   Quand j'avais 10 ans, je sortais souvent le samedi soir.
5. Maintenant, je suis souvent fatigué(e) le dimanche.
   Quand j'avais 10 ans, j'étais souvent fatigué(e) le dimanche.
6. Maintenant, je dors beaucoup le week-end.
   Quand j'avais 10 ans, je dormais beaucoup le week-end.

À VOUS!

Avec un(e) partenaire, relisez à haute voix la conversation entre Michèle et Éric. Ensuite, adaptez la conversation pour parler de ce que vous faisiez *(what you used to do)* quand vous étiez au lycée. Si vous voulez utiliser des verbes que vous n'avez pas encore appris dans cette forme du passé, demandez à votre professeur comment les conjuguer.

ce que what

PowerPoint 6-6

SAYING HOW THINGS USED TO BE

✓ Pour vérifier

1. Which form of the present tense do you use to create the stem for all verbs in the imperfect, except for **être**? What is the stem for **être**?

2. You use the **passé composé** to talk about a specific occurrence in the past. When do you use the **imparfait**?

3. Which imperfect endings are pronounced alike? What single letter distinguishes the **nous** and **vous** forms of the imperfect from the present?

iLrn Grammar Tutorials

Note de grammaire

Note that verbs like **étudier** retain the **i** of the stem before the **imparfait** endings.

j'étudi**ais**   nous étudi**ions**
vous étudi**iez**   ils étudi**aient**

Note. This **Compétence** introduces the formation of the **imparfait** and focuses on its use to express habitual, continuous, and repeated actions. The further uses of the **imparfait** and the contrast between the **passé composé** and the **imparfait** are presented in the next two **Compétences**.

Supplemental activity. Read sentences aloud about yourself at the age of twelve, some true and some false. Have students guess which ones are false. For example: **1.** J'étais marié(e). **2.** J'habitais à… **3.** J'habitais seul(e). **4.** J'avais un chien qui s'appelait… **5.** J'avais onze chats. **6.** J'étudiais le français. **7.** C'était mon cours préféré. **8.** J'étudiais à l'université. **9.** J'aimais l'école. **10.** Je jouais au basket à l'école. **11.** Mon père / Ma mère travaillait pour…

L'imparfait

Use the **passé composé** to talk about what happened on a specific occasion. To tell what things used to be like, or what happened over and over, use the **imparfait** (*imperfect*). The **imparfait** can be translated in a variety of ways in English.

I was working mornings.
I used to work mornings.   } Je travaillais le matin.
I worked mornings.

All verbs except **être** form this tense by dropping the **-ons** from the present tense **nous** form and adding the endings you see below. The stem for **être** is **ét-**.

	PARLER (nous parl**ons** → parl-)	**FAIRE** (nous fais**ons** → fais-)	**PRENDRE** (nous pren**ons** → pren-)	**ÊTRE** (ét-)
je (j')	parl**ais**	fais**ais**	pren**ais**	ét**ais**
tu	parl**ais**	fais**ais**	pren**ais**	ét**ais**
il/elle/on	parl**ait**	fais**ait**	pren**ait**	ét**ait**
nous	parl**ions**	fais**ions**	pren**ions**	ét**ions**
vous	parl**iez**	fais**iez**	pren**iez**	ét**iez**
ils/elles	parl**aient**	fais**aient**	pren**aient**	ét**aient**

Spelling changes in the present tense **nous** form of verbs like **manger** and **commencer** occur in the **imparfait** only before endings beginning with an **a**.

MANGER	**COMMENCER**
je mang**eais**	je commen**çais**
tu mang**eais**	tu commen**çais**
il/elle/on mang**eait**	il/elle/on commen**çait**
nous mang**ions**	nous commen**cions**
vous mang**iez**	vous commen**ciez**
ils/elles mang**eaient**	ils/elles commen**çaient**

Also learn these expressions in the imperfect.

c'est → c'était   il y a → il y avait   il pleut → il pleuvait   il neige → il neigeait

PRONONCIATION

Les terminaisons de l'imparfait 2-23

The **-ais**, **-ait**, and **-aient** endings of the imperfect are all pronounced alike. The **nous** and **vous** endings of the imperfect, **-ions** and **-iez**, are distinguished from the present only by the vowel **i** in the ending.

Qu'est-ce que vous faisiez?	*What did you use to do?*
Ils travaillaient pour IBM.	*They worked for IBM.*
Nous allions à la plage.	*We used to go to the beach.*

A Prononcez bien! Une amie parle de sa vie maintenant et de sa vie quand elle était au lycée. D'abord, pratiquez la prononciation de chaque phrase. Ensuite, lisez à haute voix une phrase de chaque paire. Votre partenaire va dire si vous parlez du **présent** ou du **passé**.

Maintenant	Quand j'étais au lycée
1. J'ai cours tous les jours.	J'avais cours tous les jours.
2. J'étudie beaucoup.	J'étudiais beaucoup.
3. Mon meilleur ami aime le sport.	Mon meilleur ami aimait le sport.
4. Il joue au basket.	Il jouait au basket.
5. Nous aimons sortir ensemble.	Nous aimions sortir ensemble.
6. Nous allons souvent au cinéma.	Nous allions souvent au cinéma.
7. Mes parents travaillent beaucoup.	Mes parents travaillaient beaucoup.
8. Ils sont souvent fatigués.	Ils étaient souvent fatigués.

Maintenant, changez chaque phrase pour parler de vous.

EXEMPLE Maintenant, j'ai cours le mardi et le jeudi. Quand j'étais au lycée, j'avais cours du lundi au vendredi.

Sélection musicale. Search the Web for the songs **"Comme toi"** by Jean-Jacques Goldman, **"J'aimais mieux avant"** by Christophe Cerillo, or **"Michèle"** by Gérard Lenorman to enjoy musical selections with this structure.

B La jeunesse. Interviewez un(e) partenaire pour savoir ce qu'il/elle faisait quand il/elle était au lycée.

EXEMPLE fumer / ne pas aimer ça
— Tu fumais quand tu étais au lycée ou tu n'aimais pas ça?
— Je fumais. / Je n'aimais pas ça.

1. aller presque toujours en cours / être souvent absent(e)
2. avoir beaucoup de copains / passer beaucoup de temps seul(e)
3. faire souvent du sport / préférer faire autre chose
4. pouvoir sortir tard / devoir rentrer tôt
5. aimer dormir tard le week-end / avoir beaucoup d'énergie le matin

Maintenant, avec votre partenaire, préparez six questions pour votre professeur. Demandez ce qu'il/elle faisait quand il/elle était étudiant(e) à l'université.

Quand j'avais dix ans, j'aimais jouer avec mon chien.

C Chez nous. Que faisaient ces personnes quand vous aviez dix ans? Dites au moins trois choses pour chacune.

EXEMPLE Mon père...
Mon père était très patient. Il travaillait souvent le week-end et il rentrait tard. Il n'était pas souvent à la maison.

1. Mes parents...
2. Mes amis...
3. Ma mère...
4. Mon père...
5. Dans ma famille, nous...
6. Mes copains et moi...

avoir beaucoup d'amis / un chien	arriver à l'école à... heures
être patient(e)(s) / impatient(e)(s)	rentrer à... heures
travailler le week-end	jouer au golf / à des jeux vidéo...
aimer lire / dormir…	faire souvent du roller / du sport…
être à la maison le week-end	voyager souvent
faire le ménage / du shopping…	aller souvent voir mes cousins…
aimer les maths / les sciences…	aller à la plage / au cinéma…

Supplemental activities. A. Have students write a composition to describe their life at a certain age: what they looked like, where they lived, etc. Remind them not to tell about a particular incident but to describe general characteristics. You may wish to get them started with **La meilleure époque de ma vie, c'était quand... B.** Have students bring a picture from their past (their house when they were young, their room, old friends, their high school, etc.) and describe what these things or people were like. **C.** Project pictures of yourself at various ages and have students work in groups to ask you about your life at each of those time periods. **D.** Have students work in groups to write lists of sentences comparing the advantages of growing up when their grandparents did with the advantages of growing up now. EXEMPLE **Tout était moins cher. Il n'y avait pas d'ordinateurs quand ils étaient jeunes…**

 **PowerPoint 6-7**

TALKING ABOUT ACTIVITIES

Pour vérifier

1. What are the conjugations of **sortir, partir,** and **dormir**? Which auxiliary verb is used with each one in the **passé composé**?

2. How do you say *to go out **of**? to leave **from**? to leave **for**?*

3. How do you say *to leave for the weekend? to leave on vacation? to leave on a trip?*

4. What is the difference in pronunciation between **il sort** and **ils sortent**?

Note de vocabulaire

Remember that **quitter** means *to leave* a person or a place and is *always* used with a direct object. In the **passé composé**, it is conjugated with **avoir**.

J'ai quitté la maison à midi.

Suggestion. You may wish to remind students of the use of **jusqu'à** with **dormir**.

Les verbes ***sortir, partir*** *et* ***dormir***

The verbs **sortir, partir,** and **dormir** have similar patterns of conjugation.

SORTIR (to go out)	PARTIR (to leave)	DORMIR (to sleep)
je **sors**	je **pars**	je **dors**
tu **sors**	tu **pars**	tu **dors**
il/elle/on **sort**	il/elle/on **part**	il/elle/on **dort**
nous **sortons**	nous **partons**	nous **dormons**
vous **sortez**	vous **partez**	vous **dormez**
ils/elles **sortent**	ils/elles **partent**	ils/elles **dorment**
P.C. **je suis sorti(e)**	P.C. **je suis parti(e)**	P.C. **j'ai dormi**
IMP. **je sortais**	IMP. **je partais**	IMP. **je dormais**

You have already seen that **sortir** can mean *to go out,* in the sense of going out with friends. It can also mean *to go / come out of,* in the sense of going out of a place. It is the opposite of **entrer**. Use **de** to say *of*.

Je suis sorti **de** l'appartement en pyjama pour aller chercher le journal.

Partir means *to leave* in the sense of *to go away*. It is the opposite of **arriver**. Some common expressions with **partir** are: **partir en week-end, partir en vacances, partir en voyage**. To name the place you are leaving, use **partir de**. To say where you are leaving *for*, use **partir pour**.

Il part en vacances aujourd'hui. Il est parti **de** son bureau à trois heures et il est parti **pour** l'aéroport vers cinq heures.

PRONONCIATION

Les verbes ***sortir, partir*** *et* ***dormir*** 2-24

You can distinguish aurally between the **il/elle** singular and **ils/elles** plural forms of verbs like **sortir, partir,** and **dormir**. Compare these sentences.

ALICE
Elle dort bien.
Elle sort ce soir.
Elle part demain.

ALICE ET SA FILLE
Elles dorment bien.
Elles sortent ce soir.
Elles partent demain.

When a word ends with a pronounced consonant sound in French, it must be released. Note that when you pronounce the boldfaced consonants in the following English phrases, your tongue or lips do not have to move back and release them.

What pa**rt**?   What so**rt**?   In the do**rm**.

Compare how the boldfaced consonants in the following plural verb forms are released.

Ils par**t**ent.   Ils sor**t**ent.   Ils dor**m**ent.

A Prononcez bien! Pour chaque phrase que vous entendez, dites si Alice parle d'**Éric** ou d'**Éric et de Cathy**.

B Entretien. Complétez ces questions avec la forme correcte des verbes indiqués au présent et interviewez un(e) partenaire.

EXEMPLE —Est-ce que tu **sors** (sortir) souvent en semaine avec tes amis?
— **Je sors quelquefois le mercredi soir.**

1. Est-ce que ton meilleur ami (ta meilleure amie) _____ (sortir) souvent avec toi le week-end? Est-ce que vous _____ (sortir) quelquefois en semaine?
2. Quand tu _____ (sortir) avec tes amis le samedi soir, jusqu'à quelle heure est-ce que tu _____ (dormir) le dimanche?
3. Est-ce que tes amis _____ (sortir) souvent pendant la semaine sans toi? Est-ce qu'ils _____ (dormir) quelquefois pendant leurs cours?
4. Est-ce que tu _____ (partir) souvent en week-end? Généralement, où vas-tu quand tu _____ (partir) pour quelques jours?

Maintenant, mettez les verbes à l'imparfait pour parler de ce que votre partenaire et ses amis faisaient quand il/elle était lycéen(ne).

EXEMPLE —Quand tu étais au lycée, est-ce que tu **sortais** (sortir) souvent en semaine avec tes amis?
— **Non, je ne sortais jamais en semaine.**

C Vos habitudes. Formez des phrases pour parler de ce que vous faites les jours du cours de français et quand vous sortez avec des amis. Circulez dans la classe et trouvez quelqu'un qui fait la même chose que vous.

EXEMPLES Les jours du cours de français, je / dormir jusqu'à... heures.
— **Les jours du cours de français, je dors jusqu'à 7 heures. Et toi? Tu dors jusqu'à 7 heures aussi?**
— **Non, je dors jusqu'à 8 heures.**

1. Les jours du cours de français, je / dormir jusqu'à... heures.
2. Aujourd'hui, je / sortir de mon dernier cours à... heures.
3. Mes amis et moi / sortir le plus souvent le... soir.
4. D'habitude, je / dormir jusqu'à... le dimanche.
5. Je / partir le plus souvent en vacances au mois de...

Maintenant, dites à la classe qui fait les mêmes choses que vous.

EXEMPLES **Les jours du cours de français, Courtney dort jusqu'à 7 heures, comme moi.**
Luis et ses amis sortent le plus souvent le samedi soir, comme mes amis et moi.

D Toujours des questions! Parlez avec votre partenaire de la dernière fois qu'il/elle est sorti(e) avec des amis. Posez les questions indiquées.

EXEMPLE quand / sortir ensemble
— **Quand est-ce que vous êtes sortis ensemble?**
— **On est sortis ensemble hier.**

1. quand / sortir ensemble
2. où / aller ensemble
3. qu'est-ce que / faire
4. à quelle heure / partir de la maison
5. jusqu'à quelle heure / dormir le lendemain

Script for A. Prononcez bien! 1. Ils dorment bien en général. 2. Il dort ce matin. 3. Il ne sort pas ce soir. 4. Ils sortent souvent le week-end. 5. Ils partent vers six heures. 6. Il part pour la campagne.

Follow-up for A. Prononcez bien! Give students similar sentences as dictation.

Follow-up for B. Entretien. Dites si ces personnes font souvent les choses indiquées. **EXEMPLE** je (dormir sur le canapé) **Je dors souvent sur le canapé. / Je dors quelquefois sur le canapé. / Je ne dors jamais sur le canapé.** 1. je (sortir avec des amis le mercredi, partir de chez moi avant 9 heures du matin, dormir toute la journée le samedi) 2. mon meilleur ami / ma meilleure amie (partir en vacances, sortir le vendredi soir, dormir jusqu'à 11 heures le week-end) 3. mes amis et moi (partir en week-end, sortir ensemble le dimanche soir, dormir en cours le lundi) 4. mes parents (sortir danser, partir en week-end pour leur anniversaire de mariage, dormir tard le week-end) Maintenant, dites si ces personnes faisaient souvent les choses indiquées quand vous étiez lycéen(ne). **EXEMPLE** je (dormir sur le canapé) **Je dormais quelquefois sur le canapé.**

Compétence 2 | *deux cent trente-cinq* 235

COMPÉTENCE 3

Talking about the past

 PowerPoint 6-8

Note culturelle

Aujourd'hui en France, un repas sur sept est pris en dehors du domicile *(away from home)*, comparé à un repas sur deux aux États-Unis. À votre avis, pourquoi est-ce que les Américains mangent plus souvent en dehors du domicile que les Français? Est-ce une question de prix? de qualité? de temps? de tradition?

Warm-ups. A. Questions orales. **1.** Dormez-vous bien ou mal, en général? Jusqu'à quelle heure dormez-vous le *[current day of the week]*, d'habitude? Jusqu'à quelle heure avez-vous dormi ce matin? **2.** À quelle heure partez-vous de la maison le *[current day of the week]* d'habitude? À quelle heure êtes-vous parti(e) de la maison aujourd'hui? **3.** Quand aimez-vous sortir avec des copains? Êtes-vous sortis ensemble hier soir? **B.** Répondez à l'imparfait. Qu'est-ce que vous faisiez hier… **1.** à 8h du matin? **2.** à midi? **3.** à 3h de l'après-midi? **4.** à 6h du soir? **5.** à minuit?

Suggestion. Point out the contrast between the use of the **passé composé** to tell *what happened* and the **imparfait** to tell *what things were like*.

Supplemental activity. Have students answer these questions about Cathy's day with short answers. **1.** Quel temps faisait-il quand Cathy a quitté son appartement? **2.** Quelle heure était-il quand elle est arrivée au restaurant? **3.** Combien de copains étaient au restaurant avec Cathy? Est-ce qu'ils ont mangé tout de suite? **4.** Comment était le repas? **5.** Est-ce que Cathy et ses copains ont continué la soirée après le repas? **6.** Vers quelle heure est-ce que Cathy est rentrée? **7.** Jusqu'à quelle heure est-ce qu'elle a dormi le lendemain?

UNE SORTIE

Cathy parle de la dernière fois qu'elle a dîné avec des amis. Et vous? La dernière fois que vous êtes sorti(e) avec des ami(e)s, comment était la soirée? **Qu'est-ce qui s'est passé?**

Il pleuvait quand j'ai quitté l'appartement.

Il était sept heures et demie quand je suis arrivée au restaurant.

On n'avait pas très faim et on n'a pas mangé **tout de suite.**

Le repas était **délicieux** et j'ai beaucoup mangé.

Après le repas, nous étions fatigués et nous sommes partis.

Quand je suis rentrée chez moi, il était environ dix heures.

Le lendemain, c'était dimanche et je suis restée au lit jusqu'à dix heures.

Line art on this page: © Cengage Learning

Qu'est-ce qui s'est passé? *What happened?*   **tout de suite** *right away*   **Le repas** *The meal*   **délicieux (délicieuse)** *delicious*

Cathy et une amie parlent de leurs activités du week-end dernier.

MANON: Je suis allée au restaurant avec des copines ce week-end.
CATHY: Vous êtes allées où?
MANON: Au Bistro Romain.
CATHY: **Ça t'a plu?**
MANON: Beaucoup. C'était délicieux. On a bien mangé et on a beaucoup parlé. C'était vraiment bien!
CATHY: Et qu'est-ce que tu as fait après?
MANON: **Rien du tout.** J'étais fatiguée et je suis rentrée. Et toi, qu'est-ce que tu as fait ce week-end?
CATHY: Moi aussi, je suis sortie avec des copains. On est allés au cinéma.

A   Au restaurant.
La dernière fois que vous êtes allé(e) au restaurant, qu'est-ce qui s'est passé? Changez les mots en italique pour parler de votre sortie.

1. Quand j'ai quitté *la maison*, il était *huit heures* et il *faisait froid*.
2. Quand je suis arrivé(e) au restaurant, il était *neuf heures*.
3. On *avait très faim* et on *a mangé tout de suite*.
4. Le repas était vraiment *médiocre* et j'ai *peu* mangé.
5. Après le repas, nous avions envie de *continuer la soirée* et nous *sommes allés en boîte*.
6. Quand je suis rentré(e), il était *onze heures* et j'*étais fatigué(e)*.
7. Le lendemain, c'était *dimanche* et je *suis resté(e) au lit*.

Note *de grammaire*

You usually answer a question in the same tense in which it is asked.

B   La journée d'Alice.
Décrivez la journée d'Alice vendredi dernier.

1. Alice était seule quand elle a quitté l'appartement? Quelle heure était-il? Est-ce qu'il pleuvait? Est-ce qu'il faisait froid? Quels vêtements est-ce qu'elle portait?
2. Alice était seule au café? Elle a mangé quelque chose? Elle a bu quelque chose?
3. Quelle heure était-il quand elle est rentrée chez elle?

À VOUS!

Avec un(e) partenaire, relisez à haute voix la conversation entre Manon et Cathy. Ensuite, adaptez la conversation pour parler de la dernière fois que vous avez mangé avec des copains.

Ça t'a plu? *Did you like it?*   **Rien du tout.** *Nothing at all.*

PowerPoint 6-10

TELLING WHAT HAPPENED AND DESCRIBING THE CIRCUMSTANCES

✓ Pour vérifier

1. Do you generally use the **passé composé** or the **imparfait** to say what happened at a specific moment, for a specific duration, or a specific number of times? to describe how things were or used to be or to talk about actions in progress?

2. Which would you use to talk about how you were feeling? to describe a change in a mental or physical state?

3. Which tense do you use to say what was going to happen?

Note de grammaire

You generally use the verb **vouloir** in the **imparfait** to say what someone wanted to do.

*Je **voulais** aller voir un film.*
I wanted to go see a movie.

Use **pouvoir** in the **imparfait** to say what people could do if they might have wanted to, but use it in the **passé composé** to say what they managed to do on an occasion when they tried.

*Ma copine ne **pouvait** pas sortir.*
My girlfriend couldn't go out.

*J'**ai pu** persuader un autre ami d'y aller.*
I was able to persuade another friend to go.

Use **devoir** in the **imparfait** to say what one was supposed to do, but in the **passé composé** for what one must have done, or had to do on a specific occasion.

*Il **devait** déjà être ici.*
He was supposed to be here already.

*Il **a dû** travailler tard.*
He had to work late. / He must have worked late.

🌐 **Sélection musicale.** Search the Web for the songs "**Il avait les mots**" by Sheryfa Luna or **On savait** by La Grande Sophie to enjoy musical selections with these structures.

Note. In this section, students are introduced to various uses of the **passé composé** and the **imparfait** and are given opportunities to practice each distinction. In the next **Compétence**, they will practice narrating stories in the past.

Le passé composé et l'imparfait

You know to use the **imparfait** to tell how things used to be or what was going on when something else occurred. The **imparfait** is used to describe continuing actions or states, whereas the **passé composé** is used for actions that happened and were finished.

USE THE *IMPARFAIT* TO SAY:	USE THE *PASSÉ COMPOSÉ* TO SAY:
1. HOW THINGS USED TO BE OR WHAT USED TO HAPPEN • continuing actions, states, or situations • repeated or habitual actions of an unspecified duration	**1. WHAT HAPPENED AT A PRECISE MOMENT OR FOR A SPECIFIC DURATION OR NUMBER OF TIMES** • completed actions • actions that occurred for a specific duration or a specific number of times

Notre amie habitait à côté de chez nous.
Our friend lived next to us.
Elle invitait toujours des amis chez elle.
She always invited friends over.

Elle a fait une soirée le mois dernier.
She had a party last month.
Nous sommes allées à cinq de ses soirées.
We went to five of her parties.

2. WHAT THINGS WERE LIKE OR HOW SOMEONE FELT • physical or mental states	**2. WHAT CHANGED** • changes in states

Tout le monde allait bien, mais moi, j'étais fatiguée.
Everyone was doing fine, but I was tired.

Tout à coup, j'ai eu peur.
All of a sudden, I got frightened.

Watch for words like **tout d'un coup** (*all at once*), **tout à coup** (*all of a sudden*), **soudain** (*suddenly*), **une fois** (*once*), and **un jour** (*one day*) indicating changes in states.

3. WHAT SOMEONE WAS GOING TO DO	**3. WHAT ONE WENT TO DO**

On allait partir.
We were going to leave.

Je suis allée chercher mon sac.
I went to get my purse.

240 deux cent quarante | **CHAPITRE 6**

A Pourquoi? Expliquez pourquoi Cathy a fait ou n'a pas fait ces choses. Quel verbe doit être au passé composé et lequel *(which one)* doit être à l'imparfait?

EXEMPLE Cathy **était** (être) malade, alors elle **n'a pas travaillé** (ne pas travailler).

1. Cathy _____ (ne pas sortir) parce qu'elle _____ (être) malade.
2. Elle _____ (être) trop fatiguée, alors elle _____ (ne pas faire) ses devoirs.
3. Elle _____ (faire) du shopping parce qu'elle _____ (vouloir) acheter une nouvelle robe.
4. Elle _____ (mettre) un pull parce qu'elle _____ (avoir) froid.
5. Elle _____ (avoir) besoin de réviser ses cours, alors elle _____ (ne pas sortir) avec ses amis.

B Ce matin chez les Pérez. Alice Pérez décrit la journée de sa famille. Qu'est-ce qu'elle dit? Mettez les verbes au passé composé ou à l'imparfait.

EXEMPLE Moi, j'ai fait du jogging ce matin. Je voulais dormir.

1.

Moi...
faire du jogging ce matin
vouloir dormir
avoir sommeil
ne pas avoir envie de sortir
sortir à sept heures
rentrer une heure plus tard
avoir besoin d'un bain *(bath)*
aller dans la salle de bains
prendre un long bain

2.

Éric et Cathy...
préparer le déjeuner aujourd'hui
vouloir faire du shopping
déjeuner avant de sortir
aller au centre commercial à une heure
avoir l'intention d'acheter des vêtements
rentrer vers cinq heures
avoir faim
retrouver des amis au restaurant
rentrer à neuf heures

C Entretien. Parlez à votre partenaire de la dernière fois qu'il/elle est allé(e) au restaurant avec des amis.

La dernière fois que tu es allé(e) au restaurant avec des amis,...

1. Quel temps faisait-il? Qu'est-ce que tu as mis pour sortir? un jean? une robe?
2. Quelle heure était-il quand tu es arrivé(e) au restaurant?
3. Avais-tu très faim? As-tu mangé tout de suite? Comment était le repas?
4. Qu'est-ce que tu as fait après le repas?
5. Quelle heure était-il quand tu es rentré(e)? Étais-tu fatigué(e)? Est-ce que tu es allé(e) tout de suite au lit? As-tu bien dormi?
6. Le lendemain, jusqu'à quelle heure es-tu resté(e) au lit?

COMPÉTENCE 4

Narrating in the past

PowerPoint 6-11

Note culturelle

Le cinéma est né en France, inventé par les frères Lumière en 1895. Le premier film, montré à Lyon, représente la sortie de l'usine Lumière *(the end-of-day departure from the Lumière factory)*. Aujourd'hui, le cinéma français va très bien. *Intouchables* (2011) est le film français qui a été le plus vu à l'étranger, suivi par *Le Fabuleux Destin d'Amélie Poulain* (2001). Quels films français connaissez-vous? Comment est-ce que ces films diffèrent des films hollywoodiens?

Vocabulaire sans peine!

Most nouns referring to people that end with *-tor* in English are similar in French, but end with **-teur** in the masculine and **-trice** in the feminine.

actor = **acteur / actrice**
educator = **éducateur / éducatrice**

How would you say these words in French?

protector
procrastinator

Most English adjectives ending with *-ible* are similar in French.

horrible = **horrible**
terrible = **terrible**

How would you say these words in French?

accessible
compatible

2-29

Warm-up. Questions orales. Avec qui est-ce que vous avez dîné au restaurant récemment? À quel restaurant êtes-vous allé(e)s? Quelle heure était-il quand vous êtes arrivé(e)s? Est-ce que le repas était bon? Est-ce que vous avez beaucoup mangé? Combien de temps est-ce que vous êtes resté(e)s au restaurant? À quelle heure est-ce que vous êtes parti(e)s? Quel temps est-ce qu'il faisait?

Note for the conversation. New vocabulary includes all glossed words and **il m'a plu, un acteur (une actrice), excellent,** and **la violence.**

Suggestion for the conversation. Have students first listen with books closed and answer this question: Qu'est-ce qu'Éric a fait le week-end dernier?

LES CONTES

Éric et Michèle sont allés voir le film classique ***La Belle et la Bête*** de Jean Cocteau. **Connaissez-vous** ce film? Connaissez-vous **le conte de fées** sur **lequel** ce film est basé?

Il était une fois un vieux **marchand** qui avait trois filles. Sa plus jeune fille, Belle, était très jolie, **douce** et **gracieuse**.

Un jour, la Bête a emprisonné le marchand. Belle **a promis** à la Bête de venir prendre la place de son père.

Le monstre était horrible! Il était grand et laid et il avait l'air **féroce. Au début,** Belle avait très peur de lui. Mais elle était toujours gentille et patiente avec lui.

Petit à petit, les choses ont changé. Belle et la Bête ont commencé à **se parler.** La Bête a beaucoup changé et Belle a appris à apprécier le monstre. Finalement, Belle **est tombée amoureuse de** lui! Et la Bête a aussi appris à aimer.

À suivre...

Cathy parle à son frère de ses activités du week-end dernier.

CATHY : Tu es sorti ce week-end?
ÉRIC : Oui, je suis allé au cinéclub avec Michèle.
CATHY : Quel film est-ce que vous avez vu?
ÉRIC : Nous avons vu *La Belle et la Bête* de Cocteau.
CATHY : C'est un classique! Il t'a plu?
ÉRIC : Oui, il m'a beaucoup plu. Les acteurs **ont bien joué, les effets spéciaux** étaient excellents **pour l'époque** et il n'y avait pas **trop de** violence.

---

un conte *a story* (for children)   ***La Belle et la Bête*** *Beauty and the Beast*   **Connaissez-vous...?** *Do you know...?*   **un conte de fées** *a fairy tale*   **lequel (laquelle)** *which*   **Il était une fois...** *Once upon a time there was...*   **un marchand** *a merchant, a shopkeeper*   **doux (douce)** *sweet, soft, gentle*   **gracieux (gracieuse)** *gracious*   **elle a promis** (**promettre** *to promise* [past participle **promis**])   **féroce** *ferocious*   **Au début** *At the beginning*   **se parler** *to talk to each other*   **tomber amoureux (amoureuse) de** *to fall in love with*   **À suivre** *To be continued*   **bien jouer** *to act well* (in movies and theater)   **les effets spéciaux** *the special effects*   **pour l'époque** *for that time (period)*   **trop de** *too much*

A **C'est qui?** Décidez lequel des personnages les adjectifs suivants décrivent: **le père de Belle, Belle** ou **la Bête**. N'oubliez pas d'utiliser l'imparfait pour faire une description!

EXEMPLE douce **Belle était douce.**

1. jolie   2. grande et laide   3. vieux   4. gracieuse   5. horrible

Maintenant, dites qui a fait les choses suivantes. N'oubliez pas d'utiliser le passé composé pour décrire le déroulement de l'action *(sequence of events)*!

EXEMPLE promettre de venir prendre la place de son père
Belle a promis de venir prendre la place de son père.

1. emprisonner le marchand
2. prendre la place de son père
3. commencer à parler avec la Bête
4. apprendre à apprécier la Bête
5. tomber amoureuse de Belle
6. beaucoup changer

B **Contes de fées.** En 1697, l'écrivain *(the writer)* français Charles Perrault a publié les contes de fées suivants dans son livre *Histoires ou contes du temps passé*. Choisissez la forme correcte des verbes entre parenthèses pour compléter les descriptions qui suivent. Ensuite, dites quel titre de la liste correspond à chacune.

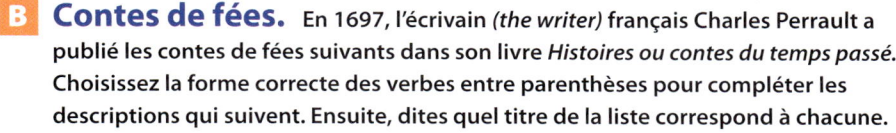

1. Les parents d'une princesse (n'ont pas invité / n'invitaient pas) une vieille fée à la fête pour le baptême de leur fille. Vexée, la vieille fée (a jeté / jetait) un sort *(cast a spell)* à la princesse.
2. Une petite fille qui (a porté / portait) toujours un chaperon *(hood)* rouge (a traversé / traversait) *(was crossing)* la forêt en allant voir sa grand-mère quand elle (a rencontré / rencontrait) un grand méchant loup *(wolf)*.
3. Un homme pauvre (a laissé / laissait) un chat à son fils comme seul héritage *(inheritance)*. Mais le chat (a eu / avait) des pouvoirs magiques *(magical powers)* et, avec son aide, le jeune homme (est devenu / devenait) riche.
4. Après la mort de son père, une belle jeune fille vivait *(lived)* avec sa belle-mère et ses deux demi-sœurs. Sa belle-mère (a été / était) cruelle et ses demi-sœurs (ont été / étaient) laides. Le prince (a invité / invitait) les filles des alentours *(surrounding area)* à un bal magnifique.

C **Une sortie au cinéma.** Alice parle du week-end à une amie. Complétez la conversation en mettant les verbes au passé composé ou à l'imparfait. Ensuite, adaptez la conversation pour parler de votre week-end avec un(e) partenaire.

— Tu __1__ (passer) un bon week-end?
— Assez bon. Mon amie __2__ (vouloir) aller voir un film, alors je __3__ (aller) au cinéma avec elle et je __4__ (rentrer) tard.
— Quelle heure __5__ (être)-il quand tu __6__ (rentrer)?
— On __7__ (rester) au cinéma jusqu'à 10h30 et après, on __8__ (avoir) faim, alors on __9__ (aller) manger quelque chose. Il y __10__ (avoir) beaucoup de gens au restaurant et on __11__ (devoir) attendre pour avoir une table. Il __12__ (être) environ 1h00 quand on __13__ (partir) du restaurant.

À VOUS!

Avec un(e) partenaire, relisez à haute voix la conversation entre Cathy et Éric. Ensuite, adaptez la conversation pour parler d'un film que vous avez vu récemment.

 **PowerPoint 6-12**

NARRATING WHAT HAPPENED

Le passé composé et l'imparfait (reprise)

When telling a story in the past, you use both the **passé composé** and the **imparfait**.

USE THE *IMPARFAIT* TO SAY:	USE THE *PASSÉ COMPOSÉ* TO SAY:
WHAT WAS ALREADY GOING ON	WHAT HAPPENED NEXT / WHAT CHANGED
• descriptions of the scene / setting • background information about the characters • interrupted actions in progress	• sequence of events that advance the storyline • actions interrupting something in progress

✓ **Pour vérifier**

If you were describing a play that you saw, would you use the **passé composé** or the **imparfait** to describe the setting and what was happening on stage when the curtain went up? Which tense would you use to explain the actions of the actors that advanced the story?

For a chart summarizing all of the uses of the **passé composé** and the **imparfait**, see the *Résumé de grammaire* on page 253.

🌐 **Sélection musicale.** Search the Web for the songs **"Nathalie"** by Gilbert Bécaud or **"La Rua Madureira"** by Nino Ferrer to enjoy musical selections with these structures.

If you were telling the old French tale **Cendrillon** *(Cinderella)*, you might begin . . .

Il **était** une fois une belle jeune fille qui **s'appelait** Cendrillon. Son père **était** mort et elle **habitait** avec sa belle-mère et ses deux demi-sœurs. Sa belle-mère **était** cruelle et ses demi-sœurs **étaient** laides et très gâtées *(spoiled)*. C'**était** Cendrillon qui **faisait** tout le travail, mais elle **était** toujours belle et gracieuse. Un jour, le prince **a décidé** de donner un bal au palais et un messager **est allé** chez Cendrillon avec une invitation.

There are only two events that occur advancing the story: the prince decided to give a ball and the messenger went to Cinderella's house. These two verbs are in the **passé composé**. All the rest of the paragraph is background information, setting the scene, so the verbs are in the **imparfait**.

When deciding whether to put a verb in the **passé composé** or the **imparfait**, learn to ask yourself whether you are talking about background information or something that was already in progress **(imparfait)**, or the next thing that happened in the story **(passé composé)**.

Suggestion for A. La journée d'Alice. Before beginning the exercise, point out that this exercise focuses on the distinction between setting the scene and narrating events. Ask students which tense you use to do each.

A **La journée d'Alice.** Alice parle de sa journée. Décidez si chaque phrase décrit la scène / la situation ou raconte le déroulement de l'action *(sequence of events)*. Décidez dans quelle colonne va chaque phrase.

Il est sept heures. Il pleut. Je quitte la maison. Il y a beaucoup de voitures sur la route. J'arrive au bureau en retard. Mon patron *(boss)* n'est pas content. Je travaille beaucoup. Je ne déjeune pas. Je rentre à cinq heures. Je suis fatiguée. Il n'y a rien à manger. Nous allons au restaurant. Nous rentrons. Je prends un bain. Il est 11 heures. Je vais au lit.

EXEMPLE

LA SCÈNE / LA SITUATION	LE DÉROULEMENT DE L'ACTION
Il est sept heures.	Je quitte la maison.

Maintenant, réécrivez le paragraphe en mettant les verbes qui présentent le déroulement de l'action au passé composé et les verbes qui décrivent la scène ou la situation à l'imparfait.

B Il était une fois... Réécrivez le début de l'histoire de *La Belle et la Bête* au passé en mettant les verbes en caractères gras à l'imparfait ou au passé composé.

EXEMPLE Il y **avait** un marchand très riche...

Il y (1) **a** un marchand très riche qui (2) **a** trois filles. Ils (3) **habitent** tous ensemble dans une belle maison en ville. Mais un jour, des voleurs *(thieves)* (4) **prennent** toute sa fortune et le marchand et ses filles (5) **doivent** aller habiter dans une petite maison à la campagne.

Ses deux filles aînées (6) **sont** très malheureuses *(unhappy)*. Elles (7) **parlent** constamment des choses qu'elles (8) **veulent.** Belle (9) **est** la plus jeune de ses filles. Elle (10) **est** très jolie et aussi très douce. Elle (11) **accepte** sa nouvelle vie et elle (12) **est** heureuse *(happy)*.

Un jour, le marchand (13) **part** pour la ville voisine *(neighboring)*. Il (14) **neige** et il (15) **fait** très froid et en route, il ne (16) **peut** rien voir dans la forêt. Le marchand (17) **pense** qu'il (18) **va** mourir quand, soudain, il (19) **trouve** un château. La porte du château (20) **est** ouverte et il (21) **décide** d'entrer. Il (22) **remarque** [remarquer *to notice*] une grande table couverte de plats délicieux. Il (23) **mange,** puis il (24) **fait** une sieste *(nap)*.

Après sa sieste, il (25) **sort** dans le jardin où il (26) **trouve** une jolie rose qu'il (27) **veut** rapporter *(to bring back)* à Belle. À ce moment-là, un monstre horrible (28) **arrive** et (29) **commence** à crier *(to shout)* qu'il (30) **veut** que Belle vienne habiter chez lui, sinon *(otherwise)*, la Bête (31) **va** tuer *(to kill)* le marchand.

Suggestion for B. Il était une fois... Encourage students to read a story in its entirety before selecting the proper tenses. You may first wish to work with them to pick out the verbs that narrate the action and those that set the scene.

C La Belle et la Bête. Continuez l'histoire de *La Belle et la Bête* en mettant les verbes entre parenthèses au passé composé ou à l'imparfait.

Quand le marchand __1__ (rentrer), il __2__ (raconter *[to recount]*) ses aventures à ses filles et Belle __3__ (décider) d'aller habiter chez la Bête. Quand elle __4__ (arriver) au château, elle __5__ (trouver) tout ce dont *(that)* elle __6__ (avoir) besoin. Chaque jour, elle __7__ (avoir) tout ce qu'elle __8__ (vouloir). Mais pendant les cinq premiers jours, elle __9__ (ne pas voir) la Bête.

Un jour, elle le (l') __10__ (voir) pour la première fois pendant *(while)* qu'elle __11__ (faire) une promenade dans le jardin. Elle le (l') __12__ (trouver) horrible et elle __13__ (crier). Belle __14__ (avoir) peur et elle __15__ (ne pas pouvoir) regarder la Bête dans les yeux, mais elle __16__ (aller) faire une promenade avec lui. La conversation __17__ (être) agréable. Quand la Bête __18__ (demander) à Belle de faire une promenade deux jours plus tard, elle __19__ (accepter).

Après ce jour-là, ils __20__ (faire) une promenade chaque après-midi. Ils __21__ (parler) de tout. Au début, Belle __22__ (avoir) très peur de la Bête mais, finalement, Belle __23__ (apprendre) à avoir confiance en lui. Après un certain temps, Belle __24__ (commencer) à aimer le monstre et un jour, elle l' __25__ (embrasser *[to kiss]*). Tout à coup, le visage *(face)* de la Bête __26__ (changer) et il __27__ (devenir) un beau et jeune prince.

Line art on this page: © Cengage Learning

VIDÉOREPRISE

Les Stagiaires

Dans *l'Épisode 6*, Matthieu essaie de dominer sa timidité pour inviter Amélie à sortir avec lui. Avant de regarder l'épisode, faites ces activités pour réviser ce que vous avez appris dans le *Chapitre 6*.

Rappel!
Dans l'épisode précédent de la vidéo, Matthieu et Christophe ont parlé d'une soirée que Christophe avait passée avec Amélie et Rachid, et Matthieu lui a posé *(asked him)* beaucoup de questions au sujet d'Amélie et de ce qu'elle aimait faire.

See the *Résumé de grammaire* section at the end of each chapter for a review of all the grammar presented in the chapter.

Follow-up for A. Invitations. Have students make the same invitations to a group. EXEMPLE aller au cinéma demain **Vous voudriez aller au cinéma demain?**

The entire *Vidéoreprise* section is designed to be a pre-viewing series for the video, as well as a chapter review that can be used independently from the video. There are also additional grammar review exercises on the Instructor's Companion Website and on iLrn.

A Invitations. Matthieu voudrait inviter Amélie à sortir avec lui. Comment est-ce qu'on invite un(e) ami(e) à aller quelque part *(to go somewhere)*? Invitez un(e) partenaire à faire les choses suivantes. Il/Elle va accepter une de vos invitations, refuser une de vos invitations et suggérer une autre activité pour la troisième. Utilisez des expressions variées.

EXEMPLE aller au cinéma demain
— **Tu voudrais aller au cinéma demain?**
— **Oui, d'accord.**

1. aller prendre un verre après les cours
2. aller danser samedi soir
3. aller voir une exposition au musée dimanche après-midi

B On ne peut pas toujours faire ce qu'on veut! Camille explique ce que ses collègues ont envie de faire et ce qu'ils ont besoin de faire. Répétez ce qu'elle dit, en utilisant les verbes **vouloir**, **pouvoir** et **devoir**.

EXEMPLE Christophe a envie de lire un manga, mais il a besoin de faire des photocopies pour son père.
Christophe veut lire un manga, mais il ne peut pas parce qu'il doit faire des photocopies pour son père.

1. M. Vieilledent a envie de boire du café, mais il a besoin de réduire *(reduce)* sa consommation de caféine.
2. Rachid et Amélie ont envie de partir tôt du bureau aujourd'hui, mais ils ont besoin de finir leur travail.
3. J'ai envie de prendre une longue pause pour le déjeuner *(lunch break)* aujourd'hui pour faire du shopping, mais j'ai besoin de rentrer au bureau.
4. Nous avons tous envie de moins travailler, mais nous avons besoin de terminer *(to finish)* ce projet pour des clients.

C Au bureau. Camille décrit les habitudes de ses collègues. Complétez chaque phrase en mettant le verbe donné à la forme correcte du présent. Ensuite, dites si les autres personnes indiquées font la même chose.

EXEMPLE Le lundi matin, M. Vieilledent **part** (partir) pour le travail avant huit heures. Et vous?
Moi aussi, je pars pour le travail avant huit heures le lundi matin.

1. Céline _____ (partir) souvent en week-end. Et vous? Et vos amis?
2. Christophe _____ (dormir) souvent jusqu'à midi le week-end. Et vous? Et vos amis?
3. Rachid et Amélie _____ (sortir) souvent danser le samedi soir. Et vos amis et vous?
4. Amélie _____ (sortir) avec ses amis. Et vous?
5. Amélie ne _____ (dormir) jamais en cours. Et le professeur de français? Et les autres étudiants et vous?

D Hier soir. Matthieu parle de ce qu'il a fait hier soir. Complétez ce qu'il dit en mettant les verbes donnés au passé composé ou à l'imparfait.

J'aime beaucoup faire la cuisine et hier, j' __1__ (inviter) des amis à dîner chez moi. Vers quatre heures, je __2__ (sortir) pour aller faire les courses. J' __3__ (acheter) tout ce dont *(that)* j' __4__ (avoir) besoin et je __5__ (rentrer). Je/J' __6__ (commencer) à préparer le repas *(meal)* quand le téléphone __7__ (sonner *[to ring]*). C' __8__ (être) un de mes amis qui __9__ (vouloir) me dire *(to tell me)* qu'ils __10__ (aller) arriver un peu en retard *(late)*. Il __11__ (être) déjà huit heures quand ils __12__ (arriver) et nous __13__ (avoir) tous très faim, alors, nous __14__ (commencer) à manger tout de suite. Après, nous __15__ (jouer) à des jeux vidéo jusqu'à minuit. Quand mes amis __16__ (partir), j' __17__ (être) fatigué et je/j' __18__ (aller) au lit.

 E Quelle soirée! Amélie est allée à une fête chez des amis, les Fédor. Par petits groupes, regardez l'illustration et racontez *(tell)* ce qui s'est passé à la fête. Utilisez **le voleur** pour *the thief*, **voler** pour *to steal* et **entrer par la fenêtre** pour *to come in through the window*. Avant de commencer, réfléchissez *(think)* aux questions suivantes.

- What night was it?
- What time was it?
- What was the weather like?
- How many people were in the Fédors' living room?
- Why were they there?
- What was each person doing?
- What was in the bedroom?
- What happened?
- What happened next?

Les Dupont Hassan Amélie   le voleur Les Fédor

 **▶ Épisode 6: Je t'invite…**

AVANT LA VIDÉO
Dans cet épisode, Matthieu invite Amélie à sortir avec lui. Avant de regarder l'épisode, faites une liste de trois phrases qu'on peut utiliser pour inviter quelqu'un.

APRÈS LA VIDÉO
Regardez l'épisode pour déterminer quand Matthieu et Amélie vont sortir ensemble et où ils vont aller.

LECTURE ET COMPOSITION

LECTURE

POUR MIEUX LIRE: Using standard formats

You are going to read summaries of the two French movies that are so far the biggest box-office hits in France. Such summaries generally have similar formats. There is a presentation of the characters; a description of a conflict or a struggle between characters, cultures, or with oneself; and a resolution. Most movie plots can be categorized into one of the following categories: 1) a triumph of good over evil (a villain or a monster), 2) a rags to riches story, 3) a comically awkward attempt to acquire or get rid of something, 4) a quest for an object or a place, 5) a spiritual journey or a rebirth, or 6) a tragic spiral towards death or destruction. Can you think of movies that fit in each of these categories? How would you categorize the last three movies you saw? Keeping these common formats in mind will help you understand better as you watch or read about movies in French.

Intrigues. Lisez les résumés des films français *Bienvenue chez les Ch'tis* et *Intouchables* et décidez si on peut les classer *(categorize)* comme: 1) un triomphe du bien sur le mal, 2) une histoire d'ascension de la pauvreté à la richesse, 3) une comédie où quelqu'un veut obtenir ou se débarrasser de *(to get rid of)* quelque chose, 4) la quête d'un objet ou d'un endroit, 5) une quête spirituelle ou une renaissance ou 6) une spirale tragique vers la mort ou la destruction.

Deux films français

Résumé du film *Bienvenue chez les Ch'tis*

Philippe Abrams est directeur d'un bureau de poste et il veut **se faire muter** sur la Côte d'Azur. **De façon à** être prioritaire pour **la mutation,** il essaie de se faire passer pour un handicapé. **Découvrant sa supercherie,** l'administration l'envoie dans le Nord pour une mutation disciplinaire de deux ans. **Croyant** que le Nord est une région froide et inhospitalière, sa femme, Julie, décide de rester dans le Sud avec leur fils, et Philippe part seul pour son nouveau poste chez les «Ch'tis», les habitants du Nord. **Contre toute attente,** Philippe trouve les «Ch'tis» **chaleureux** et charmants. **En outre,** il considère la séparation temporaire positive pour sa relation avec sa femme et il essaie de **lui faire croire** que la vie dans la petite ville du Nord est **un cauchemar** pour la dissuader de venir le rejoindre. Persuadée que son mari est **déprimé,** Julie annonce finalement qu'elle va aller le voir. Avec la complicité de ses amis, Philippe essaie de faire croire à Julie que tous les clichés qu'elle a sur les gens du Nord sont vrais. Découvrant **les mensonges** de son mari et vexée, Julie retourne dans le Sud. Finalement, Philippe redescend dans le Sud pour lui demander de venir le rejoindre dans le Nord. Deux ans plus tard, Philippe doit quitter les «Ch'tis» parce qu'il est muté dans le Sud.

se faire muter *to be transferred* **De façon à** *In order to* **la mutation** *the transfer* **Découvrant sa supercherie** *Discovering his deception* **Croyant** *Believing* **Contre toute attente** *Unexpectedly* **chaleureux** *warm* **En outre** *Moreover* **lui faire croire** *to make her believe* **un cauchemar** *a nightmare* **déprimé** *depressed* **les mensonges** *the lies*

Résumé du film *Intouchables*

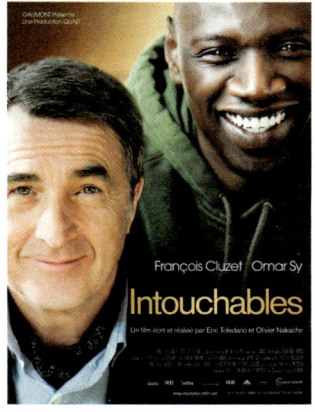

Après six mois de prison, Driss, un jeune homme d'origine sénégalaise de la banlieue parisienne, trouve du travail comme **aide à domicile** chez Philippe, un riche aristocrate devenu **tétraplégique** après un accident de **parapente**. Driss **n'a aucune formation,** mais sa confiance, sa manière franche et spontanée de parler et son énergie impressionnent Philippe, qui est fatigué de la pitié de ses anciens aides. Les différences entre les univers des deux hommes **donnent lieu** à des situations pleines d'humour, et une amitié **inattendue** entre les deux hommes **naît.** Ce film est basé sur une histoire vraie.

---

aide à domicile *personal assistant, home helper*   **tétraplégique** *quadriplegic*
parapente *paragliding*   **n'a aucune formation** *has no training*
donnent lieu *give rise*   **inattendue** *unexpected*   **naît** *is born*

Compréhension

A Répondez aux questions suivantes.

1. Dans quelle catégorie classez-vous ces deux films?
2. Qui sont les personnages *(characters)* du film *Bienvenue chez les Ch'tis*? Quels conflits surgissent *(arise)* dans ce film? Comment est-ce que le film finit?
3. Qui sont les personnages du film *Intouchables*? Quels conflits de culture y a-t-il entre les deux hommes? Est-ce qu'ils deviennent amis? Pourquoi est-ce qu'on pourrait dire *(might you say)* qu'il y a «une renaissance *(a rebirth)*» des personnages?
4. Voudriez-vous plutôt voir *Bienvenue chez les Ch'tis* ou *Intouchables*? Pourquoi?

B On peut résumer un film au présent ou au passé. Changez ces résumés du présent au passé en mettant les verbes au passé composé ou à l'imparfait.

COMPOSITION

POUR MIEUX ÉCRIRE: Using standard formats

You are going to write a brief summary of one of your favorite films using the **passé composé** and the **imparfait.** Such summaries usually begin with one or two sentences introducing the characters and setting the scene; a few sentences stating the main events that create a conflict or a struggle; and a sentence or two explaining how it is (or is not) resolved. Following this format will help you organize a clear and concise summary.

Organisez-vous. Suivez les étapes *(steps)* suivantes pour organiser votre résumé.

1. Écrivez une ou deux phrases pour présenter les personnages *(characters)* et la situation. Allez-vous utiliser le passé composé ou l'imparfait pour décrire les personnages et la scène?
2. Faites une liste des actions les plus importantes des personnages. Allez-vous utiliser le passé composé ou l'imparfait pour décrire le déroulement de l'action *(the sequence of events)*?
3. Écrivez une ou deux phrases pour expliquer comment le film se termine *(ends)*. Commencez par **À la fin...**

Process-writing follow-up for *Un film à voir!* Have students read their composition aloud one sentence at a time without naming the film to see how long it takes classmates to guess what film is being described.

Un film à voir

Utilisez les phrases que vous avez préparées dans la section ***Organisez-vous*** pour écrire un résumé du film que vous avez choisi.

iLrn Share It!

COMPARAISONS CULTURELLES

LE CINÉMA: LES PRÉFÉRENCES DES FRANÇAIS

Le cinéma, **que ce soit** les films vus au cinéma, à la télévision ou en DVD, occupe une place centrale dans le temps libre des Français. Avant de lire les renseignements **qui suivent** sur le cinéma en France, essayez de **deviner** comment compléter les phrases. Est-ce que la situation du cinéma en France est comparable à la situation dans votre région?

The Artist, un film français, muet en noir et blanc, est un hommage aux films muets hollywoodiens des années 1920. Au Festival de Cannes en 2011, l'acteur Jean Dujardin obtient le Prix d'interprétation masculine *(best leading actor).* Le film remporte aussi trois Golden Globes, sept BAFTA, six Césars, un Goya et cinq Oscars.

LES FILMS

Les Français préfèrent...

❏ les films français. ❏ les films étrangers.

Les Français aiment **autant** les films étrangers **que** les films français. En général, les films français représentent à peu près 40% des entrées au cinéma.

Comme films étrangers, ils préfèrent...

❏ les films américains. ❏ les films européens.

Parmi les films étrangers, ce sont les films américains qui sont les plus populaires. Des dix films les plus populaires en France depuis 1945, sept sont des productions américaines.

Comme genre, les Français préfèrent...

❏ les drames. ❏ les films d'aventure.

Ce sont les films qui **attirent** un public jeune qui sont les plus populaires en France: films d'aventure, d'horreur... Les Français aiment aussi les comédies et les films à grand spectacle et on assiste à la popularité **croissante** des films à message social et des films d'amour.

D'après les Français, **les cinéastes** français font les meilleurs...

❏ films à grand spectacle ❏ films comiques et satires sociales

tandis que les Américains font les meilleurs...

❏ films à grand spectacle. ❏ films comiques et satires sociales.

D'après les sondages auprès des Français, les cinéastes français font les meilleures comédies et satires sociales et les Américains sont plus forts pour le grand spectacle.

LES SPECTATEURS

La majorité des spectateurs...

❏ ont plus de 50 ans. ❏ ont entre 25 et 34 ans. ❏ ont moins de 25 ans.

---

que ce soit *whether it be* **qui suivent** *that follow* **deviner** *to guess* **autant que** *as much as* **attirent** *attract* **croissante** *growing* **D'après** *According to* **les cinéastes** *film-makers* **tandis que** *whereas* **D'après les sondages auprès des** *According to surveys of the*

Les moins de 25 ans représentent 35 % des spectateurs et deux-tiers (2/3) des gens qui vont au cinéma au moins une fois par mois.

En général, les Français vont au cinéma...

- ❑ pendant la semaine.
- ❑ le week-end.
- ❑ le mercredi, jour de sortie en salle des nouveaux films.
- ❑ en hiver.
- ❑ en été.
- ❑ de façon égale en toute saison.

En France, la saison du cinéma est l'hiver et on y va le plus souvent le week-end.

Source: Gérard Mermet, *Francoscopie 2010*, Éditions Larousse.

Voici une liste des dix films les plus vus au cinéma en France depuis 1945. Qu'est-ce que vous remarquez?

Les plus grands succès du cinéma en France depuis 1945, en millions d'entrées.	
TITANIC (ÉTATS-UNIS)	21,77
BIENVENUE CHEZ LES CH'TIS (FRANCE)	20,49
INTOUCHABLES (FRANCE)	19,44
BLANCHE-NEIGE ET LES SEPT NAINS (ÉTATS-UNIS)	18,32
LA GRANDE VADROUILLE (FRANCE, G.-B.)	17,27
AUTANT EN EMPORTE LE VENT (ÉTATS-UNIS)	16,72
IL ÉTAIT UNE FOIS DANS L'OUEST (ÉTATS-UNIS)	14,86
AVATAR (ÉTATS-UNIS)	14,77
LE LIVRE DE LA JUNGLE (ÉTATS-UNIS)	14,70
LES 101 DALMATIENS (ÉTATS-UNIS)	14,66

Source: www.jpbox-office.com

Compréhension

1. Qu'est-ce que vous pouvez dire au sujet des spectateurs français et de leurs préférences en matière de *(with regards to)* films? Quelles sont les préférences des gens là où vous habitez?

2. Combien de films du tableau ci-dessus *(chart above)* sont américains? français? Certains Français trouvent qu'il y a trop d'influence américaine dans les salles de cinéma en France et que la culture française est menacée *(is threatened)*. Est-ce que ce sentiment est justifié? Quel est le rôle du gouvernement dans la préservation de la culture? Est-ce qu'il doit y avoir une censure? des quotas? des subventions *(subsidies)*?

3. D'après la majorité des Français, quels genres de films est-ce que les cinéastes français font le mieux? Et les cinéastes américains? Est-ce que l'industrie cinématographique d'un pays est un reflet de *(a reflection of)* sa culture? Si oui, quelles comparaisons culturelles peut-on faire entre les Français et les Américains?

Follow-up for *Compréhension*. You may also wish to give students the following discussion question: **Le dynamisme de la production cinématographique française est en partie lié *(is tied)* au système de financement du cinéma. Le cinéma français est financé par des taxes sur les places de cinéma *(ticket sales)*, les revenus des chaînes de télévision et des éditeurs vidéo. Ces taxes retournent à l'industrie du cinéma sous forme de subventions *(subsidies)* à l'écriture *(writing)*, à la production, à la distribution et à l'exportation. Que pensez-vous de ce système?**

iLrn Share It!

Visit www.cengagebrain.com for additional cultural information and activities.

RÉSUMÉ DE GRAMMAIRE

THE VERBS *VOULOIR*, *POUVOIR*, AND *DEVOIR*

Je **veux** sortir ce soir, mais je ne **peux** pas. Je **dois** travailler.

Here are the conjugations of **vouloir** *(to want)*, **pouvoir** *(can, may, to be able)*, and **devoir** *(must, to have to, to owe)*.

VOULOIR	POUVOIR	DEVOIR
je **veux**	je **peux**	je **dois**
tu **veux**	tu **peux**	tu **dois**
il/elle/on **veut**	il/elle/on **peut**	il/elle/on **doit**
nous **voulons**	nous **pouvons**	nous **devons**
vous **voulez**	vous **pouvez**	vous **devez**
ils/elles **veulent**	ils/elles **peuvent**	ils/elles **doivent**
P.C. **j'ai voulu**	P.C. **j'ai pu**	P.C. **j'ai dû**
IMP. **je voulais**	IMP. **je pouvais**	IMP. **je devais**

Nous **voulions** partir en vacances, mais nous n'**avons** pas **pu**. Nous **avons dû** travailler.

Elle **a dû** quitter la maison très tôt. Elle **devait** arriver à sept heures.
She must have left / had to leave the house very early. She was supposed to arrive at seven o'clock.

You generally use the verb **vouloir** in the **imparfait** to say what someone wanted to do. Use **pouvoir** in the **imparfait** to say what people could do if they might have wanted to, but use it in the **passé composé** to say what they managed to do on an occasion when they tried. Use **devoir** in the **imparfait** to say what one was supposed to do, but in the **passé composé** for what one must have done, or had to do on a specific occasion.

THE VERBS *SORTIR*, *PARTIR*, AND *DORMIR*

Je **dors** jusqu'à sept heures et je **pars** pour l'université à huit heures.

Ce matin, j'**ai dormi** jusqu'à sept heures et demie et je **suis partie** pour l'université en retard *(late)*.

Here are the conjugations of **sortir** *(to go out)*, **partir** *(to leave)*, and **dormir** *(to sleep)*.

SORTIR	PARTIR	DORMIR
je **sors**	je **pars**	je **dors**
tu **sors**	tu **pars**	tu **dors**
il/elle/on **sort**	il/elle/on **part**	il/elle/on **dort**
nous **sortons**	nous **partons**	nous **dormons**
vous **sortez**	vous **partez**	vous **dormez**
ils/elles **sortent**	ils/elles **partent**	ils/elles **dorment**
P.C. **je suis sorti(e)**	P.C. **je suis parti(e)**	P.C. **j'ai dormi**
IMP. **je sortais**	IMP. **je partais**	IMP. **je dormais**

Avant, je **sortais** souvent avec des amis, mais nous ne **sommes** pas **sortis** le week-end dernier.

Il **quitte** Paris pour aller travailler à Nice. Il **part** demain.

Je sors **de** la maison à neuf heures.
Je pars **pour** Nice demain.
Je pars **de** chez moi à huit heures.

Sortir means *to go out* both in the sense of going out with friends and going out of a place. Use **partir** to say *to leave* in the sense of *to go away*. **Quitter** means *to leave* a person or a place and *must* be used with a direct object.

Use these prepositions with these verbs:

to go out (of) = **sortir (de)**
to leave (from) = **partir (de)**
to leave (for) = **partir (pour)**

L'IMPARFAIT AND LE PASSÉ COMPOSÉ

All verbs except **être** form the **imparfait** by dropping the **-ons** from the present tense **nous** form and adding these endings. The stem for **être** is **ét-**.

	PARLER (nous parl~~ons~~ → parl-)	FAIRE (nous fais~~ons~~ → fais-)	PRENDRE (nous pren~~ons~~ → pren-)	ÊTRE (ét-)
je (j')	parl**ais**	fais**ais**	pren**ais**	ét**ais**
tu	parl**ais**	fais**ais**	pren**ais**	ét**ais**
il/elle/on	parl**ait**	fais**ait**	pren**ait**	ét**ait**
nous	parl**ions**	fais**ions**	pren**ions**	ét**ions**
vous	parl**iez**	fais**iez**	pren**iez**	ét**iez**
ils/elles	parl**aient**	fais**aient**	pren**aient**	ét**aient**

Quand j'**avais** 16 ans, j'**allais** au lycée. Je **passais** beaucoup de temps avec mes copains. On **aimait** faire du roller.

Verbs with spelling changes in the present tense **nous** form, like **manger** and **commencer**, retain the spelling changes in the **imparfait** only before endings beginning with an **a**.

Note these expressions in the **imparfait**:

il y a	→	il y avait
il pleut	→	il pleuvait
il neige	→	il neigeait

Nous **mangions** bien, mais je **mangeais** peu.

Vous **commenciez** vos cours à midi, mais moi, je **commençais** mes cours à 11 heures.

Il y avait du vent, il **pleuvait** et **il faisait** froid, mais **il ne neigeait** pas.

When talking about the past, you use both the **passé composé** and the **imparfait**. Note their uses:

USE THE *IMPARFAIT* TO SAY:	USE THE *PASSÉ COMPOSÉ* TO SAY:
1. **HOW THINGS USED TO BE OR WHAT USED TO HAPPEN** • continuous actions or states • repeated or habitual actions of an unspecified duration	1. **WHAT HAPPENED AT A PRECISE MOMENT, FOR A SPECIFIC DURATION, OR A SPECIFIC NUMBER OF TIMES** • completed actions • actions within a specific duration • actions done a specific number of times
2. **WHAT WAS GOING ON** • scene or setting • interrupted actions in progress	2. **WHAT HAPPENED NEXT** • sequence of events • actions interrupting something in progress
3. **WHAT THINGS WERE LIKE OR HOW SOMEONE FELT** • physical or mental states	3. **WHAT CHANGED** • changes in states
4. **WHAT SOMEONE WAS GOING TO DO**	4. **WHAT SOMEONE WENT TO DO**

Cendrillon **pleurait** *(was crying)* quand sa marraine *([fairy] godmother)* **est arrivée**. La marraine **a aidé** Cendrillon et Cendrillon **est allée** au bal du prince. Le prince **est** immédiatement **tombé** amoureux de Cendrillon. Ils **ont dansé** et ils **ont** beaucoup **parlé**. À minuit, Cendrillon **est partie** sans dire au prince qui elle **était**, mais elle **a laissé** tomber *(dropped)* une de ses chaussures.

Résumé de grammaire | *deux cent cinquante-trois*

VOCABULAIRE

 Audio Flashcards

COMPÉTENCE 1

Inviting someone to go out

NOMS MASCULINS

l'amour	love
un film d'amour	a romantic movie, a love story
un groupe	a group
un horaire	a schedule

NOMS FÉMININS

une comédie	a comedy
une façon	a way
l'heure d'ouverture	opening time
l'heure officielle	official time
une idée	an idea
une invitation	an invitation
une personne	a person
une séance	a showing

EXPRESSIONS VERBALES

appeler	to call
devoir	must, to have to, to owe
dire	to say, to tell
passer un film	to show a movie
pouvoir	can, may, to be able
regretter	to regret, to be sorry
répondre (à)	to answer, to respond (to)
suggérer	to suggest
téléphoner (à)	to phone
utiliser	to use, to utilize
vouloir	to want

DIVERS

allô	hello (on the telephone)
avec plaisir	gladly, with pleasure
Je pensais	I was thinking
Je t'invite…	I'm inviting you …
Je voudrais vous inviter…	I'd like to invite you …
Quelle bonne idée!	What a good idea!
quelqu'un	someone, somebody
tellement	so much, so
uniquement	uniquely, only
Vous voudriez…?	Would you like … ?

COMPÉTENCE 2

Talking about how you spend and used to spend your time

NOMS MASCULINS

un copain	a (boy)friend, a pal
un lycée	a high school
un lycéen	a high school student
un resto U	a university cafeteria

NOMS FÉMININS

une copine	a (girl)friend, a pal
une école	a school
une lycéenne	a high school student
une soirée	a party
la vie	life

EXPRESSIONS VERBALES

avoir cours	to have class
comparer	to compare
dormir	to sleep
faire du roller	to go in-line skating
faire du skateboard	to skateboard
partir (de/pour)	to leave (from/for), to go away (from/to)
partir en vacances	to leave on vacation
partir en voyage	to leave on a trip
partir en week-end	to go away for the weekend
quitter	to leave
sortir (de)	to go out (of)

DIVERS

ce que	what
dans le passé	in the past
fatigué(e)	tired
rien de spécial	nothing special

254 *deux cent cinquante-quatre* | **CHAPITRE 6**

COMPÉTENCE 3

Talking about the past

NOMS MASCULINS

un bistro	a pub, a restaurant
un repas	a meal

NOMS FÉMININS

une fois	once, one time
une sortie	an outing

EXPRESSIONS ADVERBIALES

un jour	one day
soudain	suddenly
tout à coup	all of a sudden
tout de suite	right away
tout d'un coup	all at once

DIVERS

Ça t'a plu?	Did you like it?
délicieux (délicieuse)	delicious
Qu'est-ce qui s'est passé?	What happened?
rien du tout	nothing at all
tout le monde	everybody, everyone

COMPÉTENCE 4

Narrating in the past

NOMS MASCULINS

un acteur	an actor
un bal	a ball
un classique	a classic
un conte	a story (for children)
un conte de fées	a fairy tale
les effets spéciaux	special effects
un marchand	a merchant, a shopkeeper
un messager	a messenger
un monstre	a monster
un palais	a palace
le travail	work

NOMS FÉMININS

une actrice	an actress
une bête	a beast
une demi-sœur	a stepsister
une époque	a time (period)
une marchande	a merchant, a shopkeeper
une messagère	a messenger
la violence	violence

EXPRESSIONS VERBALES

apprécier	to appreciate
à suivre	to be continued
changer	to change
Connaissez-vous...?	Do you know...?
décider	to decide
emprisonner	to imprison
jouer	to act (in movies and theater)
se parler	to talk to each other
prendre la place de	to take the place of
promettre (promis)	to promise (promised)
tomber amoureux (amoureuse) de	to fall in love with

ADJECTIFS

amoureux (amoureuse) (de)	in love (with)
basé(e) (sur)	based (on)
cruel(le)	cruel
doux (douce)	sweet, soft, gentle
excellent(e)	excellent
féroce	ferocious
gâté(e)	spoiled
gracieux (gracieuse)	gracious
horrible	horrible
patient(e)	patient

DIVERS

au début (de)	at the beginning (of)
finalement	finally, in the end
Il était une fois...	Once upon a time there was...
il/elle m'a plu	I liked it
lequel (laquelle)	which, which one
petit à petit	little by little
trop de	too much

INTERLUDE MUSICAL

LA GARDE-ROBE D'ÉLIZABETH

AMÉLIE-LES-CRAYONS

Amélie-les-crayons, la chanteuse *(singer)* de la troupe du même nom, a fait ses débuts dans les cafés et bars de Lyon. Plus tard, elle s'est jointe aux trois autres musiciens, Heiko, Michel et Laurent, pour former la troupe. Dans leurs chansons, ils parlent de la vie de tous les jours, souvent sur un ton humoristique. Dans *La garde-robe d'Élizabeth,* Élizabeth désespère *(becomes exasperated)* parce qu'elle n'arrive pas à choisir quels vêtements elle veut mettre. Faites les activités qui suivent pour comprendre plus facilement les paroles *(lyrics)*.

Amélie-les-crayons est connue pour la qualité de son spectacle ainsi que *(as well as)* pour la qualité de sa musique.

🌐 You can find these songs on iTunes. You can also search the Internet to hear them performed and to find the lyrics.

A Élizabeth devant sa garde-robe. Voici de nouveaux mots qui se trouvent dans les paroles de *La garde-robe d'Élizabeth.* Organisez ces mots en trois listes: noms de vêtements, verbes et divers. Quels sont les vêtements que vous mettez le plus souvent?

EXEMPLE

VÊTEMENTS	VERBES	DIVERS
un anorak	**s'arracher**	**allumé(e)**
des bas	**attendre**	**à pois**

allumé(e) *turned on*
un anorak *a ski jacket*
à pois *polka-dotted*
s'arracher *to pull out*
attendre *to wait*
attraper *to grab*
des bas *hose, stockings*
des baskets *tennis shoes*
les bras *the arms*
des bretelles *suspenders*
un body *a body suit*
un cadeau *a gift*
un châle *a shawl*
le choix *the choice*
un col roulé *a turtleneck sweater*
un col V *a V-necked sweater*
se coucher *to lie down*
craquer *to crack*

criser *to panic*
croire *to believe*
une culotte *panties*
un débardeur *a tank top*
se dérober *to give way*
désespérer *to despair*
en boule *in a ball*
en croix *crossed*
s'énerver *to get upset*
enlever *to take off*
entendre *to hear*
en train de *in the process of*
fagoté(e) *done up, dressed*
un fer *an iron*
fouiller *to dig around*
un foulard *a scarf*
un froc *a frock*
une garde-robe *a wardrobe*
un gilet *a vest*

de grandes manches *puffy sleeves*
s'habiller *to dress oneself*
les info(rmation)s *news*
les jambes *legs*
des jambières *leggings*
lâcher *to let go, to release*
laver *to wash*
louper *to miss*
un maillot *a jersey*
la météo *the weather forecast*
mitigé(e) *mixed, uncertain*
un nu-dos *an open-backed outfit*
un pantalon *slacks*
repasser *to iron*
se ressaisir *to get hold of oneself*
sentir *to feel*
un tablier *an apron*
une tache *a spot*

B Qu'est-ce qu'elle fait? Complétez les phrases suivantes avec le choix logique.

1. Élizabeth s'arrache _____ (les jambes / les cheveux). Elle ne sait pas comment s'habiller!
2. Elle se couche par terre devant sa garde-robe, les _____ (bras / cheveux) en croix, le regard en l'air.
3. Élizabeth attrape quelque chose dans sa garde-robe, les _____ (bras / yeux) fermés.
4. Elle se regarde dans le miroir et elle n'en croit pas _____ (ses yeux / ses bras)! Elle voit une tache sur son gilet!

PREMIER AMOUR

TONY PARKER / RICKWEL

Tony Parker, célèbre joueur de basket des San Antonio Spurs, est aussi fana et chanteur de *(fan and singer of)* musique rap et hip-hop. Il est né en Belgique et a grandi *(grew up)* en France. Dans la chanson *Premier amour,* qu'il interprète avec l'artiste martiniquais Rickwel, il parle de son premier amour, un amour qu'il n'oubliera jamais *(he will never forget)*.

Dans la chanson *Premier amour,* c'est Tony Parker qui chante les strophes *(stanzas)* en français et Rickwel qui chante les strophes en anglais.

A **Comment c'était.** Dans la chanson *Premier amour,* le chanteur *(singer)* parle d'une copine de sa jeunesse et de leur relation. Pour mieux comprendre, faites des phrases logiques en utilisant un élément de chaque colonne.

Tu	étais / était	mon seul amour
On	aimais / aimait	mon porte-bonheur *(lucky charm)*
J'		mon avenir *(future)* et mon chemin *(path)*
		gosses *(kids)*
		fous *(crazy)*
		te serrer dans mes bras *(hold you in my arms)*
		toujours ensemble

B **Ce qui s'est passé.** Le chanteur parle aussi de ce qui leur est arrivé *(what happened to them)*. Mettez les verbes entre parenthèses au passé composé pour compléter les phrases et mieux comprendre les paroles de la chanson.

1. On s'est connus *(met)* trop jeunes et on _____ (grandir *[to grow up]*) trop vite.
2. On _____ (évoluer *[to evolve]*) dans la vie et notre amour s'est dissipé *(dissipated)*.
3. On s'est quittés *(We left each other)*, les années _____ (passer) et j'ai perdu le fil *(I lost track)*.
4. On _____ (rester) amis et on _____ (garder *[to keep]*) de beaux souvenirs de notre amour.

La Normandie
La vie quotidienne

- iLrn Heinle Learning Center
- www.cengagebrain.com
- *Horizons* Video: Les Stagiaires
- Audio
- Internet web search
- Pair work
- Group work

7

COMPÉTENCE

1 Describing your daily routine
La vie de tous les jours

Describing your daily routine
Les verbes réfléchis au présent

Stratégies et Lecture
- **Pour mieux lire:** *Using word families and watching out for* **faux amis**
- **Lecture:** *Il n'est jamais trop tard!*

2 Talking about relationships
La vie sentimentale

Saying what people do for each other
Les verbes réciproques au présent et les verbes réfléchis et réciproques au futur immédiat

Talking about activities
Les verbes en **-re**

3 Talking about what you did and used to do
Les activités d'hier

Saying what people did
Les verbes réfléchis et réciproques au passé composé

Saying what people did and used to do
Les verbes réfléchis et réciproques à l'imparfait et reprise de l'usage du passé composé et de l'imparfait

4 Describing traits and characteristics
Les traits de caractère

Specifying which one
Les pronoms relatifs **qui, que** *et* **dont**

Vidéoreprise *Les Stagiaires*

Lecture et Composition
- **Pour mieux lire:** *Recognizing conversational style*
- **Lecture:** *Conte pour enfants de moins de trois ans*
- **Pour mieux écrire:** *Organizing a paragraph*
- **Composition:** *Le matin chez moi*

Comparaisons culturelles *L'amour et le couple*

Résumé de grammaire

Vocabulaire

deux cent cinquante-neuf | 259

LA FRANCE ET SA DIVERSITÉ

Existe-t-il une identité française? Quand vous pensez à la culture française et au peuple français, comment est-ce que vous les imaginez?

En réalité, la France n'a pas **une seule** identité ou une seule culture. La France est un pays riche en diversité où chaque région a son **propre** héritage culturel.

In the **Culture Modules** in the video library, see **The Regions of France**.

Chacune des régions de la France a ses traditions, sa cuisine, sa musique, ses danses et même parfois sa langue.

Pourtant, malgré cette diversité, les Français **se sentent** bien français! Une histoire qui date de plus de 2 000 ans, **un patrimoine** riche en architecture et en culture et une tradition **à la fois laïque** et catholique donnent aux Français leur unité, le sens d'être «français».

---

une seule *a single*   **propre** *own*   **Pourtant, malgré** *However, in spite of*   **se sentent** *feel*   **un patrimoine** *a heritage*   **à la fois** *at the same time, both*   **laïque** *secular*

Récemment, l'immigration a beaucoup changé le visage de la France. Les nouveaux immigrés cherchent à **maintenir** leurs langues et leurs traditions.

Ainsi, aujourd'hui la France **fait face à** des questions importantes: Comment peut-on préserver l'identité de la culture française **tout en respectant** les divers groupes ethniques qui habitent dans le pays? Est-il possible de combiner l'unité et la diversité?

🌐 Chaque région de la France a sa propre histoire et sa propre culture. Choisissez une région de la France et recherchez des informations sur Internet au sujet de son héritage culturel. Partagez vos renseignements avec la classe.

Quick-reference answers. 1. régions/divers groupes ethniques, immigration 2. breton, corse, niçois 3. laïque, catholique 4. unité, diversité, divers groupes ethniques

maintenir *to maintain*   **Ainsi** *Thus*   **fait face à** *is facing*   **tout en respectant** *while still respecting*

La Normandie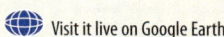

NOMBRE D'HABITANTS:
**3 500 000 habitants
(les Normands)**

CAPITALE: **Rouen**

Le savez-vous?

Qu'est-ce que vous avez appris au sujet de l'identité française? Existe-t-il une seule identité culturelle dans votre région? Complétez ces phrases.

> **breton   régions   diversité   immigration
> niçois   corse   laïque   catholique   unité
> divers groupes ethniques**

1. La France n'a pas une seule identité ou une seule culture. C'est un pays riche en diversité culturelle, grâce à *(due to)* la variété d'héritages culturels de ses _____ et à l'_____ récente.

2. Dans certaines régions de la France, les gens parlent non seulement *(not only)* français, mais aussi une langue régionale. De ces trois langues régionales – corse, niçois, breton, devinez laquelle *(guess which one)* est parlée dans chacune des régions suivantes.

   En Bretagne, certains parlent _____.

   En Corse, il y a des gens qui parlent _____.

   À Nice et dans sa région, on entend *(hears)* parfois parler _____.

3. Malgré cette diversité, les Français se sentent bien français. La France a un héritage culturel «français» basé surtout sur son histoire, son patrimoine et sa tradition à la fois _____ et _____.

4. À cause de la diversité des cultures qui font aujourd'hui partie de la culture française, les Français cherchent à trouver une réponse à deux questions importantes:

   Est-il possible de combiner l'_____ et la _____?

   Comment peut-on préserver l'identité de la culture française tout en respectant les _____ qui habitent dans le pays?

COMPÉTENCE 1

Describing your daily routine

 PowerPoint 7-2

LA VIE DE TOUS LES JOURS

Note culturelle

Les Français consacrent *(devote)* une heure par jour à leur toilette, c'est-à-dire à se laver et se préparer. Et vous, combien de temps consacrez-vous à votre routine quotidienne?

Note de vocabulaire

When saying that people are doing something to a part of their body, you generally use the definite article (**le, la, l', les**) in French, rather than a possessive adjective as in English.

Je me lave **les** mains.
*I'm washing **my** hands.*

Note de grammaire

After the expression **avant de,** use an infinitive rather than a conjugated verb.

Before I eat (Before eating), I wash my hands.
Avant de manger, je me lave les mains.

Quelle est votre **routine quotidienne**?

D'habitude le matin...

Je me réveille vers six heures. | Je me lève tout de suite et je **fais ma toilette**. | Je me lave **la figure** et **les mains** *(f)*. | Je prends un bain ou **une douche**.

  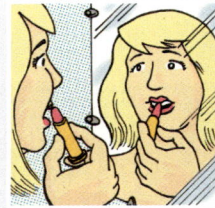 

Je me brosse les cheveux. | Je me brosse les dents. | Je me maquille **avant de m'habiller**. | Je m'habille.

Le soir...

Quelquefois, **je me repose**. | **D'autres fois**, je m'amuse avec des amis. | Parfois, quand je suis seule, **je m'ennuie**.

Je me déshabille. | Je me couche et **je m'endors** facilement.

Warm-up activity. Have students complete these sentences with an appropriate time. **EXEMPLE** Le *[current day of the week]*, je quitte la maison vers **huit heures et demie. 1.** J'ai mon premier cours à... **2.** Le cours de français est de... à... **3.** J'ai mon dernier cours à... **4.** Je rentre à la maison vers... **5.** Je dîne vers... **6.** Je vais au lit vers... **7.** Le *[tomorrow's day of the week]*, je peux dormir jusqu'à...

Supplemental activity. Review the vocabulary for rooms of the house on page 108 and have students say where you might logically be if you are doing the following things. **1.** Je me lève. **2.** Je me lave les mains. **3.** Je m'habille. **4.** Je prépare le dîner. **5.** Je prends mon dîner. **6.** Je m'endors sur le canapé. **7.** Je me déshabille. **8.** Je prends une douche. **9.** Je me brosse les dents. **10.** Je me couche.

Sélection musicale. Search the Web for the song "**C'est lundi**" by Jesse Garon to enjoy a musical selection related to this vocabulary.

Line art on this page: © Cengage Learning

la routine quotidienne *the daily routine* **faire sa toilette** *to wash up* **la figure** *the face* **les mains** *(f) the hands* **une douche** *a shower* **avant de m'habiller** *before I dress, before dressing* **je me repose (se reposer)** *to rest* **D'autres fois** *Other times* **je m'ennuie (s'ennuyer)** *to be bored, to get bored* **je m'endors (s'endormir** *to fall asleep*)

Rosalie Toulouse-Richard, d'origine française, habite à Atlanta **depuis** son mariage avec un Américain. **Veuve** maintenant, elle retourne en France avec sa **petite-fille** Rose qui ne **connaît** pas du tout la France. **Comme** elles partagent une chambre **pendant** leur **séjour**, elles parlent de leurs routines le matin.

ROSALIE: Tu te lèves vers quelle heure d'habitude?

ROSE: Entre six heures et six heures et demie. Je fais **vite** ma toilette, je m'habille et puis je me maquille. Je suis prête en une demi-heure.

ROSALIE: C'est parfait. Moi, je prends quelquefois une douche le matin, mais je préfère prendre mon bain le soir. Je peux très bien **attendre** jusqu'à sept heures pour faire ma toilette.

ROSE: Et moi, je ne quitte jamais la maison avant huit heures et demie. Alors si tu veux, on peut prendre le petit déjeuner ensemble tous les matins.

A Et ensuite... Trouvez la suite logique pour compléter chaque phrase.

Je me lève…	avec des amis.
Je me brosse…	je me couche.
Je prends…	vers huit heures.
L'après-midi, je m'amuse…	les dents.
Je me déshabille et puis…	une douche ou un bain.
Je me couche et…	je m'endors.

B Ma routine. Complétez les phrases avec une expression de la liste.

EXEMPLE Je me réveille avant six heures.
Je me réveille rarement avant six heures.
Je ne me réveille jamais avant six heures.

toujours	ne… jamais
souvent	tous les jours
quelquefois	le lundi, le mardi…
de temps en temps	le matin, l'après-midi, le soir
rarement	une (deux…) fois par jour (semaine…)

1. Je me réveille après neuf heures.
2. Je me lève tout de suite.
3. Je prends une douche ou un bain.
4. Je me lave les mains.
5. Je me lave les cheveux.
6. Je me brosse les dents.
7. Je m'habille vite.
8. Je m'ennuie.
9. Je me repose.
10. Je m'amuse bien.
11. Je me couche tard.
12. Je m'endors sur le canapé.

À VOUS!

Avec un(e) partenaire, relisez à haute voix la conversation entre Rosalie et Rose. Ensuite, imaginez que vous voyagez ensemble et adaptez la conversation pour parler de votre routine le matin.

---

depuis since **Veuve (Veuf)** Widow (Widower) **une petite-fille (un petit-fils)** a granddaughter (a grandson) **elle connaît (connaître** to know) **Comme** Since, As **pendant** during **un séjour** a stay **vite** quickly, fast **attendre** to wait (for)

PowerPoint 7-3

✓ **Pour vérifier**

1. What is the difference in usage between the reflexive verb **se laver** and the non-reflexive verb **laver**?
2. What are the different reflexive pronouns that are used with each subject pronoun when you conjugate a reflexive verb like **se laver**?
3. Where do you place **ne... pas** when negating reflexive verbs?
4. How is **s'endormir** conjugated?
5. In which forms do verbs like **se lever, s'appeler,** and **s'ennuyer** have spelling changes? What are the changes? Which forms do not have spelling changes?

iLrn Grammar Tutorials

Suggestion. Have students conjugate one of the verbs listed to check comprehension.

Supplemental activities. A. Ask students **Qui fait les choses suivantes, M. Élégant ou M. Négligé? 1.** Qui se lave les cheveux une fois par mois? **2.** Qui se lave les cheveux tous les jours? **3.** Qui ne se brosse jamais les cheveux? **4.** Qui ne se rase presque jamais? **5.** Qui se lève l'après-midi? **6.** Qui s'habille bien? **7.** Qui prend rarement un bain? **8.** Qui se brosse les dents trois fois par jour? **9.** Qui a les dents jaunes? **10.** Qui se lave toujours les mains avant de manger? **11.** Avec qui est-ce que vous préférez habiter? **B.** Distribute slips of paper with a reflexive verb on each one and have students mime the action. The rest of the class guesses which verb is being mimed.

DESCRIBING YOUR DAILY ROUTINE

Les verbes réfléchis au présent

You can do something to or for yourself or to or for another person or thing. When someone performs an action on or for himself/herself, a reflexive verb is generally used in French. Compare these sentences.

REFLEXIVE

Je me lave les mains.

NON-REFLEXIVE

Je lave la voiture.

The infinitive of reflexive verbs is preceded by the reflexive pronoun **se.** When you conjugate these verbs, change the reflexive pronoun according to the subject. In the negative, place **ne** directly after the subject and **pas** after the conjugated verb.

SE LAVER (to wash [oneself])		NE PAS SE LAVER	
je me lave	nous nous lavons	je ne me lave pas	nous ne nous lavons pas
tu te laves	vous vous lavez	tu ne te laves pas	vous ne vous lavez pas
il/elle/on se lave	ils/elles se lavent	il/elle/on ne se lave pas	ils/elles ne se lavent pas

Me, te, and **se** change to **m', t',** and **s'** before a vowel sound: **je m'habille, tu t'habilles, elle s'habille, ils s'habillent.**

Here are some reflexive verbs you can use to talk about your daily life:

s'amuser	to have fun
s'appeler	to be named
se brosser (les cheveux, les dents)	to brush (one's hair, one's teeth)
se coucher / se recoucher	to go to bed / to go back to bed
s'endormir	to fall asleep
s'ennuyer	to be bored, to get bored
s'habiller / se déshabiller	to get dressed / to get undressed
se laver (les mains, la figure)	to wash (one's hands, one's face)
se lever	to get up
se maquiller	to put on make-up
se raser	to shave
se reposer	to rest
se réveiller	to wake up

The verb **s'endormir** is conjugated like **dormir.**

S'ENDORMIR (to fall asleep)	
je m'endors	nous nous endormons
tu t'endors	vous vous endormez
il/elle/on s'endort	ils/elles s'endorment

264 *deux cent soixante-quatre* | **CHAPITRE 7**

Remember that in verbs ending in **-yer**, such as **s'ennuyer**, the letter **y** changes to **i** in all forms except those of **nous** and **vous**.

S'ENNUYER (to be bored, to get bored)

je m'ennuie	nous nous ennuyons
tu t'ennuies	vous vous ennuyez
il/elle/on s'ennuie	ils/elles s'ennuient

There is an accent spelling change in the conjugation of **se lever**. Its conjugation is similar to that of **acheter**. **S'appeler** changes its spelling by doubling the final consonant of the stem in all present tense forms except those of **nous** and **vous**.

SE LEVER (to get up)

je me lève	nous nous levons
tu te lèves	vous vous levez
il/elle/on se lève	ils/elles se lèvent

S'APPELER (to be named)

je m'appelle	nous nous appelons
tu t'appelles	vous vous appelez
il/elle/on s'appelle	ils/elles s'appellent

A **Équivalents.** Trouvez le verbe réfléchi correspondant à chaque définition.

> s'endormir   s'ennuyer
> se reposer   se lever
> s'habiller   s'amuser
> se coucher   se maquiller

1. aller au lit
2. sortir du lit
3. mettre des vêtements
4. faire quelque chose d'amusant
5. faire quelque chose d'ennuyeux
6. ne rien faire
7. commencer à dormir
8. mettre du mascara

B **D'abord...** Indiquez l'ordre logique des activités données.

EXEMPLE prendre un bain / se lever
D'abord, on se lève et puis on prend un bain.

1. se réveiller / se lever
2. se laver la figure / se maquiller
3. s'habiller / prendre un bain ou une douche
4. quitter la maison / s'habiller
5. se reposer / rentrer à la maison après les cours
6. s'amuser / retrouver des amis
7. se déshabiller / se coucher
8. s'endormir / se coucher

Mes amis et moi, on s'amuse toujours bien le week-end.

C **Un samedi typique.** Voilà la routine de Rose le samedi. Qu'est-ce qu'elle fait?

EXEMPLE Le samedi matin, ... vers neuf heures.
Le samedi matin, **elle se réveille** vers neuf heures.

EXEMPLE 1. 2. 3.

1. ... tout de suite.
2. ... la figure et les mains.
3. ... avant le petit déjeuner.

4. 5. 6. 7.

4. Après le petit déjeuner, …
5. …. les cheveux juste avant de quitter la maison.
6. Le samedi soir, … avec des amis.
7. … vers deux heures du matin et… facilement.

D **Et vous?** Regardez les illustrations de **C. Un samedi typique.** Est-ce que vous faites les mêmes choses le samedi?

EXEMPLE  ... vers 9h
Je me réveille vers 9h.
Je ne me réveille pas vers 9h.
Je me réveille vers 10h.

E **Ma routine.** Complétez ces phrases pour parler de vous.

1. En semaine *(During the week)*, je me réveille...
2. Je me lève...
3. Mes amis et moi, nous nous amusons beaucoup quand...
4. Nous nous ennuyons quand...
5. En semaine, je me couche...
6. Je m'endors...

Warm-ups for E. Ma routine. A. Est-ce que vous faites ces choses **le matin, l'après-midi** ou **le soir**? **1.** Je prends un bain ou une douche... **2.** Je me brosse les dents... **3.** Je me lave la figure... **4.** Je me brosse les cheveux... **5.** Je prépare mon petit déjeuner... **6.** Je dîne... **7.** Je me lave les cheveux... **8.** Je me repose... **9.** Je m'amuse... **10.** Je me lève... **B.** Make statements like the following ones about yourself. Have students say whether they do the same. **1.** Je m'ennuie souvent le week-end. **2.** Je m'amuse quand je vais à un match de football américain. **3.** Je m'ennuie quand mes amis parlent de leurs problèmes. **4.** Je me réveille toujours facilement. **5.** Je me lève toujours tout de suite. **6.** Je me lave les cheveux tous les jours. **7.** Je me repose toujours le soir. **8.** Je prends un bain le matin et le soir.

Line art on this page: © Cengage Learning

F   Questions. Travaillez en groupes pour préparer autant de questions que possible à poser au professeur au sujet de sa routine quotidienne. Utilisez les éléments donnés ou d'autres expressions logiques. Le groupe avec le plus grand nombre de questions logiques gagne.

> s'amuser   s'ennuyer   se réveiller   se lever
> se coucher   s'endormir   se laver la figure et les mains
> se brosser les dents/les cheveux

> à quelle heure   tôt / tard   facilement   tout de suite
> combien de fois par jour   avant / après le petit déjeuner   quand

EXEMPLE   Est-ce que vous vous couchez tôt d'habitude?

G   Beaucoup de questions! Circulez parmi les étudiants. Posez chaque paire de questions à un(e) étudiant(e) différent(e). Notez leurs réponses et ensuite, dites à la classe ce que vous avez appris.

EXEMPLE   —Eva, à quelle heure est-ce que tu te réveilles le samedi matin?
—Je me réveille vers 10h.

Après, à la classe: **Eva se réveille vers 10h.**

> À quelle heure est-ce que tu te réveilles le samedi matin?
> Est-ce que tu te lèves tout de suite?

> Tu préfères prendre un bain ou une douche?
> Est-ce que tu prends ton bain ou ta douche le matin ou le soir?

> Quand est-ce que tu te reposes?
> Tu te couches tôt pendant la semaine?

> Tu t'amuses ou tu t'ennuies quand tu es seul(e) le soir?
> Quand est-ce que tu t'amuses?

> Vers quelle heure est-ce que tu te couches le samedi soir?
> Est-ce que tu t'endors tout de suite?

H   Vous faites du baby-sitting. Imaginez que vous allez faire du baby-sitting pour les deux enfants d'un(e) ami(e). Demandez ces renseignements à votre ami(e). Votre partenaire va jouer le rôle de votre ami(e) et imaginer ses réponses. Préparez une scène à présenter à la classe.

Find out . . .

EXEMPLE   *what time they wake up*
—À quelle heure est-ce qu'ils se réveillent?
—Ils se réveillent vers huit heures.

1. *if they get up right away*
2. *if they take a bath or a shower in the morning or the evening*
3. *if they rest in the afternoon*
4. *at what time they eat dinner*
5. *at what time they go to bed*
6. *if they fall asleep easily*

STRATÉGIES ET LECTURE

POUR MIEUX LIRE: Using word families and watching out for *faux amis*

Recognizing words that belong to the same word family can make reading easier. Can you supply the missing meanings below?

la vie	vivre	se marier	le mariage
life	to live	to marry	marriage
l'arrêt	s'arrêter	espérer	l'espoir
the stop	???	to hope	???

Using cognates and word families can help you understand new texts more easily. However, beware of **faux amis,** words that look like cognates but have different meanings. For example, **rester** does not mean *to rest,* but *to stay.* Use cognates, but if a word does not seem right in the context, look it up.

A Familles de mots. Vous allez voir ces mots dans l'histoire qui suit. Servez-vous du sens des mots donnés pour déterminer le sens des autres mots.

rêver	un rêve	dire	dit(e)
to dream	a dream	to say, to tell	said, told
se souvenir de	des souvenirs	connaître	connu(e)
to remember	???	to know	???
saluer	une salutation	reconnaître	reconnu(e)
to greet	???	to recognize	???

B Faux amis. Donnez le sens des faux amis en caractères gras selon le contexte.

Supplemental pre-reading activity. Before reading *Il n'est jamais trop tard!* have students find the verbs in the text and tell whether each one is in the present or in the past.

M. Dupont se repose dans un fauteuil au jardin quand une jolie jeune fille qui passe **attire** son attention. Il la **salue** et lui dit bonjour. Cette fille ressemble à quelqu'un qu'il connaissait dans le passé et il commence à rêver. Il a de beaux **souvenirs** du temps où il était jeune. Il aimait une jeune fille et il **garde** toujours l'espoir de la revoir un jour.

Lecture: *Il n'est jamais trop tard!*

🔊 2-31 *Rosalie Toulouse-Richard, qui habite à Atlanta depuis son mariage avec un Américain, retourne à Rouen avec sa petite-fille Rose. Son vieil ami, André Dupont, ne sait pas encore que Rosalie est à Rouen.*

André Dupont a toujours aimé passer des heures à travailler dans son jardin. Il a une passion pour les roses et depuis des années, il plante des rosiers de toutes les variétés et de toutes les couleurs dans son jardin.

Ses rosiers font l'admiration de tous les gens du quartier et beaucoup d'entre eux passent devant chez lui pour regarder son beau jardin. Aujourd'hui, trois jeunes filles s'arrêtent devant son jardin et lui disent bonjour. Il reconnaît deux d'entre elles, ce sont les petites-filles de son ami Jean Toulouse, mais c'est la troisième qui attire son attention. Il ne l'a jamais vue, et pourtant il a l'impression de la connaître! Elle ressemble à quelqu'un... quelqu'un qu'il a connu il y a très longtemps.

Les souvenirs lui reviennent, comme si c'était hier. C'était il y a longtemps, il avait dix-huit ans et il était amoureux fou d'une jolie jeune fille de son âge. Elle s'appelait Rosalie... ! Il voulait lui dire combien il l'aimait, mais il n'en avait pas le courage. Il était trop timide. Un beau jour, il s'est décidé à tout lui dire. Il a choisi des fleurs de son jardin pour en faire un bouquet, il a pris son vélo et il est allé chez Rosalie. Mais en arrivant, il a trouvé Rosalie en compagnie d'un jeune Américain et elle regardait ce jeune homme d'un regard de femme amoureuse. André, lui, est rentré chez lui sans jamais parler à Rosalie.

Quelques mois après, Rosalie s'est mariée avec le jeune Américain et ils sont partis vivre aux États-Unis. De temps en temps, André avait des nouvelles, car le frère de Rosalie et lui étaient de bons amis. Il savait qu'elle habitait à Atlanta, qu'elle avait eu trois enfants, et il y a trois ans, il a appris que son mari était mort. Il gardait toujours l'espoir de la revoir, mais les années passaient et elle ne revenait toujours pas.

—Vos rosiers sont magnifiques, monsieur!
C'est Rosalie qui parle! En un instant, André Dupont revient au présent et ouvre les yeux. C'est la jeune fille qui parle... celle qu'il ne connaît pas.
—Rosalie???
—Moi, monsieur? Non, je m'appelle Rose. Rosalie, c'est ma grand-mère.
—Ta grand-mère?
—Oui. Vous connaissez ma grand-mère?
—Rosalie Toulouse? Oui, je la connais, mais...
—Eh bien, venez la voir, elle est chez son frère Jean! Je suis sûre qu'elle sera contente de revoir un ami d'ici! Allez, venez donc avec nous!

Line art on this page: © Cengage Learning

Quoi? C'est trop beau! Est-ce qu'il rêve? Rosalie, ici à Rouen! Comme la vie est à la fois belle et bizarre! Va-t-elle le reconnaître? A-t-il le courage de lui dire qu'il l'aime toujours, après toutes ces années? André Dupont choisit les plus belles roses de son jardin et en fait un magnifique bouquet. Il va enfin pouvoir les offrir à la femme pour qui il a planté tous ces rosiers au cours des années.

Qui parle? Qui parle: **André**, **Rosalie** ou **Rose**?

1. J'adore les fleurs et j'aime faire du jardinage.
2. J'ai eu trois enfants et mon mari est mort il y a trois ans.
3. Je suis passée devant une maison où il y avait des roses splendides.
4. Un monsieur m'a parlé. Il connaît ma grand-mère mais il ne l'a pas vue depuis longtemps.
5. J'ai invité ce monsieur à venir nous voir.
6. Je me suis mariée avec un Américain et je suis allée vivre aux États-Unis.
7. J'étais amoureux de Rosalie mais je n'ai jamais eu le courage de le lui dire.
8. Je garde toujours l'espoir de dire à Rosalie que je l'aime.

COMPÉTENCE 2

Talking about relationships

 PowerPoint 7-4

LA VIE SENTIMENTALE

Note culturelle

En France, on se marie tard: 30 ans et 7 mois pour les femmes et 32 ans et 11 mois pour les hommes. Les jeunes vivent *(live)* en couple avant de se marier et plus de 50% des naissances ont lieu hors *(births take place outside of)* mariage. Beaucoup de couples choisissent le Pacte civil de solidarité (Pacs), une sorte de contrat pour former une union civile. En 2010, il y a eu 251 654 mariages et 205 558 Pacs, (soit 5 mariages pour 4 Pacs). Le Pacs est populaire chez les cadres *(professionals)* parce que la séparation est moins chère qu'un divorce. Est-ce que la situation est la même dans votre région?

André va chez les Toulouse et André et Rosalie **se rencontrent** pour la première fois depuis des années. Voilà **ce qui se passe.**

André et Rosalie se regardent.

Ils s'embrassent. C'est **le coup de foudre!**

Ils se parlent pendant des heures.

Ils se quittent vers sept heures.

Pendant les semaines qui **suivent,** André et Rosalie passent beaucoup de temps ensemble. Ils **se souviennent de** leur **jeunesse** ensemble. C'est **le grand amour!**

Ils se retrouvent en ville chaque après-midi.

Quelquefois, ils se disputent.

Mais **la plupart du temps, ils s'entendent** bien.

Note de grammaire

Se souvenir de is conjugated like **venir.**

je me souviens
tu te souviens
il/elle/on se souvient
nous nous souvenons
vous vous souvenez
ils/elles se souviennent

Enfin, André et Rosalie **prennent une décision.** Ils vont se marier et vont **s'installer à** Rouen. Ils vont être très **heureux.**

Un soir, Rosalie parle à sa petite-fille Rose de sa relation avec André.

Warm-up activity. Vous êtes avec l'homme ou la femme de vos rêves. **1.** Quand vous sortez en couple, que faites-vous? **2.** Allez-vous plus souvent au théâtre ou au cinéma? **3.** Aimez-vous faire de l'exercice à deux? Quels sports faites-vous ensemble? **4.** Préférez-vous sortir en groupe ou en amoureux à deux *(as a couple)*? **5.** Aimez-vous mieux aller dîner au restaurant ou préparer le dîner à la maison? **6.** Préférez-vous aller en boîte ou aller au cinéma? **7.** Qu'est-ce que vous aimez faire avec des amis?

Note for the conversation. New vocabulary includes all glossed words and **une relation.**

Sélection musicale. Search the Web for the song **"Ils s'aiment"** by the Lost Fingers to enjoy a musical selection related to this vocabulary.

ROSE:	Alors, **mamie,** tu as passé une bonne journée?
ROSALIE:	Oui. André et moi, nous sommes allés visiter le Mont-Saint-Michel.
ROSE:	Alors, vous vous entendez bien?
ROSALIE:	Très bien. Nous nous retrouvons tous les jours, nous passons des heures ensemble et nous parlons de tout.
ROSE:	**Formidable!** Moi, je **rêve d'une telle** relation.
ROSALIE:	Et ton copain et toi, ça va?
ROSE:	Pas très bien. On ne s'entend pas très bien. On se dispute souvent.
ROSALIE:	**C'est dommage!**

Suggestion for the conversation. Set the scene and have students listen with books closed for three pieces of information about the relationship between Rosalie and André.

Line art on this page: © Cengage Learning

---

se rencontrer to meet each other (by chance), to run into each other   **ce qui** what   **se passer** to happen   **le coup de foudre** love at first sight   **suivent (suivre** to follow)   **se souvenir de** to remember   **la jeunesse** youth   **le grand amour** true love   **la plupart du temps** most of the time   **s'entendre** to get along   **Enfin** Finally   **prendre une décision** to make a decision   **s'installer (à / dans)** to settle (in), to move (into)   **heureux (heureuse)** happy   **mamie** grandma   **Formidable!** Great!   **rêver (de)** to dream (of)   **un(e) tel(le)** such a   **C'est dommage!** That's too bad!

A Test. Faites ce test pour savoir si vous êtes romantique.

Êtes-vous romantique?

I. Indiquez vos opinions sur ces sujets.

1. Pensez-vous que le grand amour...
   a. arrive une fois dans la vie?
   b. n'existe pas?
   c. est sans importance?

2. Pensez-vous qu'un couple peut s'aimer pour toujours?
   a. Certainement.
   b. Je ne sais pas, on peut essayer.
   c. Probablement pas: la vie est trop longue.

3. Au restaurant, **vous voyez** des amoureux qui se regardent dans les yeux pendant tout le dîner. Vous trouvez ça...
   a. assez charmant.
   b. ridicule.
   c. adorable.

II. Comment êtes-vous en couple?

1. Vous vous rencontrez **par hasard** et c'est le coup de foudre. Que pensez-vous?
   a. C'est juste **une attirance** physique.
   b. C'est peut-être l'amour.
   c. **Attention!**

2. Vous vous disputez. Quelle est la meilleure manière de vous réconcilier?
   a. Nous devons nous embrasser.
   b. Nous devons essayer de parler calmement du problème.
   c. Nous devons nous quitter pendant un certain temps.

3. Vous vous adorez. Vous voulez...
   a. essayer de vous voir tous les jours.
   b. vous téléphoner tous les jours et vous voir trois ou quatre fois par semaine.
   c. vous retrouver le week-end, si vous n'avez pas d'autres projets.

SCORE: Partie I. 1. a–2 points 2. a–2 points, b–1 point 3. c–2 points, a–1 point
Partie II. 1. b–2 points, a–1 point 2. a–2 points, b–1 point 3. a–2 points, b–1 point

- Si vous avez entre 10 et 12 points, vous êtes une personne très (peut-être même un peu trop?) romantique. Attention! **Ne perdez pas votre temps** à attendre un amour parfait. Essayez d'être un peu plus réaliste, quand même.
- Si vous avez entre 6 et 9 points, vous êtes romantique, mais vous n'exagérez pas. Vous êtes prêt(e) à aimer quand le bon moment arrivera, mais vous ne perdez pas votre temps à chercher l'amour idéal partout.
- Si vous avez entre 0 et 5 points, vous êtes réaliste, cynique même! Ne voulez-vous pas mettre un peu plus de poésie dans votre vie?

© Cengage Learning

B En couple. Est-ce qu'on fait ces choses **dans un couple heureux** ou **dans un couple malheureux** (unhappy)?

EXEMPLE On se dispute rarement.
On se dispute rarement **dans un couple heureux.**

1. On se dispute tout le temps.
2. On se parle de tout.
3. On ne s'entend pas bien du tout.
4. On s'amuse ensemble.
5. On s'ennuie ensemble.
6. On s'embrasse tout le temps.

À VOUS!

Avec un(e) partenaire, relisez à haute voix la conversation entre Rose et Rosalie. Ensuite, adaptez la conversation pour parler de votre relation avec votre mari, votre femme, votre copain, votre copine, votre meilleur(e) ami(e) ou votre colocataire.

Suggestion for À vous! Point out the sentence **On ne s'entend pas très bien** in the dialogue and tell students to use it as a model for their negative sentences.

You can find a list of the new words from this **Compétence** on page 298 and access the audio online.

---

vous voyez you see **par hasard** by chance **une attirance** an attraction **Attention!** Watch out! **Ne perdez pas votre temps** Don't waste your time

 **PowerPoint 7-5**

SAYING WHAT PEOPLE DO FOR EACH OTHER

✓ **Pour vérifier**

1. When do you use a reciprocal verb?

2. What verbs can be made into reciprocal verbs? How would you say *to look at each other* or *to listen to each other*?

3. When a reflexive or reciprocal verb is used in the infinitive, does the reflexive pronoun change with the subject? How would you say *I am going to get up at 6:00*? *I am not going to get up at 6:00*?

iLrn Grammar Tutorials

Note *de grammaire*

Note that although the verbs **se fiancer** and **se marier** are reflexive, **divorcer** is not.

Note *de vocabulaire*

Use **(se) retrouver** to talk about getting together with someone (by plan). Use **(se) rencontrer** to say someone runs into someone else (by accident).

Suggestions. A. Remind students of the spelling change in verbs ending in **-cer**, such as **divorcer**. **B.** You may wish to point out that some of these verbs are also used reflexively, in which case they require a preposition: **se marier (avec), se fiancer (à), se disputer (avec), s'entendre bien / mal (avec), se réconcilier (avec).**

Supplemental activities. A. Associez-vous ces mots à **se marier** ou à **divorcer**? 1. se détester 2. s'embrasser 3. se disputer 4. se quitter 5. s'aimer 6. s'entendre bien **B.** Indiquez le contraire: se disputer, s'aimer, divorcer, s'entendre mal, se quitter.

🌐 **Sélection musicale.** Search the Web for the song **"C'est quoi, c'est l'habitude"** by Isabelle Boulay to enjoy a musical selection illustrating the use of this structure.

Les verbes réciproques au présent et les verbes réfléchis et réciproques au futur immédiat

You have seen that reflexive verbs are used when someone is doing something to or for himself/herself. You use similar verbs to describe reciprocal actions; that is, to indicate that people are doing something to or for each other. Here are some reflexive and reciprocal verbs commonly used to describe relationships:

s'aimer	to like each other, to love each other
se détester	to hate each other
se disputer	to argue
s'embrasser	to kiss each other, to embrace each other
s'entendre (bien / mal)	to get along (well / badly) with each other
se fiancer	to get engaged
se marier	to get married
se quitter	to leave each other
se réconcilier	to make up
se regarder	to look at each other
se rencontrer	to meet (for the first time), to run into each other (by chance)
se retrouver	to meet (by design)
se téléphoner	to telephone each other

The verb **s'entendre** *(to get along)* is a regular **-re** verb. You will learn how to conjugate other **-re** verbs in the next section on page 276. The forms of **s'entendre** are:

S'ENTENDRE (to get along)

je m'entends	nous nous entendons
tu t'entends	vous vous entendez
il/elle/on s'entend	ils/elles s'entendent

Most verbs indicating actions done to other people can be used reciprocally.

retrouver quelqu'un *(to meet someone)*	Je retrouve **Jim** au café.
se retrouver *(to meet each other)*	Nous **nous** retrouvons souvent au café.

As with other verbs, use **aller** + an infinitive to form the immediate future of reflexive and reciprocal verbs. When reflexive or reciprocal verbs are used in the infinitive, the pronoun is placed before the infinitive, and it matches the subject. In the negative, place **ne** after the subject and **pas, jamais,** or **rien** after the first verb.

SE LEVER (to get up)

je vais me lever	nous allons nous lever
tu vas te lever	vous allez vous lever
il/elle/on va se lever	ils/elles vont se lever

Je ne vais pas **me** lever tôt.   **Nous** aimons **nous** retrouver au café.

A Une histoire d'amour. Isabelle, la cousine de Rose, rencontre Luc et ils tombent amoureux. Qu'est-ce qui se passe?

> se regarder   se rencontrer au parc   se marier
> s'embrasser   s'installer dans une maison   se fiancer
> se réconcilier   se disputer

EXEMPLE      Ils se rencontrent au parc.

1.
2.
3.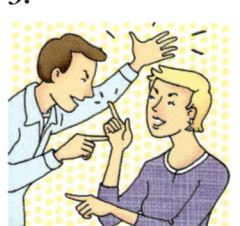
4.

5.
6.
7.

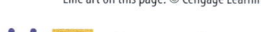

B Questions. Un(e) ami(e) veut en savoir plus *(to know more)* sur Isabelle et Luc. Avec un(e) partenaire, posez ses questions et imaginez les réponses qu'Isabelle lui donne.

EXEMPLE   s'aimer beaucoup
—Est-ce que vous vous aimez beaucoup?
—Oui, nous nous aimons beaucoup.
   Oui, on s'aime beaucoup.

1. se téléphoner tous les jours
2. se disputer souvent
3. se réconcilier facilement
4. s'entendre mal quelquefois
5. s'envoyer des textos plusieurs *(several)* fois par jour

C Isabelle et Luc. Tout va très bien entre Isabelle et Luc. Ils se retrouvent en ville tous les jours. Est-ce qu'ils vont faire les choses suivantes demain?

EXEMPLE   se disputer
   Non, ils ne vont pas se disputer.

1. se téléphoner
2. se retrouver en ville
3. se parler de tout
4. bien s'entendre
5. s'ennuyer ensemble
6. s'embrasser

Warm-up for A. Une histoire d'amour. Qu'est-ce qu'on fait d'abord? **1.** On se rencontre. / On se parle. **2.** On se marie. / On s'aime. **3.** On s'embrasse. / On se rencontre. **4.** On se dispute. / On se réconcilie. **5.** On divorce. / On se marie.

Warm-up for B. Questions. Dites si on fait ou on ne fait pas ces choses dans un couple idéal. **EXEMPLE** se disputer souvent **Dans un couple idéal, on ne se dispute pas souvent. 1.** se retrouver tous les jours **2.** se téléphoner tous les jours **3.** s'entendre mal la plupart du temps **4.** se disputer tous les jours **5.** se réconcilier facilement **6.** s'embrasser souvent

Follow-up for C. Isabelle et Luc. Tell students that Isabelle and Luc have not yet met each other, but are going to, and have them redo the sentences in *A. Une histoire d'amour* in the immediate future. **EXEMPLE Ils vont se rencontrer au parc.**

D **Et demain chez Rose.** Dites ce que Rose va faire demain d'après les illustrations.

EXEMPLE  ... vers neuf heures.
Elle va se réveiller vers neuf heures.

1. ... tout de suite. 2. ... la figure et les mains. 3. ... les cheveux.

4. ... avant de manger. 5. ... vers deux heures du matin.

E **Ce week-end.** Dites si ces personnes vont probablement faire ces choses ce week-end.

EXEMPLE Moi, je... (se lever tôt)
Moi, je vais me lever tôt. / Moi, je ne vais pas me lever tôt.

1. Samedi matin, moi, je...
   se réveiller tard
   se lever tout de suite
   rester au lit quelques minutes
2. Samedi matin, mon meilleur ami / ma meilleure amie...
   se réveiller tôt
   se lever facilement
   prendre son petit déjeuner avec moi
3. Ce week-end, cet(te) ami(e) et moi, nous...
   se retrouver en ville
   s'amuser
   s'ennuyer
   s'entendre bien

F Partons en week-end. Vous allez partir avec un groupe d'amis ce week-end. Travaillez avec un petit groupe d'étudiants et faites des projets. Ensuite, dites à la classe ce que vous allez faire. Dites:

- si vous allez à la campagne, à la montagne ou à la plage
- à quelle heure vous allez partir
- comment vous allez voyager
- si vous allez faire du camping, descendre à l'hôtel ou rester chez des parents/amis
- si vous allez vous lever tôt ou tard tous les jours
- ce que vous allez faire pendant la journée pour vous amuser
- quand vous allez vous reposer
- ce que vous allez faire le soir
- à quelle heure vous allez vous coucher

EXEMPLE On va aller à la plage. On va partir vers 8h.

G Beaucoup de questions! Circulez parmi les étudiants et posez les questions suivantes pour trouver quelqu'un qui fait la même chose que vous. Après, dites à la classe ce que vous avez en commun avec d'autres étudiants.

EXEMPLE —Eva, à quelle heure est-ce que tu te réveilles en semaine?
—Je me réveille vers 8h.

Après, à la classe:

Eva et moi, nous nous réveillons vers 8h. / Eva et moi, on se réveille vers 8h.

À quelle heure est-ce que tu te réveilles en semaine?	À quelle heure est-ce que tu vas te réveiller demain?	Est-ce que tu préfères te lever tôt ou tard?
Après les cours, est-ce que tu préfères te reposer ou t'amuser avec des amis?	Est-ce que tu vas te reposer aujourd'hui après les cours?	À quelle heure est-ce que tu vas te coucher ce soir?

H Entretien. Posez ces questions à votre partenaire au sujet de ses relations avec son meilleur ami (sa meilleure amie).

1. Est-ce que vous vous parlez tous les jours? Est-ce que vous préférez vous téléphoner ou vous envoyer des textos?
2. Combien de fois par semaine est-ce que vous vous retrouvez? Où aimez-vous vous retrouver?
3. Qu'est-ce que vous faites ensemble pour vous amuser? Est-ce que vous vous ennuyez quelquefois ensemble?
4. Est-ce que vous vous entendez toujours bien? Est-ce que vous vous disputez de temps en temps?

Supplemental activities. A. Are these good things to tell a young child to do? **1.** Tu dois te lever, il y a un bon film à la télé à minuit. **2.** Tu dois te coucher, il est neuf heures du soir. **3.** Tu ne dois pas manger beaucoup de pizza. **4.** Tu ne dois pas fumer de cigarettes. **5.** Tu ne dois pas te coucher tôt. **6.** Tu ne dois pas souvent te brosser les dents. **7.** Tu dois te laver les mains avant de manger. **8.** Tu dois t'habiller avant de sortir. **9.** Tu ne dois pas te brosser les cheveux le matin. **10.** Tu dois te brosser les dents après le dîner. **B.** L'enfant d'un ami se prépare pour aller à l'école le matin. Dites-lui *(Tell him)* s'il doit ou ne doit pas faire ces choses. **EXEMPLE** se brosser les dents **Tu dois te brosser les dents. 1.** se lever **2.** se recoucher **3.** prendre un bain **4.** s'habiller **5.** se brosser les cheveux **6.** prendre un café **7.** prendre un bon petit déjeuner

PowerPoint 7-6

TALKING ABOUT ACTIVITIES

✓ Pour vérifier

1. What ending do you add for each subject pronoun after dropping the **-re** from the infinitive of these verbs? What is the conjugation of **perdre**?
2. Which of these **-re** verbs are conjugated with **être** in the **passé composé**?

Les verbes en **-re**

Many verbs that end in **-re** follow a regular pattern of conjugation.

ATTENDRE (to wait for)	
j'attend**s**	nous attend**ons**
tu attend**s**	vous attend**ez**
il/elle/on attend	ils/elles attend**ent**

PASSÉ COMPOSÉ: **j'ai attendu**
IMPARFAIT: **j'attendais**

The following are some common **-re** verbs.

attendre	to wait (for)
descendre (de) (à)	to go down, to get off (of), to stay (at)
entendre	to hear
s'entendre (bien / mal) avec	to get along (well / badly) with
perdre	to lose, to waste
perdre du temps	to waste time
se perdre	to get lost
rendre quelque chose à quelqu'un	to return something to someone, to turn in something to someone
rendre visite à quelqu'un	to visit someone
répondre (à)	to answer, to respond (to)
vendre / revendre	to sell / to sell back, to resell

In the **passé composé, descendre** and the reflexive verbs are conjugated with **être** as the auxiliary verb. The other verbs in this list are all conjugated with **avoir**.

J'ai rendu visite à une amie à Paris.   Je suis descendu(e) à l'hôtel Étoile.

Note *de vocabulaire*

1. Do not use **pour** after **attendre** to say *for* whom or what you are waiting.

   J'attends des amis.
   I'm waiting for friends.

2. Notice the difference in meaning between the reflexive and non-reflexive forms of **entendre** and **perdre**.

   entendre *to hear*
   s'entendre *to get along*
   perdre *to lose*
   se perdre *to get lost*

3. Use **rendre visite à** or **aller voir** to say that you visit a person, but use **visiter** to say that you visit a place.

 Grammar Tutorials

Sélection musicale. Search the Web for the song **"J'attends l'amour"** by Jenifer to enjoy a musical selection related to this vocabulary.

Suggestion. Point out the use of **à** in **répondre à** and **rendre visite à** and the use of **de** and **à** with **descendre**.

Note. Students are not expected to use the verbs **se perdre** and **s'entendre** in the **passé composé** until they are taught to form the **passé composé** of reflexive / reciprocal verbs in the next **Compétence**.

Warm-ups for A. Votre vie. A. Quel verbe en **-re** est l'antonyme de... ? **1.** trouver **2.** poser une question **3.** acheter **4.** monter **B.** À quel(s) verbe(s) en **-re** associez-vous... ? **1.** le téléphone **2.** le bus **3.** un magasin **4.** la patience **5.** la musique **6.** une question **7.** un hôtel **8.** des amis

Follow-up for A. Votre vie. Have students use the cues given for item **1** of this exercise to ask partners questions. They can also use the cues for item **2** to ask their partners if they often do these things with their friends.

A **Votre vie.** Est-ce que ces personnes font toujours (souvent, quelquefois, rarement, jamais...) les choses suivantes?

EXEMPLE Moi, je... (attendre le bus pour aller en cours)
Moi, je n'attends jamais le bus pour aller en cours.

1. Moi, je...
   rendre visite à mes parents
   attendre le week-end avec impatience
   revendre mes livres à la fin *(end)* du semestre / trimestre

2. Mes amis...
   descendre en ville le week-end
   s'entendre bien
   se rendre visite

3. Mon meilleur ami / Ma meilleure amie...
   perdre patience avec moi
   s'entendre bien avec mes autres amis
   se perdre

4. En cours de français, nous...
   perdre du temps
   répondre correctement aux questions du prof
   rendre les devoirs au professeur à la fin *(end)* du cours

B La routine de Rose. En vous servant des illustrations et des phrases proposées, décrivez la routine de Rose quand elle est à Atlanta.

EXEMPLE Rose: attendre le bus le matin / aller en cours à pied
Rose attend le bus le matin. Elle ne va pas en cours à pied.

1.
2.
3.
4. (image)

1. Rose: perdre patience quand le bus est en retard *(late)* / attendre patiemment
2. Rose: perdre son temps dans le bus / préférer lire
3. Rose: descendre chez un ami / descendre à l'université
4. Rose: s'entendre bien avec ses profs / s'entendre mal avec ses profs

5.
6.
7.
8.

5. Les étudiants: travailler bien en cours / perdre leur temps
6. Les étudiants: perdre leurs devoirs / rendre leurs devoirs au professeur
7. Après les cours, Rose: rentrer chez elle / rendre visite à son ami Daniel
8. Rose et son ami: s'entendre mal / s'entendre bien

Line art on this page: © Cengage Learning

C Et toi? Choisissez le verbe logique et complétez les questions. Ensuite, posez les questions à votre partenaire. Utilisez le présent ou le passé composé comme indiqué.

AU PRÉSENT

1. Tu _____ souvent visite à tes parents? (rendre, entendre) Ta famille et toi, vous _____ bien la plupart du temps? (perdre, s'entendre) Est-ce que tu _____ souvent patience avec tes parents? (perdre, répondre) Est-ce qu'ils _____ souvent patience avec toi? (perdre, répondre)
2. Tu _____ tes prochaines vacances avec impatience? (attendre, entendre) Tu _____ facilement quand tu es dans une autre ville? (se perdre, vendre) Quand tu voyages avec des amis, vous _____ quelquefois dans un hôtel de luxe? (vendre, descendre)

AU PASSÉ COMPOSÉ

3. Tu _____ visite à tes parents récemment? (revendre, rendre) La dernière fois que tu as vu tes parents, est-ce qu'ils _____ patience avec toi? (perdre, vendre)
4. La dernière fois que vous êtes partis en week-end ensemble, est-ce que vous _____ à l'hôtel? (descendre, entendre)

COMPÉTENCE 3

Talking about what you did and used to do

 PowerPoint 7-7

LES ACTIVITÉS D'HIER

Note *culturelle*

«Métro-boulot-dodo». Cette expression populaire illustre la monotonie de la routine quotidienne des Parisiens et par extension de la majorité des Français. De plus en plus de Français habitent loin de leur travail. Par conséquent, ils ont de moins en moins de temps à consacrer *(to dedicate)* à leur vie personnelle. Malgré *(Despite)* la semaine de 35 heures, ils passent leur vie dans les transports (**métro**), au travail (**boulot**) et ils rentrent chez eux juste pour dormir (**dodo**). Est-ce que dans votre région, vous avez une expression spécifique pour exprimer cette routine?

Note *de grammaire*

Se promener is a spelling change verb like **se lever** and **acheter**:

je me promène
tu te promènes
il/elle/on se promène
nous nous promenons
vous vous promenez
ils/elles se promènent

Warm-ups. A. Nommez trois activités qu'on fait aux moments indiqués: le matin, l'après-midi, le soir, le week-end. **B.** Est-ce que vous faites souvent ou rarement ces choses? **1.** se lever très tôt **2.** se réveiller facilement **3.** prendre une douche **4.** préparer le petit déjeuner **5.** prendre le petit déjeuner au lit **6.** préparer le dîner **7.** se coucher tard **C.** Questions orales. **1.** Qui a un(e) camarade de chambre ou un(e) colocataire? Comment s'appelle-t-il/elle? **2.** Est-ce qu'il/elle se lève tôt? Il/Elle se lève avant vous ou après vous généralement? **3.** Il/Elle s'habille avant le petit déjeuner? **4.** Il/Elle prend sa douche le matin ou le soir? Il/Elle passe beaucoup de temps dans la salle de bains? **5.** Vous vous amusez ensemble? **6.** Vous vous entendez bien? **7.** Vous vous disputez de temps en temps? **8.** Qui se couche en premier d'habitude?

Rose parle de ce qu'elle a fait hier.

Le réveil a sonné et je me suis réveillée.

Je me suis levée.

J'ai pris un bain.

Je me suis brossé les dents.

Je me suis peignée.

Je me suis habillée.

J'ai passé le reste de la journée avec ma cousine et son nouvel ami.

Nous nous sommes promenés.

Nous nous sommes arrêtés au restaurant pour manger.

Nous nous sommes bien amusés.

Nous nous sommes quittés vers 10 heures et je me suis couchée vers 11 heures.

Line art on this page: © Cengage Learning

Le réveil *The alarm clock*   **sonner** *to ring*   **se promener** *to go for a walk*   **s'arrêter** *to stop*

Rose parle à sa cousine, Isabelle, qui **raconte** comment elle a rencontré son ami, Luc.

ROSE: Alors, Luc et toi, vous vous êtes rencontrés où?
ISABELLE: J'étais au parc et Luc était à côté de moi. On s'est vus et on s'est parlé un peu. Quelques jours plus tard, il était dans une librairie où j'achetais un livre et **on s'est reconnus.** Il m'a demandé si je voulais aller prendre un verre et j'ai accepté son invitation. On a passé le reste de la journée ensemble.
ROSE: Vous vous êtes bien entendus, **donc**?
ISABELLE: **Parfaitement** bien. On s'est très bien amusés et on s'est retrouvés le lendemain pour aller au cinéma. Depuis, on s'est téléphoné ou on s'est vus presque tous les jours.

A Récemment. Quand avez-vous fait ces choses?

ce matin	hier soir	il y a deux semaines
cet après-midi	hier matin	il y a un mois
???	lundi dernier	il y a longtemps

1. Le réveil a sonné et je me suis levé(e) tout de suite…
2. J'ai pris un bain / une douche…
3. Je me suis brossé les cheveux / je me suis peigné(e)…
4. Mes amis et moi, nous nous sommes bien amusés ensemble…
5. Nous nous sommes promenés en ville…
6. Je me suis arrêté(e) dans un fast-food pour manger…
7. Je me suis couché(e) après minuit…

B Ils se sont retrouvés. Décrivez la première fois que Rosalie et André se sont revus après toutes ces années en mettant ces phrases dans l'ordre logique.

_____ Ils se sont embrassés.
___1___ André et Rosalie se sont vus.
_____ Ils se sont quittés.
_____ Ils se sont reconnus.
_____ Ils se sont parlé pendant plusieurs heures et ils se sont souvenus du passé.

À VOUS!

Avec un(e) partenaire, relisez à haute voix la conversation entre Rose et Isabelle. Ensuite, parlez avec votre partenaire de comment vous avez rencontré votre meilleur(e) ami(e) ou votre copain (copine).

---

raconter to tell   **on s'est reconnus** (passé composé of **se reconnaître** to recognize each other)   **donc** then, thus, so
Parfaitement Perfectly

PowerPoint 7-8

SAYING WHAT PEOPLE DID

Les verbes réfléchis et réciproques au passé composé

All reflexive and reciprocal verbs have **être** as the auxiliary verb in the **passé composé.** Always place the reflexive pronoun directly before the auxiliary verb.

SE LEVER

je me suis levé(e)	nous nous sommes levé(e)s
tu t'es levé(e)	vous vous êtes levé(e)(s)
il s'est levé	ils se sont levés
elle s'est levée	elles se sont levées
on s'est levé(e)(s)	

✓ **Pour vérifier**

1. Do you use **être** or **avoir** as the auxiliary verb with reflexive and reciprocal verbs in the **passé composé**?

2. Where are reflexive pronouns placed with respect to the auxiliary verb? How do you conjugate **s'amuser** in the **passé composé**?

3. Where do you place **ne... pas** in the negative? How do you say *I didn't wake up early*?

4. When does the past participle agree with the reflexive pronoun and subject? When does it not agree? What are three verbs that you know that do not have agreement?

To negate a reflexive or reciprocal verb in the **passé composé,** place **ne** directly after the subject and **pas** or **jamais** directly after the conjugated form of **être.**

Je me suis réveillé(e) tôt mais je **ne** me suis **pas** levé(e) tout de suite.

In the **passé composé,** the past participle agrees in gender and number with the reflexive pronoun (and the subject) when it is the direct object of the verb.

Rosalie **s**'est levé**e** tôt.   André et Rosalie **se** sont marié**s.**

In this chapter, make the past participle agree except in these cases:

- There is no agreement when a reflexive verb is followed by a noun that is the direct object of the verb. Past participles of verbs like **se laver, se maquiller,** or **se brosser** do not agree with the subject when they are followed by the name of a part of the body.

  Rose et Rosalie se sont lavé**es.**   BUT   Rose et Rosalie se sont lavé **les mains.**
  Rose s'est maquillé**e.**   Rose s'est maquillé **les yeux.**

- With the verbs **se parler, se téléphoner,** and **s'écrire,** there is no agreement because the reflexive pronoun is an *indirect* object, not a *direct* object.

  Ils se sont parlé.   Nous nous sommes téléphoné.   Ils se sont écrit.

Note *de grammaire*

1. Remember that the past participles of regular **-er** verbs end in **-é (je me suis ennuyé[e]),** those of regular **-ir** verbs end in **-i (je me suis endormi[e]),** and those of regular **-re** verbs end in **-u (nous nous sommes entendu[e]s).**

2. When **on** means *we*, its verb may either be left in the masculine singular form **(on s'est levé)** or it may agree **(on s'est levé[e][s]).** Either form is considered correct.

3. **Se souvenir (de)** is conjugated like **venir: je me souviens, je me suis souvenu(e).**

Grammar Tutorials

Sélection musicale. To enjoy a musical selection illustrating the use of this structure, search the Web for the song **"Une belle histoire"** by Michel Fugain, which has been sung by numerous artists, including Charles Benevuto.

A **Hier chez Henri et Patricia.** Voilà ce que Patricia, la cousine de Rose, a fait hier. Qu'est-ce qu'elle a fait?

EXEMPLE   Patricia **s'est réveillée à six heures.**

EXEMPLE Patricia...   **1.** Elle...   **2.** Son mari Henri et elle...

  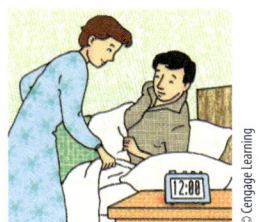

3. Ils…   4. Patricia…   5. Patricia et Henri…

B Qu'est-ce qu'ils ont fait?

Travaillez avec un groupe d'étudiants pour créer autant de *(create as many)* questions que possible au sujet de ce que Patricia et Henri ont fait hier. Basez vos questions sur les illustrations dans **A. Hier chez Henri et Patricia**. Chaque groupe gagne 1 point pour chaque question bien formée et 1 point chaque fois que les étudiants du groupe répondent correctement à la question d'un autre groupe.

EXEMPLE À quelle heure est-ce que Patricia s'est réveillée?

C Et toi?

Demandez à votre partenaire s'il/si elle a fait les choses suivantes hier.

EXEMPLE se lever tôt
— Tu t'es levé(e) tôt hier?
— Oui, je me suis levé(e) tôt hier.
   Non, je ne me suis pas levé(e) tôt hier.

1. se réveiller tôt
2. se lever tout de suite
3. prendre un bain ou une douche
4. passer la soirée à la maison
5. se reposer
6. s'ennuyer
7. s'amuser
8. se coucher tard

D Je veux tout savoir.

Utilisez les verbes suivants pour poser des questions à votre partenaire sur ses interactions avec son meilleur ami (sa meilleure amie) cette semaine.

EXEMPLE se téléphoner
— Est-ce que vous vous êtes téléphoné cette semaine?
— Oui, on s'est téléphoné hier.
   Non, on ne s'est pas téléphoné cette semaine.

se retrouver en ville	se disputer
se promener au parc	s'envoyer des textos
beaucoup se voir	s'amuser ensemble

E Entretien.

Posez ces questions à votre partenaire.

1. À quelle heure est-ce que tu t'es couché(e) hier soir? Tu as bien dormi? Tu as dormi jusqu'à quelle heure ce matin? Tu t'es levé(e) facilement?
2. Avec qui est-ce que tu es sorti(e) récemment? Où est-ce que vous vous êtes retrouvé(e)s? Qu'est-ce que vous avez fait? Vous vous êtes bien amusé(e)s?

PowerPoint 7-9

SAYING WHAT PEOPLE DID AND USED TO DO

✓ **Pour vérifier**

1. How do you form the **imparfait** of all verbs except **être**? What is the **imparfait** of **je m'amuse**? of **je ne m'amuse pas**?

2. Do you use the **imparfait** or the **passé composé** to say what happened on a specific occasion? to say how things used to be?

Note *de grammaire*

Before doing the exercises in this section, review the specific uses of the **passé composé** and the **imparfait** on page 253.

Les verbes réfléchis et réciproques à l'imparfait et reprise de l'usage du passé composé et de l'imparfait

As with all other verbs (except **être**), the **imparfait** of reflexive verbs is formed by dropping the **-ons** from the present tense **nous** form and adding the endings shown.

SE LEVER	NE PAS SE LEVER
je me lev**ais**	je ne me lev**ais** pas
tu te lev**ais**	tu ne te lev**ais** pas
il/elle/on se lev**ait**	il/elle/on ne se lev**ait** pas
nous nous lev**ions**	nous ne nous lev**ions** pas
vous vous lev**iez**	vous ne vous lev**iez** pas
ils/elles se lev**aient**	ils/elles ne se lev**aient** pas

Remember to use the **imparfait** to tell *what things were like in general* or *what was going on when something else happened* and the **passé composé** to tell *what happened on specific occasions* or to recount *a sequence of events*.

Ce matin, **je me suis levé(e)** à 6h.

Quand j'étais au lycée, **je me levais** à 7h.

Follow-up for A. À 16 ans. Un couple va divorcer. Est-ce qu'ils faisaient probablement ces choses en couple? **EXEMPLE** s'entendre bien **Non, ils ne s'entendaient pas bien. 1.** se disputer souvent **2.** s'entendre mal **3.** s'amuser bien ensemble **4.** s'embrasser souvent

A À 16 ans. Parlez de votre routine quotidienne à l'âge de 16 ans.

EXEMPLE se réveiller souvent tôt
À l'âge de 16 ans, je me réveillais souvent tôt.
Je ne me réveillais pas souvent tôt.

1. se réveiller souvent avant 6h
2. se lever facilement
3. prendre un bain / une douche le matin
4. se laver les cheveux tous les jours
5. prendre toujours le petit déjeuner
6. aller toujours en cours
7. sécher mes cours *(to cut class)* quelquefois
8. s'ennuyer quelquefois en cours

Follow-ups for B. Et hier? A. Have students say when they last did these things. (You may wish to provide some possible answers: **hier, ce matin, la semaine dernière, il y a cinq minutes, il y a longtemps, ne... jamais,...**) **1.** travailler jusqu'à minuit **2.** se lever avant 7h **3.** se disputer avec un ami **4.** se brosser les dents **5.** se laver les cheveux **6.** s'amuser **7.** s'ennuyer **8.** se promener au parc **B.** Give students the following list. Have them circulate in the class to find at least two people who did each of these things yesterday. **1.** se réveiller avant 7h **2.** se laver les cheveux **3.** se lever tard **4.** se reposer **5.** se disputer avec un(e) ami(e) **6.** se coucher après minuit

B Et hier? Utilisez les verbes de l'exercice précédent pour parler de ce que vous avez fait hier.

EXEMPLE se réveiller tôt
Hier, je me suis réveillé(e) tôt.
Hier, je ne me suis pas réveillé(e) tôt.

C Alors?
Rosalie parle de ce qui s'est passé hier. Complétez ses phrases logiquement en mettant les verbes donnés au passé composé ou à l'imparfait.

EXEMPLE Hier matin, j' _____ (être) fatiguée, alors je _____ (rester) au lit.
Hier matin, j'**étais** fatiguée, alors je **suis restée** au lit.

1. Je (J') _____ (vouloir) préparer le petit déjeuner, alors je _____ (se laver) les mains.
2. Vers midi, André et moi, nous _____ (avoir) faim, alors on _____ (se préparer) des sandwichs.
3. Nous _____ (boire) deux bouteilles d'eau minérale aussi parce que nous _____ (avoir) très soif.
4. Après, André _____ (se coucher) une demi-heure parce qu'il _____ (être) fatigué.
5. Il _____ (se lever) vers trois heures parce qu'il _____ (vouloir) travailler un peu dans le jardin.
6. Il _____ (faire) très beau, alors nous _____ (se promener) dans le quartier.
7. Quand nous _____ (rentrer), Rose et ses copains _____ (être) à la maison.
8. Nous _____ (se quitter) assez tôt parce que nous _____ (vouloir) nous lever tôt le lendemain pour aller au Mont-Saint-Michel.

D Le mariage d'André et de Rosalie.
André et Rosalie se sont enfin mariés. Décrivez le jour de leur mariage en mettant les verbes donnés au passé composé ou à l'imparfait.

Le jour de son mariage, Rosalie __1__ (se lever) tôt. André __2__ (arriver) vers 9h mais, tout de suite après, il __3__ (se souvenir) d'une course qu'il __4__ (devoir) faire et il __5__ (repartir). Il __6__ (aller) acheter une nouvelle cravate.

Il __7__ (être) 3h quand André __8__ (revenir). La cérémonie __9__ (commencer) à 4h. Tous les invités *(guests)* __10__ (être) dans le jardin. Il __11__ (faire) beau et Rosalie et André __12__ (être) contents. Rosalie __13__ (porter) une jolie robe beige et André __14__ (porter) un costume noir. Rosalie __15__ (être) très jolie! Après la cérémonie, les amis __16__ (rester) et ils __17__ (manger) du gâteau *(cake)*. Ils __18__ (s'amuser) bien quand tout d'un coup il __19__ (commencer) à pleuvoir, alors ils __20__ (rentrer) dans la maison.

André __21__ (partir) et il __22__ (revenir) avec assez de chaises pour tout le monde. Vers 8h, les invités __23__ (partir). André et Rosalie __24__ (se regarder) et ils __25__ (commencer) à sourire *(to smile)*. Ils __26__ (être) fatigués mais très, très heureux.

E Entretien.
Interviewez votre partenaire.

1. Est-ce que tu te réveillais facilement quand tu étais ado *(teenager)*? À quelle heure est-ce que tu te réveillais pour aller au lycée? Tu prenais l'autocar *(schoolbus)*, une voiture ou tu y allais à pied? Tu y arrivais souvent en retard *(late)*?
2. Quand tu étais lycéen(ne), tu t'ennuyais ou tu t'amusais la plupart du temps *(most of the time)*? Qu'est-ce que tu faisais pour t'amuser le week-end? Comment s'appelait ton meilleur ami (ta meilleure amie)? Qu'est-ce que vous aimiez faire ensemble?
3. À quelle heure est-ce que tu t'es réveillé(e) ce matin? Tu t'es levé(e) tout de suite? Qu'est-ce que tu as fait ensuite?
4. La dernière fois que tu es sorti(e) avec des amis, est-ce que tu t'es bien amusé(e) ou est-ce que tu t'es un peu ennuyé(e)? Qu'est-ce que vous avez fait ensemble?

Suggestion for E. Entretien. Remind students that questions are normally answered using the same tense as the one used in the questions.

Supplemental activity. Have students list five things they did last weekend. Then have them list five things they used to do on the weekend when they were in high school.

COMPÉTENCE 4

Describing traits and characteristics

PowerPoint 7-10

LES TRAITS DE CARACTÈRE

Note culturelle

Ridicule ou romantique? 60 % des Français donnent un petit surnom *(nickname)* amoureux à leur partenaire. Parmi *(Among)* les plus utilisés, il y a mon chéri (ma chérie) *(darling)*, mon cœur *(heart)*, mon bébé, mon amour et ma puce *(flea)*, suivi par *(followed by)* mon doudou *(cuddly toy)*, ma biche *(doe)* et mon minou *(kitten)*. Trouvez-vous ces surnoms amoureux romantiques ou ridicules? Quels sont les surnoms les plus populaires dans votre région?

 **Sélection musicale.** Search the Web for the song **"À nos actes manqués"** by M. Pokora to enjoy a musical selection related to this vocabulary.

Vocabulaire sans peine!

English words ending in *-ance*, *-ence*, or *-ion* often have corresponding cognates in French. Such nouns are often feminine.

-ance = **-ance**
tolerance = **la tolérance**
-ence = **-ence**
innocence = **l'innocence**
-ion = **-ion**
comprehension = **la compréhension**

How would you say these words in French?

ignorance
indulgence
assertion

Warm-ups. A. Un couple s'est marié et plus tard a divorcé. Est-ce qu'ils faisaient les choses suivantes probablement juste avant de se marier ou juste avant de divorcer? **EXEMPLE** Ils s'entendaient bien. **Ils s'entendaient bien juste avant de se marier.** **1.** Ils s'entendaient mal. **2.** Ils se disputaient tout le temps. **3.** Ils s'embrassaient tout le temps. **4.** Ils s'amusaient ensemble. **5.** Ils s'ennuyaient ensemble. **6.** Ils ne se quittaient jamais. **7.** Ils se parlaient de tout. **8.** Ils ne se parlaient pas beaucoup. **9.** Ils s'aimaient. **10.** Ils ne s'aimaient plus *(no longer)*. **B.** Hier, votre meilleur(e) ami(e) et vous, est-ce que vous vous êtes... (vu[e]s à l'université, parlé au téléphone, téléphoné plus d'une fois, retrouvé[e]s au café, amusé[e]s ensemble, disputé[e]s, envoyé des textos)?

Rencontres en ligne: Test de compatibilité

Rangez chaque groupe de réponses de 1 (la réponse qui **exprime** le mieux vos sentiments) à 4 (la réponse qui exprime le moins bien vos sentiments).

Je préfère partager la vie avec quelqu'un qui **s'intéresse**...

1 2 3 4   à l'art
1 2 3 4   au sport
1 2 3 4   à la politique
1 2 3 4   à la nature

Je préfère quelqu'un qui cultive...

1 2 3 4   sa spiritualité
1 2 3 4   son **corps**
1 2 3 4   son **esprit**
1 2 3 4   sa vie professionnelle

Le trait de caractère que j'apprécie le plus chez un(e) partenaire, c'est...

1 2 3 4   un bon sens de l'humour
1 2 3 4   la passion
1 2 3 4   la beauté
1 2 3 4   **la tolérance**

Un **défaut** que je ne **supporte** pas chez une autre personne, c'est...

1 2 3 4   l'indécision *(f)*
1 2 3 4   l'inflexibilité *(f)*
1 2 3 4   **l'insensibilité** *(f)*
1 2 3 4   la vanité

Ce que je supporte le moins dans une relation, c'est...

1 2 3 4   la jalousie
1 2 3 4   l'indifférence *(f)*
1 2 3 4   l'infidélité *(f)*
1 2 3 4   la violence

Chez un(e) partenaire, ce qui a le moins d'importance pour moi, c'est...

1 2 3 4   son argent
1 2 3 4   sa profession
1 2 3 4   sa religion
1 2 3 4   son **aspect physique**

---

ranger to arrange, to order   **exprimer** to express   **s'intéresser à** to be interested in   **le corps** the body   **l'esprit** *(m)* the mind, the spirit   **la tolérance** tolerance, acceptance   **un défaut** a fault   **supporter** to bear, to tolerate, to put up with   **l'insensibilité** *(f)* insensitivity   **l'aspect physique** *(m)* physical appearance

Rose parle à sa cousine, Isabelle, de son copain, Luc.

ROSE: Alors, tu as trouvé **le bonheur** avec ton nouvel ami, Luc? Il est comment?

ISABELLE: Il a un bon sens de l'humour et il est sympa. Son seul défaut, c'est qu'il est un peu **jaloux** si je ne passe pas tout mon temps avec lui.

ROSE: Vous vous intéressez aux mêmes choses?

ISABELLE: Oui et non. On aime plus ou moins la même musique et les mêmes films et il s'intéresse à la politique comme moi, mais il est **de droite** et moi, tu sais, je suis plutôt **de gauche**.

A Et vous? Changez les mots en italique pour parler de vous.

1. J'ai beaucoup d'amis qui s'intéressent *au sport / à la nature / à la politique…*
2. Je ne m'intéresse pas du tout *à la politique / au sport / à l'art…*
3. Je préfère cultiver *mon esprit / mon corps et mon aspect physique / ma spiritualité…*
4. Chez un(e) partenaire, ce qui a le plus d'importance pour moi, c'est *sa beauté / son intelligence / sa religion…*
5. Chez un(e) partenaire, je ne supporte pas bien *la vanité / l'indécision / l'inflexibilité…*
6. Dans une relation, je ne supporterai *(will never tolerate)* jamais *la jalousie / la violence / l'infidélité…*

B Entretien. Interviewez votre partenaire.

1. Tu t'intéresses au sport? à l'art? au cinéma? à la politique? à la philosophie? Est-ce que tu t'ennuies si quelqu'un parle de ces choses-là?
2. Tu passes plus de temps à cultiver ton corps, ton esprit, ta spiritualité ou ta vie professionnelle? Qu'est-ce que tu fais pour le (la) cultiver?

C Test de compatibilité. Travaillez en groupes pour écrire deux questions pour un nouveau test de compatibilité. Ensuite, utilisez les questions de tous les groupes pour créer *(to create)* le nouveau test.

EXEMPLE Quelle activité aimez-vous le moins faire avec une autre personne?
1 2 3 4   faire la cuisine
1 2 3 4   faire de l'exercice
1 2 3 4   faire du shopping
1 2 3 4   voyager

À VOUS!

Avec un(e) partenaire, relisez à haute voix la conversation entre Rose et Isabelle. Ensuite, adaptez la conversation pour parler d'un(e) ami(e), de votre copain (copine) ou de votre mari ou femme. Commencez la conversation en disant: **Alors, tu passes beaucoup de temps avec…** (au lieu de dire *[instead of saying]*: **Alors, tu as trouvé le bonheur avec…**).

---

le bonheur *happiness*   **jaloux (jalouse)** *jealous*   **de droite** *conservative*   **de gauche** *liberal*

SPECIFYING WHICH ONE

PowerPoint 7-11

✓ Pour vérifier

1. Can **qui, que,** and **dont** all be used for both people and things?

2. Which relative pronoun functions as the subject of a verb? Which one functions as the direct object of a verb? Which one replaces the preposition **de** and its object? Does **qui** or **que** change to **qu'** before a vowel sound?

3. Where are relative clauses placed with respect to the noun they describe?

Note de grammaire

Remember that past participles agree with preceding direct objects and therefore agree with the noun that **que** represents: **Je sors avec une femme que j'ai rencontrée pendant mes vacances.**

Sélection musicale. Search the Web for the song **"Quelqu'un que j'aime, quelqu'un qui m'aime"** by Céline Dion to enjoy a musical selection illustrating the use of this structure.

iLrn Grammar Tutorials

Suggestion. You may wish to point out that **ce** is inserted before relative clauses when no antecedent is stated: **ce qui, ce que, ce dont.** Such phrases are usually translated in English as *what (= that which).* Provide the following sentences and have students complete them with a noun. **1.** Ce qui est le plus important pour moi dans une relation, c'est… **2.** Ce qui a peu d'importance pour moi dans une relation, c'est… **3.** Ce que je ne supporte pas dans une relation, c'est… **4.** Ce dont j'ai le plus envie chez un(e) partenaire, c'est… **5.** Ce dont j'ai le plus peur, c'est… **6.** Ce que je veux surtout dans la vie, c'est…

Les pronoms relatifs *qui, que* et *dont*

A relative clause gives more information about a person or object you are talking about in a sentence. A relative clause begins with a relative pronoun, a word like *who, that,* or *which* that refers back to the noun being described.

Je sors avec une femme { **qui** est beaucoup plus âgée que moi.
{ **que** j'ai rencontrée pendant mes vacances.
{ **dont** je suis amoureux.

I'm going out with a woman { **who** is a lot older than I am.
{ **whom** I met during my vacation.
{ **with whom** I'm in love.

The relative pronouns **qui, que,** and **dont** are all used for both people and things. The choice depends on how the pronoun functions in the relative clause. Note how relative pronouns are used to combine two sentences talking about the same thing. The relative clause is placed immediately after the noun it describes.

- Use **qui** for both people or things when they are the *subject* of the relative clause. Since **qui** is the subject, it is followed by a verb and it can mean *that, which,* or *who.* Note that **qui** does not make elision before a vowel sound.

  Comment s'appelle ton ami? **Ton ami** habite à New York.
  Comment s'appelle ton ami **qui** habite à New York?

- Use **que (qu')** for people or things when they are the *direct object* in the relative clause. **Que (qu')** can mean *that, which,* or *whom,* or it may be omitted in English. Note that the pronoun **que** makes elision **(qu')** before a vowel sound.

  Comment s'appelle ton ami? Tu as invité **cet ami** hier.
  Comment s'appelle ton ami **que** tu as invité hier?

- Use **dont** to replace the preposition **de** + *a person or thing* in relative clauses with verbs such as the following. It can mean *whom, of (about, with) whom, whose, that,* or *of (about, with) which.*

avoir besoin de	se souvenir de
avoir envie de	parler de
avoir peur de	rêver de
être amoureux (amoureuse) de	tomber amoureux (amoureuse) de
être jaloux (jalouse) de	faire la connaissance de (*to make the acquaintance of, to meet* [for the first time])

  Comment s'appelle ton ami? Ta sœur parlait **de cet ami** hier.
  Comment s'appelle ton ami **dont** ta sœur parlait hier?

A Préférences. Complétez ces phrases comme dans les exemples. Pour chaque section, utilisez le pronom relatif indiqué.

Utilisez le pronom relatif **qui** et conjuguez le verbe.

EXEMPLE Je préfère les personnes… (avoir un bon sens de l'humour, avoir beaucoup d'argent)
Je préfère les personnes qui ont un bon sens de l'humour.

1. Je préfère un(e) colocataire… (sortir tout le temps, rester souvent à la maison)
2. Je préfère les films… (avoir beaucoup d'action, avoir peu de violence)
3. Je préfère un(e) partenaire… (cultiver son corps, cultiver son esprit)

Utilisez le pronom relatif **que (qu')**.

EXEMPLE Je préfère les personnes… (je rencontre en cours, je rencontre en boîte)
Je préfère les personnes que je rencontre en boîte.

1. Je préfère les personnes… (on rencontre dans une salle de gym, on rencontre à la bibliothèque)
2. Je préfère les activités… (je fais seul[e], je fais en groupe)
3. Je préfère la musique… (on fait maintenant, on faisait il y a vingt ans)

Utilisez le pronom relatif **dont**.

EXEMPLE L'argent est une chose… (j'ai très envie, je n'ai pas très envie)
L'argent est une chose dont je n'ai pas très envie.

1. L'amour est quelque chose… (j'ai très besoin dans ma vie, je n'ai pas vraiment besoin pour le moment)
2. La ville où je suis né(e) est un endroit *(place)*… (je me souviens bien, je ne me souviens pas bien)
3. Ma vie amoureuse, c'est une chose… (j'aime bien parler, je n'aime pas beaucoup parler)

B Identification. Complétez les descriptions suivantes avec **qui**, **que** ou **dont**. Ensuite, donnez les renseignements demandés.

EXEMPLE Un film _____ j'aime beaucoup, c'est…
Un film que j'aime beaucoup, c'est *Le Maître*.

1. Un film _____ a gagné beaucoup d'Oscars, c'est…
2. Un film _____ j'ai vu plusieurs fois, c'est…
3. Un film _____ on parle beaucoup en ce moment, c'est…
4. Un acteur (Une actrice) _____ je trouve beau (belle), c'est…
5. Un acteur (Une actrice) _____ tout le monde parle souvent, c'est…
6. Un acteur (Une actrice) _____ n'a vraiment pas de talent, c'est…
7. Une émission *(program)* de télévision _____ est à la télé depuis longtemps, c'est…
8. Une émission de télévision de mon enfance *(childhood)* _____ je me souviens, c'est…
9. Une émission de télévision _____ j'aime beaucoup regarder, c'est…

Follow-up for B. Identification. C'est André qui parle de sa vie avec Rosalie. Complétez les phrases avec **qui**, **que** ou **dont**. Ensuite, dites de qui ou de quoi il parle: **Rose, Rosalie, le premier mari de Rosalie** ou **le Mont-Saint-Michel**. **EXEMPLE** C'est quelqu'un **dont** je suis tombé amoureux il y a longtemps. C'est quelqu'un **que** j'ai revu récemment chez des amis. C'est **Rosalie**. **1.** C'est quelqu'un _____ j'ai fait la connaissance récemment. C'est quelqu'un _____ voyage avec Rosalie. C'est quelqu'un _____ j'aimerais mieux connaître. C'est _____. **2.** C'est un site touristique spectaculaire _____ se trouve *(is located)* sur une île en Normandie. C'est un endroit *(place)* _____ Rosalie se souvenait bien. C'est un endroit _____ j'ai visité avec Rosalie récemment. C'est _____. **3.** C'est quelqu'un _____ est venu en France il y a longtemps. C'est quelqu'un _____ Rosalie a trouvé très beau. C'est quelqu'un _____ j'étais jaloux. C'est _____.

VIDÉOREPRISE

Les Stagiaires

See the **Résumé de grammaire** section at the end of each chapter for a review of all the grammar presented in the chapter.

The entire **Vidéoreprise** section is designed to be a pre-viewing series for the video, as well as a chapter review that can be used independently from the video. There are also additional grammar review exercises on the Instructor's Companion Website and on iLrn.

Rappel!
Matthieu a enfin dominé sa timidité et a invité Amélie à sortir. Maintenant, Céline, l'amie et la colocataire d'Amélie, veut qu'Amélie lui raconte tout sur *(to tell her everything about)* sa sortie avec Matthieu.

Dans l'*Épisode 7* de la vidéo *Les Stagiaires,* Amélie et Céline parlent de la soirée qu'Amélie a passée avec Matthieu. Avant de regarder l'épisode, faites ces exercices pour réviser ce que vous avez appris dans le *Chapitre 7.*

A **Au bureau.** Amélie parle à une amie de ses collègues et de son travail à Technovert. Complétez chaque phrase avec la forme correcte du verbe logique entre parenthèses.

EXEMPLE Technovert **vend** (perdre / vendre) des produits technologiques verts.

1. Je prends le bus pour aller au travail et je _____ (descendre / entendre) juste en face du bureau.
2. M. Vieilledent est le directeur, mais son assistante Camille _____ (s'entendre / répondre) à toutes nos questions sur le fonctionnement de l'entreprise.
3. Christophe est un peu paresseux et il _____ (rendre / attendre) toujours le dernier moment pour faire son travail.
4. Camille et Céline _____ (perdre / vendre) souvent patience avec Christophe.
5. Je (J') _____ (entendre / s'entendre) souvent Camille parler de ses frustrations concernant le travail de Christophe.
6. Il _____ (perdre / descendre) beaucoup de temps au bureau en lisant *(reading)* des mangas.
7. J'habite avec la responsable des ventes, Céline. Nous _____ (entendre / s'entendre) bien. Il n'y a jamais de problèmes entre nous.
8. Céline _____ (attendre / rendre) souvent visite à ses parents le week-end, alors je suis seule dans l'appartement.

B **Chez Christophe.** Christophe parle de ses parents. Complétez les phrases suivantes avec la forme correcte du verbe réfléchi ou réciproque indiqué entre parenthèses.

EXEMPLE Je **m'entends** *(get along)* mieux avec mon père qu'avec ma mère.

1. Ma mère et moi, on _____ *(argue)* souvent.
2. Mon père et moi, nous ne _____ *(talk to each other)* pas beaucoup.
3. Le week-end, mon père est toujours très occupé. Il ne _____ *(rests)* jamais.
4. Mon père _____ *(wakes up)* à 6h le samedi.
5. Moi, je _____ *(get up)* vers midi.
6. Le samedi soir, mes amis et moi, on _____ *(meet one another)* presque toujours en ville.
7. Je _____ *(get bored)* si je reste à la maison le week-end.
8. Je _____ *(have fun)* plus avec mes amis qu'avec ma famille.

Maintenant changez les phrases précédentes pour décrire votre situation.

EXEMPLE Je m'entends aussi bien avec mon père qu'avec ma mère. / Je m'entends bien avec ma mère, mais je m'entends moins bien avec mon père.

C Conseils.
Matthieu pose des questions à un ami à propos des relations sociales. Complétez ses questions avec le pronom relatif (**qui, que, dont**) approprié.

1. Quand tu sors avec des amis, quels sont les sujets de conversation _____ vous parlez le plus souvent?
2. As-tu plus d'amis _____ s'intéressent à l'art, au sport ou à la politique?
3. Tu penses que c'est une bonne idée de sortir en couple avec quelqu'un _____ on a rencontré au travail?
4. Est-ce que tu as beaucoup d'amis _____ sont mariés?
5. Est-ce qu'on doit se marier avec la première personne _____ on tombe amoureux?
6. Est-ce que le mariage est quelque chose _____ tu trouves important ou _____ n'est pas important pour toi?

Maintenant interviewez un(e) autre étudiant(e) en utilisant les questions précédentes.

D Hier soir.
Après sa soirée avec Amélie, Matthieu parle à son ami. Complétez le paragraphe suivant en mettant les verbes entre parenthèses au passé composé ou à l'imparfait.

Amélie et moi, on __1__ (se retrouver) au restaurant. J' __2__ (être) déjà au restaurant quand elle __3__ (arriver). Au début, quand j' __4__ (attendre), j' __5__ (être) nerveux, mais après, on __6__ (commencer) à parler et j'ai découvert *(discovered)* qu'elle aimait les mêmes choses que moi. Après le dîner, on __7__ (se promener) un peu et on __8__ (s'arrêter) dans un café pour prendre un verre. Il __9__ (être) assez tard quand on __10__ (se quitter).

Suggestion for the video. Tell students not to worry about understanding every word, but to use what they do know and the context to guess what is being said. The video is available on DVD and on *iLrn*. The videoscript is available on the Instructor's Companion Website, **www.cengage.com/french/horizons6e,** and on iLrn.

Access the Video *Les Stagiaires* on

▶ Épisode 7: Vous vous êtes amusés?

AVANT LA VIDÉO
Dans cet épisode, Céline parle à Amélie de son rendez-vous d'hier soir avec Matthieu. Avant de le regarder, imaginez trois choses dont Amélie et Matthieu ont peut-être parlé.

APRÈS LA VIDÉO
Regardez l'épisode et répondez aux questions suivantes:
- De quoi est-ce que Matthieu et Amélie ont parlé?
- Vers quelle heure est-ce qu'ils se sont quittés?

LECTURE ET COMPOSITION

LECTURE

POUR MIEUX LIRE:
Recognizing conversational style

You are going to read a story by Eugène Ionesco (1912–1994), in which a father finds himself alone one morning with his two- or three-year-old daughter.

Sometimes a writer uses language that is not completely "correct" to portray how someone speaks. To appreciate this style and how it tells something about the character who is speaking, you can compare this conversational language with the more "correct" version of the language. In Ionesco's story, the author modifies his language to represent the way a little girl would speak or how someone might speak to a young child.

Du vocabulaire enfantin. Regardez ces phrases. Comment dit-on la même chose d'une façon plus correcte?

1. Tu laves ta figure.
2. Je rase ma barbe.
3. Tu laves ton «dérère» *(backside)*.

Conte pour enfants de moins de trois ans

Ce matin, comme d'habitude, Josette **frappe** à la porte de la chambre à coucher de ses parents. Papa n'a pas très bien dormi. Maman est partie à la campagne pour quelques jours. Alors papa a profité de cette absence pour manger beaucoup de **saucisson,** pour boire de la bière, pour manger du **pâté de cochon** et beaucoup d'autres choses que maman **l'empêche de** manger parce que c'est pas bon pour **la santé.** Alors, voilà, papa **a mal au foie, il a mal à l'estomac, il a mal à la tête,** et ne voudrait pas se réveiller. Mais Josette frappe toujours à la porte. Alors, papa **lui dit** d'entrer. Elle entre, elle va chez son papa. Il n'y a pas maman. Josette demande:

—Où elle est maman?

Papa répond: *Ta maman est allée se reposer à la campagne chez sa maman à elle.*

Josette répond: *Chez Mémée?*

Papa répond: *Oui, chez Mémée.*

—Écris à maman, dit Josette. *Téléphone à maman*, dit Josette.

Papa dit: **Faut pas** *téléphoner.* Et puis papa dit pour **lui-même:** *Parce qu'elle est peut-être* **autre part**...

Josette dit: **Raconte** *une histoire avec maman et toi, et moi.*

—Non, dit papa, *je vais aller au travail. Je me lève, je vais m'habiller.*

---

frappe knocks **saucisson** salami **pâté de cochon** pork pâté **l'empêche de** keeps him from **la santé** health
a mal au foie, il a mal à l'estomac, il a mal à la tête has indigestion, he has a stomachache, he has a headache
lui dit tells her **Faut pas** We must not **lui-même** himself **autre part** somewhere else **Raconte** Tell

Et papa se lève. Il met **sa robe de chambre** rouge, **par dessus** son pyjama, il met les **pieds** dans ses **pantoufles**. Il va dans la salle de bains. Il ferme la porte de la salle de bains. Josette est à la porte de la salle de bains. Elle frappe avec ses petits **poings**, elle **pleure**.

Josette dit: *Ouvre-moi la porte.*

Papa répond: *Je ne peux pas. Je suis **tout nu**, je me lave, après je me rase.*

Josette dit: *Et tu fais pipi-caca.*

—*Je me lave,* dit papa.

Josette dit: *Tu laves ta figure, tu laves tes **épaules**, tu laves tes **bras**, tu laves ton **dos**, tu laves ton «dérère», tu laves tes pieds.*

—*Je rase ma barbe,* dit papa.

—*Tu rases ta barbe avec **du savon**,* dit Josette. *Je veux entrer. Je veux voir.*

Papa dit: *Tu ne peux pas me voir, parce que je **ne** suis **plus** dans la salle de bains.*

Josette dit (derrière la porte): *Alors, où tu es?*

Papa répond: *Je ne sais pas, va voir. Je suis peut-être dans la salle à manger, va me chercher.*

Josette **court** dans la salle à manger, et papa commence sa toilette. Josette court avec ses petites **jambes**, elle va dans la salle à manger. Papa est tranquille, mais pas pour longtemps. Josette arrive **de nouveau** devant la porte de la salle de bains, elle **crie à travers** la porte:

Josette dit: *Je t'ai cherché. Tu n'es pas dans la salle à manger.*

Papa dit: *Tu n'as pas bien cherché. Regarde sous la table.*

Josette retourne dans la salle à manger. Elle revient.

Elle dit: *Tu n'es pas sous la table.*

Papa dit: *Alors va voir dans le salon. Regarde bien si je suis sur le fauteuil, sur le canapé, derrière les livres, à la fenêtre.*

Josette s'en va. Papa est tranquille, mais pas pour longtemps.

Josette revient.

Elle dit: *Non, tu n'es pas dans le fauteuil, tu n'es pas à la fenêtre, tu n'es pas sur le canapé, tu n'es pas derrière les livres, tu n'es pas dans la télévision, tu n'es pas dans le salon.*

Papa dit: *Alors, va voir si je suis dans la cuisine.*

Josette dit: *Je vais te chercher dans la cuisine.*

---

sa robe de chambre *his robe* **par dessus** *over* **pieds** *feet* **pantoufles** *slippers* **poings** *fists* **pleure** *cries* **tout nu** *completely naked* **épaules** *shoulders* **bras** *arms* **dos** *back* **du savon** *soap* **ne... plus** *no longer* **court** *runs* **jambes** *legs* **de nouveau** *again* **crie à travers** *yells through*

Josette court à la cuisine. Papa est tranquille, mais pas pour longtemps. Josette revient.

Elle dit: *Tu n'es pas dans la cuisine.*

Papa dit: *Regarde bien, sous la table de la cuisine, regarde bien si je suis dans le buffet, regarde bien si je suis dans **les casseroles**, regarde bien si je suis dans **le four** avec le poulet.*

Josette va et vient. Papa n'est pas dans le four, papa n'est pas dans les casseroles, papa n'est pas dans le buffet, papa n'est pas sous **le paillasson,** papa n'est pas dans **la poche** de son pantalon, dans la poche du pantalon il y a **seulement le mouchoir.**

Josette revient devant la porte de la salle de bains.

Josette dit: *J'ai cherché partout. Je ne t'ai pas trouvé. Où tu es?*

Papa dit: *Je suis là*.

Et papa, qui a eu le temps de faire sa toilette, qui s'est rasé, qui s'est habillé, ouvre la porte.

Il dit: *Je suis là.*

Il prend Josette **dans ses bras,** et voilà aussi la porte de la maison qui s'ouvre, **au fond** du couloir, et c'est maman qui arrive. Josette **saute** des bras de son papa, elle **se jette** dans les bras de sa maman, elle l'embrasse, elle dit:

*Maman, j'ai cherché papa sous la table, dans l'armoire, sous le tapis, derrière **la glace,** dans la cuisine, dans **la poubelle,** il n'était pas là.*

Papa dit à maman: ***Je suis content que tu sois revenue.*** *Il faisait beau à la campagne? Comment va ta mère?*

Josette dit: *Et Mémée, elle va bien? On va chez elle?*

Eugène Ionesco, *Conte No 4* © Éditions GALLIMARD, www.gallimard.fr

---

les casseroles the pans   **le four** the oven   **le paillasson** the doormat   **la poche** the pocket   **seulement le mouchoir** only the handkerchief   **dans ses bras** in his arms   **au fond** at the end   **saute** jumps   **se jette** throws herself   **la glace** the mirror   **la poubelle** the trash can   **Je suis content que tu sois revenue.** *I'm glad you came back.*

Avez-vous des enfants? Si non (If not), voulez-vous avoir des enfants un jour? Pourquoi ou pourquoi pas?

COMPOSITION

POUR MIEUX ÉCRIRE: Organizing a paragraph

You know how to use words like **d'abord, ensuite, alors,** and **et puis** to connect your sentences into a well-ordered paragraph. Another way to link ideas is to use **pour** to say *in order to*. In this case, **pour** is followed by an infinitive.

Je pars à 7h pour arriver à 8h.
I leave at 7:00 (in order) to arrive at 8:00.

To say that you do something *before* you do something else, use **avant de** followed by an infinitive.

Avant de m'habiller, je mange.
Before I get dressed (Before getting dressed), I eat.

Organisez-vous. Vous allez décrire votre routine matinale. Avant de commencer, traduisez les phrases qui suivent.

1. *I'm tired in the morning, so I don't wake up easily.*
2. *First, I eat breakfast. Next, I take a shower. Then, I get dressed. And then, I leave.*
3. *I eat quickly in order to be on time.*
4. *Before I eat, I get dressed.*
5. *I take a bath before I dress.*

Compréhension

1. Pourquoi est-ce que le père de Josette a mal à la tête et à l'estomac?
2. Quel jeu invente-t-il pour pouvoir faire sa toilette?
3. Dans quelles pièces est-ce que la petite fille cherche son papa?
4. Où est-ce qu'elle le cherche dans la cuisine?
5. Qui rentre à la fin du conte? Quelle est la réaction du papa?

Le matin chez moi

Décrivez votre routine du matin. Utilisez des mots comme **d'abord, ensuite** et **avant de** pour indiquer l'ordre de vos actions.

EXEMPLE Le matin, je me lève vers six heures. D'abord...

Process-writing follow-up for *Le matin chez moi*. Échangez votre description avec celle d'un(e) autre étudiant(e). Comparez votre routine matinale avec celle de votre partenaire et décrivez-les aux autres étudiants.

COMPARAISONS CULTURELLES

PowerPoint 7-12

Suggestion. Have students anonymously answer the questions to these polls. Calculate the responses for the class, compare them to those of the French, and discuss the reasons for any similarities and differences.

L'AMOUR ET LE COUPLE

Voici les résultats de **sondages** d'opinion des Français sur le couple et les relations entre hommes et femmes. Quelles sont vos opinions?

À quoi croit-on en amour?

Question: Pour chacune des choses suivantes, **diriez-vous que vous y croyez** ou que vous n'y croyez pas?

	Vous y croyez	Vous n'y croyez pas	Sans opinion
À la possibilité d'aimer **plusieurs** fois dans la vie	80	16	4
Au coup de foudre	68	28	4
À l'amour qui **dure** toute la vie	68	29	3
À la possibilité d'être heureux sans être amoureux	56	41	3
À la possibilité de retrouver un amour perdu ou un amour de jeunesse	53	41	6

© TNS Sofres

Jusqu'où va-t-on par amour?

Question: Pour chacune des choses suivantes, lesquelles **seriez-vous prêt(e)** à faire par amour?

	Prêt(e) à le faire	Pas prêt(e) à le faire	Sans opinion
Quitter votre travail pour **suivre** votre **conjoint**	64	29	7
Pratiquer avec lui des activités que vous n'aimez pas	59	37	4
Changer votre manière de vous habiller	49	47	4
Pardonner une infidélité	43	47	10
Vous **soumettre à ses fantasmes** romantiques	39	47	14
Accepter de **vivre** séparément	35	59	6
Renoncer à voir un ami ou une amie	31	64	5
Adopter sa religion	20	75	5
Avoir recours à **la chirurgie esthétique**	11	85	4

© TNS Sofres

sondages polls **À quoi croit-on en amour?** What does one believe about love? **diriez-vous que vous y croyez** would you say that you believe in it **plusieurs** several **dure** lasts **seriez-vous prêt(e) à faire par amour** would you be ready to do out of love **suivre** to follow **conjoint** partner **soumettre** to submit **à ses fantasmes** to his/her fantasies **vivre** to live **la chirurgie esthétique** plastic surgery

Ce qui menace le couple

Question: Aujourd'hui, dans votre vie, qu'est-ce qui pourrait mettre en danger votre couple?

	Ensemble	Vivent en couple
L'infidélité	35	42
L'habitude	23	27
Les disputes	18	21
Les difficultés matérielles ou d'argent	14	17
La jalousie	14	15
Le vieillissement	6	8
Le travail	5	6
Le chômage	4	4
Avoir des enfants	2	1
Rien	7	10

© TNS Sofres

Compréhension

A Vrai ou faux. D'abord, complétez les phrases suivantes avec le pronom relatif convenable: **que** ou **qui**. Ensuite, dites si les phrases sont vraies ou fausses et corrigez les phrases fausses.

1. Pour la majorité des Français, c'est le chômage *(unemployment)* _____ menace le plus le couple.
2. Les Français _____ croient au coup de foudre sont peu nombreux.
3. Avoir recours à la chirurgie esthétique est quelque chose _____ la plupart des Français trouvent normal de faire par amour pour l'autre.
4. L'infidélité est quelque chose _____ la majorité des Français acceptent dans un couple.
5. Pour la majorité des Français, l'amour _____ dure toute la vie n'existe pas.

B Comparaisons. Discutez les questions suivantes.

1. Dans les réponses des Français au sondage, qu'est-ce qui vous surprend *(surprises you)*? Qu'est-ce qui ne vous surprend pas? Pourquoi?
2. Dans un sondage sur ce sujet fait dans votre pays, quelles autres questions est-ce qu'on poserait *(would one ask)*? Quelles questions est-ce qu'on ne poserait probablement pas? Voyez-vous des attitudes différentes sur ce sujet?

---

menace *threatens*   **Ensemble** *The whole group*   **Vivent en couple** *(Just those who) live as a couple*
le vieillissement *aging*   **le chômage** *unemployment*

RÉSUMÉ DE GRAMMAIRE

REFLEXIVE VERBS

Reflexive verbs are used to say that people do something to or for themselves. In French, the reflexive pronoun corresponding to the subject is placed before the verb.

SE COUCHER (to go to bed)	
je **me** couche	nous **nous** couchons
tu **te** couches	vous **vous** couchez
il/elle/on **se** couche	ils/elles **se** couchent

Je **me** réveille à six heures et puis, je réveille mes enfants à sept heures.
*I wake **(myself)** up at six o'clock, and then I wake up my children at seven.*
Mon fils de trois ans **s'**habille tout seul.
My three-year-old son dresses all by himself.

The reflexive pronouns **me**, **te**, and **se** become **m'**, **t'**, and **s'** before vowel sounds. Also note the spelling changes with **s'ennuyer**, **s'appeler**, and **se lever**. Remember that all verbs ending with **-yer**, such as **envoyer**, **essayer**, and **payer**, follow the same pattern as **s'ennuyer**. **Se promener** is conjugated like **se lever**.

S'ENNUYER (to be / get bored)	S'APPELER (to be named)	SE LEVER (to get up)
je m'ennuie	je m'appelle	je me lève
tu t'ennuies	tu t'appelles	tu te lèves
il/elle/on s'ennuie	il/elle/on s'appelle	il/elle/on se lève
nous nous ennuyons	nous nous appelons	nous nous levons
vous vous ennuyez	vous vous appelez	vous vous levez
ils/elles s'ennuient	ils/elles s'appellent	ils/elles se lèvent

—Tu **ne** t'ennuies **pas** dans ce cours?
—Non, mes camarades et moi, nous **ne** nous y ennuyons **jamais**!
—Comment vous appelez-vous?
—Je m'appe**ll**e Catherine Faure.
—À quelle heure est-ce que vous vous levez?
—Je me lève très tôt.

To negate reflexive verbs, place **ne** directly after the subject and **pas** or **jamais** directly after the conjugated verb.

Verbs that are reflexive in English, such as *to amuse **oneself*** or *to buy **oneself** something* will generally also be reflexive in French. Many other verbs are reflexive in French that are not in English. Consult the end-of-chapter vocabulary list to find all the reflexive verbs learned in this chapter.

Mon père **s'**achète une nouvelle voiture chaque année.
*My father buys **himself** a new car each year.*
Je me brosse **les** dents trois fois par jour.
*I brush **my** teeth three times a day.*

Verbs indicating that people are doing something to their own body are generally reflexive in French. After such verbs, in French, you generally use the definite article (**le, la, l', les**) with a body part, rather than the possessive adjective (*my, your, his . . .*).

RECIPROCAL VERBS

Vous **vous** retrouvez après les cours?
*Do you meet **each other** after class?*
Mes voisins ne **se** parlent pas.
*My neighbors don't talk **to one another**.*

Reciprocal verbs indicate that two or more people do something to or for one another. Most verbs naming something one person might do to another can be made reciprocal by adding a reciprocal pronoun.

aimer	*to love*	s'aimer	*to love each other*
détester	*to hate*	se détester	*to hate each other*
regarder	*to look at*	se regarder	*to look at each other*

—**Vous** voulez **vous** marier?
—Oui, et **nous** allons **nous** installer dans un petit appartement.

When reflexive / reciprocal verbs are used in the infinitive, the reflexive / reciprocal pronoun changes to match the subject of the conjugated verb.

PAST TENSES OF REFLEXIVE AND RECIPROCAL VERBS

All reflexive / reciprocal verbs are conjugated with **être** in the **passé composé**. The past participle agrees in gender and number with the reflexive / reciprocal pronoun (and the subject) when it is the *direct* object of the verb.

S'AMUSER	
je me suis amusé(e)	nous nous sommes amusé(e)s
tu t'es amusé(e)	vous vous êtes amusé(e)(s)
il s'est amusé	ils se sont amusés
elle s'est amusée	elles se sont amusées
on s'est amusé(e)(s)	

—Tous tes amis se sont retrouvé**s** chez toi?
—Oui, et on s'est bien amusé**s** jusqu'à très tard. Mon amie Rose s'est endormi**e** sur le canapé.

With negated verbs, place **ne** directly after the subject and **pas** after the conjugated form of **être**.

Past participles do not agree with reflexive / reciprocal pronouns that are *indirect* objects. For this reason, there is no agreement with **se parler, se téléphoner, s'écrire,** or when a reflexive verb is followed directly by a noun that is the direct object of the verb, such as a part of the body.

—Vous **ne** vous êtes **pas** vus hier?
—Non, mais nous nous sommes téléphoné trois fois.

Ma petite sœur s'est maquillé**e**.
Ma petite sœur s'est maquillé **les yeux**.

As with all verbs except **être**, form the imperfect of reflexive verbs by dropping the **-ons** from the **nous** form of the verb and adding the imperfect endings: **-ais, -ais, -ait, -ions, -iez, -aient**.

—Tu te levais plus tôt l'année dernière?
—Oui, je me levais à six heures.

REGULAR -RE VERBS

The following verbs are conjugated like **répondre: descendre, entendre, s'entendre (bien / mal) (avec), perdre, se perdre, rendre visite à quelqu'un, rendre quelque chose à quelqu'un, vendre, revendre.** They all take **avoir** in the **passé composé** except **descendre** and the reflexive verbs.

RÉPONDRE (to answer)	
je répond**s**	nous répond**ons**
tu répond**s**	vous répond**ez**
il/elle/on répond	ils/elles répond**ent**
PASSÉ COMPOSÉ: **j'ai répondu**	
IMPARFAIT: **je répondais**	

—Tu ne rends jamais visite à ton ex-copine?
—Non, on a perdu contact. On ne s'entend pas très bien. Si je téléphone chez elle, elle ne répond pas au téléphone.

RELATIVE PRONOUNS

A relative clause is a phrase that describes a noun. The word that begins the phrase, referring back to the noun described is a relative pronoun. The relative pronouns **qui, que,** and **dont** are all used for both people and things. The choice of relative pronoun depends on the pronoun's function in the relative clause. **Qui** replaces the subject of the relative clause, **que (qu')** replaces the direct object, and **dont** replaces the preposition **de** and its object.

Place relative clauses directly after the noun they describe. When **que** is the object of a verb in the **passé composé,** the past participle agrees in number and gender with the noun it represents.

La femme **qui** habite à côté est française. (= La femme est française. **Cette femme** habite à côté.)
La femme **que** j'ai invité**e** est française. (= La femme est française. J'ai invité **cette femme**.)
La femme **dont** je parle souvent est française. (= La femme est française. Je parle souvent **de cette femme**.)

Résumé de grammaire | *deux cent quatre-vingt-dix-sept* **297**

VOCABULAIRE

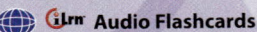 Audio Flashcards

COMPÉTENCE 1

Describing your daily routine

NOMS MASCULINS

un bain	a bath
le mariage	marriage
un petit-fils	a grandson
un séjour	a stay
un veuf	a widower

NOMS FÉMININS

une demi-heure	a half hour
les dents	the teeth
une douche	a shower
la figure	the face
la main	the hand
une petite-fille	a granddaughter
une routine	a routine
une veuve	a widow

EXPRESSIONS VERBALES

s'amuser	to have fun
s'appeler	to be named / called
attendre	to wait (for)
se brosser (les cheveux / les dents)	to brush (one's hair / one's teeth)
connaître	to be familiar with, to be acquainted with, to know
se coucher / se recoucher	to go to bed / to go back to bed
s'endormir	to fall asleep
s'ennuyer	to be bored, to get bored
faire sa toilette	to wash up
s'habiller / se déshabiller	to get dressed / to get undressed
se laver (la figure / les mains)	to wash (one's face / one's hands)
se lever	to get up
se maquiller	to put on makeup
prendre un bain / une douche	to take a bath / a shower
se raser	to shave
se reposer	to rest
se réveiller	to wake up

DIVERS

avant de	before
comme	since, as
d'autres fois	other times
depuis	since (then), for
d'origine…	of … origin
facilement	easily
parfait(e)	perfect
pendant	during
quotidien(ne)	daily
vite	quick(ly), fast

COMPÉTENCE 2

Talking about relationships

NOMS MASCULINS

le coup de foudre	love at first sight
le grand amour	true love

NOMS FÉMININS

la jeunesse	youth
une relation	a relationship

EXPRESSIONS VERBALES

s'aimer	to like each other, to love each other
descendre	to go down, to get off, to stay (at a hotel)
se détester	to hate each other
se disputer	to argue
s'embrasser	to kiss each other, to embrace each other
entendre	to hear
s'entendre (bien / mal) (avec)	to get along (well / badly) (with)
se fiancer	to get engaged
s'installer (dans / à)	to move (into), to settle (in)
se marier (avec)	to get married (to)
se parler	to talk to each other
se passer	to happen
perdre	to lose
perdre du temps	to waste time
se perdre	to get lost
prendre une décision	to make a decision
se quitter	to leave each other
se réconcilier	to make up with each other
se regarder	to look at each other
se rencontrer	to meet each other (by chance, for the first time), to run into each other
rendre quelque chose à quelqu'un	to return something to someone
rendre visite à quelqu'un	to visit someone
répondre (à)	to answer, to respond (to)
se retrouver	to meet each other (by design)
revendre	to sell back / resell
rêver (de)	to dream (of, about)
se souvenir de	to remember
suivre	to follow
se téléphoner	to phone each other
vendre	to sell

DIVERS

ce qui	what
C'est dommage!	That's too bad!
enfin	finally
formidable	great
heureux (heureuse)	happy
la plupart du temps	most of the time
mamie	grandma
sentimental(e) (mpl sentimentaux)	sentimental, emotional
un(e) tel(le)	such a

COMPÉTENCE 3

Talking about what you did and used to do

NOMS MASCULINS

le reste (de)	the rest (of)
un réveil	an alarm clock

EXPRESSIONS VERBALES

accepter	to accept
s'arrêter	to stop
se peigner	to comb one's hair
se promener	to go walking
raconter	to tell
se reconnaître	to recognize each other
sonner	to ring
se voir	to see each other

DIVERS

ce que	what
donc	then, so, thus, therefore
parfaitement	perfectly

COMPÉTENCE 4

Describing traits and characteristics

NOMS MASCULINS

l'aspect physique	physical appearance
le bonheur	happiness
le corps	the body
un défaut	a fault
l'esprit	the mind, the spirit
un groupe	a group
un partenaire	a partner
un sens de l'humour	a sense of humor
un sentiment	a feeling
un test	a test
un trait (de caractère)	a (character) trait

NOMS FÉMININS

la beauté	beauty
la compatibilité	compatibility
l'importance	the importance
l'indécision	indecision
l'indifférence	indifference
l'infidélité	infidelity
l'inflexibilité	inflexibility
l'insensibilité	insensitivity
la jalousie	jealousy
la nature	nature
une partenaire	a partner
la passion	passion
la politique	politics
la profession	the profession
la religion	religion
une rencontre	an encounter
la spiritualité	spirituality
la tolérance	tolerance, acceptance
la vanité	vanity

VERBES

cultiver	to cultivate
exprimer	to express
faire la connaissance de	to make the acquaintance of, to meet (for the first time)
s'intéresser à	to be interested in
ranger	to arrange, to order
supporter	to bear, to tolerate, to put up with

DIVERS

chez (une personne)	with, in (a person)
de droite	conservative
de gauche	liberal
dont	whom, of (about, with) whom, whose, that, of (about, with) which
jaloux (jalouse)	jealous
le mieux	the best
professionnel(le)	professional
que	that, which, whom
qui	that, which, who

En Normandie
La bonne cuisine

 iLrn Heinle Learning Center
 www.cengagebrain.com
 Horizons Video: Les Stagiaires
Audio

 Internet web search
 Pair work
 Group work

8

COMPÉTENCE

1 Ordering at a restaurant
Au restaurant

Talking about what you eat
Le partitif

Stratégies et Compréhension auditive
- **Pour mieux comprendre:** *Planning and predicting*
- **Compréhension auditive:** *Au restaurant*

2 Buying food
Les courses

Saying how much
Les expressions de quantité

Talking about foods
L'usage des articles

3 Talking about meals
Les repas

Saying what you eat and drink
Le pronom **en** *et le verbe* **boire**

Talking about choices
Les verbes en **-ir**

4 Choosing a healthy lifestyle
La santé

Saying what you would do
Le conditionnel

Vidéoreprise *Les Stagiaires*

Lecture et Composition
- **Pour mieux lire:** *Reading a poem*
- **Lecture:** *Déjeuner du matin*
- **Pour mieux écrire:** *Finding the right word*
- **Composition:** *Une critique gastronomique*

Comparaisons culturelles: *À table!*

Résumé de grammaire

Vocabulaire

trois cent un | 301

LA NORMANDIE

 PowerPoint 8-1

Que savez-vous de la Normandie? Comment imaginez-vous cette région? Pensez-vous à…

des bateaux de pêche?

des fermes normandes?

des villes anciennes?

---

de pêche *fishing* **des fermes normandes** *Norman farms*

des falaises isolées?

des villes au bord de la mer?

La Normandie, **c'est tout cela! Et encore plus!**

🌐 Élargissez vos connaissances (Broaden your knowledge) sur l'histoire de la Normandie en recherchant les sujets suivants sur Internet: Guillaume le Conquérant et l'invasion normande de l'Angleterre; Jeanne d'Arc; le Jour J (D-Day).

Suggestion. You may wish to point out that the term *D-day* is a military term predating World War II used to indicate a day selected for a military event. The *D* is a repetition of the first letter of the word *day* (*the day of days*). It is translated into French by taking the first letter of the word *jour* and and labeling the day with it: **le Jour J**.

Rouen 🌐 Visit it live on Google Earth!

NOMBRE D'HABITANTS:
113 000 habitants
(avec ses agglomérations
[*metropolitan region*]:
650 000) (les Rouennais)

Quick-reference answers. 1. b 2. c 3. d 4. a

Le savez-vous?

Que savez-vous de *(What do you know about)* l'histoire de la Normandie? Trouvez la date qui correspond à chacun de ces événements historiques.

a. 1066	c. 820–911
b. le 6 juin 1944	d. 1453

1. le Jour J, jour du débarquement en Normandie des forces alliées (américaines, anglaises, canadiennes et françaises)
2. la conquête de la région par les Vikings (Normandie veut dire «*Land of the Northmen*».)
3. la fin de la guerre de Cent Ans entre la France et l'Angleterre *(England)* (que la France a gagnée grâce surtout aux batailles remportées [*thanks especially to the battles won*] par Jeanne d'Arc)
4. la conquête de l'Angleterre par Guillaume le Conquérant, duc de Normandie

La tapisserie de Bayeux raconte en images la conquête de l'Angleterre par Guillaume le Conquérant, duc de Normandie.

---

des falaises *cliffs*   **au bord de la mer** *at the seaside*   **c'est tout cela! Et encore plus!** *it's all that! And even more!*

La Normandie | *trois cent trois* **303**

COMPÉTENCE 1

Ordering at a restaurant

 PowerPoint 8-2

Note culturelle

Malgré *(Despite)* le succès des fast-foods en France, pour un repas traditionnel au restaurant, la majorité des Français continuent à prendre une entrée, un plat principal et un fromage et/ou un dessert. Les repas se prennent entre 12h et 14h, et le soir jamais avant 19 heures. Beaucoup de restaurants en France (sauf les fast-foods) sont fermés entre 14 heures et 19 heures. Est-ce la même chose dans votre région?

Warm-up activity. Qu'est-ce que vous aimez mieux… ? le jus de fruit ou le coca? le thé ou le café? les sandwichs au jambon ou au fromage? les hamburgers ou les sandwichs? les frites ou le fromage? le jambon ou le fromage? la bière ou le vin? l'eau ou le coca?

iLrn In the **Culture Modules** in the video library, see **Cuisine**.

Note de grammaire

1. The article you see in front of many of these nouns is called the partitive. It expresses the idea of *some* or *any*. Why are there four different forms?

   du pâté *some pâté*
   de la soupe *some soup*
   de l'eau *some water*
   des œufs *some eggs*

   You will learn more about how to use the partitive article in the next section.

2. The irregular verb **servir** *(to serve)* is conjugated like **sortir**: je sers, tu sers, il/elle/on sert, nous servons, vous servez, ils/elles servent; PASSÉ COMPOSÉ: j'ai servi; IMPARFAIT: je servais.

Suggestions for the presentation. Point out: the contrast in the meaning of **entrée** in French and in English; that **hors-d'œuvre** is invariable; that **la salade** is often eaten after the main course and is usually just Boston lettuce with **vinaigrette;** the pronuciation of **œuf** [œf] and **œufs** [ø] and of **yaourt** [jauRt]; and that one hears **haricots verts** both with and without **h aspiré**.

AU RESTAURANT

Les Français aiment bien les grands repas traditionnels.

On commence par **une entrée** ou **un hors-d'œuvre**:

de la soupe à l'oignon   du pâté   des œufs *(m)* durs à la mayonnaise   **des crudités** *(f)*

de la salade de tomates   des escargots *(m)*

Sur la table, il y a aussi…

du sel et du poivre   du pain   de l'eau minérale

Ensuite, **on sert** le plat principal:

DE LA VIANDE   **DU POISSON**

du rosbif   une côte de porc   **du thon**   **du saumon**   un bifteck

DE LA VOLAILLE   **DES FRUITS** *(m)* **DE MER**

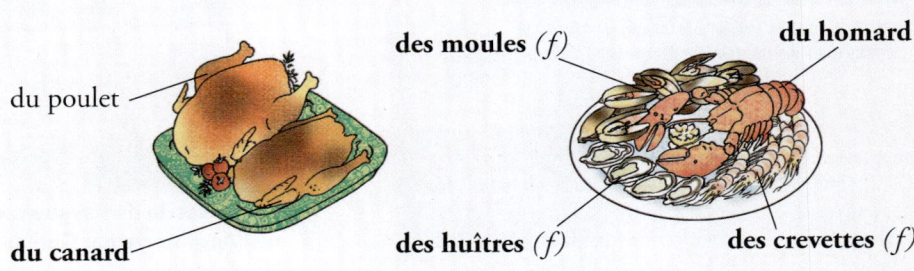

du poulet   **du canard**   **des moules** *(f)*   **du homard**   **des huîtres** *(f)*   **des crevettes** *(f)*

Line art on this page: © Cengage Learning

une entrée *a first course*   **un hors-d'œuvre** *an appetizer*   **des crudités** *(f) raw vegetables*   **on sert (servir** *to serve)*   **de la viande** *meat*   **du poisson** *fish*   **du thon** *tuna*   **du saumon** *salmon*   **de la volaille** *poultry*   **du canard** *duck*   **des fruits** *(m)* **de mer** *shellfish*   **des moules** *(f) mussels*   **du homard** *lobster*   **des huîtres** *(f) oysters*   **des crevettes** *(f) shrimp*

Le plat principal **comprend** aussi **du riz** et des légumes (m):

des haricots verts — des pommes de terre (f) — des petits pois

On sert généralement la salade verte après le plat principal. On sert le fromage après ou avec la salade.

une salade — du fromage

On finit le repas avec des fruits – ou un dessert.

du gâteau au chocolat — des fruits (m) — de la tarte aux pommes — de la glace à la vanille — un yaourt

Pour finir, on sert le café. Prenez-vous **du sucre,** du lait ou de la crème dans votre café?

du café

Line art on this page: © Cengage Learning

Vocabulaire sans peine!

Most foreign names of food items borrowed into English from other languages will be the same words in French. They tend to be masculine, unless they are borrowed from another romance language such as Spanish and Italian and end with **-a,** or sometimes **-e.** Italian pasta dishes ending with **-i** are plural, as in Italian.

du sushi   **une enchilada**
du curry   **des spaghetti**
un baklava

How would you say the following in French?
a taco   *tofu*
chow mein   *macaroni*

Vocabulaire supplémentaire

bleu(e) *very rare*
saignant(e) *rare*
à point *medium*
bien cuit(e) *well-done*
végétarien(ne) *vegetarian*
végétalien(ne) *vegan*
D'AUTRES PLATS (DISHES):
   de l'agneau (m) *lamb*
   du bifteck haché *ground meat*
   des coquilles St-Jacques (f) *scallops*
   de la dinde *turkey*
   des pâtes (f) *pasta, noodles*
   du rôti de porc *pork roast*
   de la sole *sole*
   de la truite *trout*
   du veau *veal*
POUR METTRE LA TABLE (TO SET THE TABLE):
   une assiette *a plate*
   un bol *a bowl*
   un couteau *a knife*
   une cuillère / cuiller *a spoon*
   une fourchette *a fork*
   une nappe *a tablecloth*
   une serviette *a napkin*
   une tasse *a cup*
   un verre *a glass*

Pour une liste de fruits et de légumes, voir la page 315.

Note. Additional food vocabulary is taught in *Compétences 2* and *3.*

PRONONCIATION

Le **h** aspiré 3-2

In French, **h** is never pronounced and there is usually liaison or elision before it.

     J'aime les͡ huîtres.   Il y a beaucoup **d'**huile (*oil*) dans la salade.

Before a few words beginning with **h,** there is no liaison or elision, even though the **h** is silent. These words are said to begin with **h aspiré.** In vocabulary lists, they are indicated by an asterisk (*). English words that begin with *h* often have an **h aspiré** when used in French. The following words have **h aspiré:**

     le homard   **les haricots**   **les hors-d'œuvre**   **les hot-dogs**   **les hamburgers**

---

comprend (**comprendre** *to include*)   **du riz** *rice*   **du sucre** *sugar*

Note culturelle

Dans un restaurant français, on peut commander «à la carte», ce qui permet de choisir *(which allows one to choose)* les plats qu'on préfère, ou on peut choisir un menu «à prix fixe». Dans ce cas, on a un choix plus limité, mais à un prix plus raisonnable. Regardez la carte à la page 309. Choisissez *(Choose)* une entrée, un plat principal et un dessert et faites le total. Comparez le prix de votre repas à la carte avec le prix des menus à prix fixe (à la page 308). Est-il moins cher de commander un menu à prix fixe ou de commander à la carte? Est-ce qu'il y a des restaurants chez vous qui servent des menus à prix fixe?

Note for the conversation. New vocabulary includes all glossed words and **Aimeriez-vous... ?, décider, fumé,** and **une carafe.**

Suggestion for the conversation. Before playing the conversation, set the scene, then go over the menu on pp. 308–309 with students. Have them guess the meaning of unknown words and say whether they like each item. Have them look at the menu as they listen to the conversation to determine what André and Rosalie order. As you go over the conversation, point out that the customers use the definite article here, rather than the partitive, to order the specific items on the menu *(I'll take the oysters).*

André a invité Rosalie au restaurant La Jardinière. Regardez **la carte** de ce restaurant aux pages 308–309.

LE SERVEUR:	Bonsoir, monsieur. Bonsoir, madame. Aimeriez-vous **un apéritif** avant de commander?
ANDRÉ:	Rosalie?
ROSALIE:	Non, merci, pas ce soir.
ANDRÉ:	Pour moi non plus.
LE SERVEUR:	Et pour dîner? Est-ce que vous avez décidé?
ANDRÉ:	Nous allons prendre le menu à 22 euros.
LE SERVEUR:	Très bien, monsieur. Et qu'est-ce que vous désirez **comme** entrée?
ANDRÉ:	Pour madame, le saumon fumé, s'il vous plaît. Et pour moi, les huîtres.
LE SERVEUR:	Et comme plat principal?
ROSALIE:	**La raie** pour moi, s'il vous plaît.
ANDRÉ:	Et pour moi, **le pavé de saumon.**
LE SERVEUR:	Bien, monsieur. Et comme boisson?
ANDRÉ:	Une carafe de vin blanc et **une bouteille d'**eau minérale.
LE SERVEUR:	Évian ou Perrier?
ROSALIE:	Évian, s'il vous plaît.
LE SERVEUR:	Très bien, madame.

A   Prononcez bien! Demandez à votre partenaire s'il/si elle aime ces choses. Faites attention à la prononciation du **h aspiré** et du **h non-aspiré.**

1. *le homard   2. *les haricots verts   3 *les hamburgers   4. les‿huîtres

B   Préférences. Circulez parmi les étudiants et pour chaque question trouvez quelqu'un qui préfère la même chose que vous. Pour répondre *neither . . . nor . . . ,* utilisez **ne... ni... ni...** comme dans l'exemple.

EXEMPLE   la viande ou le poisson
— Est-ce que tu aimes mieux la viande ou le poisson?
— J'aime mieux la viande. Et toi?
— Moi aussi, je préfère la viande. / Je n'aime ni la viande ni le poisson. / J'aime les deux.

1. la viande rouge ou la volaille
2. les légumes ou la viande
3. le poisson ou les fruits de mer
4. les crudités ou la salade verte
5. les pommes de terre ou le riz
6. les haricots verts ou les petits pois
7. les escargots ou les œufs durs
8. les crevettes ou le homard

C   Catégories logiques. Quel mot ne va pas logiquement avec les autres? Pourquoi?

EXEMPLE   le thé, le jus de fruit, le sel, le lait, l'eau
Le sel, parce que ce n'est pas une boisson.

1. le pain, les petits pois, les pommes de terre, les haricots verts
2. le gâteau au chocolat, le poivre, la tarte aux pommes, la glace
3. la salade de tomates, le pâté, la soupe à l'oignon, le rosbif
4. le déjeuner, le dîner, le petit déjeuner, le sel
5. le homard, le rosbif, les crevettes, les huîtres, les moules
6. les pommes de terre, les petits pois, les haricots verts, le gâteau

---

la carte *the menu*   **un apéritif** *a before-dinner drink*   **comme** *for, as a(n)*   **la raie** *skate, rayfish*   **le pavé de saumon** *the salmon steak*   **une bouteille de** *a bottle of*

D Aujourd'hui on sert... Regardez la liste et indiquez ce qu'il y a par catégorie.

> de l'eau minérale   du vin   du canard   du thon
> du saumon   des crevettes   des huîtres
> des petits pois   des pommes de terre   du gâteau
> de la tarte aux pommes   des côtes de porc
> du bifteck   du pâté   des œufs durs   du poulet

EXEMPLE viande
Comme viande, il y a des côtes de porc et...

1. entrée   3. viande   5. dessert   7. boisson
2. volaille   4. poisson   6. légume   8. fruits de mer

E Comparaisons culturelles. Pour chaque catégorie, est-ce que vous préférez la même chose que les Français (indiquée par un X)?

1. Je préfère...
   - X le café noir ou avec du sucre.
   - __ le café au lait.
   - __ le café vanille ou le café noisette *(hazelnut)*.

2. Je préfère prendre la salade...
   - __ avant le plat principal.
   - __ avec le plat principal.
   - X après le plat principal.

3. Pour terminer un repas, je préfère...
   - __ du gâteau ou de la tarte.
   - __ un fruit.
   - X un yaourt ou un fromage blanc.

4. Comme glace, je préfère...
   - X la glace à la vanille.
   - __ la glace au chocolat.
   - __ la glace à la fraise *(strawberry)*.

Suggestions for E. Comparaisons culturelles. Point out that a **café noisette** has two meanings. It can be a flavored coffee or it can be an espresso with just a dollop of milk (making it turn the color of a hazelnut). Also tell students that **un fromage blanc** is a creamy soft cheese.

F Un dîner. Voici ce que Rosalie a mangé hier soir. Qu'est-ce qu'elle a mangé? Dans quel ordre? Utilisez **du** *(m. sing.)*, **de la** *(f. sing.)* ou **des** *(pl.)* pour dire *some* ou **un(e)** pour dire *a* avant chaque substantif *(noun)*.

 À VOUS!

Avec deux autres étudiant(e)s, relisez à haute voix la conversation au restaurant. Ensuite, imaginez que vous dînez au restaurant La Jardinière avec un(e) ami(e). Commandez un repas complet. Le (La) troisième étudiant(e) va jouer le rôle du serveur (de la serveuse).

Sélection musicale. Search the Web for the song **"Les cornichons"** by Nino Ferrer to enjoy a musical selection containing food vocabulary.

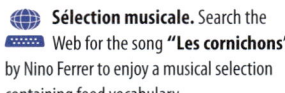 You can find a list of the new words from this *Compétence* on page 342 and access the audio online.

BISTROT DE MICHEL
RESTAURANT LA JARDINIÈRE
37   **37**

Servis Jusqu'à 23 H.

Le Bistrot - 15 €.
Service 15% Compris
Michel vous propose son petit Menu Bistrot composé uniquement de produits frais de saison

Première Assiette
- 9 Huîtres "Fines de Claires n°3" Sur lit de glace
- Assiette de Coquillages farcis à l'ail
- Cocotte de moules marinières
- Salade aux Lardons, Œuf poché
- Terrine de canard maison, au poivre vert
- Plateau de fruits de mer "L'Écailler" +10 €

Deuxième Assiette
- Brochette de poissons, beurre blanc
- Moules de pays, frites
- Sardines grillées aux herbes
- Langue de bœuf, sauce piquante
- Poêlée de Rognon de bœuf, flambée au cognac
- Bavette poêlée à la fondue d'oignons

Troisième Assiette
- Crème Caramel
- Fraises au vin ou fraises au sucre
- Feuillantine aux pommes
- Glace et sorbet artisanaux
- Île flottante
- Coupe normande

Arrivage Journalier de Poissons, d'Huîtres et de Fruits de Mer

LA JARDINIÈRE - 22 €.
Service 15% Compris
Les plus beaux produits du Terroir Sélectionnés et cuisinés dans la grande tradition de la Jardinière

Première Assiette
- 12 Huîtres "Fines de Claires n°3" Sur lit de glace
- Saumon fumé par nos soins, Toasts chauds
- Poêlon de 12 Escargots de Bourgogne à l'ail
- Beignets de Langoustines, Sauce tartare
- Salade de cervelle d'agneau poêlée
- Plateau de fruits de mer "L'Écailler" +10 €

Deuxième Assiette
- Aile de Raie capucine
- Daurade entière au lard fumé
- Pavé de Saumon Rôti, beurre de moules
- Filet de Canard à la Rouennaise
- Andouillette à la ficelle "du Père Tafournel"
- Faux-filet grillé ou Sauce Poivre

Troisième Assiette
- Salade de Saison, ou plateau de fromages

Quatrième Assiette
- Tarte Tatin chaude, crème fraîche
- Bavarois ananas coco
- Symphonie aux trois chocolats
- Feuillantine aux fraises ou fraises Melba
- Glace et Sorbet artisanaux
- Crème Brûlée

BISTROT DE MICHEL
RESTAURANT LA JARDINIÈRE
37 — **37**

La Carte
Service 15% Compris — **Servie Jusqu'à Minuit**

Nos Huîtres et Fruits de Mer (Arrivage Journalier)

12 Huîtres "Fines de claires" Sur lit de glace n°3 14€ n°2 16€
12 Huîtres "Spéciales St Vaast" Sur lit de glace n°3 15€ n°2 17€
Plateau de fruits de mer "L'Écailler" 18€ "Le marayeur" 30€ "Le Royal" 60€ (1 ou 2 personnes avec 1 Homard frais)

Fraîcheur du Marché & Préparations Maison

Soupe de poissons maison, sa rouille et ses croûtons, 6€   Assiette de coquillages farcis 6€
Moules à la crème 7€ — Salade aux lardons, œuf poché 6€   Terrine de canard maison au poivre 6€
Salade de cervelle d'agneau poêlée 8€   Beignets de langoustines, Sauce Tartare 10€
Saumon fumé par nos soins toasts chauds 10€   Poêlon de 12 Escargots de Bourgogne à l'ail 10€

Poissons Frais d'Arrivage

— Brochette de poissons frais, beurre blanc 7,50€ Moules de pays frites 7,50€
— Sardines grillées aux herbes 7,50€ Pavé de Saumon Rôti, Beurre de Moules 10,50€
— Aile de Raie capucine 10,50€ Daurade entière au lard fumé 10,50€
— Sole Meunière ou Sole Normande 19€

Traditionnels & Spécialités

Langue de Bœuf, sauce piquante 7,50€   Tête de veau Ravigote 7,50€   Bavette poêlée
à la fondue d'oignons 7,50€ Poêlée de Rognon de bœuf Flambée au cognac 7,50€ Faux filet
Grillé ou Sauce Poivre 10,50€ Filet de canard à la Rouennaise 10,50€ Andouillette à la ficelle 10,50€
Cœur de filet au Poivre Flambé au calvados 15€ Chateaubriand Grillé Beurre Persillé 14,50€

Desserts

Plateau de Fromages 5,50€
Île flottante au caramel 4€   Crème au Caramel 4€   Baiser de vierge 5€   Glace et Sorbet
artisanaux 5€   Fraises au vin ou sucrées 5€   After eight 5€   Coupe normande 5€   Feuillantine aux
Pommes 5,50€ Tarte Tatin crème fraîche 5,50€ Crème Brûlée 5,50€ Bavarois ananas coco 5,50€
Feuillantine aux fraises 6€   Fraises Melba 6€   Symphonie aux trois chocolats 6,50€

 PowerPoint 8-3

TALKING ABOUT WHAT YOU EAT

Le partitif

To express the idea of *some* or *any*, use the partitive article (**du, de la, de l', des**).

MASCULINE SINGULAR BEFORE A CONSONANT SOUND	FEMININE SINGULAR BEFORE A CONSONANT SOUND	SINGULAR BEFORE A VOWEL SOUND	PLURAL
du pain	de la glace	de l'eau	des fruits

The words *some* or *any* may be left out in English, but the partitive article must be used in French.

| Je voudrais **du** café. | I'd like **(some)** coffee. |
| Tu as **du** temps libre? | Do you have **(some)** free time? |

The partitive article becomes **de (d')**:

- after negated verbs (except after the verb **être**).

| Tu **ne** veux **pas de** café? | Don't you want **(any)** coffee? |
| Je **n'**ai **pas de** temps libre. | I don't have **(any)** free time. |

- after expressions of quantity like **beaucoup, combien,** and **trop**.

| J'ai acheté **trop de** café. | I bought **too much** coffee. |
| J'ai **peu de** temps libre. | I have **little** free time. |

✓ Pour vérifier

1. How do you express the idea of *some* in French? What are the forms of the partitive and when do you use each? Can you drop the word for *some* or *any* in French, as you can in English?

2. In what two circumstances do you use **de** instead of the partitive?

Warm-up for A. Je prends... Est-ce que les végétariens mangent les choses suivantes? **EXEMPLES** des fruits Ils mangent des fruits. / du rosbif Ils ne mangent pas de rosbif. **1.** du jambon **2.** de la soupe de légumes **3.** du bifteck **4.** du riz **5.** des pommes de terre **6.** du gâteau au chocolat **7.** du pâté **8.** des sandwichs au jambon **9.** des petits pois **10.** des côtes de porc

Suggestion for A. Je prends... Point out the use of the partitive and the use of **de** with **ne... jamais**.

Follow up for B. Comparaisons culturelles. En France... **1.** Comme entrée, on sert de la soupe ou de la glace? **2.** Comme entrée, on sert des œufs durs ou des petits pois? **3.** Comme plat principal on sert du pâté ou du saumon? **4.** Comme plat principal, on sert du gâteau ou des crevettes? **5.** Comme légume, on sert des petits pois ou des huîtres? **6.** Comme légume, on sert des pommes ou des pommes de terre? **7.** Après le plat principal, on sert de la salade verte ou de la soupe? **8.** Après le plat principal, on sert des fruits de mer ou du fromage?

A Je prends...
Complétez les espaces avec la forme correcte de l'article partitif. Ensuite, demandez à un(e) partenaire s'il/si elle prend souvent ces choses le soir.

EXEMPLE <u>du</u> vin
— Est-ce que tu prends souvent du vin le soir?
— Oui, je prends souvent du vin.
   Je prends du vin quelquefois.
   Non, je ne prends jamais de vin.

1. ___ pain
2. ___ œufs
3. ___ eau minérale
4. ___ viande rouge
5. ___ crevettes
6. ___ poisson
7. ___ volaille
8. ___ soupe

B Comparaisons culturelles.
Indiquez si les Français prennent souvent ces choses **comme entrée, comme plat principal, comme boisson, comme dessert** ou **comme légume**. Ensuite, dites si vous faites souvent la même chose.

EXEMPLE pâté
Les Français prennent souvent du pâté comme entrée.
Moi aussi, je prends souvent du pâté comme entrée.
Moi, je ne prends jamais de pâté comme entrée.

1. salade de tomates
2. eau minérale
3. petits pois
4. saumon
5. canard
6. tarte
7. gâteau
8. vin
9. pâté

C Sur la table. Rose est invitée à une fête où il y a beaucoup à manger et à boire. Voici la table de la salle à manger et la table de la cuisine. Travaillez en groupes pour faire des comparaisons entre les deux.

EXEMPLE Il y a des chips dans la cuisine et dans la salle à manger.
Il y a de l'eau minérale dans la salle à manger mais il n'y a pas d'eau minérale dans la cuisine.

la salle à manger   la cuisine

D Entretien. Complétez les questions avec l'article qui convient: **du, de la, de l', des** ou **de**. Ensuite, utilisez ces questions pour interviewer un(e) partenaire.

1. Qu'est-ce que tu préfères faire quand tu as _____ temps libre: faire _____ sport, écouter _____ musique, faire _____ shopping, faire _____ jardinage ou jouer à _____ jeux vidéo? Est-ce que tu as beaucoup _____ temps libre ou est-ce que tu as beaucoup _____ travail? Tu invites souvent _____ amis à dîner chez toi?

2. Est-ce que tu prends beaucoup _____ repas au restaurant avec tes amis? Quand tu vas au restaurant, tu commandes plus souvent _____ viande, _____ poisson, _____ légumes ou _____ fruits de mer? Tu prends _____ vin quelquefois avec tes repas? Tu manges beaucoup _____ légumes? Est-ce que tu prends plus souvent _____ glace, _____ tarte ou _____ gâteau comme dessert?

E Préparatifs. Vous allez inviter des amis pour un grand repas traditionnel à la française. Avec un(e) partenaire, faites des projets pour ce dîner.

Parlez de:
- quand et où vous allez faire ce dîner et qui vous allez inviter.
- ce que vous allez servir. (Imaginez que tout le monde n'aime pas les mêmes choses et proposez au moins trois possibilités pour l'entrée, le plat principal, le dessert et la boisson.)

STRATÉGIES ET COMPRÉHENSION AUDITIVE

> **POUR MIEUX COMPRENDRE:** Planning and predicting
>
> Since no two cultures are identical, you may sometimes find yourself lacking the cultural knowledge to understand what you hear in French. For example, if the waiter asks «**Évian ou Perrier?**», you will not be able to answer unless you recognize that these are brand names of French mineral waters. In such situations, try to infer what is being asked from the context. Also, when possible, prepare and predict from previous experiences what might be asked or said. For example, before ordering mineral water, glance at the menu to see what kinds are sold.

Suggestion. As an example of predicting, tell students to imagine they are at a restaurant with a friend. Ask them to guess what they are being asked in these situations: **1.** The hostess greets them and asks: «**Combien de personnes?**» **2.** The hostess points at two different sections and asks: «**À l'intérieur ou en terrasse?**» **3.** A waiter immediately comes to their table, without menus, and asks: «**Vous désirez un apéritif?**»

Script for A. Pendant le repas. **1.** Une table pour combien de personnes? **2.** Comme dessert, nous avons des glaces, des millefeuilles et du flan. **3.** Vous pouvez choisir le saumon avec le menu à 18 euros mais pas avec le menu à 15 euros. **4.** Voudriez-vous un café? **5.** Comme soupe, nous avons de la bouillabaisse ou de la soupe à l'oignon. **6.** Préférez-vous une table à l'intérieur ou en terrasse?

A **Pendant le repas.** Vous êtes au restaurant. Est-ce qu'on vous dit les choses que vous entendez **avant le repas** ou **à la fin du repas**?

B **Questions.** Faites une liste de trois questions qu'un(e) client(e) pose souvent au serveur ou à la serveuse dans un restaurant.

Compréhension auditive: *Au restaurant*

Deux touristes sont dans un restaurant français. Écoutez leur conversation. Qu'est-ce qu'ils commandent? Nommez au moins quatre choses.

Que demandent-ils? Écoutez encore une fois la conversation au restaurant et écrivez deux questions que les clients posent à la serveuse.

Script for *Au restaurant*
La serveuse: Bonsoir, messieurs, vous désirez?
Jean-Marc: Quelle est la soupe du jour, s'il vous plaît?
La serveuse: C'est la soupe à l'oignon.
Jean-Marc: Alors, je vais prendre le menu à 18 euros avec la soupe à l'oignon, le poulet à la crème et les carottes au beurre.
La serveuse: Très bien. Et pour vous, monsieur?
Étienne: Moi, j'hésite entre le poulet et le poisson. Quel est le poisson du jour?
La serveuse: C'est du saumon avec une sauce hollandaise.
Étienne: Je vois qu'il y a un supplément pour le poisson. C'est combien?
La serveuse: Le supplément est de 3 euros, monsieur.
Étienne: Bon. Alors, pour moi, la soupe à l'oignon, le saumon et des frites.
La serveuse: Et comme boisson?
Étienne: Du vin blanc. Vous avez du Chablis?
La serveuse: Oui, monsieur. Vous préférez en carafe ou en bouteille?
Étienne: En carafe.
La serveuse: Très bien, messieurs.

COMPÉTENCE 2

Buying food

 PowerPoint 8-4

Note culturelle

Dans le passé, les Français faisaient leurs courses presque tous les jours chez les petits commerçants. Aujourd'hui, certains Français font leurs achats *(purchases)* dans les hard-discount *(discount supercenters)*, d'autres dans les hypermarchés *(supercenters)* et supermarchés et d'autres encore chez les petits commerçants et au marché. Ces habitudes varient en partie selon les ressources financières, le niveau d'éducation, la situation géographique (milieu urbain ou rural) et l'attitude envers la nourriture *(towards food)*. Combien de fois par semaine faites-vous vos courses? Où préférez-vous les faire?

Vocabulaire supplémentaire

la confiserie *the candy shop, the confectioner's shop*
la fromagerie *the cheese shop*
le marchand de fruits et légumes *the fruit and vegetable market*
le traiteur *the caterer*

Warm-up activity. Pour un repas traditionnel en France, qu'est-ce qu'on sert d'abord? **1.** le plat principal / l'entrée **2.** le rosbif / la salade **3.** le fromage / les légumes **4.** le vin / le café **5.** le poisson / le dessert **6.** la soupe / le plat principal **7.** le pâté / le gâteau **8.** le riz / la glace

Suggestion. Explain to students that **une boucherie** sells raw meat and that **une charcuterie** is similar to a delicatessen and sells cured meats and prepared foods, although not sandwiches, cheese, or drinks.

Sélection musicale. Search the Web for the song **"Sur la table"** by Charles Aznavour to enjoy a musical selection related to this vocabulary.

LES COURSES

De plus en plus de Français font leurs courses dans les supermarchés et **les grandes surfaces** où on vend de tout. Mais beaucoup préfèrent aller chez les petits **commerçants** du quartier où le service est plus personnalisé.

À la boulangerie-pâtisserie, on peut acheter du pain et **des pâtisseries** *(f)*:

une baguette   un pain au chocolat   **un pain complet**   une tarte aux **cerises**   une tartelette aux **fraises**

À la boucherie, on achète de la viande:

du poulet   du bœuf   du porc

À la charcuterie, on achète **de la charcuterie** et **des plats préparés**:

du saucisson   du jambon   des saucisses *(f)*   des plats préparés

On achète du poisson et des fruits de mer à la poissonnerie.

Et on va à l'épicerie pour acheter des fruits, des légumes, **des conserves** *(f)* et des produits **surgelés**.

Line art on this page: © Cengage Learning

---

une grande surface *a superstore*   **un(e) commerçant(e)** *a shopkeeper*   **une pâtisserie** *a pastry*   **un pain complet** *a loaf of whole-grain bread*   **une cerise** *a cherry*   **une fraise** *a strawberry*   **de la charcuterie** *deli meats, cold cuts*   **un plat préparé** *a ready-to-serve dish*   **des conserves** *(f) canned goods*   **surgelé(e)** *frozen*

Beaucoup de Français **disent** que pour avoir un bon **choix** de légumes et de fruits vraiment **frais, il faut** aller au marché.

Au marché, on peut acheter:

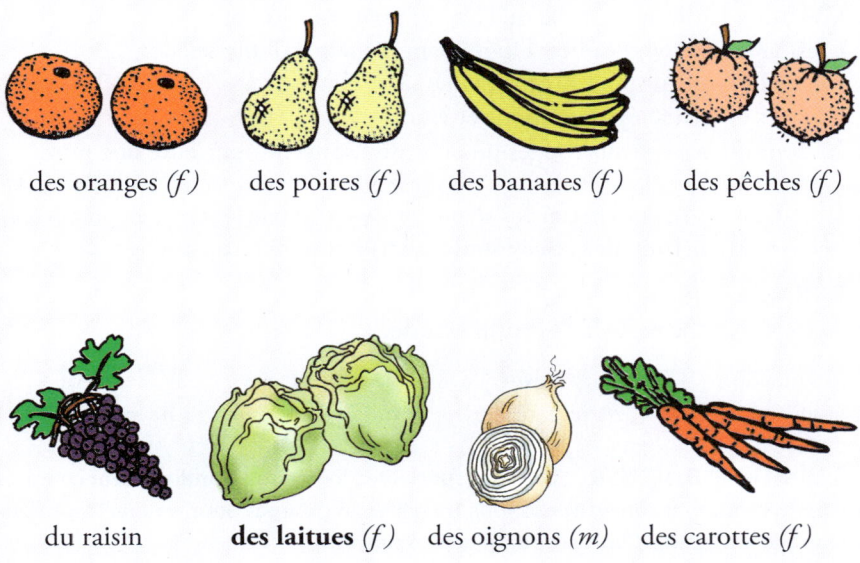

des oranges (f)   des poires (f)   des bananes (f)   des pêches (f)

du raisin   **des laitues** (f)   des oignons (m)   des carottes (f)

---

disent (**dire** *to say, to tell*)   **un choix** *a choice*   **frais (fraîche)** *fresh*   **il faut** *it is necessary, one needs, one must*
une laitue *a head of lettuce*

Vocabulaire supplémentaire

LÉGUMES
un artichaut *an artichoke*
des asperges (f) *asparagus*
une aubergine *an eggplant*
du brocoli
des champignons (m) *mushrooms*
du chou *cabbage*
du chou-fleur *cauliflower*
des choux de Bruxelles (m) *Brussels sprouts*
un concombre *a cucumber*
une courgette *a zucchini*
des épinards (m) *spinach*
du maïs *corn*
un radis *a radish*

FRUITS
un abricot *an apricot*
un ananas *a pineapple*
des bleuets (m) *blueberries* (Canada)
un citron vert *a lime*
des framboises (f) *raspberries*
un kiwi
une mandarine *a tangerine*
un melon
des myrtilles (f) *blueberries* (France)
une nectarine
un pamplemousse *a grapefruit*
une pastèque *a watermelon*
une prune *a plum*
un pruneau *a prune*
des raisins secs (m) *raisins*

Suggestion. Point out the feminine gender of nearly all fruits and vegetables ending in **-e** and the use of the singular with **du raisin**.

Supplemental activities. A. 1. On achète ces choses à la boucherie? Répondez par **oui** ou par **non**. (un pain au chocolat, des conserves, du porc, des produits surgelés, des plats préparés, du saucisson, du bœuf, des saucisses, du saumon) **2.** On peut acheter ces choses dans une boulangerie-pâtisserie? (du pain, des légumes, une tarte, des tartelettes, une baguette, des cerises, un pain complet) **3.** On peut acheter ces choses dans une poissonnerie? (des moules, des crevettes, des haricots, du poisson, de la volaille, des fruits de mer) **4.** On achète ces choses dans une charcuterie? (du jambon, un pain complet, du saucisson, du poivre, du sucre, des tartes, des saucisses) **B.** Have students ask a partner if he/she likes each of the fruits and vegetables pictured. Remind them to use the definite article when talking about likes and dislikes.

Note culturelle

En France, on utilise le système métrique.

1 kilo (kg) = 1 000 grammes = 2.2 pounds

500 grammes (g) = 1.1 pounds

1 litre (l) = 1.057 quarts

Pour désigner 500 grammes de quelque chose, on dit souvent aussi **une livre** *(a pound)*.

Si vous achetiez les choses suivantes en France, quelle quantité devriez-vous *(should you)* préciser (grammes, kilos, litres...)?

trois _____ d'oranges
deux _____ de lait
800 _____ de cerises

Rosalie fait ses courses au marché.

ROSALIE: Bonjour, monsieur.
LE MARCHAND: Bonjour, madame. **Qu'est-ce qu'il vous faut aujourd'hui?**
ROSALIE: Euh... voyons... un kilo de pommes de terre, **une livre** de tomates... Vous avez des haricots verts?
LE MARCHAND: Non, madame, pas aujourd'hui. Mais j'ai des petits pois. Regardez comme ils sont beaux.
ROSALIE: Non, merci, pas de petits pois aujourd'hui.
LE MARCHAND: Alors, qu'est-ce que je peux vous proposer d'autre?
ROSALIE: Donnez-moi aussi 500 grammes de fraises.
LE MARCHAND: Et voilà, 500 grammes. Et avec ça?
ROSALIE: C'est tout, merci. Ça fait combien?
LE MARCHAND: Voilà... Alors, un kilo de pommes de terre – 1,20 €, une livre de tomates – 1,36 € et 500 grammes de fraises – 1,50 €. Ça fait 4,06 €.
ROSALIE: Voici 5 euros.
LE MARCHAND: Et voici votre monnaie. Merci, madame, et à bientôt!
ROSALIE: Merci. Au revoir, monsieur.

A. Devinettes. Qu'est-ce que c'est?

EXEMPLE C'est un fruit rond, orange et plein de vitamine C.
C'est une orange.

1. C'est le légume préféré de Bugs Bunny.
2. C'est un fruit long et jaune que les chimpanzés adorent.
3. C'est le légume vert qui est l'ingrédient principal d'une salade.
4. On utilise ce fruit pour faire du vin.
5. Ce sont de petits légumes ronds et verts.
6. Ce sont de petits fruits rouges qu'on utilise souvent pour faire une tarte.

B. C'est... Est-ce que chacun des aliments suivants est **un légume, un plat préparé, une viande, un fruit, de la charcuterie, un fruit de mer** ou **un produit surgelé**?

EXEMPLE le rosbif
Le rosbif, c'est une viande.

1. le saucisson
2. la glace
3. le raisin
4. le pâté
5. le porc
6. la laitue
7. le bœuf
8. le homard

C. Cuisine française. Voici des spécialités françaises mondialement connues *(French specialties known worldwide)*. Travaillez en groupes pour trouver le mot qui manque à chacune. Choisissez dans la liste suivante.

EXEMPLE un **pain** au chocolat

> bœuf   canard   chocolat   crème   oignon   pain   quiche   salade   vin

1. de la mousse au _____
2. du coq au _____
3. de la _____ lorraine
4. de la _____ brûlée
5. une _____ niçoise
6. du _____ à l'orange
7. de la soupe à l'_____
8. du _____ bourguignon

Qu'est-ce qu'il vous faut aujourd'hui? *What do you need today?*   **une livre** *half a kilo (≈ a pound)*

D Un dîner. Votre classe va préparer un dîner. Qu'est-ce que vous allez servir? Chaque étudiant doit répéter de mémoire les choses déjà mentionnées et ajouter *(add)* quelque chose.

EXEMPLE Étudiant 1: **On va servir du pain.**
Étudiant 2: **On va servir du pain et du pâté.**
Étudiant 3: **On va servir du pain, du pâté et du bifteck…**

Maintenant travaillez en groupes pour dire ce que vous allez acheter de cette liste dans chaque magasin. Vous allez faire les courses chez les petits commerçants au lieu d'aller au supermarché. Le premier groupe à compléter la liste de courses gagnera.

EXEMPLE À la boulangerie-pâtisserie, on va acheter du pain…

À la charcuterie

E Entretien. Interviewez votre partenaire.

1. Aimes-tu faire les courses? Combien de fois par semaine est-ce que tu fais les courses? Où est-ce que tu fais tes courses d'habitude? Est-ce que tu achètes quelquefois des choses chez les petits commerçants?
2. Aimes-tu les fruits? les légumes? Préfères-tu les fruits ou les légumes? Quels légumes préfères-tu? Quels légumes est-ce que tu n'aimes pas? Quels fruits préfères-tu? Quels fruits est-ce que tu n'aimes pas?

À VOUS!

Avec un(e) partenaire, relisez à haute voix la conversation entre Rosalie et le marchand. Ensuite, imaginez que vous êtes à la boulangerie-pâtisserie. Achetez au moins trois choses.

Warm-ups for *D. Un dîner*. A. Dans quel magasin est-ce qu'on vend ces produits? **EXEMPLE** du rosbif **On vend du rosbif à la boucherie. 1.** de la viande **2.** des tartes **3.** des produits surgelés **4.** des plats préparés **5.** du saucisson **6.** des pommes de terre **B.** Nommez au moins quatre choses qu'on vend dans les endroits suivants. **EXEMPLE** À la charcuterie: **À la charcuterie, on vend du jambon… 1.** à la charcuterie **2.** à l'épicerie **3.** à la boucherie **4.** à la boulangerie-pâtisserie **5.** au marché **6.** à la poissonnerie
With books closed and a time limit, have groups of students list as many items as possible for each place.

Suggestion for *D. Un dîner*. When doing this type of chain activity, you may allow students to take notes or require them to list items from memory. You may also assign a student to make a shopping list, writing down the items and helping students who forget something by giving them forgotten words or cues, such as their initial letters.

Supplemental activity. C'est logique? **1.** Je prépare une tarte aux pommes. J'ai besoin de pommes de terre. **2.** Pour faire un gâteau au chocolat, j'ai besoin de chocolat et de sucre. **3.** Pour faire une salade de fruits, j'ai besoin d'oranges, de fraises et de pommes. **4.** Pour faire une omelette, j'ai besoin d'œufs, de chocolat et de sel. **5.** Pour faire un sandwich au fromage, j'ai besoin de petits pois.

You can find a list of the new words from this *Compétence* on page 342 and access the audio online.

PowerPoint 8-5

✓ **Pour vérifier**

What word follows quantity expressions before nouns? Do you use **de** or **des** after a quantity expression followed by a plural noun?

Suggestion. Point out that cheese is often bought by the **morceau**, since many cheeses come in a round shape.

SAYING HOW MUCH

Les expressions de quantité

Use these expressions to specify how much you want at the market or in a restaurant.

un verre de	a glass of	une boîte de	a box of, a can of
un litre de	a liter of	un pot de	a jar of
une carafe de	a carafe of	un paquet de	a bag of, a sack of
une bouteille de	a bottle of	une douzaine de	a dozen
une tranche de	a slice of	300 grammes de	300 grams of
un morceau de	a piece of	un kilo (et demi) de	a kilo (and a half) of
		une livre de	a half a kilo (1.1 pounds) of

After quantity expressions like those above, use **de (d')** before a noun instead of **du, de la, de l'**, or **des**. This is also true for less specific quantities such as:

combien de	how much, how many
(un) peu de	(a) little
assez de	enough
beaucoup de	a lot of
trop de	too much, too many
beaucoup trop de	much too much, much too many
plus de	more
moins de	less

J'ai acheté une bouteille **de** vin rouge, un kilo **de** viande et beaucoup **de** légumes!

A **C'est assez?** Dans chaque situation, est-ce que la quantité indiquée est suffisante?

EXEMPLE Vous prenez le petit déjeuner seul(e) le matin et il y a un verre de lait dans le réfrigérateur.
Il y a trop de lait. / Il y a assez de lait. / Il y a trop peu de lait.

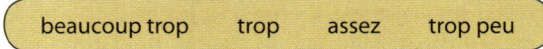

beaucoup trop   trop   assez   trop peu

1. Vous êtes quatre au restaurant et il y a une demi-bouteille d'eau.
2. Vous allez préparer une salade de tomates pour deux personnes. Vous avez un kilo de tomates.
3. Vous allez faire une omelette pour deux personnes et vous avez un seul œuf.
4. C'est le matin et il y a un verre de lait dans le réfrigérateur chez vous.
5. Vous dînez seul(e) au restaurant et il y a trois carafes d'eau.
6. Vous voulez préparer des carottes pour six personnes et vous avez deux carottes.

B Je voudrais... Complétez de façon logique chaque quantité proposée.

> thon   cerises   jambon   vin   tomates   fromage
> jus de fruit   rosbif   lait   sel   sucre   riz

Je voudrais...

1. une bouteille de
2. un paquet de
3. une boîte de
4. une livre de
5. deux kilos de
6. un morceau de
7. un litre de
8. dix tranches de

Je voudrais six tranches de jambon, s'il vous plaît.

C Donnez-moi... Demandez les quantités indiquées des produits suivants.

EXEMPLE  Une bouteille de vin, s'il vous plaît.

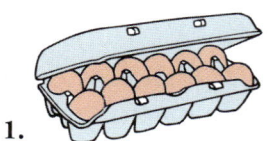   
1.   2.   3.   4.

5.   6.   7.   8.

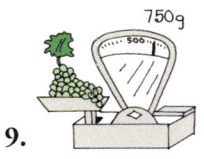  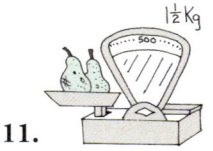
9.   10.   11.

Line art on this page: © Cengage Learning

D Ces courses. Avec un(e) partenaire, faites une liste de choses qu'on achète dans les endroits suivants. Utilisez une expression de quantité logique avec chacune.

EXEMPLE   à la charcuterie
une tranche de pâté, une livre de jambon, trois cents grammes de saucisson, un kilo de saucisses

1. à la boucherie
2. au marché de fruits et légumes

Maintenant, préparez une conversation avec un(e) commerçant(e) dans laquelle vous achetez trois choses d'une de ces listes.

PowerPoint 8-6

✓ Pour vérifier

1. Which article do you use to say *a* in French? Which articles do you use to express the idea of *some* or *any*?

2. Which article do you use to say *the*? to talk about likes, dislikes, and preferences? to make statements about entire categories?

3. Which articles change to **de**? When do they make this change? Which articles do not change to **de**?

Note *de grammaire*

Note that **je voudrais** expresses a want or desire, not a preference, and is often followed by a partitive article: **Je voudrais** *du* **jambon et** *des* **légumes.**

TALKING ABOUT FOODS

L'usage des articles

Each article you use with a noun conveys a different meaning.

 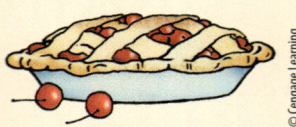

Vous voulez **de la** tarte?
Do you want (some) pie?
(This refers to a portion.)

Vous voulez **une** tarte?
Do you want a pie?
(This refers to a whole pie.)

- To say *a* or talk about a whole, use **un** or **une**. To say *some* or *any*, use **du, de la, de l'**, or **des**.

  J'ai acheté **un** croissant et **du** thé.   *I bought a croissant and (some) tea.*

- Remember that after a negative or an expression of quantity, **un, une, du, de la, de l'**, and **des** all change to **de (d')**.

  Elle ne mange jamais **de** viande.   *She never eats meat.*
  Elle mange beaucoup **de** légumes.   *She eats a lot of vegetables.*

- To say *the* or refer to a specific item, such as on a menu, use **le, la, l'**, or **les**. Also use these articles to talk about likes and dislikes, and to talk about something as a general category.

  Comme entrée, je voudrais **le** pâté.   *As an appetizer, I'd like the pâté.*
  Le pâté qu'ils servent ici est bon.   *The pâté that they serve here is good.*
  J'aime **la** viande mais je n'aime pas   *I like meat, but I don't like fish.*
    le poisson.
  Mais **le** poisson a moins de calories   *But fish has fewer calories than*
    que **la** viande.   *meat.*

- Remember that **le, la, l'**, and **les** do *not* change to **de** after a negative or an expression of quantity.

  Je n'aime pas **le** poisson, mais j'aime   *I don't like fish, but I like*
    beaucoup **les** fruits de mer.   *shellfish a lot.*

	IN AFFIRMATIVE STATEMENTS, USE:	IN NEGATIVE STATEMENTS AND AFTER QUANTITY EXPRESSIONS, USE:
To say *a* or to talk about a whole:	**un, une** (J'achète **une** tarte.)	**de (d')** (Je n'achète pas **de** tarte.) (Je mange trop **de** tarte.)
To say *some* or *any*:	**du, de la, de l', des** (J'achète **du** lait.)	**de (d')** (Je n'achète pas **de** lait.) (J'achète beaucoup **de** lait.)
To say *the*, to talk about likes and dislikes, or to make generalizations about categories:	**le, la, l', les** (**Le** thon est bon.) (J'aime **le** thon.) (**Le** thon est un poisson.)	**le, la, l', les** (**Le** thon n'est pas bon.) (Je n'aime pas **le** thon.) (**Le** thon n'est pas une viande.) (Je n'aime pas trop **le** thon.)

A **Manges-tu bien?** Demandez à votre partenaire s'il/si elle mange souvent les choses suivantes.

EXEMPLE pâté
— Manges-tu souvent du pâté?
— Je mange rarement du pâté. / Je ne mange jamais de pâté.

1. escargots
2. tarte
3. légumes
4. viande rouge
5. poulet
6. crudités
7. glace
8. tarte aux pommes
9. carottes

Maintenant, demandez à votre partenaire s'il/si elle aime ces mêmes choses.

EXEMPLE pâté
— Aimes-tu le pâté?
— J'aime assez le pâté. / Je n'aime pas le pâté.

B **Vos préférences.** Dites si vous achetez souvent les choses suivantes et expliquez pourquoi.

EXEMPLE café
J'achète souvent du café parce que j'aime le café.
Je n'achète jamais de café parce que je n'aime pas le café.

1. fromage
2. bananes
3. viande rouge
4. raisin
5. eau minérale
6. jambon
7. huîtres
8. jus de fruit
9. crevettes

C **Vos goûts.** Complétez les phrases suivantes avec le nom d'un aliment *(food)* ou d'une boisson logique. Utilisez les articles appropriés.

1. Moi, j'adore…
2. J'aime bien…
3. Comme viande, je mange souvent…
4. Chez moi, il n'y a jamais…
5. Pour le déjeuner, je prends souvent…

D **Ce soir.** Rosalie parle du dîner qu'elle va préparer ce soir. Complétez ses phrases avec l'article qui convient: **un, une, du, de la, de l', des, le, la, l', les** ou **de (d')**.

Ce soir, je vais servir __1__ soupe de légumes, __2__ poulet, __3__ riz et __4__ petits pois. Et comme dessert, je pense préparer __5__ tarte aux cerises. Moi, je préfère __6__ gâteau, mais André aime beaucoup __7__ tarte! Cet après-midi, je dois aller acheter __8__ sucre, 500 grammes __9__ cerises et beaucoup __10__ légumes. Il y a un marché tout près où __11__ légumes sont toujours très frais! Je ne mets pas __12__ oignons dans la soupe parce qu'André n'aime pas __13__ oignons. C'est dommage parce que __14__ oignons sont bons pour la santé *(health)*.

E **Entretien.** Interviewez votre partenaire.

1. Quels fruits de mer aimes-tu? Quelles viandes? Est-ce que tu manges plus de fruits de mer ou plus de viande?
2. Manges-tu plus souvent des fruits ou des légumes? Quel fruit préfères-tu? Quel légume préfères-tu? Quels fruits et légumes est-ce que tu n'aimes pas? Est-ce que tu achètes plus de légumes surgelés, frais ou en conserve?

COMPÉTENCE 3

Talking about meals

 PowerPoint 8-7

LES REPAS

Note culturelle

La grande majorité des Français prennent le petit déjeuner tous les matins et généralement chez eux. La plupart *(Most)* des adultes boivent une boisson chaude (café, café au lait, thé ou chocolat) accompagnée d'une tartine (de beurre, confiture ou miel [*honey*]) ou d'une viennoiserie *(pastry)* (croissant, pain au chocolat). Un jeune sur quatre préfère manger des céréales avec du lait ou un yaourt. Les fruits et les jus de fruit ne sont pas très présents au petit déjeuner des Français! Dans votre région, qu'est-ce que les gens prennent le matin?

Warm-ups. A. C'est bon ou mauvais pour la santé *(health)*? les boissons alcoolisées, le poisson, les desserts, les légumes, le sucre, les carottes, la laitue, les fruits
B. Lequel des deux mots indique la plus grande quantité? une bouteille ou une demi-bouteille, un litre ou un verre, une carafe ou un verre, une livre ou un kilo

Suggestions. A. Point out the plurality of **céréales** and the pronunciation of **bacon** [bekɔn]. Remind students of the pronunciation of **œuf** [œf] and **œufs** [ø]. Suggested mnemonic device: — Why did the Frenchman eat only one egg? — Because one egg was **un œuf** *(enough)*.
B. Tell students that at breakfast in France, many people drink **café au lait** from a bowl.

En France, le petit déjeuner est généralement un repas **léger**. On prend:

du café au lait   du thé

des tartines *(f)* ou des croissants *(m)*

du chocolat   du beurre   de la confiture

De plus en plus de Français, **surtout** les jeunes, prennent aussi des céréales le matin.

Les Américains et les Canadiens prennent souvent un petit déjeuner plus **copieux**. Ils prennent:

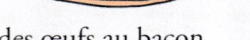

des œufs au bacon   des céréales *(f)*   du pain grillé   des fruits

À midi, certains Français prennent un déjeuner complet. D'autres prennent un repas rapide. Dans les cafés, les fast-foods et les self-services, on peut manger:

une soupe	une salade	une pizza
une omelette	un hamburger	un sandwich
un steak-frites		

Les gens qui prennent un repas rapide à midi mangent souvent un repas plus complet le soir. **Ceux** qui mangent un repas plus copieux à midi mangent **seulement** de la soupe, des légumes, de la charcuterie, une salade, du fromage ou une omelette comme dîner.

Line art on this page: © Cengage Learning

---

léger (légère) *light*   **une tartine** *bread with butter and jelly*   **surtout** *especially*   **copieux (copieuse)** *copious, large*   **un steak-frites** *steak and fries*   **Ceux (Celles)** *Those*   **seulement** *only*

Rose prépare le petit déjeuner avec sa cousine Lucie.

LUCIE: Tu as faim? Je peux te faire des œufs au bacon si tu veux – un vrai petit déjeuner à l'américaine.
ROSE: Merci, c'est gentil, mais je mange très peu le matin. **Pourtant, je prendrais bien** des céréales et du thé si tu **en** as.
LUCIE: Ah, je suis **désolée**... il **n'**y a **plus** de thé. Mais il y a du café. Tu en veux?
ROSE: Oui, je veux bien. Et toi? Qu'est-ce que tu vas prendre?
LUCIE: Le matin, **je bois** toujours du chocolat chaud et quelquefois je prends des tartines.
ROSE: Oh, regarde! **Il n'y a presque plus** de pain.
LUCIE: Mais **si**! Il y a **encore** une baguette, **là**.

Vocabulaire supplémentaire

des gaufres (f) waffles
des muffins (m) anglais
des pancakes (m)
des petites saucisses breakfast sausages
du sirop d'érable maple syrup
du porridge d'avoine oatmeal
une barre de céréales a granola bar
du pain perdu French toast

A. Vrai ou faux? Est-ce que ces phrases sont vraies ou fausses?

1. En France, on prend plus souvent des œufs le soir ou à midi que le matin.
2. Les Français prennent un repas copieux le matin.
3. Beaucoup de Français prennent seulement du pain et du café le matin.
4. Certains, surtout les jeunes, aiment prendre des céréales.

B. Chez nous. Aux États-Unis et au Canada, à quel(s) repas mange-t-on le plus souvent ces choses: au petit déjeuner, au déjeuner ou au dîner?

EXEMPLE une omelette
On mange plus souvent une omelette au petit déjeuner.

1. des croissants
2. des céréales
3. du poisson
4. un hamburger
5. de la soupe
6. du pain grillé
7. du saumon
8. des œufs au bacon
9. des légumes

C. Comparaisons culturelles. Avec d'autres étudiant(e)s, devinez comment le plus grand nombre de Français ont répondu aux questions suivantes dans des sondages (polls). Après, faites un sondage parmi (among) les étudiants de votre classe.

1. Combien de temps prenez-vous pour le petit déjeuner tous les matins? (moins de 10 minutes / de 10 à 15 minutes / plus de 15 minutes / Je ne prends pas de petit déjeuner.)
2. Que mangez-vous au petit déjeuner? (des céréales / du pain ou des biscottes *[melba toast]* / des viennoiseries *[pastries]* / des œufs / rien)
3. Quelle est votre confiture préférée? (cerises / oranges / fraises / abricots / framboises *[raspberry]*)
4. Qu'est-ce que vous aimez manger quand vous avez un peu faim entre les repas? (un fruit / des chips / du fromage / des biscuits *[cookies, crackers]* / du yaourt)

À VOUS!

Avec un(e) partenaire, relisez à haute voix la conversation entre Rose et Lucie. Ensuite, imaginez que vous passez des vacances avec un(e) ami(e) français(e). Parlez de ce que vous mangez d'habitude le matin.

Pourtant However **je prendrais bien** I would gladly have **en** some, any **désolé(e)** sorry **ne... plus** no more, no longer **je bois (boire** to drink) **Il n'y a presque plus** There is almost no more **si** yes (in response to a question / statement in the negative) **encore** still, again, more **là** there

PowerPoint 8-8

✓ Pour vérifier

1. In what three instances do you use the pronoun **en**? How is **en** usually translated in English? Can you omit **en** in French as you often can its equivalent in English?

2. How do you say *to drink* in French? What is the conjugation of this verb? How do you say *I drank some coffee this morning? I used to drink a lot of coffee*?

SAYING WHAT YOU EAT AND DRINK

Le pronom **en** *et le verbe* **boire**

Use the pronoun **en** *(some, any, of it, of them)* to replace a noun preceded by a partitive article, an expression of quantity, **un, une, des,** or a number. Although the equivalent expression may be omitted in English, **en** is always used in French.

— Tu veux un croissant? — *Do you want a croissant?*
— Oui, j'**en** veux un. — *Yes, I want one (of them).*

En is placed *immediately* before the verb. It goes before the infinitive if there is one. If not, it goes before the conjugated verb. In the **passé composé,** it is placed before the auxiliary verb.

— Tu prends du gâteau?
— Oui, je vais **en** prendre. / Oui, j'**en** prends. / Non, merci, j'**en** ai déjà pris.

Use **en** to replace:

- a noun preceded by **du, de la, de l', des,** or **de (d')**.
  — Tu veux **du café**? — *Do you want some coffee?*
  — Non merci, je n'**en** veux pas. — *No thanks, I don't want any.*

- a noun preceded by an expression of quantity. (In this case, repeat the expression of quantity in the sentence containing **en,** unless it is negative.)
  — Vous voulez un kilo **de cerises**? — *Do you want a kilo of cherries?*
  — Oui, j'**en** veux un kilo. — *Yes, I want a kilo (of them).*
  Non, je n'**en** veux pas. *No, I don't want any.*

- a noun preceded by **un, une,** or a number. (In this case, include **un, une,** or the number in the sentence containing **en,** unless it is negative.)
  — Tu as mangé **une tartelette**? — *You ate a tart?*
  — Oui, j'**en** ai mangé une. — *Yes, I ate one (of them).*
  Non, je n'**en** ai pas mangé. *No, I didn't eat any (of them).*

Here is the conjugation of **boire** *(to drink)*.

BOIRE *(to drink)*	
je **bois**	nous **buvons**
tu **bois**	vous **buvez**
il/elle/on **boit**	ils/elles **boivent**
PASSÉ COMPOSÉ: j'**ai bu**	
IMPARFAIT: je **buvais**	

Vous avez bu du vin hier soir? Je buvais du lait quand j'étais petit.

A À table. Un(e) ami(e) vous propose les choses suivantes au petit déjeuner. Comment répondez-vous? Utilisez le pronom **en** dans vos réponses.

EXEMPLE du café
— Tu veux du café?
— Non merci, je n'en veux pas. / Oui, j'en veux bien.

Sélection musicale. Search the Web for the song **"Bois ton café"** by L'Affaire Louis' trio to enjoy a musical selection containing the verb **boire**.

1. du café
2. du thé
3. des œufs
4. de l'eau
5. des tartines
6. des céréales

B Des courses. Voici la liste de Rosalie pour les courses. Combien va-t-elle acheter de chaque chose? Utilisez le pronom **en** dans vos réponses.

EXEMPLE du sucre
Elle va en acheter un paquet.

1. des pommes
2. du bœuf
3. du lait
4. des œufs
5. du vin rouge
6. des cerises
7. du pâté
8. des céréales

Follow-up for *B. Des courses.* Rosalie préfère faire ses courses chez les petits commerçants. Dites où elle va pour acheter chaque chose sur sa liste. **EXEMPLE** du sucre **Elle va à l'épicerie pour en acheter.**

C Et toi? Posez ces questions à un(e) partenaire pour savoir s'il/si elle fait attention à sa santé. Il/Elle va répondre avec le pronom **en**.

EXEMPLE —Tu manges des œufs?
 —Oui, j'en mange trop / beaucoup / assez / peu.
  Oui, mais je n'en mange pas assez.
  Non, je n'en mange pas.

1. Tu bois de l'eau?
2. Tu manges des desserts?
3. Tu fais de l'exercice?
4. Tu manges des fruits?
5. Tu manges du poisson?
6. Tu fumes des cigarettes?
7. Tu manges des légumes?
8. Tu manges de la viande?

D Boissons. Complétez les phrases logiquement en utilisant le verbe **boire**.

EXEMPLE Le matin, je **bois du lait.**

1. Au petit déjeuner, les Français…
2. Au petit déjeuner, les Américains / Canadiens…
3. Le matin, je…
4. Quand j'étais jeune, le matin, je…
5. Ce matin, j'…
6. Avec un hamburger, on…
7. Dans cette région, quand il fait chaud, nous…
8. Quand j'ai très soif, je…
9. *[À un(e) autre étudiant(e)]* À une fête, qu'est-ce que tu… ?
10. *[Au professeur]* Est-ce que vous… beaucoup de café?

E Entretien. Interviewez votre partenaire. Utilisez le pronom **en** dans les réponses.

1. Manges-tu souvent des légumes? Est-ce que tu en as déjà mangé aujourd'hui? Manges-tu souvent de la viande rouge? En manges-tu tous les jours? Est-ce que tu vas en manger aujourd'hui ou demain?
2. Fais-tu souvent de l'exercice? Combien de fois par semaine est-ce que tu en fais?
3. Est-ce que tu bois du café? En bois-tu trop? Quand est-ce que tu en bois? Et tes amis, est-ce qu'ils en boivent souvent?

COMPÉTENCE 4

Choosing a healthy lifestyle

 PowerPoint 8-10

LA SANTÉ

Note culturelle

La plupart des Français ont conscience du lien étroit *(close link)* entre la nourriture et la santé. Ils estiment qu'une alimentation variée, saine et équilibrée *(healthy and balanced)* contribue à préserver la santé. Ils pensent aussi qu'il est important de pratiquer un sport et de bien dormir. Qu'est-ce qu'on fait pour rester en bonne santé dans votre région?

Note de grammaire

1. **Se sentir** *(to feel)* is conjugated like **sortir** (je me sens, tu te sens, il/elle/on se sent, nous nous sentons, vous vous sentez, ils/elles se sentent).

2. Note that **prendre** and **faire** are often followed by an indefinite or partitive article (**prendre des vitamines, faire de l'aérobic**), whereas **éviter** and **contrôler** are often followed by the definite article (**éviter le tabac, contrôler le stress**).

Warm-up. Est-ce que vous mangez ou buvez **trop, assez, peu** ou **trop peu** de ces choses? EXEMPLE du café J'en bois trop / assez / peu / trop peu. / Je n'en bois pas. (du café, du jus de fruit, des fruits, des légumes, de l'eau, des frites)

Note for the conversation. New vocabulary includes glossed words and **content(e)** and **régulièrement**.

Suggestion for the conversation. Have students listen for two pieces of advice that Rosalie gives Patricia.

Faites-vous attention à votre santé? **À votre avis,** qu'est-ce qu'il faut faire pour rester en bonne santé?

Pour rester en bonne santé, est-ce qu'**on devrait...**

- manger des plats **sains** et légers?
- manger plus de produits **bio**?
- manger moins de **matières grasses** *(f)*?
- manger plus **lentement**?
- prendre des vitamines?
- **éviter** l'alcool et le tabac?
- contrôler le stress? (faire du yoga ou de la méditation, parler avec des ami[e]s...)

Pour être en forme et pour devenir plus **fort,** est-ce qu'on devrait...

- **marcher** et faire des randonnées?
- faire de l'aérobic?
- **faire de la muscu(lation)**?

Patricia demande **des conseils** à Rosalie.

PATRICIA: **Je me sens** toujours fatiguée ces jours-ci. J'ai besoin d'être en meilleure santé. Toi, tu as l'air toujours en forme. **Tu pourrais** me donner des conseils?
ROSALIE: Tu dors assez la nuit?
PATRICIA: Je me couche assez tôt, mais je dors très mal. Je me réveille **plusieurs** fois pendant la nuit. Si je pouvais mieux dormir, **je serais** contente.
ROSALIE: Tu devrais boire moins de café pendant la journée. **Tu ferais mieux de** bien manger aussi et de faire de l'exercice régulièrement.
PATRICIA: J'aime bien marcher. Si j'avais plus de temps libre, **j'aimerais** bien faire du sport tous les jours.
ROSALIE: Si tu marchais tous les jours et si tu mangeais mieux, **tu te sentirais sans doute** mieux. Et **n'oublie pas** de boire moins de café et plus d'eau!

---

la santé health   **faire attention (à)** to pay attention (to), to watch out (for)   **À votre avis** In your opinion   **on devrait** one should   **sain(e)** healthy   **bio (biologiques)** organic   **les matières grasses** (f) fats   **lentement** slowly   **éviter** to avoid   **fort(e)** strong   **marcher** to walk   **faire de la muscu(lation)** to do weight training, to do bodybuilding   **des conseils** (m) advice   **Je me sens (se sentir** to feel)   **Tu pourrais... ?** Could you . . . ?   **plusieurs** several   **je serais** I would be   **Tu ferais mieux de** You would do better to   **j'aimerais** I would like   **tu te sentirais** you would feel   **sans doute** without doubt, doubtlessly   **n'oublie pas** don't forget (**oublier** to forget)

A Des conseils. C'est **un bon conseil** ou **un mauvais conseil** pour la santé?

1. Il faut faire de l'exercice plusieurs fois par semaine.
2. On devrait manger plus de viande rouge et moins de légumes.
3. Il est important de faire de l'aérobic.
4. On devrait éviter les matières grasses.
5. Les plats sains et légers sont bons pour la santé.
6. On peut devenir plus fort si on fait de la muscu.
7. On devrait manger plus vite pour éviter de trop manger.
8. On devrait manger des produits bio.
9. On ferait mieux de rester très stressé, ça donne de l'énergie.
10. Si vous voulez être en bonne santé, n'oubliez pas de boire assez d'eau.

B Habitudes. Deux amis parlent de ce qu'ils font pour être en meilleure santé. Mettez chaque verbe entre parenthèses à la forme correcte dans l'espace qui convient.

EXEMPLE Je **maigris** parce que je **choisis** des plats sains et légers. (choisir, maigrir)

1. Les enfants _____ si on les _____ mal. (grossir, nourrir)
2. Je _____ à ne pas fumer, mais je _____ parce que je mange quand j'ai envie d'une cigarette. (réussir, grossir)
3. Mon meilleur ami _____ parce qu'il _____ toujours des desserts avec beaucoup de sucre. (choisir, grossir)
4. Dans notre famille, nous _____ beaucoup à notre régime *(diet)*: on _____ bien et on _____ rarement le dîner par un dessert. (réfléchir, finir, se nourrir)
5. Nos enfants _____ toujours et ils _____ tous leurs légumes. (obéir, finir)
6. Tu ne _____ pas à contrôler ton stress parce que tu _____ trop à tes problèmes. (réussir, réfléchir)

C Entretien. Interviewez votre partenaire.

1. Est-ce que tu te sens souvent fatigué(e)? Dors-tu assez?
2. Fais-tu attention à ta santé? Que fais-tu pour ta santé?
3. Manges-tu bien? Manges-tu beaucoup de fruits et de légumes? beaucoup de plats sains et légers? beaucoup de produits bio? Est-ce que tu prends des vitamines?
4. Est-ce que tu évites l'alcool ou est-ce que tu en bois? Est-ce que tu fumes?
5. Es-tu stressé(e)? Que fais-tu pour contrôler le stress?
6. Aimes-tu faire de l'exercice? Fais-tu de l'aérobic? de la muscu? des randonnées?

À VOUS!

Avec un(e) partenaire, relisez à haute voix la conversation entre Rosalie et Patricia. Ensuite, imaginez que vous voulez faire plus attention à votre santé. Demandez des conseils à votre partenaire.

 **PowerPoint 8-11**

SAYING WHAT YOU WOULD DO

✓ Pour vérifier

1. What other verb tense has the same endings as the conditional? What is the stem for the conditional of most verbs? What are 13 verbs with irregular stems in the conditional? What is the stem of each? Do they use the regular conditional endings?

2. How do you say *there would be? it would rain? it would be necessary?*

3. How do you express *could* and *should* in French?

4. When do you use the conditional?

Note *de prononciation*

An unaccented **e** is usually not pronounced if you can drop it without bringing three pronounced consonants together (**sam**e**di**). This is called **e caduc** and often occurs in the pronunciation of conditional verb forms (**j'habit**e**rais**).

This occurs in many words in English, as in the words réf**e**rence, diff**e**rence, and rev**e**rence.

🌐 **Sélection musicale.** Search the Web for the song **"Mourir demain"** by Natasha St Pier and Pascal Obispo to enjoy a musical selection containing verbs in the conditional form.

iLrn Grammar Tutorials

Le conditionnel

To say what one **would** do, use the conditional form of the verb.

> To say **would** + verb, use the conditional form of the verb.

I would like to lose weight.   **J'aimerais** maigrir.
If he cooked, **he'd eat** better.   S'il faisait la cuisine, **il mangerait** mieux.

The verb stem used to form the conditional of all regular and most irregular verbs is the verb's infinitive. If an infinitive ends in **-e**, the **e** is dropped. The endings are identical to those used in the **imparfait: -ais, -ais, -ait, -ions, -iez, -aient.**

REGULAR -ER VERBS	REGULAR -IR VERBS	REGULAR -RE VERBS
je parler**ais**	je finir**ais**	je perdr**ais**
tu parler**ais**	tu finir**ais**	tu perdr**ais**
il/elle/on parler**ait**	il/elle/on finir**ait**	il/elle/on perdr**ait**
nous parler**ions**	nous finir**ions**	nous perdr**ions**
vous parler**iez**	vous finir**iez**	vous perdr**iez**
ils/elles parler**aient**	ils/elles finir**aient**	ils/elles perdr**aient**

All regular and most irregular verbs follow this same pattern.

dormir → je dormirais...   prendre → je prendrais...   boire → je boirais...

Spelling change verbs like **acheter, appeler,** and **payer** have spelling changes in *all* forms of the conditional; but verbs like **préférer** or **répéter** do not change their accent marks in any conditional form.

j'achèterais / nous achèterions   je préférerais / nous préférerions
j'appellerais / nous appellerions   je répéterais / nous répéterions
je paierais / nous paierions

The following verbs have irregular stems in the conditional. The endings are regular.

STEM ENDS WITH *R*		STEM ENDS WITH *DR / VR*		STEM ENDS WITH *RR*	
aller	**ir-**	venir	**viendr-**	voir	**verr-**
avoir	**aur-**	revenir	**reviendr-**	envoyer	**enverr-**
être	**ser-**	devenir	**deviendr-**	pouvoir	**pourr-**
faire	**fer-**	vouloir	**voudr-**	mourir	**mourr-**
		devoir	**devr-**		

Also note these conditional forms:

il y a	→	**il y aurait**	*there would be*
falloir	→	**il faudrait**	*it would be necessary*
il pleut	→	**il pleuvrait**	*it would rain*

In the conditional, use **devoir** to say what one *should* do and **pouvoir** to say what one *could* do.

> To say *should* + verb, use the conditional of **devoir** plus an infinitive.
> To say *could* + verb, use the conditional of **pouvoir** plus an infinitive.

You should eat more vegetables.   **Tu devrais manger** plus de légumes.
You could eat better.   **Tu pourrais** mieux **manger**.

Use the conditional:

- to make polite requests or offers.

    Pourrais-tu me passer le sel?   *Could you pass me the salt?*
    Voudriez-vous du café?   *Would you like some coffee?*

- to say what someone would do if circumstances were different (to make hypothetical or contrary-to-fact statements).

    Si je faisais la cuisine, **je mangerais** mieux.
    *If I cooked, **I would eat** better.*

In statements such as the one above, the **si** clause is in the imperfect and the result clause is in the conditional. Note that either clause can come first.

si + imperfect → conditional

Si **nous avions** plus de temps libre, **nous nous reposerions** plus.
*If **we had** more free time, **we would rest** more.*

Nous nous reposerions plus si **nous avions** plus de temps libre.
We would rest more if we had more free time.

PRONONCIATION

*La consonne **r** et le conditionnel*
3-11

The conditional stem of all verbs in French ends in **-r**. To pronounce a French **r**, arch the back of the tongue firmly in the back of the mouth, as if to pronounce a *g*, and pronounce a strong English *h* sound.

je pourrais   tu trouverais   nous serions   il reviendrait   ils devraient

A Prononcez bien! Dites ce que les personnes indiquées feraient dans les circonstances données. Faites attention à la prononciation de la consonne **r**.

1. Si j'avais plus de temps,...
   je ferais / je ne ferais pas plus souvent de l'exercice.
   je mangerais / je ne mangerais pas mieux.
   je me reposerais / je ne me reposerais pas plus.
   je dormirais / je ne dormirais pas plus.

2. Si mes amis et moi pouvions passer plus de temps ensemble,...
   nous dînerions / nous ne dînerions pas plus au restaurant.
   nous voyagerions / nous ne voyagerions pas plus ensemble.
   nous ferions / nous ne ferions pas plus d'exercice ensemble.
   nous irions / nous n'irions pas danser ensemble.

3. Si on voulait être en meilleure santé,...
   on éviterait / on n'éviterait pas le tabac.
   on irait / on n'irait pas souvent à la salle de gym.
   on mangerait plus / moins de matières grasses.
   on devrait / on ne devrait pas manger plus de légumes.

B Scrupules. Que feriez-vous dans ces circonstances?

1. Si vous voyiez *(saw)* la fiancée de votre frère embrasser un autre garçon, est-ce que vous…
   a. le diriez *(would tell)* à votre frère?
   b. ne feriez rien?
   c. demanderiez 50 dollars à sa fiancée pour garder le silence?
2. Si vous voyiez une copie de l'examen de fin de semestre / trimestre sur le bureau du prof deux jours avant l'examen, est-ce que vous…
   a. la prendriez?
   b. ne feriez rien?
   c. liriez l'examen tout de suite?
3. Si vous trouviez un chien perdu dans la rue, est-ce que vous…
   a. téléphoneriez à la Société protectrice des animaux?
   b. prendriez le chien et chercheriez son maître *(owner)*?
   c. ne feriez rien?
4. Si vous ne veniez pas en cours le jour d'un examen important parce que vous n'étiez pas préparé(e), est-ce que vous…
   a. expliqueriez *(would explain)* la situation au professeur?
   b. diriez au professeur que vous étiez malade?
   c. accepteriez d'avoir un zéro à l'examen?
5. Si vous voyiez quelqu'un qui attaquait votre professeur de français, est-ce que vous…
   a. téléphoneriez à la police?
   b. resteriez là pour aider votre professeur?
   c. resteriez là pour aider l'agresseur?

Follow-up for C. Temps libre. Have students name two other things they would do.

 C Temps libre. Demandez à votre partenaire s'il/si elle ferait les choses suivantes s'il/si elle avait plus de temps libre.

EXEMPLE préparer plus souvent des plats sains
— Si tu avais plus de temps libre, préparerais-tu plus souvent des plats sains?
— Oui, je préparerais plus souvent des plats sains.
Non, je ne préparerais pas plus souvent des plats sains.

1. dormir plus
2. être moins stressé(e)
3. pouvoir plus te reposer
4. partir souvent en week-end
5. aller plus souvent au parc
6. faire plus d'exercice
7. voir plus souvent tes amis
8. rendre plus souvent visite à ta famille

D Une interview. Un journaliste vous interviewe. Comment lui répondez-vous? Jouez les deux rôles avec votre partenaire.

1. Si vous habitiez dans une autre ville, où voudriez-vous habiter?
2. Si vous étiez un animal, quel animal seriez-vous: un chien, un chat, un poisson, un rat ou un oiseau *(a bird)*?
3. Si vous étiez une saison, quelle saison seriez-vous: l'hiver, l'été, le printemps ou l'automne?
4. Si votre vie était un morceau de musique, est-ce que ce serait de la musique populaire, de la musique classique, du rock, du blues… ?
5. Si votre vie était un film, est-ce que ce serait un drame, une comédie, un film d'horreur ou un film d'aventure?

E Situations. Qu'est-ce que ces gens feraient ou ne feraient pas dans les situations suivantes?

> **EXEMPLE** Si nous n'avions pas cours aujourd'hui, mes amis et moi... (aller au parc)
> **Si nous n'avions pas cours aujourd'hui, nous irions au parc.**
> **Si nous n'avions pas cours aujourd'hui, nous n'irions pas au parc.**

1. Si nous n'avions pas cours aujourd'hui, mes amis et moi... (être ici, aller prendre un verre, passer l'après-midi ensemble, se reposer)
2. Si Rose voulait être en meilleure santé, elle... (fumer beaucoup, devoir faire plus d'exercice, prendre des vitamines, boire assez d'eau)
3. Si les étudiants voulaient mieux réussir en cours de français, ils... (faire tous les devoirs, aller à tous les cours, dormir en cours, boire plus de vin français)
4. Si mes parents avaient des vacances cette semaine, ils... (être contents, faire un voyage, rester chez eux, aller en France)

F Décisions. Qu'est-ce que ces gens feraient dans les circonstances données?

> **EXEMPLE** Si je pouvais quitter le cours maintenant, **je rentrerais chez moi.**

1. Si je pouvais faire ce que je voulais en ce moment, je (j')...
2. Si j'avais des vacances la semaine prochaine, je (j')...
3. Si mon meilleur ami (ma meilleure amie) pouvait faire ce qu'il/elle voulait en ce moment, il/elle...
4. S'il/Si elle gagnait au loto *(the lottery)*, il/elle...
5. Si nous pouvions sortir ensemble ce soir, nous...
6. Si nous avions envie de faire de l'exercice, nous...
7. Si mes parents gagnaient au loto, ils...
8. S'ils pouvaient partir en vacances maintenant, ils...
9. Si le professeur nous disait *(told us)* qu'il n'y aurait plus d'examens dans ce cours, nous...

G Par politesse. Mettez ces phrases au conditionnel pour être plus poli(e) *(polite)*.

> **EXEMPLE** Veux-tu rester en forme?
> **Voudrais-tu rester en forme?**

1. Tu veux faire de l'exercice?
2. Quand as-tu le temps d'aller à la salle de gym avec moi?
3. Peux-tu passer chez moi vers dix heures?
4. Ton amie veut venir aussi?
5. Qu'est-ce que vous voulez faire après?
6. On peut aller au restaurant végétarien?
7. Est-ce que vous voulez manger leur nouvelle salade?

Warm-up for E. Situations. Qu'est-ce que ces gens demanderaient s'ils trouvaient la lampe d'Aladin? (You may wish to show students these cues: **un bon travail** *[job]*, **de l'argent, une maison, une voiture, des voyages...**) 1. Mes parents... 2. *[Au professeur]* Vous... 3. *[À un(e) autre étudiant(e)]* Tu... 4. Nous, la classe de français,... 5. Mon meilleur ami (Ma meilleure amie)... 6. Moi, je...

Follow-up for F. Décisions. Si vous pouviez transformer ces personnes, comment seraient-elles? Que feraient-elles différemment? **EXEMPLE** Mon colocataire (Ma colocataire)... **Mon colocataire (Ma colocataire) se coucherait plus tôt et il/elle ferait plus souvent le ménage. / Je ne changerais rien.** 1. Mes professeurs... 2. Mon meilleur ami (Ma meilleure amie)... 3. Moi, je... 4. Nous, les étudiants... 5. Mes parents...

VIDÉOREPRISE

Les Stagiaires

Rappel!
Amélie a tout raconté *(told)* à Céline sur sa sortie avec Matthieu. Maintenant tout le monde semble *(seems)* être au courant *(aware)* de cette sortie.

Dans l'*Épisode 8,* Amélie parle à Rachid du restaurant où elle a dîné avec Matthieu. Avant de regarder la vidéo, faites ces activités pour réviser ce que vous avez appris dans le *Chapitre 8.*

A Un grand dîner. Matthieu va préparer un grand dîner avec un groupe d'amis. Qu'est-ce qu'ils pourraient servir? Travaillez avec un(e) partenaire pour nommer autant de choses que possible pour chaque catégorie.

EXEMPLE Comme entrée, **ils pourraient servir du pâté...**

Comme entrée...   Comme légumes...   Comme boisson...
Comme plat principal...   Comme dessert...

Matthieu fait les courses pour le dîner. Dites où il va aller pour acheter chacune des choses indiquées.

EXEMPLE Il va aller à l'épicerie pour acheter un pot de confiture.

1.   2.   3.   4.

B La bonne santé. Camille fait très attention à sa santé, mais elle n'arrive pas à convaincre *(she's not able to convince)* Monsieur Vieilledent de boire moins de café et de manger moins de croissants. Répondez à ces questions en employant le pronom **en**.

EXEMPLE Camille mange beaucoup *de pâtisseries*?
Non, elle n'en mange pas beaucoup.

1. Camille mange *de la viande rouge* tous les soirs?
2. Elle fait *de l'exercice* tous les jours?
3. Elle a bu beaucoup *de vin* hier soir?
4. Monsieur Vieilledent va boire moins *de café*?
5. Il va prendre *des croissants* ce matin?

C Comparaisons culturelles. Monsieur Vieilledent dîne avec un client américain. Son client parle des différences entre les habitudes alimentaires des Américains et les habitudes alimentaires des Français. Nommez autant de choses que possible pour chaque repas ou situation.

EXEMPLE au petit déjeuner
En France, au petit déjeuner, vous mangez des tartines ou des croissants et vous buvez du café. Chez nous, on mange...

1. au petit déjeuner
2. dans un fast-food
3. pour un dîner léger
4. pour un repas traditionnel

D À table! Continuez à faire des comparaisons culturelles en complétant ces phrases avec la forme correcte de l'article qui convient.

Ce qu'on mange varie d'une culture à l'autre. Aux États-Unis, par exemple, on prend __1__ petit déjeuner copieux. On mange souvent __2__ œufs au bacon et __3__ pain grillé. En France, __4__ petit déjeuner est un repas léger. On boit __5__ café au lait, __6__ thé ou __7__ chocolat chaud et on mange __8__ tartines.

À midi, on peut manger dans un café où on peut prendre __9__ omelette, __10__ salade ou __11__ sandwich avec __12__ vin ou __13__ eau minérale. __14__ vins français sont très bons, mais __15__ eau minérale est très populaire aussi. On peut finir son repas avec __16__ café avec un peu __17__ sucre ou un peu __18__ lait.

E Qu'est-ce qu'ils font? Amélie parle à Rachid des habitudes alimentaires des gens à Technovert. Complétez ses phrases de façon logique.

EXEMPLE Je ne veux pas grossir. Alors, je (finir) tous mes repas par un dessert.
Je ne veux pas grossir. Alors, je **ne finis pas** tous mes repas par un dessert.

1. Céline et moi faisons attention à notre santé. Alors, nous (choisir) des plats sains.
2. Céline et son chien (maigrir) parce qu'ils marchent tous les jours.
3. Toi, tu n'aimes pas les boissons alcoolisées. Alors, tu (boire) beaucoup de bière.
4. Camille et Céline veulent rester en bonne forme. Alors, elles (boire) très rarement de la bière.
5. Monsieur Vieilledent ne fait pas attention à sa santé. Il (boire) beaucoup de café et il (choisir) toujours des croissants au petit déjeuner.
6. Tes amis et toi, vous voulez rester en forme. Alors, vous (choisir) de bien manger et vous (boire) trop de café.

F Si... Amélie dit ce que tous les gens de Technovert feraient s'ils avaient plus de temps libre. Qu'est-ce qu'elle dit?

EXEMPLE Monsieur Vieilledent (voyager plus, passer plus de temps avec ses enfants)
Si Monsieur Vieilledent avait plus de temps libre, il voyagerait plus et il passerait plus de temps avec ses enfants.

1. Matthieu (inventer des jeux vidéo, apprendre à danser)
2. Moi, je (réfléchir plus à mon avenir, sortir plus souvent)
3. Camille et Céline (faire de l'exercice, se reposer plus)
4. Christophe (dormir plus, lire plus de mangas, aller plus souvent au cinéma)
5. Rachid et moi (réussir mieux à nos cours, être moins stressés)

Suggestion for the video. Tell students not to worry about understanding every word, but to use what they do know and the context to guess what is being said. The video is available on DVD and on *iLrn*. The videoscript is available on the Instructor's Companion Website, **www.cengage.com/french/horizons6e,** and on iLrn.

Access the Video *Les Stagiaires* on iLrn.

▶ Épisode 8: Qu'est-ce qu'ils servent?

AVANT LA VIDÉO
Dans cet épisode, Amélie parle du restaurant où elle est allée avec Matthieu. Avant de le regarder, citez au moins trois choses qu'on sert dans un restaurant que vous aimez bien.

APRÈS LA VIDÉO
Regardez la vidéo et déterminez ce que Matthieu et Amélie ont commandé au restaurant.

LECTURE ET COMPOSITION

LECTURE

POUR MIEUX LIRE: Reading a poem

To appreciate a poem, it is important to read it with the right rhythm. Traditionally, French poems have verses with an even number of syllables, with regular pauses in the middle. Modern poets such as Jacques Prévert often use more irregular rhythms to create different moods. Prévert's poem *Déjeuner du matin* can be read in more than one way, creating different impressions. Do the following activity to help you read it.

Sentiments. Jacques Prévert (1900–1977), l'un des poètes les plus célèbres du vingtième siècle *(century)*, aimait parler de la vie de tous les jours dans sa poésie. Lisez les phrases suivantes du poème *Déjeuner du matin* en faisant une pause à la fin de chaque vers *(line)*. Ensuite, relisez les phrases sans pause. Pour vous, quels sentiments sont évoqués par les différentes manières de lire les vers?

l'hésitation	l'angoisse	le calme
la patience	la confusion	le désaccord
la décision	l'accord	???
l'indifférence	l'indécision	
l'impatience	la réflexion	

Il a mis
Son chapeau *(hat)* sur sa tête *(head)*

Il a fait des ronds *(rings)*
Avec la fumée *(smoke)*

Et moi, j'ai pris
Ma tête *(head)* dans ma main
Et j'ai pleuré *(cried)*

Déjeuner du matin

Jacques Prévert

Il a mis le café
Dans **la tasse**
Il a mis le lait
Dans la tasse de café
Il a mis le sucre
Dans le café au lait
Avec la petite **cuiller**
Il a tourné
Il a bu le café au lait
Et il a reposé la tasse
Sans me parler
Il a allumé
Une cigarette
Il a fait des ronds
Avec la fumée
Il a mis **les cendres**
Dans **le cendrier**
Sans me parler
Sans me regarder
Il s'est levé
Il a mis
Son **chapeau** sur sa **tête**
Il a mis
Son manteau de pluie
Parce qu'il pleuvait
Et il est parti
Sous la pluie
Sans **une parole**
Sans me regarder
Et moi j'ai pris
Ma tête dans ma main
Et **j'ai pleuré.**

Jacques Prévert, "Déjeuner du matin" in *Paroles* © Éditions GALLIMARD
© Fatras / succession Jacques Prévert pour les droits électroniques réservés.

| **la tasse** *the cup* | **cuiller** *spoon* | **les cendres** *the ashes* | **le cendrier** *the ashtray* |
| **chapeau** *hat* | **tête** *head* | **une parole** *a word* | **j'ai pleuré** *I cried* |

Compréhension

Qu'est-ce qui s'est passé? Qu'est-ce qui s'est passé dans le poème?

1. Faites une liste des choses qu'il a faites.
2. Nommez deux choses qu'il n'a pas faites.
3. Quelle a été la réaction de l'autre personne?
4. Qui sont ces personnages? Sont-ils amis? parents? Sont-ils mariés, divorcés... ?
5. Pourquoi est-ce qu'ils ne se parlent pas? Qu'est-ce qui s'est passé?

COMPOSITION

POUR MIEUX ÉCRIRE:
Finding the right word

You are going to write a review of a restaurant. When you write, try to use the most precise word possible to get your message across. Note how, in the following sentence, the word *small* can convey different messages.

It is a *small* restaurant with only fifteen tables.
Positive: It is a *cozy (intimate)* restaurant with only fifteen tables.
Negative: It is a *cramped (crowded)* restaurant with only fifteen tables.

To find the right word to express your meaning in French, you may need to use a synonym dictionary. Once you select a French word from an English-French dictionary, double check that you understand its use by looking it up in a French-English or French-French dictionary, or search for it on the Internet in the context in which you wish to use it.

Organisez-vous. Dans les phrases suivantes, voici quelques mots qu'on pourrait utiliser au lieu des mots en italique pour décrire un restaurant. Trouvez un mot supplémentaire pour chaque liste en cherchant dans un dictionnaire de synonymes sur Internet ou à la bibliothèque.

Le décor est *joli* (beau, charmant, harmonieux, pittoresque, ???).
Le décor est *laid* (atroce, hideux, grotesque, vulgaire, ???).
Le menu est *intéressant* (exotique, varié, extraordinaire, sensationnel, phénoménal, ???).
Le menu est *ennuyeux* (médiocre, ordinaire, limité, commun, insuffisant, banal, ???).
La cuisine est *bonne* (délicieuse, appétissante, savoureuse, délectable, exquise, succulente, ???).
La cuisine est *mauvaise* (insipide, déplorable, révoltante, fade, désastreuse, ???).
L'ambiance est *agréable* (sympathique, chaleureuse, intime, charmante, confortable, ???).
L'ambiance est *désagréable* (déplaisante, inhospitalière, froide, ???).
Le service est *bon* (rapide, animé, enthousiaste, immédiat, plaisant, gracieux, ???).
Le service est *mauvais* (lent, impoli, hostile, inconsistant, honteux, exaspérant, ???).

Une critique gastronomique

Écrivez une critique gastronomique d'un restaurant de votre ville. Parlez du décor, du menu, de la cuisine, de l'ambiance et du service.

iLrn Share It!

COMPARAISONS CULTURELLES

À TABLE!

Ce qui est considéré «normal» ou «**poli**» diffère souvent d'une culture à l'autre. Chaque société a ses **propres coutumes,** ses plats préférés, et même sa propre **façon** de manger.

Par exemple, lorsqu'on est invité chez des Français, pour **éviter de venir les mains vides,** on offre généralement un bouquet de fleurs (mais pas de chrysanthèmes, qui sont des fleurs de cimetières en France) ou des chocolats. Il est préférable d'éviter d'**apporter** un dessert ou une bouteille de vin, **car** cela voudrait dire que votre hôte ou hôtesse a oublié ou les a peut-être mal choisis!

À table, **on garde** toujours les deux mains sur la table, mais on ne met pas **les coudes** sur la table. **Après avoir coupé** la viande, on garde sa **fourchette** dans la main gauche. On ne boit jamais de lait avec les repas comme le font certains Américains et le café est servi à la fin du repas, après le dessert. De nombreux restaurants et cafés acceptent que leurs clients viennent en compagnie de leur chien, du moment qu'il **se comporte** correctement.

Regardez ces photos. Qu'est-ce que vous **remarquez**?

Suggestion for the photos. Draw attention to how the French use their silverware. Point out that both hands always remain above the table.

poli polite   **propres coutumes** own customs   **façon** way, manner   **éviter de venir les mains vides** to avoid coming empty-handed   **apporter** to bring, bringing   **car** because   **on garde** one keeps   **les coudes** elbows   **Après avoir coupé** After cutting   **fourchette** fork   **se comporte** behaves   **remarquez** notice

Lisez ces phrases concernant les coutumes et les bonnes manières. Lesquelles sont vraies dans votre région? Et en France?

	CHEZ NOUS	EN FRANCE
1. On boit quelquefois du lait aux repas.	☐	☐
2. On mange souvent des œufs le matin.	☐	☐
3. On mange plus souvent des œufs le soir ou à midi.	☐	☐
4. On mange assez souvent dans des fast-foods.	☐	☐
5. La présentation est presque aussi importante que la saveur *(taste)* d'un plat.	☐	☐
6. Le pain est presque indispensable à tous les repas.	☐	☐
7. Le pain se mange généralement sans beurre, sauf le matin.	☐	☐
8. On fait assez souvent les courses chez les petits commerçants.	☐	☐
9. On mange beaucoup de choses avec les mains.	☐	☐
10. On mange très peu de choses avec les mains et certains mangent même les fruits avec un couteau et une fourchette.	☐	☐
11. Quand on mange, on garde toujours les deux mains sur la table.	☐	☐
12. On met le pain directement sur la table, pas sur l'assiette *(plate)*.	☐	☐
13. Au restaurant, on peut commander à la carte ou on peut choisir un menu à prix fixe.	☐	☐
14. La carte est toujours affichée *(posted)* à l'extérieur d'un restaurant.	☐	☐

> Pour la France – Vrai: 3, 4, 5, 6, 7, 8, 10, 11, 12, 13, 14

Compréhension

1. Quelles différences est-ce qu'il y a entre ce qu'on fait chez vous et ce qu'on fait en France? Quelles ressemblances?
2. Les opinions des Français ne sont pas toujours reflétées *(reflected)* dans leur vie de tous les jours. Comment pouvez-vous expliquer ce contraste entre ce que les Français pensent et ce qu'ils font?

Opinions	Actions
Manger, c'est un art et un plaisir et les qualités esthétiques d'un plat *(dish)* (son apparence, sa présentation, sa fraîcheur,...) sont presque aussi importantes que sa saveur *(taste)*.	Aujourd'hui, les Français se contentent de menus plus simples et passent moins de temps à table. On passe de moins en moins de temps à préparer les repas en se servant *(using)* de produits tout prêts, de produits surgelés et du four à micro-ondes *(microwave)*.
Les repas sont un moment pour se retrouver en famille ou entre amis et pour apprécier la bonne cuisine.	Les repas sont pris moins souvent en famille et plus souvent devant la télé.
Le service et la qualité sont meilleurs chez les petits commerçants que dans les grandes surfaces.	On fait de plus en plus souvent les courses dans les grandes surfaces.

RÉSUMÉ DE GRAMMAIRE

THE PARTITIVE AND REVIEW OF ARTICLE USE

Je vais acheter **de l'**eau, **du** pain, **de la** crème et **des** légumes.

I'm going to buy (some) water, (some) bread, (some) cream and (some) vegetables.

In French, use the partitive to convey the idea of *some* or *any*, even when *some* or *any* can be omitted in English.

MASCULINE SINGULAR BEFORE A CONSONANT SOUND	FEMININE SINGULAR BEFORE A CONSONANT SOUND	SINGULAR BEFORE A VOWEL SOUND	PLURAL
du pain	de la glace	de l'eau	des fruits

— Je vais prendre **un** sandwich et **des** frites.
— Je **ne** prends **pas de** frites parce qu'elles ont **trop de** calories.
— Tu **n'**aimes **pas les** frites?
— Mais si, j'aime **beaucoup les** frites, mais **le** riz est meilleur pour **la** santé.
— Mais **les** frites qu'ils servent ici sont délicieuses.

Un and **une** mean *a* and **du, de la, de l',** and **des** express the idea of *some* or *any*. All of these forms change to **de (d')** after most negated verbs and after expressions of quantity. (See page 318 for a list of quantity expressions.)

Use the definite article (**le, la, l', les**) to say *the*, to express likes, dislikes, and preferences, or to make statements about entire categories. The definite article does *not* change to **de** after a negative or quantity expression.

THE VERB *BOIRE* AND REGULAR *-IR* VERBS

Le matin, je **bois** du thé mais mon mari **boit** du café. À midi, nous **buvons** de l'eau.
Qu'est-ce que tu **as bu** ce matin?
Qu'est-ce qu'tu **buvais** quand tu étais petit?

The verb **boire** *(to drink)* is irregular.

BOIRE *(to drink)*	
je **bois**	nous **buvons**
tu **bois**	vous **buvez**
il/elle/on **boit**	ils/elles **boivent**
PASSÉ COMPOSÉ: **j'ai bu**	
IMPARFAIT: **je buvais**	

Les étudiants **réussissent** bien au cours. Tu **réussis** à tes cours?
J'ai fini mes devoirs.
Je ne **réfléchissais** pas beaucoup à mon avenir *(future)* quand j'étais jeune.

The stem for the present tense of regular **-ir** verbs is obtained by dropping the **-ir**. Add the following endings for the present tense.

RÉUSSIR *(to succeed)*	
je réuss**is**	nous réuss**issons**
tu réuss**is**	vous réuss**issez**
il/elle/on réuss**it**	ils/elles réuss**issent**
PASSÉ COMPOSÉ: **j'ai réussi**	
IMPARFAIT: **je réussissais**	

See page 326 for a list of common **-ir** verbs. All **-ir** verbs presented in this chapter form the **passé composé** with **avoir**, except the reflexive verb **se nourrir**.

THE PRONOUN *EN*

— Tu veux **de l'**eau?
— Oui, j'**en** veux bien. Non merci, je n'**en** veux pas.

— Tu prends un **sandwich**?
— Oui, j'**en** prends **un**. Non, j'**en** prends **deux**. Non, je n'**en** prends pas.

— Tu as acheté un kilo **de carottes**?
— Oui, j'**en** ai acheté **un kilo**. Non, j'**en** ai acheté **une livre**. Non, je n'**en** ai pas acheté.

En replaces a noun preceded by a partitive article, an expression of quantity, **un, une,** or a number. When replacing a noun preceded by **un, une,** a number, or an expression of quantity, repeat the **un, une,** number, or expression of quantity in the sentence containing **en,** unless it's negative. In English, **en** is usually translated by *some, any, of it,* or *of them*. Although the equivalent expression may be omitted in English, **en** is always used in French.

En is placed *immediately* before the verb. It goes before the infinitive if there is one. If not, it goes before the conjugated verb. In the **passé composé,** place it before the auxiliary verb.

Je vais **en** prendre.
J'**en** prends.
J'**en** ai pris.

THE CONDITIONAL (LE CONDITIONNEL)

Use the conditional to say what someone *would, could,* or *should* do. To form the conditional of most verbs, add the same endings as the **imparfait** to the infinitive of the verb. If an infinitive ends in **-e,** drop the **e** before adding the endings.

PARLER	FINIR	PERDRE
je parler**ais**	je finir**ais**	je perdr**ais**
tu parler**ais**	tu finir**ais**	tu perdr**ais**
il/elle/on parler**ait**	il/elle/on finir**ait**	il/elle/on perdr**ait**
nous parler**ions**	nous finir**ions**	nous perdr**ions**
vous parler**iez**	vous finir**iez**	vous perdr**iez**
ils/elles parler**aient**	ils/elles finir**aient**	ils/elles perdr**aient**

Si j'avais plus de temps, **je réviserais** plus mes cours. **Je finirais** tous mes devoirs et **le prof perdrait** moins souvent patience avec moi.

Most irregular verbs follow this same pattern.

dormir → je dormirais, tu dormirais...
prendre → je prendrais, tu prendrais...
boire → je boirais, tu boirais...

Si tu voulais être en forme, **tu dormirais** plus, **tu prendrais** des vitamines et **tu boirais** assez d'eau.

Spelling-change verbs like **se lever, appeler,** and **payer** have spelling changes in *all* forms of the conditional; but verbs like **préférer** or **répéter** do not change their accent marks in any conditional form.

Si nous étions en vacances, **nous nous lèverions** plus tard. **Mon ami préférerait** se lever vers neuf heures.

The following verbs have irregular stems in the conditional. The endings are regular.

aller → j'irais, tu irais...
avoir → j'aurais, tu aurais...
être → je serais, tu serais...
faire → je ferais, tu ferais...
devoir → je devrais, tu devrais...
vouloir → je voudrais, tu voudrais...
venir → je viendrais, tu viendrais...
devenir → je deviendrais, tu deviendrais...
revenir → je reviendrais, tu reviendrais...
voir → je verrais, tu verrais...
envoyer → j'enverrais, tu enverrais...
pouvoir → je pourrais, tu pourrais...
mourir → je mourrais, tu mourrais...

Si j'avais plus de temps libre, **je ferais** beaucoup de choses. **J'irais** plus souvent au parc, **je verrais** plus souvent mes amis et **je serais** content!

Also learn the following:

il y a → il y aurait   il pleut → il pleuvrait   il faut → il faudrait

Si tu visitais la Normandie au printemps, **il y aurait** du vent et **il pleuvrait. Il** te **faudrait** un parapluie!

To say *should,* use the conditional of **devoir** plus an infinitive. To say *could,* use the conditional of **pouvoir** plus an infinitive.

Use the conditional:
- to make polite requests or offers.
- to say what someone would do if circumstances were different.

— **Pourrais-tu** me donner des conseils pour rester en bonne santé?
— **Tu devrais** bien manger et faire de l'exercice.

Voudrais-tu y aller avec moi?

S'il faisait la cuisine, **il mangerait** mieux.

VOCABULAIRE

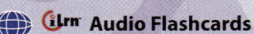 Audio Flashcards

COMPÉTENCE 1

Ordering at a restaurant

NOMS MASCULINS
un apéritif	a before-dinner drink
un dessert	a dessert
un fruit	a fruit
des fruits de mer	shellfish, crustaceans
*des haricots (verts)	(green) beans
*un hors-d'œuvre	an hors d'œuvre, an appetizer
du lait	milk
des légumes	vegetables
un menu à prix fixe	a set-price menu
du pain	bread
un pavé (de)	a thick slice (of)
des petits pois	peas
le plat (principal)	the (main) dish
du poisson (fumé)	(smoked) fish
du poivre	pepper
un repas	a meal
du riz	rice
du sel	salt
du sucre	sugar

NOMS FÉMININS
une bouteille (de)	a bottle (of)
une carafe (de)	a carafe (of)
la carte	the menu
de la crème	cream
une entrée	a first course
une pomme	an apple
une pomme de terre	a potato
de la raie	rayfish, skate
une salade	a salad
de la viande	meat
de la volaille	poultry

DIVERS
Aimeriez-vous… ?	Would you like … ?
comme	for, as (a)
comprendre	to include
décider	to decide
du, de la, de l', des	some, any
finir	to finish
fumé(e)	smoked
généralement	generally
servir	to serve
traditionnel(le)	traditional

Pour les noms des différentes sortes d'entrées, voir la page 304.
Pour les noms des différentes sortes de viandes, de volailles, de poissons et de fruits de mer, voir la page 304.
Pour voir les différentes possibilités pour finir un repas, voir la page 305.

COMPÉTENCE 2

Buying food

NOMS MASCULINS
du bœuf	beef
un choix	a choice
un commerçant	a shopkeeper
un marché	a market
un oignon	an onion
un pain au chocolat	a chocolate-filled croissant
un pain complet	a loaf of whole-grain bread
un plat préparé	a ready-to-serve dish
du porc	pork
un produit	a product
du raisin	grapes
du saucisson	salami
le service personnalisé	personal service
un supermarché	a supermarket

NOMS FÉMININS
une baguette	a loaf of French bread
une banane	a banana
la boucherie	the butcher's shop
la boulangerie-pâtisserie	the bakery-pastry shop
une calorie	a calorie
une carotte	a carrot
une cerise	a cherry
la charcuterie	the deli
de la charcuterie	deli meats, cold cuts
une commerçante	a shopkeeper
des conserves	canned goods
l'épicerie	the grocery store
une fraise	a strawberry
une grande surface	a superstore
une laitue	a head of lettuce
une orange	an orange
une pâtisserie	a pastry
une pêche	a peach
une poire	a pear
la poissonnerie	the fish market
des saucisses	sausages
une tartelette (aux fraises / aux cerises)	a (strawberry / cherry) tart

DIVERS
C'est tout.	That's all.
de plus en plus (de)	more and more (of)
dire	to say, to tell
frais (fraîche)	fresh
il faut	it is necessary, one needs, one must
Qu'est-ce que je peux vous proposer d'autre?	What else can I get you?
Qu'est-ce qu'il vous faut?	What do you need?
surgelé(e)	frozen

Pour les expressions de quantité, voir la page 318.

COMPÉTENCE 3

Talking about meals

NOMS MASCULINS

du bacon	bacon
du beurre	butter
du chocolat	chocolate
un croissant	a croissant
le déjeuner	lunch
le dîner	dinner
*un hamburger	a hamburger
du pain grillé	toast
un self-service	a self-service restaurant
un steak-frites	a steak and fries

NOMS FÉMININS

des céréales	cereal
de la confiture	jelly
une omelette	an omelet
une pizza	a pizza
une tartine	bread with butter and jelly

EXPRESSIONS VERBALES

boire	to drink
choisir (de faire)	to choose (to do)
finir (de faire)	to finish (doing)
grandir	to grow, to grow up, to get taller
grossir	to get fatter
maigrir	to get thinner, to slim down
(se) nourrir	to feed, to nourish, to nurture (oneself)
obéir (à)	to obey
réfléchir (à)	to think (about)
réussir (à)	to succeed (at, in), to pass [a test]

DIVERS

à l'américaine	American-style
certains	some (people)
ceux (celles)	those
complet (complète)	complete
copieux (copieuse)	copious, large
désolé(e)	sorry
en	some, any, of it, of them
encore	still, again, more
grillé(e)	toasted, grilled
je prendrais	I would have, I would take
là	there
léger (légère)	light
ne... plus	no more, no longer
pourtant	however
rapide	rapid, fast, quick
seulement	only
si	yes (in response to a question or statement in the negative)
surtout	especially
vrai(e)	true

COMPÉTENCE 4

Choosing a healthy lifestyle

NOMS MASCULINS

l'alcool	alcohol
des conseils	advice
des produits bio	organic products
le stress	stress
le tabac	tobacco

NOMS FÉMININS

des matières grasses	fats
la santé	health
des vitamines	vitamins

EXPRESSIONS VERBALES

contrôler	to control
éviter	to avoid
faire attention (à)	to pay attention (to), to watch out (for)
faire de l'aérobic	to do aerobics
faire de la méditation	to meditate
faire de la muscu(lation)	to do weight training, to do bodybuilding
faire du yoga	to do yoga
faire mieux (de)	to do better (to)
marcher	to walk
on devrait	one should
oublier	to forget
se sentir	to feel

DIVERS

à votre avis	in your opinion
content(e)	content, happy
en forme	in shape
fort(e)	strong
lentement	slowly
plusieurs	several
régulièrement	regularly
sain(e)	healthy
sans doute	without doubt, doubtlessly

INTERLUDE MUSICAL

RETOMBER AMOUREUX

Née en banlieue parisienne, Chimène Badi a grandi en Aquitaine, dans le sud-ouest *(southwest)* **de la France.**

You can find these songs on iTunes. You can also search the Internet for videos to hear them performed and to find the lyrics.

Preview all songs for appropriateness of content for your students.

CHIMÈNE BADI

Chimène Badi chante du *rhythm and blues*. Elle est connue pour sa voix puissante *(known for her powerful voice)*. Dans **Retomber amoureux,** elle chante la joie de retomber amoureux de quelqu'un qu'on avait cessé *(had ceased)* d'aimer. Faites l'activité qui suit pour comprendre plus facilement les paroles *(lyrics)*.

Retomber amoureux. Pour mieux comprendre cette chanson, lisez les phrases suivantes. Indiquez si chacune d'elles s'applique à…

a. quand ils ne s'aimaient plus
ou
b. quand ils sont retombés amoureux

_____ On ne se parlait plus.
_____ On ne se faisait plus de dîners aux chandelles *(candlelight)*.
_____ On était heureux d'être heureux.
_____ On ne se plaisait *(didn't please each other)* plus.
_____ On ne se parlait plus des prénoms possibles pour les enfants.
_____ Tout a recommencé.
_____ On ne se prenait pas pour Adam et Ève.
_____ On ne croquait *(didn't bite into)* plus dans le même pain.
_____ On s'est dit «on se quitte».
_____ On s'est dit de nouveau «je t'aime».
_____ On ne s'est plus jamais quittés.
_____ On était heureux d'être deux, différents mais toujours les mêmes.

POUR TOI

PRINCESS SARAH

Dans la chanson **Pour toi,** Princess Sarah regrette *(misses)* un amour perdu. Elle parle de ce qu'elle aurait dû faire *(what she should have done)* pour garder *(to keep)* cet amour et de ce qu'elle ferait si son amour revenait. Faites l'activité qui suit pour comprendre plus facilement les paroles *(lyrics)*.

Princess Sarah s'est fait connaître d'abord *(first made herself known)* par Internet.

Pour toi. Imaginez que vous voulez qu'un ancien amour *(a former love)* revienne. Est-ce que vous feriez ou ne feriez pas les choses suivantes? Faites des phrases au conditionnel.

Si tu revenais, je...
rester à tes côtés *(by your side)*
prendre le temps de te comprendre
être prêt(e) à aimer
gâcher *(to spoil)* notre amour
te donner la terre entière *(give you the whole world)*
t'oublier *(forget you)*
faire tout pour toi

Interlude musical | *trois cent quarante-cinq* **345**

Aux Antilles
En vacances

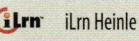 iLrn Heinle Learning Center
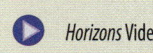 www.cengagebrain.com
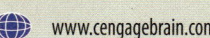 *Horizons* Video: Les Stagiaires
 Audio
 Internet web search
 Pair work
 Group work

9

COMPÉTENCE

1 Talking about vacation
Les vacances

Talking about how things will be
Le futur

Stratégies et Lecture
- **Pour mieux lire:** *Recognizing compound tenses*
- **Lecture:** *Quelle aventure!*

2 Preparing for a trip
Les préparatifs

Communicating with people
*Les verbes **dire**, **lire** et **écrire***

Avoiding repetition
*Les pronoms compléments d'objet indirect (**lui**, **leur**) et reprise des pronoms compléments d'objet direct (**le**, **la**, **l'**, **les**)*

3 Buying your ticket
À l'agence de voyages

Saying what people know
*Les verbes **savoir** et **connaître***

Indicating who does what to whom
*Les pronoms **me**, **te**, **nous** et **vous***

4 Deciding where to go on a trip
Un voyage

Saying where you are going
Les expressions géographiques

Vidéoreprise *Les Stagiaires*

Lecture et Composition
- **Pour mieux lire:** *Understanding words with multiple meanings*
- **Lecture:** *Ma grand-mère m'a appris à ne pas compter sur les yeux des autres pour dormir*
- **Pour mieux écrire:** *Revising what you write*
- **Composition:** *Un itinéraire*

Comparaisons culturelles *La culture créole aux Antilles*

Résumé de grammaire

Vocabulaire

trois cent quarante-sept | **347**

LA FRANCE D'OUTRE-MER

PowerPoint 9-1

Saviez-vous qu'on peut visiter la France **sans jamais** aller en Europe? que la France partage **une frontière** avec le Brésil? que la France **possède** une partie du continent antarctique?

En effet, la République française **comprend:**

- la France métropolitaine (la France en Europe plus l'île de Corse)
- cinq départements d'outre-mer (les DOM)
- plusieurs collectivités d'outre-mer (les COM)
  - la Nouvelle-Calédonie
  - les **Terres australes** et antarctiques françaises et l'île de Clipperton

La Guadeloupe et la Martinique sont les deux plus grandes îles françaises aux Caraïbes. Leur beauté naturelle **attire** un grand nombre de touristes.

Les cinq DOM – la Guadeloupe, la Martinique, la Guyane, La Réunion et Mayotte – **font partie de** la France **tout comme** Hawaii fait partie des États-Unis.

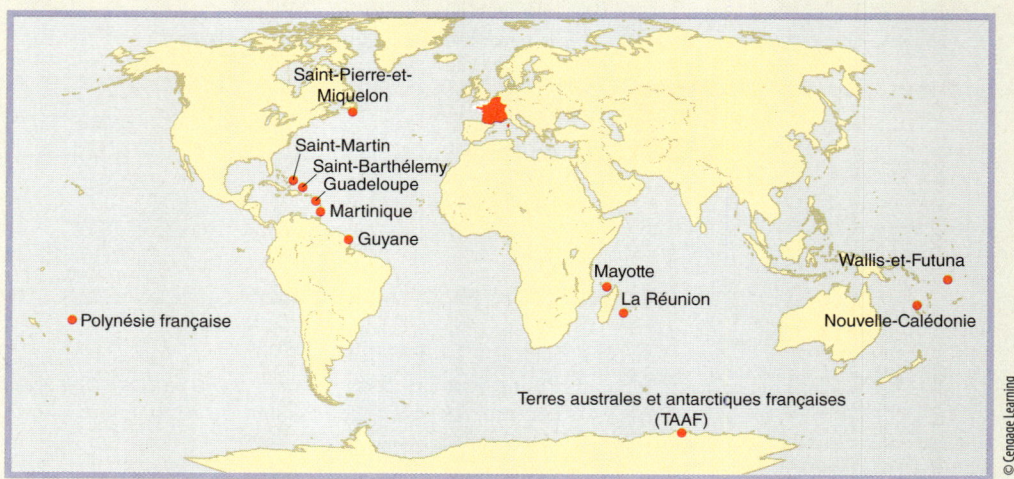

Les Outre-Mer

---

d'outre-mer *overseas* **Saviez-vous** *Did you know* **sans jamais** *without ever* **une frontière** *a border* **possède** *possesses*
En effet *In fact* **comprend** *includes* **Terres australes** *Southern Lands* **font partie de** *are part of*
tout comme *just as* **attire** *attracts*

La Guyane est caracterisée par sa biodiversité. Le tourisme vert s'y développe, mais l'économie se base surtout sur l'industrie spatiale.

Les collectivités d'outre-mer – la Polynésie française, Wallis-et-Futuna, Saint-Pierre-et-Miquelon, Saint-Barthélemy et Saint-Martin – sont comparables aux territoires américains de Puerto Rico et Guam.

L'ancien territoire de la Nouvelle-Calédonie est maintenant une collectivité presque **autonome** et ses **citoyens** vont bientôt voter sur l'indépendance.

La Réunion est le départment français d'outre-mer le plus peuplé, avec une société multiethnique.

La Guadeloupe

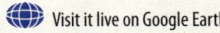 Visit it live on Google Earth!

NOMBRE D'HABITANTS: **466 000 (les Guadeloupéens)**

CHEF-LIEU *(ADMINISTRATIVE CENTER)*: **Basse-Terre**

La Martinique

NOMBRE D'HABITANTS: **409 000 (les Martiniquais)**

CHEF-LIEU: **Fort-de-France**

Quick-reference answers. 1. départements d'outre-mer, collectivités d'outre-mer 2. Guadeloupe, Martinique 3. Guyane 4. Réunion 5. Nouvelle-Calédonie

Le savez-vous?

Quelles régions de la République française voudriez-vous visiter? Servez-vous de la carte *(map)*, des photos et des renseignements donnés sur ces pages pour compléter les phrases qui suivent.

**Nouvelle-Calédonie   Guyane   Réunion
collectivités d'outre-mer   Guadeloupe
départements d'outre-mer   Martinique**

1. Les _____ font partie de la France, tout comme Hawaii fait partie des États-Unis. Les _____ sont comparables aux territoires américains de Puerto Rico et Guam.

2. La _____ et la _____ sont deux îles dans la mer des Caraïbes. La majorité des habitants de ces deux départements sont des descendants d'esclaves africains amenés *(African slaves brought)* dans ces îles pour travailler dans les plantations.

3. La _____, en Amérique du Sud, est connue *(known)* pour sa beauté naturelle et pour sa base du programme spatial français.

4. La _____ est située dans l'océan Indien près de Madagascar. C'est le département d'outre-mer le plus peuplé, avec une société multiethnique: des Africains, des Européens, des Indiens, des Chinois et des Malgaches *(inhabitants of Madagascar)*.

5. Les habitants de la _____ vont bientôt voter sur l'indépendance.

Connaissez-vous bien la France d'outre-mer? Regardez la liste des départements d'outre-mer et des collectivités d'outre-mer de la France. Choisissez une des régions nommées et faites des recherches sur Internet pour trouver des informations à son sujet. Préparez une présentation sur un aspect de cette région que vous trouvez intéressant.

---

se base surtout sur *is largely based on*   **L'ancien** *The former*   **autonome** *autonomous*   **citoyens** *citizens*
le plus peuplé *the most populous*

La France d'outre-mer

COMPÉTENCE 1

Talking about vacation

PowerPoint 9-2

Note culturelle

En vacances, les Français aiment le plus souvent visiter d'autres régions de France où ils préfèrent aller (par ordre de préférence) à la mer, à la campagne, en ville ou à la montagne. Et vous? Où aimez-vous partir en vacances?

 In the **Culture Modules** in the video library, see **Work**.

Note de grammaire

The verb **courir** is irregular: **je cours, tu cours, il/elle/on court, nous courons, vous courez, ils/elles courent**. Passé composé: **j'ai couru**; Imparfait: **je courais**; Conditionnel: **je courrais**.

Vocabulaire supplémentaire

faire de la plongée avec masque et tuba *to go snorkeling*
faire de la plongée sous-marine *to go scuba diving*
faire de la planche à voile *to go windsurfing*
faire du wakeboard *to go wakeboarding*

 **Sélection musicale.** Search the Web for the song "**Tes vacances avec moi**" by Sonia Dersion from Martinique to enjoy a musical selection related to this vocabulary.

Warm-up. Aimez-vous faire les choses suivantes en vacances? Est-ce que vous les avez faites pendant vos dernières vacances? **1.** manger au restaurant **2.** lire **3.** travailler **4.** aller voir des amis **5.** faire du shopping **6.** voir une exposition **7.** dormir jusqu'à midi **8.** sortir avec des amis

Note for the conversation. New vocabulary includes all glossed words.

Suggestion for the conversation. Set the scene for the conversation and have students listen for the following information with books closed. **1.** Quand est-ce que Lucas va partir? **2.** Combien de temps est-ce qu'il va rester en Guadeloupe?

LES VACANCES

Lucas, un jeune Parisien, va passer ses vacances en Guadeloupe. Et vous? Où aimez-vous passer vos vacances?

dans un pays étranger ou exotique | sur une île tropicale ou **à la mer** | dans une grande ville | à la montagne

Qu'est-ce qu'on peut faire dans chaque **endroit**?

admirer **les paysage**s *(m)* | visiter des sites *(m)* historiques et touristiques | profiter des activités culturelles (aller à l'opéra, au ballet…)

bronzer ou **courir** sur la plage | **goûter** la cuisine locale **assis** à la terrasse d'un restaurant | faire des randonnées

Lucas parle à son ami Alex de ses prochaines vacances en Guadeloupe.

LUCAS: Je vais bientôt partir en vacances.
ALEX: Et tu vas où?
LUCAS: Je vais en Guadeloupe.
ALEX: En Guadeloupe? Quelle chance! Tu pars quand?
LUCAS: Je pars le 20 juillet et je **compte** y passer trois semaines.
ALEX: Génial! J'espère que **ça te plaira**!

Line art on this page: © Cengage Learning

à la mer *at the coast, by the sea* • **un endroit** *a place* • **les paysages** *(m) the scenery, the landscape* • **bronzer** *to tan*
courir *to run* • **goûter** *to taste* • **assis(e)** *seated* • **compter** *to plan on, to count on* • **ça te plaira** *you'll like it*

350 trois cent cinquante | **CHAPITRE 9**

A. Activités.
Lesquelles des activités nommées fait-on normalement à l'endroit indiqué?

EXEMPLE dans une grande ville: faire du shopping / faire des randonnées / profiter des activités culturelles
Dans une grande ville, on fait du shopping et on profite des activités culturelles. On ne fait pas de randonnées.

1. sur une île tropicale: manger beaucoup de fruits de mer / courir sur la plage / faire du snowboard
2. à la montagne: profiter des activités culturelles / faire des randonnées / admirer les paysages
3. dans un pays étranger: visiter des sites historiques et touristiques / goûter la cuisine locale / voyager sans passeport
4. à la mer: faire du ski / bronzer / nager

B. Que feriez-vous?
Imaginez où vous iriez et ce que vous feriez si vous aviez assez d'argent pour faire un beau voyage. Choisissez une des destinations données et indiquez trois choses que vous y feriez.

> à la montagne à la campagne dans un pays étranger
> sur une île tropicale dans une grande ville chez moi

EXEMPLE Si j'avais assez d'argent, je passerais mes vacances **sur une île tropicale** où **je bronzerais, je nagerais et je prendrais beaucoup de photos.**

Maintenant, circulez dans la classe et demandez à plusieurs personnes où elles iraient et ce qu'elles feraient si elles pouvaient faire un beau voyage.

EXEMPLE —Si tu pouvais faire un beau voyage, où passerais-tu tes vacances et qu'est-ce que tu ferais?
—Je passerais mes vacances sur une île tropicale où je bronzerais, je nagerais et je prendrais beaucoup de photos. Et toi?
—Moi, je…

Après, dites à la classe ce que vous avez appris.

EXEMPLE Clarence passerait ses vacances sur une île tropicale où il…

C. Entretien.
Interviewez votre partenaire.

1. Préférerais-tu visiter une île tropicale ou visiter une grande ville? aller à la mer ou à la montagne? faire une randonnée ou faire du ski? faire de l'exercice à l'hôtel ou courir sur la plage? bronzer ou nager?
2. Où est-ce que tu aimerais passer tes prochaines vacances? Qu'est-ce qu'on peut faire dans cette région? Où est-ce que tu as passé tes meilleures vacances? Pourquoi as-tu trouvé ces vacances agréables? Qu'est-ce que tu as fait?

À VOUS!

Avec un(e) partenaire, relisez à haute voix la conversation entre Lucas et Alex. Ensuite, imaginez que vous allez faire le voyage de vos rêves *(dreams)* et changez la conversation pour dire où vous allez, avec qui, quand et combien de temps vous comptez rester.

Au parc national de la Guadeloupe, on peut profiter de tous les loisirs de la nature: randonnées, promenades, VTT…

 PowerPoint 9-3

TALKING ABOUT HOW THINGS WILL BE

Le futur

You have used **aller** + *infinitive* to say what someone *is going* to do. You can use the future tense to say what someone *will* do. Form the future tense by adding the boldfaced endings below to the same stem you use for the conditional.

PARLER	ÊTRE	VENIR
je parler**ai**	je ser**ai**	je viendr**ai**
tu parler**as**	tu ser**as**	tu viendr**as**
il/elle/on parler**a**	il/elle/on ser**a**	il/elle/on viendr**a**
nous parler**ons**	nous ser**ons**	nous viendr**ons**
vous parler**ez**	vous ser**ez**	vous viendr**ez**
ils/elles parler**ont**	ils/elles ser**ont**	ils/elles viendr**ont**

The future is generally used in French as it is in English. However, one difference is its use in clauses with **quand** referring to the future. English has the present in such clauses.

quand + future → future

Quand j'**arriverai** en Guadeloupe, je **prendrai** un taxi à l'hôtel.
*When I **arrive** in Guadeloupe, I'**ll take** a taxi to the hotel.*

As in English, use the future tense to say what will happen if another event occurs. Use the present tense in the clause with **si.**

si + present → future

Si je **peux** visiter la Martinique, je **serai** vraiment content!
*If I **can** visit Martinique, I **will be** really happy!*

✓ Pour vérifier

1. What do most verbs have as the stem in the future tense? Which verbs have irregular stems? What other verb form has the same stem as the future?

2. What endings do you use to form the future tense in French?

3. In French, what verb tense is used in clauses with **quand** referring to the future? How do you say *When I finish, I'll go home?*

iLrn Grammar Tutorials

Note *de grammaire*

The future/conditional stem always ends with **-r.** Do you remember these irregular ones?

aller	ir-
avoir	aur-
être	ser-
faire	fer-
devoir	devr-
vouloir	voudr-
venir	viendr-
revenir	reviendr-
devenir	deviendr-
voir	verr-
envoyer	enverr-
pouvoir	pourr-
mourir	mourr-
courir	courr-

Note these forms in the future:

il y a	il y aura
il faut	il faudra
il pleut	il pleuvra
c'est	ce sera

As in the conditional, verbs like **se lever, payer,** and **appeler** have spelling changes in *all* forms of the future (**je me lèverai, je paierai, j'appellerai**). Those like **préférer** do not (**je préférerai**).

Note *de prononciation*

As in the conditional forms, an unaccented **e** is usually not pronounced in future tense forms if you can drop it without bringing together three pronounced consonants (**j'habit∕erai, nous invit∕erons**).

🌐 **Sélection musicale.** Search the Web for the song **"Mon île"** by Sonia Dersion to enjoy a musical selection illustrating the use of this structure.

A **Boule de cristal.** Vous pouvez voir l'avenir *(the future)* dans une boule de cristal. Comment sera la vie des personnes suivantes dans cinq ans?

EXEMPLE Moi, je… (être riche)
Je serai riche. / Je ne serai pas riche.

1. Moi, je (j')…
   habiter ici
   avoir mon diplôme
   devoir travailler
   aller souvent en France

2. Mon meilleur ami (Ma meilleure amie)…
   venir souvent me voir
   réussir dans la vie
   sortir souvent avec moi
   faire souvent des voyages

3. La personne de mes rêves et moi, nous...
   se marier
   avoir des enfants
   acheter une maison
   faire beaucoup de voyages ensemble

4. Tous les membres de ma famille...
   s'entendre bien
   se rendre souvent visite
   se voir souvent
   voyager souvent ensemble

5. [à un(e) autre étudiant(e)]
   Toi, tu...
   finir tes études
   trouver un bon travail
   apprendre beaucoup
   avoir beaucoup de problèmes

6. [au professeur]
   avoir toujours cours à 7 heures du matin
   pouvoir prendre votre retraite *(retirement)*
   Vous... travailler toujours *(still)* ici
   être heureux (heureuse)

B **Je... quand...** Lucas parle à un ami avant de partir en Guadeloupe. Complétez la phrase suivante en mettant les deux actions dans l'ordre logique. Mettez les deux verbes au futur.

Je... quand...

EXEMPLE partir en vacances / pouvoir se reposer
Je pourrai me reposer quand je partirai en vacances.

1. aller en Guadeloupe / être dans l'avion pendant onze heures
2. arriver / envoyer des textos à mes amis
3. s'amuser / être en Guadeloupe
4. faire des excursions / ne pas être à la plage
5. visiter les sites touristiques / voir des choses intéressantes
6. aller voir le volcan la Soufrière / prendre beaucoup de photos
7. écrire un blog de voyage sur ma page Internet / rentrer à l'hôtel chaque soir
8. faire le blog / mettre mes photos sur Facebook

C **Si...** Complétez logiquement ces phrases.

EXEMPLE S'il pleut ce week-end, je **resterai à la maison.**

1. S'il fait beau ce week-end, je (j')...
2. S'il fait mauvais ce week-end, je (j')...
3. Si je sors avec des amis ce week-end, on...
4. Si je peux partir en vacances cette année, je (j')...
5. Si un jour je peux visiter la France, je (j')...
6. Si mes amis et moi décidons de visiter une autre ville, nous...

D **Entretien.** Pensez à un voyage (réel ou imaginaire) que vous ferez pendant les prochaines vacances. Votre partenaire vous posera des questions au sujet de ce voyage. Après, changez de rôles.

1. Où iras-tu? Comment est-ce que tu voyageras?
2. Quand est-ce que tu partiras? Quand est-ce que tu reviendras?
3. Qui fera le voyage avec toi? Quels vêtements est-ce que vous devrez emporter?
4. Où descendrez-vous?
5. Qu'est-ce que vous ferez pendant le voyage? Qu'est-ce que vous verrez d'intéressant? Quels sites touristiques est-ce que vous visiterez?

Suggestion for B. Je... quand... Remind students that they have to put the actions in the logical order.

Follow-ups for B. Je... quand...
A. Complétez les phrases suivantes de façon logique. **1.** Je serai content(e) quand... **2.** Les étudiants étudieront plus quand... **3.** Le professeur de français sera content quand... **4.** Je parlerai souvent français quand... **5.** J'aurai plus de temps libre quand... **6.** Je serai moins stressé(e) quand... **B.** Quand ferez-vous les choses suivantes? **1.** se marier **2.** acheter une maison **3.** aller en Europe **4.** comprendre tout **5.** être surpris(e) **6.** être content(e) **7.** avoir des enfants

Visiterez-vous la Martinique ou la Guadeloupe un jour?

STRATÉGIES ET LECTURE

POUR MIEUX LIRE: Recognizing compound tenses

French has other compound tenses, like the **passé composé,** which are formed with the auxiliary verb **avoir** or **être** and a past participle (**dansé, mangé, vu,** etc.). To translate these tenses, change the auxiliary verb *have* in English to the same tense as in French (imperfect, future, conditional): *They had (will have, would have) arrived.*

In the **passé composé,** where the auxiliary verb is in the *present* tense, translate it as the simple past or as *has/have + past participle.*

J'**ai** commencé.   Elle **est** rentrée.
*I began. / I **have** begun.*   *She returned. / She **has** returned.*

If the auxiliary verb is in the *imperfect,* translate it as *had + past participle.*

J'**avais** déjà commencé.   Il **n'était pas** encore rentré.
*I **had** already begun.*   *He **hadn't** returned yet.*

If the auxiliary verb is in the *conditional,* translate it as *would have + past participle.*

J'**aurais** déjà commencé.   Nous **ne serions pas** encore rentrés.
*I **would have** already begun.*   *We **wouldn't have** returned yet.*

If it is in the *future,* translate it as *will have + past participle.*

J'**aurai** déjà commencé.   Tu **ne seras pas** encore rentré(e).
*I **will have** already begun.*   *You **will not have** returned yet.*

Note *de grammaire*

Note the names of these compound tenses.

plus-que-parfait: auxiliary verb in the *imperfect + past participle*
J'avais fini. *I had finished.*

conditionnel passé: auxiliary verb in the *conditional + past participle*
J'aurais fini. *I would have finished.*

futur antérieur: auxiliary verb in the *future + past participle*
J'aurai fini. *I will have finished.*

Suggestion. Remind students that these tenses are presented for recognition only to allow them to read more advanced texts.

A   **Et vous?**   Traduisez les phrases suivantes en anglais.

1. J'ai déjà visité la Guadeloupe.
2. L'année dernière, j'y suis resté un mois.
3. Avant de partir en vacances, j'avais réservé une chambre d'hôtel.
4. J'ai visité la Martinique aussi. J'y étais déjà allé(e) deux fois avant.
5. Si j'avais eu assez d'argent, j'aurais passé mes vacances en Europe.
6. Mes vacances auraient été plus agréables s'il n'avait pas plu tout le temps.
7. Après ce voyage, j'aurai visité la Martinique trois fois.
8. J'aurai fini quatre semestres de français avant d'y aller.

B   **Le temps des verbes.**   Dans le texte qui suit, traduisez tous les verbes *en italique*.

Lecture: *Quelle aventure!*

Lucas, un jeune Parisien qui passe ses vacances en Guadeloupe, raconte ses aventures dans un mail à son ami Alex.

Salut Alex,

Je passe des vacances formidables ici en Guadeloupe! *Je t'aurais écrit* plus tôt si *je n'avais pas été* si occupé. Ici, tout est à mon goût… la cuisine, le paysage, les femmes! En fait, j'ai rencontré une jeune Guadeloupéenne très sympa. Elle s'appelle Anaïs et nous passons beaucoup de temps ensemble depuis notre rencontre assez comique au parc naturel.

J'étais allé au parc pour faire l'escalade de la Soufrière, un énorme volcan en repos… mais comme j'allais bientôt le comprendre, pas si «en repos» que ça! En montant vers le volcan, *j'avais remarqué* qu'il y avait un peu de vapeur qui sortait du cratère, mais *je n'avais pas fait trop attention*. Quand j'étais presque au sommet du volcan, je me suis assis par terre pour me reposer un peu et c'est là que la scène comique a commencé. Là où j'étais assis, la terre était toute chaude, mais vraiment chaude, et je voyais des jets de vapeur qui sortaient du sommet! J'ai pensé que le volcan allait exploser!

La Soufrière

J'ai commencé à crier aux autres touristes: «Attention! Attention! Le volcan entre en éruption, il va exploser!» Heureusement, Anaïs était parmi le groupe et elle nous a expliqué calmement: «Mais non, mais non… calmez-vous! C'est tout à fait normal. Le volcan est en repos, il n'y a pas de danger!» Si *elle n'avait pas été* avec nous, *on aurait* tous *commencé* à courir, paniqués.

Sur le moment, j'ai eu l'impression d'être complètement ridicule! Mais cette impression n'a pas duré. On a commencé à parler et nous avons continué l'escalade du volcan ensemble. Arrivés au sommet, nous avons découvert une vue impressionnante… la lave…, les fissures…, l'odeur… C'était un paysage presque irréel. Pendant un instant, j'ai eu l'impression d'être sur une autre planète!

Alors, tout est bien qui finit bien. Si *je n'avais pas fait* cette bêtise, *Anaïs et moi n'aurions jamais commencé à parler* et *je n'aurais pas fait* la connaissance de cette femme extraordinaire. Elle est super sympa et nous passons presque tous les soirs ensemble!

À bientôt,
Lucas

Compréhension. Répondez aux questions suivantes d'après la lecture.

1. Quel site touristique est-ce que Lucas visitait quand il a rencontré Anaïs?
2. Qu'est-ce que Lucas avait vu avant de commencer à crier que le volcan allait exploser?
3. Qu'est-ce que tous les touristes auraient fait si Anaïs n'avait pas été là pour les calmer?
4. Pourquoi est-ce que Lucas dit que «tout est bien qui finit bien»?

COMPÉTENCE 2

Preparing for a trip

 PowerPoint 9-4

LES PRÉPARATIFS

Note culturelle

Succès de l'e-tourisme! La majorité des Français vont sur Internet pour préparer leurs vacances et ils font leurs réservations en ligne. La possibilité de se connecter quand on veut, de comparer les prestations *(services)*, de trouver les promotions *(deals)* et des tarifs compétitifs sont des avantages importants. Comment est-ce que les gens dans votre région préparent leurs vacances?

Note de grammaire

Obtenir is conjugated like **venir**: j'obtiens, tu obtiens, il/elle/on obtient, nous obtenons, vous obtenez, ils/elles obtiennent. PASSÉ COMPOSÉ: j'ai obtenu; IMPARFAIT: j'obtenais; FUTUR/CONDITIONNEL: j'obtiendrai/j'obtiendrais.

Leur *(them, to them)* is an indirect object pronoun. Like direct object pronouns, it is placed before a verb. You will learn more about these pronouns in this chapter.

Je *leur* envoie des textos.
I send *them* text messages.

Avant de faire un voyage **à l'étranger**, il faut faire beaucoup de préparatifs *(m)*.

Avant **le départ**, il faut…

obtenir votre passeport *(m)* (bien à l'avance!) et acheter votre **billet** *(m)* **d'avion**.

vous informer sur la région sur Internet ou lire **un guide**.

réserver une chambre d'hôtel.

dire à votre famille où vous allez.

demander à **vos voisins** de **donner à manger à** votre chien.

faire vos valises *(f)*.

À votre **arrivée** *(f)*, vous devez…

montrer votre passeport.

passer **la douane**.

changer de l'argent.

Pour rester en contact pendant le voyage, vous pouvez…

envoyer des textos ou téléphoner à vos amis par Skype.

leur écrire des cartes postales.

mettre vos photos sur Facebook ou écrire un blog.

Line art on this page: © Cengage Learning

Warm-ups. A. Dites si vous ferez ou si vous ne ferez pas les choses suivantes la prochaine fois que vous partirez en voyage. **1.** visiter une île tropicale **2.** aller dans un pays étranger **3.** faire du ski **4.** prendre l'avion **5.** descendre dans un hôtel de luxe **6.** faire du camping **7.** inviter vos parents **8.** aller à la montagne **B.** Give students the following situation. Vous avez gagné 10 000 dollars et un billet d'avion *(plane ticket)* pour le pays francophone de votre choix. Racontez ce que vous y ferez. Utilisez le futur. **1.** Le jour de mon arrivée, je… **2.** Comme activités culturelles, je… **3.** Comme sport, je… **4.** Mon hôtel… **5.** Le soir, je… **6.** Au restaurant, je… **7.** Comme souvenirs, je… **8.** Comme sites touristiques, je… **C. Questions orales.** Quand vous aurez votre diplôme… **1.** Est-ce que vous ferez un voyage? **2.** Est-ce que vous visiterez l'Europe? **3.** Est-ce que vous vous marierez? **4.** Est-ce que vous achèterez une maison? Où ? **5.** Est-ce que vous trouverez du travail?

les préparatifs *(m)* preparations **à l'étranger** in another country, abroad **le départ** the departure **obtenir** to obtain **un billet d'avion** a plane ticket **s'informer** to find out information **un guide** a guidebook, a guide **dire** to say, to tell **un(e) voisin(e)** a neighbor **donner à manger à** to feed **faire une valise** to pack a suitcase **l'arrivée** *(f)* the arrival **la douane** customs **leur** them, to them

🔊 3-14   Alex parle à sa femme d'un mail qu'**il a reçu** de son ami Lucas.

CATHERINE: Qu'est-ce que **tu lis**?
ALEX: C'est un mail que j'ai reçu de Lucas. Il **m'**écrit de la Guadeloupe où il passe ses vacances.
CATHERINE: Et **ça lui plaît**, la Guadeloupe?
ALEX: Ça lui plaît beaucoup.
CATHERINE: La Guadeloupe, ça doit être beau. J'aimerais bien voir les plages et les paysages tropicaux.
ALEX: Lucas dit qu'il aime beaucoup le paysage, la cuisine et le climat. Il me parle aussi d'une «jeune femme extraordinaire» qu'il a rencontrée là-bas.

A Avant le départ ou après l'arrivée? Quand on voyage à l'étranger, est-ce qu'il faut faire les choses suivantes **avant le départ** ou **après l'arrivée**?

EXEMPLE acheter un billet d'avion
Il faut acheter un billet d'avion avant le départ.

1. passer la douane
2. obtenir un passeport
3. s'informer sur Internet
4. réserver une chambre
5. montrer son passeport
6. lire des guides
7. faire ses valises
8. mettre des photos sur Facebook
9. demander à un ami de donner à manger à son chien

B Et vous? Quelle sorte de voyageur (voyageuse) êtes-vous? Dites ce que vous feriez si vous voyagiez à l'étranger.

1. J'achèterais mon billet d'avion *sur Internet / dans une agence de voyages*.
2. Pour préparer le voyage, *je m'informerais sur Internet / je lirais un guide / je ne m'informerais pas beaucoup avant de partir*.
3. J'obtiendrais mon passeport *bien à l'avance / au dernier moment*.
4. Je réserverais ma chambre *par téléphone / sur Internet*.
5. *Je dirais / Je ne dirais pas* à ma famille où j'allais.
6. Je ferais ma valise *bien à l'avance / au dernier moment*.
7. Je changerais de l'argent *avant mon départ / à l'arrivée*.
8. Pour rester en contact avec mes amis, *j'écrirais un blog / je leur enverrais des textos / je leur téléphonerais / je leur parlerais par Skype*.
9. Je mettrais les photos du voyage sur Facebook *pendant le voyage / après mon retour* (return). *(Je ne mettrais pas mes photos sur Facebook.)*

À VOUS!

Avec un(e) partenaire, relisez à haute voix la conversation entre Alex et Catherine. Ensuite, imaginez que vous recevez un mail d'un(e) ami(e) qui visite une autre région francophone. Parlez avec votre partenaire de vos impressions de cette région et dites pourquoi vous voudriez ou ne voudriez pas y aller.

---

il a reçu (*recevoir* to receive)   **tu lis** (*lire* to read)   **me (m')** me, to me   **ça lui plaît?** (*plaire* to please) does he like it?

Compétence 2 | *trois cent cinquante-sept* **357**

 PowerPoint 9-5

COMMUNICATING WITH PEOPLE

Les verbes *dire*, *lire* et *écrire*

You have already seen the verbs **dire** *(to say, to tell)*, **lire** *(to read)*, and **écrire** *(to write)*. Here are their full conjugations. The verb **décrire** *(to describe)* is conjugated like **écrire**.

DIRE (to say, to tell)	LIRE (to read)	ÉCRIRE (to write)
je **dis**	je **lis**	j' **écris**
tu **dis**	tu **lis**	tu **écris**
il/elle/on **dit**	il/elle/on **lit**	il/elle/on **écrit**
nous **disons**	nous **lisons**	nous **écrivons**
vous **dites**	vous **lisez**	vous **écrivez**
ils/elles **disent**	ils/elles **lisent**	ils/elles **écrivent**
PASSÉ COMPOSÉ: j'**ai dit**	PASSÉ COMPOSÉ: j'**ai lu**	PASSÉ COMPOSÉ: j'**ai écrit**
IMPARFAIT: je **disais**	IMPARFAIT: je **lisais**	IMPARFAIT: j'**écrivais**
CONDITIONNEL: je **dirais**	CONDITIONNEL: je **lirais**	CONDITIONNEL: j'**écrirais**
FUTUR: je **dirai**	FUTUR: je **lirai**	FUTUR: j'**écrirai**

Here are some things you might want to read or write.

un article *an article*
une carte postale *a postcard*
un mail *an e-mail*
une histoire *a story*
un journal *(pl* **des journaux***) a newspaper*

une lettre *a letter*
un magazine *a magazine*
un poème *a poem*
une rédaction *a composition*
un roman *a novel*

✓ Pour vérifier

1. What are the conjugations of **dire**, **lire**, and **écrire**? What do you need to remember about the **vous** form of **dire**? What are the future and conditional stems of these verbs?

2. Which two of these verbs have similar past participles? What are they? What is the past participle of **lire**?

Grammar Tutorials

Suggestion. Point out the form **vous dites** and remind students of the similar forms **vous êtes** and **vous faites**.

A En cours de français. Est-ce que ces personnes font souvent les choses indiquées en cours de français?

> souvent   quelquefois   rarement   ne… jamais

EXEMPLE je / écrire des poèmes
> **Je n'écris jamais de poèmes en cours de français.**

1. le professeur / écrire au tableau
2. les étudiants / écrire au tableau
3. je / écrire quelque chose dans mon cahier
4. les autres étudiants et moi / s'écrire des mails après le cours
5. je / lire le journal
6. le professeur / lire des poèmes à la classe
7. nous / lire des phrases à haute voix *(aloud)*
8. les étudiants / lire des romans en français

Maintenant, dites si ces personnes ont fait ces choses en cours la semaine dernière.

EXEMPLE je / écrire des poèmes
> **Je n'ai pas écrit de poèmes en cours de français la semaine dernière.**

Warm-ups for A. En cours de français.
A. Est-ce que vous préférez lire…? **1.** le journal ou un roman **2.** un roman de science-fiction ou un roman d'amour **3.** une histoire d'amour ou un article sur le sport **4.** un magazine sur la politique ou un poème **5.** un roman historique ou un roman d'amour **B.** Have students complete the following statements: **1.** J'aime lire… **2.** Je lis souvent… **3.** Je ne lis jamais… **4.** Je n'aime pas lire… **5.** J'aime écrire… **6.** Je n'aime pas écrire… **7.** J'écris souvent… **8.** J'écris quelquefois… **9.** Je n'écris jamais…

Follow-up for A. En cours de français. Have students redo the activity in the **futur** to talk about what these people will or will not probably do next week.

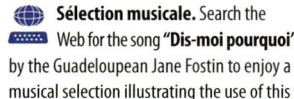 **Sélection musicale.** Search the Web for the song **"Dis-moi pourquoi"** by the Guadeloupean Jane Fostin to enjoy a musical selection illustrating the use of this structure.

B Qu'est-ce qu'on dit? Dites si ces personnes font les choses indiquées.

EXEMPLE je / dire «merci» quand le professeur me rend mes devoirs
Je (ne) dis (pas) «merci» quand le professeur me rend mes devoirs.

1. le prof / dire «bonjour» quand il arrive en cours
2. les autres étudiants et moi / se dire «bonjour» en cours
3. les étudiants / dire la vérité *(the truth)* au prof
4. nous / se dire «au revoir» quand nous quittons la classe
5. je / dire «merci» au prof

Maintenant, dites si ces personnes ont dit les choses indiquées pendant le dernier cours.

EXEMPLE je / dire «merci» quand le professeur me rend mes devoirs
J'ai dit (Je n'ai pas dit) «merci» quand le professeur m'a rendu mes devoirs.

C En vacances. Vous faites le voyage de vos rêves avec un(e) ami(e). Avec un(e) partenaire, faites des phrases logiques en utilisant un élément de chaque colonne. Faites au moins deux phrases pour chaque sujet.

EXEMPLE Je lis des guides.

Je... Nous... L'agent de voyages *(The travel agent)*...	dire écrire lire	un blog sur le voyage des mails un mail pour réserver une chambre des guides à des voisins de donner à manger aux animaux «au revoir» à nos amis le nom de notre hôtel à ma famille le prix *(price)* du voyage

Suggestion for C. En vacances. Put students into teams to see which team can create the largest number of logical and correct sentences within a set time limit.

D Entretien. Interviewez votre partenaire.

1. Est-ce que tu écris plus de textos ou plus de mails? Est-ce que tu as écrit un mail ce matin? À qui? Quand tu voyages, est-ce que tu écris des cartes postales? un blog? Est-ce que tu envoies des textos ou des mails? Tu mets tes photos sur Facebook?
2. Lis-tu le journal tous les jours? Est-ce que tu lis un journal en ligne? Quel journal préfères-tu lire? Le liras-tu ce soir? Est-ce que tu l'as lu ce matin? Quel magazine lis-tu le plus souvent? Est-ce que tu l'as lu ce mois-ci?
3. Lis-tu beaucoup de romans? Quel est le dernier roman que tu as lu? Quand est-ce que tu l'as lu?

Follow-up for D. Entretien. Vous partez en vacances avec un(e) ami(e) qui veut savoir si vous avez tout préparé. Préparez une conversation où vous dites si vous avez fait les choses suivantes. • écrire pour réserver une chambre • dire à votre famille où vous allez • acheter votre billet • faire vos valises • demander à un(e) ami(e) de donner à manger à vos animaux • lire des guides

 **PowerPoint 9-6**

AVOIDING REPETITION

Les pronoms compléments d'objet indirect **(lui, leur)** *et reprise des pronoms compléments d'objet direct* **(le, la, l', les)**

✓ Pour vérifier

1. What are the French direct object pronouns for *him, her, it, them*? What are the indirect object pronouns for *(to) him, (to) her, (to) them*?

2. How can you often recognize a noun that is an indirect object in French? What types of verbs are frequently followed by indirect objects?

3. Where do you place the object pronoun when there is an infinitive in the same clause? Where does it go otherwise?

4. Where do you place the object pronoun in the **passé composé**? When does the past participle agree with an object pronoun?

iLrn Grammar Tutorials

Note *de grammaire*

In French, a noun that is a direct object generally follows the verb directly, whereas a noun that is an indirect object is preceded by a preposition, usually **à**.

J'invite **mes amis** chez moi. (direct object)
Je **les** invite chez moi.
Je téléphone **à mes amis**. (indirect object)
Je **leur** téléphone.

In **Chapitre 5**, you learned that you can replace the direct object of the verb with the direct object pronouns **le, la, l'**, and **les**.

—Tu fais **ta valise** maintenant? —Tu as acheté **ton billet**?
—Oui, je **la** fais. —Oui, je **l'**ai acheté.

Replace the indirect object of the verb with the indirect object pronouns **lui** *([to] him, [to] her)* and **leur** *([to] them)*. Generally, indirect objects in French can only be people or animals, not places or things. You can recognize a noun that is an indirect object because it is usually preceded by the preposition **à** (**à, au, à la, à l', aux**).

Verbs indicating communication or exchanges, such as **parler à, téléphoner à, dire à, écrire à, demander à, rendre visite à,** and **donner à,** are often followed by indirect objects.

—Tu écris **à ta mère**? —Tu vas rendre visite **à tes parents**?
—Oui, je **lui** écris un mail. —Oui, je vais **leur** rendre visite ce week-end.

DIRECT OBJECT PRONOUNS		INDIRECT OBJECT PRONOUNS	
le (l')	*him, it* (m)	lui	*(to) him*
la (l')	*her, it* (f)	lui	*(to) her*
les	*them*	leur	*(to) them*

Indirect object pronouns follow the same placement rules as direct object pronouns. Generally, place them *immediately* before the verb. They go before the infinitive if there is one in the same clause. If not, they go before the conjugated verb. In the **passé composé,** they go before the auxiliary verb.

—Lucas va téléphoner **à Anaïs**? —*Is Lucas going to call Anaïs?*
—Oui, il va **lui** téléphoner. —*Yes, he's going to call* **her**.
—Il écrit **à son ami**? —*Is he writing* **to his friend**?
—Oui, il **lui** écrit. —*Yes, he is writing* **(to) him**.
—Il a parlé **à ses parents**? —*Has he talked* **to his parents**?
—Non, il ne **leur** a pas parlé. —*No, he hasn't talked* **to them**.

In negated sentences, place **ne** immediately after the subject and **pas, rien,** or **jamais** immediately after the first verb.

Je **ne** veux **pas lui** écrire.
Je **ne lui** écris **jamais**.
Je **ne lui** ai **pas** écrit.

In the **passé composé,** the past participle agrees with direct object pronouns, but not with indirect objects.

Lucas a invité Anaïs. Lucas **l'**a invité**e**.
Lucas a téléphoné à Anaïs. Lucas **lui** a téléphoné.

Suggestion. Give students these exercises to review the direct object pronouns and familiarize students with the indirect object pronouns before doing the exercises in the book. **A.** Dites si on fait ces choses **avant son départ** ou **après son arrivée**. Remplacez les noms en italique par les pronoms **le, la, l', les**. **EXEMPLE** On passe *la douane*. **On la passe après son arrivée**. 1. On montre *son passeport*. 2. On fait *sa valise*. 3. On admire *les paysages*. 4. On change *son argent*. **B.** Est-ce qu'un bon guide fait les choses suivantes pour les touristes? Utilisez le pronom **leur**. **EXEMPLE** parler de ses problèmes personnels **Non, il ne leur parle pas de ses problèmes personnels.** 1. dire son nom 2. montrer les sites historiques 3. répondre poliment *(politely)* 4. parler de choses ennuyeuses 5. demander un pourboire *(tip)* 6. parler de l'histoire de la région 7. parler dans une langue qu'ils ne comprennent pas 8. décrire la culture **C.** Maintenant, dites si les touristes sympas font les choses suivantes au guide. Utilisez le pronom **lui**. **EXEMPLE** demander son nom **Oui, ils lui demandent son nom.** 1. téléphoner à minuit 2. parler 3. obéir 4. donner un pourboire *(tip)* 5. poser des questions 6. dire «merci»

A En voyage. Quel genre de voyageur (voyageuse) êtes-vous? Formez des phrases pour parler de vos habitudes en voyage. Utilisez les pronoms **le, la, l', les**.

> EXEMPLE Je réserve *ma chambre* (sur Internet / par téléphone).
> **Je la réserve sur Internet.**

1. J'achète *mon billet* (dans une agence de voyages *[travel agency]* / sur Internet).
2. Je fais *ma valise* (au dernier moment / à l'avance).
3. Je lis *mon guide* (avant de partir / à l'hôtel au dernier moment).
4. Je visite *les sites touristiques* (avec un guide / sans guide).

Maintenant, utilisez les pronoms **lui** et **leur** pour remplacer les noms compléments d'objet indirect.

5. Je dis (toujours / quelquefois / rarement) *à mes parents* où je vais.
6. J'écris (souvent / quelquefois / rarement) des mails *à mes amis*.
7. (Je téléphone / Je ne téléphone pas) *à mon meilleur ami (à ma meilleure amie)*.
8. (J'envoie / Je n'envoie pas) mes photos *à mon meilleur ami (à ma meilleure amie)*.

Aimez-vous faire de l'écotourisme?

B La prochaine fois. Refaites les phrases de *A. En voyage* pour parler de ce que vous allez probablement faire la prochaine fois que vous partirez en voyage.

> EXEMPLE Je réserve *ma chambre* (sur Internet / par téléphone).
> **La prochaine fois, je vais la réserver sur Internet.**

Maintenant, refaites ces mêmes phrases au passé composé pour dire ce que vous avez fait la dernière fois que vous êtes parti(e) en voyage.

> EXEMPLE Je réserve *ma chambre* (sur Internet / par téléphone).
> **La dernière fois, je l'ai réservée sur Internet.**

C Habitudes de voyage. Parlez de vos voyages en répondant à ces questions. Utilisez **le, la, l', les, lui** ou **leur**.

> EXEMPLE Vous demandez de l'argent *à vos parents*?
> **Non, je ne leur demande pas d'argent.**

En général...

1. Vous réservez *votre chambre d'hôtel* sur Internet?
2. Vous achetez *votre billet* sur Internet ou dans une agence de voyages *(travel agency)*?
3. Vous proposez *à vos parents* de partir en vacances avec vous?
4. Vous demandez *à votre meilleur(e) ami(e)* de donner à manger à votre chien ou à votre chat?
5. Vous lisez *le magazine de la compagnie aérienne* dans l'avion?

Et la dernière fois que vous êtes parti(e) en voyage...

6. Vous avez téléphoné *à votre mère* pendant le voyage?
7. Vous avez envoyé des textos *à votre meilleur(e) ami(e)*?
8. Vous avez passé *vos soirées* à l'hôtel?
9. À votre retour *(return)*, vous avez parlé du voyage *à vos parents*?
10. Vous avez mis *vos photos* sur Facebook?

Compétence 2 | *trois cent soixante et un* **361**

COMPÉTENCE 3

Buying your ticket

PowerPoint 9-7

À L'AGENCE DE VOYAGES

Note culturelle

En France, vous pouvez trouver des distributeurs automatiques de billet (des DAB *[ATMs]*) un peu partout. Les DAB sont un moyen pratique de retirer *(withdraw)* de l'argent en utilisant votre propre *(own)* carte bancaire, surtout parce que de nos jours, les banques n'ont pas toujours de bureau de change *(foreign currency exchange counter)* et les bureaux de change sont quelquefois difficiles à trouver.

Mais faites attention! Normalement, il faut faire savoir *(to inform)* à votre banque que vous avez l'intention de visiter un autre pays avant de pouvoir utiliser votre carte de crédit ou votre carte bancaire à l'étranger. Avez-vous utilisé un DAB dans un pays étranger?

3-15

Warm-up. Dites si vous ferez ou ne ferez probablement pas les choses suivantes la prochaine fois que vous partirez en voyage. **1.** acheter votre billet sur Internet **2.** lire un guide **3.** vous informer sur Internet **4.** réserver une chambre **5.** demander à un ami de donner à manger à vos animaux **6.** dire à votre famille où vous allez

Note for the conversation. New vocabulary includes the glossed words and **l'agent de voyages, un billet aller-retour, un aller simple, classe économique, le retour,** and **une réservation.**

Suggestion for the conversation. Point out that there is a six-hour time difference between Paris and Guadeloupe. Have students first listen with books closed for the answers to these questions. **1.** À quelle date est-ce que Lucas va partir? **2.** À quelle date est-ce qu'il va rentrer? **3.** Combien coûte son billet?

Pour voyager à l'étranger, il faut avoir... Il faut aussi **savoir**...

un passeport
un billet d'avion
une carte de crédit
(une carte bleue)
une carte bancaire

le numéro du **vol**
l'heure de départ
l'heure d'arrivée

Aimez-vous préparer vos voyages à l'avance? Il faut lire des infos *(f)* sur Internet pour mieux **connaître**...

l'histoire, la géographie et la culture régionale

le réseau de **transports** *(m)* **en commun**

Avant son voyage, Lucas achète son billet à l'agence de voyages.

LUCAS: Bonjour, monsieur. Je voudrais acheter un billet Paris – Pointe-à-Pitre.

L'AGENT DE VOYAGES: Très bien, monsieur. Vous voulez un billet aller-retour ou un aller simple?

LUCAS: Un billet aller-retour.

L'AGENT DE VOYAGES: À quelle date est-ce que vous voulez partir?

LUCAS: Le 20 juillet.

L'AGENT DE VOYAGES: Quand est-ce que vous voulez rentrer?

LUCAS: Le 12 août.

L'AGENT DE VOYAGES: Vous voulez un billet en première classe ou en classe économique?

LUCAS: En classe économique.

L'AGENT DE VOYAGES: Très bien. Il y a un vol le 20 juillet, départ Paris-Orly à 15h15, arrivée à Pointe-à-Pitre à 17h30, heure locale. Pour le retour, il y a un vol qui part de Pointe-à-Pitre le 12 août à 20h15 et qui arrive à Paris-Orly à 10h15 le 13 août. **Ça vous convient?**

LUCAS: Oui, c'est parfait. Combien coûte le billet?

L'AGENT DE VOYAGES: C'est 759 euros.

LUCAS: Bon. Alors, faites ma réservation. Voilà ma carte bancaire.

Line art on this page: © Cengage Learning

---

savoir *to know* **une carte bancaire** *a bank/debit card* **un vol** *a flight* **connaître** *to know, to be familiar with, to be acquainted with* **le réseau** *the network* **les transports** *(m)* **en commun** *public transportation* **Ça vous convient?** *Is that good for you?*

A Le voyage de Lucas.
Lisez le récapitulatif *(itinerary)* du voyage de Lucas et répondez à ces questions.

1. Est-ce que Lucas a acheté un billet aller-retour ou un aller simple?
2. Est-ce que Lucas voyagera en première classe ou en classe économique?
3. Quelle est la date de son départ? de son retour? De quel aéroport partira-t-il?
4. Il devra arriver à l'aéroport combien d'heures avant le départ?
5. À quelle heure est son départ de Paris? À quelle heure est son arrivée à Pointe-à-Pitre?
6. Est-ce qu'un repas sera servi en route?
7. Quelle est la date de son retour à Paris? C'est quel jour de la semaine?

RÉCAPITULATIF DE VOTRE VOYAGE

Passager: Moreau/Lucas

Aller: Mardi 20 juillet:

Départ de Paris-Orly	15h15
Air France-Vol 624	Classe économique
Arrivée à Pointe-à-Pitre	17h30

- Un repas et une collation seront servis en vol.

Retour: Jeudi 12 août:

Départ de Pointe-à-Pitre	20h15
Air France-Vol 625	Classe économique
Arrivée à Paris-Orly	10h15

- Un repas et une collation seront servis en vol.

Prix du billet aller-retour: 759€.

Prévoyez d'arriver à l'aéroport deux heures avant l'heure de départ et n'oubliez pas de reconfirmer votre retour 72 heures avant le départ.

BON VOYAGE!

B Et vous?
Choisissez la phrase qui vous décrit le mieux quand vous voyagez.

1. a. Je préfère préparer mes voyages bien à l'avance.
   b. Je prépare tout quelques jours avant de partir.
   c. Je préfère voyager sans prévoir *(without planning)*.
2. a. J'arrive à l'aéroport bien en avance.
   b. J'arrive à l'aéroport au dernier moment.
   c. Je manque *(miss)* quelquefois mon vol.
3. a. Pendant le voyage, je préfère payer par carte de crédit.
   b. Je préfère payer par carte bancaire.
   c. Pendant le voyage, je préfère payer en espèces *(in cash)*.
4. a. Dans une grande ville comme Paris, j'utilise les moyens de transport en commun.
   b. Je prends toujours un taxi ou je loue une voiture.
   c. Je ne sors pas de l'hôtel.
5. a. J'aime lire un guide pour connaître l'histoire et la culture d'une région.
   b. J'aime mieux m'informer sur Internet pour connaître la région.
   c. Je préfère tout découvrir *(discover)* pendant le voyage.

À VOUS!

Avec un(e) partenaire, relisez à haute voix la conversation entre Lucas et l'agent de voyages. Ensuite, imaginez que vous êtes dans une agence de voyages d'une ville francophone et que vous achetez un billet pour rentrer chez vous. Votre partenaire jouera le rôle de l'agent de voyages.

 **PowerPoint 9-8**

✓ Pour vérifier

1. What is the conjugation of **savoir**? of **connaître**?

2. Do you use **savoir** or **connaître** when *to know* is followed by a verb? by a question word, **si, que,** or **ce que**? to say that one knows a language? if *to know* is followed by a noun that indicates a fact or information? by a noun that indicates that someone is familiar with a person, place or thing?

Note *de grammaire*

1. When saying what someone knows how to do, use **savoir** + *an infinitive*. Since **savoir** means *to know how,* you do not need to add a word for *how*.

   Il sait parler italien.
   Je sais jouer de la guitare.

2. Notice that in the conjugation of **connaître,** there is a circumflex on the **i** only when it appears before the letter **t**.

SAYING WHAT PEOPLE KNOW

Les verbes *savoir* et *connaître*

Both **savoir** and **connaître** mean *to know*. The verb **reconnaître** *(to recognize)* has the same conjugation as **connaître**.

SAVOIR (to know [how])	CONNAÎTRE (to know, to be familiar with, to be acquainted with)
je **sais** nous **savons** tu **sais** vous **savez** il/elle/on **sait** ils/elles **savent**	je **connais** nous **connaissons** tu **connais** vous **connaissez** il/elle/on **connaît** ils/elles **connaissent**
PASSÉ COMPOSÉ: j'**ai su** *(I found out)* IMPARFAIT: je **savais** *(I knew)* CONDITIONNEL: je **saurais** FUTUR: je **saurai**	PASSÉ COMPOSÉ: j'**ai connu** *(I met)* IMPARFAIT: je **connaissais** *(I knew)* CONDITIONNEL: je **connaîtrais** FUTUR: je **connaîtrai**

Use **savoir** to say you *know* . . .

FACTS OR INFORMATION:
Est-ce que tu **sais** la réponse?
Nous ne **savons** pas où ils sont.

A LANGUAGE:
Je **sais** le français.
Je ne **sais** pas l'allemand.

HOW TO DO SOMETHING:
Je **sais** nager.
Je ne **sais** pas danser.

Use **connaître** to say you *know (of)* or *are familiar* or *acquainted with* . . .

PEOPLE:
Vous **connaissez** mon amie Anaïs?
Je la **connais** bien.

PLACES:
Tu **connais** bien la Guadeloupe?
Qui **connaît** ce quartier?

THINGS:
Je ne **connais** pas ce monument.
Tu **connais** l'histoire de la Guadeloupe?

Use **savoir** when *to know* is followed by a verb, a question word **(qui, où...),** or by **si, que,** or **ce que.** When *to know* is followed by a noun, use **savoir** to say one *knows a language, a fact,* or *information,* and **connaître** to say one is *familiar with a person, place,* or *thing.*

Follow-up for *A. Quel pays?* (Give students the following cues and allow them a few minutes to think of places to name before beginning.) Demandez à un(e) autre étudiant(e) s'il/si elle connaît bien différents endroits de votre ville. Donnez un nom précis. Utilisez le pronom **le, la, l'** ou **les** dans la réponse. EXEMPLE la rue... —Est-ce que tu connais la rue Canyon? —Oui, je la connais. / Non, je ne la connais pas. **1.** le magasin... **2.** le centre commercial... **3.** la librairie... **4.** la rue... **5.** le parc... **6.** le restaurant... **7.** le cinéma...

🌐 **Sélection musicale.** Search the Web for the song **"Je voudrais la connaître"** by Patricia Kaas to enjoy a musical selection illustrating the use of this structure.

A   Quel pays?   Quels pays est-ce que ces personnes connaissent bien? Quelles langues savent-elles parler?

EXEMPLE   Lucas habite à Paris.
Il connaît bien la France. Il sait parler français.

> la France   l'Allemagne   le Canada
> l'Espagne   les États-Unis   le Sénégal

> français   anglais   allemand   espagnol

1. Sophie habite à Berlin. Elle…
2. Ana et Luis habitent à Barcelone. Ils…
3. Edouard habite à Dakar. Il…
4. Nous habitons à *[votre ville]*. Nous…
5. *[au professeur]* Et vous, vous habitez à *[votre ville]*. Alors, vous… ?

B Qui sait faire ça?
Dites qui sait faire les choses suivantes dans votre famille. Dites **Personne ne sait…** pour dire *No one knows how to…*

EXEMPLE nager
Tout le monde sait nager dans ma famille.
Moi, je sais nager mais les autres ne savent pas nager.
Personne ne sait nager dans ma famille.

1. bien faire la cuisine
2. faire du ski
3. bien danser
4. jouer au tennis
5. bien chanter
6. parler français

Maintenant demandez aux autres étudiants s'ils savent faire ces choses.

EXEMPLE nager
—Marc, tu sais nager?
—Oui, je sais nager. / Non, je ne sais pas nager.

C Et vous?
Complétez ces phrases avec **je sais / je ne sais pas** ou avec **je connais / je ne connais pas** pour parler de vos connaissances.

1. _____ bien le campus. _____ où se trouvent *(is located)* la bibliothèque et d'autres endroits importants.
2. D'habitude, _____ répondre aux questions du prof. _____ très bien le français. _____ bien les conjugaisons des verbes que nous avons étudiés. _____ qu'il est très important de bien apprendre toutes les conjugaisons.
3. _____ le nom de tous les autres étudiants. _____ bien ces étudiants. _____ ce qu'ils vont tous faire après les cours aujourd'hui.
4. _____ bien la bibliothèque. _____ où se trouvent tous les livres en français.
5. _____ utiliser Internet pour trouver comment dire ce que je veux en français. _____ des / de sites Web avec de bons dictionnaires.

Connaissez-vous la Guadeloupe? Savez-vous parler français?

D Ici et en voyage.
Complétez chaque question avec la forme correcte de **connaître** ou de **savoir** et posez-la à votre partenaire.

1. _____-tu un bon agent de voyages? _____-tu une bonne agence de voyages dans notre ville?
2. _____-tu acheter un billet sur Internet? Est-ce que tu _____ combien coûte un billet d'ici à Paris? _____-tu s'il y a un vol direct d'ici à Paris? _____-tu combien de temps dure *(lasts)* un vol d'ici à Paris?
3. _____-tu la Guadeloupe? Est-ce que tu _____ quelle ville est le chef-lieu *(administrative center)* de la Guadeloupe? _____-tu bien l'histoire et la géographie de la Guadeloupe?
4. Tu parles français et anglais. _____-tu parler d'autres langues? Est-ce que tu _____ bien un pays étranger?

Supplemental activity. Questions orales. **1.** Dans quels cours est-ce que vous connaissez bien les autres étudiants? **2.** Est-ce que vous connaissez d'autres professeurs de français à l'université? **3.** Est-ce que vous savez si le prochain semestre/trimestre de français va être plus difficile? **4.** Savez-vous si on va avoir le même livre? **5.** Est-ce que vous savez quand le prochain semestre/trimestre va commencer?

 PowerPoint 9-9

INDICATING WHO DOES WHAT TO WHOM

Les pronoms *me, te, nous* et *vous*

The pronouns **me** *(me, to me)*, **te** *(you, to you)*, **nous** *(us, to us)*, and **vous** *(you, to you)* are used as both direct and indirect objects.

me (m')	me, to me	Tu ne **m'**attends pas?
te (t')	you, to you (familiar)	Nous **t'**avons attendu(e) une heure.
nous	us, to us	Tu peux venir **nous** chercher?
vous	you, to you (plural / formal)	Je **vous** téléphonerai plus tard.

All object pronouns go immediately before an infinitive if there is one in the same clause; otherwise they go before the conjugated verb. In the **passé composé,** they go before the auxiliary verb.

Je vais **te** voir demain.   Il ne **nous** connaît pas bien.   Je **vous** ai vu(e)(s).

In the **passé composé,** the past participle agrees with preceding *direct* objects, but not with *indirect* objects.

Il **nous** a *vus* mais il ne **nous** a pas *parlé.*

The expression **il faut** followed by an infinitive generally means *it is necessary* or *one must.*

Il faut arriver une heure à l'avance.
It is necessary to arrive (One must arrive) one hour in advance.

Use **il faut** with the indirect object pronouns **me, te, nous, vous, lui,** and **leur** to say that someone needs something or needs to do something.

Il me faut aller au consulat. Il me faut un passeport.
I need to go to the consulate. I need a passport.

✓ Pour vérifier

What four pronouns are used for both direct and indirect objects? Where are they usually placed in a sentence with an infinitive in the same clause? Where are they placed otherwise?

iLrn Grammar Tutorials

Suggestions. A. Point out that with the object pronouns **nous** and **vous,** the verb form matches the subject: **Je vous parle. B.** Remind students of the **e caduc** and point out that the unaccented **e** in **me, te,** and **le** is usually not pronounced if you can drop it without bringing three pronounced consonants together (**Tu mę parles?**).

A Que voulez-vous? Dites la même chose en utilisant une des expressions données.

> il me faut   il te faut   il lui faut   il nous faut   il vous faut   il leur faut

EXEMPLE J'ai besoin d'un passeport.
Il me faut un passeport.

1. Tu as besoin d'une carte bancaire.
2. Nous avons besoin d'un guide.
3. Vous avez besoin d'un billet.
4. J'ai besoin d'un nouveau bikini.
5. Tu as besoin d'une pièce d'identité *(identification).*
6. Vous avez besoin d'une réservation.
7. Il a besoin d'un passeport.
8. Ils ont besoin d'une carte d'embarquement *(boarding pass).*

🌐 **Sélection musicale.** Search the Web for the song **"Radiologie"** by Malajube to enjoy a musical selection illustrating the use of this structure.

Maintenant, expliquez pourquoi chacun a besoin de ces choses.

EXEMPLE J'ai besoin d'un passeport.
Il me faut un passeport pour faire un voyage à l'étranger.

> changer de l'argent   avoir une chambre d'hôtel   faire un voyage à l'étranger
> payer le voyage   monter dans l'avion   préparer un itinéraire
> aller à la plage

B Meilleurs amis. Demandez à votre partenaire si son meilleur ami (sa meilleure amie) fait les choses suivantes. Utilisez le pronom **te (t')** dans vos questions.

EXEMPLE téléphoner souvent
—Il/Elle te téléphone souvent?
—Non, il/elle ne me téléphone pas souvent.
 Oui, il/elle me téléphone souvent.

1. parler tous les jours
2. retrouver souvent en ville
3. écouter toujours
4. comprendre bien
5. rendre souvent visite
6. donner de l'argent

C Je te promets! Un jeune homme dit à sa fiancée qu'il fait ou qu'il va faire tout ce qu'elle veut. Elle lui pose les questions suivantes. Comment répond-il?

EXEMPLE Tu m'aimes vraiment beaucoup?
Oui, je t'aime vraiment beaucoup.

1. Tu m'adores?
2. Tu me trouves belle?
3. Tu me comprends?
4. Tu veux me voir tous les jours?
5. Tu vas venir me voir demain?
6. Tu vas m'abandonner?
7. Tu vas m'aimer pour toujours?

Est-ce que ton meilleur ami t'écoute quand tu lui parles?

D Professeurs et étudiants. En groupes, dites au professeur trois choses que les autres étudiants et vous faites pour lui et trois choses que le professeur fait pour vous. Faites deux listes sur une feuille de papier.

EXEMPLES Nous vous écoutons...
Vous nous donnez trop de devoirs...

E Entretien. Interviewez votre partenaire.

1. Est-ce que tes amis t'invitent souvent à partir en voyage avec eux?
2. As-tu des amis qui te téléphonent d'un autre pays de temps en temps?
3. De tous les endroits où tu as passé tes vacances, quelle ville est-ce que tu me recommandes de visiter? Pourquoi?

Follow-up for *D. Professeurs et étudiants*. Questions orales. **1.** Vous me comprenez quand je vous parle? **2.** Je vous parle plus en français ou en anglais? **3.** Vous me répondez toujours en français? **4.** Je vous comprends? **5.** Vous m'attendez quand je suis en retard *(late)*? **6.** Vous m'écoutez en cours? **7.** Vous me rendez les devoirs à l'avance? **8.** Vous me rendez visite dans mon bureau?

COMPÉTENCE 4

Deciding where to go on a trip

 PowerPoint 9-10

Note culturelle

La grande majorité des Français passent leurs vacances en France. Mais pour les séjours *(stays)* à l'étranger, 70 % ont lieu en Europe et l'Espagne est leur première destination. Quels pays voudriez-vous visiter?

Vocabulaire sans peine!

Most countries, states, or regions ending with **-ia** in English end with **-ie** in French, and are feminine (except *India* [**l'Inde**]). Also, the words for the nationalities of the people from these countries end with **-ien(ne)** (except *Russian* [**russe**]).

Australia = **l'Australie**
Australian = **australien(ne)**

How would you say the following in French?

Tunisia / Tunisian

Vocabulaire supplémentaire

EN AFRIQUE	l'Afrique (f) du Sud
	la Tunisie
EN ASIE	la Corée (du Nord / du Sud)
	l'Inde (f)
	l'Iran (m)
	l'Irak (m)
EN EUROPE	le Danemark
	la Pologne
	le Portugal
	la République tchèque

Warm-up. Vous allez visiter la France avec un(e) ami(e). Est-ce que vous savez… (parler français, combien de temps il faut pour aller à Paris en avion, prendre le métro)? Est-ce que vous connaissez… (la ville de Paris, des gens en France, un hôtel à Paris, quelques sites touristiques)?

UN VOYAGE

Lucas visite la Guadeloupe. Et vous? Quels continents et pays aimeriez-vous visiter?

Moi, j'aimerais visiter…

l'Afrique *(f)*: **le Maroc,** l'Algérie *(f)*, l'Égypte *(f)*, le Sénégal, la Côte d'Ivoire

L'oasis Kerzaz, Algérie

l'Asie *(f)* et **le Moyen-Orient:** la Chine, Israël *(m)*, le Japon, le Viêt Nam

l'Amérique *(f)* **du Nord ou l'Amérique centrale:** **les Antilles** *(f)*, le Canada, les États-Unis *(m)*, le Mexique

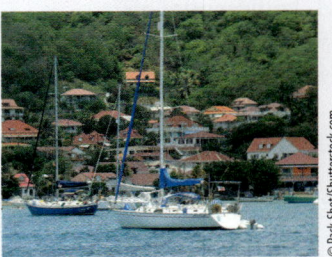
La Guadeloupe

l'Amérique *(f)* **du Sud:** l'Argentine *(f)*, le Brésil, le Chili, la Colombie, la Guyane, le Pérou

l'Océanie *(f)*: l'Australie *(f)*, la Nouvelle-Calédonie, la Polynésie française

Le Parlement européen, Bruxelles

l'Europe *(f)*: l'Allemagne *(f)*, la Belgique, la Croatie, l'Espagne *(f)*, la France, la Grèce, l'Irlande *(f)*, l'Italie *(f)*, **le Royaume-Uni,** la Russie, la Suisse

Line art on this page: © Cengage Learning

---

le Maroc *Morocco*   **le Moyen-Orient** *the Middle East*   **les Antilles** *(f pl)* *the West Indies*   **le Royaume-Uni** *the United Kingdom*

Lucas et Anaïs parlent des voyages qu'ils ont faits.

ANAÏS: Pourquoi es-tu venu tout seul en Guadeloupe? Tu aimes voyager?
LUCAS: Oui, j'adore ça!
ANAÏS: Quels pays as-tu visités?
LUCAS: J'ai visité les États-Unis, la Chine et le Canada. Et toi? Tu aimes voyager?
ANAÏS: Je n'ai jamais quitté la Guadeloupe, mais j'aimerais bien visiter l'Afrique un jour.
LUCAS: Où aimerais-tu aller en Afrique?
ANAÏS: Moi, j'aimerais surtout visiter le Sénégal et la Côte d'Ivoire.

A Quel continent? Où se trouvent *(are located)* ces pays?

> en Amérique du Nord   en Afrique   en Amérique du Sud
> en Océanie   en Asie   en Europe

EXEMPLE la Chine
La Chine se trouve en Asie.

1. les États-Unis
2. l'Algérie
3. le Japon
4. l'Australie
5. l'Allemagne
6. le Sénégal
7. la Guyane
8. le Maroc

B Quels pays? Dites quels pays vous aimeriez visiter dans la région indiquée.

EXEMPLE en Europe
En Europe, j'aimerais visiter la France, l'Espagne...

1. en Asie et au Moyen-Orient
2. en Amérique du Nord et centrale
3. en Amérique du Sud
4. en Afrique
5. en Europe
6. en Océanie

C Associations. Travaillez avec un(e) partenaire pour trouver quel pays de chaque groupe ne va pas avec les autres. Expliquez pourquoi.

EXEMPLE l'Allemagne, les États-Unis, la France, la Suisse
les États-Unis: Tous les autres sont en Europe.

1. le Canada, l'Argentine, l'Espagne, le Pérou, le Mexique
2. l'Australie, la Polynésie française, la Martinique, le Sénégal
3. la France, les États-Unis, l'Australie, le Royaume-Uni
4. le Sénégal, l'Égypte, le Brésil, l'Algérie, le Maroc
5. la France, la Belgique, le Sénégal, la Suisse, le Mexique

À VOUS!

Avec un(e) partenaire, relisez à haute voix la conversation entre Anaïs et Lucas. Ensuite, changez la conversation pour parler des régions et pays que vous avez visités et de ceux que vous aimeriez visiter.

Note for the conversation. *Adorer* is the only new vocabulary.

Suggestion for the conversation. Have students listen to the conversation with books closed for the answers to these questions. **1.** Quels pays est-ce que Lucas a visités? **2.** Quels pays est-ce qu'Anaïs aimerait visiter?

In the **Culture Modules** in the video library, see **Vacations**.

Supplemental activity. C'est logique? **1.** Je vais aller au Royaume-Uni où on parle anglais. **2.** J'adore la plage et je vais passer mes vacances à la mer. **3.** Je n'aime pas les activités de plein air, alors je vais passer mes vacances à la montagne. **4.** Je préfère rester à l'hôtel mais je vais faire du camping parce que c'est moins cher. **5.** Si tu aimes la mer, tu peux passer tes vacances à Las Vegas. **6.** Je vais aller au Mexique parce que je voudrais visiter un pays francophone.

Quick-reference answers for C. Associations. 1. le Canada: On parle espagnol dans les autres. OR l'Espagne: Tous les autres sont en Amérique. **2.** le Sénégal: Tous les autres sont des îles. OR l'Australie: On parle français dans les autres. **3.** la France: On parle anglais dans les trois autres. **4.** le Brésil: Tous les autres sont en Afrique. **5.** le Mexique: Tous les autres sont francophones.

You can find a list of the new words from this *Compétence* on page 381 and access the audio online.

 PowerPoint 9-11

SAYING WHERE YOU ARE GOING

Les expressions géographiques

When a place name is used as the subject or object of a verb, you generally need to use the definite article with continents, countries, states, and provinces, but not with cities. Most continents, countries, states, and provinces ending in **-e** are feminine, whereas most others are masculine. **Le Mexique** and **le Royaume-Uni** are exceptions.

J'adore **l'**Europe. **La** France est très belle. Nous allons visiter Londres, Paris et Nice. J'aimerais aussi voir **les** États-Unis: **la** Californie, **le** Texas et **la** Floride.

To say *to* or *in* with a geographical location, the preposition you use varies.

to / in

à	with cities		à Paris
aux	with any plural country or region		aux États-Unis
en	with any feminine country or region and with any masculine one beginning with a vowel		en France / en Ontario
au	with any masculine country or region beginning with a consonant		au Canada

✓ Pour vérifier

1. With which one of the following do you generally not use a definite article when it is the subject or direct object of a verb: cities, states, provinces, countries, or continents? Would you use **le, la, l',** or **les** before the following place names:

_____ Italie, _____ Antilles, _____ Ohio, _____ Japon, _____ France?

2. Which countries, states, or provinces are generally feminine? masculine?

3. How do you say *to* or *in* with a city? with a feminine country? with a masculine country beginning with a vowel sound? with a masculine country beginning with a consonant? with plural countries?

Note *de grammaire*

1. The following places are exceptions to the rule that countries and states ending in **-e** are feminine: **le Royaume-Uni, le Mexique, le Delaware, le Maine, le New Hampshire, le Nouveau-Mexique, le Rhode Island, le Tennessee.**

2. You also say **dans le** with masculine states (**dans le Vermont**).

3. You say **(dans) l'état de New York** and **(dans) l'état de Washington** to clarify that you are talking about the states rather than the cities with the same names.

Supplemental activities. A. Quels pays ont une frontière *(border)* avec… ? **1.** les États-Unis (le Canada, le Mexique) **2.** la France (l'Espagne, Andorre, la Belgique, le Luxembourg, l'Allemagne, la Suisse, l'Italie, Monaco) **3.** le Canada (les États-Unis) **B.** Combien de pays est-ce que vous pouvez nommer en Asie / en Europe / en Amérique du Nord / en Amérique du Sud / en Afrique? **C.** Play a chain game. Start off by saying **Nous allons faire le tour du monde. Nous allons en France et ensuite…** Each student lists all the places named before and adds another. Check that the correct preposition is used with each country.

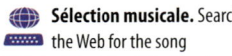 **Sélection musicale.** Search the Web for the song **"Sénégal fast-food"** by Amadou & Mariam to enjoy a musical selection illustrating the use of this structure.

A C'est connu!
D'abord, mettez la forme convenable de l'article défini devant le nom de chaque pays. Ensuite, demandez à votre partenaire quel pays est connu *(known)* pour les choses indiquées.

_____ Royaume-Uni _____ Égypte _____ Suisse
_____ Colombie _____ États-Unis _____ France
_____ Mexique _____ Italie _____ Brésil

EXEMPLE —Quel pays est connu pour le café?
—La Colombie.

Quel pays est connu pour… ?

1. le fromage et le vin
2. le carnaval
3. le chocolat
4. le thé
5. les spaghetti
6. les pyramides
7. la musique rock
8. le sphinx

B Leçon de géographie.
Votre ami(e) n'est pas très fort(e) en géographie et il/elle vous pose des questions. Répondez-lui. D'abord, donnez la préposition convenable pour dire *to / in* avec chaque pays. Ensuite, jouez les deux rôles avec votre partenaire.

EXEMPLE Londres (_____ Royaume-Uni, _____ Canada)
—Londres se trouve *(is located)* au Royaume-Uni ou au Canada?
—Londres se trouve au Royaume-Uni.

1. Tokyo (_____ Chine, _____ Japon)
2. Mexico (_____ Mexique, _____ Pérou)
3. Moscou (_____ Italie, _____ Russie)
4. Berlin (_____ Croatie, _____ Allemagne)
5. Hanoi (_____ Viêt Nam, _____ Chine)
6. Alger (_____ Algérie, _____ Maroc)

7. Le Caire (_____ Maroc, _____ Égypte)
8. Dakar (_____ Sénégal, _____ Côte d'Ivoire)
9. La Nouvelle-Orléans (_____ États-Unis, _____ Irlande)
10. Abidjan (_____ Côte d'Ivoire, _____ Sénégal)

C C'est où? Devinez où dans le monde francophone se trouvent *(are located)* ces sites touristiques.

Quick-reference answers for C. C'est où?
1. à Bruxelles, en Belgique **2.** à Québec, au Canada **3.** à Fès, au Maroc **4.** à Papeete, en Polynésie française **5.** à Dakar, au Sénégal

EXEMPLE Le château de Versailles
Le château de Versailles se trouve à Versailles en France.

Dakar (Sénégal)   Versailles (France)
Bruxelles (Belgique) Fès (Maroc)
Québec (Canada)   Papeete (Polynésie française)

Le château de Versailles

1.
La Grand-Place

4.
Le marché de Papeete

2.
Le Château Frontenac

3.
La Médina

5.
La Grande Mosquée

VIDÉOREPRISE

Les Stagiaires

See the **Résumé de grammaire** section at the end of each chapter for a review of all the grammar of the chapter.

Rappel!
Dans l'épisode précédent de la vidéo, Amélie a parlé avec Rachid du restaurant où elle a dîné avec Matthieu.

Dans l'**Épisode 9** de la vidéo **Les Stagiaires**, M. Vieilledent fait des projets pour des vacances en Martinique. Avant de regarder l'épisode, faites ces exercices pour réviser ce que vous avez appris dans le **Chapitre 9**.

The entire **Vidéoreprise** section is designed to be a pre-viewing series for the video, as well as a chapter review that can be used independently from the video. There are also additional grammar review exercises on the Instructor's Companion Website and on iLrn.

A Qu'est-ce qu'on fait? Avant de décider où aller en vacances, M. Vieilledent parle à ses amis de ce qu'il pourrait faire dans les différents endroits où il pense peut-être aller. Avec un(e) partenaire, faites une liste de ce qu'il pourrait faire dans les endroits suivants: **dans une grande ville, à la mer, à la montagne.**

EXEMPLE dans une grande ville
Dans une grande ville, il pourrait profiter des activités culturelles...

Follow-ups for **B. Destinations**. **A.** Dites l'endroit que vous préféreriez visiter pour chaque proposition. **EXEMPLE —On va au Sénégal ou en Égypte? —Allons en Égypte! 1.** On va au Maroc ou en Algérie? **2.** On va aux Antilles ou en Polynésie française? **3.** On va au Canada ou au Mexique? **4.** On va en France ou en Suisse? **5.** On va en Argentine ou au Brésil? **6.** On va en Allemagne ou au Royaume-Uni? **7.** On va en Israël ou en Chine? **8.** On va au Japon ou en Grèce? **B.** Questions orales. **1.** Dans quels pays avez-vous voyagé? Quels pays voulez-vous visiter? Pourquoi? **2.** Dans quelles villes avez-vous habité? Quelles grandes villes avez-vous visitées? Est-ce que vous aimeriez habiter dans ces villes? Pourquoi (pas)? **3.** Qu'est-ce qu'on peut faire en vacances à Washington, D.C.? au Colorado? en Floride?

B Destinations. Tout le monde à Technovert parle des vacances. Complétez chaque espace avec la préposition appropriée (**en, au, aux**).

EXEMPLE Christophe veut aller **au** Japon parce qu'il adore les mangas.

1. Matthieu veut aller _____ États-Unis pour pratiquer son anglais.
2. Rachid est marocain. Il est né _____ Maroc. Il a déjà voyagé _____ Algérie et _____ Égypte.
3. Amélie aime passer les vacances d'hiver _____ Suisse.
4. M. Vieilledent va bientôt partir pour la Martinique, _____ Antilles.

C En Martinique. M. Vieilledent dit à Camille qu'il va partir en vacances. Complétez les phrases suivantes en mettant les verbes au futur dans l'espace le plus logique.

EXEMPLE (être, prendre) Je **prendrai** des vacances à la fin de ce mois, alors je ne **serai** pas au bureau.

1. (partir, rentrer) Je _____ pour la Martinique le quinze et je _____ le vingt-neuf.
2. (arriver, décider, visiter) Je _____ peut-être la Guadeloupe aussi, mais je _____ ça quand j'_____ en Martinique.
3. (être, faire) Céline _____ mon travail et elle _____ responsable du bureau pendant mon absence.
4. (pouvoir, lire) Je _____ mes mails pendant les vacances et vous _____ aussi me téléphoner.

D Renseignements. M. Vieilledent parle à Camille de son voyage en Martinique. Complétez chaque phrase avec la forme correcte du verbe **savoir** ou **connaître**.

1. Vous _____ à quel hôtel je vais descendre en Martinique?
2. _____-vous un bon site Web où on peut comparer des hôtels?
3. Je ne _____ pas la région. Ce sera mon premier voyage aux Antilles.
4. Je _____ qu'il y a des plantations de café que je voudrais voir.
5. _____-vous combien d'heures dure (lasts) le vol d'ici en Martinique?

E Un mail. Lisez la conversation suivante entre Céline et Amélie et complétez-la avec la forme correcte du verbe indiqué entre parenthèses.

CÉLINE: Qu'est-ce que tu 1 (lire)?
AMÉLIE: C'est un mail de Matthieu.
CÉLINE: Vous 2 (s'écrire) beaucoup de mails, on dirait, non?
AMÉLIE: Oui, Matthieu m' 3 (écrire) souvent. Il est un peu timide quand on est face à face et il 4 (dire) plus facilement ce qu'il pense dans un mail.
CÉLINE: Alors, ça devient sérieux entre vous deux si vous 5 (se dire) tous vos secrets.
AMÉLIE: Je ne lui 6 (dire) pas encore tous mes secrets,... mais je le trouve sympa.

F Interactions. Matthieu pense souvent à Amélie et rêve de leur relation. Décrivez tout ce que Matthieu fait dans ses rêves en faisant des phrases avec les verbes suivants et le pronom convenable, **la (l')** ou **lui**.

EXEMPLES écouter avec attention quand elle parle
Il l'écoute avec attention quand elle parle.
envoyer beaucoup de textos
Il lui envoie beaucoup de textos.

1. parler de tout
2. téléphoner tous les jours
3. inviter à sortir le week-end
4. retrouver en ville
5. acheter des fleurs *(flowers)*
6. dire tous ses secrets

Maintenant parlez à un(e) autre étudiant(e) de sa relation avec son meilleur ami (sa meilleure amie). Posez des questions avec les verbes précédents et le pronom **te (t')** comme dans les exemples.

EXEMPLES écouter avec attention quand elle parle
—**Est-ce que ton meilleur ami (ta meilleure amie) t'écoute avec attention quand tu parles?**
—**Il/Elle m'écoute en général.**

Suggestion for the video. Tell students not to worry about understanding every word, but to use what they do know and the context to guess what is being said. The video is available on DVD and on iLrn. The videoscript is available on the Instructor's Companion Website, www.cengage.com/french/horizons6e, and on iLrn.

Access the Video **Les Stagiaires** on **iLrn**.

▶ **Épisode 9: J'ai acheté vos billets**

AVANT LA VIDÉO
Dans ce clip, Camille aide M. Vieilledent à choisir un hôtel pour son voyage en Martinique et elle lui donne les renseignements sur les réservations pour son billet d'avion. Avant de regarder l'épisode, imaginez quel genre d'hôtel M. Vieilledent pourrait préférer et les services qu'il aimerait y trouver.

APRÈS LA VIDÉO
Regardez le clip et répondez aux questions suivantes:
- Quel genre d'hôtel est-ce que M. Vieilledent a choisi?
- À quelle heure partira son vol pour la Martinique et à quelle heure arrivera-t-il?

LECTURE ET COMPOSITION

LECTURE

POUR MIEUX LIRE:
Understanding words with multiple meanings

You are going to read an extract from a work by Dany Bébel-Gisler (1935–2003), whose stories depict the culture of the Antilles. As you will find in this reading, words often have more than one meaning. Learning to be flexible about the meanings of words will help you read more easily. Consider the multiple meanings of these words.

apprendre	*to learn*	*to teach*
la terre	*the ground*	*the earth*
serrer	*to squeeze*	*to wrap around*
une berceuse	*a lullaby*	*a rocking chair*
soigner	*to care for*	*to treat*
frais (fraîche)	*cool*	*fresh*
finir	*to finish*	**finir par** *to end up*
compter	*to count, to plan*	**compter sur** *to depend on, to count on*

Quel sens? Traduisez les phrases suivantes. Choisissez selon le contexte le sens le plus logique pour les mots en italique. Voir la liste ci-dessus. *(See the above list.)*

1. Ma grand-mère *m'a appris* à ne pas trop *compter sur* les autres.
2. Elle m'a appris le travail de *la terre*, à reconnaître les plantes qui *soignent* les maladies.
3. Je *serre* ma tête *(head)* avec ce madras [a type of Caribbean scarf].
4. Quand ma grand-mère avait la tête *fraîche*, elle s'asseyait *(used to sit)* dans sa *berceuse*.
5. Ils *finissaient par* devenir riches.

Ma grand-mère m'a appris à ne pas compter sur les yeux des autres pour dormir

Je suis restée avec grand-mère moins longtemps qu'avec maman. Maman était en meilleure santé, elle ne buvait pas, mais grand-mère a plus fait pour moi que maman. Elle m'a beaucoup appris. Et surtout à ne pas compter sur les yeux des autres pour dormir.

Elle m**'a enseigné** le travail de la terre, à organiser un jardin, à planter des légumes. À reconnaître aussi les plantes qui soignent, celles qui sont bonnes pour **le ventre,** pour **la toux,** pour **les blessures.**

[Quand **j'ai très mal,** ma grand-mère m'avait donné **un mouchoir.** Alors je prends ce mouchoir – ce que l'on appelle un madras chez nous ici – et je serre **ma tête** avec ce madras et **je me sens très forte.**]

La nuit venue, quand grand-mère **était d'attaque, debout** sur ses deux pieds, la tête bien fraîche, elle s'asseyait dans sa berceuse et me lançait: *Yékrik!* Je répondais: *Yékrak!* et allais m'installer **sur ses genoux.** Ma petite main dans **la sienne, j'enfouissais** ma tête entre ses deux **seins.** Alors grand-mère me faisait voyager dans **un monde étrange, celui** des contes… J'aimais beaucoup les contes où les **enfants orphelins, pauvres, à force de lutter contre la misère,** de marcher, de marcher, de marcher, **d'employer la ruse comme Compère Lapin,** finissaient, une fois grands, par devenir riches et respectés par tous.

In the **Culture Modules** in the video library, see **Francophone Literature.**

Dany Bébel-Gisler, À la recherche d'une odeur de grand-mère © Éditions Jasor, 2000.

---

a enseigné taught   **le ventre** the belly   **la toux** coughing   **les blessures** injuries   **j'ai très mal** I hurt very badly   **un mouchoir** a handkerchief   **ma tête** my head   **je me sens très forte** I feel very strong   **était d'attaque, debout** was feeling fit, standing   **Yékrik! Yékrak!** a cry used to begin a story   **sur ses genoux** on her lap   **la sienne** hers   **j'enfouissais** I buried   **seins** breasts   **un monde étrange, celui** a strange world, the one   **enfants orphelins, pauvres** orphaned children, poor   **à force de lutter contre la misère** by fighting poverty   **d'employer la ruse comme Compère Lapin** using trickery like Compère Lapin (equivalent of Brer Rabbit)

Compréhension

1. Avec qui est-ce que la petite fille aimait passer son temps? Pourquoi?
2. Qu'est-ce qu'elle a appris de sa grand-mère?
3. Quelle sorte de contes est-ce qu'elle aimait?

COMPOSITION

POUR MIEUX ÉCRIRE:
Revising what you write

Editing and revising what you write is an important final step in the writing process. Once you finish a composition, reread it and make sure you have an introductory and a concluding sentence and that your sentences and paragraphs are clear and well organized. Then, check each sentence against this checklist:

- Are the verbs in the proper form for the subject and the tense?
- Do all of your adjectives agree (masculine, feminine, singular, plural) with the nouns they modify?
- Are all the words spelled correctly (including accents) and do the nouns have the correct article (**un, une, le, du, de,…**), possessive adjective (**mon, ton, ses,…**),…?
- Did you use the correct forms of the prepositions **de (du, de la,…)** and **à (au, à la,…)**?

Révisons! Lisez ce paragraphe. D'abord, trouvez une phrase pour commencer le paragraphe et une autre pour le terminer. Ensuite, corrigez les 16 erreurs *(errors)* (marqués en italique) dans le paragraphe.

Philippe préfère *voyagé* à l'étranger, mais Marie préfère *reste* dans son propre *(own)* pays. Quand ils *voyage* ensemble, Philippe passe très peu *du* temps *au* hôtel mais Marie aime passer toutes les soirées dans *son* chambre. Philippe préfère visiter une *grand* ville et profiter *de les* activités culturelles. Marie préfère les activités de plein air et elle aime passer *sa* vacances à la *montage* ou à la *mère*. L'année *prochain*, ils visiteront Nice *ou* Philippe *iront au* musées et Marie passera *sa* temps à la plage.

Un itinéraire

Imaginez que votre classe de français va faire un voyage d'une semaine dans un pays francophone. Écrivez une description détaillée du voyage que la classe fera ensemble. Dans la description, donnez les renseignements suivants:

- où vous irez, quand vous partirez et quand vous reviendrez
- comment vous voyagerez et combien coûtera le voyage par personne
- où vous descendrez et où vous prendrez les repas
- ce que vous ferez chaque jour de la semaine

N'oubliez pas de relire votre composition et de la réviser si nécessaire.

iLrn: Share It!

Process-writing follow-up for *Un itinéraire*. Comparez votre itinéraire et celui d'un(e) partenaire. Ensuite, préparez une conversation basée sur cette situation: Un agent de voyages décrit les deux itinéraires à un client qui fait des projets de vacances. Le client lui pose des questions sur chaque voyage et choisit l'un des deux.

COMPARAISONS CULTURELLES

LA CULTURE CRÉOLE AUX ANTILLES

La culture **antillaise** est une culture créole qui reflète l'histoire de ces îles et la diversité de leurs peuples. La majorité des habitants sont les descendants d'**esclaves africains amenés** dans ces îles pour travailler dans les plantations. Il y a aussi des Amérindiens, des Indiens, des Chinois, des békés (les descendants des premiers **colons** français), des métros (les Français plus récemment arrivés d'Europe) et bien d'autres.

Le français est la langue officielle des Antilles françaises mais la population locale parle aussi créole. Le créole antillais est **un mélange de** français, de langues **indigènes** et africaines, d'espagnol, de portugais, d'anglais et de hindi. D'origine une langue orale, il y a de nos jours un fort mouvement littéraire créole et un mouvement de **créolité** pour encourager et protéger la langue et la culture créoles.

Aux Antilles, les fêtes traditionnelles sont nombreuses. Le Tour des Yoles Rondes au mois d'août est une fête très populaire en Martinique: une semaine de compétition avec les bateaux typiques de l'île. C'est aussi l'occasion de **déguster** des plats antillais accompagnés de rhum dans une ambiance de musique et de fête.

La cuisine créole antillaise est un mélange délicieux de fruits tropicaux, de poissons et fruits de mer, de rhum et d'**épices d'Inde**, avec des influences africaines et françaises.

La Fête des **Cusinières** est une grande tradition guadeloupéenne. Au mois d'août, à l'occasion de la St Laurent, **patron** des cuisinières, 200 cuisinières **vêtues** de leurs plus belles robes et **parées** de leurs plus beaux **bijoux,** se rendent en procession à la cathédrale de Pointe-à-Pitre. Elles portent des **paniers remplis de** plats typiquement créoles (**écrevisses, boudin…**) pour **les faire bénir**. Après **la messe, elles défilent** dans les rues, puis passent à table. La fête se termine le soir avec le Bal des Cuisinières.

---

antillaise of the Antilles   **esclaves africains amenés** African slaves brought   **des colons** colonists   **un mélange de** a mixture of   **indigènes** indigenous   **créolité** "Creoleness"   **déguster** to savor   **épices d'Inde** Indian spices   **Cuisinières** Cooks   **patron** patron saint   **vêtues** dressed   **parées** adorned   **bijoux** jewels   **paniers remplis de** baskets filled with   **écrevisses** crawfish   **boudin** blood sausage   **les faire bénir** to have them blessed   **la messe** the mass   **elles défilent** they parade

Le créole, c'est plus qu'une langue, c'est «également une façon de vivre, et l'histoire d'un peuple, évoquant à la fois l'Afrique, l'esclavage, mais aussi la danse, la musique, les îles, la fête... »[1]

La musique et la danse antillaises, **dérivées d'**un mélange de **sons** et de rythmes européens, américains et africains, reflètent l'histoire des îles caraïbes et sont connues partout dans le monde: le zouk, le zouk-love, la biguine, la Cadence-lypso et d'autres. **Parmi** les artistes antillais les plus connus sont Expérience 7, Zouk Machine et Kassav'.

Compréhension

1. La majorité des habitants des Antilles sont de quelle origine?
2. Quelle est la langue officielle des Antilles françaises? Quelle autre langue est-ce que la population locale parle?
3. Par définition une langue créole est une langue formée d'une combinaison de plusieurs langues. Le créole antillais est un mélange de quelles langues?
4. Comment s'appelle le mouvement qui a pour but *(goal)* la préservation et le développement de la culture créole?
5. Aimeriez-vous mieux participer au Tour des Yoles Rondes ou à la Fête des Cuisinières? Pourquoi?
6. Comment est la cuisine créole?
7. La musique et la danse antillaises sont dérivées d'un mélange de sons et de rythmes de quelles origines?
8. Quelles sont les cultures importantes dans votre région? Est-ce qu'il y a des traditions, des fêtes, de la musique ou une cuisine que vous associez à chacune?

[1] http://www.webcaraibes.com/guadeloupe/culture.htm

une façon *a way*   **évoquant à la fois** *evoking at the same time*   **l'esclavage** *slavery*   **dérivées de** *derived from*
sons *sounds*   **Parmi** *Among*

RÉSUMÉ DE GRAMMAIRE

THE FUTURE TENSE (LE FUTUR)

Use the future tense to say what someone *will* do. Form it by adding the bold-faced endings below to the same stem that you used for the conditional. For most verbs, it is the infinitive, but drop the final **e** of infinitives ending with **-re**.

Je prendrai des vacances en été.
Tu resteras ici?
Tu partiras tout seul?
Mes parents voyageront avec moi.

VISITER	CONNAÎTRE	FINIR
je visiter**ai**	je connaîtr**ai**	je finir**ai**
tu visiter**as**	tu connaîtr**as**	tu finir**as**
il/elle/on visiter**a**	il/elle/on connaîtr**a**	il/elle/on finir**a**
nous visiter**ons**	nous connaîtr**ons**	nous finir**ons**
vous visiter**ez**	vous connaîtr**ez**	vous finir**ez**
ils/elles visiter**ont**	ils/elles connaîtr**ont**	ils/elles finir**ont**

The following verbs have irregular stems.

J'irai en Europe.
Combien de temps **serez-vous** en Europe?
On reviendra après trois semaines.

-r-		-vr- / -dr-		-rr-	
aller:	ir-	devoir:	devr-	voir:	verr-
être:	ser-	pleuvoir:	pleuvr-	pouvoir:	pourr-
faire:	fer-	vouloir:	voudr-	mourir:	mourr-
avoir:	aur-	venir:	viendr-	courir:	courr-
savoir:	saur-	devenir:	deviendr-	envoyer:	enverr-
		revenir:	reviendr-		
		obtenir:	obtiendr-		

S'il peut, mon frère **ira** en vacances avec nous.
Il décidera quand **on saura** la date exacte de notre départ.

As in English, use the future tense in *if / then* sentences to say what will happen if something else occurs. Use the present tense in the clause with **si**. Unlike English, use the future in French in clauses with **quand** referring to the future. English has the present tense in such clauses.

THE VERBS *DIRE*, *LIRE*, AND *ÉCRIRE*

The verbs **dire, lire,** and **écrire** are irregular in the present tense and the **passé composé (j'ai dit, j'ai lu, j'ai écrit)**. As with other verbs, use the stem for **nous** in the present tense to form the imperfect (**je disais, je lisais, j'écrivais**). Obtain the future / conditional stem by dropping the final **e** of the infinitive (**je dirai, je lirai, j'écrirai**).

Est-ce que **tu lis** tes mails quand tu voyages?
J'écris à mes amis et je leur montre des photos de mon voyage.
Mes parents disent que la Méditerranée est très jolie.

DIRE	LIRE	ÉCRIRE
je **dis**	je **lis**	j' **écris**
tu **dis**	tu **lis**	tu **écris**
il/elle/on **dit**	il/elle/on **lit**	il/elle/on **écrit**
nous **disons**	nous **lisons**	nous **écrivons**
vous **dites**	vous **lisez**	vous **écrivez**
ils/elles **disent**	ils/elles **lisent**	ils/elles **écrivent**

THE VERBS *SAVOIR* AND *CONNAÎTRE*

Savoir and **connaître** both mean *to know*. Use **savoir** when *to know* is followed by a verb, a question word **(qui, où…)**, or by **si, que,** or **ce que,** or to say that one knows a language. When *to know* is followed by a noun, use **savoir** to say one *knows a fact or information*, and **connaître** to say one is *familiar with a person, place, or thing*.

	SAVOIR		CONNAÎTRE
	je **sais**		je **connais**
	tu **sais**		tu **connais**
	il/elle/on **sait**		il/elle/on **connaît**
	nous **savons**		nous **connaissons**
	vous **savez**		vous **connaissez**
	ils/elles **savent**		ils/elles **connaissent**
PASSÉ COMPOSÉ:	j'ai **su** *(I found out)*		j'ai **connu** *(I met)*
IMPARFAIT:	je **savais** *(I knew)*		je **connaissais** *(I knew)*
CONDITIONNEL:	je **saurais**		je **connaîtrais**
FUTUR:	je **saurai**		je **connaîtrai**

Quelles langues **sais-tu**?
Je sais parler français et **mes parents savent** l'allemand.

Savez-vous si vous allez visiter l'Allemagne?
On ira à Berlin, où **mes parents connaissent** beaucoup de gens.

Je ne connais pas du tout l'Europe. Est-ce que **tu connais** bien l'histoire de la région?

DIRECT AND INDIRECT OBJECT PRONOUNS

Direct object pronouns replace nouns that are the direct object of the verb. Indirect object pronouns replace nouns that are the indirect object of the verb. Generally, indirect objects are people or animals, not things, and they follow the preposition **à.** They often are used with verbs indicating communication or exchanges **(parler à, téléphoner à, dire à, écrire à, demander à, rendre visite à, donner à).**

DIRECT OBJECT PRONOUNS				INDIRECT OBJECT PRONOUNS			
me (m')	*me*	**nous**	*us*	**me (m')**	*(to) me*	**nous**	*(to) us*
te (t')	*you*	**vous**	*you*	**te (t')**	*(to) you*	**vous**	*(to) you*
le (l')	*him, it* (m)	**les**	*them*	**lui**	*(to) him*	**leur**	*(to) them*
la (l')	*her, it* (f)			**lui**	*(to) her*		

Est-ce que tu **m'**écriras si je **te** donne mon adresse mail?

Mon frère habite à Paris. Je vais **te** donner son numéro de téléphone et tu pourras **lui** téléphoner quand tu seras en France.

Both direct and indirect object pronouns have the same placement rules. They go immediately before the infinitive if there is one in the same clause. If not, they go before the conjugated verb. In the **passé composé,** they go before the auxiliary verb. The past participle agrees with direct object pronouns, but not with indirect objects.

Les amis de mes parents **nous** ont demandé de **leur** rendre visite. Mes parents ne **les** ont pas vus depuis vingt ans, la dernière fois qu'ils **leur** ont rendu visite.

GEOGRAPHICAL EXPRESSIONS

Use the definite article with names of continents, countries, states, and provinces used as the subject or object of a verb, but not with cities. Most continents, countries, states, and provinces ending in **e** are feminine, whereas most others are masculine.

Je voudrais visiter **les** États-Unis, **le** Canada et **la** Colombie.

To say *to* or *in* with a geographical location, use…

à	with cities
aux	with any plural country or region
en	with any feminine country or region and with any masculine one beginning with a vowel sound
au	with any masculine country or region beginning with a consonant

Pendant notre voyage, on ira à Berlin **en** Allemagne, à Copenhague **au** Danemark, à Amsterdam **aux** Pays-Bas et à Paris et à Nice **en** France.

Résumé de grammaire | *trois cent soixante-dix-neuf*

VOCABULAIRE

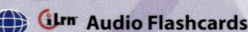

COMPÉTENCE 1

Talking about vacation

NOMS MASCULINS

le ballet	the ballet
un endroit	a place
l'opéra	the opera
un Parisien	a Parisian
le paysage	the landscape, the scenery
un site	a site, a spot

NOMS FÉMININS

une île	an island
la mer	the sea
une Parisienne	a Parisian
une terrasse	a terrace

EXPRESSIONS VERBALES

admirer	to admire
bronzer	to tan
compter	to count on, to plan on
courir	to run
goûter	to taste
profiter de	to take advantage of

ADJECTIFS

assis(e)	seated
exotique	exotic
historique	historic
local(e) (*mpl* locaux)	local
touristique	touristic
tropical(e) (*mpl* tropicaux)	tropical

DIVERS

Ça te plaira.	You'll like it.

COMPÉTENCE 2

Preparing for a trip

NOMS MASCULINS

un article	an article
un billet (d'avion)	a (plane) ticket
un blog	a blog
le climat	the climate
le départ	the departure
un guide	a guidebook, a guide
un magazine	a magazine
un passeport	a passport
un poème	a poem
des préparatifs	preparations
un roman	a novel
un voisin	a neighbor

NOMS FÉMININS

une arrivée	an arrival
une carte postale	a postcard
la douane	customs
une histoire	a story
une lettre	a letter
une rédaction	a composition
une région	a region, an area
une valise	a suitcase
une voisine	a neighbor

EXPRESSIONS VERBALES

changer	to change, to exchange
décrire	to describe
dire	to say, to tell
donner à manger à	to feed
écrire	to write
faire sa valise	to pack one's bag
s'informer	to find out information
lire	to read
obtenir	to obtain
passer	to pass (through)
recevoir	to receive
réserver	to reserve

DIVERS

(bien) à l'avance	(well) in advance
à l'étranger	in another country, abroad
Ça lui plaît?	Does he/she like it?
en contact	in contact
extraordinaire	extraordinary, great
leur	(to) them
lui	(to) him, (to) her
me (m')	(to) me

COMPÉTENCE 3

Buying your ticket

NOMS MASCULINS

un agent de voyages	a travel agent
un aller simple	a one-way ticket
un billet aller-retour	a round-trip ticket
un réseau	a network
le retour	the return
les transports en commun	public transportation
un vol	a flight

NOMS FÉMININS

une agence de voyages	a travel agency
une carte bancaire	a bank card, a debit card
une carte de crédit (une carte bleue)	a credit card
la classe économique	economy class, coach
la culture	the culture
la géographie	the geography
l'heure d'arrivée	the arrival time
l'heure de départ	the departure time
l'heure locale	local time
des infos	info
la première classe	first class

EXPRESSIONS VERBALES

connaître	to know, to be familiar with, to be acquainted with
faire une réservation	to make a reservation
reconnaître	to recognize
savoir	to know

DIVERS

Ça te/vous convient?	Does that work for you?
il me (te/nous/vous/lui/leur) faut	I (you/we/you/he [she]/they) need
me	(to) me
nous	(to) us
te	(to) you
vous	(to) you

COMPÉTENCE 4

Deciding where to go on a trip

NOMS MASCULINS

le Brésil	Brazil
le Canada	Canada
le Chili	Chile
un continent	a continent
les États-Unis	the United States
Israël	Israel
le Japon	Japan
le Maroc	Morocco
le Mexique	Mexico
le Moyen-Orient	the Middle East
l'Ontario	Ontario
le Pérou	Peru
le Royaume-Uni	the United Kingdom
le Sénégal	Senegal
le Texas	Texas
le Viêt Nam	Vietnam

NOMS FÉMININS

l'Afrique	Africa
l'Algérie	Algeria
l'Allemagne	Germany
l'Amérique centrale	Central America
l'Amérique du Nord	North America
l'Amérique du Sud	South America
les Antilles	the West Indies
l'Argentine	Argentina
l'Asie	Asia
l'Australie	Australia
la Belgique	Belgium
la Californie	California
la Chine	China
la Colombie	Colombia
la Côte d'Ivoire	Ivory Coast
la Croatie	Croatia
l'Égypte	Egypt
l'Espagne	Spain
l'Europe	Europe
la Floride	Florida
la France	France
la Grèce	Greece
la Guyane	French Guiana
l'Irlande	Ireland
l'Italie	Italy
la Nouvelle-Calédonie	New Caledonia
l'Océanie	Oceania
la Polynésie française	French Polynesia
la Russie	Russia
la Suisse	Switzerland

DIVERS

adorer	to adore, to love

Aux Antilles
À l'hôtel

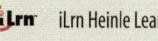 iLrn Heinle Learning Center
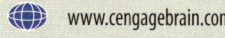 www.cengagebrain.com
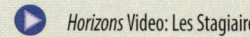 *Horizons* Video: Les Stagiaires
 Audio

 Internet web search
 Pair work
 Group work

10

COMPÉTENCE

1 Deciding where to stay
Le logement

Giving general advice
  Les expressions impersonnelles et l'infinitif

Stratégies et Compréhension auditive
  • **Pour mieux comprendre:** *Anticipating a response*
  • **Compréhension auditive:** *À la réception*

2 Going to the doctor
Chez le médecin

Giving advice to someone in particular
  Les expressions impersonnelles et les verbes réguliers au subjonctif

Giving advice
  Les verbes irréguliers au subjonctif

3 Running errands on a trip
Des courses en voyage

Expressing wishes and emotions
  Les expressions d'émotion et de volonté et le subjonctif

Saying who you want to do something
  Le subjonctif ou l'infinitif?

4 Giving directions
Les indications

Telling how to go somewhere
  Reprise de l'impératif et les pronoms avec l'impératif

Vidéoreprise *Les Stagiaires*

Lecture et Composition
  • **Pour mieux lire:** *Using word families*
  • **Lecture:** *Avis de l'hôtel*
  • **Pour mieux écrire:** *Making suggestions*
  • **Composition:** *Suggestions de voyage!*

Comparaisons culturelles *La musique francophone: les influences africaines et antillaises*

Résumé de grammaire

Vocabulaire

trois cent quatre-vingt-trois | **383**

LES ANTILLES

PowerPoint 10-1

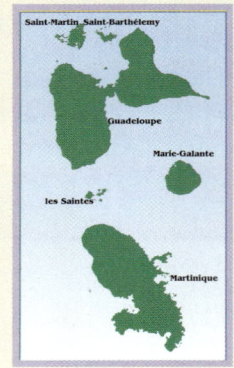

Les Antilles françaises **comprennent** la Martinique, la Guadeloupe et son **archipel**, Saint-Barthélemy et Saint-Martin. La Guadeloupe et la Martinique sont des **départements d'outre-mer** de la France, ce qui donne à leurs **citoyens** tous les **droits** et toutes les responsabilités des citoyens français. Ces deux îles offrent donc aux visiteurs **un monde** caraïbe **à la française**. Est-ce que vous aimeriez les visiter? Qu'est-ce qu'un touriste pourrait y faire?

La Martinique est connue pour la beauté de ses paysages et **la chaleur** de son peuple.

Fort-de-France, **le chef-lieu** de la Martinique, est une ville **pleine d'**activité.

Saint-Pierre, son **ancien** chef-lieu, a été **détruit** par une éruption volcanique en 1902. Près de 30 000 personnes sont mortes. Un seul habitant **a survécu**, un prisonnier protégé par les murs de la prison. **Au milieu de** la ville d'aujourd'hui, on peut voir des ruines de l'ancienne ville.

Additional information. The islands of the Guadeloupe archipelago (Marie-Galante, les Saintes, la Désirade and Petite-Terre) are administered by Guadeloupe, but the islands of Saint-Martin and Saint-Barthélemy are **collectivités territoriales,** separate from Guadeloupe.

comprennent include   **archipel** archipelago   **départements d'outre-mer** overseas departments   **citoyens** citizens   **droits** rights   **un monde** a world   **à la française** French-style   **la chaleur** the warmth   **le chef-lieu** the administrative center   **pleine de** full of   **ancien** former   **détruit** destroyed   **a survécu** survived   **Au milieu de** In the middle of

384 trois cent quatre-vingt-quatre | CHAPITRE 10

La Guadeloupe est composée de deux îles en forme de **papillon:** Grande-Terre et Basse-Terre.

Grande-Terre a un climat sec et aride. Ses plages sont couvertes d'un sable blanc comme le marbre. Cette île est recouverte de nombreuses plantations de canne à sucre.

Basse-Terre est montagneuse et volcanique. C'est une île au climat tropical recouverte de forêt dense et humide. Pour protéger sa biodiversité unique, un parc national a été établi en 1989. La Soufrière, un volcan actif, domine la partie sud de l'île.

Quick-reference answers for Le savez-vous? **1.** Martinique, Guadeloupe **2.** départements **3.** Fort-de-France, une éruption volcanique **4.** Basse-Terre, Grande-Terre **5.** Pointe-à-Pitre, (la ville de) Basse-Terre

Aux Antilles, on parle français aussi en Haïti. Faites des recherches sur cette région sur Internet. Préparez une présentation sur un aspect de cette région que vous trouvez intéressant.

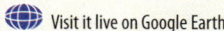

La Guadeloupe

NOMBRE D'HABITANTS:
466 000 (les Guadeloupéens)

CHEF-LIEU *(ADMINISTRATIVE CENTER):* **Basse-Terre**

La Martinique

NOMBRE D'HABITANTS:
409 000 (les Martiniquais)

CHEF-LIEU: **Fort-de-France**

Le savez-vous?

Complétez ces phrases en vous servant des expressions données.

> Basse-Terre   Grande-Terre   Fort-de-France
> Martinique   Guadeloupe   départements
> une éruption volcanique   Pointe-à-Pitre
> la ville de Basse-Terre

1. Les Antilles françaises comprennent la _____, la _____ et son archipel, Saint-Barthélemy et Saint-Martin.

2. Les citoyens de ces deux îles ont tous les droits et toutes les responsabilités des citoyens français parce que la Guadeloupe et la Martinique sont des _____ français.

3. _____ est aujourd'hui le chef-lieu de la Martinique. Son ancien chef-lieu a été détruit par _____.

4. La Guadeloupe est composée de deux îles. _____ est montagneuse et volcanique, mais _____ a un climat sec et aride.

5. _____ est la plus grande ville de la Guadeloupe, mais _____ est son chef-lieu.

Pointe-à-Pitre, la plus grande ville de la Guadeloupe, se trouve sur Grande-Terre.

---

papillon *a butterfly*   **sec** *dry*   **couvertes d'un sable** *covered with a sand*   **le marbre** *marble*   **recouverte de** *covered with*
canne à sucre *sugar cane*   **établi** *established*   **sud** *south*   **se trouve** *is located*

COMPÉTENCE 1

Deciding where to stay

PowerPoint 10-2

LE LOGEMENT

Note culturelle

Les hôtels en France sont répartis en 5 catégories de 1 à 5 étoiles *(stars)*. Un hôtel une étoile est simple et bon marché *(inexpensive)*: la chambre est petite et les W.-C. ne sont pas toujours dans la chambre. L'hôtel n'est pas obligé d'accepter les cartes de crédit. Dans un hôtel trois étoiles, la chambre de taille moyenne vient avec salle de bains, téléphone et télévision. Il y a l'accès Internet dans les parties communes et quelquefois dans les chambres. Un hôtel cinq étoiles est un hôtel de luxe. La chambre vient avec mini-bar, coffre-fort *(a safe)*, accès Internet et télévision avec chaînes internationales. Aux États-Unis, est-ce qu'il y a un système de classement similaire pour les hôtels?

Note de vocabulaire

Les auberges de jeunesse *(youth hostels)* offer inexpensive basic accommodations throughout the world and are good places for meeting other young travelers.

3-17

Warm-up activity. Quand vous partez en vacances, est-ce que vous préférez…? **1.** visiter un pays étranger ou rester dans votre pays **2.** réserver une chambre d'hôtel avant votre départ ou chercher une chambre après votre arrivée **3.** voyager en avion ou en voiture **4.** dire à votre famille où vous allez être ou partir sans rien dire **5.** voyager seul(e), en famille ou avec des amis **6.** avoir beaucoup de bagages ou prendre seulement une valise **7.** préparer vos repas ou manger au restaurant

Note for the conversation. New vocabulary includes all glossed words and **la réception, l'hôtelier (l'hôtelière), privé(e), quelque chose de moins cher, calme, un supplément, recommander.**

Suggestion for the conversation. Have students listen with books closed for the answers to these questions. **1.** Combien coûte la chambre avec salle de bains? **2.** Combien coûte la chambre avec douche? **3.** Quelle chambre est-ce que Lucas a choisie?

Quand vous êtes en vacances, est-ce que vous aimez mieux descendre dans…?

un hôtel (de luxe)

une auberge de jeunesse

un chalet à la montagne

Préférez-vous avoir une chambre… ?

simple ou double / avec balcon

avec ou sans salle de bains et **W.-C.**

avec mini-bar, télé et accès Wi-Fi **gratuit**

Préférez-vous **régler la note en espèces,** par carte bancaire ou par carte de crédit?

Lucas a quitté la Guadeloupe pour aller passer quelques jours en Martinique. Il arrive à la réception d'un hôtel.

LUCAS:	Bonjour, monsieur.
L'HÔTELIER:	Bonjour, monsieur.
LUCAS:	Avez-vous une chambre pour ce soir?
L'HÔTELIER:	Eh bien… nous avons une chambre avec salle de bains et W.-C. privés.
LUCAS:	C'est combien la nuit?
L'HÔTELIER:	108 euros, monsieur.
LUCAS:	Vous avez quelque chose de moins cher?
L'HÔTELIER:	Voyons… nous avons une chambre avec douche et **lavabo** à 88 euros, si vous préférez.
LUCAS:	Je préfère une chambre calme.
L'HÔTELIER:	Alors, **il vaut mieux** prendre la chambre avec douche. C'est **côté cour** et il y a moins de **bruit.**

Line art on this page: © Cengage Learning

une auberge de jeunesse *a youth hostel* **une chambre simple** *a single room* **un W.-C.** *a toilet, a restroom* **gratuit** *free* **régler la note** *to pay the bill* **en espèces** *(f) in cash* **un lavabo** *a sink* **il vaut mieux** *it's better* **côté cour** *on the courtyard side* **le bruit** *noise*

386 trois cent quatre-vingt-six | CHAPITRE 10

LUCAS:	Bon, d'accord. Le petit déjeuner est **compris**?
L'HÔTELIER:	Non, monsieur. Il y a un supplément de 6 euros. Il est servi entre sept heures et neuf heures dans la salle à manger.
LUCAS:	Eh bien, je vais prendre la chambre avec douche. Vous préférez que je vous paie maintenant?
L'HÔTELIER:	Non, monsieur. Vous pouvez régler la note à votre départ. Voici **la clé**. C'est la chambre 210. C'est au bout du couloir.
LUCAS:	Y a-t-il un restaurant dans le quartier?
L'HÔTELIER:	Je vous recommande Le Tropical.
LUCAS:	Est-ce qu'il faut réserver?
L'HÔTELIER:	Oui, il vaut mieux.
LUCAS:	Merci, monsieur.
L'HÔTELIER:	**Bon séjour.**

A **Auberges de jeunesse.** À votre avis, est-ce que chacun des aspects suivants de ce genre de logement est un avantage, un inconvénient *(disadvantage)* ou est-ce que ça vous est égal *(you don't care)*?

> C'est un (petit / gros) avantage.   Ça m'est égal.   C'est un (petit / gros) inconvénient.

EXEMPLE Il y a des douches en commun.
   Pour moi, c'est un gros inconvénient. / Ça m'est égal.

1. Ce n'est pas cher.
2. D'habitude, on y rencontre des voyageurs du monde *(world)* entier.
3. On partage souvent une chambre avec des gens qu'on ne connaît pas.
4. Il y a souvent une atmosphère de fête.
5. Il y a quelquefois beaucoup de bruit.
6. On peut rencontrer beaucoup de jeunes célibataires.
7. Généralement, il y a le Wi-Fi gratuit.
8. La décoration et les meubles sont souvent vieillots *(outdated)*.

B **Votre chambre.** Un(e) ami(e) et vous allez passer six jours dans un hôtel en Martinique. Répondez aux questions de l'hôtelier selon vos goûts. Jouez les deux rôles avec un(e) partenaire.

1. Vous voulez une chambre pour combien de personnes?
2. C'est pour combien de nuits?
3. Vous voulez une chambre à deux lits ou avec un grand lit?
4. Vous préférez une chambre avec salle de bains à 125 euros ou sans salle de bains à 85?
5. Voulez-vous prendre le petit déjeuner? Il y a un supplément de 10 euros.
6. Comment voulez-vous régler?
7. C'est à quel nom?

À VOUS!

Avec un(e) partenaire, relisez à haute voix la conversation entre Lucas et l'hôtelier. Ensuite, imaginez que vous allez visiter la Martinique ensemble. Parlez de la sorte de chambre que vous voulez et comment vous allez régler la note.

Une auberge de jeunesse

Follow-up for A. Auberges de jeunesse. Questions orales. **1.** Quand vous partez en vacances, préférez-vous visiter une grande ville, aller à la montagne ou aller à la mer? **2.** Préférez-vous descendre dans un hôtel pas cher, un hôtel de luxe, une auberge de jeunesse ou un chalet à la montagne? **3.** À votre avis, est-ce qu'il vaut mieux réserver une chambre d'hôtel à l'avance ou est-ce qu'il vaut mieux trouver un hôtel à son arrivée pour voir la chambre d'abord? **4.** Préférez-vous une chambre avec mini-bar, balcon et Wi-Fi gratuit ou la chambre la moins chère? **5.** Dans un hôtel, préférez-vous prendre votre petit déjeuner dans votre chambre, dans le restaurant de l'hôtel, dans un autre restaurant ou dans un fast-food? **6.** Préférez-vous régler la note en espèces, par carte bancaire ou par carte de crédit?

You can find a list of the new words from this ***Compétence*** on page 418 and access the audio online.

compris(e) included   **la clé** the key   **Bon séjour.** Enjoy your stay.

GIVING GENERAL ADVICE

 PowerPoint 10-3

✔ Pour vérifier

1. What are two ways to say *it is necessary*? How do you say *it's not necessary*? What does **il ne faut pas** mean? How do you say *it's better? it's important? it's good? it's bad?*

2. When offering general advice, what form of the verb do you use following these impersonal expressions? How do you negate an infinitive?

Note *de grammaire*

1. Note that the expressions that have **être (Il est important / essentiel / bon…)** require the preposition **de (d')** before an infinitive.

2. **C'est bien…** is less formal than **Il est bon…** and is more likely to be used when talking with a friend. You will also hear **C'est important / essentiel / bon…** in less formal conversation.

3. When negating an infinitive, remember to place both parts of a negative expression before it: **Il est important de ne pas perdre la clé.**

Les expressions impersonnelles et l'infinitif

Use the following expressions to give advice and state opinions. When making generalizations, follow them with an infinitive.

Notice that although **il faut** means *it is necessary*, **il ne faut pas** means *one should not* or *one must not*. Use **il n'est pas nécessaire** to say *it is not necessary*.

Il faut	Il faut réserver bien à l'avance.
Il ne faut pas	Il ne faut pas attendre jusqu'au dernier moment.
Il est essentiel (de)	Il est essentiel de vérifier les prix.
Il est nécessaire (de)	Il est nécessaire de confirmer la réservation.
Il n'est pas nécessaire (de)	Il n'est pas nécessaire de payer à l'avance.
Il vaut mieux	Il vaut mieux s'informer sur les hôtels avant.
Il est possible (de)	Il est possible de comparer les prix sur Internet.
Il est préférable (de)	Il est préférable d'être près des transports.
Il est important (de)	Il est important de ne pas perdre la clé.
Il est bon (de)	Il est bon de choisir une chambre calme.
C'est bien (de)…	C'est bien de profiter de la piscine.
Il est mauvais (de)	Il est mauvais de faire trop de bruit.

A **À l'étranger.** Qu'est-ce qu'on doit faire pour être un bon touriste quand on voyage à l'étranger? Complétez chaque phrase avec **il faut, il vaut mieux** ou **il ne faut pas**.

1. _____ apprendre quelques mots de la langue avant de partir.
2. _____ supposer que tout le monde parle sa langue.
3. _____ s'informer sur la culture avant de partir.
4. _____ s'adapter aux différences culturelles.
5. _____ toucher aux objets d'art dans les musées.
6. _____ utiliser le flash pour prendre une photo d'une peinture *(painting)* au musée.
7. _____ demander la permission avant de prendre des photos de quelqu'un.
8. _____ respecter les traditions.
9. _____ faire beaucoup de bruit dans les endroits sacrés *(sacred)*.
10. _____ être poli(e).

B **Préparatifs.** Un ami fait les préparatifs pour un voyage que vous allez faire ensemble. Utilisez un élément de chaque colonne pour lui expliquer ce qu'il faut faire.

EXEMPLE Il vaut mieux réserver une chambre à l'avance.

Il faut	réserver une chambre à l'avance
Il vaut mieux	obtenir les passeports bien à l'avance
Il est bon de	oublier les billets
Il n'est pas bon de	savoir le numéro et l'heure de départ du vol
Il est important de	tout payer par carte de crédit
Il n'est pas important de	choisir une chambre côté rue / cour
Il ne faut pas	faire beaucoup de bruit dans l'hôtel

🌐 **Sélection musicale.** Search the Web for the song **"Il faut tout oublier"** by the zouk artist Jamice to enjoy a musical selection illustrating the use of this structure.

C **Forum de voyages.** Lisez le forum de voyages suivant dans lequel un Français demande des conseils pour un voyage à New York. Ensuite, complétez ces phrases avec des conseils qu'on lui donne.

1. Il vaut mieux…
2. Il est possible de… mais il est difficile.
3. Il faut…
4. Il est préférable de…
5. Il est bon de…
6. C'est bien de…

> Je pense passer un week-end à New York, peut-être vers la fin de l'année. Est-ce que je pourrai trouver un hôtel pas trop cher quand j'arriverai à New York ou est-ce que je ferais mieux de réserver une chambre à l'avance? Merci!

D'abord, un week-end, c'est trop court après un vol de 8 heures! Il vaut mieux rester une semaine (minimum!) – il y a un tas de choses à faire et à voir à NYC! On peut trouver un hôtel sur place, bien sûr, mais ce n'est pas facile, surtout en période de fêtes. En plus, à votre arrivée, l'immigration vous demandera quelle sera votre adresse pendant votre séjour. Il est donc préférable de trouver un hôtel avant votre départ pour ne pas rencontrer de problème. Faites votre réservation en ligne avant votre départ et tout sera réglé! Bon voyage et amusez-vous bien!

Pour un week-end, il est bon de réserver à l'avance pour ne pas perdre de temps en cherchant un hôtel et pour avoir un hôtel près de ce qui vous intéresse, et il vaut mieux réserver de France car toutes les taxes sont comprises = pas de surprise. C'est bien de trouver un hôtel vers Times Square. Si vous voulez visiter Manhattan, c'est parfaitement bien placé.

D **Conseils.** Donnez des conseils sur un forum pour des voyageurs francophones qui vont visiter votre région. Travaillez en petits groupes pour compléter les phrases suivantes. Ensuite, comparez vos suggestions à celles des autres groupes.

EXEMPLE Il est essentiel d'aller **au City Arts Museum.**

1. Il vaut mieux venir au mois de (d')…
2. Il ne faut pas venir au mois de (d')…
3. Il est essentiel de ne pas oublier…
4. Il est bon de descendre à l'hôtel…
5. Pour goûter la cuisine locale, il est bon d'aller au restaurant…
6. Il est essentiel de voir…

Supplemental activities. A. Give students the following French proverbs and have them give the English equivalent. **1.** Il vaut mieux tard que jamais. *Better late than never.* **2.** Il ne faut pas mettre la charrue *(cart)* avant les bœufs. *Don't put the cart before the horse.* **3.** Il vaut mieux prévenir que guérir *(to cure)*. *Prevention is the best medicine. / An ounce of prevention is worth a pound of cure.* **4.** Entre deux maux il faut choisir le moindre. *It's better to choose the lesser of two evils.* **5.** Il ne faut jamais dire jamais. *Never say never.* **6.** Il ne faut pas se fier *(to trust)* aux apparences. *You shouldn't judge a book by its cover.* **7.** Il ne faut pas remettre au lendemain ce qu'on peut faire le jour même. *Don't put off until tomorrow what you can do today.* **8.** Il ne faut pas mettre tous ses œufs dans le même panier. *Don't put all your eggs in the same basket.* **B.** Un nouvel étudiant veut réussir ses études universitaires. Dites-lui si **il vaut mieux** ou si **il ne faut pas** faire ces choses. **EXEMPLES** On copie les réponses des autres étudiants? **Non, il ne faut pas copier les réponses des autres étudiants.** On va toujours en cours? **Oui, il vaut mieux toujours aller en cours.** **1.** On arrive en classe à l'heure? **2.** On va en boîte tous les soirs? **3.** On prépare les examens bien à l'avance? **4.** On dort en classe? **5.** On écoute le professeur? **6.** On fait attention en cours? **7.** On lit le journal en classe? **8.** On prend des notes en cours?

STRATÉGIES ET COMPRÉHENSION AUDITIVE

Script for A. Quel hôtel? 1. Nous avons 132 chambres. Toutes sont climatisées et offrent tout confort. 2. Nous avons aussi des suites. 3. Le restaurant sert des spécialités créoles et françaises. 4. Toutes nos chambres ont une terrasse ou un balcon. 5. Notre style colonial vous charmera. 6. La spécialité de notre restaurant, La Paillote Bleue, est une langouste style créole. 7. Il y a deux bars et deux restaurants. 8. Nous sommes situés à trois kilomètres du bourg du Diamant.

Script for B. Le ton de la voix

1. — Nous cherchons une chambre pour deux nuits.
— J'ai une chambre avec salle de bains à 123 euros la nuit.
— *(Said with shock and disbelief in voice.)* 123 euros la nuit! Vraiment?

2. — Je voudrais une chambre pour une semaine.
— Voyons... J'ai une chambre sans salle de bains pour 75 euros la nuit.
— *(Said with satisfaction in voice.)* Ah... 75 euros la nuit!

3. — Je m'appelle Georges Massé. J'ai réservé une chambre pour trois nuits.
— *(Said with confusion.)* Massé? Ça s'écrit comment?
— M-A-S-S-É... Voici ma carte de crédit.
— *(Said with hesitation in voice.)* Voyons... euh..

Script for À la réception

— Bonjour, monsieur. Nous cherchons une chambre.
— Voyons... il ne reste plus grand-chose. C'est pour combien de nuits?
— C'est pour trois nuits. Nous préférerions avoir une chambre à deux lits si possible.
— J'ai une chambre à 125 euros la nuit.
— *(Said with slight disappointment in voice.)* Vous n'avez pas quelque chose de moins cher?
— Euh, voyons... j'ai une chambre avec un grand lit à 105 euros la nuit.
— Le petit déjeuner est compris?
— Non, madame. Il y a un supplément de sept euros par personne. Il est servi dans votre chambre entre 7h et 9h30.
— La chambre est avec salle de bains, n'est-ce pas?
— Oui, madame.
— Bon, c'est bien. Nous allons la prendre.
— Bon, très bien. Voilà votre clé. Vous avez la chambre 38. C'est au troisième étage au bout du couloir. L'ascenseur est derrière vous, à droite.
— Merci, monsieur.
— Je vous en prie, madame.

POUR MIEUX COMPRENDRE: Anticipating a response

When you cannot understand everything you hear, use what you can understand, as well as non-verbal cues such as circumstances, tone of voice, and written materials such as ads or signs to anticipate what someone will say. Read the two hotel ads at the bottom of this page and on the next page and list five things you learned about each hotel from its ad.

A Quel hôtel? On parle de l'hôtel de l'Anse Bleue ou de l'hôtel Belle Époque?

B Le ton de la voix. Écoutez le début de ces conversations dans un hôtel. Pour chacune, écoutez le ton de la voix *(tone of voice)* pour deviner la suite *(what follows)*, **a** ou **b**.

1. **a.** C'est bien. Nous allons prendre la chambre.
   b. Est-ce que vous avez quelque chose de moins cher?
2. **a.** Nous préférons une chambre avec salle de bains.
   b. Bon, c'est bien. Je vais prendre cette chambre.
3. **a.** Voici votre clé, monsieur. Vous avez la chambre numéro 385.
   b. Je regrette, mais nous n'avons pas de réservation à votre nom.

Compréhension auditive: *À la réception*

Deux touristes arrivent dans un hôtel. Écoutez cette conversation pour déterminer le prix de leur chambre.

À l'hôtel. Écoutez la conversation une seconde fois et répondez à ces questions.

1. Pourquoi est-ce que les touristes ne veulent pas la première chambre?
2. Combien coûte le petit déjeuner? Où est-ce qu'il est servi?
3. Quel est le numéro de leur chambre?

COMPÉTENCE 2

Going to the doctor

 PowerPoint 10-4

CHEZ LE MÉDECIN

Note culturelle

Les trois principes de l'assurance maladie universelle *(universal health insurance)* en France sont l'égalité d'accès aux soins *(care)*, la qualité des soins et la solidarité. Que vous soyez *(Whether you are)* salarié, artisan, commerçant, étudiant, jeune ou vieux, riche ou pauvre… vos frais médicaux sont pris en charge *(your medical costs are covered)* par l'Assurance Maladie, qui est une branche de la Sécurité sociale. Est-ce que le régime *(system)* des assurances maladie est le même dans votre région?

iLrn In the **Culture Modules** in the video library, see **Health**.

Vocabulaire sans peine!

Notice the cognate patterns for these endings used to name illnesses and types of doctors.

-ite (f) = -itis
l'appendicite (f) appendicitis
-ose (f)= -osis
la mononucléose mononucleosis
-ologue (m / f) = -ologist
le/la dermatologue dermatologist

How would you say the following in French?

bronchitis, arthritis
tuberculosis, osteoporosis
neurologist, pychologist

🔊 3-21

Warm-up activity. Questions orales. Faites-vous attention à votre santé? Qu'est-ce que vous faites pour rester en bonne santé? Est-ce que vous faites de l'exercice tous les jours? Est-ce que vous faites de la musculation? Qu'est-ce qu'il faut manger si on veut rester en bonne santé?

Note for the conversation. New vocabulary includes all glossed words and **exactement, tout simplement, des médicaments,** and **des liquides.**

Suggestion for the conversation. Have students listen for the answers to these questions. **1.** Quels sont deux des symptômes de Lucas? **2.** Quels sont les conseils du médecin?

Lucas tombe **malade** pendant son séjour en Martinique. Savez-vous communiquer avec le médecin si vous tombez malade **au cours d'**un voyage?

— Où est-ce que vous **avez mal**?
— J'ai mal à la tête et au ventre.
— Quels autres symptômes avez-vous?

LE CORPS

la tête, l'œil (m) (pl les yeux), le nez, les dents (f), l'oreille (f), la bouche, **la gorge**, le dos, les doigts (m), le ventre, le pied, la main, le bras, la jambe, les doigts (m) de pied

— Je tousse.

— J'éternue.

— J'ai une indigestion et j'ai envie de vomir.

Avez-vous **la grippe**? **un rhume**? un virus? des allergies? Êtes-vous **enceinte**?

Lucas va chez le médecin.

LE MÉDECIN:	Bonjour, monsieur. **Qu'est-ce qui ne va pas** aujourd'hui?
LUCAS:	Je ne sais pas exactement. Je me sens mal. Je tousse, j'**ai des frissons** et j'ai mal un peu partout.
LE MÉDECIN:	Vous avez mal à la gorge?
LUCAS:	Oui, très.
LE MÉDECIN:	Eh bien, vous avez tout simplement la grippe.
LUCAS:	Qu'est-ce que je dois faire?
LE MÉDECIN:	Je vais vous donner **une ordonnance.** Prenez ces médicaments trois fois par jour. Il est important que vous les finissiez tous. N'oubliez pas de boire beaucoup de liquides, mais ne buvez pas d'alcool. Et il est essentiel que vous restiez au lit.

Line art on this page: © Cengage Learning

le médecin *the doctor* **malade** *sick* **au cours de** *in the course of, during, while on* **avoir mal (à)...** *one's … hurts* **la gorge** *the throat* **la grippe** *the flu* **un rhume** *a cold* **enceinte** *pregnant* **Qu'est-ce qui ne va pas?** *What's wrong?* **avoir des frissons** *to have the shivers* **une ordonnance** *a prescription*

A **J'ai mal partout!** Un hypocondriaque va voir son médecin. Selon lui *(According to him)*, il a mal partout, de la tête jusqu'aux pieds. De quoi se plaint-il? *(What does he complain about?)*

EXEMPLE Au secours *(Help)*, docteur! J'ai mal à la tête, j'ai mal aux yeux...

B **Associations.** Quelle(s) partie(s) du corps associez-vous aux verbes suivants?

EXEMPLE écrire   la main et les doigts

1. fumer
2. se brosser
3. écouter
4. voir
5. éternuer
6. faire du jogging
7. toucher
8. embrasser

C **Qu'est-ce qui ne va pas?** Quels symptômes ont-ils?

EXEMPLE Il a mal aux yeux.

1.

2.

3.

4.

5.

Line art on this page: © Cengage Learning

D **Des symptômes.** Nommez autant de symptômes que possible pour chaque situation.

EXEMPLE Quand on a la grippe, **on a mal partout. On a des frissons et...**

1. Quand on a un rhume...
2. Quand on a un virus intestinal...

E **Entretien.** Posez ces questions à votre partenaire pour parler de la dernière fois qu'il/elle a été malade.

1. La dernière fois que tu as été malade, est-ce que tu avais mal à la tête? à la gorge? Est-ce que tu avais des frissons? Quels symptômes avais-tu? Qu'est-ce que tu avais? *(What was wrong?)*
2. Est-ce que tu es allé(e) chez le médecin? Est-ce que le médecin t'a donné une ordonnance? Est-ce que tu as pris des médicaments?

À VOUS!

Avec un(e) partenaire, relisez à haute voix la conversation entre Lucas et le médecin. Ensuite, imaginez que vous êtes malade et créez une conversation entre le médecin et vous.

Warm-ups for A. J'ai mal partout!
A. Play Simon Says (**Jacques a dit**), instructing students to touch different parts of their body. **B.** Name an article of clothing and have students name what body part they associate with it.

Suggestion for A. J'ai mal partout!
Do this as a chain game to see who is the biggest hypochondriac in the class. Choose a student to begin, who says he/she hurts somewhere. The next person has to say he/she hurts there, as well as somewhere else. Each new person has all the pains previously mentioned plus something else.

Vocabulaire supplémentaire
un antibiotique an antibiotic
un antihistaminique an antihistamine
une aspirine an aspirin
des pastilles *(f)* **contre la toux** cough drops
du sirop contre la toux cough syrup
avoir de la fièvre to have a fever
avoir le nez bouché to have a stuffy nose
avoir le nez qui coule to have a runny nose
se brûler / se casser / se couper / se fouler la cheville to burn / break / cut / sprain one's ankle
faire une piqûre to give a shot

You can find a list of the new words from this **Compétence** on page 418 and access the audio online.

PowerPoint 10-5

✓ **Pour vérifier**

1. When do you use the subjunctive?
2. For most verbs, the **nous** and **vous** forms of the subjunctive look like what other verb tense? How do you form them?
3. What do you use as the subjunctive stem for all verb forms other than **nous** and **vous**? What endings do you use?

Note *de grammaire*

1. The **de** in expressions like **il est important de** is replaced by **que** in these structures.
2. Remember that verbs ending in **-ier**, like **étudier** and **oublier**, will have two **i**'s in the **nous** and **vous** forms of the subjunctive, just as they did in the **imparfait**: **nous oubliions, vous étudiiez.**

iLrn Grammar Tutorials

Note. Irregular verbs in the subjunctive are presented in the next section. There is additional practice of both the regular and irregular verbs in the subjunctive in the next two **Compétences.**

Suggestion. Point out that **1.** the subjunctive of regular **-er** verbs is the same as the present tense indicative, except in the **nous** and **vous** forms **2.** in all forms of the regular subjunctive, except **nous** and **vous**, one usually hears a pronounced consonant sound at the end.

GIVING ADVICE TO SOMEONE IN PARTICULAR

Les expressions impersonnelles et les verbes réguliers au subjonctif

You know you can use impersonal expressions like **il faut** and **il est important de** followed by an infinitive to give general advice or state opinions. When talking to or about a particular person, you can use these same expressions followed by **que** and a second clause with a conjugated verb.

Il est important **de bien manger.** Il est important **que tu manges mieux.**
It's important **to eat well.** It's important **that you eat better.**

Up to now, you have used verbs in the present indicative mode to say what happens. Another verb mode called the subjunctive is generally used in the second clause of a sentence, when the first clause expresses a feeling, attitude, or opinion about what should or might be done, rather than simply stating what is happening. The present subjunctive is used after the following expressions, and it may imply either present or future actions.

Il faut que	Il vaut mieux que	Il est possible que
Il ne faut pas que	Il est préférable que	Il est bon que
Il est nécessaire que	Il est essentiel que	C'est bien que
Il n'est pas nécessaire que	Il est important que	Il est mauvais que

Il faut que tu te **reposes.**
Il vaut mieux que tu ne **sortes** pas.
Il est important que tu **finisses** ces médicaments.

For most verbs, the subjunctive is formed as follows:

- For **nous** and **vous,** the subjunctive looks like the imperfect. Drop the **-ons** ending of the **nous** form of the present indicative and use the endings: **-ions, iez.**
- For the other forms, find the subjunctive stem by dropping the **-ent** ending of the **ils/elles** form of the present indicative and use the endings: **-e, -es, -e, -ent.**

	PARLER	FINIR	RENDRE
que je	parl**e**	finiss**e**	rend**e**
que tu	parl**es**	finiss**es**	rend**es**
qu'il/elle/on	parl**e**	finiss**e**	rend**e**
que nous	parl**ions**	finiss**ions**	rend**ions**
que vous	parl**iez**	finiss**iez**	rend**iez**
qu'ils/elles	parl**ent**	finiss**ent**	rend**ent**

Most irregular verbs follow the same rule.

connaître	que je connaiss**e**	que nous connaiss**ions**
dire	que je dis**e**	que nous dis**ions**
dormir	que je dorm**e**	que nous dorm**ions**
écrire	que j'écriv**e**	que nous écriv**ions**
lire	que je lis**e**	que nous lis**ions**
partir	que je part**e**	que nous part**ions**
sortir	que je sort**e**	que nous sort**ions**

These verbs follow the same rule, but have a different stem for the **nous** and **vous** forms.

acheter	que j'achète	que nous achetions
boire	que je boive	que nous buvions
devoir	que je doive	que nous devions
payer	que je paie	que nous payions
prendre	que je prenne	que nous prenions
venir	que je vienne	que nous venions

A **Précautions de santé.** Un guide touristique donne des conseils à des voyageurs pour éviter des problèmes de santé à l'étranger. Est-ce qu'il leur dit qu'**il faut** ou qu'**il ne faut pas** que les personnes suivantes fassent *(do)* les choses indiquées?

EXEMPLE vous: prendre des précautions / tomber malades pendant le voyage
Il faut que vous preniez des précautions.
Il ne faut pas que vous tombiez malades pendant le voyage.

1. les voyageurs: partir sans assurances *(insurance)* / vérifier leur couverture *(coverage)* à l'étranger
2. les voyageurs: oublier leurs médicaments / en apporter assez pour tout le voyage
3. nous: se reposer un peu à l'hôtel après le long vol / sortir trop fatigués
4. nous: essayer de trop faire tout de suite / s'adapter au décalage horaire *(time difference)*
5. vous: manger des plats légers / choisir des plats difficiles à digérer *(to digest)*
6. vous: risquer une infection gastro-intestinale / commander des plats bien cuits *(cooked)*
7. on: prendre trop d'alcool / boire beaucoup d'eau

Follow-up for A. Précautions de santé. Dites s'il faut ou s'il ne faut pas que votre ami fasse *(do)* ces choses dans les situations indiquées. **EXEMPLE:** Votre ami est fatigué. (se reposer, sortir): **Il faut qu'il se repose. Il ne faut pas qu'il sorte.** 1. Votre ami a la grippe. (se reposer, rendre visite à sa famille, acheter des médicaments, prendre de l'aspirine, boire beaucoup d'eau, venir en cours, finir ses médicaments, fumer) 2. Votre ami veut réussir en cours de français. (finir tous ses devoirs, le dire au professeur quand il ne comprend pas, apprendre toutes les conjugaisons, obéir au prof, dormir en cours, écouter en cours)

B **Préparatifs.** Une amie va bientôt partir en vacances. Donnez-lui des conseils. Basez vos réponses sur les illustrations et utilisez une de ces expressions:

il (n')est (pas) essentiel / nécessaire / important / bon / mauvais que…
il vaut mieux que…   il faut que…   il ne faut pas que…

EXEMPLE  **Il vaut mieux que tu t'informes sur la région sur Internet.**

apporter des bagages légers
passer la douane
t'informer sur la région sur Internet
dire à tes parents où tu vas
lire des guides
téléphoner à l'hôtel pour confirmer ta réservation

1.
2.
3.
4.
5.

PowerPoint 10-6

✓ **Pour vérifier**

1. What are seven verbs that are irregular in the subjunctive?
2. Which four of these verbs have a different stem for the **nous** and **vous** forms?
3. What are the conjugations of these seven verbs in the subjunctive?
4. What is the subjunctive of **il y a**? of **il pleut**?

iLrn Grammar Tutorials

Suggestions. A. Point out that the subjunctive forms of **être** and **avoir** are similar to the imperative, and that the **nous** and **vous** forms of only **aller** and **vouloir** are like the imperfect. **B.** Model the difference in pronunciation between **que j'aie** and **que j'aille**.

Follow-up for B. La grossesse. Vous êtes conseiller (conseillère) familial(e). Expliquez à des parents s'**il faut** ou s'**il ne faut pas** que leurs enfants fassent ces choses. EXEMPLE dormir assez **Il faut qu'ils dorment assez.** 1. faire de l'exercice 2. savoir que vous les aimez 3. aller toujours en cours 4. pouvoir faire tout ce qu'ils veulent 5. manger toujours dans un fast-food 6. vouloir réussir à l'école 7. avoir des responsabilités à la maison 8. être toujours sages

GIVING ADVICE

Les verbes irréguliers au subjonctif

The following seven verbs are irregular in the subjunctive. Note that **être**, **avoir**, **aller**, and **vouloir** have a different stem for the **nous** and **vous** forms. All except **être** and **avoir** have the regular subjunctive endings.

	ÊTRE	AVOIR	ALLER	VOULOIR
	soi- / soy-	ai- / ay-	aill- / all-	veuill- / voul-
que je (j')	sois	aie	aille	veuille
que tu	sois	aies	ailles	veuilles
qu'il/elle/on	soit	ait	aille	veuille
que nous	soyons	ayons	allions	voulions
que vous	soyez	ayez	alliez	vouliez
qu'ils/elles	soient	aient	aillent	veuillent

	FAIRE	POUVOIR	SAVOIR
	fass-	puiss-	sach-
que je	fasse	puisse	sache
que tu	fasses	puisses	saches
qu'il/elle/on	fasse	puisse	sache
que nous	fassions	puissions	sachions
que vous	fassiez	puissiez	sachiez
qu'ils/elles	fassent	puissent	sachent

The subjunctive of **il y a** is **qu'il y ait**.
The subjunctive of **il pleut** is **qu'il pleuve**.

A **On a perdu mes bagages!** Pour ne pas perdre leurs bagages pendant un voyage en avion, vaut-il mieux que les passagers fassent ou qu'ils ne fassent pas les choses suivantes?

> **EXEMPLE** avoir beaucoup de petites valises
> **Il vaut mieux que les passagers n'aient pas beaucoup de petites valises.**

1. être à l'aéroport bien à l'avance
2. faire des correspondances de vol *(flight connections)* trop courtes
3. choisir des vols directs si possible
4. avoir un bagage à main dans l'avion pour les choses les plus importantes
5. pouvoir rapidement identifier leurs bagages
6. faire une marque sur les valises pour les rendre *(to make them)* uniques
7. savoir où aller pour reprendre les bagages à la fin du vol
8. aller directement à la zone de retrait des bagages *(baggage claim area)* après le vol

B **La grossesse.** Une femme enceinte parle avec son médecin. Lui dit-il qu'**il faut** ou qu'**il ne faut pas** qu'elle fasse les choses indiquées?

> **EXEMPLES** Il faut que vous mangiez bien.
> Il ne faut pas que vous fumiez.

manger bien   fumer   se reposer assez   avoir beaucoup de stress
faire attention à votre santé   être très agitée   boire de l'alcool
savoir contrôler le stress   grossir beaucoup   prendre des vitamines

Sélection musicale. Search the Web for the song **"Il faut que tu t'en ailles"** by Marie-Mai to enjoy a musical selection illustrating the use of this structure.

C Réactions. Une amie vous parle des habitudes de sa famille. Réagissez *(React)* à ce qu'elle dit avec **c'est bien que...** ou **ce n'est pas bien que...** Jouez les deux rôles avec un(e) partenaire.

> **EXEMPLE** — Je ne fume plus.
> — C'est bien que tu ne fumes plus.

1. Je veux mieux manger.
2. Je vais souvent à la salle de gym.
3. Mes enfants font très attention à leur santé.
4. Mon mari n'est pas en forme.
5. Il a souvent mal à la tête.
6. Le médecin ne sait pas pourquoi.
7. Mon mari ne veut pas arrêter de fumer.
8. Nous sommes stressés.
9. Nous avons beaucoup de problèmes.
10. Nous ne pouvons pas bien dormir la nuit.
11. Nous faisons des promenades ensemble.

D Encore des conseils. Avec un(e) partenaire, préparez des suggestions pour quelqu'un qui dit les choses suivantes. Utilisez des expressions qui exigent *(that require)* le subjonctif.

> **EXEMPLE** — Je suis toujours fatigué(e). Qu'est-ce que je devrais faire?
> — Il est important que tu... / Il ne faut pas que tu...

- Je suis toujours fatigué(e).
- Je mange mal et j'ai souvent mal au ventre.
- Je prépare un voyage à l'étranger.

E L'ange et le diable. Un groupe de jeunes touristes fait un tour d'Europe. Donnez-leur des conseils dans les situations suivantes. Un(e) étudiant(e) jouera le rôle d'un ange *(angel)* et l'autre le rôle du diable *(devil)*. Utilisez des expressions telles que les suivantes: **Il faut que... / Il ne faut pas que... / Il vaut mieux que... / Il n'est pas bon que...**, etc.

> **EXEMPLE** Un très bel homme que je viens de rencontrer *(I just met)* m'a invitée au restaurant ce soir.
> **LE DIABLE:** Il faut que tu ailles avec lui! Il est possible que ce soit le grand amour!
> **L'ANGE:** Il faut que tu fasses attention! Il vaut mieux que des amis aillent avec toi.

1. Notre car touristique va partir dans dix minutes, mais je veux vite entrer dans ce magasin pour acheter des souvenirs.
2. Je veux monter sur cette statue pour une photo pendant que le policier ne regarde pas.
3. J'ai de la fièvre, mais je ne veux pas passer la journée à l'hôtel.
4. Je ne veux pas perdre mon temps avec le reste du groupe. Je veux faire un tour de la ville seul.
5. Mes amis veulent sortir en boîte ce soir, mais notre vol est à huit heures demain et je dois faire mes valises.

Follow-up for E. L'ange et le diable. Votre partenaire et vous êtes chaperons d'un groupe de jeunes étudiants pendant un voyage à l'étranger. Préparez deux listes de règles. Qu'est-ce qu'il faut qu'ils fassent et qu'est-ce qu'il ne faut pas qu'ils fassent?

Supplemental activity. Qu'est-ce que chacun doit ou ne doit pas faire dans ces circonstances? **EXEMPLE** Je suis très malade. (dormir beaucoup, aller danser) **Il faut que tu dormes beaucoup. Il ne faut pas que tu ailles danser! 1.** Mes collègues et moi, nous sommes très stressé(e)s. (être plus calmes, travailler plus, faire plus d'exercice) **2.** Mon frère fait une dépression. (sortir plus, penser à ses problèmes, être seul tout le temps) **3.** Mes parents ne sont pas en forme. (faire de l'exercice, regarder la télé toute la journée, manger plus de légumes et moins de sucre) **4.** Ma sœur est enceinte. (boire de l'alcool, dormir assez, aller chez le médecin)

COMPÉTENCE 3

Running errands on a trip

PowerPoint 10-7

Note culturelle

En plus de la distribution du courrier *(mail)*, la poste française offre des services supplémentaires comme, par exemple, dans les domaines des opérations bancaires, des sites Web et des téléphones portables. La Banque postale gère les comptes *(manages the accounts)* de plus de 11 millions de Français et est classée parmi les banques les moins chères du marché. La poste a un site Web: laposte.net, qui inclut un Webmail, des pages d'actualités *(news)* et des sites d'e-commerce. Quels services offre la poste dans votre région?

Note de grammaire

1. Remember that **envoyer** is a spelling change verb (**j'envoie, nous envoyons**). The stem for the future and conditional is **enverr-**.
2. Remember that nouns ending in **-eau**, like **cadeau**, form their plurals with **-x (des cadeaux)**.

3-22

Warm-up activity. Questions orales. **1.** La dernière fois que vous êtes parti(e) en vacances, où est-ce que vous êtes allé(e)? **2.** Combien de temps est-ce que vous êtes resté(e)? **3.** Quand est-ce que vous êtes parti(e)? **4.** Avec qui est-ce que vous avez fait ce voyage? **5.** Qu'est-ce que vous avez fait? **6.** Avez-vous envie d'y retourner?

Note for the conversation. New vocabulary includes all glossed words and **l'aéroport, insister, principal**.

Suggestion for the conversation. Have students listen with books closed for the answer to this question: **Où et quand est-ce que Lucas et Anaïs vont se retrouver?**

DES COURSES EN VOYAGE

Où va-t-on pour faire les choses suivantes en voyage? Il faut qu'on aille...

au **distributeur de billets** pour **retirer** de l'argent

à la banque ou au **bureau de change** pour changer de l'argent

à la pharmacie pour acheter de l'aspirine *(f)*

dans une boutique de **cadeaux** pour acheter un cadeau

au kiosque pour acheter le journal et une carte téléphonique

au bureau de poste pour envoyer des cartes postales et acheter **des timbres** *(m)*

Lucas quitte la Martinique pour retourner en Guadeloupe. Il parle au téléphone avec Anaïs.

ANAÏS: Je suis contente que tu reviennes bientôt de Martinique. Quand penses-tu arriver en Guadeloupe?

LUCAS: Je prends l'avion vendredi matin.

ANAÏS: Voudrais-tu que j'**aille** te **chercher** à l'aéroport?

LUCAS: Non, non, je ne veux pas que tu perdes ton temps à l'aéroport si l'avion arrive **en retard. J'aimerais autant** prendre **la navette.**

ANAÏS: Mais non, j'insiste! L'avion arrive à quelle heure?

LUCAS: À 10 heures.

ANAÏS: Alors, je viendrai te chercher devant la porte principale de l'aéroport vers dix heures et quart. Et si tu n'as pas d'autres projets, nous pouvons passer la journée à Pointe-à-Pitre.

LUCAS: Bonne idée! J'aimerais faire un tour de la ville.

ANAÏS: Parfait. À demain, alors.

LUCAS: Oui, au revoir, à demain.

Line art on this page: © Cengage Learning

un distributeur de billets *an ATM machine* **retirer** *to withdraw* **un bureau de change** *a currency exchange* **un cadeau** *a gift* **un timbre** *a stamp* **aller / venir chercher** *to go / come pick up* **en retard** *late* **J'aimerais autant...** *I would just as soon...* **la navette** *the shuttle*

398 trois cent quatre-vingt-dix-huit | **CHAPITRE 10**

A Des courses. Où dit-on les choses suivantes?

EXEMPLE C'est combien pour envoyer cette carte postale en Belgique?
au bureau de poste

1. Une carte téléphonique de dix euros, s'il vous plaît.
2. Qu'est-ce que vous recommandez contre les allergies? J'éternue beaucoup.
3. Je voudrais changer des dollars, s'il vous plaît.
4. C'est combien pour ces paniers *(baskets)* traditionnels? Je cherche un cadeau pour ma femme.
5. Avez-vous des magazines africains?
6. Trois timbres à 60 centimes, s'il vous plaît.

> à la banque
> au bureau de change
> dans un restaurant
> au distributeur de billets
> à la pharmacie
> au bureau de poste
> à la réception de l'hôtel
> à la boutique de cadeaux
> au kiosque
> à l'aéroport

B Où faut-il aller? Complétez ces phrases d'une façon logique.

EXEMPLE Notre vol va partir dans deux heures. Il faut que nous **allions à l'aéroport.**

1. Vous voulez changer de l'argent. Il faut que vous…
2. Tu as perdu la clé de ta chambre? Il faut que tu…
3. Tes amis ont besoin d'acheter une carte téléphonique. Il faut qu'ils…
4. J'ai besoin de retirer de l'argent. Il faut que j'…
5. Nous voulons envoyer des cartes postales. Il faut que nous…
6. Lucas veut acheter de l'aspirine. Il faut qu'il…
7. Anaïs a besoin d'acheter des timbres. Il faut qu'elle…
8. Lucas veut acheter un cadeau pour Anaïs. Il faut qu'il…

C Une journée chargée. Pourquoi est-ce que Lucas est probablement allé aux endroits indiqués?

EXEMPLE Lucas est allé au marché pour **acheter des fruits.**

1. Lucas est allé au bureau de poste pour…
2. Il est allé à la pharmacie pour…
3. Il a cherché un distributeur de billets pour…
4. Il est allé à la banque pour…
5. Il est allé au restaurant pour…
6. Il est allé au kiosque pour…
7. Il est allé à l'agence de voyages pour…
8. Il est allé à la boutique de cadeaux pour…

À VOUS!

Avec un(e) partenaire, relisez à haute voix la conversation entre Lucas et Anaïs. Ensuite, imaginez qu'un(e) ami(e) va venir vous rendre visite. Créez une conversation dans laquelle vous parlez de quel jour il/elle va arriver, de l'endroit où vous allez vous retrouver et de ce que vous allez faire ensemble.

PowerPoint 10-8

✓ Pour vérifier

1. What are eight expressions that indicate feelings that trigger the subjunctive? What expressions do you know that indicate desires, doubts, fears, opinions, and requests that trigger the subjunctive?

2. Do you use the subjunctive after the verb **espérer** (to hope)?

3. Does the present subjunctive always indicate present time?

Note de grammaire

1. Although most verbs that express desires trigger the subjunctive, **espérer** (to hope) does not.
   J'espère que tu **es** heureuse ici.

2. Traditionally, **ne** was always used in a clause following the expression **avoir peur que**. This **ne explétif** does not change the meaning of the clause and is now optional.
   J'ai peur qu'il **n'**arrive en retard. =
   J'ai peur qu'il arrive en retard. =
   I'm afraid he'll arrive late.

iLrn Grammar Tutorials

EXPRESSING WISHES AND EMOTIONS

Les expressions d'émotion et de volonté et le subjonctif

The indicative mood is used to talk about reality. The subjunctive mood conveys subjectivity: feelings, desires, opinions, requests, doubts, and fears about what should or might happen.

You know to use the subjunctive to give advice and state opinions about someone in particular after impersonal expressions like **il faut que** and **il vaut mieux que**.

You also use the subjunctive in a second clause beginning with **que** when:
- the verb in the first clause "triggers" the subjunctive in the second clause by expressing a feeling, desire, doubt, fear, opinion, or request.
- the subject of the first clause is not the same as the subject of the second clause.

Verbal expressions such as these will "trigger" the subjunctive in the second clause.

FEELINGS	DESIRES
être content(e) que *to be glad that*	vouloir que *to want that*
être heureux (heureuse) que *to be happy that*	préférer que *to prefer that*
être furieux (furieuse) que *to be furious that*	aimer mieux que *to prefer that*
être surpris(e) que *to be surprised that*	souhaiter que *to wish that*
être étonné(e) que *to be astonished that*	**DOUBTS AND FEARS**
être triste que *to be sad that*	douter que *to doubt that*
être désolé(e) que *to be sorry that*	avoir peur que *to be afraid that*
regretter que *to regret that*	
OPINIONS	**REQUESTS / DEMANDS**
accepter que *to accept that*	insister que *to insist that*
c'est dommage que *it's too bad that*	
il est bon / mauvais, etc., que *it's good / bad, etc., that*	

Je suis désolé que votre chambre n'ait pas de vue sur la mer.
J'ai peur que le quartier de l'hôtel ne soit pas calme.
C'est dommage que votre lit ne soit pas confortable.
J'insiste que nous changions d'hôtel.

Remember that the present subjunctive refers to either the present or the future.

Je doute qu'elle soit ici.   *I doubt she **is / will be** here.*
Je doute qu'il arrive demain.   *I doubt he **will arrive** tomorrow.*

A Écoutez la guide!
Anaïs guide un groupe de touristes au sommet du volcan la Soufrière. Dites si **elle veut** ou si **elle ne veut pas** que les touristes fassent les choses indiquées.

EXEMPLE   rester près d'elle / se perdre
              Elle veut qu'ils restent près d'elle.
              Elle ne veut pas qu'ils se perdent.

1. se perdre / venir avec elle
2. rester avec le groupe / se promener seuls
3. s'amuser / s'ennuyer
4. avoir peur / rester calmes
5. être satisfaits du tour / avoir de mauvais souvenirs du tour

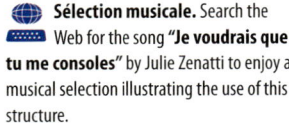

Sélection musicale. Search the Web for the song **"Je voudrais que tu me consoles"** by Julie Zenatti to enjoy a musical selection illustrating the use of this structure.

B Il se plaint!
Un des touristes qui fait partie d'un groupe guidé par Anaïs se plaint de tout *(complains about everything)*. Donnez la réaction d'Anaïs à ce qu'il lui dit. Jouez les deux rôles avec un(e) partenaire.

EXEMPLE je / se sentir mal
— Je me sens mal.
— C'est dommage que vous vous sentiez mal.

> Je regrette que…
> C'est dommage que…
> Je suis désolée que…

EXEMPLE je / se sentir mal

1. je / avoir un rhume
2. notre chambre / être vraiment laide

3. le restaurant de l'hôtel / servir une cuisine très médiocre
4. on / ne pas pouvoir acheter de beaux cadeaux à notre hôtel
5. le distributeur de billets / ne pas accepter notre carte bancaire

C Quel hôtel?
Vous allez faire un voyage. Quelle sorte d'hôtel préférez-vous? Donnez votre réaction comme indiqué.

EXEMPLE l'hôtel / être près des sites touristiques
Je préfère que l'hôtel soit près des sites touristiques.

> Je veux absolument que…
> Je préfère que…
> Il n'est pas important que…

1. quelqu'un de l'hôtel / aller nous chercher à l'aéroport
2. l'hôtel / avoir une piscine
3. le réceptionniste / parler anglais
4. l'hôtel / accepter les cartes de crédit
5. la chambre / être grande
6. la chambre / avoir un mini-bar et une télé plasma
7. on / pouvoir acheter de beaux cadeaux dans la boutique

D Réactions.
Vous êtes parti(e) en voyage organisé en Martinique et vous partagez votre chambre d'hôtel avec un(e) autre touriste. Donnez votre réaction à ce qu'il/elle vous dit. Jouez les deux rôles avec un(e) partenaire.

EXEMPLE — Je parle français couramment *(fluently)*.
— Je suis content(e) que vous parliez français couramment.

1. Notre hôtel est tout près de la mer.
2. Notre chambre a un grand balcon.
3. Je ne dors pas bien la nuit.
4. Je tousse toute la nuit.
5. L'hôtel n'accepte pas les cartes de crédit.
6. Il n'y a pas de distributeur de billets à l'hôtel.
7. Je n'ai pas assez d'argent pour payer ma part de la chambre.

> Je (ne) suis (pas) content(e) que…
> Je suis furieux (furieuse) que…
> Je suis désolé(e) que…
> Je regrette que…

E Un voyage ensemble. Votre partenaire et vous pensez peut-être partir en voyage ensemble. Posez ces questions à votre partenaire pour parler de ses habitudes quand il/elle est en vacances. Réagissez chaque fois à sa réponse.

EXEMPLE — Tu passes beaucoup de temps à l'hôtel?
— Non, je ne passe pas beaucoup de temps à l'hôtel.
— Je suis content(e) que tu ne passes pas beaucoup de temps à l'hôtel.

1. Tu préfères aller à la plage ou à la montagne?
2. Tu descends dans un hôtel de luxe ou dans un hôtel pas cher?
3. Tu sors souvent le soir ou tu restes à l'hôtel?
4. Tu préfères une chambre avec ou sans salle de bains?
5. Tu dînes dans un restaurant ou dans ta chambre?

F Un voyage en Afrique. Lucas veut qu'Anaïs et sa sœur fassent un voyage avec lui en Afrique. Qu'est-ce qu'il dit à Anaïs pour la persuader de l'accompagner? Commencez chaque phrase avec **j'aimerais que…** ou **je ne voudrais pas que…**.

EXEMPLE aller en vacances avec moi / me dire non
J'aimerais que vous alliez en vacances avec moi.
Je ne voudrais pas que vous me disiez non.

1. rater *(to lose out on)* cette occasion de voir l'Afrique / faire ce voyage avec moi
2. être timide / dire ce que vous voulez
3. visiter plusieurs pays africains avec moi / rentrer tout de suite en Guadeloupe
4. pouvoir rester au moins un mois en Afrique avec moi / prendre moins de quatre semaines de vacances
5. sortir seules dans la rue la nuit / être avec moi
6. avoir peur / se sentir à l'aise *(at ease)*
7. s'amuser / s'ennuyer
8. se souvenir de ce voyage / oublier notre voyage en Afrique

G Comparaisons culturelles. Voici les résultats de plusieurs sondages *(polls)* sur ce que les Françaises veulent chez les hommes. Complétez les phrases logiquement en mettant les verbes entre parenthèses au subjonctif.

1. (faire, être, avoir)
Pour la majorité des femmes, il est plus important qu'un homme _____ un bon sens de l'humour et qu'il les _____ rire *(laugh)*. Il est moins important qu'il _____ sexy.

2. (être, accepter)
Les femmes veulent qu'un homme _____ moderne et convaincu *(convinced)* des valeurs du féminisme, et qu'il _____ l'égalité sociale, politique et économique de la femme.

3. (avoir, montrer, payer)
Elles veulent aussi qu'il _____ des valeurs traditionnelles. Elles veulent encore qu'il _____ le chemin *(way)* et qu'il _____ l'addition au restaurant.

4. (être, avoir)

Pour 37 % (pour cent) des femmes, il faut absolument que leur partenaire _____ fidèle, mais 9 % acceptent sans problème qu'il _____ d'autres partenaires.

5. (se séparer, rester)

Si un couple avec un jeune enfant ne s'entend plus, 19 % des femmes pensent qu'il est nécessaire que le couple _____ ensemble mais 73 % disent qu'il vaut mieux que le couple _____.

6. (être, avoir)

La moitié *(half)* des Françaises veulent que leur partenaire _____ un côté spirituel, mais pour l'autre moitié il n'est pas important qu'il _____ religieux.

H Et vous? Pour vous, quels sont les traits de caractère les plus importants chez un(e) partenaire? Exprimez vos opinions en vous servant des éléments donnés.

j'insiste que		être riche
je préfère que		être intelligente
je ne voudrais pas que		avoir beaucoup d'ambition
je souhaite que	cette personne	avoir les mêmes valeurs que moi
il n'est pas très important que		fumer
je n'accepterais pas que		vouloir passer tout son temps avec moi

I Un couple heureux. Travaillez avec un groupe d'étudiants pour expliquer ce qu'il faut faire pour être un couple heureux. Complétez les phrases suivantes. Quel groupe peut faire le plus grand nombre de phrases logiques?

Il est très important qu'un couple / qu'une femme / qu'un homme…

Il est assez important qu'un couple / qu'une femme / qu'un homme…

Il n'est pas important qu'un couple / qu'une femme / qu'un homme…

 **PowerPoint 10-9**

SAYING WHO YOU WANT TO DO SOMETHING

✓ **Pour vérifier**

1. Do you use the infinitive or the subjunctive when people have feelings about what *others* should or might do? when they have feelings about what *they themselves* should or might do?

2. When do you use the infinitive after impersonal expressions such as **il faut**? When do you use the subjunctive?

iLrn Grammar Tutorials

Le subjonctif ou l'infinitif?

Use the subjunctive in a second clause when the first clause expresses feelings, desires, doubts, fears, requests, or opinions about what someone else does, might do, or should do. In this case, the subjunctive is used only when there are different subjects in the main and dependent clauses. When there is no change of subject, you normally use the infinitive.

FEELINGS ABOUT SOMEONE ELSE	FEELINGS ABOUT ONESELF
Je veux que tu le fasses. *I want you to do it.*	Je veux le faire. *I want to do it.*
Nous préférons qu'il soit à l'heure. *We prefer that he be on time.*	Nous préférons être à l'heure. *We prefer to be on time.*

Use **de** before an infinitive after the verb **regretter** or phrases that include the verb **être**.

Je regrette **de** partir demain.   Elle est contente **de** venir.

Remember to use an infinitive after expressions such as **il faut** or **il est important de** to talk about people in general, rather than someone specific.

TALKING ABOUT SOMEONE SPECIFIC	TALKING ABOUT PEOPLE IN GENERAL
Il faut que nous le fassions. *We have to do it.*	Il faut le faire. *It has to be done.*
Il est important qu'il y aille. *It's important for him to go there.*	Il est important d'y aller. *It's important to go there.*

A **De bons conseils.** Dites s'**il faut**, s'**il vaut mieux** ou s'**il ne faut pas** faire ces choses quand on voyage à l'étranger.

EXEMPLE prendre la photo d'un tableau avec un flash dans un musée
Il ne faut pas prendre la photo d'un tableau avec un flash dans un musée.

1. arriver à l'aéroport bien à l'avance
2. oublier son passeport
3. passer la sécurité
4. fumer dans l'avion
5. montrer son passeport à la douane
6. réserver une chambre avant de partir
7. faire beaucoup de bruit à l'hôtel
8. savoir parler un peu la langue

Maintenant, imaginez que vous donnez ces mêmes conseils à un groupe de jeunes qui partent en voyage.

EXEMPLE prendre la photo d'un tableau avec un flash dans un musée
Il ne faut pas que vous preniez la photo d'un tableau avec un flash dans un musée.

B Préférences.
Choisissez les mots entre parenthèses qui décrivent le mieux vos préférences quand vous voyagez. Conjuguez le verbe au subjonctif ou utilisez l'infinitif comme il convient.

1. Pour un long voyage, je préfère… (prendre l'avion, prendre le train, prendre ma voiture, ???)
2. Je préfère que mon vol… (être le matin, être l'après-midi, être le soir)
3. Pendant le vol, j'aime… (lire, voir le film, écouter de la musique, dormir, parler avec d'autres passagers, ???)
4. Je n'aime pas que les autres passagers près de moi… (parler tout le temps, avoir un petit bébé, se lever tout le temps, ???)
5. Je préfère que l'hôtel… (être près de tout, être beau mais pas trop cher, être dans une rue calme et tranquille, ???)
6. Je préfère que ma chambre d'hôtel… (avoir le Wi-Fi gratuit, être propre, avoir une belle vue, ???)
7. Généralement, j'aime… (dîner dans ma chambre d'hôtel, manger au restaurant de l'hôtel, sortir dîner dans un restaurant du quartier)
8. À l'hôtel, je préfère… (payer par carte bancaire, payer par carte de crédit, payer en espèces)

C Des courses.
Anaïs et sa sœur se préparent pour aller voir leur oncle qui habite dans une autre ville. Anaïs préfère faire ce qu'il y a à faire à la maison et elle voudrait que sa sœur aille faire des courses. Que dit-elle à sa sœur de faire?

EXEMPLE faire le ménage / faire des courses
Je voudrais que tu fasses des courses. Moi, je préfère faire le ménage.

1. aller retirer de l'argent au distributeur de billets / faire les valises
2. acheter un cadeau pour l'oncle Jean / lui faire un gâteau
3. écrire un mail à l'oncle Jean / envoyer ces lettres
4. téléphoner à l'hôtel / aller à la pharmacie
5. chercher des renseignements sur la région sur Internet / acheter un plan de la ville
6. aller en ville / rester à la maison

D Entretien.
Interviewez votre partenaire sur un voyage qu'il/elle voudrait faire.

1. Où est-ce que tu voudrais faire un voyage? Quand est-ce que tu voudrais le faire? Est-ce que tu aimerais que ta famille ou que tes amis voyagent avec toi?
2. Est-ce que tu préfères que ton hôtel soit un hôtel de luxe ou un hôtel pas cher? Est-il important qu'il y ait une piscine? Aimes-tu nager dans la piscine d'un hôtel?
3. Aimes-tu voyager en avion? Aimes-tu parler avec les personnes à côté de toi dans l'avion ou préfères-tu dormir? Quand tu arrives, préfères-tu prendre la navette ou un taxi pour te rendre à ta destination ou préfères-tu que quelqu'un vienne te chercher?

Follow-up for C. Des courses. Dites si vos parents veulent que vous fassiez les choses suivantes. Ensuite, dites si vous voulez les faire. **EXEMPLE** travailler cet été **Mes parents veulent que je travaille cet été. Moi, je ne veux pas travailler cet été. 1.** habiter avec eux **2.** leur téléphoner plus souvent **3.** leur dire tous vos secrets **4.** les accompagner en vacances **5.** aller à l'université cet été **6.** avoir un A en français

Supplemental activities. A. Have students list three things that someone else wants them to do that they don't want to do. For example: **Mon copain veut que j'aille chez ses parents ce week-end mais moi, je ne veux pas y aller. / Mes parents veulent que j'habite avec eux, mais je préfère habiter avec un(e) ami(e).** Afterward, have them work with a partner to create a conversation in which they discuss one of their three situations. The partners should give each other advice about what to do. **B.** Have students prepare a role play in groups of three in which a couple goes to a marriage counselor. The husband and wife both complain that their spouse always wants them to do things they do not want to do. They also describe things the spouse does that they do not like. The marriage counselor advises them on what to do to save their marriage.

COMPÉTENCE 4

Giving directions

 PowerPoint 10-10

LES INDICATIONS

Note culturelle

Sur le plan de Pointe-à-Pitre, vous pouvez voir le musée Schœlcher. Victor Schœlcher, homme politique français, était à la tête du mouvement pour l'abolition de l'esclavage *(slavery)* dans les colonies françaises. En 1848, il a réussi à faire accomplir son but *(goal)* et par le décret d'abolition de l'esclavage du 27 avril 1848, l'esclavage a été aboli. Que savez-vous de l'histoire de l'abolition de l'esclavage?

Lucas et Anaïs visitent Pointe-à-Pitre. Ils sont à l'office de tourisme. Voici un plan du centre-ville. Qu'est-ce qu'il y a dans le quartier?

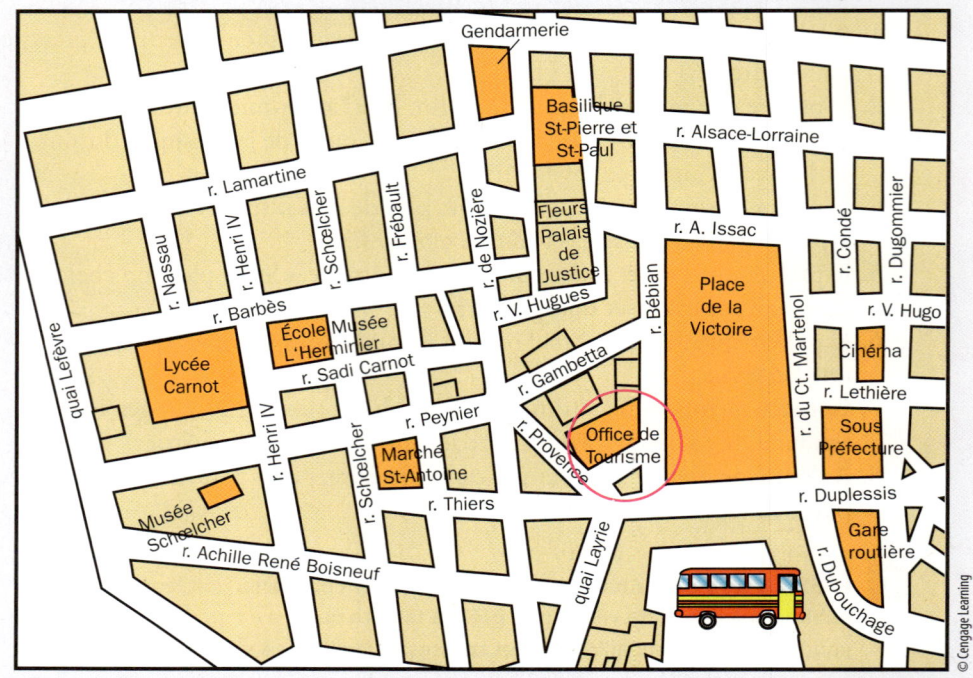

L'employé à l'office de tourisme va **expliquer** à Lucas et à Anaïs comment arriver au musée Schœlcher. Voici quelques expressions **utiles** pour **indiquer le chemin**.

Prenez la rue…	**Traversez la place…**
Continuez **tout droit jusqu'à…**	C'est dans la rue…
Tournez à droite.	sur le boulevard…
Tournez à gauche.	sur l'avenue…
Descendez la rue…	sur la place…
Montez la rue…	C'est **au coin de** la rue.

Warm-up activity. Give the expressions **je suis content(e) que…**, **je suis surpris(e) que…**, **c'est dommage que…** Then, read the following imaginary changes on campus and have students react: **1.** On ne peut plus fumer sur le campus. **2.** On ne peut plus avoir de voiture sur le campus. **3.** L'équipe de football américain gagne tous les matchs. **4.** Il y a un ordinateur gratuit pour chaque étudiant. **5.** Le français devient la langue officielle pour tous les cours. **6.** Il n'y a plus de football américain ni de basket à l'université. **7.** La bibliothèque ferme à 18 heures. **8.** Il y a trois semaines de plus chaque semestre/trimestre. **9.** Nous n'avons pas cours demain.

Supplemental activity. Have students stand, then use these commands to practice following directions with TPR (total physical response). **1.** Tournez à droite. **2.** Tournez à gauche. **3.** Regardez droit devant vous. **4.** Regardez derrière vous. **5.** Allez à côté de la porte. **6.** Allez devant la classe. **7.** Allez au mur en face de moi. **8.** Venez à côté de moi. **9.** Retournez à votre place.

expliquer to explain   **utile** useful   **indiquer le chemin** to give directions, to show the way   **tout droit jusqu'à…** straight ahead until / as far as / up to …   **traverser** to cross, to go across   **la place** the square   **au coin de** on the corner of

Anaïs **se renseigne** à l'office de tourisme pour savoir comment aller au musée Schœlcher.

ANAÏS: S'il vous plaît, monsieur, pourriez-vous m'expliquer comment aller au musée Schœlcher?
L'EMPLOYÉ: Bien sûr, madame, il n'y a rien de plus simple. C'est tout près. Montez la rue Provence jusqu'à la rue Peynier. Tournez à gauche...
ANAÏS: À gauche dans la rue Peynier?
L'EMPLOYÉ: Oui, c'est ça. Continuez tout droit et le musée Schœlcher est sur votre gauche, juste après la rue Henri IV.
ANAÏS: Je vous remercie, monsieur.
L'EMPLOYÉ: Je vous en prie, madame.

Où allez-vous? Imaginez que vous êtes à l'office de tourisme avec Lucas et Anaïs. D'abord, complétez les explications suivantes en traduisant les mots entre parenthèses. Ensuite, regardez le plan à la page précédente et dites où vous arrivez.

1. _____ *(Go up)* la rue Provence _____ *(as far as)* la rue Peynier. _____ *(Turn left)*. _____ *(Continue straight ahead)* et il est sur votre gauche, juste après la rue Henri IV.

2. _____ *(Cross)* la place de la Victoire et prenez la rue Lethière. _____ *(Continue straight ahead)* jusqu'à la rue Condé et _____ *(turn left)*. Il est sur votre _____ *(right)* entre la rue Victor Hugo et la rue Lethière.

3. _____ *(Go up)* la rue Bébian _____ *(as far as)* la rue Alsace-Lorraine. _____ *(Turn left)*. Elle est juste devant vous.

4. _____ *(Go up)* la rue Provence, _____ *(turn left)* dans la rue Peynier. _____ *(Continue straight ahead)* et il est sur votre gauche, entre la rue Frébault et la rue Schœlcher.

À VOUS!

D'abord, avec un(e) partenaire, relisez à haute voix la conversation entre Anaïs et l'employé. Ensuite, votre partenaire va vous demander comment aller à votre restaurant préféré en partant de *(leaving from)* l'université. Expliquez-lui comment y aller. Il/Elle va dessiner un plan selon vos indications.

Vous pouvez aussi utiliser ces mots:
au feu *at the light*
au stop *at the stop sign*
Prenez l'autoroute 35. *Take freeway 35.*
Prenez la sortie 7. *Take exit 7.*
vers le nord / le sud / l'est / l'ouest *toward the north / the south / the east / the west*

se renseigner *to inquire, to get information*

 **PowerPoint 10-11**

✓ **Pour vérifier**

1. How do you form the imperative of most verbs? Which verbs drop the final **s** in the **tu** form of the imperative? Which two verbs are irregular in the imperative and what are their forms?

2. Where do you place **y, en,** and object and reflexive pronouns in negative commands? Where do you place **y, en,** and object and reflexive pronouns in affirmative commands? What happens to **me** and **te** in an affirmative command?

3. When do you reattach the **s** to a **tu** form command?

iLrn Grammar Tutorials

Suggestions. Before beginning, review the imperative. Then do these warm-up activities: **A.** Acceptez ou refusez ces suggestions. **EXEMPLE** On va à la mer pour les vacances? Oui, allons à la mer. / Non, n'allons pas à la mer! Allons à Paris. **1.** On va à la montagne? **2.** On fait du bateau? **3.** On reste à la maison? **4.** On visite l'Europe? **5.** On descend dans un hôtel de luxe? **6.** On fait du ski? **B.** Je vais bientôt partir à l'étranger. Donnez-moi trois conseils. **EXEMPLE Achetez un guide! C.** Un de vos amis part en voyage aussi. Donnez-lui des conseils. **EXEMPLE Réserve une chambre bien à l'avance! D.** Review the forms, uses, and positions of the reflexive, direct, and indirect object pronouns, and of **y** and **en.** Then give students this warm-up activity: Vous êtes en vacances et vous rencontrez l'homme ou la femme de vos rêves. Est-ce que vous faites les choses suivantes? **1.** Est-ce que vous lui parlez? **2.** Qu'est-ce que vous lui demandez? (son numéro de téléphone? s'il/si elle est marié[e]?) **3.** Qu'est-ce que vous lui dites? (votre nom? qu'il/elle est beau/belle?) **4.** Est-ce que vous lui donnez le nom de votre hôtel? votre numéro de téléphone?

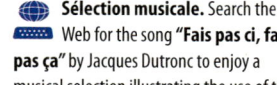 **Sélection musicale.** Search the Web for the song **"Fais pas ci, fais pas ça"** by Jacques Dutronc to enjoy a musical selection illustrating the use of this structure.

TELLING HOW TO GO SOMEWHERE

Reprise de l'impératif et les pronoms avec l'impératif

You use the **impératif** (command) form of the verb to give directions. As you have seen, the imperative of most verbs is the **tu, vous,** or **nous** form of the verb without the subject pronoun.

Descends cette rue!	*Go down this street!*
Traversez la place!	*Cross the square!*
Allons à la banque!	*Let's go to the bank!*

Remember to drop the final **s** of **-er** verbs and of **aller,** but not of other verbs, in **tu** form commands.

| | Tourne à gauche! | *Turn left!* | Va en ville! | *Go to town!* |
| BUT: | Prend**s** la navette! | *Take the shuttle!* | Fai**s** ta valise! | *Pack your bag!* |

Review the irregular command forms of **être** and **avoir.**

Sois calme!	*Be calm!*	Aie de la patience!	*Have patience!*
Soyons gentils!	*Let's be nice!*	Ayons confiance!	*Let's have confidence!*
Soyez à l'heure!	*Be on time!*	Ayez pitié!	*Have pity!*

In negative commands, reflexive pronouns, direct and indirect object pronouns, **y,** and **en** are placed before the verb.

Ne te perds pas!	*Don't get lost!*
Ne les prends pas!	*Don't take them!*
N'y va pas!	*Don't go there!*

In affirmative commands, pronouns are attached to the end of the verb with a hyphen.

| Attends-le à l'aéroport. | *Wait for him at the airport.* |
| Dis-lui que nous arriverons bientôt. | *Tell her that we will arrive soon.* |

When **me** and **te** are attached to the end of the verb, they become **moi** and **toi.**

| Attendez-moi! | *Wait for me!* | Lève-toi! | *Get up!* |

When **y** or **en** follows a **tu** form command, the final **s** is reattached to the end of the verb and it is pronounced in liaison.

| Va**s**-y! | *Go ahead!* | Mange**s**-y! | *Eat there!* |
| Achète**s**-en! | *Buy some!* | Mange**s**-en! | *Eat some!* |

A **Le chemin.** Consultez le plan à la page 406 et expliquez comment aller...

- de l'office de tourisme à la gendarmerie *(police station)*
- de la gendarmerie au musée Schœlcher
- du musée Schœlcher à la sous-préfecture *(administrative building)*

B Une drôle de touriste. Une extraterrestre passe ses vacances ici. Dites-lui ce qu'il faut et ce qu'il ne faut pas faire pour s'adapter à la culture terrienne *(earthling)*.

EXEMPLE Je m'habille avant de prendre une douche?
Non, ne t'habille pas avant de prendre une douche. Habille-toi après.

1. Je me couche sur la table?
2. Je m'habille sur le balcon?
3. Je me couche à midi?
4. Je me lève à minuit?
5. Je me maquille le ventre?
6. Je me déshabille dans l'ascenseur?
7. Je me lave les mains avec du vin?
8. Je me brosse les dents avec l'eau de la piscine?

C Lucas est amoureux. Lucas est tombé amoureux d'Anaïs et il ne veut pas qu'elle l'oublie quand il sera rentré en France. Vous êtes son ami(e). Répondez à ses questions. Dites-lui de faire ou de ne pas faire chaque chose.

EXEMPLE — Est-ce que je devrais lui écrire des mails de France?
— **Oui, écris-lui des mails.**
Non, ne lui écris pas de mails. Téléphone-lui.

1. Est-ce que je devrais l'inviter à venir me voir l'été prochain?
2. Je devrais lui téléphoner deux fois par jour?
3. Est-ce que je devrais lui dire que je suis amoureux d'elle?
4. Est-ce que je devrais lui envoyer des fleurs *(flowers)*?
5. Est-ce que je devrais l'oublier?
6. Je ferais mieux de la quitter pour toujours?
7. Est-ce que je devrais l'embrasser avant de partir?

D Anaïs aussi! Anaïs aussi est amoureuse de Lucas. Est-ce qu'elle lui dirait de faire les choses indiquées dans **C. Lucas est amoureux**?

EXEMPLE Écris-moi des mails.
Ne m'écris pas de mails. Téléphone-moi.

E Conseils. Répondez aux questions d'un touriste. Utilisez l'impératif et le pronom convenable. Jouez les deux rôles avec un(e) partenaire.

EXEMPLE — Quand est-ce que je devrais confirmer mon vol?
— **Confirmez-le 72 heures avant votre départ.**

1. Quand est-ce que je règle la note de la chambre?
2. Comment est-ce que je peux régler la note?
3. Où est-ce que je peux prendre le petit déjeuner?
4. Où est-ce que je peux changer de l'argent?
5. Où est-ce que je peux acheter des timbres?
6. Où est-ce que je peux acheter un plan de la ville?
7. Comment est-ce que je peux aller à l'aéroport?
8. Où est-ce que je peux acheter de l'aspirine?

Warm-up for B. Une drôle de touriste. Qu'est-ce qu'on dit de faire d'abord? **1.** Levez-vous. / Habillez-vous. **2.** Habillez-vous. / Prenez un bain. **3.** Endormez-vous. / Couchez-vous. **4.** Habillez-vous. / Sortez de la maison. **5.** Prenez le petit déjeuner. / Lavez-vous les mains. **6.** Mangez. / Brossez-vous les dents. **7.** Levez-vous. / Allez travailler.

Follow-up for B. Une drôle de touriste. Un ami part en voyage à l'étranger. Utilisez l'impératif pour lui dire de faire ou de ne pas faire les choses suivantes. EXEMPLE s'informer sur la région avant de partir **Informe-toi sur la région avant de partir! 1.** s'amuser **2.** se coucher tard la nuit avant le départ **3.** se reposer après le long vol **4.** s'informer sur la culture de la région **5.** s'adapter à la culture **6.** s'habiller comme il faut **7.** se souvenir d'emporter son passeport **8.** se donner assez de temps pour changer de vols à l'aéroport **9.** se perdre

VIDÉOREPRISE

Les Stagiaires

See the *Résumé de grammaire* section at the end of each chapter for a review of all the grammar presented in the chapter.

Rappel!
Dans l'épisode précédent de la vidéo, M. Vieilledent a fait des projets pour des vacances en Martinique.

The entire *Vidéoreprise* section is designed to be a pre-viewing series for the video, as well as a chapter review that can be used independently from the video. There are also additional grammar review exercises on the Instructor's Companion Website and on iLrn.

Follow-up for A. À l'étranger. Have students work together to come up with three or four more suggestions of what Monsieur Vieilledent needs to do to get ready for his trip abroad.

Comme vous l'avez découvert dans l'épisode précédent de la vidéo, Monsieur Vieilledent va partir en voyage aux Antilles. Faites les exercices qui suivent pour en savoir un peu plus sur son voyage et pour réviser ce que vous avez appris dans ce chapitre avant de regarder le dernier épisode de la vidéo.

A À l'étranger.
C'est le grand jour: Monsieur Vieilledent part en vacances! D'abord, dites ce qu'il vaut mieux faire en général quand on part en voyage.

EXEMPLE emporter beaucoup de choses ou emporter une seule valise?
Il vaut mieux emporter une seule valise.

1. chercher un hôtel à l'arrivée ou réserver une chambre à l'avance?
2. faire les valises à l'avance ou faire les valises au dernier moment?
3. arriver à l'aéroport juste avant le départ ou être à l'aéroport au moins deux heures avant le départ?
4. se souvenir de prendre ses médicaments ou oublier ses médicaments à la maison?

Maintenant, dites à Monsieur Vieilledent ce qu'il vaut mieux qu'il fasse. Utilisez les phrases précédentes.

EXEMPLE **Il vaut mieux que vous emportiez une seule valise.**

B Des préparatifs.
Vous aussi, vous partez à l'étranger avec un(e) ami(e) et vous faites les préparatifs. Dites à votre ami(e) ce que vous préférez faire et ce que vous préférez qu'il/elle fasse.

EXEMPLE choisir l'hôtel / choisir le vol
Je préfère choisir le vol et je préfère que tu choisisses l'hôtel.

1. faire les réservations d'hôtel / louer une voiture
2. lire le guide touristique / chercher des renseignements sur Internet
3. dormir dans le lit / dormir sur le canapé
4. acheter des timbres au bureau de poste / aller à la banque pour changer de l'argent
5. payer le voyage / ne rien payer

C En voyage.
Votre ami(e) vous pose les questions suivantes pendant votre voyage. Répondez en utilisant l'impératif avec un pronom complément d'objet direct. Jouez les deux rôles avec un(e) partenaire.

EXEMPLE —Je mets le réveil *(set the alarm)* pour six heures ou pour huit heures?
—**Ne le mets pas pour six heures. Mets-le pour huit heures.**

1. Je paie l'hôtel avec ma carte de crédit ou avec ta carte de crédit?
2. Je fais le lit ou je le laisse pour la femme de chambre *(maid)*?
3. Je prends la clé avec moi ou je la laisse à la réception?
4. J'appelle le taxi une heure ou deux heures avant le vol?
5. J'écris ces cartes postales avant de partir ou je les écris dans l'avion?

D Il est malade!
Monsieur Vieilledent tombe malade pendant son voyage. Il dit les choses suivantes à Camille au téléphone. Donnez les réactions de Camille à ce qu'il dit.

EXEMPLE Je me sens très malade et j'ai très mal à la tête.
Je suis désolée que vous vous sentiez très malade et que vous ayez très mal à la tête.

| Je regrette que... | Je suis désolée que... | C'est dommage que... |
| Il est bon que... | Il n'est pas bon que... | Il est important que... |

1. Je n'ai pas d'appétit et je ne mange presque rien.
2. Je reste au lit et je me repose.
3. L'hôtelier connaît un très bon médecin et il va lui téléphoner.
4. Je tousse toute la nuit et je ne peux pas dormir.
5. Je bois beaucoup de liquides et je prends de l'aspirine.

E Quelques ennuis.
Monsieur Vieilledent se trouve dans les situations suivantes pendant son voyage. Avec un(e) partenaire, préparez une conversation pour chacun de ces scénarios.

Pauvre Monsieur Vieilledent! On a perdu sa réservation d'hôtel, alors il cherche un autre hôtel. Il discute des choses suivantes avec le (la) réceptionniste.

- *He says that he is looking for a room for two weeks.*
- *He describes what sort of room he is looking for.* [Use your imagination!]
- *They discuss the price, including breakfast.*

Monsieur Vieilledent est toujours malade. Préparez la conversation suivante entre le médecin et lui.

- *The doctor greets him and asks what is wrong.*
- *He says that he is coughing and has a sore throat and a headache.*
- *The doctor says he has the flu and gives him a prescription for medicine. The doctor says that it is important that he take it every morning and gives him other advice on what else to do.*

Monsieur Vieilledent va enfin mieux et il a décidé de passer deux ou trois jours en Guadeloupe. Il est perdu dans Pointe-à-Pitre. Consultez le plan de Pointe-à-Pitre à la page 406. Monsieur Vieilledent est à la gare routière dans la rue Dubouchage. (Cherchez le petit bus.) Il veut aller au marché St-Antoine et il demande son chemin à un(e) passant(e). Jouez la scène avec un(e) partenaire. Ensuite, changez de rôles. Cette fois, Monsieur Vieilledent voudrait aller de la gare routière au lycée Carnot.

Suggestion for the video. Tell students not to worry about understanding every word, but to use what they do know and the context to guess what is being said. The video is available on DVD and on iLrn. The videoscript is available on the Instructor's Companion Website, **www.cengage.com/french/horizons6e** and on iLrn.

Access the Video *Les Stagiaires* on iLrn.

Épisode 10: Au revoir et merci!

AVANT LA VIDÉO

Dans ce dernier épisode, c'est le dernier jour de stage pour Rachid et Amélie. Monsieur Vieilledent, de retour de *(back from)* vacances, et tous leurs collègues de Technovert se réunissent *(get together)* pour leur dire au revoir. C'est surtout difficile pour Matthieu! Est-ce qu'il reverra Amélie?

Avant de regarder le clip, pensez à une chose que vous pourriez leur dire si vous étiez Monsieur Vieilledent et à une chose que vous pourriez dire si vous étiez Amélie ou Rachid.

APRÈS LA VIDÉO

Regardez le clip et répondez aux questions qui suivent:
- Qu'est-ce que chaque personne dit à Rachid et Amélie à la fin de leur stage à Technovert?
- Qu'est-ce qui se passe – ou non – entre Matthieu et Amélie?

LECTURE ET COMPOSITION

LECTURE

POUR MIEUX LIRE:
Using word families

When looking for a hotel for a trip, it is useful to read comments by former guests on Internet hotel booking services. You are going to read three opinions of former guests of a hotel in Guadeloupe.

Learning to recognize new words with the same root as vocabulary you already know will help you guess their meaning. Before reading the comments about the hotel, do the following activity to help make your reading easier.

Familles de mots. Servez-vous des mots donnés que vous avez déjà appris pour deviner les sens des mots en caractères gras.

1. vieille: La déco est un peu **vieillotte.**
2. vert: L'hôtel est à côté d'un parc **verdoyant.**
3. servir: Le personnel de l'hôtel est très **serviable.**
4. fraîche: L'hôtel a besoin d'un **rafraîchissement.**
5. le climat / un bruit: **La climatisation** était un peu **bruyante** dans la chambre.
6. propre / douter: La salle de bains était d'une **propreté douteuse.**

Avis de l'hôtel

Christophe: Caen, France

J'ai passé huit jours dans cet hôtel. La déco est un peu vieillotte mais les chambres sont en bon état et propres. À proximité de belles plages, l'hôtel est très calme et tranquille et à côté d'un parc verdoyant. Le personnel de l'hôtel est sympa et très serviable. Il y a tout ce dont on a besoin: balcon pour chaque chambre, salle de sport, télé XXL, petit déjeuner copieux. Bref, un séjour très agréable.

Florence: Liège, Belgique

Les prix sont trop élevés pour un établissement à rénover. L'ensemble de l'hotel est vieillot et a besoin d'un rafraîchissement. La déco de l'hôtel n'a aucun charme. La climatisation était bruyante et difficilement réglable. Par contre, son personnel est absolument charmant! Les femmes de ménage sont adorables! Sa situation géographique est excellente.

Annick: Montréal, Canada

L'hôtel n'avait pas notre réservation. Nous avons perdu beaucoup de temps à la réception dans une atmosphère de suspicion. Deux semaines avant notre nuitée, j'avais téléphoné pour demander une chambre avec vue sur la plage: «Oui, oui, c'est noté.» On a eu une chambre bruyante côté rue. La déco ancienne pourrait passer, mais la salle de bains était d'une propreté douteuse: odeur de toilettes dans la chambre.

Line art on this page: © Cengage Learning

COMPOSITION

POUR MIEUX ÉCRIRE: Making suggestions

When making suggestions in French or trying to persuade someone to do something, you can stress importance by using the imperative or certain expressions with the subjunctive (**il faut que…, il est essentiel que…**), or you can give less emphatic suggestions by using the conditional (**vous devriez…, vous pourriez…**) or other expressions with the subjunctive (**il vaut mieux que…, il est préférable que…**). Choosing the correct verb form sets the right tone for expressing the necessity of something.

Organisez-vous. Vous allez écrire des suggestions pour un blog pour des touristes français qui voudraient visiter votre pays. D'abord complétez les phrases suivantes pour parler d'une région qu'ils devraient visiter et de ce qu'ils devraient faire dans cet endroit.

1. Visitez…
2. Allez voir…
3. Il faut absolument que vous…
4. Il est essentiel que vous…
5. Il vaut mieux que vous…
6. Il est préférable que vous…
7. Vous devriez…
8. Vous pourriez…

Suggestions de voyage!

Écrivez une entrée pour un blog en français dans laquelle vous donnez des suggestions pour des voyageurs qui vont visiter une région de votre pays. Qu'est-ce qu'il faut absolument faire? Quelles autres choses les voyageurs pourraient-ils faire s'ils avaient le temps? Où est-ce qu'ils devraient se loger *(to stay)* et manger? Qu'est-ce qu'ils devraient éviter?

iLrn Share It!

Follow-up for reading. Have students search for comments about well-known hotels in your area on an online hotel booking service in French.

Process-writing follow-up for *Suggestions de voyage!* Have students exchange compositions and compare what they wrote. Then have them prepare a conversation in which one of them is working at the front desk of a hotel and the other is a French tourist asking about where to go and what to do in one of the regions they wrote about.

Compréhension

1. Quelles descriptions se répètent dans les avis de ces voyageurs?
2. D'après les descriptions, comment est la décoration de l'hôtel? le personnel? l'emplacement? la propreté?
3. Est-ce que vous voudriez descendre dans cet hôtel? Pourquoi (pas)?

COMPARAISONS CULTURELLES

LA MUSIQUE FRANCOPHONE: LES INFLUENCES AFRICAINES ET ANTILLAISES

En moyenne, un Français écoute au moins deux heures de musique par jour et la diversité **croissante** de la société française est reflétée dans la musique. La chanson française traditionnelle reste la musique préférée de la plupart des Français, mais la musique africaine et antillaise est de plus en plus populaire.

Angélique Kidjo

Youssou N'Dour

LA MUSIQUE FRANCOPHONE AFRICAINE

Dans la musique francophone d'Afrique, on trouve cinq genres d'influence régionale importants.

la rumba
Pays francophones d'origine: la République démocratique du Congo, le Congo
Instruments typiques: **les tambours, les trompes,** les flûtes et les xylophones
Artistes: Papa Wemba, Zao, Tabu Ley Rochereau, Wendo Kolosoy

la musique Sahel
Pays francophones d'origine: le Sénégal, le Burkina Faso, la Mauritanie, le Mali, le Niger
Instruments typiques: les luths et les tambours
Artistes: Youssou N'Dour, Wasis Diop, Ismaël Lô, Ali Farka Touré

l'Afro-beat
Pays francophones d'origine: le Togo, le Bénin, le Cameroun, la République centrafricaine
Instruments typiques: les percussions
Artistes: Fela Kuti, Angélique Kidjo, Francis Bebey, Lapiro de Mbanga, Sally Nyolo

la musique Mandingue
Pays francophones d'origine: le Sénégal, la Côte d'Ivoire, la Guinée
Instruments typiques: **la kora, le balafon,** les percussions
Artistes: Amadou et Mariam, Tiken Jah Fakoly, Alpha Blondy, Salif Keïta

la musique Maloya
Pays francophones d'origine: Madagascar, l'Île Maurice, La Réunion, les Seychelles et les Comores
Instruments typiques: **la cithare** et l'accordéon
Artistes: René Lacaille, Danyel Waro, Abou Chihabi

Suggestion. At http://www.lehall.com/galerie/africains, students can listen to clips of the African francophone singers named here, as well as others.

iLrn In the Culture Modules in the video library, see **Francophone music**.

---

croissante growing   **les tambours** drums   **les trompes** horns   **la kora** the kora (a 21 string harp lute)   **le balafon** the balaphone (an instrument similar to the xylophone)   **la cithare** the zither

LA MUSIQUE FRANCOPHONE ANTILLAISE

Quand on pense à la musique antillaise, on pense surtout au reggae et au zouk.

Le reggae, né en Jamaïque pendant les années 60, est devenu populaire auprès des Français. Dans un sondage sur les genres de musique les plus appréciés en France, 38% des jeunes hommes de 15 à 24 ans mentionnent le reggae.

Le zouk, né en Guadeloupe et en Martinique dans les années 80, est chanté en français ou en créole et le verbe *zouker* est devenu un synonyme de *danser* dans la région. Comme beaucoup de musiques aux Caraïbes, ce genre possède des influences de la rumba africaine.

Le succès du reggae et des artistes du zouk antillais, comme Jocelyne Béroard, Sonia Dersion, Zouk Machine et surtout du groupe Kassav', a servi d'inspiration pour une renaissance de la musique populaire en Afrique. L'interaction artistique entre les Antilles et l'Afrique est signe des **liens** culturels forts entre leurs peuples.

Compréhension

1. Quels sont cinq genres de musique africaine qui ont influencé la musique francophone? Est-ce que la musique africaine a influencé la musique de votre pays? Quels genres de musique?
2. Quels sont deux genres de musique antillaise populaires en France? Dans lequel de ces genres est-ce qu'on trouve souvent des chansons en créole? Qui est Kassav'? Est-ce qu'on écoute ces genres de musique dans votre région?

Zouker, c'est danser!

Jean-Philippe Marthély avec le groupe Kassav' et Jocelyne Béroard.

liens *ties*

RÉSUMÉ DE GRAMMAIRE

IMPERSONAL EXPRESSIONS AND THE INFINITIVE

Use an infinitive after the following expressions to state general advice and opinions. Notice that **il faut** means *it is necessary,* **il ne faut pas** means *one should / must not,* and **il n'est pas nécessaire** means *it is not necessary.*

> Il faut… / Il ne faut pas…
> Il est nécessaire de… / Il n'est pas nécessaire de…
> Il vaut mieux…
> Il est essentiel / important / bon / mauvais / possible / préférable de…
> C'est bien de…

Pour préparer un voyage à l'étranger, **il faut obtenir** des passeports.
Il vaut mieux réserver une chambre à l'avance.
Il ne faut pas attendre le dernier moment.

THE SUBJUNCTIVE (LE SUBJONCTIF)

The indicative mood expresses reality. The subjunctive mood conveys subjectivity; that is, feelings, desires, doubts, fears, opinions, and requests about what happens or might happen. The present subjunctive may imply either present or future actions.

The subjunctive is used in a second clause preceded by **que:**

- to give advice for someone in particular after impersonal expressions like those listed above. (In expressions like **il est bon de, que** replaces **de.**)
- when the verb in the first clause "triggers" the subjunctive in the second clause by expressing feelings, desires, doubts, fears, opinions, or requests; provided that the subject of the first clause is not the same as the subject of the second clause. (See page 400 for a list of such "trigger" verbs.)

S'il est malade, il faut **qu'il téléphone** au médecin.
J'ai peur **qu'il soit** très malade.
Je suis content **qu'il aille** chez le médecin.

For most verbs, form the subjunctive as follows.

- For **nous** and **vous,** the subjunctive looks like the imperfect. Form it by dropping the **-ons** ending of the **nous** form of the present indicative and use the endings: **-ions, iez.**
- For the other forms, find the subjunctive stem by dropping the **-ent** ending of the **ils/elles** form of the present indicative and use the endings: **-e, -es, -e, -ent.**

Le médecin veut **qu'il reste** au lit et **qu'il finisse** tous ses médicaments.
Il vaut mieux **qu'il ne rende pas visite** à ses amis.

	PARLER	**FINIR**	**RENDRE**
que je	parl**e**	finiss**e**	rend**e**
que tu	parl**es**	finiss**es**	rend**es**
qu'il/elle/on	parl**e**	finiss**e**	rend**e**
que nous	parl**ions**	finiss**ions**	rend**ions**
que vous	parl**iez**	finiss**iez**	rend**iez**
qu'ils/elles	parl**ent**	finiss**ent**	rend**ent**

416 *quatre cent seize* | CHAPITRE 10

Most irregular verbs follow the same rule.

connaître	que je connaisse	que nous connaiss**ions**
dire	que je dise	que nous dis**ions**
dormir	que je dorme	que nous dorm**ions**
écrire	que j'écrive	que nous écriv**ions**
lire	que je lise	que nous lis**ions**
partir	que je parte	que nous part**ions**
sortir	que je sorte	que nous sort**ions**

Il ne veut pas **que je dise** à ses parents qu'il est malade.

Il faut **qu'il dorme** beaucoup. Il ne faut pas **qu'il sorte** ce soir.

These verbs follow the same rule, but have a different stem for the **nous** and **vous** forms.

acheter	que j'achète	que nous achet**ions**
boire	que je boive	que nous buv**ions**
devoir	que je doive	que nous dev**ions**
payer	que je paie	que nous pay**ions**
prendre	que je prenne	que nous pren**ions**
venir	que je vienne	que nous ven**ions**

Il faut **que nous achetions** ces médicaments à la pharmacie.

Il veut **que tu viennes** le voir.

Only seven verbs are irregular in the subjunctive: **avoir, être, aller, faire, vouloir, savoir,** and **pouvoir.** Memorize their conjugations from the charts on page 396. The subjunctive of **il y a** is **qu'il y ait** and the subjunctive of **il pleut** is **qu'il pleuve.**

Je regrette **qu'il soit** malade mais je suis content **qu'il aille** voir le médecin.

THE SUBJUNCTIVE OR THE INFINITIVE?

The subjunctive is used when there are different subjects in the main and dependent clauses. When there is no change of subject, you normally use the infinitive. Also remember to use an infinitive after expressions such as **il faut** or **il est important de** to talk about what should be done as a general rule, rather than what specific people should do. Use **de** before an infinitive after the verb **regretter** or phrases that include the verb **être.**

Je ne veux pas le **faire** seul. Je préfère **que tu** le **fasses** avec moi.

COMMANDS AND USING PRONOUNS WITH COMMANDS

The imperative (command form) of most verbs is the **tu, nous,** or **vous** form of the verb without the subject pronoun. Remember to drop the final **s** of **-er** verbs and of **aller,** but not of other verbs, in **tu** form commands.

Être and **avoir** have irregular command forms: **sois, soyons, soyez** and **aie, ayons, ayez.**

In negative commands, reflexive and object pronouns, **y,** and **en** are placed before the verb. In affirmative commands, pronouns are attached to the end of the verb with a hyphen, and **me** and **te** become **moi** and **toi.** When **y** or **en** follows a **tu** form command, the final **s** is reattached to the end of the verb.

Prends la rue Provence, **va** jusqu'à la rue Thiers et **tourne** à gauche.

Prenons la rue Provence.

Prenez la rue Provence.

Sois à l'heure.

Aie de la patience.

Ne lui achète pas de cadeau dans la boutique de l'aéroport.

Achète-lui un cadeau au marché.

Réveille-toi tôt et **vas-y** le matin.

VOCABULAIRE

Audio Flashcards

COMPÉTENCE 1

Deciding where to stay

NOMS MASCULINS

l'accès Wi-Fi	Wi-Fi access
un balcon	a balcony
un bruit	a noise
un chalet à la montagne	a ski cabin
un hôtelier	a hotel manager
un lavabo	a washbasin, a sink
le logement	lodging
un mini-bar	a mini-bar
un supplément	an extra charge, a supplement
un W.-C.	a toilet

NOMS FÉMININS

une auberge de jeunesse	a youth hostel
une chambre simple / double	a single / double room
une clé	a key
une hôtelière	a hotel manager
la réception	the front desk

EXPRESSIONS VERBALES

C'est bien de…	It's good to …
confirmer	to confirm
Il est bon de…	It's good to …
Il est essentiel de…	It's essential to …
Il est important de…	It's important to …
Il est mauvais de…	It's bad to …
Il est nécessaire de…	It's necessary to …
Il n'est pas nécessaire de…	It's not necessary to …
Il est possible de…	It's possible to …
Il est préférable de…	It's preferable to …
Il faut…	One must…, It's necessary to …
Il ne faut pas…	One shouldn't…, One must not …
Il vaut mieux…	It's better to …
recommander	to recommend
régler la note	to pay the bill
vérifier	to check, to verify

ADJECTIFS

calme	calm
compris(e)	included
gratuit(e)	free
privé(e)	private
servi(e)	served

DIVERS

Bon séjour!	Enjoy your stay!
côté cour	on the courtyard side
de luxe	deluxe
en espèces	in cash

COMPÉTENCE 2

Going to the doctor

NOMS MASCULINS

les frissons	the shivers
un liquide	a liquid
un médecin	a doctor
un médicament	a medicine, a medication
un rhume	a cold
un symptôme	a symptom
un virus	a virus

NOMS FÉMININS

une allergie	an allergy
la grippe	the flu
une indigestion	indigestion
une ordonnance	a prescription

LES PARTIES DU CORPS

la bouche	the mouth
le bras	the arm
le corps	the body
les dents (f)	the teeth
les doigts (m)	the fingers
les doigts (m) de pied	the toes
le dos	the back
la gorge	the throat
la jambe	the leg
la main	the hand
le nez	the nose
l'œil (m) (pl les yeux)	the eye
l'oreille (f)	the ear
le pied	the foot
la tête	the head
le ventre	the stomach

EXPRESSIONS VERBALES

avoir des frissons	to have the shivers
avoir mal à…	one's … hurt(s)
communiquer	to communicate
éternuer	to sneeze
tomber malade	to get sick
tousser	to cough
vomir	to vomit, to throw up

DIVERS

au cours de	in the course of, during, while on
enceinte	pregnant
exactement	exactly
Qu'est-ce qui ne va pas?	What's wrong?
tout simplement	quite simply

COMPÉTENCE 3

Running errands on a trip

NOMS MASCULINS

un aéroport	an airport
un bureau de change	a currency exchange
un bureau de poste	a post office
un cadeau (*pl* des cadeaux)	a present
un distributeur de billets	an ATM machine
un kiosque	a kiosk
un timbre	a stamp

NOMS FÉMININS

de l'aspirine	some aspirin
une banque	a bank
une boutique (de cadeaux)	a (gift) shop
une carte téléphonique	a telephone card
une navette	a shuttle
une pharmacie	a pharmacy

EXPRESSIONS VERBALES

accepter que…	to accept that…
aller / venir chercher quelqu'un	to go / come pick someone up
c'est dommage que…	it's too bad that…
douter que…	to doubt that…
être content(e) que…	to be happy that…
être désolé(e) que…	to be sorry that…
être étonné(e) que…	to be astonished that…
être furieux (furieuse) que…	to be furious that…
être heureux (heureuse) que…	to be happy that…
être surpris(e) que…	to be surprised that…
être triste que…	to be sad that…
insister que…	to insist that…
j'aimerais autant…	I would just as soon…
regretter que…	to regret that…
retirer de l'argent	to withdraw money
souhaiter que…	to wish that…

DIVERS

en retard	late
principal(e) (*mpl* principaux)	principal, main

COMPÉTENCE 4

Giving directions

NOMS MASCULINS

un employé	an employee
l'office de tourisme	the Tourist Office
un plan	a map

NOMS FÉMININS

une employée	an employee
une expression	an expression
les indications	the directions
une place	a (town) square, a plaza

EXPRESSIONS VERBALES

avoir pitié (de)	to have pity (on)
continuer (tout droit)	to continue (straight ahead)
descendre la rue…	to go down … Street
expliquer	to explain
indiquer le chemin	to give directions, to show the way
monter la rue…	to go up … Street
prendre la rue…	to take … Street
remercier	to thank
se renseigner	to inquire, to get information
tourner (à droite / à gauche)	to turn (right / left)
traverser	to cross, to go across

EXPRESSIONS PRÉPOSITIONNELLES

au coin de	on the corner of
dans la rue…	on … Street
jusqu'à	until, up to, as far as
sur l'avenue / le boulevard / la place…	on … Avenue / Boulevard / Square

DIVERS

juste	just
tout droit	straight (ahead)
utile	useful

Vocabulaire | quatre cent dix-neuf **419**

INTERLUDE MUSICAL

DONNE-MOI UNE VIE

YANNICK NOAH

Les problèmes sociaux sont un thème commun dans les chansons. Dans la chanson **Donne-moi une vie,** Yannick Noah lance un appel en faveur des enfants pauvres dans le monde. Avant d'écouter la chanson, faites les activités suivantes pour pouvoir mieux comprendre la chanson.

Yannick Noah, d'origine française et camerounaise, est musicien et ancien champion de tennis à Roland Garros. Il a fondé une organisation caritative *(charitable)* pour aider les enfants pauvres.

🌐 You can search the Internet for videos to hear these songs performed and to find the lyrics.

A. Enfants perdus. En petits groupes, parlez de comment devrait être la vie *(life)* des enfants suivants, tous mentionnés dans la chanson **Donne-moi une vie.** Parlez aussi du sens du titre de la chanson.

les mendiants	*beggars*
les gosses à la colle	*kids sniffing glue*
les filles qu'on solde / les gamins vendus	*girls who are sold / sold kids*
les enfants soldats	*child soldiers*

B. C'est où? Identifiez, en anglais, les endroits suivants qui sont tous nommés dans la chanson et parlez avec vos camarades de classe de ce que vous savez de ces régions.

le Pérou	Manille	Calcutta	Haïti	Moscou	la Roumanie	Darfour
Grosnyï	Bali	Gaza	l'Irak	l'Éthiopie	Kaboul	

JE SAIS

SHY'M

Shy'm est passionnée par la musique depuis qu'elle est très jeune, mais elle doit dominer sa timidité avant de pouvoir se présenter devant le public. D'après elle, son pseudonyme Shy'm reflète sa timidité.

«C'est *Shy* pour *timide* en anglais et le *M* de *Martinique* pour rendre hommage à mes origines. Timide, parce que je voulais que ce soit un pseudo qui me corresponde, c'est l'un de mes principaux traits de caractère… Quant à la Martinique, c'est mon père qui est martiniquais et ma mère métropolitaine»[1].

Dans la chanson *Je sais,* Shy'm parle des difficultés qu'on a quelquefois en couple. Faites les activités qui suivent pour mieux comprendre les paroles de cette chanson.

Je te rends fou! Dans la chanson, Shy'm dit à son copain qu'elle sait qu'elle le rend fou *(she drives him crazy)* quelquefois. Choisissez le mot ou l'expression qui finit logiquement chacune des phrases suivantes pour exprimer ce qu'elle pourrait lui dire.

1. Je ne suis pas toujours…   d'être toi!
2. Quelquefois, je te rends…   un peu difficile parfois.
3. Et je rends ta vie   fou.
4. C'est dur…   facile.

Née d'un père qui est chanteur et d'une mère danseuse, Shy'm a grandi entourée de *(surrounded by)* musique.

[1]From http://teemix.aufeminin.com/mag/musique/d1669/x11722.html

BIENVENUE EN AFRIQUE FRANCOPHONE

 PowerPoint BV-2

Le Français est une langue importante dans 22 pays d'Afrique et plus de 200 millions d'habitants de ce continent parlent français. Allons visiter trois régions africaines francophones!

Suggestion. Point out that the existence of French-speaking countries in Africa is largely due to the history of French colonialism and that the various colonization and decolonization processes led to the creation of nations in Africa without any true ethnic, linguistic, cultural, or historic unity. This has rendered stability and democratization more difficult.

Afrique

- Pays et régions où le français est langue officielle, co-officielle ou administrative
- Pays et régions où le français est langue d'enseignement privilégiée

0 500 1000 1500 km

Sahara occidental, Maroc, Tunisie, Algérie, Libye, Égypte, Mauritanie, Mali, Niger, Tchad, Soudan, Érythrée, République de Djibouti, Sénégal (Dakar), Gambie, Guinée-Bissau, Guinée, Sierra Leone, Libéria, Burkina Faso, Côte d'Ivoire (Abidjan), Ghana, Togo (Lomé), Bénin (Porto Novo), Nigéria, Cameroun, République centrafricaine, Soudan du Sud, Éthiopie, Somalie, Guinée équatoriale, São Tomé & Principe, Gabon (Libreville), Congo (Brazzaville), République démocratique du Congo (Kinshasa), Ouganda, Kenya, Rwanda, Burundi, Tanzanie, Angola (Luanda), Zambie, Malawi, Mozambique, Zimbabwe, Namibie, Botswana, Swaziland, Afrique du Sud, Lesotho, Comores, Mayotte, Seychelles, Île Maurice, Réunion, Madagascar

© Cengage Learning

422 quatre cent vingt-deux | BIENVENUE EN AFRIQUE FRANCOPHONE

La Côte d'Ivoire est un pays fascinant par sa diversité géographique et culturelle. Dans ce seul pays, vous pouvez voir des régions géographiques très variées.

Le long de **la côte**, il y a des plages et **des falaises**. Au centre, il y a la jungle et des forêts tropicales. Dans le nord, il y a la savane.

Il y a plus de 60 **tribus** différentes en Côte d'Ivoire, **chacune** avec ses **propres** traditions.

En Afrique, on trouve le moderne juxtaposé au traditionnel. Abidjan, la plus grande ville ivoirienne, est une belle ville moderne qu'on appelait **autrefois** le «Paris de l'Afrique».

la côte *the coast*   **des falaises** *cliffs*   **tribus** *tribes*   **chacune** *each one*   **propres** *own*   **autrefois** *in the past*

Bienvenue en Afrique francophone | *quatre cent vingt-trois*

L'île de La Réunion, **qui se trouve** près de Madagascar dans l'océan Indien et à plus de 10 000 kilomètres de Paris, est un département de la France, tout comme Hawaii est un État des États-Unis.

La Réunion est une société riche de différentes cultures: française, africaine, hindoue, **malaisienne**, chinoise, créole... toutes au parfum tropical! Cette diversité se révèle dans une variété de traditions, de styles architecturaux, de musique et de cuisine.

La Réunion offre aussi une grande variété géographique de villes, petits villages, **stations balnéaires**, plages, forêts...

---

qui se trouve *which is located*   **malaisienne** *Malaysian*   **stations balnéaires** *seaside resorts*

Le Maroc, aussi appelé «le pays du soleil couchant» *(al-Maghrib al-aqsa)*, est l'État le plus occidental de l'Afrique du Nord. Par sa situation entre la Méditerranée, l'Atlantique et le Sahara, le Maroc **appartient à la fois** au monde méditerranéen, occidental et berbère.

Composé de montagnes, de déserts, de plages, de **côtes escarpées** et de forêts, et **doté de** villes fascinantes (Rabat, Casablanca, Marrakech), le Maroc est un des plus beaux pays du monde.

Le Maroc est un trésor de sites historiques et archéologiques.

Encore plus **attirante** que la beauté de ses paysages, la culture marocaine est très riche **car** elle reflète l'histoire et les traditions du peuple marocain, **tant d'**origine arabe que berbère et saharienne.

---

appartient à la fois *belongs at the same time*   **côtes escarpées** *rocky coasts*   **doté de** *endowed with*   **attirante** *attractive*   **car** *because*   **tant de (d')** *as much*

Bienvenue en Afrique francophone

Chapitre de révision
La vie moderne

iLrn Heinle Learning Center

www.cengagebrain.com

 Pair work

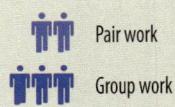 Group work

CHAPITRE DE RÉVISION

Révision: Chapitres 1–2
Les profils en ligne

Révision: Chapitres 3–4
Vivre vert

Révision: Chapitres 5–6
Ma vie, c'est une BD!

Révision: Chapitres 7–8
La vie saine

Révision: Chapitres 9–10
L'écotourisme

Note. This *Chapitre de révision* is broken into five sections, each of which reviews a pair of chapters. You may do it all together after *Chapitre 10* as a review of the whole book, or you may do each section after the corresponding pair of chapters. New vocabulary in the review chapter is not considered active. Encourage students to use the strategies they have learned to understand new words.

iLrn You can access an alternate/supplementary end-of-book review *Un drôle de mystère* on iLrn.

Note. With the alternate/supplementary end-of-book review, *Un drôle de mystère,* students review grammar from throughout *Horizons* while solving a mystery story. The electronic version allows students to do it alone online. You can access it on iLrn.

RÉVISION: CHAPITRES 1–2

Les profils en ligne

Ànous2
Faites-vous de nouveaux amis et cherchez des relations sentimentales sur notre site de rencontres.

MEMBRES

Email

Mot de passe

Je suis [un homme / une femme] de ☐ ans.

Je cherche [une femme / un homme] de ☐ à ☐ ans.

AHMAD LB13
35 ans
Salut, mon nom est Ahmad. Je suis un homme sincère, sensible, un peu geek. **Formation** en informatique. J'aime la musique, la nature et les animaux et les jeux vidéo. Recherche relation durable et honnête. Si tu aimes les promenades dans la nature et les dîners romantiques, contacte-moi.

ENZO JF77
25 ans
Salut! Je suis un homme sportif mais civilisé et romantique. Je suis éducateur. Je cherche une femme qui s'intéresse beaucoup au sport, surtout au foot. Vive les Bleus!

CASSANDRA SNS45
23 ans
Passionnée de musique, j'aime aussi le cinéma, la littérature et tous les arts, surtout la danse. J'aime sortir en boîte de nuit, danser, aller aux spectacles. Je cherche un homme avec qui partager mes intérêts.

LILOU JM100
32 ans
Je suis de nature indépendante, mais j'aimerais passer les beaux après-midis au parc avec un homme sympa qui aime la nature.

CHAN MP21
30 ans
Je suis calme et plutôt réservé. Cultivé, j'aime la littérature, le cinéma et les arts. Pourtant, je suis aussi sportif et j'aime surtout **la course à pied.** Je cherche une femme avec qui partager des moments tendres.

MONICA TTR38
20 ans
Jeune femme cool passionnée de musique. Profession: DJ. Contacte-moi si tu aimes sortir entre amis, aller prendre un verre et aller danser. Recherche relation sincère et sérieuse.

Formation *Education*   **la course à pied** *running, racing*

AVANT DE LIRE

Mots apparentés. Regardez les six profils à la page précédente. Servez-vous des mots que vous connaissez, des mots apparentés et du contexte pour compléter le tableau suivant.

	DESCRIPTIONS	ACTIVITÉS/ INTÉRÊTS	RECHERCHE
Ahmad			
Enzo			
Cassandra			
Lilou			
Chan			
Monica			

LECTURE ET COMPRÉHENSION

Comprenez-vous? Lisez les six profils à la page précédente. Décidez avec qui chacune des personnes décrites devraient prendre contact *(should get in touch)* et dites pourquoi.

> **EXEMPLE** Ahmad
> **Ahmad devrait *(should)* contacter Lilou parce qu'ils aiment tous les deux la nature et il a 35 ans et elle a 32 ans. Je ne trouve pas *(I don't find)* de contact pour Ahmad.**

> **Note** *de vocabulaire*
>
> To express someone's age, use **Il/Elle a... ans.**
> *He is 21.* **Il a 21 ans.**

À VOUS LA PAROLE!

Personnes célèbres. Recréez le formulaire suivant sur une feuille de papier. Ensuite, imaginez que vous êtes une personne célèbre et complétez le formulaire au nom de cette personne.

Nom: Antoine Beaujolais

Sexe: ● homme ○ femme

État civil: ○ célibataire ○ séparé(e) ● divorcé(e) ○ veuf/veuve
○ avec enfants ● sans enfants

Fumer: ○ fumeur ● non-fumeur

Intérêts: Sport, Musique, Politique, Associations caritatives, Bonne cuisine, Sorties

Données personnelles: Homme sportif et dynamique, j'aime le sport (surtout le basket) et la musique (surtout le rap et le hip-hop). Recherche une femme d'esprit ouvert qui aime la musique, le sport et l'humour.

Maintenant, toujours dans le rôle de votre célébrité, présentez-vous à la classe.

> **EXEMPLE** Bonjour, je suis Antoine Beaujolais et je suis... J'aime...

PRATIQUE

A Qui est-ce?
Complétez les descriptions suivantes avec **c'est** ou **il/elle est**. Ensuite, relisez les profils à la page 428 et identifiez la personne décrite.

EXEMPLE <u>C'est</u> une femme qui aime tous les arts. <u>Elle est</u> passionnée de musique.
C'est Cassandra.

Review the *Résumé de grammaire* sections on pages 60–61 and 98–99 at the end of *Chapitre 1* and *Chapitre 2* before doing these activities.

Quick reference answers for A. *Qui est-ce?* 1. Chan 2. Enzo 3. Monica 4. Lilou

1. _____ un homme réservé qui voudrait partager des moments tendres. _____ cultivé, mais _____ sportif aussi.
2. _____ un homme. _____ sportif. _____ éducateur.
3. _____ une femme qui voudrait une relation sincère. _____ passionnée de musique. _____ DJ.
4. _____ une personne indépendante. _____ une femme qui aime la nature.

B Préférences.
Deux jeunes Français indiquent leurs préférences sur leurs profils en ligne. Que disent-ils? Faites des phrases complètes. Attention à la forme et à la position de l'adjectif!

EXEMPLE la littérature *(modern)*
J'aime la littérature moderne.

1. les activités (f) *(intellectual)*
2. les loisirs *(athletic)*
3. les amis *(outgoing)*
4. les restaurants *(good)*
5. les femmes *(pretty)*
6. la cuisine *(French)*
7. les films *(old)*
8. les hommes *(tall)*
9. la musique *(classical)*
10. les hommes *(handsome)*

C Activités.
Utilisez le verbe **être** avec l'adjectif indiqué pour poser des questions à votre partenaire. Ensuite, demandez si ces personnes font souvent une activité logique de la liste.

> jouer au tennis et au foot   aimer lire   inviter des amis à la maison
> rester au lit jusqu'à midi   penser à tes problèmes   aimer sortir
> jouer du piano ou de la guitare   envoyer des textos
> passer beaucoup de temps seul(e)

EXEMPLE tu / sociable
— Tu es sociable? Tu envoies souvent des textos?
— Je suis sociable, mais je n'envoie pas beaucoup de textos. Je préfère parler au téléphone.

1. tes amis et toi / sportifs
2. tu / musicien(ne) *(musical)*
3. tes parents / sociables
4. ta meilleure amie / paresseuse
5. ton meilleur ami / timide
6. tes amis / intellectuels
7. tes amis et toi / très extravertis
8. tu / pessimiste

À VOUS LA PAROLE!

A Faisons connaissance! D'abord, complétez la description suivante avec vos informations. Ensuite, interviewez votre partenaire pour compléter une description de lui/d'elle.

> (avec) qui   que (qu')   quand   où
> pourquoi   comment   quels jours   jusqu'à quelle heure

EXEMPLE — Qu'est-ce que tu étudies? / Qu'étudies-tu?
— J'étudie le français et...

MOI	MON/MA PARTENAIRE
EXEMPLE J'étudie **le français et les maths.**	Il/Elle étudie le français et...
Je m'appelle...	
J'étudie...	
Je suis en cours *[say which days]*...	
Le samedi, je reste au lit jusqu'à...	
J'aime sortir *[say when]*...	
Je préfère passer la soirée avec...	
J'aime passer mon temps avec lui/elle parce que (qu')...	
Nous aimons aller *[say where]*...	

B Mon profil. Écrivez votre profil en français pour un site de correspondants *(penpals)* en ligne.

C Des questions. Avec un(e) partenaire, préparez une liste de 6–8 questions que vous voudriez poser à quelqu'un que vous rencontrez en ligne.

EXEMPLES   Tu es célibataire, marié(e), divorcé(e) ou séparé(e)?
Tu habites seul(e)?

À VOUS!

Imaginez un premier rendez-vous au café entre deux des personnes décrites dans les profils à la page 428. En groupe de trois, préparez une conversation dans laquelle vous commandez quelque chose à boire et chacun pose trois ou quatre questions à l'autre. Un(e) étudiant jouera *(will play)* le rôle du serveur/de la serveuse.

RÉVISION: CHAPITRES 3–4

Vivre vert

Vivre vert est un jeu en ligne où vous gagnez des points pour chaque geste vert que vous faites dans la réalité. Recyclez, compostez, donnez, partagez… Bref! Vivez votre vie, gagnez des points, devenez plus **écolo** et amusez-vous! Comptez vos points et comparez votre score à celui de vos amis pour voir qui est le/la plus écolo!

1. Je recycle ma bouteille d'eau en plastique: 10 points

Recyclez le plastique ou le papier dans des containers spéciaux et gagnez des points facilement. Quand **on** ne **jette** pas tout à la poubelle, **on gaspille** moins.
 Une idée pour aller plus loin: Compostez! Réduisez la taille de votre poubelle, c'est bon pour l'environnement.

2. On échange des choses: 10 points

Donnez une deuxième vie à vos objets! Quand vous avez besoin de quelque chose, n'allez pas au centre commercial. Demandez à vos amis s'ils ont ce que vous cherchez.
 Une idée pour aller plus loin: Soyez créatifs et transformez les objets récupérés en œuvres d'art!

3. Je donne des vêtements à une famille dans le besoin: 25 points

Vous avez des vêtements **que vous ne mettez plus**? Donnez ces vêtements à une famille dans le besoin.
 Une idée pour aller plus loin: À chaque fois qu'on achète un vêtement, on donne un vêtement. Comme ça, notre placard est toujours en ordre!

4. Je n'utilise pas ma voiture: 50 points

Prenez le bus, le métro ou le train! Ou même mieux, allez en ville à vélo – arrivez à votre destination et faites de l'exercice en même temps.
 Une idée pour aller plus loin: Faites du covoiturage dans la semaine. Aller au travail avec un collègue, c'est sympa et c'est vert.

5. J'utilise des énergies renouvelables: 100 points

Avec les énergies renouvelables telles que l'énergie solaire, on préserve les ressources naturelles et on réduit les émissions de CO2.
 Une idée pour aller plus loin: Achetez des appareils qui consomment moins d'électricité et qui ne gaspillent pas l'eau.

Vivre vert *Living green*   **écolo** *ecological*   **on jette** *one throws (away/out)*   **on gaspille** *one wastes*   **que vous ne mettez plus** *that you no longer wear*

AVANT DE LIRE

A **Familles de mots.** Utilisez le vocabulaire en caractères gras *(boldface)* pour deviner le sens des mots en italique dans les phrases suivantes.

> Review the reading strategies in the *Pour mieux lire* sections on pages 132 of *Chapitre 3* and 268 of *Chapitre 7* before beginning these activities.

EXEMPLE vivre *(to live)*: **Vivez** votre *vie* de façon écologique!
Live your life in an ecological way!

1. **amusant:** Jouez à ce jeu en ligne, *amusez-vous* et vivez une vie verte.
2. **la voiture:** Faites du *covoiturage* pour aller au travail.
3. **de taille moyenne:** Réduisez *la taille* de votre poubelle *(trash)*.
4. **le compost:** *Compostez* tout pour réduire la taille de votre poubelle.
5. **nouveau (nouvelle):** Utilisez les énergies *renouvelables* pour réduire les émissions de CO2.

Voyager en métro, c'est agréable et c'est vert!

B **Parcourez le texte!** Regardez la page précédente. Servez-vous des images, des phrases principales et de vos idées sur le thème de l'écologie pour prédire *(to predict)* si le programme *Vivre vert* vous proposerait *(would suggest)* de faire ces choses.

Quick-reference answers for B. Parcourez le texte! 1. oui 2. non 3. oui 4. oui 5. oui 6. non

Pour être plus écologique, est-ce que le programme *Vivre vert* vous proposerait de (d')... ?

	OUI	NON
EXEMPLE acheter de nouveaux vêtements		X
1. recycler vos bouteilles d'eau en plastique		
2. acheter beaucoup de nouvelles choses		
3. échanger des choses		
4. donner les vêtements que vous ne portez pas		
5. prendre votre vélo		
6. utiliser beaucoup de ressources naturelles		

LECTURE ET COMPRÉHENSION

Et vous? Lisez la page précédente. Quels gestes verts présentés sur le site *Vivre vert* est-ce que vous faites déjà et quels gestes est-ce que vous ne faites pas? Écrivez deux listes.

À VOUS LA PAROLE!

A **Entretien.** Interviewez votre partenaire sur les listes qu'il/elle a préparées.

1. Quel geste est-ce que tu fais le plus souvent?
2. Quel est un geste que tu ne fais pas, mais que tu voudrais faire?
3. Quel geste est le plus difficile à faire pour toi? Pourquoi?

B **Suggestions.** Travaillez en groupes pour créer une autre suggestion (avec une nouvelle image) pour le site *Vivre vert*. Servez-vous d'un dictionnaire (en ligne) si nécessaire. Ensuite, présentez vos idées à la classe.

Review the *Résumé de grammaire* sections on pages 136–137 and 172–173 at the end of **Chapitre 3** and **Chapitre 4** before doing these activities.

PRATIQUE

A **Vivre vert!** Complétez ce que dit un étudiant membre de *Vivre vert* en français avec l'expression avec **avoir** indiquée dans le premier espace et la forme convenable des autres verbes donnés en anglais dans les autres.

1. Quand j'_____ *(am thirsty)*, je n'_____ *(buy)* jamais de bouteille d'eau en plastique. Je _____ *(take)* de l'eau du robinet *(tap)*. Je _____ *(understand)* l'importance de protéger l'environnement.

2. Quand nous _____ *(need)* de recycler un vieil ordinateur, nous _____ *(go)* au centre de recyclage. Nous _____ *(learn)* tous les jours une nouvelle manière de recycler.

3. Beaucoup de gens _____ *(are cold)* en hiver. Alors, on _____ *(go)* au magasin d'une organisation caritative *(charitable organization)* pour donner des vêtements aux gens qui en ont besoin.

4. Beaucoup d'étudiants _____ *(feel like)* de vivre plus vert et ils _____ *(become)* plus écologiques parce qu'ils _____ *(understand)* l'importance de protéger l'environnement. Ils _____ *(come)* à la fac en bus ou à vélo.

5. Vous _____ *(are right)* de toujours prendre le métro ou le bus pour aller en ville. Comment est-ce que vous _____ *(come)* ici en cours? Est-ce que vous _____ *(take)* le bus?

6. Quand mon ami _____ *(is hungry)*, il _____ *(goes)* au restaurant d'à côté parce qu'il peut *(can)* y aller à pied. Il _____ *(understands)* l'importance de conserver nos ressources naturelles.

7. Tu _____ *(are wrong)* de gaspiller l'eau. Tu _____ *(take)* de trop longues douches *(showers)*! Tu ne _____ *(understand)* pas l'importance de conserver l'eau!

B **On échange?** Votre partenaire et vous êtes à une grande troc party *(swap party)* et vous parlez de ce que *(what)* vous voulez échanger. Demandez à votre partenaire s'il/si elle aime mieux ses propres *(own)* choses ou les choses indiquées.

EXEMPLE vélo / Thomas
— **Tu aimes mieux ton vélo ou le vélo de Thomas?**
— **Je préfère mon vélo. / Je préfère son vélo. / Je n'ai pas de vélo.**

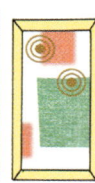

1. voiture / Alain et David 2. tableaux / ami de Sonia 3. canapé / sœur de Gabriel 4. étagère / frère de Malika

Maintenant, utilisez **ce, cet, cette** ou **ces** pour dire comment vous trouvez ces choses.

EXEMPLE **Ce vélo est en bon état.**

| élégant | laid | moderne | en bon état | un peu bizarre |
| très joli | trop vieux / petit… | ??? |

À VOUS LA PAROLE!

A **Des renseignements.** Imaginez que vous êtes un(e) Québécois(e) et que vous désiriez vous inscrire dans l'organisation *Vivre vert*. Créez votre nouvelle identité. Ensuite, votre partenaire va vous aider à vous inscrire. Il/Elle va vous poser des questions avec **quel /quelle** pour savoir: **votre nom, votre prénom, votre date de naissance, votre adresse mail** et **votre numéro de téléphone.**

EXEMPLE — Quel est ton nom?
— Mon nom, c'est Dupont.

B **Des solutions.** Utilisez l'impératif pour dire à un(e) ami(e) de faire ou de ne pas faire les choses suivantes pour vivre vert.

EXEMPLE conserver l'eau / prendre de longues douches *(showers)*
Conserve l'eau! Ne prends pas de longues douches!

1. prendre le bus ou le métro / venir toujours en ville en voiture
2. acheter beaucoup de choses / prendre seulement *(only)* les choses nécessaires
3. avoir peur de changer d'habitudes / apprendre à changer petit à petit
4. être pessimiste / comprendre que vivre vert, c'est facile

Maintenant, avec un(e) partenaire, créez trois autres conseils pour votre ami(e).

C **Ma vie verte.** Pour chaque activité, trouvez quelqu'un qui la fait déjà ou quelqu'un qui va la faire à l'avenir *(someone who already does it or someone who is going to do it in the future).*

EXEMPLE — Austin, est-ce que tu utilises déjà des ampoules LED ou est-ce que tu vas utiliser des ampoules LED à l'avenir?
— Je vais utiliser des ampoules LED à l'avenir.

	MAINTENANT	À L'AVENIR
utiliser des ampoules LED *(LED lightbulbs)*		Austin
acheter des produits régionaux		
venir en cours à pied ou à vélo		
aller sur Craigslist pour acheter des meubles		
composter		
acheter des cahiers en papier recyclé		
prendre des douches *(showers)* rapides		
recycler le papier et le plastique		

Note for A. Des renseignements. Students are instructed to create fake identities so that they do not give out personal information.

Follow-up for A. Des renseignements. To practice the date and large numbers, have students answer aloud the question **Quelle est votre date de naissance?** with a real or imaginary date. The rest of the class will write down each date in numerals **(12/2/1999).**

Follow-ups for B. Des solutions. A. Have students make the same suggestions to a group using **vous** form commands. **B.** Display the items that follow and tell students to make **nous** form commands to suggest whether or not to do the following: **composter, planter plus d'arbres, gaspiller les ressources naturelles, manger bio** *(organic)*, **utiliser des ampoules** *(lightbulbs)* **LED, utiliser des produits qui sont testés sur les animaux.**

Suggestions for C. Ma vie verte. A. Pass out copies of the activity for students to write on. **B.** If you are using this review at the end of the book rather than immediately after *Chapitre 4,* you may wish to encourage students to use direct object pronouns and **en** in this activity.

RÉVISION: CHAPITRES 5–6

Ma vie, c'est une BD!

Lucile Gomez, auteur de BD et de blog

Lucile Gomez

Qui es-tu?

Lucile Gomez. Je suis une «mademoiselle» qu'**on appelle** de plus en plus souvent «madame». Je n'ai pas de chat et pourtant je parle avec lui. Je ne sais pas vraiment bien pourquoi mais j'aime bien **tenir** mon blog. :)

Peux-tu présenter ton blog?

Sur mon blog, **je mets en scène un personnage** que j'appelle mystérieusement «Mademoiselle». Ce personnage, ce n'est pas moi. C'est juste une fille de mon âge, avec les mêmes cheveux et souvent les mêmes problèmes. La Mademoiselle du blog a un chat noir nommé Méphistofélix. C'est son confident, sa conscience, son Jiminy Cricket…

Pourquoi as-tu commencé à bloguer?

On était au mois de janvier. **À peine** rentrée d'un voyage, j'ai dû **rompre avec** mon copain. **Déboussolée**, j'ai quitté l'appartement que je partageais avec «lui» et j'ai trouvé une toute petite chambre en ville. **Bien qu'**au 6ème étage, j'étais **au fond du trou**. **Je pleurais dedans**, il pleuvait **dehors**. Bref, la seule fenêtre qui m'offrait **de la lumière** était celle de mon ordinateur. À cette période, **j'ai découvert** beaucoup de blogs. Comme j'aimais **dessiner**, j'ai pensé: MONTRER DES DESSINS À DES GENS est peut-être une bonne façon de me changer les idées.

Où peut-on voir ton travail en dehors des blogs?

Dans le monde matériel, sur des cartes postales, jeux, petits livres illustrés… et puis dans mes albums de BD.

Parle-nous d'un truc qui n'a rien à voir avec la BD et que tu aimes.

J'aime faire du vélo en ville et chanter, boire **des apéros** entre amis, aller au cinéma, le chocolat, les voyages, la randonnée en montagne, les chats, les pistaches, le vin, les fleurs au printemps, l'été tout entier, **le bruit** de la pluie, mes baskets noires, boire du thé chez une copine, un expresso à une terrasse, observer les gens, mes amis, mon sac à dos, mon ordinateur, la musique, recevoir un gentil texto ou une carte postale, **rire**, faire rire, rire…

Ma vie My life **une BD (une bande dessinée)** a comic (strip) **on appelle** one calls **tenir** to keep **je mets en scène un personnage** I present a character **À peine** Barely **rompre avec** to break up with **Déboussolée** Disoriented **Bien que** Although **au fond du trou** at the bottom of the hole **Je pleurais dedans** I was crying inside **dehors** outside **de la lumière** light **j'ai découvert** I discovered **dessiner** to draw **des apéros** drinks **le bruit** the noise **rire** to laugh

AVANT DE LIRE

Dans quel ordre? Avant de lire l'interview avec Lucile Gomez à la page précédente, parcourez *(scan)* le texte et regardez les questions qu'on lui pose pour déterminer dans quel paragraphe elle parle des choses suivantes: **le premier, le deuxième, le troisième, le quatrième** ou **le cinquième.**

1. Elle se présente dans le _____ paragraphe.
2. Elle parle de ce qui *(what)* l'a inspirée à bloguer dans le _____ paragraphe.
3. Elle parle de ses autres activités (en dehors de *[outside of]* son blog) dans le _____ paragraphe.
4. Elle parle de ses publications en dehors de l'Internet dans le _____ paragraphe.
5. Elle décrit son blog dans le _____ paragraphe.

Review the reading strategy in the **Pour mieux lire** section on page 56 of **Chapitre 1** before beginning these activities.

Quick-reference answers for *Dans quel ordre?* **1.** premier **2.** troisième **3.** cinquième **4.** quatrième **5.** deuxième

LECTURE ET COMPRÉHENSION

Lucile et son blog. Lisez l'interview à la page précédente et répondez aux questions.

1. Qui est «Mademoiselle»?
2. Qui est Méphistofélix?
3. Qui était «lui»?
4. Qu'est-ce que Lucile voulait faire quand elle a commencé son blog?

À VOUS LA PAROLE!

Préférences. Relisez le dernier paragraphe de l'interview et indiquez quelque chose que Lucile aime bien dans chacune de ces catégories. Ensuite, pour ces mêmes catégories, indiquez quelque chose que vous aimez.

	LUCILE	MOI	MON/MA PARTENAIRE
quelque chose qu'on fait dehors			
quelque chose qu'on fait entre amis			
quelque chose qu'on mange ou qu'on boit			
quelque chose qu'on admire dans la nature			

Maintenant, interviewez un(e) autre étudiant(e) pour compléter la dernière colonne du tableau.

EXEMPLE — Qu'est-ce que tu aimes faire dehors?
— J'aime faire du vélo. Et toi?

Review the *Résumé de grammaire* sections on pages 212–213 and 252–253 at the end of *Chapitre 5* and *Chapitre 6* before doing these activities.

PRATIQUE

A. On blogue!
Comme Lucile, ces gens parlent de leur expérience sur les blogs. Complétez leurs phrases avec la forme correcte du verbe logique.

EXEMPLE Pourquoi est-ce que vous **faites** (partir/faire) un blog, vous?

1. Sur un blog, on _____ (sortir/devoir) de son silence. En général, les blogueurs écrivent pour leurs amis et leur famille, mais certains _____ (vouloir/partir) aussi écrire pour le grand public.

2. Pendant que *(While)* le blogueur _____ (dormir/pouvoir), des gens de l'autre côté de la planète _____ (pouvoir/dormir) lire ses histoires *(stories)*.

3. Nous, les lecteurs *(readers)*, nous _____ (pouvoir/faire) aussi laisser des commentaires. Mais on ne _____ (devoir/partir) pas écrire des textes trop longs. Les gens préfèrent lire des commentaires plutôt courts.

4. Mon blog s'appelle: «Elle ne _____ (faire/dormir) rien!». Quand je _____ (partir/faire) en vacances, cela me donne de nouvelles idées de sujets pour bloguer. Ma sœur et moi, nous _____ (faire/pouvoir) aussi un blog ensemble. C'est génial!

B. Une histoire personnelle.
Dans son interview, Lucile raconte comment son blog est né. Utilisez le **passé composé** ou **l'imparfait** des verbes entre parenthèses pour compléter son histoire.

Lucile ___1___ (partir) en voyage puis, quand elle ___2___ (rentrer) à Paris en janvier, elle et son copain ___3___ (avoir) une grosse rupture amoureuse *(break-up)*.

Lucile ___4___ (devoir) quitter son appartement. Elle ___5___ (louer) une petite chambre au 6ème étage.

Elle ___6___ (commencer) son premier blog parce qu'elle ___7___ (vouloir) montrer ses dessins à des gens. Avant de commencer à bloguer, elle ___8___ (être) déprimée *(depressed)* et elle ___9___ (passer) beaucoup de temps devant son ordinateur. Elle ___10___ (ne pas sortir) beaucoup et elle ___11___ (dormir) mal.

Peu après, son blog ___12___ (avoir) du succès et sa nouvelle vie et sa carrière dans la BD ___13___ (commencer)!

C. Le monde de Lucile.
À tour de rôle, posez les questions suivantes à un(e) partenaire. Utilisez un pronom complément d'objet direct dans la réponse.

EXEMPLE — Comment Lucile appelle-t-elle *le chat* de son blog?
— Elle l'appelle Méphistofélix.

1. Est-ce que «Mademoiselle» écoute *son chat*?
2. Pourquoi est-ce que Lucile a commencé *son blog*?
3. Elle aime bien montrer *ses dessins* aux gens?
4. Où est-ce qu'on trouve *les dessins* de Lucile dans le monde matériel?
5. Où est-ce que Lucile a trouvé *sa nouvelle chambre* après sa rupture *(break-up)*?
6. Selon vous *(In your opinion)*, est-ce que Lucile va continuer *son blog*?

À VOUS LA PAROLE!

Le destin d'une lycéenne. Lisez la bande déssinée suivante de Lucile Gomez. Ensuite, en groupes, racontez l'histoire de cette lycéenne amoureuse en utilisant le **passé composé** et l'**imparfait**.

RÉVISION: CHAPITRES 7–8

La vie saine

Le beurre de cacahuète, c'est pour les sportifs!

Le beurre de cacahuète: un super aliment!

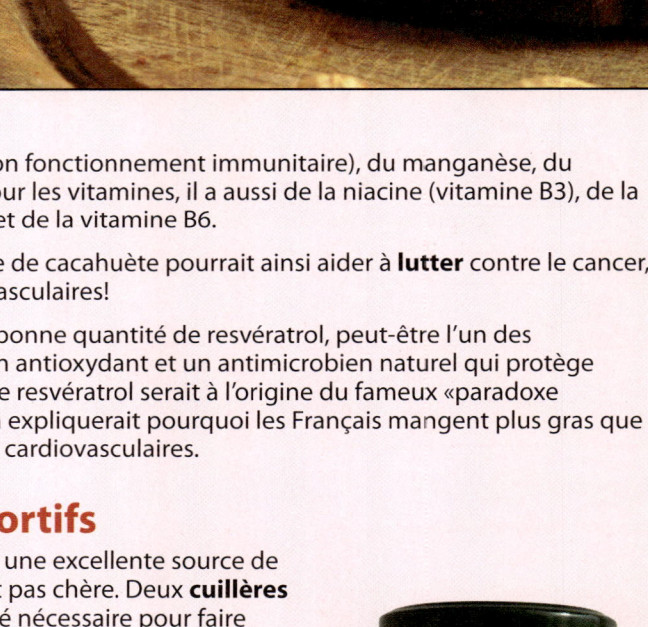

Le beurre de cacahuète est un super aliment. Pourquoi? Parce qu'il est délicieux, nourrissant et bon pour la santé! Beaucoup de personnes l'évitent, parce qu'elles pensent qu'il est trop calorique. Mais nous allons vous montrer pourquoi on devrait tous en manger.

Ses bienfaits pour la santé

Ce super aliment contient beaucoup de fibres. Il est aussi riche en minéraux et apporte du zinc (qui aide au bon fonctionnement immunitaire), du manganèse, du **cuivre,** du phosphore et du magnésium. Pour les vitamines, il a aussi de la niacine (vitamine B3), de la vitamine E, de l'acide folique (vitamine B9) et de la vitamine B6.

Grâce à tous ces micronutriments, le beurre de cacahuète pourrait ainsi aider à **lutter** contre le cancer, le diabète de type 2 et les maladies cardiovasculaires!

Enfin, le beurre de cacahuète contient une bonne quantité de resvératrol, peut-être l'un des micronutriments les plus fascinants. C'est un antioxydant et un antimicrobien naturel qui protège contre les bactéries et les virus. On dit que le resvératrol serait à l'origine du fameux «paradoxe français». Sa présence dans le vin et le raisin expliquerait pourquoi les Français mangent plus gras que les Américains, mais ont moins de maladies cardiovasculaires.

Des protéines pour les sportifs

Pour les sportifs, le beurre de cacahuète est une excellente source de calories et de protéines, à la fois naturelle et pas chère. Deux **cuillères à soupe** de beurre de cacahuète (la quantité nécessaire pour faire une tartine de taille moyenne) contiennent environ sept grammes de protéines. Quelle bonne nouvelle pour les sportifs végétariens!

De bons acides gras

Les graisses présentes dans le beurre de cacahuète sont des acides gras insaturés: elles sont donc «bonnes» et ne donnent pas de mauvais cholestérol. Mais attention! Tous les beurres de cacahuète ne sont pas **égaux.** Quand on y **rajoute** des huiles végétales, ils peuvent avoir quelques acides gras trans, qu'il vaut mieux éviter. Choisissez donc de préférence des beurres non raffinés, c'est-à-dire naturels ou bio.

cacahuète peanut   **cuivre** copper   **Grâce à** Thanks to   **lutter** to fight   **cuillères à soupe** soup spoonfuls   **égaux** equal   **rajoute** adds

AVANT DE LIRE

Mots apparentés. Les Français mangent très peu de beurre de cacahuète. Parcourez *(Scan)* l'article à la page précédente qui fait la promotion de cet aliment *(food)* et servez-vous des mots apparentés pour trouver les expressions indiquées ci-dessous *(below)*.

Review the reading strategies in the *Pour mieux lire* sections on pages 56 of **Chapitre 1** and 132 of **Chapitre 3** before beginning these activities.

DANS LA SECTION	TROUVEZ:
Le beurre de cacahuète: un super aliment!	deux mots qui indiquent pourquoi le beurre de cacahuète est un super aliment *(food)*
Ses bienfaits pour la santé	• les noms de trois minéraux qu'on trouve dans le beurre de cacahuète • les noms de trois vitamines qu'on y trouve • les noms de trois maladies *(illnesses)* • le nom d'un antioxydant qui protège *(protects)* contre les virus
De bons acides gras	les deux différentes sortes de graisses *(fats)* mentionnées

LECTURE ET COMPRÉHENSION

Pourquoi le beurre de cacahuète? Une amie française ne connaît pas bien le beurre de cacahuète. Répondez à ses questions d'après le texte.

1. Ne devrait-on pas éviter le beurre de cacahuète parce qu'il a trop de calories?
2. Pourquoi est-ce que le beurre de cacahuète serait «un super aliment»?
3. Quels minéraux est-ce que le beurre de cacahuète apporterait au régime *(diet)* de quelqu'un? Pourquoi est-ce que le zinc serait bon pour la santé? Quelles autres substances nutritives prendrait-on si on mangeait du beurre de cacahuète?
4. Contre quelles maladies est-ce que le beurre de cacahuète pourrait lutter?
5. Pourquoi est-ce que le beurre de cacahuète aiderait les sportifs?
6. Pourquoi faudrait-il choisir un beurre de cacahuète non raffiné?

À VOUS LA PAROLE!

Sport et nutrition. Posez ces questions à votre partenaire.

1. Est-ce que tu manges du beurre de cacahuète? Pourquoi est-ce que tu en manges? (Pourquoi est-ce que tu n'en manges pas?) Est-ce que tu conseillerais *(would advise)* à tous les sportifs de manger du beurre de cacahuète? Pourquoi (pas)?
2. Qu'est-ce que tu manges avant de faire du sport? Qu'est-ce que tu bois quand tu fais du sport? Qu'est-ce que tu ne bois pas ou ne manges pas avant de faire du sport?
3. D'après toi, qu'est-ce que les sportifs devraient manger ou boire parce que c'est bon pour eux? Qu'est-ce qu'ils devraient éviter?

À VOUS!

Vous êtes nutritionniste. Votre partenaire est un sportif (une sportive) qui n'a jamais entendu parler du *(has never heard of)* beurre de cacahuète. Préparez une conversation dans laquelle votre partenaire vous pose des questions à ce sujet et vous lui expliquez pourquoi il/elle devrait en manger. Est-ce que vous réussissez à le/la convaincre *(to convince)*?

Review the *Résumé de grammaire* sections on pages 296–297 and 340–341 at the end of *Chapitre 7* and *Chapitre 8* before doing these activities.

Quick-reference answers for *A. Que de bonnes choses!* **1.** Oui, il y en a. **2.** Oui, il en a. **3.** Non, on n'en trouve pas. **4.** Non, il n'en a pas. **5.** Oui, il y en a beaucoup. **6.** Il y en a (environ) sept.

PRATIQUE

A Que de bonnes choses!
Relisez l'article à la page 440. Ensuite, répondez aux questions en utilisant **en**.

EXEMPLE Est-ce qu'on trouve des protéines dans le beurre de cacahuète?
Oui, on en trouve.

1. Est-ce qu'il y a de la vitamine B6 dans le beurre de cacahuète?
2. Est-ce que le beurre de cacahuète a des minéraux?
3. Est-ce qu'on trouve de la vitamine C dans le beurre de cacahuète?
4. Est-ce que le beurre de cacahuète a du lactose?
5. Est-ce qu'il y a beaucoup de fibres dans le beurre de cacahuète?
6. Combien de grammes de protéines est-ce qu'il y a dans deux cuillères à soupe de beurre de cacahuète?

B Une pub.
La pub *(ad)* suivante encourage les jeunes sportifs à manger plus de beurre de cacahuète. Complétez le texte de la pub avec **qui, que** ou **dont**.

«Quand je mange du beurre de cacahuète, je mange quelque chose ____1____ me fait du bien et ____2____ les nutritionnistes recommandent aux sportifs comme moi. Tous les micronutriments ____3____ le beurre de cacahuète contient sont bons pour ma santé!

Une tartine au goûter me donne les protéines ____4____ mes muscles ont besoin pour se développer. Le beurre de cacahuète a aussi des fibres ____5____ aident à la digestion et il n'a pas de mauvaises graisses ____6____ pourraient me donner du mauvais cholestérol. Le beurre de cacahuète est un super aliment ____7____ toi aussi, tu devrais essayer!»

Follow-up for *C. Un micro-trottoir*. Give students the following activity: En groupes, imaginez en quoi votre style de vie et vos habitudes alimentaires seraient différents si vous habitiez en France. Utilisez le conditionnel. **EXEMPLES: Si on était en France, on mangerait moins de beurre de cacahuète et on mangerait plus de Nutella. On prendrait plus souvent les transports en commun et on marcherait plus.** Tell students whether you agree with their statements and discuss cultural differences in the lifestyle and diet of Americans and the French.

C Un micro-trottoir *(Street interview).*
Des Français dans la rue donnent leur avis *(opinion)* à un enquêteur *(interviewer)* sur le beurre de cacahuète. Complétez leurs déclarations en mettant un verbe au conditionnel et l'autre à l'imparfait.

EXEMPLE J'**achèterais** (acheter) du beurre de cacahuète si mon supermarché en **vendait** (vendre).

1. Je l'_____ (essayer), si je n'_____ (être) pas allergique aux cacahuètes.
2. Je _____ (pouvoir) mieux répondre à vos questions si je _____ (pouvoir) en goûter mais je ne sais pas ce que c'est.
3. J'en _____ (manger) souvent si le beurre de cacahuète _____ (avoir) moins de matières grasses.
4. Si on _____ (être) végétarien, le beurre de cacahuète _____ (être) peut-être un bon substitut à la viande.
5. Je _____ (préférer) manger du Nutella, même si le beurre de cacahuète _____ (être) meilleur pour la santé.
6. Moi, j'_____ (avoir) envie de vomir si je _____ (devoir) manger ça! Ça a l'air dégoûtant *(yucky, disgusting)*!
7. J'ai un ami américain qui _____ (mourir) de faim s'il n'y _____ (avoir) pas de beurre de cacahuète!

À VOUS LA PAROLE!

A Entretien.
Complétez les questions suivantes avec **le, la, l', les, un, une, du, de la, de l', des** ou **de (d')**.

1. Est-ce que tu aimes _____ beurre de cacahuète? Est-ce que tu manges beaucoup _____ beurre de cacahuète? Est-ce que tu aimes _____ tartines au beurre de cacahuète? Est-ce que tu préfères faire _____ tartine au beurre de cacahuète avec _____ confiture ou sans confiture? Est-ce que tu utilises _____ beurre de cacahuète pour faire _____ autres plats?

2. D'habitude, est-ce que tu bois _____ lait avec _____ tartine au beurre de cacahuète ou est-ce que tu préfères une autre boisson? Est-ce que tu aimes _____ lait? Est-ce que tu préfères _____ lait entier *(whole)* ou écrémé *(skim, low-fat)*? Est-ce que _____ lait a beaucoup _____ vitamine D? Est-ce que les Français boivent souvent _____ lait avec le déjeuner ou le dîner comme les Américains?

Maintenant, posez les questions à votre partenaire.

B Conseils.
Vous êtes conseiller (conseillère) à l'université et vous aidez les étudiants qui sont souvent fatigués ou qui ont d'autres problèmes. Avec un(e) partenaire, préparez une liste de 6–8 questions que vous poseriez aux étudiants qui viennent vous demander des conseils. Utilisez les verbes en **-re** (p. 276), **-ir** (p. 326), **boire** (p. 324) et les verbes réfléchis (p. 264) et réciproques (p. 272).

EXEMPLES Est-ce que vous vous entendez bien avec vos colocataires?
Est-ce que vous réfléchissez trop à des choses que vous ne pouvez pas changer?

Maintenant, changez de partenaire et utilisez les questions que vous avez préparées pour interviewer votre nouveau (nouvelle) partenaire. Utilisez la forme familière.

EXEMPLES — Est-ce que tu t'entends bien avec tes colocataires?
— On s'entend bien en général, mais on se dispute de temps en temps.
— Est-ce que tu réfléchis trop à des choses que tu ne peux pas changer?
— Oui, je réfléchis souvent à des choses que je ne peux pas contrôler.

C Le week-end dernier.
Avec un(e) partenaire, préparez 6–8 questions au passé composé ou à l'imparfait pour interviewer un(e) autre étudiant(e) sur sa routine et ses activités du week-end dernier. Utilisez les verbes en **-ir**, les verbes en **-re**, **boire** et les verbes réfléchis et réciproques.

EXEMPLES — Est-ce que tu t'es levé(e) tôt ou tard samedi?
— Tes amis et toi, est-ce que vous vous êtes retrouvés en ville samedi soir?

Maintenant, changez de partenaire et utilisez les questions que vous avez préparées pour interviewer votre nouveau (nouvelle) partenaire. Ensuite, décrivez le week-end de votre partenaire à la classe.

EXEMPLE Christine s'est levée vers onze heures samedi matin. Samedi soir, ses amis et elle se sont retrouvés au cinéma…

Suggestion for A. Entretien. Encourage students to respond to the questions using **en** or direct object pronouns.

RÉVISION: CHAPITRES 9–10

L'écotourisme

Tours Guadeloupe Nature

Savez-vous comment **les Caraïbes des Petites Antilles** appelaient la Guadeloupe? *Karukera* ou «l'île aux belles eaux». Si vous venez faire de l'écotourisme en Guadeloupe, vous comprendrez pourquoi ce nom lui va si bien.

Les Chutes du Carbet

Les Bains jaunes

Au pied du volcan la Soufrière, vous trouverez les Bains jaunes, un petit bassin d'eau sulfureuse chaude et bien agréable à visiter avant ou après l'ascension du volcan.

Des cocotiers sur la plage du Gosier

Vous préférez la mer? Pas de problème! Nos guides vous feront visiter les plus belles plages de l'île, du sable blanc fin et des cocotiers de la plage du Gosier au sable noir volcanique de Grande-Anse. Et près de Port-Louis, vous pourrez faire de la plongée sous-marine.

Venez avec nous faire des randonnées en pleine nature dans le Parc national de la Guadeloupe. Vous y observerez l'incroyable biodiversité de la forêt tropicale et vous verrez plusieurs sites naturels remarquables, comme les magnifiques Chutes du Carbet! Vous nagerez au pied de ces cascades, en pleine forêt tropicale, dans de petites piscines naturelles. Si la température est un peu trop fraîche, vous pourrez aussi essayer les sources d'eau chaude.

Le soir? Nous voulons que vous finissiez votre journée en toute tranquillité. Nos bungalows sont dans un grand jardin botanique où vous serez au calme. Nous vous y proposons des massages relaxants et une délicieuse cuisine de plats antillais authentiques.

Alors, qu'attendez-vous? Il faut absolument que vous visitiez la Guadeloupe! Nous voulons que vous ayez une expérience formidable et que vous appreniez à connaître notre belle île. Faites-nous confiance. Vous verrez, vous ne le regretterez pas!

---

les Caraïbes *the Kalinagos* (an early Amerindian population of the Antilles)   **des Petites Antilles** *of the Lesser Antilles*

AVANT DE LIRE

Devinez! Regardez la page précédente et utilisez les photos, le titre et l'organisation du texte pour répondre aux questions suivantes.

Review the reading strategy in the *Pour mieux lire* section on page 208 of *Chapitre 5* before beginning these activities.

1. Le texte est une publicité pour quelle sorte de tourisme?
2. Qu'est-ce qu'on verra sur le tour offert?
3. Quelles activités est-ce qu'on fera dans les endroits illustrés sur les photos?
4. En vous basant sur le thème de l'écotourisme et sur les photos à la page précédente, devinez le sens des mots et des expressions suivants.

> une chute   une source d'eau chaude   une cascade
> du sable blanc et des cocotiers   faire de la plongée sous-marine

LECTURE ET COMPRÉHENSION

À mon avis. Lisez le texte, puis répondez aux questions.

1. Quel genre de paysages peut-on voir à la Guadeloupe? Sont-ils variés?
2. Comprenez-vous pourquoi la Guadeloupe s'appelle «l'île aux belles eaux»?
3. Est-ce que la Guadeloupe est une bonne destination pour faire de l'écotourisme? Pourquoi (pas)?
4. Connaissez-vous des endroits qui ressemblent à *(look like)* la Guadeloupe?

À VOUS LA PAROLE!

 A Et toi? Votre partenaire va visiter la Guadeloupe cet été avec Tours Guadeloupe Nature. Demandez-lui où il/elle ira et ce qu'il/elle fera. Est-ce qu'il y a des endroits où il/elle n'ira pas du tout? Des choses qu'il/elle n'essaiera pas? Posez-lui au moins cinq questions en utilisant des verbes au futur.

> EXEMPLE — Est-ce que tu iras à la plage?
> — Oui, j'irai voir le sable noir de Grande-Anse.

 B Itinéraire de voyage. En groupes, identifiez un endroit que vous connaissez bien (votre quartier, votre campus, votre ville ou un autre endroit), puis créez un itinéraire de tourisme pour cet endroit.

- Faites une liste de sites naturels ou culturels à visiter.
- Décidez quelles sortes d'activités vous allez proposer aux touristes.

Finalement, créez la publicité pour votre voyage et présentez-la à la classe.

Review the *Résumé de grammaire* sections on pages 378–379 and 416–417 at the end of *Chapitre 9* and *Chapitre 10* before doing these activities.

PRATIQUE

A On part bientôt!
Anna parle avec des amis de recherches qu'elle fait pour un séjour qu'ils vont tous faire en Guadeloupe. Complétez ses phrases avec le verbe logique au *présent*.

| dire | lire | écrire | connaître | savoir |

EXEMPLE Je <u>sais</u> qu'on peut faire de la plongée à Port-Louis.

1. Maintenant je _____ beaucoup mieux la culture guadeloupéenne parce que je _____ un bon guide sur la Guadeloupe.
2. Sur ce site de tourisme, ils _____ que les plages sont extraordinaires.
3. Vous ne _____ pas encore la cuisine créole? Je _____ préparer quelques plats.
4. Si nous _____ ensemble ces descriptions d'hôtels, nous pourrons trouver quelque chose qui plaira à tout le monde, d'accord?
5. Sur ce site, les voyageurs _____ des commentaires sur des hôtels.
6. Toi, tu _____ bien tes amis. Est-ce que tu _____ s'ils voudront aller à la plage tous les jours?

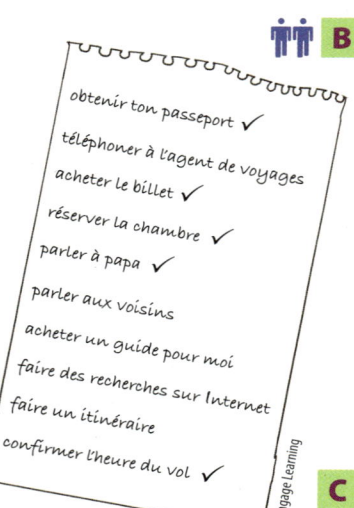

B Tout est prêt?
Anna a donné à une amie une liste de choses à faire avant le voyage. Maintenant, elle demande à cette amie ce qu'elle a déjà fait. Avec un(e) partenaire, jouez les deux rôles en suivant les exemples. Utilisez un pronom complément d'objet direct ou indirect ou **en** dans les réponses.

EXEMPLES obtenir *ton passeport*
— Tu as obtenu ton passport?
— Oui, je l'ai obtenu.

téléphoner *à l'agent de voyages*
— Tu as téléphoné à l'agent de voyages?
— Non, je ne lui ai pas encore téléphoné.
— Alors, téléphone-lui.
— Je lui téléphonerai demain.

C Réactions.
Anna parle de son voyage en Guadeloupe. Donnez votre réaction à ce qu'elle dit. Utilisez des expressions comme **il faut, il ne faut pas, il vaut mieux, c'est bien, ce n'est pas bien, c'est mauvais, c'est dommage…**

EXEMPLE Je m'amuse bien en Guadeloupe.
C'est bien que tu t'amuses bien en Guadeloupe.

1. Ma sœur ne mange pas la cuisine locale.
2. Je veux goûter la cuisine locale.
3. Ce monsieur fait des photos sans autorisation.
4. Le guide a beaucoup de patience.
5. Je ne dors pas bien.
6. On choisit de beaux souvenirs.
7. Nous nous levons très tôt.
8. Beaucoup de touristes ne savent pas respecter la nature.
9. Les enfants n'obéissent pas au guide.
10. Nous apprenons beaucoup sur la culture créole.

À VOUS LA PAROLE!

A Un voyage idéal. Vous allez faire le voyage de vos rêves avec quelques amis. Travaillez en petits groupes et déterminez les choses suivantes entre vous.

- quels pays / villes vous visiterez
- comment vous voyagerez
- quand vous partirez
- combien de temps vous resterez
- ce que vous ferez
- quels vêtements vous apporterez
- quand vous rentrerez
- quels préparatifs il vous faudra faire et qui fera chacun de ces préparatifs

> **EXEMPLE** On ira en France, au Maroc et en Martinique.
> On prendra l'avion et on partira…

B Conseils. Chaque groupe va présenter les détails du voyage qu'il a préparé dans **A. Un voyage idéal** à un autre groupe. L'autre groupe va donner au moins cinq réactions ou conseils.

> **EXEMPLE** C'est bien que vous visitiez des pays étrangers.
> Il faut que vous obteniez vos passeports bien à l'avance.
> Il vaut mieux que…

Au Maroc, on goûtera la cuisine locale.

En Martinique, on nagera et on fera de la plongée.

En France, on visitera tous les sites touristiques et historiques comme la cathédrale de Chartres.

C Touristes responsables. En groupes, préparez une liste de 3–4 choses qu'il faut faire pour être un touriste responsable et une autre liste de 3–4 choses qu'il ne faut pas faire.

> **EXEMPLES** Il faut respecter la nature.
> Il ne faut pas marcher sur les plantes dans les jardins.

Follow-up for C. Touristes responsables. Have students use their recommendations to give advice to a group of tourists. **Il faut que vous respectiez la nature.**

Tableaux des verbes

VERBES AUXILIAIRES

VERBE INFINITIF	INDICATIF PRÉSENT	PASSÉ COMPOSÉ	IMPARFAIT	FUTUR	CONDITIONNEL PRÉSENT	SUBJONCTIF PRÉSENT	IMPÉRATIF
avoir	ai	ai eu	avais	aurai	aurais	aie	
to have	as	as eu	avais	auras	aurais	aies	aie
	a	a eu	avait	aura	aurait	ait	
	avons	avons eu	avions	aurons	aurions	ayons	ayons
	avez	avez eu	aviez	aurez	auriez	ayez	ayez
	ont	ont eu	avaient	auront	auraient	aient	
être	suis	ai été	étais	serai	serais	sois	
to be	es	as été	étais	seras	serais	sois	sois
	est	a été	était	sera	serait	soit	
	sommes	avons été	étions	serons	serions	soyons	soyons
	êtes	avez été	étiez	serez	seriez	soyez	soyez
	sont	ont été	étaient	seront	seraient	soient	

VERBES RÉGULIERS

VERBE INFINITIF	INDICATIF PRÉSENT	PASSÉ COMPOSÉ	IMPARFAIT	FUTUR	CONDITIONNEL PRÉSENT	SUBJONCTIF PRÉSENT	IMPÉRATIF
-er verbs							
parler	parle	ai parlé	parlais	parlerai	parlerais	parle	
to talk,	parles	as parlé	parlais	parleras	parlerais	parles	parle
to speak	parle	a parlé	parlait	parlera	parlerait	parle	
	parlons	avons parlé	parlions	parlerons	parlerions	parlions	parlons
	parlez	avez parlé	parliez	parlerez	parleriez	parliez	parlez
	parlent	ont parlé	parlaient	parleront	parleraient	parlent	
-ir verbs							
finir	finis	ai fini	finissais	finirai	finirais	finisse	
to finish	finis	as fini	finissais	finiras	finirais	finisses	finis
	finit	a fini	finissait	finira	finirait	finisse	
	finissons	avons fini	finissions	finirons	finirions	finissions	finissons
	finissez	avez fini	finissiez	finirez	finiriez	finissiez	finissez
	finissent	ont fini	finissaient	finiront	finiraient	finissent	
-re verbs							
vendre	vends	ai vendu	vendais	vendrai	vendrais	vende	
to sell	vends	as vendu	vendais	vendras	vendrais	vendes	vends
	vend	a vendu	vendait	vendra	vendrait	vende	
	vendons	avons vendu	vendions	vendrons	vendrions	vendions	vendons
	vendez	avez vendu	vendiez	vendrez	vendriez	vendiez	vendez
	vendent	ont vendu	vendaient	vendront	vendraient	vendent	

VERBES RÉFLÉCHIS

VERBE INFINITIF	INDICATIF PRÉSENT	PASSÉ COMPOSÉ	IMPARFAIT	FUTUR	CONDITIONNEL PRÉSENT	SUBJONCTIF PRÉSENT	IMPÉRATIF
se laver *to wash oneself*	me lave	me suis lavé(e)	me lavais	me laverai	me laverais	me lave	
	te laves	t'es lavé(e)	te lavais	te laveras	te laverais	te laves	lave-toi
	se lave	s'est lavé(e)	se lavait	se lavera	se laverait	se lave	
	nous lavons	nous sommes lavé(e)s	nous lavions	nous laverons	nous laverions	nous lavions	lavons-nous
	vous lavez	vous êtes lavé(e)(s)	vous laviez	vous laverez	vous laveriez	vous laviez	lavez-vous
	se lavent	se sont lavé(e)s	se lavaient	se laveront	se laveraient	se lavent	

VERBES À CHANGEMENTS ORTHOGRAPHIQUES

VERBE INFINITIF	INDICATIF PRÉSENT	PASSÉ COMPOSÉ	IMPARFAIT	FUTUR	CONDITIONNEL PRÉSENT	SUBJONCTIF PRÉSENT	IMPÉRATIF
préférer *to prefer*	préfère	ai préféré	préférais	préférerai	préférerais	préfère	
	préfères	as préféré	préférais	préféreras	préférerais	préfères	préfère
	préfère	a préféré	préférait	préférera	préférerait	préfère	
	préférons	avons préféré	préférions	préférerons	préférerions	préférions	préférons
	préférez	avez préféré	préfériez	préférerez	préféreriez	préfériez	préférez
	préfèrent	ont préféré	préféraient	préféreront	préféreraient	préfèrent	
acheter *to buy*	achète	ai acheté	achetais	achèterai	achèterais	achète	
	achètes	as acheté	achetais	achèteras	achèterais	achètes	achète
	achète	a acheté	achetait	achètera	achèterait	achète	
	achetons	avons acheté	achetions	achèterons	achèterions	achetions	achetons
	achetez	avez acheté	achetiez	achèterez	achèteriez	achetiez	achetez
	achètent	ont acheté	achetaient	achèteront	achèteraient	achètent	
appeler *to call*	appelle	ai appelé	appelais	appellerai	appellerais	appelle	
	appelles	as appelé	appelais	appelleras	appellerais	appelles	appelle
	appelle	a appelé	appelait	appellera	appellerait	appelle	
	appelons	avons appelé	appelions	appellerons	appellerions	appelions	appelons
	appelez	avez appelé	appeliez	appellerez	appelleriez	appeliez	appelez
	appellent	ont appelé	appelaient	appelleront	appelleraient	appellent	
essayer *to try*	essaie	ai essayé	essayais	essaierai	essaierais	essaie	
	essaies	as essayé	essayais	essaieras	essaierais	essaies	essaie
	essaie	a essayé	essayait	essaiera	essaierait	essaie	
	essayons	avons essayé	essayions	essaierons	essaierions	essayions	essayons
	essayez	avez essayé	essayiez	essaierez	essaieriez	essayiez	essayez
	essaient	ont essayé	essayaient	essaieront	essaieraient	essaient	
manger *to eat*	mange	ai mangé	mangeais	mangerai	mangerais	mange	
	manges	as mangé	mangeais	mangeras	mangerais	manges	mange
	mange	a mangé	mangeait	mangera	mangerait	mange	
	mangeons	avons mangé	mangions	mangerons	mangerions	mangions	mangeons
	mangez	avez mangé	mangiez	mangerez	mangeriez	mangiez	mangez
	mangent	ont mangé	mangeaient	mangeront	mangeraient	mangent	
commencer *to begin*	commence	ai commencé	commençais	commencerai	commencerais	commence	
	commences	as commencé	commençais	commenceras	commencerais	commences	commence
	commence	a commencé	commençait	commencera	commencerait	commence	
	commençons	avons commencé	commencions	commencerons	commencerions	commencions	commençons
	commencez	avez commencé	commenciez	commencerez	commenceriez	commenciez	commencez
	commencent	ont commencé	commençaient	commenceront	commenceraient	commencent	

VERBES IRRÉGULIERS

VERBE INFINITIF	INDICATIF PRÉSENT	PASSÉ COMPOSÉ	IMPARFAIT	FUTUR	CONDITIONNEL PRÉSENT	SUBJONCTIF PRÉSENT	IMPÉRATIF
aller *to go*	vais	suis allé(e)	allais	irai	irais	aille	
	vas	es allé(e)	allais	iras	irais	ailles	va
	va	est allé(e)	allait	ira	irait	aille	
	allons	sommes allé(e)s	allions	irons	irions	allions	allons
	allez	êtes allé(e)(s)	alliez	irez	iriez	alliez	allez
	vont	sont allé(e)s	allaient	iront	iraient	aillent	
s'asseoir *to sit (down)*	m'assieds	me suis assis(e)	m'asseyais	m'assiérai	m'assiérais	m'asseye	
	t'assieds	t'es assis(e)	t'asseyais	t'assiéras	t'assiérais	t'asseyes	assieds-toi
	s'assied	s'est assis(e)	s'asseyait	s'assiéra	s'assiérait	s'asseye	
	nous asseyons	nous sommes assis(es)	nous asseyions	nous assiérons	nous assiérions	nous asseyions	asseyons-nous
	vous asseyez	vous êtes assis(e)(s)	vous asseyiez	vous assiérez	vous assiériez	vous asseyiez	asseyez-vous
	s'asseyent	se sont assis(es)	s'asseyaient	s'assiéront	s'assiéraient	s'asseyent	
battre *to beat*	bats	ai battu	battais	battrai	battrais	batte	
	bats	as battu	battais	battras	battrais	battes	bats
	bat	a battu	battait	battra	battrait	batte	
	battons	avons battu	battions	battrons	battrions	battions	battons
	battez	avez battu	battiez	battrez	battriez	battiez	battez
	battent	ont battu	battaient	battront	battraient	battent	
boire *to drink*	bois	ai bu	buvais	boirai	boirais	boive	
	bois	as bu	buvais	boiras	boirais	boives	bois
	boit	a bu	buvait	boira	boirait	boive	
	buvons	avons bu	buvions	boirons	boirions	buvions	buvons
	buvez	avez bu	buviez	boirez	boiriez	buviez	buvez
	boivent	ont bu	buvaient	boiront	boiraient	boivent	
conduire *to drive*	conduis	ai conduit	conduisais	conduirai	conduirais	conduise	
	conduis	as conduit	conduisais	conduiras	conduirais	conduises	conduis
	conduit	a conduit	conduisait	conduira	conduirait	conduise	
	conduisons	avons conduit	conduisions	conduirons	conduirions	conduisions	conduisons
	conduisez	avez conduit	conduisiez	conduirez	conduiriez	conduisiez	conduisez
	conduisent	ont conduit	conduisaient	conduiront	conduiraient	conduisent	
connaître *to be acquainted with, to know*	connais	ai connu	connaissais	connaîtrai	connaîtrais	connaisse	
	connais	as connu	connaissais	connaîtras	connaîtrais	connaisses	connais
	connaît	a connu	connaissait	connaîtra	connaîtrait	connaisse	
	connaissons	avons connu	connaissions	connaîtrons	connaîtrions	connaissions	connaissons
	connaissez	avez connu	connaissiez	connaîtrez	connaîtriez	connaissiez	connaissez
	connaissent	ont connu	connaissaient	connaîtront	connaîtraient	connaissent	
courir *to run*	cours	ai couru	courais	courrai	courrais	coure	
	cours	as couru	courais	courras	courrais	coures	cours
	court	a couru	courait	courra	courrait	coure	
	courons	avons couru	courions	courrons	courrions	courions	courons
	courez	avez couru	couriez	courrez	courriez	couriez	courez
	courent	ont couru	couraient	courront	courraient	courent	
croire *to believe*	crois	ai cru	croyais	croirai	croirais	croie	
	crois	as cru	croyais	croiras	croirais	croies	crois
	croit	a cru	croyait	croira	croirait	croie	
	croyons	avons cru	croyions	croirons	croirions	croyions	croyons
	croyez	avez cru	croyiez	croirez	croiriez	croyiez	croyez
	croient	ont cru	croyaient	croiront	croiraient	croient	

VERBES IRRÉGULIERS (SUITE)

VERBE INFINITIF	INDICATIF PRÉSENT	PASSÉ COMPOSÉ	IMPARFAIT	FUTUR	CONDITIONNEL PRÉSENT	SUBJONCTIF PRÉSENT	IMPÉRATIF
devoir	dois	ai dû	devais	devrai	devrais	doive	
must,	dois	as dû	devais	devras	devrais	doives	
to have to,	doit	a dû	devait	devra	devrait	doive	
to owe	devons	avons dû	devions	devrons	devrions	devions	
	devez	avez dû	deviez	devrez	devriez	deviez	
	doivent	ont dû	devaient	devront	devraient	doivent	
dire	dis	ai dit	disais	dirai	dirais	dise	
to say,	dis	as dit	disais	diras	dirais	dises	dis
to tell	dit	a dit	disait	dira	dirait	dise	
	disons	avons dit	disions	dirons	dirions	disions	disons
	dites	avez dit	disiez	direz	diriez	disiez	dites
	disent	ont dit	disaient	diront	diraient	disent	
dormir	dors	ai dormi	dormais	dormirai	dormirais	dorme	
to sleep	dors	as dormi	dormais	dormiras	dormirais	dormes	dors
	dort	a dormi	dormait	dormira	dormirait	dorme	
	dormons	avons dormi	dormions	dormirons	dormirions	dormions	dormons
	dormez	avez dormi	dormiez	dormirez	dormiriez	dormiez	dormez
	dorment	ont dormi	dormaient	dormiront	dormiraient	dorment	
écrire	écris	ai écrit	écrivais	écrirai	écrirais	écrive	
to write	écris	as écrit	écrivais	écriras	écrirais	écrives	écris
	écrit	a écrit	écrivait	écrira	écrirait	écrive	
	écrivons	avons écrit	écrivions	écrirons	écririons	écrivions	écrivons
	écrivez	avez écrit	écriviez	écrirez	écririez	écriviez	écrivez
	écrivent	ont écrit	écrivaient	écriront	écriraient	écrivent	
envoyer	envoie	ai envoyé	envoyais	enverrai	enverrais	envoie	
to send	envoies	as envoyé	envoyais	enverras	enverrais	envoies	envoie
	envoie	a envoyé	envoyait	enverra	enverrait	envoie	
	envoyons	avons envoyé	envoyions	enverrons	enverrions	envoyions	envoyons
	envoyez	avez envoyé	envoyiez	enverrez	enverriez	envoyiez	envoyez
	envoient	ont envoyé	envoyaient	enverront	enverraient	envoient	
faire	fais	ai fait	faisais	ferai	ferais	fasse	
to do,	fais	as fait	faisais	feras	ferais	fasses	fais
to make	fait	a fait	faisait	fera	ferait	fasse	
	faisons	avons fait	faisions	ferons	ferions	fassions	faisons
	faites	avez fait	faisiez	ferez	feriez	fassiez	faites
	font	ont fait	faisaient	feront	feraient	fassent	
falloir	faut	a fallu	fallait	faudra	faudrait	faille	
to be necessary							
lire	lis	ai lu	lisais	lirai	lirais	lise	
to read	lis	as lu	lisais	liras	lirais	lises	lis
	lit	a lu	lisait	lira	lirait	lise	
	lisons	avons lu	lisions	lirons	lirions	lisions	lisons
	lisez	avez lu	lisiez	lirez	liriez	lisiez	lisez
	lisent	ont lu	lisaient	liront	liraient	lisent	
mettre	mets	ai mis	mettais	mettrai	mettrais	mette	
to put (on),	mets	as mis	mettais	mettras	mettrais	mettes	mets
to place,	met	a mis	mettait	mettra	mettrait	mette	
to set	mettons	avons mis	mettions	mettrons	mettrions	mettions	mettons
	mettez	avez mis	mettiez	mettrez	mettriez	mettiez	mettez
	mettent	ont mis	mettaient	mettront	mettraient	mettent	

VERBES IRRÉGULIERS (SUITE)

VERBE INFINITIF	INDICATIF PRÉSENT	PASSÉ COMPOSÉ	IMPARFAIT	FUTUR	CONDITIONNEL PRÉSENT	SUBJONCTIF PRÉSENT	IMPÉRATIF
obtenir	obtiens	ai obtenu	obtenais	obtiendrai	obtiendrais	obtienne	
to obtain	obtiens	as obtenu	obtenais	obtiendras	obtiendrais	obtiennes	obtiens
	obtient	a obtenu	obtenait	obtiendra	obtiendrait	obtienne	
	obtenons	avons obtenu	obtenions	obtiendrons	obtiendrions	obtenions	obtenons
	obtenez	avez obtenu	obteniez	obtiendrez	obtiendriez	obteniez	obtenez
	obtiennent	ont obtenu	obtenaient	obtiendront	obtiendraient	obtiennent	
ouvrir	ouvre	ai ouvert	ouvrais	ouvrirai	ouvrirais	ouvre	
to open	ouvres	as ouvert	ouvrais	ouvriras	ouvrirais	ouvres	ouvre
	ouvre	a ouvert	ouvrait	ouvrira	ouvrirait	ouvre	
	ouvrons	avons ouvert	ouvrions	ouvrirons	ouvririons	ouvrions	ouvrons
	ouvrez	avez ouvert	ouvriez	ouvrirez	ouvririez	ouvriez	ouvrez
	ouvrent	ont ouvert	ouvraient	ouvriront	ouvriraient	ouvrent	
partir	pars	suis parti(e)	partais	partirai	partirais	parte	
to leave	pars	es parti(e)	partais	partiras	partirais	partes	pars
	part	est parti(e)	partait	partira	partirait	parte	
	partons	sommes parti(e)s	partions	partirons	partirions	partions	partons
	partez	êtes parti(e)(s)	partiez	partirez	partiriez	partiez	partez
	partent	sont parti(e)s	partaient	partiront	partiraient	partent	
pleuvoir	pleut	a plu	pleuvait	pleuvra	pleuvrait	pleuve	
to rain							
pouvoir	peux	ai pu	pouvais	pourrai	pourrais	puisse	
to be able,	peux	as pu	pouvais	pourras	pourrais	puisses	
can	peut	a pu	pouvait	pourra	pourrait	puisse	
	pouvons	avons pu	pouvions	pourrons	pourrions	puissions	
	pouvez	avez pu	pouviez	pourrez	pourriez	puissiez	
	peuvent	ont pu	pouvaient	pourront	pourraient	puissent	
prendre	prends	ai pris	prenais	prendrai	prendrais	prenne	
to take	prends	as pris	prenais	prendras	prendrais	prennes	prends
	prend	a pris	prenait	prendra	prendrait	prenne	
	prenons	avons pris	prenions	prendrons	prendrions	prenions	prenons
	prenez	avez pris	preniez	prendrez	prendriez	preniez	prenez
	prennent	ont pris	prenaient	prendront	prendraient	prennent	
recevoir	reçois	ai reçu	recevais	recevrai	recevrais	reçoive	
to receive	reçois	as reçu	recevais	recevras	recevrais	reçoives	reçois
	reçoit	a reçu	recevait	recevra	recevrait	reçoive	
	recevons	avons reçu	recevions	recevrons	recevrions	recevions	recevons
	recevez	avez reçu	receviez	recevrez	recevriez	receviez	recevez
	reçoivent	ont reçu	recevaient	recevront	recevraient	reçoivent	
rire	ris	ai ri	riais	rirai	rirais	rie	
to laugh	ris	as ri	riais	riras	rirais	ries	ris
	rit	a ri	riait	rira	rirait	rie	
	rions	avons ri	riions	rirons	ririons	riions	rions
	riez	avez ri	riiez	rirez	ririez	riiez	riez
	rient	ont ri	riaient	riront	riraient	rient	
savoir	sais	ai su	savais	saurai	saurais	sache	
to know	sais	as su	savais	sauras	saurais	saches	sache
	sait	a su	savait	saura	saurait	sache	
	savons	avons su	savions	saurons	saurions	sachions	sachons
	savez	avez su	saviez	saurez	sauriez	sachiez	sachez
	savent	ont su	savaient	sauront	sauraient	sachent	

VERBES IRRÉGULIERS (SUITE)

VERBE INFINITIF	INDICATIF PRÉSENT	PASSÉ COMPOSÉ	IMPARFAIT	FUTUR	CONDITIONNEL PRÉSENT	SUBJONCTIF PRÉSENT	IMPÉRATIF
sortir *to go out*	sors	suis sorti(e)	sortais	sortirai	sortirais	sorte	
	sors	es sorti(e)	sortais	sortiras	sortirais	sortes	sors
	sort	est sorti(e)	sortait	sortira	sortirait	sorte	
	sortons	sommes sorti(e)s	sortions	sortirons	sortirions	sortions	sortons
	sortez	êtes sorti(e)(s)	sortiez	sortirez	sortiriez	sortiez	sortez
	sortent	sont sorti(e)s	sortaient	sortiront	sortiraient	sortent	
suivre *to follow*	suis	ai suivi	suivais	suivrai	suivrais	suive	
	suis	as suivi	suivais	suivras	suivrais	suives	suis
	suit	a suivi	suivait	suivra	suivrait	suive	
	suivons	avons suivi	suivions	suivrons	suivrions	suivions	suivons
	suivez	avez suivi	suiviez	suivrez	suivriez	suiviez	suivez
	suivent	ont suivi	suivaient	suivront	suivraient	suivent	
venir *to come*	viens	suis venu(e)	venais	viendrai	viendrais	vienne	
	viens	es venu(e)	venais	viendras	viendrais	viennes	viens
	vient	est venu(e)	venait	viendra	viendrait	vienne	
	venons	sommes venu(e)s	venions	viendrons	viendrions	venions	venons
	venez	êtes venu(e)(s)	veniez	viendrez	viendriez	veniez	venez
	viennent	sont venu(e)s	venaient	viendront	viendraient	viennent	
vivre *to live*	vis	ai vécu	vivais	vivrai	vivrais	vive	
	vis	as vécu	vivais	vivras	vivrais	vives	vis
	vit	a vécu	vivait	vivra	vivrait	vive	
	vivons	avons vécu	vivions	vivrons	vivrions	vivions	vivons
	vivez	avez vécu	viviez	vivrez	vivriez	viviez	vivez
	vivent	ont vécu	vivaient	vivront	vivraient	vivent	
voir *to see*	vois	ai vu	voyais	verrai	verrais	voie	
	vois	as vu	voyais	verras	verrais	voies	vois
	voit	a vu	voyait	verra	verrait	voie	
	voyons	avons vu	voyions	verrons	verrions	voyions	voyons
	voyez	avez vu	voyiez	verrez	verriez	voyiez	voyez
	voient	ont vu	voyaient	verront	verraient	voient	
vouloir *to want, to wish*	veux	ai voulu	voulais	voudrai	voudrais	veuille	
	veux	as voulu	voulais	voudras	voudrais	veuilles	veuille
	veut	a voulu	voulait	voudra	voudrait	veuille	
	voulons	avons voulu	voulions	voudrons	voudrions	voulions	veuillons
	voulez	avez voulu	vouliez	voudrez	voudriez	vouliez	veuillez
	veulent	ont voulu	voulaient	voudront	voudraient	veuillent	

VOCABULAIRE français–anglais

This list contains words appearing in **Horizons,** except for absolute cognates. The definitions of active vocabulary words are followed by the number of the chapter where they are first presented. A (P) refers to the ***Chapitre préliminaire.*** When several translations, separated by commas, are listed before a chapter number, they are all considered active. Since verbs are sometimes introduced lexically in the infinitive before the conjugation of the present indicative is presented, consult the ***Index*** to find out the chapter where a conjugation is introduced. An (m), (f), or (pl) following a noun indicates that it is masculine, feminine, or plural. *Inv* means that a word is invariable. An asterisk before a word beginning with an **h** indicates that the **h** is aspirate.

A

à to, at, in (P); **À bientôt.** See you soon. (P); **à cause de** due to, because of; **À ce soir.** See you tonight/this evening. (2); **à côté (de)** next to (3); **À demain.** See you tomorrow. (P); **à… heure(s)** at . . . o'clock (P); **à la campagne** in the country (3); **à la française** French-style; **à la maison** at home (P); **à la page…** on page . . . (P); **à l'avance** in advance (9); **à l'étranger** abroad (9); **à l'heure** on time (4); **à l'université** at the university (P); **à peu près** about; **à pied** on foot (4); **À plus (tard)!** See you later! (P); **À quelle heure?** At what time? (P); **à suivre** to be continued (6); **À tout à l'heure.** See you in a little while. (P); **au café** at the café (2); **au coin de** on the corner of (10); **au cours de** in the course of, during, while on (10); **au-dessus de** above; **au premier étage** on the second floor (3); **Au revoir.** Good-bye. (P); **à votre avis** in your opinion (8); **café** (m) **au lait** coffee with milk (2); **du lundi au vendredi** from Monday to Friday (*every week*) (P); **j'habite à** (+ *city*) I live in (+ *city*) (P)
abandonner to abandon, to leave
abolir to abolish
abonnement (m) subscription
abonner: s'abonner à to subscribe to
abord: d'abord first (2)
abricot (m) apricot
abriter to shelter
absolument absolutely
Acadie (f) Acadia
accent (m) accent (P); **accent aigu / circonflexe / grave** acute / circumflex / grave accent (P); **Ça s'écrit avec ou sans accent?** That's written with or without an accent? (P)
accepter to accept (7)
accès (m) access (10); **accès Wi-Fi** (m) Wi-Fi access (10)
accessoire (m) accessory
accidentellement accidentally
accompagner to accompany
accomplir to accomplish
accord (m) agreement; **D'accord!** Okay! (2), Agreed!; **se mettre d'accord** to come to an agreement
accorder to give; **s'accorder** to grant each other
achat (m) purchase
acheter to buy (4)
acide gras (trans) (m) (trans) fatty acid
acteur (m) actor (6)
actif (active) active, working
activité (f) activity (2)
actrice (f) actress (6)
actuellement currently
adapter: s'adapter to adapt

addition (f) check, bill
adjectif (m) adjective (3)
administratif(-ive): centre administratif (m) administration building
admirer to admire (9)
adorer to adore, to love (5)
adresse (f) address (3); **adresse** (f) **mail** e-mail address (3)
aérien(ne) aerial
aérobic (f) aerobics: **faire de l'aérobic** to do aerobics (8)
aéroport (m) airport (10)
affaire (f) thing, belonging, business; **femme d'affaires** businesswoman (5); **homme d'affaires** businessman (5)
affiché(e) posted
africain(e) African
Afrique (f) Africa (9); **Afrique** (f) **du Sud** South Africa
âge (m) age (4); **Quel âge a… ?** How old is . . . ? (4)
âgé(e) old (4)
agence (f) **de voyages** travel agency (9)
agent (m) agent; **agent** (m) **de police** police officer; **agent** (m) **de voyages** travel agent (9)
agir to act, to take action
agité(e) agitated
agneau (m) lamb
agréable pleasant (1)
aider to help (5); **Je peux vous aider?** May I help you? (5)
aïe ouch
aigu(ë) acute (P), shrill
ail (m) garlic
aile (f) wing
ailleurs elsewhere; **par ailleurs** furthermore
aimable kind, amiable
aimer to like, to love (2); **Aimeriez-vous… ?** Would you like . . . ? (8); **aimer mieux** to like better, to prefer (2); **Est-ce que tu aimes/vous aimez… ?** Do you like . . . ? (1); **J'aime/Je n'aime pas…** I like/I don't like . . . (1); **J'aimerais…** I would like . . . (8); **J'aimerais autant…** I would just as soon . . . (10); **s'aimer** to love each other (7)
aîné(e) oldest (*child*)
ainsi thus; **ainsi que** as well as
air (m) air, look, appearance; **avoir l'air** (+ *adjective*) to look / to seem (+ *adjective*) (4); **Ça a l'air bien.** It/That seems nice. (3); **de plein air** outdoor (4)
aise (f) ease; **mal à l'aise** ill at ease
aisé(e): classe aisée (f) upper class
ajouter to add
alcool (m) alcohol (8)
alcoolisé(e) alcoholic
Algérie (f) Algeria (9)
algérien(ne) Algerian
aliment (m) food

alimentaire food
Allemagne (f) Germany (9)
allemand (m) German (1)
allemand(e) German
aller (à) to go (to) (2); **aller à la chasse** to go hunting; **aller à la pêche** to go fishing; **aller à pied** to walk, to go on foot (4); **aller simple** (m) one-way ticket (9); **aller très bien à quelqu'un** to look very good on someone; **aller voir** to go see, to visit (*a person*) (4); **Allez au tableau.** Go to the board. (P); **Allons…!** Let's go…! (2); **billet aller-retour** (m) round-trip ticket (9); **Ça va?** How's it going? (*familiar*) (P); **Ça va.** It's going fine. (P); **Comment allez-vous?** How are you? (*formal*) (P); **Comment ça va?**, How's it going? (*familiar*) (P); **Comment vas-tu?** How are you? (*informal*) (P); **je vais** I go, I am going (2); **Je vais très bien** I'm doing very well. (P); **On va…** ? Shall we go . . . ? (2); **Qu'est-ce que vous allez prendre?** What are you going to have? (2); **Qu'est-ce qui ne va pas?** What's wrong? (10); **s'en aller** to go away
allergie (f) allergy (10)
allié(e) allied
allô hello (*on the telephone*) (6)
allumer to light
alors so, then, therefore (1); **alors que** whereas
alpinisme (m) mountain climbing; **faire de l'alpinisme** to go mountain climbing
amande (f) almond
amant(e) (mf) lover
améliorer to improve
amener to take, to bring
américain(e) American (P); **à l'américaine** American-style (8)
Amérindien(ne) (mf) Native American
Amérique (f) America (9); **Amérique centrale** (f) Central America (9); **Amérique** (f) **du Nord** North America (9); **Amérique** (f) **du Sud** South America (9)
ami(e) (mf) friend (P)
amitié (f) friendship
amour (m) love (6); **film** (m) **d'amour** romantic movie (6); **le grand amour** (m) true love (7)
amoureux(-euse) (de) in love (with) (6); **tomber amoureux(-euse) de** to fall in love with (6); **vie amoureuse** (f) love life
amphithéâtre (m) lecture hall (1)
ampoule (f) light bulb
amusant(e) fun (1)
amuser to amuse; **s'amuser** to have fun (7)
an (m) year (5); **avoir… ans** to be . . . years old (4); **jour** (m) **de l'An** (m) New Year's Day
ananas (m) pineapple
anchois (m) anchovy
ancien(ne) former, old, ancient

andouillette *(f)* small sausage of chitterlings
ange *(m)* angel
anglais *(m)* English (P)
anglais(e) English
Angleterre *(f)* England; **Nouvelle-Angleterre** *(f)* New England
anglophone English-speaking
angoisse *(f)* anguish
animal *(m)* *(pl* **animaux***)* animal (3)
animé(e) animated; **dessin animé** *(m)* cartoon
année *(f)* year (4); **les années** *(fpl)* **trente** the thirties
annexion *(f)* annexation
anniversaire *(m)* birthday (4); **anniversaire** *(m)* **de mariage** wedding anniversary
annonce *(f)* advertisement, announcement
anorak *(m)* ski jacket, anorak (5)
antillais(e) West Indian
Antilles *(fpl)* West Indies (9)
antimicrobien(ne) antimicrobial
antipathique disagreeable, unpleasant (1)
antique ancient
août *(m)* August (4)
apéritif (apéro) *(m)* (before-dinner) drink (8)
appareil *(m)* device, apparatus, appliance
apparence *(f)* appearance
apparenté(e) related
appartement *(m)* apartment (3)
appartenir (à) to belong (to)
appeler to call; **appelé(e)** called; **Comment s'appelle... ?** What is . . . 's name? (4); **Comment t'appelles-tu?** What's your name? *(informal)*; **Comment vous appelez-vous?** What's your name? *(formal)* (P); **Il/Elle s'appelle...** His/Her name is . . . (4); **Je m'appelle...** My name is . . . (P); **s'appeler** to be named (7), to be called; **Tu t'appelles comment?** What's your name? *(informal)* (P)
appétit *(m)* appetite
apporter to bring
apprécier to appreciate (6), to like
apprendre to learn (4); **Apprenez les mots de vocabulaire.** Learn the vocabulary words. (P)
apprentissage *(m)* apprenticeship
approcher: s'approcher (de) to approach
approprié(e) appropriate
approximatif(-ive) approximate
après after (P), afterwards (2); **après les cours** after class (2); **d'après** according to
après-demain the day after tomorrow (4)
après-midi *(m)* afternoon (P); **cet après-midi** this afternoon (4); **Il est une heure de l'après-midi.** It's one o'clock in the afternoon. (P); **l'après-midi** in the afternoon, afternoons (P)
arabe *(m)* Arabic
arbre *(m)* tree (1)
arc *(m)* arch, bow
archéologique archeological
archipel *(m)* archipelago
argent *(m)* money, silver (2)
Argentine *(f)* Argentina (9)
armée *(f)* army
arracher: s'arracher les cheveux to pull out your hair
arrêt *(m)* stop; **arrêt** *(m)* **de bus** bus stop (3)
arrêter to arrest, to stop; **s'arrêter** to stop (7)
arrivée *(f)* arrival (9)
arriver to arrive (3), to happen
art *(m)* art (1); **les arts** the arts (1); **les beaux-arts** the fine arts
article *(m)* article (9)

artisanal(e) *(mpl* **artisanaux***)* handcrafted
artiste *(mf)* artist, performer
ascenseur *(m)* elevator (3)
Asie *(f)* Asia (9)
aspect physique *(m)* physical appearance (7)
asperge *(f)* asparagus
aspirine *(f)* aspirin (10)
assassiner to murder, to assassinate
asseoir: Asseyez-vous. Sit down.; **s'asseoir** to sit (down)
assez fairly, rather (P); **assez (de)** enough (of) (1)
assiette *(f)* plate
assis(e) seated (9)
assister à to attend
association caritative *(f)* charitable organization
associer to associate; **associé(e)** associated
assurance *(f)* insurance
Atlantique *(m)* Atlantic
atroce atrocious, dreadful
attaque *(f)* attack; **attaque** *(f)* **d'apoplexie** stroke; **être d'attaque** to feel fit
attendre to wait (for) (7); **s'attendre à** to expect to
attente *(f)* waiting
attention: faire attention (à) to pay attention (to), to watch out (for) (8)
attirant(e) attractive
attirer to attract
attraper to catch, to get hold of
aube *(f)* dawn
auberge *(f)* inn; **auberge** *(f)* **de jeunesse** youth hostel (10)
aubergine *(f)* eggplant
auburn *(inv)* auburn (7)
aucun(e): ne... aucun(e) no, none, not one
audacieux(-euse) audacious, bold
au-dessus above
auditif(-ive) auditory
augmenter to augment, to raise
aujourd'hui today (P)
auparavant beforehand
auprès de among
auquel (à laquelle, auxquels, auxquelles) to which
aussi too, also (P); **aussi... que** as . . . as (1)
austral(e) *(mpl* **austraux***)* southern
Australie *(f)* Australia (9)
autant (de)... (que) as much . . . (as), as many . . . (as); **J'aimerais autant...** I would just as soon . . . (10)
autobus *(m)* bus (4); **arrêt** *(m)* **d'autobus** bus stop (3); **en autobus** by bus (4)
autocar *(m)* bus (4); **en autocar** by bus (4)
automne *(m)* autumn, fall (5); **en automne** in autumn (5)
autoportrait *(m)* self-portrait (P)
autour de around
autre other (P); **dans un autre cours** in another class (P); **quelquefois... d'autres fois** sometimes . . . other times (7); **Qu'est-ce que je peux vous proposer d'autre?** What else can I get you? (8); **autre part** somewhere else
autrefois formerly, in the past
Autriche *(f)* Austria (9)
auxiliaire auxiliary
avance *(f)* advance; **à l'avance** in advance (9); **en avance** early
avancer to advance
avant before (P); **avant de (faire)** before (doing) (7); **avant tout** above all
avantage *(m)* advantage

avec with (P); **avec elle / lui / elles / eux** with her / him / them *(f)* / them *(m)* (2); **avec ma famille** with my family (P); **Avec plaisir!** With pleasure! (6)
avenir *(m)* future
aventure *(f)* adventure; **film** *(m)* **d'aventure** adventure movie
avenue *(f)* avenue (10)
avion *(m)* airplane (4); **en avion** by airplane (4)
avis *(m)* opinion; **à votre avis** in your opinion (8)
avoir to have (3); **avoir... ans** to be . . . years old (4); **avoir besoin de** to need (4); **avoir chaud** to be hot (4); **avoir cours** to have class (6); **avoir de la fièvre** to have fever; **avoir du mal à...** to have difficulty . . . , to have a hard time . . . ; **avoir envie de** to feel like, to want (4); **avoir faim** to be hungry (4); **avoir froid** to be cold (4); **avoir l'air** (+ *adjective*) to look / to seem (+ *adjective*) (4); **avoir le nez bouché** to have a stopped-up nose; **avoir le nez qui coule** to have a runny nose; **avoir les cheveux/les yeux...** to have . . . hair/eyes (4); **avoir lieu** to take place; **avoir l'intention de** to plan on, to intend to (4); **avoir mal (à)** one's . . . hurts (10), to ache; **avoir peur (de)** to be afraid (of), to fear (4); **avoir pitié (de)** to have pity (on / for) (10); **avoir raison** to be right (4); **avoir soif** to be thirsty (4); **avoir sommeil** to be sleepy (4); **avoir tort** to be wrong (4); **j'ai faim** I'm hungry (2); **j'ai soif** I'm thirsty (2); **il y a...** there is/there are . . . (1), ago (5); **Quel âge a... ?** How old is . . . ? (4)
avril *(m)* April (4)
ayant having

B

baccalauréat (bac) *(m)* a comprehensive examination at the end of secondary school
bacon *(m)* bacon (8)
bagages *(mpl)* baggage
baguette *(f)* loaf of French bread (8)
baie *(f)* bay
bain *(m)* bath (7); **maillot** *(m)* **de bain** swimsuit (5); **prendre un bain** *(m)* **de soleil** to sunbathe (4); **salle** *(f)* **de bains** bathroom (3)
baiser *(m)* kiss
baisser to lower
bal *(m)* ball, dance (6)
balcon *(m)* balcony (10)
baleine *(f)* whale
ballet *(m)* ballet (9)
ballon *(m)* ball
banal(e) *(mpl* **banaux***)* commonplace, banal
banane *(f)* banana (8)
bancaire banking; **carte** *(f)* **bancaire** bank card, debit card (9)
bande-annonce *(f)* movie trailer
bande dessinée *(f)* comic strip, comic book
banlieue *(f)* suburbs (3); **en banlieue** in the suburbs (3)
banque *(f)* bank (10)
banquier *(m)* banker
barbe *(f)* beard (4)
barrer to cross out
bas *(m)* bottom
bas(se) low; **table basse** *(f)* coffee table
basant: en vous basant sur based on
basé(e) sur based on (6)
baseball *(m)* baseball (2)
basilique *(f)* basilica

basket *(m)* basketball (1)
baskets *(fpl)* tennis shoes (5)
bataille *(f)* battle
bateau *(m)* boat (4); **en bateau** by boat (4); **faire du bateau** to go boating (5)
bâtiment *(m)* building (1)
batterie *(f)* drums (2)
battre to beat; **se battre** to fight
bavarois *(m)* Bavarian cream
bavette *(f)* flank steak
bazar: Quel bazar! *(familiar)* What a mess! (3)
BD (bande déssinée) *(f)* comic strip, comic book
beau (bel, belle, *pl* **beaux, belles)** beautiful, handsome (1); **beau-frère** *(m)* brother-in-law (4); **beau-père** *(m)* father-in-law (4); **beaux-arts** *(mpl)* fine arts; **beaux-parents** *(mpl)* stepparents, in-laws (4); **belle-mère** *(f)* mother-in-law (4); **belle-sœur** *(f)* sister-in-law; **Il fait beau.** The weather's nice. (5)
beaucoup a lot (P); **beaucoup (de)** a lot (of) (1)
beauté *(f)* beauty (7)
bébé *(m)* baby
beige beige (3)
beignet *(m)* fritter
belge Belgian
Belgique *(f)* Belgium (9)
bénéfique beneficial
bénévole benevolent, volunteer
berbère Berber
berceuse *(f)* lullaby
besoin *(m)* need; **avoir besoin de** to need (4)
bête *(f)* beast (6), animal
bête stupid, dumb (1)
bêtise *(f)* foolish thing, stupidity
beurre *(m)* butter (8); **beurre** *(m)* **de cacahuète** peanut butter
beurré(e) buttered
bibliothèque *(f)* library (1), bookcase
bien *(m)* good; **biens** *(mpl)* goods
bien well (P), very; **à bien des égards** in many regards; **bien d'autres** many others; **bien que** although; **Bien sûr!** Of course! (5); **Ça a l'air bien.** It/That seems nice. (3); **c'est bien de…** it's good to . . . (10)
bien-être *(m)* well-being
bienfait *(m)* benefit
bienfaiteur *(m)*, **bienfaitrice** *(f)* benefactor
bientôt soon (P); **À bientôt.** See you soon. (P)
bienvenu(e) welcome
bière *(f)* beer (2)
bifteck *(m)* steak (8); **bifteck hâché** *(m)* ground meat
bikini *(m)* bikini (5)
bilan *(m)* assessment
bilingue bilingual
billet *(m)* ticket (9), bill; **billet** *(m)* **d'avion** plane ticket (9); **distributeur** *(m)* **de billets** ATM machine (10)
bio organic; **produits bio** *(mpl)* organic products (8)
biologie *(f)* biology (1)
biscotte *(f)* melba toast
bise *(f)* kiss
bistro(t) *(m)* restaurant, pub (6)
blanc(he) white (3); **vin blanc** *(m)* white wine (2)
blanquette *(f)* stew *(usually veal)*
blessure *(f)* injury
bleu(e) blue (3); **carte** *(f)* **bleue** credit card (9)
blog *(m)* blog (9)
bloguer to blog
blond(e) blond (4)
blouson *(m)* windbreaker, jacket

Blu-ray: lecteur *(m)* **Blu-ray** Blu-ray player (3)
bœuf *(m)* beef (8); **bœuf bourguignon** *(m)* beef burgundy
bohème bohemian
boire to drink (4)
boisson *(f)* drink (2)
boîte *(f)* box, can (8); **boîte** *(f)* **de nuit** nightclub (1)
bol *(m)* bowl
bon (ne) good (1); **Bon anniversaire!** Happy birthday!; **Bonne année!** Happy New Year!; **Bonne idée!** Good idea! (4); **Bonne journée!** Have a good day!; **Bon séjour!** Enjoy your stay! (10); **Bon week-end!** Have a good weekend!
bonbon *(m)* candy
bonheur *(m)* happiness (7)
bonhomme *(m)* man, guy, fellow
Bonjour. Hello., Good morning. (P)
bonne *(f)* maid, nanny
Bonsoir. Good evening. (P)
bord *(m)* edge; **à bord** on board; **au bord de** at the edge of; **bord** *(m)* **de la mer** seaside
border to border
botanique botanical
botte *(f)* boot (5)
bouche *(f)* mouth (10)
bouché(e) stopped-up; **cidre bouché** *(m)* bottled cider
boucherie *(f)* butcher's shop (8)
boudin *(m)* blood sausage
bouillabaisse *(f)* fish soup
bouillir to boil
bouillon *(m)* broth
boulangerie *(f)* bakery (8); **boulangerie-pâtisserie** bakery-pastry shop (8)
boule *(f)* ball
boulevard *(m)* boulevard (10)
bouleversant(e) overwhelming, very touching
boulot *(m)* *(familiar)* work
bouquiniste *(mf)* secondhand bookseller
bourg *(m)* town
bout *(m)* end (3); **au bout (de)** at the end (of) (3)
bouteille (de) *(f)* bottle (of) (8)
boutique *(f)* shop (10); **boutique** *(f)* **de cadeaux** gift shop (10)
bras *(m)* arm (10)
bref (brève) short, brief; **Bref,…** In short, . . ., To be brief, . . .
Brésil *(m)* Brazil (9)
Bretagne *(f)* Brittany
breton *(m)* Breton *(language)*
brevet *(m)* certificate, diploma
bricoler to do handiwork (2)
brioche *(f)* brioche *(a type of soft bread)*
brique *(f)* brick
britannique British
brochette *(f)* skewer
brocoli *(m)* broccoli
bronzer to tan (9)
brosser to brush; **se brosser (les cheveux / les dents)** to brush (one's hair / one's teeth) (7)
brouillard *(m)* fog, mist, haze
bruit *(m)* noise (10)
brûler to burn; **se brûler la main** to burn your hand
brun(e) *(with hair)* medium/dark brown (4), brunette, darkhaired
Bruxelles Brussels
bruyant(e) noisy
bulletin *(m)* **d'abonnement** subscription form

bureau *(m)* desk (3), office (1); **bureau** *(m)* **de change** currency exchange (10); **bureau** *(m)* **de poste** post office (10); **bureau** *(m)* **de tabac** tobacco shop
bus *(m)* bus (3); **arrêt** *(m)* **de bus** bus stop (3); **en bus** by bus (4)
but *(m)* goal

C

ça that (P); **Ça fait combien?** How much is it? (2); **Ça fait… euros.** That's . . . euros. (2); **Ça lui plaît?** Does he/she like it? (9); **Ça s'écrit comment?** How is that written? (P); **Ça s'écrit…** That's written . . . (P); **Ça te/vous dit?** How does that sound to you? (2); **Ça te plaît.** You like it. (3); **Ça va?** How's it going? *(familiar)* (P); **Ça va.** It's going fine. (P); **C'est ça!** That's right! (1); **comme ci comme ça** so-so (P); **Comment ça va?** How's it going? *(familiar)* (P); **Qu'est-ce que ça veut dire?** What does that mean? (P)
cabine *(f)* **d'essayage** fitting room (5); **cabine** *(f)* **téléphonique** telephone booth
cacahuète *(f)* peanut; **beurre** *(m)* **de cacahuète** peanut butter
cacher to hide; **se cacher** to hide oneself, to be hidden
cadeau *(m)* gift, present (10); **boutique** *(f)* **de cadeaux** gift shop (10)
cadien(ne) Cajun (4)
cadre *(m)* frame, surroundings
café *(m)* café (1), coffee (2); **café** *(m)* **au lait** coffee with milk (2)
cahier *(m)* workbook (P), notebook; **Faites les devoirs dans le cahier.** Do the homework in the workbook. (P)
calcul *(m)* calculation, calculus
calculer to calculate
Californie *(f)* California (9)
calme calm (4)
calmement calmly
calmer: se calmer to calm down
calorie *(f)* calorie (8)
calorique high in calories
camarade *(mf)* pal; **camarade** *(mf)* **de chambre** roommate (P); **camarade** *(mf)* **de classe** classmate
camerounais(e) Cameroonian
campagne *(f)* country (3), campaign; **à la campagne** in the country (3)
camping *(m)* camping, campground (5); **faire du camping** to go camping (5)
campus *(m)* campus (1)
Canada *(m)* Canada (9)
canadien(ne) Canadian (P)
canapé *(m)* couch (3), open-faced sandwich
canard *(m)* duck (8)
candidat(e) *(mf)* candidate, applicant
canne à sucre *(f)* sugar cane
canoë *(m)* canoeing
caprice *(m)* whim
car *(m)* bus (4); **en car** by bus (4)
car because
caractère *(m)* character; **en caractères gras** boldfaced; **trait** *(m)* **de caractère** character trait (7)
carafe (de) *(f)* carafe (of) *(a decanter)* (8)
caraïbe Caribbean; **mer** *(f)* **des Caraïbes** Caribbean Sea
caritatif(-ive) charitable
carotte *(f)* carrot (8)
carré *(m)* square; **Vieux Carré** *(m)* French Quarter (4)
carrière *(f)* career

carte *(f)* menu (8), card, map; **carte** *(f)* **bancaire** bank card, debit card (9); **carte** *(f)* **bleue** credit card (9); **carte** *(f)* **de crédit** credit card (9); **carte** *(f)* **d'identité** identity card; **carte** *(f)* **postale** postcard (9); **carte** *(f)* **téléphonique** telephone card (10)
cas *(m)* case; **dans tous les cas** in any case
cascade *(f)* waterfall
casquette *(f)* cap
casser to break; **se casser la jambe** to break one's leg
casserole *(f)* pan
catégorie *(f)* category
cathédrale *(f)* cathedral
catholique *(mf)* Catholic (1)
cauchemar *(m)* nightmare
cause *(f)* cause; **à cause de** because of
CD *(m)* CD (3); **lecteur** *(m)* **CD** CD player (3)
ce (cet, cette) this, that (3); **ce (cet, cette)...ci** this . . . over here (3); **ce (cet, cette)... là** that . . . over there (3); **ce que** what, that which (7); **ce qui** what, that which (7); **ces** these, those (3); **ce semestre** this semester (P); **ce soir** tonight, this evening (2); **Ce sont…** They are . . ., These are . . ., Those are . . . (1); **C'est…** It's . . . (P), He / She / This / That is . . . (1); **c'est-à-dire** in other words, that is to say; **Qu'est-ce que c'est?** What is it? (2); **Qui est-ce?** Who is it? (2)
céder to give up
ceinture *(f)* belt
cela that; **depuis cela** since then
célèbre famous (4)
célébrer to celebrate
céleri *(m)* celery
célibataire single, unmarried (1)
celtique Celtic
celui (celle) the one
cendre *(f)* ash
cendrier *(m)* ashtray
censé(e) supposed
censure *(f)* censorship
cent *(m)* one hundred (3)
centime *(m)* centime *(one hundredth part of a euro)* (2)
central(e) *(mpl* **centraux)** central; **Amérique** *(f)* **centrale** Central America (9)
centre *(m)* center; **centre administratif** *(m)* administration building; **centre commercial** *(m)* shopping center, mall (4); **centre** *(m)* **d'étudiants** student center
centre-ville *(m)* downtown (3)
cependant however
céréales *(fpl)* cereal (8)
cerise *(f)* cherry (8)
certain(e) certain; **certains** some, certain people (8)
certainement certainly
cervelle *(f)* brain
cesser to cease
ceux (celles) those (ones) (8)
chacun(e) each one
chagrin *(m)* sorrow
chaîne *(f)* chain; **chaîne de télévision** television channel; **chaîne hi-fi** *(f)* stereo (3)
chaise *(f)* chair (3)
chalet *(m)* **à la montagne** ski lodge (10)
chaleur *(f)* warmth
chaleureux(-euse) warm
chambre *(f)* bedroom (3); **camarade** *(mf)* **de chambre** roommate (P); **chambre** *(f)* **d'hôte** bed and breakfast; **chambre double** *(f)* double room (10); **chambre simple** single room *(f)* (10)
champ *(m)* field; **champ** *(m)* **de bataille** battlefield
champignon *(m)* mushroom
chance *(f)* luck (5); **Quelle chance!** What luck! (5)
change: bureau *(m)* **de change** currency exchange (10)
changement *(m)* change
changer to change (6); **changer de l'argent** to exchange money (9)
chanson *(f)* song
chanter to sing (2)
chanteur(-euse) *(mf)* singer
chapeau *(m)* hat
chapelle *(f)* chapel
chapitre *(m)* chapter
chaque each, every (3)
charcuterie *(f)* delicatessen, deli meats, cold cuts (8)
charger to charge, to load; **chargé(e) (de)** busy *(schedule)*, in charge (of); **se charger de** to take charge of
charmant(e) charming
chasse *(f)* hunt, hunting; **aller à la chasse** to go hunting
chasser to hunt, to make go away
chasseur *(m)* hunter
chat *(m)* cat (3)
châtain light/medium brown *(with hair)* (4)
château *(m)* castle
chaud(e) hot (2); **avoir chaud** to be hot (4); **chocolat chaud** *(m)* hot chocolate (2); **Il fait chaud.** It's hot. (5)
chauffeur *(m)* driver
chaussette *(f)* sock
chausson *(m)* **aux pommes** apple turnover
chaussure *(f)* shoe (5)
chef *(m)* head, boss, chief
chef-d'œuvre *(m)* masterpiece
chef-lieu *(m)* administrative center
chemin *(m)* road; **chemin** *(m)* **de fer** railroad; **indiquer le chemin** to give directions, to show the way (10)
chemise *(f)* shirt (5); **chemise** *(f)* **de nuit** nightgown
chemisier *(m)* blouse (5)
chèque *(m)* check (9); **chèque** *(m)* **de voyage** traveler's check
cher(-ère) expensive (3), dear
chercher to look for (3), to seek; **aller / venir chercher quelqu'un** to go / come pick up someone (10)
chéri(e) *(mf)* honey, darling
cheval *(m)* *(pl* **chevaux)** horse; **faire du cheval** to go horseback riding
cheveux *(mpl)* hair (4)
cheville *(f)* ankle; **se fouler la cheville** to sprain one's ankle
chèvre *(m)* goat cheese
chez… at / in / to / by . . . 's house/place (2); in *(a person)* (7)
chien *(m)* dog (3)
chiffre *(m)* number, numeral
Chili *(m)* Chile (9)
chimie *(f)* chemistry (1)
Chine *(f)* China (9)
chinois *(m)* Chinese
chirurgie *(f)* surgery
chocolat *(m)* chocolate (2); **gâteau** *(m)* **au chocolat** chocolate cake (8); **pain au chocolat** *(m)* chocolate-filled croissant (8)
choisir (de faire) to choose (to do) (8)
choix *(m)* choice (8)
chose *(f)* thing (3); **quelque chose** something (2)
chou *(m)* cabbage; **choux** *(mpl)* **de Bruxelles** Brussels sprouts
chou-fleur *(m)* cauliflower
chrysanthème *(m)* chrysanthemum
chute *(f)* waterfall
ci: ce (cet, cette)...-ci this . . . (5); **ce mois-ci** this month (4); **ces...-ci** these . . . (5); **ci-dessous** below; **ci-dessus** above; **comme ci comme ça** so-so (P)
ciao bye *(informal)*
ciel *(m)* sky
cimetière *(m)* cemetery
cinéaste *(mf)* filmmaker
ciné-club *(m)* cinema club (2)
cinéma *(m)* movie theater (1); **aller au cinéma** to go to the movies (2)
cinématographique film
cinq five (P)
cinquante fifty (2); **cinquante et un** fifty-one (2)
cinquième fifth (3)
circonstance *(f)* circumstance
circuler to circulate
cithare *(f)* zither
citoyen(ne) *(mf)* citizen
citron *(m)* lemon (2); **citron vert** *(m)* lime; **thé** *(m)* **au citron** tea with lemon (2)
civilisé(e) civilized
clair(e) light, clear; **bleu clair** light blue
claire *(f)* oyster bed
clairement clearly
classe *(f)* class (1); **classe** *(f)* **économique** economy class, coach (9); **première classe** *(f)* first class (9)
classé(e) ranked
classement *(m)* ranking
classique classical (1), classic (2)
clavier *(m)* keyboard
clé *(f)* key (10)
client(e) *(mf)* customer
climat *(m)* climate (9)
climatisation *(f)* air conditioning
climatisé(e) air-conditioned
coca *(m)* cola (2); **coca** *(m)* **light** diet cola (2)
coco *(m)* coconut
cocotier *(m)* coconut tree, palm tree
cocotte *(f)* casserole, primper
code *(m)* code; **code postal** *(m)* zip code (3)
cœur *(m)* heart; **au cœur de** in the heart of
coin *(m)* corner (3); **au coin de** on the corner of (10); **café** *(m)* **du coin** neighborhood café; **dans le coin (de)** in the corner (of) (3)
collation *(f)* snack
colle *(f)* glue, detention
collectionner to collect
collectivité *(f)* community
collège *(m)* middle school
collègue *(mf)* colleague
colline *(f)* hill
colocataire *(mf)* housemate (P)
Colombie *(f)* Colombia (9)
colon *(m)* colonist
colonne *(f)* column
combien (de) how much, how many (3); **Ça fait combien? / C'est combien?** How much is it? (2); **Combien font… et / moins… ?** How much is . . . plus / minus . . . ? (P); **Pendant combien de temps?** For how long? (5); **Vous êtes combien dans votre (ta) famille?** How many are there in your family? (4)

combinaison *(f)* slip, combination
comédie *(f)* comedy (6); **comédie musicale** *(f)* musical
comique comical
commander to order (2), to command
comme like, as, for (1), since (7); **comme ci comme ça** so-so (P); **comme tu vois** as you see (3); **tout comme** just as
commencer (à) to begin (to), to start (2); **Le cours de français commence à...** French class starts at . . . (P)
comment how (P); **Ça s'écrit comment?** How is that written? (P); **Comment allez-vous?** How are you? *(formal)* (P); **Comment ça va?** How's it going? *(familiar)* (P); **Comment dit-on... en français/en anglais?** How does one say . . . in French/in English? (P); **Comment est-il/elle (sont-ils/elles)?** What is he/she (are they) like? (1); **Comment? Répétez, s'il vous plaît.** What? Please repeat. (P); **Comment s'appelle... ?** What is . . . 's name? (4); **Comment vas-tu?** How are you? *(informal)*; **Comment vous appelez-vous?** What's your name? *(formal)* (P); **Tu t'appelles comment?** What's your name? *(informal)* (P)
commentaire *(m)* commentary
commerçant(e) *(mf)* shopkeeper (8), merchant
commerce *(m)* business (1)
commercial: centre commercial *(m)* shopping center, mall (4)
commettre to commit
commode *(f)* dresser, chest of drawers (3)
commode convenient
commodité *(f)* convenience, comfort
commun(e) common
communauté *(f)* community
communiquer to communicate (10)
compagnie *(f)* company; **en compagnie de** accompanied by
comparaison *(f)* comparison
comparer to compare (6); **comparé(e)** compared
compatibilité *(f)* compatibility (7)
compétence *(f)* skill, competency
complément d'objet direct / indirect *(m)* direct / indirect object
complet(-ète) complete (8); **avec une phrase complète** *(f)* with a complete sentence (P); **pain complet** *(m)* (loaf of) whole-grain bread (8)
complètement completely
complicité *(f)* bonding
comporter: se comporter to behave
composer to compose; **composé(e) de** composed of; **se composer de** to be made up of
compréhension *(f)* understanding
comprenant including
comprendre to understand (4), to include (8); **compris(e)** included (10); **Oui, je comprends. / Non, je ne comprends pas.** Yes, I understand. / No, I don't understand. (P); **Vous comprenez?** Do you understand? (P)
comptabilité *(f)* accounting (1)
comptable *(mf)* accountant
compte *(m)* **en banque** bank account
compter to count, to plan on (9); **Comptez de... à...** Count from . . . to . . . (P)
concentrer: se concentrer sur to concentrate on
concerner to concern; **concernant** concerning
concert *(m)* concert (1); **de concert avec** along with

concombre *(m)* cucumber
concours *(m)* competition, competitive entrance examination
confiance *(f)* confidence; **avoir confiance** to have confidence (4); **faire confiance à** to trust
confirmer to confirm (10)
confit *(m)* **de canard** conserve of duck
confiture *(f)* jam, jelly (8)
confort *(m)* comfort
confortable comfortable (3)
conforter to comfort
confus(e) confused
congé *(m)* day off
conjuguer to conjugate
connaissance *(f)* acquaintance, knowledge; **faire la connaissance de** to meet *(for the first time)* (7)
connaître to know, to get to know, to be familiar / acquainted with (4); **Connaissez-vous...?** Do you know . . . ? (6); **faire connaître** to inform
connecter to connect; **se connecter à Internet** to log on to Internet
connu(e) known
conquérant(e) *(mf)* conqueror
conquête *(f)* conquest
consacrer to devote; **consacré(e) à** devoted to
conseil *(m)* piece of advice (8), council, committee
conseiller(-ère) *(mf)* counselor, adviser
conséquent: par conséquent consequently
conserver to keep
conserves *(fpl)* canned goods (8)
considérer to consider; **se considérer** to consider oneself
consommation *(f)* consumption, drink
consommer to consume
consonne *(f)* consonant
constamment constantly
construire to construct, to build; **construit(e)** built
consulat *(m)* consulate
contact *(m)* contact; **en contact** in contact (9)
conte *(m)* story (6); **conte** *(m)* **de fées** fairy tale (6)
contempler to contemplate
contenir to contain
content(e) happy, glad (8)
contenter: se contenter de to be happy to / with
continent *(m)* continent (9)
continu(e) continuous
continuer (tout droit) to continue (straight ahead) (10)
contraire *(m)* contrary; **au contraire** on the contrary
contrat *(m)* contract, agreement
contre against; **par contre** on the other hand
contrôle *(m)* control
contrôler to control (8); **contrôlé(e)** controlled, supervised
convenable appropriate, suitable
convenir to be suitable; **Ça te/vous convient?** Does that work for you? (9)
cool: assez cool pretty cool (P)
copain *(m)* boyfriend (2), (male) friend, pal (6)
copier sur to copy from
copieux(-euse) copious, large (8)
copine *(f)* girlfriend (2), (female) friend, pal (6)
coquelicot *(m)* poppy
coquillage *(m)* shellfish

coquilles St-Jacques *(fpl)* scallops
corde *(f)* rope, cord
corporel(le) of the body
corps *(m)* body (7)
correctement correctly
correspondant(e) corresponding
correspondre (à) to correspond (to)
Corse *(f)* Corsica
corse *(m)* Corsican *(language)*
costume *(m)* suit *(for a man)* (5)
côte *(f)* coast; **Côte d'Azur** *(f)* Riviera; **côte** *(f)* **de porc** pork chop (8); **Côte d'Ivoire** *(f)* Ivory Coast
côté *(m)* side (3); **à côté (de)** next to (3); **côté cour** on the courtyard side (10); **d'à côté** next-door
cou *(m)* neck
couchant setting
coucher: se coucher to go to bed (7); **chambre à coucher** *(f)* bedroom
couler to run *(liquids)*
couleur *(f)* color (3); **De quelle couleur est/sont... ?** What color is/are . . . ? (3)
coulis *(m)* purée
couloir *(m)* hall, corridor (3)
coup *(m)* stroke, blow; **coup** *(m)* **de foudre** love at first sight (7); **coup** *(m)* **de téléphone** telephone call; **tout à coup** all of a sudden (6); **tout d'un coup** all at once (6)
coupe *(f)* dessert dish
couper to cut; **se couper le doigt** to cut one's finger
cour *(f)* court, courtyard; **côté cour** on the courtyard side (10)
couramment fluently
courant(e) present, current, common; **au courant de** aware of
courgette *(f)* zucchini
courir to run (9)
courrier *(m)* mail; **courrier électronique** *(m)* e-mail
cours *(m)* class, course (P); **au cours de** in the course of, during, while on (10); **avoir cours** to have class (6); **cours** *(m)* **de français** French class (P); **cours** *(m)* **en ligne** online course (1); **dans un autre cours** in another class (P); **en cours** in class (P); **salle** *(f)* **de cours** classroom (1); **suivre un cours** to take a course
course *(f)* errand (5), race; **faire des courses** to run errands (5); **faire les courses** to go grocery shopping (5)
court(e) short (4)
cousin(e) *(mf)* cousin (4)
coûter to cost (5)
coutume *(f)* custom
couvert(e) de covered with
couverture *(f)* blanket, cover (3)
covoiturage *(m)* carpooling
cravate *(f)* tie (5)
crayon *(m)* pencil (P); **Prenez une feuille de papier et un crayon ou un stylo.** Take out a piece of paper and a pencil or a pen. (P)
créancier(-ière) *(mf)* creditor
créatif(-ive) creative
crèche *(f)* *(government-sponsored)* day care
crédit: carte *(f)* **de crédit** credit card (9)
créer to create
crème *(f)* cream (8)
créole Creole
crevette *(f)* shrimp (8)
crier to shout
crise *(f)* crisis

critique *(f)* criticism
Croatie *(f)* Croatia (9)
croire (à) (que) to believe (in) (that); **je crois** I think
croiser to run across, to bump into
croisière *(f)* cruise
croissant *(m)* croissant (8)
croissant(e) growing
croix *(f)* cross; **en croix** crossed
croque-madame *(m)* toasted ham-and-cheese sandwich with an egg on top
croque-monsieur *(m)* toasted ham-and-cheese sandwich
cru(e) raw
crudités *(fpl)* raw vegetables (8)
cruel(le) cruel (6)
crustacé *(m)* shellfish
cuiller (cuillère) *(f)* spoon
cuir *(m)* leather
cuisine *(f)* kitchen (3), cuisine, cooking (4); **faire la cuisine** to cook (5)
cuisinier(-ère) *(mf)* cook
cuisinière *(f)* stove
cuivre *(m)* copper
cultiver to cultivate (7); **cultivé(e)** cultivated
culture *(f)* culture (9), cultivation
culturel(le) cultural (4)
curieux(-euse) curious, odd
cyclisme *(m)* cycling

D

dame *(f)* lady
Danemark *(m)* Denmark
dans in (P); **dans la rue...** on . . . Street (10)
dansant(e) dancing
danse *(f)* dance
danser to dance (2)
danseur(-euse) *(mf)* dancer
date *(f)* date (4); **C'est quelle date?** What is the date? (4); **Quelle est la date?** What is the date? (4)
dater de to date from
daurade *(f)* sea bream
de of, from, about (P); **de la, de l', du** some, any (8); **de luxe** deluxe (10); **De rien.** You're welcome. (P); **du lundi au vendredi** from Monday to Friday *(every week)* (P); **parler de** to talk about
débarquement *(m)* landing
déboussolé(e) disoriented
debout standing
début *(m)* beginning (6); **au début (de)** at the beginning (of) (6)
décédé(e) dead; deceased (4)
décembre *(m)* December (4)
décidément decidedly, for sure
décider to decide (6); **se décider** to make up one's mind
décision *(f)* decision (7); **prendre une décision** to make a decision (7)
décorer to decorate
découper to cut out
découverte *(f)* discovery
découvrir to discover; **découvrant** discovering
décret *(m)* decree
décrire to describe (9); **décrit(e)** described
dedans inside
défaut *(m)* fault (7)
défini(e) definite
définir to define
degré *(m)* degree
déguster to sample
dehors outside; **en dehors de** outside of

déjà already (5)
déjeuner *(m)* lunch; **petit déjeuner** *(m)* breakfast (5)
déjeuner to have/eat lunch (2)
délicieux(-euse) delicious (6)
délirer: faire délirer to crack up
demain tomorrow (P); **À demain!** See you tomorrow! (P)
demande *(f)* request
demander to ask (for) (2); **se demander** to wonder
demi *(m)* draft beer (2)
demi(e) half (P); **demi-heure** *(f)* half hour (7); **Il est deux heures et demie.** It's half past two. (P); **un kilo et demi de** a kilo and a half of (8)
dénoncer to denounce, to turn in
dent *(f)* tooth (7)
dentaire dental
départ *(m)* departure (9)
département *(m)* department *(a French administrative region)*
dépassement *(m)* **de soi** surpassing oneself
dépendre (de) to depend (on) (5); **Ça dépend.** That depends.
dépense *(f)* expense
dépenser to spend
déplaisant(e) unpleasant
depuis since, for (7), from; **depuis cela** since then; **depuis que** since
dérivé(e) derived
dernier(-ère) last (5)
derrière behind (3)
des some (1)
dès since, right after; **dès que** as soon as
désaccord *(m)* disagreement
désagréable unpleasant (1)
désastreux(-euse) disastrous
descendre (de) to go down, to get off (5); **descendre dans / à** to stay at *(a hotel)* (5)
déshabiller to undress; **se déshabiller** to get undressed (7)
désigner to designate, to indicate
désirer to desire; **Vous désirez?** What would you like?, May I help you? (2)
désolé(e) sorry (8); **être désolé(e) que...** to be sorry that . . . (10)
désordre: en désordre in disorder (3)
dessert *(m)* dessert (8)
dessin *(m)* drawing; **dessin animé** *(m)* cartoon
dessiner to draw
dessous: ci-dessous below
dessus: au dessus de above; **par dessus** over
destin *(m)* destiny
détaillé(e) detailed
détendre: se détendre to relax
détenir to hold, to possess
détester to hate; **se détester** to hate each other (7)
détruit(e) destroyed
dette *(f)* debt
deux two (P); **deux-tiers** two-thirds
deuxième second (3)
devant in front of (3)
développement *(m)* development
développer to develop; **se développer** to be developed.; **développé(e)** developed
devenir to become (4)
deviner to guess
devinette *(f)* riddle
devoir must, to have to, to owe (6); **il/elle doit** he/she must (3)
devoirs *(mpl)* homework (P); **Faites les devoirs dans le cahier.** Do the homework in the workbook. (P)

diabète *(m)* diabetes
diable *(m)* devil
diamant *(m)* diamond
dictée *(f)* dictation
dictionnaire *(m)* dictionary
dieu *(m)* god
différemment differently
différer to differ
difficile difficult (P)
dimanche *(m)* Sunday (P)
diminuer to diminish
dinde *(f)* turkey
dîner *(m)* dinner (8)
dîner to have dinner (2), to dine
diplôme *(m)* diploma, degree
dire to say, to tell (6); **Ça te/vous dit?** How does that sound to you? (2); **Ça veut dire...** That means . . . (P); **Comment dit-on... en français/en anglais?** How do you say . . . in French/in English? (P); **On dit...** One says . . . (P); **On dit que...** They say that . . . (4); **Qu'est-ce que ça veut dire?** What does that mean? (P)
directement directly
directeur(-trice) *(mf)* director
direction *(f)* direction, management
disciplinaire disciplinary
discothèque *(f)* dance club
discrètement discreetly
discuter to discuss
disparaître to disappear; **disparu(e)** having disappeared
disposer de to have available
disputer to dispute; **se disputer (avec)** to argue (with) (7)
disque *(m)* record; **disque compact** *(m)* compact disc
dissiper to dissipate
distraction *(f)* entertainment (5)
distributeur *(m)* **de billets** ATM machine (10)
divers(e) diverse, different
divisé(e) divided
divorcer to divorce; **divorcé(e)** divorced (1)
dix ten (P); **dix-huit** eighteen (P); **dix-huitième** eighteenth (3); **dix-neuf** nineteen (P); **dix-sept** seventeen (P)
dixième tenth (3)
doctorat *(m)* doctorate
dodo: faire dodo *(m)* to go beddy-bye *(familiar)*
doigt *(m)* finger (10); **doigt** *(m)* **de pied** toe (10)
dollar *(m)* dollar (3)
domestique *(mf)* servant
domestique domestic, household
domicile *(m)* place of residence
dominer to dominate
dommage: C'est dommage! It's a shame!, It's a pity!, That's too bad! (4)
donc so, therefore, thus, then (7)
données *(fpl)* information, data
donner to give (2); **donner à manger à** to feed (9); **donner lieu à** to give rise to; **Donnez-moi votre feuille de papier.** Give me your piece of paper. (P)
dont of which, (among) which, whose (7)
dormir to sleep (2); **je dors** I'm sleeping, I sleep (2)
dos *(m)* back (10); **sac** *(m)* **à dos** backpack
dossier *(m)* file
doté(e) endowed
douane *(f)* customs (9)
double double; **chambre double** *(f)* double room (10)

VOCABULAIRE FRANÇAIS–ANGLAIS | *quatre cent cinquante-neuf* **459**

douche *(f)* shower (7)
doute *(m)* doubt; **sans doute** without doubt, doubtlessly, probably (8)
douter to doubt (10)
douteux(-euse) doubtful
doux (douce) sweet, soft, gentle (6)
douzaine (de) *(f)* dozen (8)
douze twelve (P)
drame *(m)* drama
drap *(m)* sheet
droit *(m)* law *(field of study)*, right *(legal)*; **droits** *(mpl)* **de l'homme** human rights; **tout droit** straight (ahead) (10)
droite *(f)* right *(direction)*; **à droite (de)** to the right (of) (3); **de droite** conservative (7)
drôle funny, odd
du (de la, de l', des) some, any (8)
dû (due, dus, dues) à due to
duc *(m)* duke
duché *(m)* dukedom, duchy
dur(e) hard; **œuf dur** *(m)* hard-boiled egg (8)
durant during
durer to last
DVD *(m)* DVD (2); **lecteur** *(m)* **DVD** DVD player (3)
dynamique active (1)

E

eau *(f)* water (2)
écailler to open *(shellfish)*
échange *(m)* exchange
échanger to exchange
échapper to escape; **s'échapper** to escape
échouer to fail
école *(f)* school (6); **école** *(f)* **secondaire** secondary school
économie *(f)* economy; **faire des économies** to save money
économique economic; **classe** *(f)* **économique** economy class, coach (9); **sciences économiques** *(fpl)* economics
écossais(e) plaid
écossé(e) shelled
écouter to listen (to) (2); **Écoutez la question.** Listen to the question. (P)
écran *(m)* screen
écrevisse *(f)* crawfish
écrire to write (2); **Ça s'écrit...** That's written . . . (P); **Ça s'écrit avec un accent ou sans accent?** That's written with or without an accent? (P); **Ça s'écrit comment?** How is that written? (P); **écrit(e)** written; **Écrivez la réponse avec une phrase complète.** Write the answer with a complete sentence. (P)
écrivain *(m)* writer
éducateur *(m)*, **éducatrice** *(f)* educator
éduquer to educate
effectuer to carry out
effet *(m)* effect; **effets personnels** personal belongings (3); **effets spéciaux** special effects (6); **en effet** in fact
égal(e) *(mpl* **égaux)** equal; **Ça m'est égal.** It's all the same to me.; **sans égal** unequaled
également also, as well, equally, likewise
égalité *(f)* equality
égard *(m)* respect
église *(f)* church (4)
égoïste selfish
Égypte *(f)* Egypt (9)
électrique electrical
électronique electronic; **billet** *(m)* **électronique** e-ticket; **courrier** *(m)* **électronique** e-mail

élève *(mf)* pupil, student
élevé(e) high, elevated, raised
elle she, it (1); **avec elle** with her (2); **elles** they (1); **avec elles** with them (2); **elle-même** herself
embarquement *(m)* boarding; **porte** *(f)* **d'embarquement** departure gate
embêtant(e) annoying (3)
embrasser to kiss; **s'embrasser** to kiss each other, to embrace each other (7)
émission *(f)* broadcast, show
emmener to take
empêcher (quelqu'un de faire quelque chose) to prevent (somebody from doing something)
emplacement *(m)* location
emploi *(m)* employment, use; **emploi** *(m)* **du temps** schedule
employé(e) *(mf)* employee (10)
employer to use; **s'employer** to be used
emporter to take (along), to carry (away) (5)
emprisonner to imprison (6)
emprunter (à) to borrow (from)
en some, any, of it/them (8), about it/them; **Je vous/t'en prie.** You're welcome. (2); **s'en aller** to go away
en in (P); **de temps en temps** from time to time (4); **en avance** early; **en avion** by plane (4); **en centre-ville** downtown (3); **en désordre** in disorder (3); **en espèces** in cash (10); **en face (de)** across from, facing (3); **en ligne** online (1); **en même temps** at the same time; **en ordre** in order (3); **en outre** in addition; **en retard** late (10); **en solde** on sale (5); **en vacances** on vacation (4); **être en train de...** to be in the process of . . . ; **partir en voyage** to leave on a trip (5); **partir en week-end** to go away for the weekend (5)
enceinte pregnant (10)
enchanter to enchant; **enchanté(e)** enchanted
encore still (4), again, more (8); **ne... pas encore** not . . . yet (5)
endormir: s'endormir to fall asleep (7)
endroit *(m)* place (9)
énergique energetic
énerver to irritate
enfance *(f)* childhood
enfant *(mf)* child (4)
enfin finally (7)
enflé(e) swollen
enfouir to bury
engagé(e) involved
enlever to take off, to remove
ennui *(m)* trouble
ennuyer to bore; **s'ennuyer (de)** to get bored (with), to be bored (with) (7)
ennuyeux(-euse) boring (1)
énorme enormous
enquête *(f)* investigation, survey
enregistrer to record
enseignement *(m)* teaching, education; **enseignement supérieur** higher education
enseigner to teach
ensemble *(m)* whole group
ensemble together (2)
ensuite then, afterwards (4)
entendre to hear (7); **Entendu!** Understood!; **s'entendre bien/mal (avec)** to get along well/badly (with) (7)
enthousiaste enthusiastic
entier(-ère) entire, whole; **à part entière** complete
entièrement entirely, completely

entre between (3), among
entrée *(f)* appetizer, first course (8), entry ticket, entrance, entry; **entrée** *(f)* **au cinéma** cinema attendance
entreprise *(f)* firm, enterprise
entrer (dans) to enter (5), to go in
entretien *(m)* conversation, interview, maintenance
envahir to invade
envers towards
envie: avoir envie de to feel like, to want (4)
environ around, about (4)
envisager to consider, to imagine
envoyer to send (2); **envoyer un texto** to send a text message (2)
épaule *(f)* shoulder
épice *(f)* spice
épicerie *(f)* grocer's shop (8)
épinards *(mpl)* spinach
époque *(f)* time period (6); **à cette époque-là** at that time, in those days
épouser to marry; **s'épouser** to get married
épouvante: film *(m)* **d'épouvante** horror movie
équilibre *(m)* equilibrium, balance
équipe *(f)* team
équipé(e) equipped
escalade *(f)* (rock) climbing
escalier *(m)* stairs, staircase (3)
escargot *(m)* snail (8)
escarpé(e) steep
esclavage *(m)* slavery
esclave *(mf)* slave
Espagne *(f)* Spain (9)
espagnol *(m)* Spanish (P)
espagnol(e) Spanish
espèce: en espèces in cash (10)
espérer to hope (3)
espion(ne) *(mf)* spy
espoir *(m)* hope
esprit *(m)* mind, spirit (7)
essayage: cabine *(f)* **d'essayage** fitting room (5)
essayer to try on (5); **essayer (de faire)** to try (to do)
essentiel(le) essential; **Il est essentiel de...** It's essential to . . . (10)
est *(m)* east; **la partie est** the eastern part
est-ce que *(particle used in questions)* (1)
estomac *(m)* stomach
et and (P); **et quart/et demi(e)** a quarter past/half past (P); **Combien font... et... ?** How much is . . . plus . . . ? (P)
établir to establish; **s'établir** to establish oneself, to settle
établissement *(m)* establishment
étage *(m)* floor (3); **à l'étage** on the same floor, down the hall; **À quel étage?** On what floor? (3); **au premier étage** on the second floor (3)
étagère *(f)* shelf, bookcase (3)
étape *(f)* stopping place, step
état *(m)* condition; **État** *(m)* state (3), government; **États-Unis** *(mpl)* United States (3)
été *(m)* summer (5); **en été** in summer (5)
étendre: s'étendre to extend; **étendu(e)** stretched out
éternuer to sneeze (10)
étoile *(f)* star
étonner to amaze, to astonish; **être étonné(e) que...** to be astonished that . . . (10)

étouffant(e) stifling
étrange strange
étranger(-ère) foreign (1); **à l'étranger** abroad (9)
être to be (1); **c'est** it's (P), he is, she is, it is, this is, that is (1); **C'est ça!** That's right! (1); **C'est quel jour aujourd'hui?** What day is today? (P); **Comment est / sont... ?** What is / are . . . like? (1); **être à** to belong to; **Je suis...** I'm . . . (P) **Je ne suis pas...** I'm not . . . (P); **le français est...** French is . . . (P); **Nous sommes....** There are . . . of us. (4); **Quelle est la date?** What is the date? (4); **tu es/vous êtes** you are (P)
étroit(e) tight, narrow
études *(fpl)* studies, going to school (1)
étudiant(e) *(mf)* student (P)
étudier to study (1); **J'étudie/Je n'étudie pas...** I study/I don't study . . . (1); **Qu'est-ce que vous étudiez/tu étudies?** What are you studying?, What do you study? (1)
euro *(m)* euro (2)
Europe *(f)* Europe (9)
européen(ne) European
eux them, they; **eux-mêmes** themselves
évader: s'évader to escape
événement *(m)* event
éviter to avoid (8)
exact(e) accurate
exactement exactly (10)
examen *(m)* test, exam (P); **Préparez l'examen pour le prochain cours.** Prepare for the exam for the next class. (P)
excessivement excessively
exclamer: s'exclamer to exclaim, to cry out
excuser to excuse, to forgive; **Excusez-moi.** Excuse me. (P)
exemple *(m)* example; **par exemple** for example (2)
exercice *(m)* exercise (P); **faire de l'exercice** to exercise (2); **Faites l'exercice A à la page 21.** Do exercise A on page 21. (P)
exiger to require
exotique exotic (9)
expérience *(f)* experience, experiment
explication *(f)* explanation
expliquer to explain (10)
explorateur(-trice) *(mf)* explorer
exploser to explode
exposition *(f)* exhibit (4)
expression *(f)* expression (10)
expresso *(m)* espresso (2)
exprimer to express
expulser to throw out
exquis(e) exquisite
extérieur *(m)* outside, exterior
extra(ordinaire) great, terrific (4)
extrascolaire extracurricular
extraterrestre *(mf)* extraterrestrial
extraverti(e) outgoing, extroverted (1)

F
fac *(f)* university, campus (2)
face *(f)* face; **en face (de)** across from, facing (3); **face à** across from, confronted with; **faire face à** to face
facile easy (P)
facilement easily (7)
faciliter to facilitate, to make easy
façon *(f)* way
faculté *(f)* university, campus, school, faculty; **la fac** the university, the campus (2)
fade tasteless
faillir: il a failli avoir he almost had

faim *(f)* hunger; **avoir faim** to be hungry (4); **j'ai faim** I'm hungry (2)
faire to do, to make (2); **Ça fait... euros.** That's . . . euros. (2); **Ça ne se fait pas!** That is not done!; **Combien font… et / moins…?** How much is . . . plus / minus . . . ? (P); **faire attention (à)** to pay attention (to), to watch out (for) (8); **faire connaître** to inform; **faire de l'aérobic** to do aerobics (8); **faire de l'alpinisme** to go mountain climbing; **faire de la méditation** to meditate (8); **faire de la musculation** to do weight training, to do bodybuilding (8); **faire de la musique** to play music (2); **faire de la planche à voile** to go windsurfing; **faire de la plongée sous-marine** to go scuba diving; **faire de la varappe** to go rock climbing; **faire de l'exercice** to exercise (2); **faire des courses** to run errands (5); **faire des économies** to save up (money); **faire des projets** to make plans (4); **faire des randonnées** to go hiking (5); **faire du bateau** to go boating (5); **faire du camping** to go camping (5); **faire du cheval** to go horseback riding; **faire du jardinage** to garden (5); **faire du jogging** to jog (2); **faire du patin (à glace)** to go (ice-)skating; **faire du roller** to go in-line skating (6); **faire du shopping** to go shopping (2); **faire du skateboard(ing)** to skateboard (6); **faire du ski** to go skiing (2); **faire du sport** to play sports (2); **faire du vélo** to go bike-riding (2); **faire du VTT** to go all-terrain biking (5); **faire du yoga** to do yoga (8); **faire face à** to face; **faire la connaissance de** to meet *(for the first time)* (7); **faire la cuisine** to cook (5); **faire la fête** to party; **faire la lessive** to do laundry (5); **faire la vaisselle** to do the dishes (5); **faire le ménage** to do housework (5); **faire les courses** to go grocery shopping (5); **faire mal** to hurt; **faire mieux (de)** to do better (to) (8); **faire noir** to be dark; **faire partie de** to be a part of; **faire quelque chose** to do something (2); **faire sa toilette** to wash up (7); **faire sa valise** to pack your bag (9); **faire une promenade** to go for a walk (5); **faire une réservation** to make a reservation (9); **faire un tour** to take a tour, to go for a ride (4); **faire un voyage** to take a trip (5); **Faites les devoirs dans le cahier.** Do the homework in the workbook. (P); **Faites l'exercice A à la page 21.** Do exercise A on page 21. (P); **Il fait beau / chaud / (du) soleil / du vent / frais / froid / mauvais.** It's nice / hot / sunny / windy / cool / cold / bad. (5); **Il fait bon / du brouillard.** It's nice / foggy.; **Il va faire...** It's going to be . . . (5); **Je fais du...** I wear size. . . . (5); **Quelle taille faites-vous?** What size do you wear? (5); **Quel temps fait-il?** What's the weather like? (5); **Quel temps va-t-il faire?** What's the weather going to be like? (5); **Qu'est-ce que vous aimez faire?** What do you like to do?; **Qu'est-ce que vous faites/tu fais?** What are you doing? What do you do? (2); **se faire passer pour** to pass as
fait: en fait in fact
falaise *(f)* cliff
falloir: il faut... it is necessary . . . , one must . . . , one needs . . . (8); **il me/te/nous/vous/lui/leur faut** I/you/we/you/he (she)/they need(s) (9); **il ne faut pas** one

shouldn't, one must not . . . (10); **Qu'est-ce qu'il vous faut?** What do you need? (8)
fameux(-euse) famous
familial(e) *(mpl* **familiaux)** family
familier(-ère) familiar, informal
famille *(f)* family (P); **nom** *(m)* **de famille** family name, surname (3)
fantastique fantastic; **film fantastique** *(m)* fantasy movie
farci(e) stuffed
fascinant(e) fascinating
fast-food *(m)* fast-food restaurant (1)
fatigué(e) tired (6)
faut *See* **falloir.**
fauteuil *(m)* armchair (3)
faux (fausse) false
faux-filet *(m)* sirloin
favoriser to favor, to further
fée *(f)* fairy; **conte** *(m)* **de fées** fairy tale (6)
femme *(f)* woman (1), wife (2); **ex-femme** *(f)* ex-wife; **femme** *(f)* **d'affaires** business woman (5)
fenêtre *(f)* window (3)
fer *(m)* iron; **chemin** *(m)* **de fer** railroad
férié(e): jour férié *(m)* holiday
ferme *(f)* farm
fermer to close (2); **Fermez votre livre.** Close your book. (P)
féroce ferocious
festival *(m)* festival (4)
fête *(f)* holiday, celebration (4), party (1); **faire la fête** *(f)* to party; **fête** *(f)* **des Mères** Mother's Day; **fête** *(f)* **des Pères** Father's Day; **fête** *(f)* **du travail** Labor Day; **fête nationale** *(f)* national holiday
fêter to celebrate
feu *(m)* fire, traffic light
feuille *(f)* **de papier** sheet of paper (P); **Prenez une feuille de papier et un crayon ou un stylo.** Take out a piece of paper and a pencil or a pen. (P)
feuilleté(e) flaky (pastry)
février *(m)* February (4)
fiancé(e) engaged (1)
fiancer: se fiancer to get engaged (7)
ficelle *(f)* string
fidélité *(f)* faithfulness
fier(-ère) proud
fièvre *(f)* fever; **avoir de la fièvre** to have fever
figure *(f)* face (7)
fille *(f)* girl; daughter (4); **fille unique** *(f)* only child
film *(m)* movie, film (1); **film** *(m)* **à grand spectacle** epic film
fils *(m)* son (4); **fils unique** *(m)* only child
fin *(f)* end
fin(e) fine
finalement finally (6)
financier(-ère) financial
finir (de faire) to finish (doing) (8); **finir par faire** to end up doing; **Le cours de français finit à...** French class finishes at . . . (P)
fissure *(f)* crack, fissure
fixe fixed; **menu à prix fixe** set-price menu (8)
fixer to set, to fix
flamand *(m)* Flemish *(language)*
fleur *(f)* flower
fleuri(e) with a floral pattern
fleuve *(m)* river
flic *(m)* cop
Floride *(f)* Florida (9)
flottant(e) floating
foie *(m)* liver

fois (f) time (5), occasion; **à la fois** at the same time; **d'autres fois** other times (7); **Il était une fois...** Once upon a time there was . . . (6)
folique: acide (m) **folique** folic acid
folklore (m) folklore (4)
foncé(e) dark; **bleu foncé** dark blue
fonction (f) function; **en fonction de** according to
fonctionnement (m) functioning, operation, running
fond (m) bottom, back, background; **au fond de** at the end of; **dans le fond** really, basically
fondateur: père (m) **fondateur** founding father
fonder to found; **fondé(e)** founded
fontaine (f) fountain
football (m) soccer (1); **football américain** (m) football (1); **match** (m) **de football américain** football game (1)
force (f) force, strength; **à force de** as a result of
forcément necessarily, inevitably
forêt (f) forest
forme (f) shape; **en forme** in shape (8); **en forme de** in the shape of
former to form, to educate
formidable great (7)
formulaire (m) form
formule (f) formula, expression
fort(e) strong (8)
fort very
fou (folle) crazy
foudre (f) lightning, thunderbolt; **coup** (m) **de foudre** love at first sight (7)
foulard (m) dress scarf
fouler: se fouler la cheville to sprain one's ankle
four (à micro-ondes) (m) (microwave) oven
fourchette (f) fork
frais (fraîche) fresh (8); **Il fait frais.** It's cool. (5)
fraise (f) strawberry (8)
framboise (f) raspberry
franc (franche) frank, honest
français (m) French (P); **cours** (m) **de français** French class (P)
français(e) French (1); **à la française** French style
France (f) France (1)
franciscain(e) Franciscan
francophone French-speaking
francophonie (f) French-speaking world
frapper to strike; **frapper à la porte** to knock on the door
fréquenté(e) visited, frequented
frère (m) brother (1); **beau-frère** (m) brother-in-law; **demi-frère** (m) stepbrother, half-brother
frigo (m) refrigerator
frire to fry
frisson (m) shiver (10); **avoir des frissons** to have the shivers (10)
frit(e) fried
frites (fpl) French fries (2); **steak-frites** (m) steak and fries (8)
frivole frivolous
froid(e) cold (4); **avoir froid** to be cold (4); **Il fait froid.** It's cold. (5)
fromage (m) cheese (2)
frontière (f) border
fruit (m) fruit (8); **fruits** (mpl) **de mer** shellfish (8); **jus** (m) **de fruit** fruit juice (2)
fuir to flee, to run away
fumé(e) smoked (8)

fumée (f) smoke
fumer to smoke (3)
fumeur(-euse) (mf) smoker; **fumeur/non-fumeur** smoking/non-smoking
furieux(-euse) furious (10)
fusée (f) rocket
fusiller to shoot down
futur (m) future (tense)

G

gagner to win (2), to gain; **gagner de l'argent** to earn money, to make money
gai(e) gay, lively
gamin(e) (mf) kid
garçon (m) boy (4)
garder to keep
garde-robe (f) wardrobe
gare (f) train station; **gare routière** bus station
gaspiller to waste
gâté(e) spoiled (6)
gâteau (m) cake (8)
gauche (f) left; **à gauche (de)** to the left (of) (3); **de gauche** liberal (7)
général(e) (mpl **généraux**) general; **en général** in general (2)
généralement generally (8)
génial(e) (mpl **géniaux**) great (4)
génie (m) genius, engineering
genou (m) knee; **sur ses genoux** on one's lap
genre (m) gender, kind, type, genre
gens (mpl) people (1)
gentil(le) nice (1)
géographie (f) geography (9)
géographique geographical
germanique Germanic
geste (m) gesture
gilet (m) vest
glace (f) ice cream (8), ice; **glace à la vanille** vanilla ice cream (8)
glace (f) mirror
glacier (m) ice cream shop
golf (m) golf (2)
gommage (m) rubbing out, scrub
gorge (f) throat (10); **soutien-gorge** (m) bra
gosse (mf) kid
goût (m) taste
goûter to taste (9)
gouvernement (m) government
grâce (f) grace; **grâce à** thanks to, due to; **jour** (m) **d'Action de Grâce** Thanksgiving
gracieux(-euse) gracious (6)
graisse (f) fat, grease
grammaire (f) grammar
gramme (m) gram (8)
grand(e) big, tall (1); **grande surface** (f) superstore (8); **le grand amour** (m) true love (7)
grand-chose: ne... pas grand-chose not much, not a lot
grandir to grow, to grow up, to get taller (8)
grand-mère (f) grandmother (4)
grand-père (m) grandfather (4)
grands-parents (mpl) grandparents (4)
gras(se) fatty; **en caractères gras** boldfaced; **matière grasse** (f) fat (8)
gratuit(e) free (of charge) (10)
grave serious, grave
Grèce (f) Greece (9)
grillé(e) grilled, toasted (8); **pain grillé** (m) toast (8)
grippe (f) flu (10)
gris(e) gray (3)
grog (m) **au rhum** rum toddy

gros(se) fat (1)
grossesse (f) pregnancy
grossir to get fatter (8)
groupe (m) group (6); **en groupe** in a group
gruyère (m) Swiss cheese
guerre (f) war
guichet (m) ticket window
guide (m) guide, guidebook (9)
guitare (f) guitar (2)
Guyane (f) French Guiana (9)
gym: salle (f) **de gym** gym, fitness club (1)
gymnase (m) gym

H

habiller to dress; **s'habiller** to get dressed (7)
habitant(e) (mf) inhabitant
habiter to live ; **j'habite à** (+ *city*) I live in (+ *city*) (P); **Vous habitez... ?** Do you live . . . ? (P)
habitude (f) habit; **comme d'habitude** as usual; **d'habitude** usually (2)
habitué(e) à used to, accustomed to
*****haché(e)** chopped (up)
*****hamburger** (m) hamburger (8)
*****haricots verts** (mpl) green beans (8)
harmonieux(-euse) harmonious
*****hasard: par hasard** by chance
*****haut(e)** high; **en haut** on top; **là-haut** up there
*****hein?** huh?
héritage (m) inheritance, heritage
hériter to inherit
hésiter to hesitate
heure (f) hour, time (P); **à l'heure** on time (4); **À tout à l'heure.** See you in a little while. (P); **heure d'ouverture** opening time (6); **heure locale** local time (9); **heure officielle** official time (6), 24-hour clock; **Il est... heure(s).** It's . . . o'clock. (P); **Quelle heure est-il?** What time is it? (P); **tout à l'heure** a little while ago
heureusement luckily
heureux(-euse) happy (7)
hideux(-euse) hideous
hier yesterday (5); **hier soir** last night, yesterday evening (5)
hi-fi: chaîne (f) **hi-fi stereo** (3)
histoire (f) history (1); story (9)
historique historic (9)
hiver (m) winter (5); **en hiver** in winter (5)
*****hockey** (m) hockey (2)
*****homard** (m) lobster (8)
homme (m) man (1); **homme** (m) **d'affaires** businessman (5)
honnête honest
honnêteté (f) honesty
*****honteux (-euse)** shameful
hôpital (m) (pl **hôpitaux**) hospital
horaire (m) schedule (6)
horreur (f) horror
horrible horrible (6)
*****hors de** outside of
*****hors-d'œuvre** (m) (inv) hors d'œuvre, appetizer (8)
hôte (m) host; **chambre** (f) **d'hôte** bed and breakfast
hôtel (m) hotel (5)
hôtelier(-ère) (mf) hotel manager (10)
hôtesse (f) hostess
huile (f) oil
*****huit** eight (P); **huit jours** one week
*****huitième** eighth (3)
huître (f) oyster (8)

humain(e) human; **sciences humaines** *(fpl)* social sciences (1)
humeur *(f)* mood; **de bonne humeur** in a good mood
humour *(m)* humor; **sens** *(m)* **de l'humour** sense of humor (7)
hurlement *(m)* howl
hypermarché *(m)* superstore

I

ici here (P); **d'ici** from here (P); **par ici** this way (5)
idéaliste idealistic (1)
idée *(f)* idea (4)
identité *(f)* identity; **carte** *(f)* / **pièce** *(f)* **d'identité** identity card
ignorer to ignore; **en ignorant** while ignoring
il he (1), it (P); **il faut...** it is necessary..., one must... (8); **il ne faut pas...** one shouldn't..., one must not... (10); **ils** they (1); **il y a...** there is..., there are... (1), ago (5); **Quelle heure est-il?** What time is it? (P); **Qu'est-ce qu'il y a?** What is there? (1), What's the matter?; **s'il vous plaît** please (P)
île *(f)* island (9)
illustré(e) illustrated
image *(f)* picture
imaginaire imaginary
imaginer to imagine
immédiatement immediately
immeuble *(m)* apartment building (3)
immigré(e) *(mf)* immigrant
imparfait *(m)* imperfect
impatient(e) impatient (4)
impératif *(m)* imperative
imperméable *(m)* raincoat (5)
impoli(e) impolite
importance *(f)* importance (7)
important(e) important (10)
importer to be important; **n'importe où** (just) anywhere; **n'importe quoi** (just) anything
impressionnant(e) impressive
impressionner to impress
imprimé(e) printed
inattendu(e) unexpected
inciter à to encourage
inclure to include; **inclus(e)** included
inconnu(e) *(mf)* stranger
inconvénient *(m)* disadvantage, inconvenience
incroyable incredible
Inde *(f)* India
indécision *(f)* indecision (7)
indéfini(e) indefinite
indicatif *(m)* indicative
indications *(fpl)* directions (10)
indifférence *(f)* indifference (7)
indigène native
indigestion *(f)* indigestion (10)
indiquer to show, to indicate (3); **indiqué(e)** indicated; **indiquer le chemin** to give directions, to show the way (10)
indiscret(-ète) indiscreet
industrialisé(e) industrialized
industrie *(f)* industry
inégalé(e) unequaled
infidélité *(f)* unfaithfulness (7)
infinitif *(m)* infinitive
infirmerie *(f)* health center
inflexibilité *(f)* inflexibility
influencer to influence; **s'influencer** to influence each other
informatique *(f)* computer science (1); **salle** *(f)* **d'informatique** computer lab (1)
informer to inform; **s'informer** to find out information (9)
infos *(fpl)* info (9)
infusion *(f)* herbal tea
ingénieur *(m)* engineer
inhospitalier(-ière) inhospitable
inoubliable unforgettable
insaturé(e) unsaturated
inscrire to register; **s'inscrire** to register (3)
insensibilité *(f)* insensitivity (7)
insipide tasteless, insipid
insister to insist (10)
inspecteur *(m)* inspector
inspirer to inspire; **s'inspirer de** to draw inspiration from
installations *(fpl)* facilities
installer: s'installer (à / dans) to settle (in), to move (into) (7), to set up business
instant *(m)* instant; **Un instant!** Just a moment!
institut *(m)* institute
instrument *(m)* **de musique** musical instrument
insuffisant insufficient
intellectuel(le) intellectual (1)
intelligent(e) intelligent (1)
intention: avoir l'intention de to plan on, to intend to (4)
intéressant(e) interesting (P)
intéresser to interest; **s'intéresser à** to be interested in (7)
intérêt *(m)* interest
intérieur *(m)* inside
internaute *(mf)* Internet surfer
Internet *(m)* Internet (2); **surfer sur Internet** to surf the Internet (2); **sur Internet** on the Internet (2)
interrogatif(-ive) interrogative, question
interroger to question
interrompre to interrupt
intime intimate; **ami(e) intime** *(mf)* close friend
intrigue *(f)* plot
investir to invest
invitation *(f)* invitation (6)
invité(e) *(mf)* guest
inviter (à) to invite (to) (2)
iPod *(m)* iPod (3)
Irlande *(f)* Ireland (9)
irréel(le) unreal
irresponsable irresponsible
irriter to irritate
isolé(e) isolated
Israël *(m)* Israel (9)
Italie *(f)* Italy (9)
italien(ne) Italian
italique: en italique in italics
itinéraire *(m)* itinerary
ivoirien(ne) from Côte d'Ivoire

J

jalousie *(f)* jealousy (7)
jaloux(-ouse) jealous (7)
jamais: ne... jamais never (2)
jambe *(f)* leg (10); **se casser la jambe** to break your leg
jambon *(m)* ham (2); **sandwich** *(m)* **au jambon** ham sandwich (2)
janvier *(m)* January (4)
Japon *(m)* Japan (9)
japonais *(m)* Japanese
jardin *(m)* garden (5), yard
jardinage *(m)* gardening; **faire du jardinage** to garden (5)
jaune yellow (3)
jazz *(m)* jazz (1)
je (j') I (P)
jean *(m)* jeans (5)
jet *(m)* stream
jeter to throw
jeu *(m)* game; **jeu** *(m)* **vidéo** video game (2)
jeudi *(m)* Thursday (P)
jeune young (1); **jeunes** *(pl)* young people
jeunesse *(f)* youth (7); **auberge** *(f)* **de jeunesse** youth hostel (10)
jogging: faire du jogging to jog (2)
joie *(f)* joy
joindre: se joindre à to join
joli(e) pretty (1)
jouer to play (2), to act (in movies and theater) (6); **jouer à** to play (a sport or game) (2); **jouer de** to play (an instrument) (2)
jour *(m)* day (P); **C'est quel jour aujourd'hui?** What day is today? (P); **jour** *(m)* **de l'An** New Year's Day; **jour J** *(m)* D-day; **tous les jours** every day (P)
journal *(m)* (*pl* **journaux**) newspaper (5), journal; **journal** *(m)* **télévisé** news broadcast
journée *(f)* day (2), daytime; **Bonne journée!** Have a good day!; **journée continue** nine-to-five schedule; **toute la journée** the whole day (2)
joyeux(-euse) happy, joyful; **Joyeux Noël!** Merry Christmas!
juger to judge
juif(-ive) *(mf)* Jew
juillet *(m)* July (4)
juin *(m)* June (4)
jumeau (jumelle) twin (1)
jupe *(f)* skirt (5)
jus *(m)* **(de fruit)** (fruit) juice (2)
jusqu'à until, up to (2)
juste just (10), fair; **juste là** right there
justement precisely, exactly, as a matter of fact (3)

K

kilo (de) *(m)* kilo(gram) (of) (2.2 pounds) (8)
kilomètre *(m)* kilometer (.6 mile)
kiosque *(m)* kiosk (10)

L

la the (1), her, it (5)
là there (1); **à ce moment-là** at that time; **ce (cet, cette, ces) ...-là** that/those... over there (5); **là-bas** over there (1); **là-haut** up there
laboratoire *(m)* **de langues** language laboratory (1)
lac *(m)* lake
laid(e) ugly (1)
laïque lay, secular, civil
laisser to leave (behind) (3), to let; **laisser tomber** to drop
lait *(m)* milk (2); **café** *(m)* **au lait** coffee with milk (2)
laitue *(f)* lettuce (8)
lampe *(f)* lamp (3)
lancer to throw, to fire
langouste *(f)* spiny lobster
langue *(f)* language (1); tongue
lapin *(m)* rabbit
laqué(e) lacquered, with a gloss finish
lard *(m)* bacon
lardon *(m)* piece of bacon
large wide
largement widely
lavabo *(m)* washbasin, sink (10)

lave *(f)* lava
laver to wash; **se laver la figure/les mains** to wash one's face/one's hands (7)
lave-vaisselle *(m)* dishwasher
le the (1), him, it (5); **le lundi** on Mondays (P); **le matin** in the morning, mornings (P); **le week-end** on the weekend, weekends (P)
leçon *(f)* lesson
lecteur (lectrice) *(mf)* reader; **lecteur** *(m)* **CD / DVD / Blu-ray** CD / DVD / Blu-ray player (3); **lecteur** *(m)* **MP3** MP3 player
lecture *(f)* reading
léger(-ère) light (8)
légume *(m)* vegetable (8)
lendemain *(m)* the next day (5)
lent(e) slow
lentement slowly (8)
lequel (laquelle, lesquels, lesquelles) which, which one(s) (6)
les the (1); them (5)
lessive *(f)* laundry (5)
lettre *(f)* letter (9); **lettres** *(fpl)* study of literature
leur (to, for) them (9)
leur their (1)
lever: se lever to get up (7)
liaison *(f)* linking, link
liberté *(f)* freedom
librairie *(f)* bookstore (1)
libre free (2); **temps libre** *(m)* free time (2); **Tu es libre ce soir?** Are you free this evening? (2)
licence *(f)* *three-year university degree*
lien *(m)* link, tie
lier to connect, to link; **lié(e)** linked
lieu *(m)* place; **au lieu de** instead of; **avoir lieu** to take place
light: coca *(m)* **light** diet cola (2)
ligne *(f)* figure; line; **en ligne** online (1)
limande *(f)* dab
limiter to limit, to border; **limité(e)** limited; **se limiter à** to limit oneself to
linguistique linguistic
liquide *(m)* liquid (10)
lire to read (2); **Lisez la page 17.** Read page 17. (P)
liste *(f)* list
lit *(m)* bed (3); **rester au lit** to stay in bed (2)
litre *(m)* liter *(approximately one quart)* (8)
littéraire literary
littérature *(f)* literature (1)
livre *(m)* book (P); **Fermez votre livre.** Close your book. (P); **Ouvrez votre livre à la page 23.** Open your book to page 23. (P)
livre (de) *(f)* pound (of), half-kilo (of) (8)
livrer: se livrer à to participate in
local(e) *(mpl* **locaux)** local (9)
locataire *(mf)* renter
location *(f)* rental; **voiture** *(f)* **de location** rental car (5)
logement *(m)* lodging (3)
logique logical
logiquement logically
loi *(f)* law
loin (de) far (from) (3); **au loin** in the distance; **de loin** by far
loisir *(m)* leisure activity, pastime (2)
Londres London
long: le long de along; **de long** in length
long(ue) long (4)
longer to go alongside
longtemps a long time (5)
longueur *(f)* length

lors de at the time of
lorsque when
louer to rent (4)
Louisiane *(f)* Louisiana (3)
loyer *(m)* rent (3)
lui him (2), (to, for) him/her (9); **lui-même** himself
lumière *(f)* light
lundi *(m)* Monday (P)
lune *(f)* moon; **lune** *(f)* **de miel** honeymoon
lunettes *(fpl)* glasses (4); **lunettes** *(fpl)* **de soleil** sunglasses (5)
luth *(m)* lute
lutter to struggle, to fight
luxe *(m)* luxury; **de luxe** deluxe (10)
luxembourgeois *(m)* Luxembourgish *(native language of Luxembourg)*
lycée *(m)* high school (6)
lycéen(ne) *(mf)* high school student (6)

M

madame (Mme) *(f)* Mrs., madam (P)
mademoiselle (Mlle) *(f)* Miss (P)
magasin *(m)* store (4), shop
magazine *(m)* magazine (9)
magnifique magnificent
mai *(m)* May (4)
maigre skinny
maigrir to get thinner, to slim down (8)
mail *(m)* e-mail (2)
maillon *(m)* link
maillot *(m)* **de bain** swimsuit (5)
main *(f)* hand (7)
maintenant now (P)
maintenir to maintain
mais but (P)
maïs *(m)* corn
maison *(f)* house (1); **à la maison** (at) home (P)
maître *(m)* master
maîtrise *(f)* master's degree
majorité *(f)* majority
mal *(m)* bad, evil; **avoir mal à...** one's ... hurt(s) (10); **faire mal (à...)** to hurt (one's ...)
mal badly (P); **mal à l'aise** ill at ease; **pas mal** not bad(ly) (P)
malade *(mf)* sick person
malade ill, sick; **tomber malade** to get sick (10)
maladie *(f)* illness
malaise *(m)* discomfort
Malgache *(mf)* Madagascan
malgré in spite of
malheureux(-euse) unhappy
malhonnête dishonest
maman *(f)* mama, mom
mamie *(f)* granny, grandma (7)
Manche *(f)* English Channel
mandarine *(f)* tangerine
mandat *(m)* money order, mandate
manger to eat (2); **donner à manger à** to feed (9); **salle** *(f)* **à manger** dining room (3)
manière *(f)* manner, way
manifestation *(f)* demonstration; **manifestation sportive** *(f)* sports event
manquer to miss, to lack
manteau *(m)* overcoat (5)
maquiller: se maquiller to put on make-up (7)
marais *(m)* swamp
marbre *(m)* marble
marchand(e) *(mf)* merchant, shopkeeper (6)
marché *(m)* market (8)

marcher to walk (8), to work
mardi *(m)* Tuesday (P); **Mardi gras** *(m)* Fat Tuesday
marge *(f)* margin
mari *(m)* husband (2); **ex-mari** *(m)* ex-husband
mariage *(m)* marriage (7)
marié(e) married (1)
marier: se marier (avec) to get married (to) (7)
marinier(-ère): moules marinières *(f)* mussels cooked with onions and white wine
marionnettiste *(mf)* puppeteer
marketing *(m)* marketing (1)
Maroc *(m)* Morocco (1)
marocain(e) Moroccan
marquer to mark
marrant(e) funny (1)
marron *(inv)* brown (3)
mars *(m)* March (4)
martiniquais(e) from Martinique
masque *(m)* mask, face pack
massif *(m)* group of mountains, clump
match *(m)* match, game (1)
matelas *(m)* mattress
matérialiste materialistic
maternel(le) maternal; **école maternelle** *(f)* kindergarten
mathématiques (maths) *(fpl)* mathematics (math) (1)
matière *(f)* matter; **matières grasses** *(fpl)* fats (8)
matin *(m)* morning (P); **À huit heures du matin.** At eight o'clock in the morning. (P); **le matin** mornings, in the morning (P)
matinée *(f)* morning (2)
mauvais(e) bad (1); **Il est mauvais de...** It's bad to . . . (10); **Il fait mauvais.** The weather's bad. (5)
maxidiscompte *(m)* discount supercenter
me (to, for) me (9), myself (7); **il me faut...** I need . . . (9)
mec *(m)* *(familiar)* guy
méchant(e) mean (1)
mécontent(e) displeased
médecin *(m)* doctor (10), physician
médicament *(m)* medication, medicine (10), drugs
Méditerranée: (mer) Méditerranée *(f)* Mediterranean (Sea)
méditerranéen(ne) Mediterranean
méfiance *(f)* mistrust
meilleur(e) best (1), better
mélange *(m)* mixture
membre *(m)* member
même same (1), even; **moi-même** myself; **quand même** all the same
mémoire *(f)* memory
menacer to threaten
ménage *(m)* housework (5), household; **femme** *(f)* **de ménage** cleaning lady
mendiant(e) *(mf)* beggar
menthe *(f)* mint
mentir to lie
menu *(m)* menu; **menu à prix fixe** set-price menu (8)
mer *(f)* sea (9); **bord** *(m)* **de la mer** seaside; **fruits** *(mpl)* **de mer** shellfish (8)
merci thank you, thanks (P)
mercredi *(m)* Wednesday (P)
mère *(f)* mother (4)
mérité(e) deserved, earned
messager(-ère) *(mf)* messenger (6)
messieurs (MM.) gentlemen, sirs
mètre *(m)* meter
métrique metric

métro *(m)* subway (4); **en métro** by subway (4)
mettre to wear, to put (on) (5), to place; **mettre en place** to put in place; **mettre en scène** to stage, to present; **mettre la table** to set the table; **se mettre à** to start, to set out; **se mettre d'accord** to come to an agreement
meubles *(mpl)* furniture, furnishings (3)
meurtre *(m)* murder
Mexico Mexico City
Mexique *(m)* Mexico (9)
mi- mid-, half-; **cheveux mi-longs** *(mpl)* shoulder-length hair (4)
micronutriment *(m)* micronutrient
micro-ondes *(m)* microwave oven
midi *(m)* noon (P)
mie: pain *(m)* **de mie** soft sandwich bread
mien(ne): le/la mien(ne) mine
mieux (que) better (than) (2); **aimer mieux** to prefer (2); **il vaut mieux…** it's better . . . (10); **le mieux** the best (7)
milieu *(m)* middle, milieu, environment; **au milieu (de)** in the middle (of)
mille one thousand
mille-feuille *(m)* mille-feuille *(a layered pastry)*
million: un million (de) *(m)* one million (3)
mince thin (1)
minéral(e) *(mpl* **minéraux)**: **eau minérale** *(f)* mineral water (2)
mini-bar *(m)* mini-bar (10)
minuit *(m)* midnight (P)
minute *(f)* minute (5)
miroir *(m)* mirror
miser: en misant sur relying on
misère *(f)* misery
mobile *(m)* motive
mobilier *(m)* furnishings
mode *(f)* fashion; **mode** *(m)* **de vie** lifestyle
modèle *(m)* model
moderne modern (1)
moi me (P); **Donnez-moi votre feuille de papier.** Give me your piece of paper. (P); **Excusez-moi.** Excuse me. (P); **moi-même** myself; **Pour moi… s'il vous plaît.** For me . . . please. (2)
moindre: le moindre the least
moins minus (1); **au moins** at least; **Combien font… moins… ?** How much is . . . minus . . . ? (P); **de moins en moins** fewer and fewer, less and less; **le moins** the least; **moins de** fewer, less (8); **moins le quart** a quarter until (P); **moins… que** less . . . than (1)
mois *(m)* month (3); **ce mois-ci** this month (4); **par mois** per month (3)
moitié *(f)* half
moment *(m)* moment; **à ce moment-là** at that time; **au dernier moment** at the last minute
mon (ma, mes) my (3); **ma famille** my family (P); **mes amis** my friends (1)
monarchie *(f)* monarchy
monastère *(m)* monastery
monde *(m)* world, crowd; **faire le tour du monde** to take a trip around the world; **tout le monde** everybody, everyone (6)
mondial(e) *(mpl* **mondiaux)** world(-wide)
monétaire monetary
monnaie *(f)* change (2), currency
monotonie *(f)* monotony
monsieur (M.) *(m)* Mr., sir (P)
monstre *(m)* monster (6)
mont *(m)* mount
montagne *(f)* mountain (5); **aller à la montagne** to go to the mountains (5); **chalet** *(m)* **à la montagne** ski lodge (10)

montagneux(-euse) mountainous
monter (dans) to go up; to get on/in (5), to set up, to climb, to raise
montre *(f)* watch (5)
montrer to show (3)
morceau de *(m)* piece of (8)
mort *(f)* death
mort(e) dead (5)
mosquée *(f)* mosque
mot *(m)* word (P); **Apprenez les mots de vocabulaire.** Learn the vocabulary words. (P)
motif *(m)* reason, motive
mouchoir *(m)* handkerchief
moule *(f)* mussel (8)
moulin *(m)* mill
mourir to die (5)
moustache *(f)* mustache (4)
mouton *(m)* sheep
moyen *(m)* means; **moyen** *(m)* **de transport** means of transportation (4)
moyen(ne) medium, average; **de taille moyenne** medium-sized (4); **Moyen-Orient** *(m)* Middle East (9)
moyenne *(f)* average; **en moyenne** on average
muet(te) silent
mur *(m)* wall (3)
musculation: faire de la musculation to do weight training, to do bodybuilding (8)
musée *(m)* museum (4)
musical(e) *(mpl* **musicaux)**: **comédie musicale** *(f)* musical
musicien(ne) *(mf)* musician
musicien(ne) musical
musique *(f)* music (1); **musique zydeco** zydeco music (4)
mutation *(f)* transfer
muter to transfer
myrtille *(f)* blueberry
mystère *(m)* mystery
mystérieusement mysteriously

N

nager to swim (2)
nain(e) *(mf)* dwarf
naissance *(f)* birth
naître to be born (5); **être né(e)** to be born (5)
natation *(f)* swimming
national(e) *(mpl* **nationaux)** national (4)
nationalité *(f)* nationality (3)
nature *(f)* nature (7); **omelette nature** *(f)* plain omelet
naturel(le) natural
naturellement naturally
nautique: faire du ski nautique *(m)* to go water-skiing (5)
navette *(f)* shuttle (10)
ne: je ne travaille pas I don't work (P); **ne… aucun(e)** none, not one; **ne… jamais** never (2); **ne… ni… ni…** neither . . . nor . . .; **ne… nulle part** nowhere; **ne… pas (du tout)** not (at all) (1); **ne… pas encore** not yet (5); **ne… personne** nobody, no one; **ne… plus** no more, no longer (8); **ne… que** only; **ne… rien** nothing (5); **ne… rien que** nothing but; **n'est-ce pas?** right? (1); **n'importe où** (just) anywhere
né(e) born (5); **être né(e)** to be born (5)
nécessaire necessary (10)
néerlandais(e) Dutch
négliger to neglect
négocier to negotiate
neige *(f)* snow (5)
neiger to snow (5)

nerveux(-euse) nervous
n'est-ce pas? right? (1)
neuf nine (P)
neuf (neuve) brand-new
neutre neutral
neuvième ninth (3)
neveu *(m)* (*pl* **neveux**) nephew (4)
nez *(m)* nose (10); **avoir le nez bouché** to have a stopped-up nose
ni: ne… ni… ni… neither . . . nor . . .
niçois(e) from Nice
nièce *(f)* niece (4)
niveau *(m)* level
Noël *(m)* Christmas
noir(e) black (3); **Il faisait noir.** It was dark.
noisette *(inv)* hazel (with eyes) (4)
nom *(m)* name, noun (3); **au nom de** in the name of; **nom de famille** family name, last name (3)
nombre *(m)* number (P)
nombreux(-euse) numerous
nommer to name; **nommé(e)** named
non no (P); **non?** right? (1); **non plus** neither (3)
nord *(m)* north; **Amérique** *(f)* **du Nord** North America (9)
normalement normally
normand(e) from Normandy
Normandie *(f)* Normandy
Norvège *(f)* Norway
note *(f)* note (4), grade; **régler la note** to pay the bill (10)
noter to note, to notice
notre (*pl* **nos**) our (3)
nourrir to feed, to nourish, to nurture (8); **se nourrir** to feed oneself, to nourish oneself, to nurture oneself (8)
nourrissant(e) nourishing
nourriture *(f)* food, nourishment
nous we (1), us (2), (to, for) us (9), ourselves (7); **Nous sommes…** There are . . . of us. (4)
nouveau (nouvel, nouvelle) new (1); **de nouveau** again, anew; **Nouvelle-Angleterre** *(f)* New England; **Nouvelle-Calédonie** *(f)* New Caledonia (9); **La Nouvelle-Orléans** *(f)* New Orleans (4)
novembre *(m)* November (4)
nu(e) naked; **pieds nus** barefoot
nuage *(m)* cloud
nuit *(f)* night (5); **boîte** *(f)* **de nuit** nightclub (1)
nuitée *(f)* overnight stay
nul(le) (en) no good (at), really bad (at); **ne… nulle part** nowhere
numéro *(m)* number (3), issue
nutritif(-ive) nutritional

O

obéir (à) to obey (8)
objectif *(m)* objective
objet *(m)* object
obligatoire required, obligatory
obliger to force, to make; **obligé(e)** obliged, forced
observer to observe
obtenir to get, to obtain (9)
occasion *(f)* occasion; **vêtements** *(mpl)* **d'occasion** second-hand clothes
occasionnellement occasionally
occidental(e) *(mpl* **occidentaux)** western
occupé(e) busy
occuper to occupy; **s'occuper de** to take care of

Océanie *(f)* Oceania (9)
octobre *(m)* October (4)
odeur *(f)* odor, smell
œil *(pl* **yeux)** *(m)* eye (10); **avoir les yeux...** to have . . . eyes (4)
œuf *(m)* egg (8); **œuf dur** *(m)* hard-boiled egg (8)
œuvre *(f)* work
office *(m)* **de tourisme** tourist office (10)
offrir to offer; **offert(e)** offered; **offrant** offering
oignon *(m)* onion (8); **soupe** *(f)* **à l'oignon** onion soup (8)
oiseau *(m)* bird
omelette *(f)* omelet (8)
omniprésent(e) ever-present
on one, they, we, people, you (4); **Comment dit-on... en français/en anglais?** How does one say . . . in French/in English? (P); **On...?** Shall we . . . ?, How about we. . . ? (4); **On dit...** One says . . . (P); **On dit que...** They say that . . . (4); **On va... ?** Shall we go . . . ? (2)
oncle *(m)* uncle (4)
Ontario *(m)* Ontario (9)
onze eleven (P)
opéra *(m)* opera (9)
optimiste optimistic (1)
or *(m)* gold
orage *(m)* storm
orange *(f)* orange (8); **jus** *(m)* **d'orange** orange juice (2)
orange *(inv)* orange (3)
Orangina *(m)* Orangina *(an orange drink)* (2)
orchestre *(m)* orchestra, band (4)
ordinateur *(m)* computer (2)
ordonnance *(f)* prescription (10)
ordre *(m)* order; **en ordre** in order (3)
oreille *(f)* ear (10)
organiser to organize; **s'organiser** to get organized
origine *(f)* origin; **d'origine...** of . . . origin (7)
orné(e) (de) decorated with, adorned with
orphelin(e) orphan
orthographique spelling
os *(m)* bone
OTAN (Organisation du Traité de l'Atlantique Nord) NATO
ou or (P)
où where (1); **d'où** from where (1); **n'importe où** (just) anywhere
oublier to forget (8)
ouest *(m)* west
oui yes (P)
outre-mer overseas
ouvert(e) open
ouverture *(f)* opening; **heure** *(f)* **d'ouverture** opening time (6)
ouvrable: jour ouvrable *(m)* workday
ouvrir to open; **Ouvrez votre livre à la page 23.** Open your book to page 23. (P)

P

pacifique pacific, peaceful
page *(f)* page (P)
paiement *(m)* payment
paillasson *(m)* doormat
pain *(m)* bread (8); **pain au chocolat** *(m)* chocolate-filled croissant (8); **pain complet** *(m)* loaf of whole-grain bread (8); **pain grillé** *(m)* toast (8)
palais *(m)* palace (6)

pâle pale
palier *(m)* (floor) landing
pamplemousse *(m)* grapefruit
panique *(f)* panic
paniqué(e) panicked
panoramique panoramic
pantalon *(m)* pants (5)
pantoufles *(fpl)* slippers
papa *(m)* dad, papa
pape *(m)* pope
papier *(m)* paper; **feuille** *(f)* **de papier** sheet of paper (P)
papillon *(m)* butterfly
pâque juive *(f)* Passover
Pâques *(fpl)* Easter
paquet *(m)* package, bag (8)
par per (3), by (5); **par ailleurs** furthermore; **par conséquent** consequently; **par contre** on the other hand; **par exemple** for example (2); **par *hasard** by chance; **par ici** this way (5); **par la fenêtre** through the window; **par mois** per month (3); **par terre** on the ground / floor (3)
paradis *(m)* paradise, heaven
paraître to appear
parapluie *(m)* umbrella (5)
parc *(m)* park (1); **parc naturel** *(m)* natural park, nature reserve
parce que because (P)
parcourir to scan
Pardon. Excuse me. (P)
pardonner to forgive, to pardon
pareil(le) (à) similar (to)
parent *(m)* parent (4), relative (5); **chez mes parents** at my parents' house (3)
paresseux(-euse) lazy (1)
parfait(e) perfect (7)
parfaitement perfectly (7)
parfois sometimes (5)
parfum *(m)* perfume
Parisien(ne) *(mf)* Parisian (9)
parking *(m)* parking lot (1), parking garage
parler to talk, to speak (2); **Je parle/Je ne parle pas...** I speak/I don't speak . . . (P); **parler au téléphone** to talk on the phone (2); **se parler** to talk to each other (7); **Vous parlez... ?** Do you speak . . . ? (P)
parmi among
paroisse *(f)* parish
parole *(f)* word, lyric
part: à part... besides . . . ; **mettre à part** to set aside; **ne... nulle part** not . . . anywhere; **quelque part** somewhere
part *(f)* share
partager to share (3), to divide up; **partagé(e)** shared, divided (3)
partenaire *(mf)* partner (7)
participer (à) to participate (in)
particulier(-ère) particular, private; **en particulier** especially
partie part *(f)*; **en grande partie** mostly, in large part; **en partie** partially; **faire partie de** to be a part of
partir (de... pour...) to leave (from . . . for . . .), to go away (4); **à partir de** starting from; **partir en voyage** to leave on a trip (5)
partout everywhere (3)
pas not (P); **je ne comprends pas** I don't understand (P); **ne... pas (du tout)** not (at all) (1); **ne... pas encore** not . . . yet (5); **Pas de problème!** No problem! (3); **Pas mal.** Not badly. (P); **pas plus** no more (4); **pas tellement** not so much (1); **Pas très bien.** Not very well. (P)

passant(e) *(mf)* passer-by
passé *(m)* past (6); **dans le passé** in the past (6)
passé(e) past (5)
passeport *(m)* passport (9)
passer to spend, to pass (2); **passer chez** to go by . . .'s house (2); **passer le week-end / la matinée** to spend the weekend / the morning (2); **passer un film** to show a movie (6); **s'en passer** to do without; **se faire passer pour** to pass as; **se passer** to happen (7)
passion *(f)* passion (7)
passionnant(e) fascinating
passionné(e) (de) passionate about, fascinated by
pastèque *(f)* watermelon
patate *(f) (familiar)* idiot
pâte *(f)* paste, dough; **pâtes** *(fpl)* pasta
pâté *(m)* pâté, meat spread (8); **pâté de cochon** pork pâté
patience *(f)* patience; **avoir de la patience** to have patience (4)
patient(e) patient (6)
patin *(m)* skate; **patin** *(m)* **à glace** ice-skate, ice-skating
pâtisserie *(f)* pastry shop, pastry (8)
patrimoine *(m)* patrimony, heritage
patron(ne) *(mf)* owner, boss
pauvre poor
pauvreté *(f)* poverty
pavé (de) *(m)* thick slice (of) (8)
payer to pay (2)
pays *(m)* country (3)
paysage *(m)* landscape (9)
Pays-Bas *(mpl)* Netherlands
Pays-de-la-Loire *(mpl)* Loire Valley
pêche *(f)* peach (8), fishing; **aller à la pêche** to go fishing
peigner: se peigner to comb one's hair (7)
peine: à peine barely
peintre *(m)* painter
peinture *(f)* painting (1)
pendant during (1), for (5); **pendant que** while
penser to think (2); **je pense que le français est...** I think that French is . . . (P); **penser à** to think about; **Qu'en pensez-vous?** What do you think about it? (5)
penseur (penseuse) *(mf)* thinker
perçu(e) perceived
perdre to lose (7); **perdre du temps** to waste time (7); **perdu(e)** lost; **se perdre** to get lost (7)
père *(m)* father (4)
période *(f)* period; **à cette période** at that time
permettre (de) to permit, to allow; **permis(e)** permitted, allowed
Pérou *(m)* Peru (9)
Perse *(f)* Persia
personnage *(m)* character
personnalisé(e) personalized; **service personnalisé** personal service (8)
personnalité *(f)* personality (1)
personne *(f)* person (6); **ne... personne** nobody, no one, not . . . anyone
personnel(le) personal; **effets personnels** *(mpl)* personal belongings (3)
pessimiste pessimistic (1)
pétanque *(f)* lawn bowling, petanque
petit(e) small, short (1); **petit à petit** little by little (6); **petit déjeuner** *(m)* breakfast (5); **petite annonce** *(f)* classified ad; **petits pois** *(mpl)* peas (8)
petite-fille *(f)* granddaughter (7)

petit-fils *(m)* grandson (7)
petits-enfants *(mpl)* grandchildren
peu little (P); **à peu près** approximately, about; **un peu difficile** a little difficult/hard (P)
peuple *(m)* people
peuplé(e) populated
peur *(f)* fear; **avoir peur (de)** to be afraid (of) (4), to fear; **faire peur à** to frighten
peut-être perhaps, maybe (3)
pharmacie *(f)* pharmacy (10)
pharmacien(ne) *(mf)* pharmacist
philosophie *(f)* philosophy (1)
phrase *(f)* sentence (P); **Écrivez la réponse en phrases complètes.** Write the answer in complete sentences. (P)
physiologique physiological
physique *(f)* physics (1)
physique physical; **aspect physique** *(m)* physical appearance (7)
piano *(m)* piano (2)
pièce *(f)* room (3); **pièce** *(f)* **de monnaie** coin; **pièce** *(f)* **de théâtre** play (4); **pièce** *(f)* **d'identité** identity card
pied *(m)* foot (10); **aller à pied** to walk, to go on foot (4); **doigt** *(m)* **de pied** toe (10); **pieds nus** barefoot
pin *(m)* pine
pique-nique *(m)* picnic
pire worse
piscine *(f)* swimming pool (4)
pistache *(f)* pistachio
pitié *(f)* pity; **avoir pitié (de)** to have pity (on / for) (10)
pittoresque picturesque
pizza *(f)* pizza (8)
placard *(m)* closet (3)
place *(f)* place (3), square, plaza (10); **à sa place** in its place (3)
plage *(f)* beach (4)
plaindre: se plaindre to complain
plaine *(f)* plain
plaire to please; **Ça t'a plu?** Did you like it? (6); **Ça te plaira!** You'll like it! (9); **Ça te plaît!** You like it! (3); **Il/Elle m'a plu!** I liked it! (6); **Il/Elle me plaît.** I like it. (5); **s'il vous plaît** please (P)
plaisant(e) pleasant
plaisir *(m)* pleasure; **Avec plaisir!** With pleasure! (6); **faire plaisir à** to please
plan *(m)* map (10), level; **plan** *(m)* **d'eau** stretch of water
planche *(f)* **à voile** windsurfing; **faire de la planche à voile** to windsurf
plante *(f)* plant (3)
plastique *(m)* plastic
plat *(m)* dish (8); **plat préparé** *(m)* ready-to-serve dish (8); **plat principal** main dish (8)
plat(e) flat; **œuf** *(m)* **au plat** fried egg
plateau *(m)* tray
plein(e) full; **de plein air** outdoor (4); **plein de** full of, a lot of
pleurer to cry
pleuvoir to rain (5)
plongée sous-marine *(f)* scuba diving
pluie *(f)* rain (5)
plupart: la plupart *(f)* the most part; **la plupart de** the majority of; **la plupart du temps** most of the time (7)
plus plus; **À plus (tard)!** See you later! (P); **de plus** in addition; **de plus en plus de** more and more of (8); **en plus** besides, furthermore; **ne... plus** no more, no longer (8); **non plus** neither (3); **pas plus** no more (4); **plus de** more (8); **plus... que** more . . . than (1); **plus tard** later (4)
plusieurs several (8)
plutôt rather (1); instead (4); **plutôt que** rather than
poche *(f)* pocket
poché(e) poached
poêlée (de) *(f)* frying pan full (of)
poêlon *(m)* cast iron pan
poème *(m)* poem (9)
poésie *(f)* poetry
poing *(m)* fist
point *(m)* point; **au point de** to be about to; **point** *(f)* **de vue** viewpoint
poire *(f)* pear (8)
pois: petits pois *(mpl)* peas (8)
poisson *(m)* fish (8); **poisson fumé** smoked fish (8); **poissons** *(mpl)* **d'avril** April Fool's Day
poissonnerie *(f)* fish market (8)
poivre *(m)* pepper (8)
poli(e) polite
police *(f)* police, policy
policier(-ère) detective, police
politesse *(f)* politeness
politique *(f)* politics (7), policy; **sciences** *(fpl)* **politques** political science (1)
politique political; **homme politique** *(m)* politician
politiquement politically
polo *(m)* knit shirt (5)
Pologne *(f)* Poland
Polynésie française *(f)* French Polynesia (9)
pomme *(f)* apple (8); **pomme** *(f)* **de terre** potato (8)
populaire popular, pop (1)
porc *(m)* pork (8); **côte** *(f)* **de porc** pork chop (8)
portable: (ordinateur) portable *(m)* laptop (3); **(téléphone) portable** *(m)* cell phone (3)
porte *(f)* door (3); **porte** *(f)* **d'arrivée** arrival gate; **porte** *(f)* **d'embarquement** departure gate
portefeuille *(m)* wallet (5)
porter to wear, to carry (4)
portugais *(m)* Portuguese
poser to place; **poser une question** to ask a question (3)
posséder to possess, to own
possibilité *(f)* possibility (4)
possible possible (10); **il est possible que** it is possible that (10); **Pas possible!** I don't believe it!
postal(e) *(mpl* **postaux): carte postale** *(f)* postcard (9); **code postal** *(m)* zip code (3)
poste *(f)* post office; **bureau** *(m)* **de poste** post office (10)
poster *(m)* poster (3)
pot (de) *(m)* jar (of) (8)
pote *(m)* *(familiar)* buddy, pal
poubelle *(f)* trash can
poudre *(f)* powder
poulet *(m)* chicken (8)
poumon *(m)* lung
pour for (P), in order to (1); **pour cent** percent; **pour que** so that
pourboire *(m)* tip
pourcentage *(m)* percentage
pourquoi why (2); **Pourquoi pas?** Why not? (2)
pourtant however, yet (8)
pouvoir *(m)* power
pouvoir to be able, can, may (6); **Je peux vous aider?** May I help you? (5); **on peut** one can (4)
pratique *(f)* practice
pratique practical, convenient (3)
pratiquer to practice, to play *(a sport)*, to do
précédent(e) preceding
prêcher to preach
préciser to specify
préférable preferable (10); **il est préférable que** it's preferable that (10)
préféré(e) favorite (3)
préférence *(f)* preference
préférer to prefer (2); **je préfère** I prefer (1)
premier(-ère) first (1)
prendre to take (4); **Ça prend combien de temps?** How long does it take? (4); **Je vais prendre...** I'm going to have . . . (2); **prendre possession de** to take possession of; **prendre son petit déjeuner** to have one's breakfast (5); **prendre un bain** to take a bath (7); **prendre un bain de soleil** to sunbathe (4); **prendre une décision** to make a decision (7); **prendre un verre** to have a drink (2); **Prenez une feuille de papier et un crayon ou un stylo.** Take out a piece of paper and a pencil or a pen. (P); **Qu'est-ce que vous allez prendre?** What are you going to have? (2)
prénom *(m)* first name (3)
préoccuper to worry; **se préoccuper (de)** to worry (about)
préparatifs *(mpl)* preparations (9)
préparer to prepare (2); **plat préparé** ready-to-serve dish (8); **Préparez l'examen pour le prochain cours.** Prepare for the exam for the next class. (P)
près (de) near (1), nearly; **à peu près** approximately, about
présentation *(f)* introduction, presentation
présenter to introduce, to present; **Je vous/te présente...** I would like to introduce . . . to you.; **se présenter** to arise, to introduce oneself
presque almost, nearly (2)
prêt(e) ready (4)
prêter to loan, to lend
prier to beg, to request, to pray; **Je vous/t'en prie.** You're welcome (2).
prière *(f)* prayer
primaire: école primaire *(f)* elementary school
principal(e) *(mpl* **principaux)** main (8)
principalement mainly
principauté *(f)* principality
printemps *(m)* spring (5); **au printemps** in spring (5)
prioritaire having priority
priorité *(f)* priority
prisonnier(-ère) *(mf)* prisoner
privatif(-ive) private
privé(e) private (10)
privilégié(e) privileged, favored
prix *(m)* price; **menu** *(m)* **à prix fixe** set-price menu (8)
probablement probably
problème *(m)* problem; **pas de problème** no problem (3)
prochain(e) next (4); **le prochain cours** the next class (P)
producteur(-trice) producer
produit *(m)* product (8); **produits bio** *(mpl)* organic products (8)

professeur *(m)* professor (P); **Le professeur dit aux étudiants...** The professor says to the students . . . (P)
profession *(f)* profession (7)
professionnel(le) professional (7)
profil *(m)* profile
profiter de to take advantage of (9)
profond(e) deep
programme *(m)* program
projet *(m)* plan (4); **faire des projets** to make plans (4)
promenade *(f)* walk (5); **faire une promenade** to take a walk (5)
promener: se promener to go walking (7)
promettre (de...) to promise (to . . .) (6)
promouvoir to promote
pronom *(m)* pronoun
prononcer to pronounce
prononciation *(f)* pronunciation
propos: à propos de about
proposer to offer, to suggest, to propose; **Qu'est-ce que je peux vous proposer d'autre?** What else can I get you? (8)
propre clean (3), own
propreté *(f)* cleanliness
protéger to protect; **protégé(e) par** protected by
provençal *(m)* Provençal
Provence *(f)* Provence
provenir de to come from
province *(f)* province (3)
proviseur *(m)* principal
provoquer to cause
prune *(f)* plum
pruneau *(m)* prune
psychologie *(f)* psychology (1)
public: le grand public the public at large
publicité *(f)* advertising, advertisement
puis then (4)
puisque since
puissant(e) powerful
pull *(m)* pullover sweater (5)
pureté *(f)* purity
pyjama *(m)* pajamas

Q

quai *(m)* quay, wharf
quand when (2); **quand même** all the same
quantité *(f)* quantity
quarante forty (2); **quarante et un** forty-one (2)
quart *(m)* quarter; **Il est deux heures et quart.** It's a quarter past two. (P)
quartier *(m)* neighborhood (1)
quatorze fourteen (P)
quatre four (P)
quatre-vingts eighty (2); **quatre-vingt-un** eighty-one (2); **quatre-vingt-dix** ninety (2); **quatre-vingt-onze** ninety-one (2)
quatrième fourth (P)
que that (P), than, as (1), what (2), which, whom (7); **ce que** what, that which (7); **Je pense que...** I think that . . . (P); **ne... que** only; **ne... rien que** nothing but; **que ce soit** whether it be; **qu'est-ce que** what (1); **Qu'est-ce que ça veut dire?** What does that mean? (P); **Qu'est-ce que c'est?** What is it? (2)
quel(le) which, what (3); **À quelle heure?** At what time? (P); **C'est quel jour aujourd'hui?** What day is today? (P); **n'importe quel(le)...** (just) any . . . ; **Quel âge a... ?** How old is . . . ? (4)
quelque some; **quelque chose** something (2); **quelque part** somewhere; **quelques** a few (5); **quelques-un(e)s** *(mf)* a few; **quelqu'un** someone, somebody (6)
quelquefois sometimes (2)
quelques-un(e)s *(mf)* a few
question *(f)* question (P); **Écoutez la question.** Listen to the question. (P); **Répondez à la question.** Answer the question. (P)
quête *(f)* quest
qui who (2), that, which, who (7); **ce qui** what (7); **Qu'est-ce qui ne va pas?** What's wrong? (10); **Qu'est-ce qui s'est passé?** What happened? (6); **Qui est-ce?** Who is it? (2)
quinze fifteen (P)
quinzième fifteenth (3)
quitter to leave (4); **se quitter** to leave each other (7)
quoi what; **n'importe quoi** (just) anything; **à quoi bon** what's the point
quotidien(ne) daily (7)

R

rabbin *(m)* rabbi
raccompagner to (re)accompany
racine *(f)* root
raconter to tell (7), to recount
radio *(f)* radio (2), X-ray
raffiné(e) refined
raie *(f)* skate (fish), rayfish (8)
raisin *(m)* grape(s) (8); **raisins secs** *(mpl)* raisins
raison *(f)* reason; **avoir raison** to be right (4), **en raison de** because of
raisonnable reasonable
rajouter to add
ralentir to slow down
randonnée *(f)* hike (5); **faire une randonnée** to go for a hike (5)
rangé(e) orderly, put away, in its place (3)
ranger to arrange, to order (7)
rapide rapid (8)
rapport *(m)* relationship, report
rapporter to bring back; **se rapporter à** to be related to
rarement rarely (2)
raser: se raser to shave (7)
rassembler: se rassembler to gather
rater to miss
ravigote *(f)* a seasoned sauce
rayé(e) striped
réagir (à) to react (to)
réaliste realistic (1)
récemment recently (5)
réception *(f)* front desk (10), receiving
recevoir to receive (9)
recherche *(f)* research, search
rechercher to seek; **recherché(e)** sought
réciproque reciprocal
recoins *(mpl)* the nooks and corners
recommander to recommend (10); **recommandé(e)** recommended
réconcilier: se réconcilier to make up with each other (7)
reconnaître to recognize (9); **se reconnaître** to recognize each other (7)
recoucher: se recoucher to go back to bed (7)
recours: avoir recours à to resort to
recouvert(e) covered
recréer to recreate
récrire to rewrite
récupéré(e) recuperated, salvaged
rédaction *(f)* composition (9)
redéfinir to redefine
réduire to reduce
réel(le) real
réfléchi(e) reflexive
réfléchir (à) to think (about) (8), to reflect (on)
refléter to reflect
réflexion *(f)* reflection, thought
réfrigérateur *(m)* refrigerator
réfugié(e) *(mf)* refugee
regard *(m)* look
regarder to look at, to watch (2); **se regarder** to look at each other (7)
régime *(m)* diet; regime; **être au régime** to be on a diet
région *(f)* region (4); region, area (9)
régional(e) *(mpl* **régionaux)** regional (4)
réglable adjustable
règlement *(m)* payment
réglementé(e) regulated
régler to adjust; **régler la note** to pay the bill (10)
regretter to regret (6)
régulier(-ière) regular
régulièrement regularly (8)
rejoindre to join
relation *(f)* relationship (7)
relativement relatively
relaxant(e) relaxing
religieux(-euse) religious
religion *(f)* religion (7)
relire to reread
remarquable remarkable
remarquer to notice
rembourser to reimburse
remercier (de) to thank (for) (10)
remettre to put back
remonter to go back (up)
remplacer to replace
remplir to fill up
remporter to win
renaissance *(f)* revival, renaissance
rencontre *(f)* meeting, encounter (7)
rencontrer to meet for the first time or by chance, to run into (1); **se rencontrer** to run into each other (7)
rendez-vous *(m)* date, appointment; **Rendez-vous à...** Let's meet at . . .
rendre (quelque chose à quelqu'un), to return (something to someone) (7); **rendre (+ adjective)** to make (+ adjective); **rendre visite à quelqu'un** to visit someone (7); **se rendre (à / chez)** to go (to)
renommé(e) renowned
renommée *(f)* fame
renoncer renounce, give up
renouvelable renewable
rénover to renovate
renseignement *(m)* piece of information (3)
renseigner: se renseigner to inquire, to get information (10)
rentrer to return, to come / go back (home) (2); **rentré(e)** having returned
réparti(e) distributed
repartir to start again, to leave again
répartition *(f)* distribution
repas *(m)* meal (6)
répéter to repeat (2); **Répétez, s'il vous plaît.** Repeat, please. (P); **se répéter** to be repeated
répondre (à) to answer (6); **Répondez à la question.** Answer the question. (P)
réponse *(f)* answer (P); **Écrivez la réponse avec une phrase complète.** Write the answer with a complete sentence. (P)

reposer to set down; **se reposer** to rest (7)
reprendre to catch again
représenter to represent
république (f) republic
réseau (m) network (9)
réservation (f) reservation (9); **faire une réservation** to make a reservation (9)
réserver to reserve (9); **réservé(e)** reserved
résidence (f) dormitory (1), residence hall
résoudre to solve
respecter to respect; **se respecter** to respect one another
respiration (f) breathing
responsable responsible
ressemblance (f) similarity
ressembler à to look like, to resemble
ressortir: faire ressortir to make stand out
restaurant (m) restaurant (1); **dîner au restaurant** to have dinner in a restaurant (2)
reste (m) rest (7); **le reste (de)** the rest (of) (7)
rester to stay (2); **rester au lit** to stay in bed (2)
resto-U (m) university cafeteria (6)
résultat (m) result
résumé (m) summary
resvératrol (m) resveratrol
retard (m) delay; **en retard** late (10)
retirer (de l'argent) to take out, to withdraw (money) (10); **se retirer** to retire
retour (m) return (9); **billet aller-retour** (m) round-trip ticket (9)
retourner to return (5); **se retourner** to turn around
retrouver to meet (4), to find (again); **se retrouver** to meet each other (by design) (7)
réunion (f) meeting
réunir: se réunir to meet
réussir (à) to succeed (at/in), to pass (a test) (8)
revanche: en revanche on the other hand
rêve (m) dream
réveil (m) alarm clock (7), awakening
réveiller to wake up; **se réveiller** to wake up (7)
réveillon (m) **du jour de l'An** New Year's Eve
révélateur(-trice) revealing
révéler to reveal; **se révéler** to be revealed
revendre to resell, to sell back (7)
revenir to come back (4)
revenu (m) income
rêver (de) to dream (about, of) (7)
réviser to review (7)
révision (f) review, revision
revoir to see again; **Au revoir.** Good-bye. (P)
revue (f) magazine
rez-de-chaussée (m) ground floor (3)
rhum (m) rum
rhume (m) cold (10)
riche rich (2)
richesse (f) wealth
rideau (m) curtain (3)
ridicule ridiculous
rien nothing; **de rien** you're welcome (P); **ne... rien** nothing, not . . . anything (5); **ne... rien de spécial** nothing special (5); **ne... rien que** nothing but; **rien à voir avec** nothing to do with; **rien du tout** nothing at all (6)
rillettes (fpl) potted pork or goose
ringard(e) old-fashioned
rire to laugh
rive (f) bank

rivière (f) river
riz (m) rice (8)
robe (f) dress (5); **robe** (f) **de chambre** robe
rock (m) rock music (1)
rockeur(-euse) (mf) rock singer
rôle (m) role; **à tour de rôle** taking turns
roller: faire du roller to go in-line skating (6)
romain(e) Roman
roman (m) novel (9)
romanche (m) Romansh
romantique romantic
rompre to break (up)
rond (m) circle
rosbif (m) roast beef (8)
rose pink (3)
rosier (m) rosebush
rôti(e) roasted; **rôti** (m) **de porc** pork roast
rouennais(e) from Rouen
rouge red (3); **vin rouge** (m) red wine (2)
route (f) route, way
routine (f) routine (7)
roux (rousse) red (with hair) (4)
royaume (m) kingdom; **Royaume-Uni** (m) United Kingdom (9)
rue (f) street (3); **dans la rue...** on . . . Street (10)
ruine (f) ruin
rural(e) (mpl **ruraux**) rural
ruse (f) trick
russe Russian
Russie (f) Russia (9)
rythme (m) rhythm

S

sable (m) sand
sac (m) purse (5); **sac** (m) **à dos** backpack
sage good, well-behaved (4)
sain(e) healthy (8)
saint(e) holy
Saint-Valentin (f) Valentine's Day
saison (f) season (5)
salade (f) salad (8); **salade** (f) **de tomates** tomato salad (8)
salarié(e) (mf) wage earner
sale dirty (3)
salé(e) salted
salle (f) room; **salle** (f) **à manger** dining room (3); **salle** (f) **de bains** bathroom (3); **salle** (f) **de cours** classroom (1); **salle** (f) **de gym** gym, fitness club (1); **salle** (f) **d'informatique** computer lab (1)
salon (m) living room (3)
saluer to greet
Salut! Hi! (P)
salutation (f) greeting
samedi (m) Saturday (P)
sandale (f) sandal (5)
sandwich (m) sandwich (2)
sang (m) blood
sans without (P); **Ça s'écrit avec ou sans accent?** That's written with or without an accent? (P); **sans égal** unequaled
santé (f) health (8)
satisfaisant(e) satisfying
satisfait(e) satisfied
saucisse (f) sausage (8)
saucisson (m) salami (8)
sauf except (2)
saumon (m) salmon (8)
sauter to jump; **faire sauter** to blow up
sauver to save; **sauvé(e)** saved
savane (f) savanna
saveur (f) flavor, taste

savoir to know (how) (9); **Je ne sais pas.** I don't know. (P)
savon (m) soap
savoureux(-euse) tasty
science (f) science (1); **sciences humaines** (fpl) social sciences (1); **sciences politiques** (fpl) political science, government (1)
scientifique scientific
scolaire school; **extra-scolaire** extracurricular
scolarité (f) education
se herself, himself, itself, oneself, themselves (7); **Il/Elle s'appelle...** His/Her name is . . . (4); **Il/Elle se trouve...** It is located . . .
séance (f) showing (6)
sec (sèche) dry
sécher to dry, to skip (class)
secondaire secondary
seconde (f) second (5)
sécurité (f) security, safety
séducteur(-trice) seductive
séduire to seduce
séduisant(e) attractive
sein (m) breast; **au sein de** within
seize sixteen (P)
seizième sixteenth (3)
séjour (m) stay (7)
sel (m) salt (8)
self-service (m) self-service restaurant (8)
selon according to
semaine (f) week (P); **en semaine** weekdays; **les jours de la semaine** the days of the week (P)
semblable similar
sembler to seem
semestre (m) semester (P)
Sénégal (m) Senegal (9)
sénégalais(e) Senegalese
sens (m) meaning, sense; **sens** (m) **de l'humour** sense of humor (7)
sensible sensitive
sentiment (m) feeling (7)
sentimental(e) (mpl **sentimentaux**) sentimental, emotional (7)
sentir: se sentir to feel (8)
séparément separately
séparer to separate; **séparé(e)** separated
sept seven (P)
septembre (m) September (4)
septième seventh (3)
sérieux(-euse) serious
serrer to squeeze
serveur (m) waiter, server (2)
serveuse (f) waitress, server (2)
serviable helpful, obliging
service (m) service (8)
serviette (f) napkin, towel
servir to serve (4); **servi(e)** served (10); **se servir de** to use
seul(e) alone (P), only (1), single, lonely; **le/la seul(e)** the only one
seulement only (8)
shopping: faire du shopping to go shopping (2)
short (m) shorts (5)
si if (5), yes (in response to a question in the negative) (8); **s'il vous plaît** please (P)
siècle (m) century
siège (m) seat
sieste (f) nap
signaler to point out, to draw attention to
similaire (à) similar (to)
simple simple; **aller simple** (m) one-way ticket (9); **chambre simple** single room (f) (10)

VOCABULAIRE FRANÇAIS–ANGLAIS

simplement simply (10); **tout simplement** quite simply (10)
sinon if not, otherwise
sirène *(f)* mermaid, siren
site *(m)* site (9)
situé(e) situated
six six (P)
sixième sixth (3)
skateboard(ing): faire du skateboard(ing) to skateboard (6)
ski *(m)* skiing (2); **faire du ski** to go skiing (2); **faire du ski nautique** to go water-skiing (5)
smartphone *(m)* smartphone (3)
social(e) *(mpl* **sociaux)** social
société *(f)* company, society
sœur *(f)* sister (1); **belle-sœur** *(f)* sister-in-law; **demi-sœur** *(f)* stepsister (6), half-sister
soi oneself
soif *(f)* thirst; **avoir soif** to be thirsty (4); **j'ai soif** I'm thirsty (2)
soigner to treat, to cure
soin *(m)* care
soir *(m)* evening (P); **à huit heures du soir** at eight in the evening (P); **ce soir** tonight, this evening (2); **le soir** in the evening, evenings (P)
soirée *(f)* evening (4), party (6)
soixante sixty (2); **les années soixante** the sixties; **soixante-dix** seventy (2); **soixante et onze** seventy-one (2); **soixante et un** sixty-one (2)
sol *(m)* ground
solaire solar
soldat *(m)* soldier
solde: en solde on sale (5)
sole *(f)* sole (fish)
soleil *(m)* sun; **Il fait (du) soleil.** It's sunny. (5); **lunettes** *(fpl)* **de soleil** sunglasses (5); **prendre un bain de soleil** to sunbathe (4)
sombre dark, gloomy
sommeil *(m)* sleep; **avoir sommeil** to be sleepy (4)
sommet *(m)* summit
son *(m)* sound
son (sa, ses) her, his, its (3)
sondage *(m)* poll
sonder to poll
sonner to ring (7)
sorte *(f)* kind, sort; **en sorte que** so that
sortie *(f)* outing (6), exit
sortir to go out (2); to take out
soudain suddenly (6)
soudain(e) sudden
soudainement suddenly
souhaiter to wish (10)
soupçonner to suspect
soupe *(f)* soup (8); **soupe** *(f)* **à l'oignon** onion soup (8)
sourire to smile
sous under (3); **sous réserve de** subject to
sous-marin(e) underwater; **plongée sous-marine** *(f)* scuba diving
sous-sol *(m)* basement (3)
sous-vêtements *(mpl)* underwear
souterrain(e) underground
soutien *(m)* support
souvenir *(m)* memory
souvenir: se souvenir (de) to remember (7)
souvent often (2)
spatial(e) *(mpl* **spatiaux): industrie** *(f)* **spatiale** space industry
spécial(e) *(mpl* **spéciaux)** special; **effets spéciaux** *(mpl)* special effects (6); **ne... rien de spécial** nothing special (5)

spécialisé(e) specialized
spécialité *(f)* specialty (4)
spectacle *(m)* show
spectateur(-trice) *(mf)* spectator, viewer
spiritualité *(f)* spirituality (7)
spontané(e) spontaneous
sport *(m)* sports (1); **faire du sport** to play sports (2)
sportif *(m)* athlete
sportif(-ive) athletic (1)
stade *(m)* stadium (1)
stage *(m)* internship
stagiaire *(mf)* intern
station *(f)* station; **station-service** *(f)* service station
statistique *(f)* statistics
statut *(m)* statute, status
steak-frites *(m)* steak and fries (8)
stimuler to stimulate
stratégie *(f)* strategy
stress *(m)* stress (8)
stressé(e) stressed (out)
stylo *(m)* pen (P); **Prenez une feuille de papier et un crayon ou un stylo.** Take out a piece of paper and a pencil or a pen. (P)
subventions *(fpl)* subsidies
sucre *(m)* sugar (8)
sucré(e) sweet, sugary
sud *(m)* south; **Amérique** *(f)* **du Sud** South America (9)
Suède *(f)* Sweden
suffire to suffice; **Suffit!** That's enough!
suffisant(e) sufficient
suggérer to suggest (6)
Suisse *(f)* Switzerland (9)
suisse Swiss
suite: tout de suite right away (6)
suivant(e) following (3)
suivre to follow (7); **à suivre** to be continued (6); **suivi(e) de** followed by; **suivre un cours** to take a course
sujet *(m)* subject; **au sujet de** about
sulfureux(-euse) sulferous
super great (P)
superficie *(f)* area
supérieur(e) superior, higher
supermarché *(m)* supermarket (8)
supplément *(m)* extra charge (10)
supporter to bear, to tolerate, to put up with (7)
sur on (1); **sept jours sur sept** seven days out of seven
sûr(e) sure; **Bien sûr!** Of course! (5)
suranné(e) old-fashioned
surface: grande surface *(f)* superstore (8)
surfer sur Internet to surf the Net (2)
surgelé(e) frozen (8)
surgir to arise, to come up, to appear suddenly
surnom *(m)* nickname
surprenant(e) surprising
surprendre to surprise; **surpris(e)** surprised (10)
sursauter to jump
surtout especially (8), above all
survêtement *(m)* jogging suit (5)
survivre to survive
sympathique (sympa) nice (1)
symptôme *(m)* symptom (10)
synonyme synonymous

T

tabac *(m)* tobacco (8); **bureau** *(m)* **de tabac** tobacco shop
table *(f)* table (3); **à table** at the table; **table basse** *(f)* coffee table

tableau *(m)* board (P), painting, picture (3), scene, chart; **Allez au tableau.** Go to the board. (P); **tableau** *(m)* **d'affichage** bulletin board
tache *(f)* spot
taille *(f)* size (4); **de taille moyenne** medium-sized, of medium height (4); **Quelle taille faites-vous?** What size do you wear? (5)
tailleur *(m)* woman's suit
talon *(m)* heel; *haut talon *(m)* high heel
tambour *(m)* drum
tandis que whereas, while
tant (de) so much, so many; **tant que** as long as
tante *(f)* aunt (4)
tapis *(m)* rug (3)
tapisserie *(f)* tapestry
tard late (4); **À plus tard!** See you later! (P); **plus tard** later (4)
tarif *(m)* rate, fare
tarte *(f)* pie (8); **tarte** *(f)* **aux pommes** apple pie (8)
tartelette *(f)* **(aux fraises/aux cerises)** (strawberry/cherry) tart (8)
tartine *(f)* bread with butter and jelly (8)
tas *(m)* pile; **un tas de** a bunch of
tasse *(f)* cup
taxi *(m)* taxi (4); **en taxi** by taxi (4)
te (to, for) you (9), yourself (7); **Ça te dit?** How does that sound to you? (2); **Ça te plaît?** Do you like it? (3); **Je te présente...** I would like to introduce . . . to you.; **s'il te plaît** please; **Te voilà!** There you are!
technologie *(f)* technology (1); **technologies** *(fpl)* technical courses (1)
technologique technological
tee-shirt *(m)* T-shirt (5)
tel(le): tel(le) que such as; **un(e) tel(le)** such a (7)
télé *(f)* TV (2)
téléchargement *(m)* downloading
téléphone *(m)* telephone (2); **au téléphone** on the telephone (2); **numéro** *(m)* **de téléphone** telephone number (3)
téléphoner (à) to phone (3); **se téléphoner** to phone each other (7)
téléphonique: carte *(f)* **téléphonique** telephone card (10)
télévisé(e) televised
télévision (télé) *(f)* television (2)
tellement so much (1), so (6); **pas tellement** not so much (1)
temple *(m)* temple, Protestant church
temporaire temporary
temps *(m)* time (2), weather (5); **Ça prend combien de temps?** How long does it take? (4); **de temps en temps** from time to time (4); **emploi** *(m)* **du temps** schedule; **en même temps** at the same time; **en tout temps** at all times, at any time; **passer du temps** to spend time; **Pendant combien de temps?** For how long? (5); **Quel temps fait-il?** What's the weather like? (5); **temps libre** *(m)* free time (2); **temps verbal** *(m)* tense
tendance *(f)* tendency
tendre tender
tenir to hold, to keep; **Ah tiens!** Hey!; **tenir à** to value, to be keen on; **tenir la maison** to keep house
tennis *(m)* tennis (1); **court** *(m)* **de tennis** tennis court
terme *(m)* term; **mettre terme à** to put an end to
terminaison *(f)* ending

terminer to finish
terrasse (f) terrace (9)
terre (f) earth; **par terre** on the ground / floor (3); **pomme** (f) **de terre** potato (8)
terrine (f) earthenware bowl, terrine
territoire (m) territory
test (m) test (7)
tête (f) head (10); **prendre la tête** to take charge
Texas (m) Texas (9)
texto (m) text message (2)
thé (m) tea (2)
théâtre (m) theater, drama (1)
thon (m) tuna (8)
tiers (m) third
timbre (m) stamp (10)
timide shy, timid (1)
tiroir (m) drawer
toi you (P); **Et toi?** And you? (familiar) (P)
toilette: toilettes (fpl) toilet, restroom (3); **faire sa toilette** to wash up (7)
tolérance (f) tolerance, acceptance (7)
tomate (f) tomato (8)
tomber to fall (5); **tomber amoureux(-euse) (de)** to fall in love (with) (6); **tomber malade** to get sick (10)
ton (m) tone
ton (ta, tes) your (3); **tes amis** your friends (1)
tongs (fpl) flip-flops (5)
tort: avoir tort to be wrong (4)
tôt early (4)
touche (f) key
toucher to touch
toujours always (2), still
tour (m) tour, ride (4); **à tour de rôle** taking turns; **faire un tour** to take a tour, to go for a ride (4)
tour (f) tower
tourisme (m) tourism; **office** (m) **de tourisme** tourist office (10)
touriste (mf) tourist
touristique touristic (9)
tourner (à droite/à gauche) to turn (right/left) (10), to stir, to film; **se tourner (vers)** to turn (toward); **tourné(e)** filmed
tousser to cough (10)
tout (toute, tous, toutes) everything, all (2), whole (2); **(À) tout à l'heure** (See you) in a little while (P), a while ago; **C'est tout.** That's all. (8); **ne... pas du tout** not at all (1); **rien du tout** nothing at all (6); **tous (toutes) les deux** both; **tous les jours** every day (P); **tous les soirs** every evening; **tout à coup** all of a sudden (6); **tout à fait** completely; **tout de suite** right away (6); **tout droit** straight (10); **tout d'un coup** all at once (6); **tout en** while; **toute la journée** the whole day (2); **tout le monde** everybody, everyone (6); **tout près (de)** right by, very near (3); **tout simplement** quite simply (10)
toutefois however
toux (f) cough
traditionnel(le) traditional (8)
traduire to translate
train (m) train (4); **en train** by train (4); **être en train de...** to be in the process of . . .
trait (m) trait (7); **trait** (m) **de caractère** character trait (7)
tranche (f) slice (8)
tranquille tranquil, calm
transformer: se transformer en to change into

transmettre to transmit; to pass on
transport (m) transportation (4); **moyen** (m) **de transport** means of transportation (4); **réseau** (m) **de transports en commun** public transportation system (9)
travail (m) (pl **travaux**) work (6); **fête** (f) **du travail** Labor Day
travailler to work (2); **Je travaille...** I work . . . (P); **Je ne travaille pas...** I do not work . . . (P); **Tu travailles?/Vous travaillez?** Do you work? (P)
travers: à travers across
traverser to cross, to go across (10)
treize thirteen (P)
trekking (m) backpacking
trente thirty (P)
très very (P); **Je vais très bien.** I'm doing very well. (P)
tribu (f) tribe
trinité (f) trinity
triomphe (m) triumph
triste sad (10)
trois three (P)
troisième third (3)
trompe (f) horn
trompette (f) trumpet
trop too, too much (3); **trop de** too much, too many (6)
tropical(e) (mpl **tropicaux**) tropical (9)
trou (m) hole
trouver to find (4); **Il/Elle se trouve...** It is located . . ., He/She/It finds himself/herself/ itself
truc (m) thing (1); **Ce n'est pas mon truc.** That's not my thing. (1)
truite (f) trout
tu you (P)
tuer to kill
Tunisie (f) Tunisia
Turquie (f) Turkey
typique typical (2)
typiquement typically
tyran (m) tyrant

U

un(e) one, a (P)
uni(e) (à) close (to), united, solid-colored; **Royaume-Uni** (m) United Kingdom (9)
union: Union (f) **européenne** European Union
unique only, single, unique
uniquement only (6)
unité (f) unity, unit
universel(le) universal
universitaire university (1); **résidence** (f) **universitaire** university dorm (3)
université (f) university (P); **à l'université** at the university (P)
urbain(e) urban
urgence (f) emergency
usage (m) use
usine (f) factory
utile useful (10)
utiliser to use, to utilize

V

vacances (fpl) vacation (4); **partir en vacances** to leave on vacation (4)
vacancier(-ière) (mf) vacationer
vachement really (slang)
vadrouille (f) stroll
vague (f) wave
vaisselle (f) dishes; **faire la vaisselle** to wash dishes (5); **lave-vaisselle** (m) dishwasher
valeur (f) value

valise (f) suitcase (9); **faire sa valise** to pack your bag (9)
vallée (f) valley; **la Vallée de la Loire** the Loire Valley
valoir to be worth; **il vaut mieux (que)...** it's better (that) . . . (10)
valse (f) waltz
vanille (f) vanilla (8)
vanité (f) vanity (7)
vaniteux(-euse) vain
varié(e) varied
varier to vary
vaut See **valoir**
veau (m) veal
végétal(e) (mpl **végétaux**) **huile végétale** (f) vegetable oil
végétarien(ne) vegetarian
vélo (m) bicycle (2); **à vélo** by bike (4); **faire du vélo** to go bike-riding (2)
vendeur(-euse) (mf) salesperson (5)
vendre to sell (7)
vendredi (m) Friday (P)
venir to come (4); **venir de** (+ infinitive) to have just (+ past participle); **Viens voir!** Come see! (3)
vent (m) wind; **Il fait du vent.** It's windy. (5); **Il y a du vent.** It's windy. (5)
vente (f) sale
ventre (m) stomach (10), belly
verbe (m) verb
verdoyant(e) green, verdant
verdure (f) greenery
verglas: Il y a du verglas. It's icy.
vérifier to check, to verify (10)
vérité (f) truth
verre (m) glass (2); **prendre un verre** to have a drink (2)
vers (m) verse
vers toward(s), about, around (2)
verser to pour, to pay
vert(e) green (3)
vêtements (mpl) clothes (3); **sous-vêtements** (mpl) underwear
veuf (m) widower (7)
veuve (f) widow (7)
vexé(e) offended
viande (f) meat (8)
victime (f) victim
vidéo (f) video (2); **jeu** (m) **vidéo** video game (2)
vie (f) life (6)
vieillir to age, to get old
vieillot(te) outdated, old-fashioned
viennois(e) Viennese
viennoiserie (f) baked goods sold at a bakery
vierge (f) virgin
Viêt Nam (m) Vietnam (9)
vieux (vieil, vieille) old (1); **Vieux Carré** (m) French Quarter (4)
vif(-ive) lively, bright; **bleu vif** bright blue
village (m) village, town
villageois(e) (mf) villager
ville (f) city (3); **en ville** in town (3)
vin (m) wine (2)
vingt twenty (P)
vingtième twentieth
violence (f) violence (6)
violet(te) violet (3)
virus (m) virus (10)
visage (m) face
visite (f) visit; **rendre visite à quelqu'un** to visit someone (7)
visiter to visit (a place) (1)

VOCABULAIRE FRANÇAIS-ANGLAIS

visiteur(-euse) *(mf)* visitor
vitamine *(f)* vitamin (8)
vite quick(ly), fast (7)
vitesse *(f)* speed
vivoir *(m)* living room
vivre to live; **Vive… !** Long live… !, Hurray for… !
vocabulaire *(m)* vocabulary (P); **Apprenez les mots de vocabulaire.** Learn the vocabulary words. (P)
vœu *(m)* wish
voici here is, here are (2)
voilà there is, there are (2); **Te/Vous voilà!** There you are!
voile *(f)* sailing; **faire de la planche à voile** *(f)* to go windsurfing
voir to see (1); **aller voir** to go see, to visit (4); **comme tu vois** as you see (3); **rien à voir avec** nothing to do with; **se voir** to see each other (7); **Voyons!** Let's see! (5)
voisin(e) *(mf)* neighbor (9)
voiture *(f)* car (3); **en voiture** by car (4); **voiture** *(f)* **de location** rental car (5)
voix *(f)* voice
vol *(m)* flight (9)
volaille *(f)* poultry (8)
volcan *(m)* volcano
voleur *(m)* thief

volley *(m)* volleyball (2)
volonté *(f)* will, wish
volontiers gladly, willingly
volupté *(f)* voluptuousness
vomir to vomit (10)
voter to vote
votre *(pl* **vos)** your (2); **Ouvrez votre livre à la page 23.** Open your book to page 23. (P)
vouloir to want (6); **Ça veut dire…** That means . . . (P); **Je voudrais (bien)…** I would like . . . (2); **Qu'est-ce que ça veut dire?** What does that mean? (P); **Qu'est-ce que vous voudriez faire?** What would you like to do? (2); **Tu voudrais… ?** Would you like . . . ? (2)
vous you (P), (to, for) you (9), yourself(-selves) (7); **Ça vous dit?** How does that sound to you? (2); **Et vous?** And you? *(formal)* (P); **Je vous présente…** I would like to introduce . . . to you.; **s'il vous plaît** please (P); **vous-même** yourself; **Vous voilà!** There you are!
voyage *(m)* trip (4); **agence** *(f)* **de voyages** travel agency (9); **agent** *(m)* **de voyages** travel agent (9); **chèque** *(m)* **de voyage** traveler's check; **faire un voyage** to take a trip (5); **partir en voyage** to leave on a trip (5); **voyage** *(m)* **de noces** honeymoon
voyager to travel (2)

voyageur(-euse) *(mf)* traveler
voyelle *(f)* vowel
vrai(e) true (8)
vraiment really, truly (2)
VTT (vélo *[m]* **tout-terrain): faire du VTT** to go all-terrain biking (5)
vue *(f)* view (3); **point** *(m)* **de vue** viewpoint

W

wallon(ne) Walloon
W.-C. *(m)* toilet, restroom (10)
week-end *(m)* weekend (P); **Bon week-end!** Have a good weekend!; **le week-end** on the weekend, weekends (P)
Wi-Fi *(m)* Wi-Fi (1); **accès Wi-Fi** *(m)* Wi-Fi access (10)

Y

y there (4); **il y a** there is, there are (1), ago (5)
yaourt *(m)* yogurt (8)
yeux *(mpl)* *(sing* **œil)** eyes (4)

Z

zéro *(m)* zero (P)
zydeco: musique *(f)* **zydeco** zydeco music (4)

VOCABULAIRE anglais–français

The **Vocabulaire anglais–français** includes all words presented in *Horizons* for active use, as well as others that students may need for more personalized expression. The definitions of active vocabulary words are followed by the number of the chapter where they are first presented. A (P) refers to the **Chapitre préliminaire.** When several translations separated by commas are listed before a chapter number, they are all considered active. Since verbs are sometimes introduced lexically in the infinitive before the conjugation of the present indicative is presented, consult the **Index** to find out the chapter where a conjugation is introduced. An *(m)*, *(f)*, or *(pl)* following a noun indicates that it is masculine, feminine, or plural. *Inv* means that a word is invariable. An asterisk before a word beginning with an **h** indicates that the **h** is aspirate.

A

a un(e) (P); **a few** quelques (5); **a lot** beaucoup (P)
able: be able pouvoir (6)
about vers (2), environ (4); **about it/them** en (8); **About what?** À propos de quoi?; **talk about** parler de (1); **think about** penser à
above au-dessus de; **above all** surtout (8)
abroad à l'étranger (9)
absolutely absolument
accent accent *(m)* (P); **Is that written with or without an accent?** Ça s'écrit avec ou sans accent? (P)
accept accepter (7)
acceptance tolérance *(f)* (7)
access accès *(m)* (10); **Wi-Fi access** accès Wi-Fi *(m)* (10)
accident accident *(m)*
accompany accompagner
according to selon
account compte *(m)*
accountant comptable *(mf)*
accounting comptabilité *(f)* (1)
ache avoir mal (à) (10)
acquaintance: make the acquaintance of faire la connaissance de (7)
acquainted: be / get acquainted with connaître (4)
across from en face (de) (3); **go across** traverser (10)
act jouer *(in movies and theater)* (6); agir
active dynamique (1)
activity activité *(f)* (2)
actor acteur *(m)* (6)
actress actrice *(f)* (6)
actually en fait, réellement
adapt s'adapter
add ajouter
address adresse *(f)* (3); **e-mail address** adresse *(f)* mail (3)
adjective adjectif *(m)* (3)
administration office service administratif *(m)*
admire admirer (9)
adopted adopté(e)
adore adorer
adult adulte *(mf)*
advance avance *(f)*; **in advance** à l'avance (9)
advantage avantage *(m)*; **take advantage of** profiter de (9)
adventure aventure *(f)*; **adventure movie** film *(m)* d'aventure
advertisement publicité *(f)*; **classified ad** petite annonce *(f)*
advertising publicité *(f)*
advice conseils *(mpl)* (8); **give a piece of advice** donner un conseil
aerobics: do aerobics faire de l'aérobic (8)
afraid: be afraid (of) avoir peur (de) (4)
Africa Afrique *(f)* (9)
African africain(e)

after après (P); **after having done . . .** après avoir fait... ; **day after tomorrow** après-demain (4)
afternoon après-midi *(m)* (P); **in the afternoon, afternoons** l'après-midi (P); **It's one o'clock in the afternoon.** Il est une heure de l'après-midi. (P); **this afternoon** cet après-midi (4)
afterwards après (2), ensuite (4)
again encore (8), de nouveau
against contre (10)
age âge *(m)* (4)
agency: travel agency agence *(f)* de voyages (9)
agent agent *(m)*; **travel agent** agent *(m)* de voyages (9)
ago il y a (5); **How long ago?** Il y a combien de temps? (5)
agree être d'accord; **Agreed!** D'accord! (2)
ahead: straight ahead tout droit (10)
air air *(m)*
airplane avion *(m)* (4); **by airplane** en avion (4)
airport aéroport *(m)* (10)
alarm: alarm clock réveil *(m)* (7)
alcohol alcool *(m)* (8)
alcoholic drink boisson alcoolisée *(f)*
algebra algèbre *(f)*
Algeria Algérie *(f)* (9)
alive vivant(e)
all tout (toute, tous, toutes) (2); **above all** surtout (8); **all at once** tout à coup (6); **all day** toute la journée (2); **all of the sudden** tout d'un coup (6); **all of the time** tout le temps; **all sorts of** toutes sortes de; **all the better** tant mieux; **not . . . at all** ne... pas du tout (1); **nothing at all** rien du tout (6); **That's all.** C'est tout. (8)
allergy allergie *(f)* (10)
allow permettre (de); **allowed** permis(e)
almost presque (2)
alone seul(e) (P)
along le long de; **get along well / badly** s'entendre bien / mal (7)
already déjà (5)
also aussi (P)
although bien que, quoique
always toujours (2)
A.M. du matin (P)
amaze étonner; **amazed** étonné(e) (10)
America Amérique *(f)* (9)
American américain(e) (P); **American-style** à l'américaine (8)
among parmi
amusing amusant(e) (1)
an un(e) (1)
and et (P)
angry fâché(e); **get angry** se fâcher
animal animal *(m)* (*pl* animaux) (3)
animated animé(e)
anniversary *(wedding)* anniversaire *(m)* de mariage

annoying embêtant(e) (3)
another un(e) autre (P); **another glass of . . .** encore un verre de...; **another thing** autre chose; **one another** se, nous, vous (7)
answer réponse *(f)* (P)
answer répondre (à) (6); **Answer the question.** Répondez à la question. (P)
anthropology anthropologie *(f)*
antibiotic antibiotique *(m)*
any du, de la, de l', de, des, en (8)
anymore: not . . . anymore ne... plus (8)
anyone quelqu'un (6); **(just) anyone** n'importe qui; **not . . . anyone** ne... personne
anything quelque chose (2); **(just) anything** n'importe quoi; **not . . . anything** ne... rien (5)
anyway quand même
anywhere: (just) anywhere n'importe où; **not . . . anywhere** ne... nulle part
apartment appartement *(m)* (3); **apartment building** immeuble *(m)* (3)
appear paraître
appearance: physical appearance aspect physique *(m)* (7)
appetite appétit *(m)*
appetizer *hors-d'œuvre *(m)* (8)
apple pomme *(f)* (8); **apple pie** tarte *(f)* aux pommes (8)
appointment rendez-vous *(m)*
appreciate apprécier (6)
appropriate approprié(e), convenable
April avril *(m)* (4); **April Fool's Day** les poissons *(mpl)* d'avril
Arabic arabe *(m)*
architect architecte *(mf)*
architecture architecture *(f)*
Argentina Argentine *(f)* (9)
argue (with) se disputer (avec) (7)
arm bras *(m)* (10)
armchair fauteuil *(m)* (3)
around vers (2), environ (4), autour de
arrange ranger (7)
arranged rangé(e) (3)
arrival arrivée *(f)* (9)
arrive arriver (3)
art art *(m)* (1); **fine arts** beaux-arts *(mpl)*; **the arts** les arts (1)
article article *(m)* (9)
artist artiste *(mf)*
as comme (1); **as . . . as** aussi... que (1); **as long as** tant que; **as many . . . (as)** autant de... (que); **as much . . . (as)** autant (de)... (que); **as soon as** aussitôt que; **as you see** comme tu vois (3)
ashamed: be ashamed avoir *honte
Asia Asie *(f)* (9)
ask (for) demander (2); **ask a question** poser une question (3)
asleep: fall asleep s'endormir (7)
asparagus asperge *(f)*
aspirin aspirine *(f)* (10)

VOCABULAIRE ANGLAIS-FRANÇAIS | *quatre cent soixante-treize* **473**

associate associer
astronomy astronomie (f)
at à (P); at home à la maison (P); at . . . 's house / place chez... (2)
athletic sportif(-ive) (1)
ATM machine distributeur de billets (m) (10)
attend assister à
attention attention (f); pay attention (to) faire attention (à) (8)
attract attirer
auburn auburn (inv) (4)
August août (m) (4)
aunt tante (f) (4)
Australia Australie (f) (9)
automatic automatique; automatic teller machine distributeur (m) de billets (10)
autumn automne (m) (5); in autumn en automne (5)
available disponible
avenue avenue (f) (10)
average moyen(ne) (4)
avoid éviter (8)
away: go away partir (4), s'en aller; put away bien rangé(e) (3); right away tout de suite (6)

B

baby bébé (m)
back dos (m) (10)
back: bring back rapporter; come back revenir (4); give back rendre (7); go back rentrer (4), retourner (4); go back to bed se recoucher (7); in the back of au fond de; sell back revendre (7)
bacon bacon (m) (8)
bad mauvais(e) (1); really bad nul(le); That's too bad! C'est dommage (7); The weather's bad. Il fait mauvais. (5)
badly mal (P); not badly pas mal (P)
bag sac (m) (5), paquet (m) (8); pack your bag faire sa valise (9)
baggage bagages (mpl)
bakery boulangerie (f) (8); bakery-pastry shop boulangerie-pâtisserie (8)
balcony balcon (m)
bald chauve
ball balle (f), (inflated) ballon (m)
ballet ballet (m) (9)
banana banane (f) (8)
band orchestre (m) (4), groupe (m)
bank banque (f) (10); bank card carte bancaire (f) (9)
banker banquier (m)
bar bar (m)
baseball baseball (m) (2)
based: based on basé(e) sur (6)
basement sous-sol (m) (3)
basketball basket (m) (1)
bath bain (m) (7); take a bath prendre un bain (7)
bathe prendre un bain (7), se baigner
bathroom salle (f) de bains (3)
be être (1); be able pouvoir (6); be afraid (of) avoir peur de (4); be ashamed avoir *honte; be bored s'ennuyer (7); be born naître, (être) né(e) (5); be cold avoir froid (4); be familiar with connaître (4); be hot avoir chaud (4); be hungry avoir faim (4); be interested in s'intéresser à (7); be named s'appeler (7); be right avoir raison (4); be sleepy avoir sommeil (4); be thirsty avoir soif (4); be wrong avoir tort (4); be . . . years old avoir... ans (4); here is/are voici (2); How are you? Comment allez-vous? (P); How is it going? Comment ça va? (P); I am . . . Je suis... (P); I'm hungry. J'ai faim.

(2); I'm thirsty. J'ai soif. (2); isn't it? n'est-ce pas?, non? (1); It is located... Il/Elle se trouve... ; It's Monday. C'est lundi. (P); It's windy. Il fait du vent., Il y a du vent. (5); My name is . . . Je m'appelle... (P); There are . . . of us. Nous sommes.... (4); there is/ are il y a (1), voilà (2); The weather's nice / bad / cold / cool / hot / sunny / windy. Il fait beau / mauvais / froid / frais / chaud / (du) soleil / du vent. (5); to be continued à suivre (6); you are tu es/vous êtes (P)
beach plage (f) (4)
beans: green beans *haricots verts (mpl) (8)
bear supporter
beard barbe (f) (4)
beast bête (f) (6)
beat battre
beautiful beau (bel, belle, pl beaux, belles) (1)
beauty beauté (7)
because parce que (P); because of à cause de
become devenir (4)
bed lit (m) (2); bed and breakfast chambre (f) d'hôte; go back to bed se recoucher (7); go to bed se coucher (7); stay in bed rester au lit (2)
bedroom chambre (f) (3)
beef bœuf (m) (8); roast beef rosbif (m) (8)
beer bière (f) (2); draft beer demi (m) (2)
before avant (P); before (doing) avant de (faire) (7); before-dinner drink apéritif (m) (8)
beforehand auparavant
begin commencer (2); French class begins at . . . Le cours de français commence à... (P)
beginning début (m); at the beginning (of) au début (de) (6)
behaved: well-behaved sage (4)
behind derrière (3)
beige beige (3)
Belgium Belgique (f) (9)
believe (in) croire (à)
belong to appartenir à, être à
belongings effets personnels (mpl) (3), affaires (fpl)
belt ceinture (f)
beside à côté de (3)
besides de plus, d'ailleurs
best (le/la) meilleur(e) (adjective) (1), (le) mieux (adverb)
better meilleur(e) (adjective), mieux (adverb) (2); do better (to) . . . faire mieux (de)... (8); it's better . . . il vaut mieux... (10)
between entre (3)
beverage boisson (f) (2)
bicycle vélo (m) (3)
bicycle-riding: go bicycle-riding faire du vélo (2)
big grand(e) (1), gros(se) (1)
bike vélo (m) (2); by bike à vélo (4); ride a bike faire du vélo (2)
bikini bikini (m) (5)
bilingual bilingue
bill (restaurant) addition (f), (utilities) facture (f); pay the bill (at a hotel) régler la note (10)
billiards billard (m)
biology biologie (f) (1)
bird oiseau (m)
birth naissance (f); date of birth date (f) de naissance
birthday anniversaire (m) (4)
bizarre bizarre
black noir(e) (3)
blackboard tableau (m) (P)
blanket couverture (f) (3)
blog blog (m) (9)
blond blond(e) (4)
blood sang (m)

blouse chemisier (m) (5)
blue bleu(e) (3)
blueberry myrtille (f)
blues (music) blues (m)
Blu-ray player lecteur (m) Blu-ray (3)
board tableau (m) (P)
boat bateau (m) (4); by boat en bateau (4)
boating: go boating faire du bateau (5)
body corps (m) (7)
bodybuilding: to do bodybuilding faire de la musculation (8)
book livre (m) (P)
bookcase étagère (f) (3)
bookstore librairie (f) (1)
boot botte (f) (5)
border frontière (f)
bored: be/get bored s'ennuyer (7)
boring ennuyeux(-euse) (1)
born né(e) (5); be born naître (5); He/She was born . . . Il/Elle est né(e)... (5)
borrow emprunter
boss patron(ne) (mf)
both les deux
bottle (of) bouteille (de) (f) (8)
boulevard boulevard (m) (10)
bowl bol (m)
box (of) boîte (de) (f) (8)
boy garçon (m) (4)
boyfriend copain (m) (2), petit ami (m)
bracelet bracelet (m)
brave courageux(-euse)
Brazil Brésil (m) (9)
bread pain (m) (8); bread with butter and jelly tartine (f) (8); loaf of French bread baguette (f) (8); (loaf of) whole-grain bread pain complet (m) (8)
break casser; break down (machine) tomber en panne; break one's arm se casser le bras
breakfast petit déjeuner (m) (5); bed and breakfast chambre (f) d'hôte; to have one's breakfast prendre son petit déjeuner (5)
breathe respirer
brief bref (brève)
briefly brièvement
briefs slip (m)
bright (colors) vif(-ive)
bring (a thing) apporter, (a person) amener; bring back rapporter
Britain: Great Britain Grande-Bretagne (f)
broccoli brocoli (m)
brother frère (m) (1); brother-in-law beau-frère (m)
brown marron (inv) (3), brun(e) (4), medium/dark brown (with hair) châtain (4)
brunette brun(e)
brush (one's hair/one's teeth) se brosser (les cheveux/les dents) (7)
Brussels sprouts choux (mpl) de Bruxelles
build construire
building bâtiment (m) (1); administration building centre administratif (m); apartment building immeuble (m) (3)
burn (oneself) (se) brûler
bus (in city) (auto)bus (m) (3), (between cities) (auto)car (m) (4); bus stop arrêt (m) de bus (3)
business commerce (1); affaires (fpl) (5)
businessman homme (m) d'affaires (5)
businesswoman femme (f) d'affaires (5)
busy chargé(e) (schedule), occupé(e) (person)
but mais (P); nothing but ne... rien que
butcher's shop boucherie (f) (8)
butter beurre (m) (8); bread with butter and jelly tartine (f) (8)

buy acheter (4)
by par (5); **by bike / boat / bus / car / plane / taxi** à vélo / en bateau / en (auto)bus ([auto]car) / en voiture / en avion / en taxi (4); **by chance** par *hasard; **by the way** à propos; **go by . . .'s house** passer chez… (2); **right by** tout près (de) (3)
Bye! Salut! (P), Ciao!

C

cab taxi *(m)* (4)
cabbage chou *(m)*
café café *(m)* (1)
cafeteria cafétéria *(f)*; **university cafeteria** resto-U *(m)* (6)
Cajun cadien(ne) (4)
cake gâteau *(m)* (8); **chocolate cake** gâteau au chocolat (8)
calculator calculatrice *(f)*
Caledonia: New Caledonia Nouvelle-Calédonie *(f)* (9)
California Californie *(f)* (9)
call communication *(f)*; appel *(m)*
call téléphoner (3), appeler (6); **Who's calling?** Qui est à l'appareil?
calm calme (4), tranquille
calm down se calmer
calorie calorie *(f)*
camera appareil photo *(m)*
campground camping *(m)* (5)
camping camping *(m)* (5); **go camping** faire du camping (5)
campus campus *(m)* (1); fac(ulté) *(f)* (2)
can (of) boîte (de) *(f)* (8)
can (be able) pouvoir (6); **one can** on peut (4)
Canada Canada *(m)* (9)
Canadian canadien(ne) (P)
canceled annulé(e)
candy bonbon *(m)*
canned goods conserves *(fpl)* (8)
cap casquette *(f)*
capital capitale *(f)*
car voiture *(f)* (3); **by car** en voiture (4); **rental car** voiture *(f)* de location (5)
carafe (of) carafe (de) *(f)* (8)
card carte *(f)*; **bank card** carte bancaire *(f)* (9); **credit card** carte *(f)* de crédit, carte bleue *(f)* (9); **debit card** carte bancaire *(f)* (9); **identity card** carte *(f)* d'identité; **play cards** jouer aux cartes (6); **telephone card** carte téléphonique *(f)* (10)
care: I don't care. Ça m'est égal.; **take care of** s'occuper de, *(health)* (se) soigner
career carrière *(f)*
careful soigneux(-euse); **be careful** faire attention (à)
carefully soigneusement, attentivement
carpenter charpentier *(m)*
carrot carotte *(f)* (8)
carry porter (4); **carry (away)** emporter (5)
cartoon dessin animé *(m)*
cash: in cash en espèces (10)
cashier caissier(-ère) *(mf)*
cassette cassette *(f)*; **video cassette** vidéocassette *(f)*; **video cassette player** magnétoscope *(m)*
castle château *(m)*
cat chat *(m)* (3)
cathedral cathédrale *(f)*
Catholic catholique (1)
cauliflower chou-fleur *(m)*
cause cause *(f)*
cause causer
CD CD *(m)* (3), disque compact *(m)*; **CD player** lecteur *(m)* CD (3)

celebrate célébrer, fêter
cell phone (téléphone) portable *(m)* (3)
cent centime *(m)* (2)
center centre *(m)*; **shopping center** centre commercial *(m)* (4)
centime centime *(m)* (2)
central central(e) (mpl centraux); **Central America** Amérique centrale *(f)* (9)
century siècle *(m)*
cereal céréales *(fpl)* (8)
certain certain(e), sûr(e)
certainly certainement
certificate certificat *(m)*
chair chaise *(f)* (3)
chance: by chance par *hasard; **have the chance to** avoir l'occasion de
change monnaie *(f)* (2)
change changer (de) (6); **change one's mind** changer d'avis
character *(disposition)* caractère *(m)* (7), *(from a story)* personnage *(m)*; **character trait** trait *(m)* de caractère (7)
charge: extra charge supplément *(m)* (10); **in charge of** responsable de
cheap bon marché
check chèque *(m)*, *(restaurant)* addition *(f)*; **traveler's check** chèque *(m)* de voyage
check vérifier (10)
cheese fromage *(m)* (2); **cheese sandwich** sandwich *(m)* au fromage (2)
chemistry chimie *(f)* (1)
cherry cerise *(f)* (8)
chest poitrine *(f)*; **chest of drawers** commode *(f)* (3)
chicken poulet *(m)* (8)
child enfant *(mf)* (4)
childhood enfance *(f)*
Chile Chili *(m)* (9)
chill frisson *(m)* (10)
China Chine *(f)* (9)
Chinese chinois(e)
chips chips *(fpl)*
chocolate chocolat *(m)* (2); **chocolate cake** gâteau *(m)* au chocolat (8); **chocolate-filled croissant** pain *(m)* au chocolat (8)
choice choix *(m)* (8)
choose (to do) choisir (de faire) (8)
chore: household chore tâche domestique *(f)*
Christian chrétien(ne)
Christmas Noël *(m)*; **Merry Christmas!** Joyeux Noël!
church église *(f)* (4), *(Protestant)* temple *(m)*
cinema cinéma *(m)* (1); **cinema club** ciné-club *(m)* (2)
circumstance circonstance *(f)*
city ville *(f)* (3)
clarinet clarinette *(f)*
class cours *(m)* (P), classe *(f)* (1); **economy class** classe économique *(f)* (9); **first class** première classe *(f)* (9); **French class** cours *(m)* de français (P); **have class** avoir cours (6); **online class** cours *(m)* en ligne (1); **Prepare the exam for the next class.** Préparez l'examen pour le prochain cours. (P)
classic classique *(m)* (2)
classical classique (1)
classmate camarade *(mf)* de classe
classroom salle *(f)* de cours (1)
clean propre (3)
climate climat *(m)* (9)
climb *(tree)* grimper, *(rocks)* escalader
climbing: go mountain climbing faire de l'alpinisme; **go rock climbing** faire de l'escalade
clinic clinique *(f)*

clock horloge *(f)*; **alarm clock** réveil *(m)* (7)
close fermer (2); **Close your book.** Fermez votre livre. (P)
close (to) *(location)* près (de) (1); *(a friend)* proche
closet placard *(m)* (3)
clothes vêtements *(mpl)* (3)
cloud nuage *(m)*
cloudy nuageux(-euse); **It's cloudy.** Il y a des nuages.
club club *(m)*; **cinema club** ciné-club *(m)* (2); **fitness club** salle *(f)* de gym (1); **nightclub** boîte *(f)* de nuit (1)
coach classe économique *(f)* (9)
coast côte *(f)*
coat manteau *(m)* (5), pardessus *(m)*
code: zip code code postal *(m)* (3)
coffee (with milk) café *(m)* (au lait) (2); **coffee table** table basse *(f)*
coin pièce *(f)* de monnaie
Coke coca *(m)* (2)
cola coca *(m)* (2); **diet cola** coca light *(m)* (2)
cold froid(e); **be cold** avoir froid (4); **cold cuts** charcuterie *(f)* (8); **It's cold.** Il fait froid. (5)
cold rhume *(m)* (10)
colleague collègue *(mf)*
collect collectionner
college: go to college étudier à l'université
Colombia Colombie *(f)* (9)
color couleur *(f)* (3); **What color is/are . . . ?** De quelle couleur est/sont... ? (3)
comb one's hair se peigner (7)
come venir (4); **come back** revenir (4); **come down (from)** descendre (de) (5); **come get someone** venir chercher quelqu'un (10); **Come see!** Viens voir! (3)
comedy comédie *(f)* (6)
comfortable confortable (3)
commercial publicité *(f)*
communicate communiquer (10)
communication communication *(f)*
compact disc CD *(m)* (3), disque compact *(m)*
company société *(f)*, compagnie *(f)*, entreprise *(f)*
compare comparer (6)
compatibility compatibilité *(f)* (7)
complain se plaindre
complete complet(-ète) (8); **with a complete sentence** avec une phrase complète (P)
completely tout à fait
complicated compliqué(e)
composition rédaction *(f)* (9), composition *(f)*
computer ordinateur *(m)* (2); **computer lab** salle *(f)* d'informatique (1)
computer science informatique *(f)* (1)
concern concerner
concert concert *(m)* (1)
condition condition *(f)*
confidence confiance *(f)*; **have confidence** avoir confiance (4)
confirm confirmer (10)
confused confus(e)
congratulations félicitations *(fpl)*
conservative de droite (7)
conserve conserver
constantly constamment
contact contact *(m)*; **contact lenses** lentilles *(fpl)*; **in contact** en contact (9)
content content(e) (8)
continent continent *(m)* (9)
continue (straight ahead) continuer (tout droit) (10); **to be continued** à suivre (6)
contrary: on the contrary par contre; au contraire
control contrôler (8)

VOCABULAIRE ANGLAIS-FRANÇAIS | *quatre cent soixante-quinze* **475**

convenient pratique (3), commode
cook faire la cuisine (5); (faire) cuire
cooking cuisine (f) (4)
cool frais (fraîche); **pretty cool** assez cool (P); **The weather's cool.** Il fait frais. (5)
copious copieux(-euse) (8)
corn maïs (m)
corner coin (m) (3); **in the corner (of)** dans le coin (de) (3); **on the corner of** au coin (de) (10)
cost coûter (5)
cotton coton (m)
couch canapé (m) (3)
cough tousser (10)
count compter (2); **Count from . . . to . . .** Comptez de... à... (P)
country campagne (f) (3), pays (m) (3); **country music** musique country (f); **in the country** à la campagne (3)
couple couple (m)
course cours (m) (1); **first course** (of a meal) entrée (f) (8); **in the course of** au cours de (10); **Of course!** Bien sûr! (5), Évidemment!; **take a course** suivre un cours
court: tennis court court (m) de tennis
courtyard cour (f); **on the courtyard side** côté cour (10)
cousin cousin(e) (mf) (4)
cover couverture (f) (3)
cover couvrir
crab crabe (m)
crazy fou (folle)
cream crème (f) (8); **ice cream** glace (f) (8)
create créer
credit card carte (f) de crédit, carte bleue (f) (9)
crime crime (m), criminalité (f)
criminal criminel(le) (mf)
criticize critiquer
Croatia Croatie (f) (9)
croissant croissant (m) (8); **chocolate-filled croissant** pain (m) au chocolat (8)
cross traverser (10)
cruel cruel(le) (6)
crustaceans fruits (mpl) de mer (8)
cry pleurer
cucumber concombre (m)
cuisine cuisine (f) (4)
cultiver to cultivate (7)
cultural culturel(le) (4)
culture culture (f) (9)
cup tasse (f)
cure guérir
curly frisé(e)
currency exchange bureau (m) de change (10)
current actuel(le)
currently actuellement
curtain rideau (m) (pl rideaux) (3)
custom coutume (f)
customs (border) douane (f) (9)
cut: cold cuts charcuterie (f) (8)
cut (one's finger) (se) couper (le doigt); **cut class** sécher un cours
cycling cyclisme (m)

D

dad(dy) papa (m)
daily quotidien(ne) (7)
dairy product produit laitier (m)
dance danse (f); bal (m) (6)
dance danser (2)
dancer danseur(-euse) (mf)
danger danger (m)
dangerous dangereux(-euse)

dark foncé(e); **dark brown** (with hair) brun(e) (4); **to be dark** (outside) faire noir (4)
darling chéri(e) (mf)
date date (f) (4); rendez-vous (m); **What is the date?** Quelle est la date?, C'est quelle date? (4)
date sortir avec
daughter fille (f) (4)
day jour (m) (P), journée (f) (2); **day after tomorrow** après-demain (4); **day before yesterday** avant-hier; **every day** tous les jours (P); **Father's Day** fête (f) des Pères; **the following day** le lendemain (m) (5); **Have a good day!** Bonne journée!; **Mother's Day** fête (f) des Mères; **the next day** le lendemain (m) (5); **the whole day** toute la journée (2); **What day is today?** C'est quel jour, aujourd'hui? (P)
daycare crèche (f)
daytime journée (f)
dead mort(e) (5)
death mort (f)
debit: debit card carte bancaire (f) (9)
deceased décédé(e) (4)
December décembre (m) (4)
decide décider (de) (6)
decision décision (f); **make a decision** prendre une décision (7)
degree (temperature) degré (m), (university) diplôme (m)
delay retard (m)
deli(catessen) charcuterie (f) (8); **deli meats** charcuterie (f) (8)
delicious délicieux(-euse) (6)
delighted ravi(e); **Delighted to meet you.** Enchanté(e).
deluxe de luxe (10)
demand exiger
democratic démocratique
den salle (f) de séjour
dentist dentiste (mf)
department département (m); **department store** grand magasin (m)
departure départ (m) (9); **departure gate** porte (f) d'embarquement
depend (on) dépendre (de) (5); **That depends.** Ça dépend.
deposit déposer
depressed déprimé(e)
depressing déprimant(e)
depression déprime (f)
descend descendre (5)
describe décrire (9)
description description (f)
desire désirer (2)
desk bureau (m) (3); **front desk** réception (f) (10)
despite malgré
dessert dessert (m) (8)
destroy détruire
detective movie film policier (m)
detest (each other) (se) détester (7)
develop (se) développer
dictionary dictionnaire (m)
die mourir (5)
diet régime (m); **be on a diet** être au régime; **diet cola** coca (m) light (2)
different différent(e)
differently différemment
difficult difficile (P)
difficulty difficulté (f)
dine (out) dîner (au restaurant) (2)
dining room salle à manger (f) (3)
dinner dîner (m) (8); **before-dinner drink** apéritif (m) (8); **have dinner** dîner (2)

diploma diplôme (m)
direct diriger
direct direct(e)
directions indications (fpl) (10); **give directions** indiquer le chemin (10)
directly directement
dirty sale (3)
disadvantage inconvénient (m)
disagreeable désagréable, antipathique (1)
disappointed déçu(e)
disc: compact disc CD (m) (3), disque compact (m); **compact disc player** lecteur (m) CD (3)
discover découvrir
discuss discuter (de)
disguise (oneself) (se) déguiser
dish plat (m) (8); **do the dishes** faire la vaisselle (5); **main dish** plat principal (8); **ready-to-serve dish** plat préparé (m) (8)
dishwasher lave-vaisselle (m)
disorder désordre (m) (3); **in disorder** en désordre (3)
diversity diversité (f)
divided partagé(e) (3)
diving: scuba diving plongée sous-marine (f)
divorce divorcer
divorced divorcé(e) (1)
do faire (2); **do aerobics** faire de l'aérobic (8); **do better (to) . . .** faire mieux (de)… (8); **do handiwork** bricoler (2); **Do the homework.** Faites les devoirs. (P); **do weight training** faire de la musculation (8); **Do you . . . ?** Est-ce que vous… ? (1); **I do not . . .** Je ne… pas (P)
doctor médecin (m) (10)
doctorate doctorat (m)
dog chien (m) (3)
dollar dollar (m) (3)
domestic domestique
door porte (f) (3); **next door** à côté
dormitory résidence universitaire (f) (1)
double room chambre double (f) (10)
doubt doute (m); **without doubt** sans doute (8)
doubt that . . . douter que…(10)
doubtlessly sans doute (8)
down: go / come down descendre (5)
downtown en centre-ville (m) (3)
dozen (of) douzaine (de) (f) (8)
draft beer demi (m) (2)
drama drame (m); **drama course** cours (m) de théâtre (1)
dramatic dramatique
draw dessiner
drawer tiroir (m); **chest of drawers** commode (f) (3)
drawing dessin (m)
dream rêve (m)
dream (about, of) rêver (de) (7)
dress robe (f) (5)
dress habiller; **get dressed** s'habiller (7)
dresser commode (f) (3)
drink boisson (f) (2); **before-dinner drink** apéritif (m) (8); **have a drink** prendre un verre (2)
drink boire (4)
drive conduire; **go for a drive** faire un tour en voiture
drop laisser tomber
drums batterie (f) (2)
dry sécher; **dry cleaner's** teinturerie (f)
duck canard (m) (8)
due to à cause de
dumb bête (1)

during pendant (1), au cours de (10)
DVD DVD *(m)* (2); **DVD player** lecteur *(m)* DVD (3)

E

each chaque (3); **each one** chacun(e); **each other** se, vous, nous (7), l'un(e) l'autre
ear oreille *(f)* (10)
early tôt (4), en avance
earn gagner
earring boucle *(f)* d'oreille
earth terre *(f)*
easily facilement (7)
east est *(m)*; **Middle East** Moyen-Orient *(m)* (9)
Easter Pâques *(fpl)*
easy facile (P)
eat manger (2); **eat dinner (out)** dîner (au restaurant) (2); **eat lunch** déjeuner (2); **eat one's breakfast** prendre son petit déjeuner (5); **eat dinner** dîner (2)
eccentric excentrique
ecological écologique
economics sciences économiques *(fpl)*
economy économie *(f)*; **economy class** classe économique *(f)* (9)
editor rédacteur(-trice) *(mf)*
educate éduquer
education éducation *(f)*
effect effet *(m)* (6); **special effects** effets spéciaux *(mpl)* (6)
egg œuf *(m)* (8); **hard-boiled egg** œuf dur *(m)* (8)
Egypt Égypte *(f)* (9)
eight *huit (P)
eighteen dix-huit (P)
eighth *huitième (3)
eighty quatre-vingts (2); **eighty-one** quatre-vingt-un (2)
either . . . or . . . soit… soit…
election élection *(f)*
element élément *(m)*
elementary school école primaire/élémentaire *(f)*
elevator ascenseur *(m)* (3)
eleven onze (P)
else: What else? Quoi d'autre?; **What else can I get you?** Qu'est-ce que je peux vous proposer d'autre? (8)
elsewhere ailleurs
e-mail mail *(m)* (2), courrier électronique *(m)*; **e-mail address** adresse *(f)* mail (3)
embarrassed gêné(e)
embassy ambassade *(f)*
embrace (each other) (s')embrasser (7)
employee employé(e) *(mf)* (10); **government employee** fonctionnaire *(mf)*
encounter rencontre *(f)* (7)
end fin *(f)*; **at the end (of)** au bout (de) (3)
end finir (8), (se) terminer; **end up doing** finir par faire; **French class ends . . .** Le cours de français finit… (P)
energetic énergique
energy énergie *(f)*
engaged fiancé(e) (1); **get engaged** se fiancer (7)
engineer ingénieur *(m)*
engineering études *(fpl)* d'ingénieur, génie *(m)*
English anglais *(m)* (P)
English anglais(e)
enjoy: Enjoy your stay! Bon séjour! (10)
enough assez (de) (1)
enter entrer (dans) (5)
enterprise entreprise *(f)*
entertainment distractions *(fpl)* (5)
enthusiastic enthousiaste
entire entier(-ère)
environment environnement *(m)*
equality égalité *(f)*
equals: . . . plus . . . equals . . . … et… font… (P)
errand course *(f)* (5); **run errands** faire des courses (1)
especially surtout (8)
espresso expresso *(m)* (2)
essential essentiel(le)
establish établir
euro euro *(m)* (2)
Europe Europe *(f)* (9)
European européen(ne)
eve: New Year's Eve le réveillon *(m)* du jour de l'An
even même; **even though** bien que
evening soir *(m)* (P), soirée *(f)* (4); **At ten o'clock in the evening.** À dix heures du soir. (P); **Good evening.** Bonsoir. (P); **in the evening, evenings** le soir (P); **See you this evening.** À ce soir. (2)
every chaque (3), tout (toute, tous, toutes) (2); **every day** tous les jours (P)
everybody tout le monde (6)
everyone tout le monde (6)
everything tout (3)
everywhere partout (3)
exactly justement (3), exactement (10)
exam examen *(m)* (P)
example exemple *(m)*; **for example** par exemple (2)
excellent excellent(e) (6)
except sauf (2)
exception exception *(f)*; **with the exception of** à l'exception de
exchange: currency exchange bureau *(m)* de change (10)
exchange money changer de l'argent (9)
exciting passionnant(e)
excuse excuser; **Excuse me.** Excusez-moi, Pardon. (P)
executive cadre *(m)*
exercise exercice *(m)* (P)
exercise faire de l'exercice (2)
exhausted épuisé(e)
exhibit exposition *(f)* (4)
ex-husband ex-mari *(m)*
exotic exotique (9)
expensive cher (chère) (3)
experience expérience *(f)*
explain expliquer
express exprimer
expression expression *(f)* (10)
extra charge supplément *(m)* (10)
extracurricular extrascolaire
extraordinary extra(ordinaire) (4)
extroverted extraverti(e) (1)
ex-wife ex-femme *(f)*
eye œil *(m) (pl* yeux) (10); **to have . . . eyes** avoir les yeux… (4)

F

face figure *(f)* (7), visage *(m)*
facing en face (de) (3)
fact fait *(m)*; **in fact** en fait
fail échouer (à)
fair juste
fairly assez (P)
fairy tale conte *(m)* de fées (6)
fall automne *(m)* (5); **in (the) fall** en automne (5)
fall tomber (5); **fall asleep** s'endormir (7); **fall in love (with)** tomber amoureux(-euse) (de) (6)
false faux (fausse)
familiar: be familiar with connaître (4)
family famille *(f)* (P); **family name** nom *(m)* de famille (3); **family room** salle *(f)* de séjour
famous célèbre (4), fameux(-euse)
far (from) loin (de) (3); **as far as** jusqu'à (10)
farm ferme *(f)*
fashion mode *(f)*; **designer fashion** *haute couture *(f)*
fast vite (7), rapide (8)
fast food restaurant fast-food *(m)* (1)
fat gros(se) (1); **get fatter** grossir (8)
father père *(m)* (4); **father-in-law** beau-père *(m)* (4); **Father's Day** fête *(f)* des Pères
fats matières grasses *(fpl)* (8)
fault défaut *(m)* (7)
favorite préféré(e) (3)
fear avoir peur (de) (4)
February février *(m)* (4)
feed nourrir (8), donner à manger à (9); **to feed oneself** se nourrir (8)
feel (se) sentir (8); **feel like** avoir envie de (4)
feeling sentiment *(m)* (7)
ferocious féroce (6)
festival festival *(m)* (4)
fever fièvre *(f)*; **have fever** avoir de la fièvre
few: a few quelques (5), quelques-un(e)s
fewer moins de (8); **fewer . . . than** moins de… que
fiancé fiancé *(m)*
fiancée fiancée *(f)*
field champ *(m)*
fifteen quinze (P)
fifth cinquième (3)
fifty cinquante (2); **fifty-one** cinquante et un (2)
fight combattre, se battre; **fight (against)** lutter (contre)
fill (in) remplir
film film *(m)* (1)
finally finalement (6), enfin (7)
find trouver (4); **find out information** s'informer (9), se renseigner (10)
fine: fine arts beaux-arts *(mpl)*; **It's going fine.** Ça va. (P)
finger doigt *(m)* (10)
finish (doing) finir (de faire) (8), terminer
first premier(-ère) (1), d'abord (4); **at first** au début; **first course (of a meal)** entrée *(f)* (8); **first floor** rez-de-chaussée *(m)* (3); **first name** prénom *(m)* (3); **in first class** en première classe (9); **love at first sight** coup *(m)* de foudre (7)
fish poisson *(m)* (8); **fish market** poissonnerie *(f)* (8)
fishing pêche *(f)*; **go fishing** aller à la pêche
fitness club salle *(f)* de gym (1)
fitting room cabine *(f)* d'essayage (5)
five cinq (P)
fixed: at a fixed price à prix fixe (8)
flight vol *(m)* (9)
flip-flops tongs *(fpl)* (5)
floor étage *(m)* (3); **ground floor** rez-de-chaussée *(m)* (3); **on the floor** par terre (3); **on the second floor** au premier étage (3)
Florida Floride *(f)* (9)
flower fleur *(f)*
flu grippe *(f)* (10)
fluently couramment
flute flûte *(f)*
foggy: It's foggy. Il fait du brouillard.
folk music folk *(m)*
folklore folklore *(m)* (4)
follow suivre (7)
following suivant(e) (3)

food aliments *(mpl)*, nourriture *(f)*
foot pied *(m)* (10); **go on foot** aller à pied (4)
football football américain *(m)* (1)
for pour (P), pendant (5), depuis (7), comme (8); **for example** par exemple (2); **For how long?** Pendant combien de temps? (5); **for the last three days** depuis les trois derniers jours; **go away for the weekend** partir en week-end (5); **look for** chercher (3); **watch out for** faire attention à (8)
forbidden: It's forbidden to . . . Il est inderdit de...
foreign étranger(-ère) (1)
foreseen prévu(e)
forest forêt *(f)*
forget oublier (8)
forgive pardonner
fork fourchette *(f)*
former ancien(ne)
formerly autrefois, jadis
forty quarante (2); **forty-one** quarante et un (2)
four quatre (P)
fourteen quatorze (P)
fourth quatrième (3)
France France *(f)* (1)
frankly franchement
free libre (2), *(price)* gratuit(e) (10); **Are you free this evening?** Tu es libre ce soir? (2); **free time** temps libre *(m)* (2)
freedom liberté *(f)*
French français *(m)* (P); **French class** cours *(m)* de français (P); **French-speaking** francophone; **How do you say . . . in French?** Comment dit-on... en français? (P)
French français(e) (1); **French fries** frites *(fpl)* (8); **French Guiana** Guyane *(f)* (9); **French Polynesia** Polynésie française *(f)* (9); **French Quarter** Vieux Carré *(m)* (4); **loaf of French bread** baguette *(f)* (8)
frequently fréquemment
fresh frais (fraîche) (8)
Friday vendredi *(m)* (P)
friend ami(e) *(mf)* (P), copain *(m)*, copine *(f)* (6)
friendly amical(e) *(mpl* amicaux)
fries frites *(fpl)* (2); **steak and fries** steak-frites *(m)* (8)
frisbee: to play frisbee jouer au frisbee
from de (P), depuis; **from Monday to Friday** *(every week)* du lundi au vendredi (P)
front: front desk réception *(f)* (10); **in front of** devant (3)
frozen surgelé(e) (8)
fruit fruit *(m)* (8); **fruit juice** jus *(m)* de fruit (2)
full plein(e)
fun amusant(e) (1); **have fun** s'amuser (7); **make fun of** se moquer de
funny marrant(e) (1), drôle
furious furieux(-euse) (6); **to be furious that . . .** être furieux (furieuse) que... (10)
furnishings meubles *(mpl)* (3)
furniture meubles *(mpl)* (3)
furthermore en plus
futon futon *(m)*
future avenir *(m)*

G

gain gagner; **gain weight** prendre du poids
game match *(m)* (1), jeu *(m)* (2); **video game** jeu vidéo *(m)* (2)
garage garage *(m)*
garden jardin *(m)* (5)
garden faire du jardinage (5), jardiner
gardening jardinage *(m)*
gate: arrival gate porte *(f)* d'arrivée; **departure gate** porte *(f)* d'embarquement
general: in general en général (2)
generally généralement (8)
generous généreux(-euse)
gentle doux(-ce) (6)
gentleman monsieur *(m)*; **ladies and gentlemen** messieurs-dames
geography géographie *(f)* (9)
geology géologie *(f)*
German allemand *(m)* (1)
German allemand(-e)
Germany Allemagne *(f)* (9)
get obtenir (9), recevoir; **get along** s'entendre (7); **get bored** s'ennuyer (7); **get dressed** s'habiller (7); **get engaged** se fiancer (7); **get fatter** grossir (8); **get information** s'informer (9), se renseigner (10); **get lost** se perdre (7); **get married (to)** se marier (avec) (7); **get off** descendre (de) (5); **get older** vieillir; **get on** monter (dans) (5); **get ready** se préparer; **get sick** tomber malade (10); **get taller** grandir (8); **get thinner** maigrir (8); **get to know** connaître (4); **get undressed** se déshabiller (7); **get up** se lever (7); **get well** guérir; **go/come get someone** aller/venir chercher quelqu'un (10)
gift cadeau *(m)* (10); **gift shop** boutique *(f)* de cadeaux (10)
girl (jeune) fille *(f)* (4)
girlfriend copine *(f)* (2), petite amie *(f)*
give donner (2); **give (something) back (to someone)** rendre (quelque chose à quelqu'un) (7); **give directions** indiquer le chemin (10); **Give me your sheet of paper.** Donnez-moi votre feuille de papier. (P)
glad content(e) (8)
gladly avec plaisir (6), volontiers
glass verre *(m)* (2); **a glass of** un verre de (2)
glasses lunettes *(fpl)* (4)
global global(e) *(mpl* globaux)
glove gant *(m)*
go aller (2), se rendre (à / chez); **go across** traverser (10); **go all-terrain biking** faire du VTT (5); **go away** partir (4), s'en aller; **go back** rentrer (2), retourner (5); **go bike-riding** faire du vélo (5); **go boating** faire du bateau (5); **go by / past** passer (2); **go camping** faire du camping (5); **go down** descendre (5); **go for a ride** faire un tour (4); **go for a walk** faire une promenade (5); **go in-line skating** faire du roller (6); **go grocery shopping** faire les courses (5); **go hiking** faire des randonnées (5); **go in** entrer (dans) (5); **going to school** les études (1); **go jogging** faire du jogging (2); **go on foot** aller à pied (4); **go out** sortir (2); **go pick up someone** aller chercher quelqu'un (10); **go scuba diving** faire de la plongée sous-marine; **go see** aller voir (4); **go shopping** faire du shopping (2); **go skiing** faire du ski (2); **go to bed** se coucher (7); **Go to the board!** Allez au tableau! (P); **go to the movies** aller au cinéma (2); **go up** monter (5); **go walking** se promener (7); **go water-skiing** faire du ski nautique (5); **go windsurfing** faire de la planche à voile; **How's it going?** Comment ça va? (P); **It's going fine.** Ça va. (P); **Let's go . . . !** Allons... ! (2)
goal but *(m)*
god dieu *(m)*
golf golf *(m)* (2)
good: canned goods conserves *(fpl)* (8)

good bon(ne) (1), sage (4); **Good evening.** Bonsoir. (P); **Good idea!** Bonne idée! (4); **good in/at** fort(e) en; **Good morning.** Bonjour. (P); **Have a good day!** Bonne journée!; **Have a good weekend!** Bon week-end!; **It's good to . . .** C'est bien de..., Il est bon de... (10); **One has a good time!** On s'amuse bien!
good-bye au revoir (P)
government gouvernement *(m)*, sciences politiques (1); **government worker** fonctionnaire *(mf)*
gracious gracieux(-euse) (6)
grade note *(f)*
gram (of) gramme (de) *(m)* (8)
grammar grammaire *(f)*
grandchildren petits-enfants *(mpl)*
granddaughter petite-fille *(f)* (7)
grandfather grand-père *(m)* (4)
grandma mamie *(f)* (7)
grandmother grand-mère *(f)* (4)
grandparents grands-parents *(mpl)* (4)
grandson petit-fils *(m)* (7)
grape(s) raisin *(m)* (8)
grapefruit pamplemousse *(m)*
graphic artist dessinateur(-trice) *(mf)* (de publicité)
gray gris(e) (3)
great super (P), extra(ordinaire) (4), génial(e) *(mpl* géniaux) (4), formidable (7), magnifique; **Great Britain** Grande-Bretagne *(f)*
Greece Grèce *(f)* (9)
green vert(e) (3); **green beans** *haricots verts *(mpl)* (8)
greet saluer
grilled grillé(e) (8)
grocery: go buy groceries faire les courses (5); **grocery store** épicerie *(f)* (8)
ground terre *(f)*; **ground floor** rez-de-chaussée *(m)* (3); **on the ground** par terre (3)
ground meat bifteck *haché *(m)*
group groupe *(m)* (6)
grow (up) grandir (8)
guess deviner
Guiana: French Guiana Guyane *(f)* (9)
guide guide *(m)* (9)
guidebook guide *(m)* (9)
guilty coupable
guitar guitare *(f)* (2)
gym salle *(f)* de gym (1), gymnase *(m)*

H

hair cheveux *(mpl)* (4); **comb one's hair** se peigner (7); **hair stylist** coiffeur(-euse) *(mf)*
half moitié *(f)*
half demi(e) (P); **a kilo and a half (of)** un kilo et demi (de) (8); **half-brother** demi-frère *(m)*; **half hour** demi-heure *(f)* (7); **half-sister** demi-sœur *(f)*; **It's half past two.** Il est deux heures et demie. (P)
hall couloir *(m)* (3); **lecture hall** amphithéâtre *(m)* (1); **residence hall** résidence universitaire *(f)* (1)
ham jambon *(m)* (2); **ham sandwich** sandwich au jambon *(m)* (2)
hamburger *hamburger *(m)* (8)
hand main *(f)* (7); **on the other hand** par contre
handiwork: do handiwork bricoler (2)
handsome beau/bel (belle) (1)
hang up raccrocher
Hanukkah *Hanoukka *(f)*
happen se passer (7), arriver; **What happened?** Qu'est-ce qui s'est passé? (7)

happiness bonheur *(m)* (7)
happy content(e) (8), heureux(-euse) (7);
  Happy Birthday! Bon anniversaire!
hard dur(e); **have a hard time** avoir du mal à
hard-boiled egg œuf dur *(m)* (8)
hardly ne... guère
hard-working travailleur(-euse)
hat chapeau *(m)*
hate (each other) (se) détester (7)
hatred *haine *(f)*
have avoir (3); **have a drink** prendre un verre (2); **have breakfast** prendre le petit déjeuner (5); **have class** avoir cours (6); **have difficulty doing** avoir du mal à faire; **have dinner** dîner (2); **have fun** s'amuser (7); **have just (done)** venir de (faire); **have lunch** déjeuner (2); **have to** devoir (6)
hazel *(with eyes)* noisette *(inv)* (4)
he il (1); **he is...** c'est..., il est... (1)
head tête *(f)* (10)
health santé *(f)* (8); **health center** centre médical *(m)*
healthy sain(e) (8)
hear entendre (7)
heart cœur *(m)*
heavy lourd(e)
Hebrew hébreu *(m)*
heels: high heels *hauts talons *(mpl)*
height *hauteur *(f)*, taille *(f)*; **of medium height** de taille moyenne (4)
hello bonjour (P), *(on the telephone)* allô (6)
help aider (5); **May I help you?** Je peux vous aider? (5)
henceforth désormais
her la (5); **to her** lui (9); **with her** avec elle (2)
her son (sa, ses) (3)
here ici (P); **here is/are** voici (2); **this/these... over here** ce (cet, cette, ces) ...-ci (3)
herself se (7), elle-même
Hi! Salut! (P)
high *haut(e), élevé(e); **high fashion** *haute couture *(f)*; **high heels** *hauts talons *(mpl)*; **high school** lycée *(m)* (6); **high school student** lycéen(ne) *(mf)* (6)
hike: to go for a hike faire une randonnée (5)
hiking: to go hiking faire des randonnées (5)
him le (5); **to him** lui (9); **with him** avec lui (2)
himself se (7), lui-même
his son (sa, ses) (3)
historic historique (9)
history histoire *(f)* (1)
hobby passe-temps *(m)*
hockey *hockey *(m)* (2)
hold tenir
holiday fête *(f)* (4); **national holiday** fête nationale *(f)*
home: at home à la maison (P); **come / go back home** rentrer (2)
homework devoirs *(mpl)* (P); **Do the homework.** Faites les devoirs. (P)
honest honnête
honey miel *(m)*, *(endearment)* chéri(e)
honeymoon lune *(f)* de miel, voyage *(m)* de noces
hope espérer (3)
horrible horrible (6), affreux(-euse)
horror movie film *(m)* d'horreur
hors d'œuvre *hors-d'œuvre *(m)* *(inv)* (8), entrée *(f)*
horse cheval *(m)* *(pl* chevaux); **ride a horse** monter à cheval
horseback: go horseback riding faire du cheval
hose: panty hose collant *(m)*
hospital hôpital *(m)* *(pl* hôpitaux)

hostel: youth hostel auberge *(f)* de jeunesse (10)
hot chaud(e) (2); **be hot** avoir chaud (4); **hot chocolate** chocolat chaud *(m)* (2); **The weather's hot.** Il fait chaud. (5)
hotel hôtel *(m)* (5); **hotel manager** hôtelier(-ère) *(mf)* (10)
hour heure *(f)* (P); **half hour** demi-heure *(f)* (7)
house maison *(f)* (1); **at / to / in my house** chez moi (2); **pass by the house of...** passer chez... (2)
household ménage *(m)*; **household chore** tâche domestique *(f)*
housemate colocataire *(mf)* (P)
housework ménage *(m)* (5)
housing logement *(m)* (3)
how comment (P); **How are you?** Comment allez-vous? (P); **How does that sound?** Ça te/vous dit? (2); **How do you say...?** Comment dit-on...? (P); **How long does it take?** Ça prend combien de temps? (4); **how many** combien (de) (3); **How many people are there in your family?** Vous êtes combien dans votre (ta) famille? (4); **how much** combien (de) (3); **How much is it?** C'est combien?, Ça fait combien? (2); **How much is... plus / minus...?** Combien font... et / moins...? (P); **How old is...?** Quel âge a...? (4); **How's it going?** Comment ça va? (P); **How's the weather?** Quel temps fait-il? (5)
however pourtant (8)
human humain(e)
humid: It's humid. Il fait humide.
humor: sense of humor sens *(m)* de l'humour (7)
hundred: one hundred cent (2)
hunger faim *(f)*
hungry: be hungry avoir faim (4); **I'm hungry.** J'ai faim. (2)
hunter chasseur *(m)*
hunting chasse *(f)*; **go hunting** aller à la chasse
hurry se dépêcher (de); **hurried** pressé(e)
hurt: hurt (someone) faire mal (à quelqu'un); **one's... hurt(s)** avoir mal (à)... (10)
husband mari *(m)* (2)

I

I je, j' (P)
ice glace *(f)*; **ice cream** glace *(f)* (8)
ice-skating patin *(m)* à glace; **go ice-skating** faire du patin à glace
icy: It's icy. Il y a du verglas.
idea idée *(f)* (4)
idealistic idéaliste (1)
identify identifier
identity card carte *(f)* d'identité
if si (5)
ill malade (10)
illness maladie *(f)*
image image *(f)*
immediately immédiatement, tout de suite (6)
impatient impatient(e) (4)
importance importance *(f)* (7)
important important(e)
imprison emprisonner (6)
improve améliorer
impulsive impulsif(-ive)
in dans (P), en (P), chez *(+ a person)* (7); **go in** entrer (dans) (5); **I live in** *(+ city)* J'habite à *(+ city)* (P); **in advance** à l'avance (9); **in bed** au lit (2); **in front of** devant (3); **in love** amoureux(-euse); **in order to** pour (1); **in the country** à la campagne (3); **in the morning** le matin (P); **in your opinion** à votre avis (8)

include comprendre (8); **included** compris(e) (10)
indecision indécision *(f)* (7)
indefinite indéfini(e)
independent indépendant(e)
India Inde *(f)*
Indies: West Indies Antilles *(fpl)* (9)
indifference indifférence *(f)* (7)
indigestion indigestion *(f)* (10)
inequality inégalité *(f)*
inexpensive pas cher(-ère)
infidelity infidélité *(f)* (7)
inflexibility inflexibilité *(f)* (7)
influence influencer
inform (oneself) (s')informer (9); se renseigner (10)
information renseignements *(mpl)* (3); infos *(fpl)* (9); **find out information** s'informer (9)
in-laws beaux-parents *(mpl)*
inquire se renseigner (10)
insensitivity insensibilité *(f)* (7)
inside à l'intérieur, dedans
insist insister (10)
instant instant *(m)*
instead plutôt (4)
instructions instructions *(fpl)*
intellectual intellectuel(le) (1)
intelligent intelligent(e) (1)
intend (to) avoir l'intention de (4)
interested: be interested in s'intéresser à (7)
interesting intéressant(e) (P)
international international(e) *(mpl* internationaux)
Internet Internet *(m)* (2); **on the Internet** sur Internet (2); **to surf the Internet** surfer sur Internet (2)
interpret interpréter
interpreter interprète *(mf)*
introduce présenter; **Let me introduce... to you.** Je vous/te présente...
introverted introverti(e)
investigation enquête *(f)*
invitation invitation *(f)* (6)
invite inviter (à) (2)
iPod iPod *(m)* (3)
Irak Iraq *(m)*
Iran Iran *(m)*
Ireland Irlande *(f)* (9)
island île *(f)* (9)
Israel Israël *(m)* (9)
it ce (P), il (P), elle (1), le, la (5); **How's it going?** Comment ça va? (P); **it's...** c'est... (P); **It's going fine.** Ça va. (P); **of it** en (8)
Italian italien *(m)*
Italian italien(ne)
Italy Italie *(f)* (9)
its son (sa, ses) (3)
Ivory Coast Côte d'Ivoire *(f)* (9); **from/of the Ivory Coast** ivoirien(ne)

J

jacket veste *(f)*, blouson *(m)*; **ski jacket** anorak *(m)* (5); **windbreaker jacket** blouson *(m)*
jam confiture *(f)* (8)
January janvier *(m)* (4)
Japan Japon *(m)* (9)
Japanese japonais *(m)*
Japanese japonais(e)
jar (of) pot (de) *(m)* (8)
jazz jazz *(m)* (1)
jealous jaloux(-ouse) (7)
jealousy jalousie *(f)* (7)
jeans jean *(m)* (5)
jelly confiture *(f)* (8)
jewelry bijoux *(mpl)*

job poste (m), travail (m) (6)
jog faire du jogging (2)
jogging jogging (m) (2); **go jogging** faire du jogging (2); **jogging suit** survêtement (m) (5)
join rejoindre
journal journal (m) (pl journaux)
journalism journalisme (m)
journalist journaliste (mf)
juice jus (m) (2)
July juillet (m) (4)
June juin (m) (4)
just seulement (8), juste (10); **have just (done)** venir de (faire), **I would just as soon . . .** J'aimerais autant… (10); **just anything** n'importe quoi

K

keep garder
key clé (f) (10)
keyboard clavier (m)
kidney rein (m)
kilo (of) kilo (de) (m) (8)
kilometer kilomètre (m)
kind genre (m); **all kinds of . . .** toutes sortes de…
kindergarten école maternelle (f)
kingdom royaume (m); **United Kingdom** Royaume-Uni (m) (9)
kiosk kiosque (m) (10)
kiss baiser (m), bise (f)
kiss (each other) (s')embrasser (7)
kitchen cuisine (f) (3)
knee genou (m)
knife couteau (m)
knit shirt polo (m) (5)
know (person, place) connaître (4), (how, answers) savoir (9); **Do you know how to . . . ?** Savez-vous…? (9); **get to know** connaître (4); **I don't know.** Je ne sais pas. (P); **known** connu(e); **What do you know about . . . ?** Que savez-vous de…?
knowledge connaissance (f)

L

laboratory laboratoire (m) (1); **computer lab** salle (f) d'informatique (1); **language lab** laboratoire (m) de langues (1)
lack of manque de (m)
lady dame (f); **ladies and gentlemen** messieurs-dames; **lady's suit** tailleur (m)
lake lac (m)
lamb agneau (m)
lamp lampe (f) (3)
landscape paysage (m) (9)
language langue (f) (1); **language lab** laboratoire (m) de langues (1)
laptop (ordinateur) portable (m) (3)
large grand(e) (1); copieux(-euse) (8)
last durer
last dernier(-ère) (1)
late tard (4), en retard (10); **later** plus tard (4); **See you later.** À tout à l'heure., À plus tard!, À plus! (P)
laugh rire
laundry linge (m); **do laundry** faire la lessive (5)
law loi (f); (field) droit (m)
lawyer avocat(e) (mf)
lazy paresseux(-euse) (1)
learn apprendre (à) (4); **Learn . . .** Apprenez… (P)
leave quitter (4), partir (de) (4), sortir (de) (6), (something behind) laisser (3), s'en aller; **leave each other** se quitter (7)
lecture hall amphithéâtre (m) (1)

left gauche (f) (3); **to the left (of)** à gauche (de) (3)
leg jambe (f) (10)
leisure activity loisir (m) (2)
lemon citron (m) (2); **tea with lemon** thé (m) au citron (2)
lend prêter
lense: contact lenses lentilles (fpl)
less moins de (8); **less . . . than** moins… que (1)
let laisser; **Let's go . . . !** Allons… ! (2); **Let's see!** Voyons! (5)
letter lettre (f) (9)
lettuce laitue (f) (8)
level niveau (m)
liberal de gauche (7)
library bibliothèque (f) (1)
life vie (f) (6)
lift weights faire des haltères
light (weight) léger(-ère) (8), (color) clair(e)
like aimer (2); **Did you like it?** Ça t'a plu? (6); **Does he/she like it?** Ça lui plaît? (9); **Do you like . . . ?** Est-ce que vous aimez… ? (1); **I like . . .** J'aime… (1); **I like it!** Il/Elle me plaît! (5); **I liked it!** Il/Elle m'a plu! (6); **I would like . . .** Je voudrais (bien)… (2); **like each other** s'aimer (7); **What would you like?** Vous désirez? (2); **You like it.** Ça te plaît. (3); **You'll like it!** Ça te/vous plaira! (9); **You would like . . .** Tu voudrais…, Vous voudriez… (2)
like comme (1); **What is / are . . . like?** Comment est/sont… ? (1)
lime citron vert (m)
line ligne (f); **online** en ligne (1)
lip lèvre (f)
liquid liquide (m) (10)
listen (to) écouter (2); **Listen to the question.** Écoutez la question. (P)
liter (of) litre (de) (m) (8)
literature littérature (f) (1); **classical literature** littérature classique (1); **literature class** cours (m) de littérature (1)
little (of) peu (de) (8); **a little** un peu (P); **little by little** petit à petit (6)
little petit(e) (1)
live habiter (2); **Do you live . . . ?** Vous habitez…? (P); **I live in . . .** (+ city) J'habite à… (+ city) (P)
liver foie (m)
living room salon (m) (3)
loaf of French bread baguette (f) (8)
loafers mocassins (mpl)
loan prêter
lobster *homard (m) (8)
local local(e) (mpl locaux) (9)
located situé(e); **It is located . . .** Il/Elle se trouve…
lock fermer à clé
lodge: ski lodge chalet (m) à la montagne (10)
lodging logement (m) (3)
lonely seul(e)
long long(ue) (4); **a long time** longtemps (5); **as long as** tant que; **How long does it take?** Combien de temps est-ce que ça prend? (4); **no longer** ne… plus (8)
look (at) regarder (2); **look (+ adjective)** avoir l'air (+ adjectif) (4); **look at each other** se regarder (7); **look for** chercher (3); **look like** ressembler (7); **look very good on someone** aller très bien à quelqu'un
lose perdre (7); **get lost** se perdre (7); **lose weight** perdre du poids
lot: a lot beaucoup (P), **a lot of** beaucoup de (1); **not a lot** pas grand-chose

love amour (m) (6); **fall in love (with)** tomber amoureux(-euse) (de) (6); **love at first sight** coup (m) de foudre (7); **love story** film (m) d'amour (6); **true love** le grand amour (7)
love aimer (2), adorer (5); **love each other** s'aimer (7)
luck chance (f) (5); **What luck!** Quelle chance! (5)
lucky: be lucky avoir de la chance
luggage bagages (mpl)
lunch déjeuner (m) (8); **have lunch** déjeuner (2)
lung poumon (m)
luxury luxe (m)
lyrics paroles (fpl)

M

machine machine (f); **automatic teller machine** distributeur de billets (m) (10)
madam (Mrs.) madame (Mme) (P)
magazine magazine (m) (9)
magnificent magnifique
mail courrier (m); **e-mail** mail (m) (2), courrier électronique (m); **mail carrier** facteur (m), factrice (f)
main principal(e) (mpl principaux); **main dish** plat (m) principal (8)
major in se spécialiser en
majority: the majority of the time la plupart du temps (7)
make faire (2); **make (+ adjective)** rendre (+ adjectif); **make a decision** prendre une décision (7); **make money** gagner de l'argent; **make up with each other** se réconcilier (7); **made up of** composé(e) de
make-up maquillage (m); **put on make-up** se maquiller (7)
mall: shopping mall centre commercial (m) (4)
mama maman (f)
man homme (m) (1); monsieur (m)
management gestion (f)
manual worker ouvrier(-ère) (mf)
many beaucoup (de) (1); **how many** combien (de) (1); **How many people are there in your family?** Vous êtes combien dans votre (ta) famille? (4); **so many** tant (de); **too many** trop (de) (8)
map plan (m) (10), carte (f)
March mars (m) (4)
market marché (m) (8)
marketing marketing (m) (1)
marriage mariage (m) (7)
married marié(e) (1); **get married (to)** se marier (avec) (7)
marvelous merveilleux(-euse)
mathematics mathématiques (maths) (fpl) (1)
matter: It doesn't matter to me. Ça m'est égal.; **What's the matter?** Qu'est-ce qu'il y a?
May mai (m) (3)
may pouvoir (6); **May I help you?** Je peux vous aider? (5)
maybe peut-être (3)
me moi (P), me (9); **with me** avec moi (2); **Give me . . .** Donnez-moi… (P)
meal repas (m) (6)
mean: What does that mean? Qu'est-ce que ça veut dire? (P)
mean méchant(e) (1)
means moyen (m); **means of transportation** moyen (m) de transport (4)
meat viande (f) (8); **ground meat** bifteck *haché (m); **meat spread** pâté (m) (8)
medical médical(e) (mpl médicaux)
medication médicament (m) (10)

medicine *(studies)* médecine *(f)*, *(medication)* médicament *(m)* (10)
medium moyen(ne); **medium brown** *(with hair)* châtain (4); **medium-height** de taille moyenne (4)
meet *(by design)* retrouver (4), *(by chance, for the first time)* rencontrer (1), *(for the first time)* faire la connaissance de (7), se réunir; **Let's meet at . . .** Rendez-vous à...; **meet each other** *(by chance, for the first time)* se rencontrer, *(by design)* se retrouver (7)
meeting réunion *(f)*
melon melon *(m)*
member membre *(m)*
memory souvenir *(m)*, mémoire *(f)*
menu *(set-price)* menu *(m)* (à prix fixe), carte *(f)* (8)
merchant marchand(e) *(mf)* (6)
Merry Christmas! Joyeux Noël!
mess: What a mess! Quel bazar! *(familiar)* (3)
message message *(m)*
messenger messager(-ère) *(mf)* (6)
Mexico Mexique *(m)* (9)
microwave oven four *(m)* à micro-ondes
middle milieu *(m)*; **in the middle of** au milieu de
Middle East Moyen-Orient *(m)* (9)
midnight minuit *(m)* (P)
milk lait *(m)* (8); **coffee with milk** café *(m)* au lait (2)
million: one million un million (de) (3)
mind esprit *(m)* (7)
mine le mien (la mienne, les miens, les miennes)
mineral water eau minérale *(f)* (2)
minus: How much is . . . minus . . . ? Combien font... moins... ? (P)
minute minute *(f)* (5); **at the last minute** au dernier moment
mirror miroir *(m)*
mischievous espiègle
miss mademoiselle (Mlle) (P)
mistake erreur *(f)*; **make a mistake** se tromper
mister (Mr.) monsieur (M.) (P)
mistrust se méfier de
modern moderne (1)
mom maman *(f)*
moment instant *(m)*, moment *(m)*
Monday lundi *(m)* (P)
money argent *(m)* (2)
monster monstre *(m)* (6)
month mois *(m)* (3); **per month** par mois (3); **this month** ce mois-ci (4)
mood: in a good/bad mood de bonne/mauvaise humeur
more plus (1), encore (8), plus de (8); **more and more of** de plus en plus de (8); **more . . . than** plus... que (1); **no more** ne... plus (8), pas plus (4)
morning matin *(m)* (P); **at eight o'clock in the morning** à huit heures du matin (P); **Good morning.** Bonjour. (P); **in the morning, mornings** le matin (P); **morning hours** matinée *(f)* (2)
Morocco Maroc *(m)* (9)
mosque mosquée *(f)*
most: most of the time la plupart du temps (7), **the most** le (la) plus
mother mère *(f)* (4); **mother-in-law** belle-mère *(f)* (4); **Mother's Day** fête *(f)* des Mères
motorcycle moto *(f)*
mountain montagne *(f)* (5); **go mountain climbing** faire de l'alpinisme; **go to the mountains** aller à la montagne (5)
mouth bouche *(f)* (10)

move (into) s'installer (à/dans) (7)
movement mouvement *(m)*
movie film *(m)* (1); **go to the movies** aller au cinéma (2); **movie theater** cinéma *(m)* (1); **romantic movie** film *(m)* d'amour (6); **show a movie** passer un film (6)
MP3 player lecteur *(m)* MP3
Mr. monsieur (M.) (P)
Mrs. madame (Mme) (P)
much beaucoup (de) (1); **as much . . . (as)** autant de... (que); **how much** combien (de) (1); **How much is it?** C'est combien?, Ça fait combien? (2); **not much** ne... pas grand-chose; **so much** tellement (1), tant; **too much** trop (3)
muscular musclé(e)
museum musée *(m)* (4)
mushroom champignon *(m)*
music musique *(f)* (1); **listen to music** écouter de la musique (2)
musical *(movie)* comédie musicale *(f)*
musical musicien(ne)
musician musicien(ne) *(mf)*
mussel moule *(f)* (8)
must devoir (6); **he/she must** il/elle doit (3); **one must . . .** il faut... (8)
mustache moustache *(f)* (4)
my mon (ma, mes) (3); **at / in / to my house** chez moi (2); **my best friend** mon meilleur ami *(m)*, ma meilleure amie *(f)* (1); **my friends** mes amis (1); **My name is . . .** Je m'appelle... (P); **with my family** avec ma famille (P)
myself me (7), moi-même

N

naive naïf(-ïve)
name nom *(m)* (3); **family name** nom *(m)* de famille (3); **first name** prénom *(m)* (3); **His/Her name is . . .** Il/Elle s'appelle... (4); **last name** nom *(m)* de famille (3); **My name is . . .** Je m'appelle... (P); **What is his/her name?** Comment s'appelle-t-il/elle? (4); **What's your name?** Tu t'appelles comment? *(familiar)* (P), Comment vous appelez-vous? *(formal)* (P)
named nommé(e); **be named** s'appeler (7)
nap sieste *(f)*; **take a nap** faire la sieste
napkin serviette *(f)*
nationality nationalité *(f)* (3)
natural naturel(le)
nature nature *(f)* (7)
near près (de) (1)
nearly presque (2)
necessary nécessaire (10); **it is necessary to . . .** il faut... (8), il est nécessaire (de)... (10)
neck cou *(m)*
necklace collier *(m)*
necktie cravate *(f)* (5)
nectarine nectarine *(f)*
need avoir besoin de (4); **I/you/we/you/he/she/they need(s)** Il me/te/nous/vous/lui/leur faut (9); **one needs . . .** il faut... (8)
needy nécessiteux *(mpl)*
neighbor voisin(e) *(mf)* (9)
neighborhood quartier *(m)* (1)
neither non plus (3); **neither . . . nor** ne... ni... ni...
nephew neveu *(pl* neveux) *(m)* (4)
nervous nerveux(-euse); **feel nervous** se sentir mal à l'aise
Net: surf the Net surfer sur Internet (2)
network réseau *(m)* (9)
never ne... jamais (2)

new nouveau / nouvel (nouvelle) (1); neuf (neuve); **Happy New Year!** Bonne année!; **New Caledonia** Nouvelle-Calédonie *(f)* (9); **New Orleans** La Nouvelle-Orléans (4); **New Year's Eve** le réveillon *(m)* du jour de l'An
news nouvelles *(fpl)*, *(television program)* informations *(fpl)*
newspaper journal *(m)* (5)
next prochain(e) (4), ensuite (4); **next to** à côté (de) (3); **the next class** le prochain cours (P); **the next day** le lendemain *(m)* (5)
nice sympathique (sympa) (1), gentil(le) (1); **It/That seems nice.** Ça a l'air bien. (3); **The weather's nice.** Il fait beau. (5)
niece nièce *(f)* (4)
night nuit *(f)* (5); **night stand** table *(f)* de chevet
nightclub boîte *(f)* de nuit (1); **to go to a club** aller en boîte (de nuit) (2)
nightgown chemise *(f)* de nuit
nine neuf (P)
nineteen dix-neuf (P)
ninety quatre-vingt-dix (2); **ninety-one** quatre-vingt-onze (2)
ninth neuvième (3)
no non (P); **no longer** ne... plus (8); **no more** ne... plus (8), pas plus (4); **no one** ne... personne; **No problem!** Pas de problème! (3)
nobody ne... personne
noise bruit *(m)* (10)
none ne... aucun(e)
non-smoking section section non-fumeur *(f)*
noon midi *(m)* (P)
nor: neither . . . nor . . . ne... ni... ni...
normal normal(e) *(mpl* normaux)
normally normalement
north nord *(m)*; **North America** Amérique *(f)* du Nord (9)
nose nez *(m)* (10)
not ne... pas (P); **I do not work.** Je ne travaille pas. (P); **not . . . at all** ne... pas du tout (1); **not badly** pas mal (P); **not . . . one** ne... aucun(e); **not . . . so much** pas tellement (1); **not yet** ne... pas encore (5), **Why not?** Pourquoi pas? (2)
notebook cahier *(m)*
nothing ne... rien (5); **nothing at all** rien du tout (6); **nothing but** ne... rien que; **nothing special** ne... rien de spécial (5)
notice remarquer
noun nom *(m)* (3)
nourish nourrir (8); **nourish oneself** se nourrir (8)
nourishment nourriture *(f)*
novel roman *(m)* (9)
November novembre *(m)* (4)
now maintenant (P)
nowadays de nos jours
nowhere ne... nulle part
number nombre *(m)* (P), numéro *(m)* (3), chiffre *(m)*; **telephone number** numéro *(m)* de téléphone (3)
numeral chiffre *(m)* (P)
numerous nombreux(-euse)
nurse infirmier(-ière) *(mf)*
nurture nourrir (8); **nurture oneself** se nourrir (8)

O

obey obéir (à) (8)
object objet *(m)*
observe observer
obtain obtenir (9)

obvious évident(e)
obviously évidemment
ocean océan (m)
Oceania Océanie (f) (9)
o'clock: It's . . . o'clock. Il est... heure(s). (P)
October octobre (m) (4)
of de (1); **Of course!** Bien sûr! (5); Évidemment!; **of it/them** en (8)
off: get off descendre (de) (5)
offer proposer (8), offrir
office bureau (m) (1); **post office** bureau (m) de poste (10); **tourist office** office (m) de tourisme (10)
official time l'heure officielle (f) (6)
often souvent (2)
oil huile (f)
okay d'accord (2); **It's going okay.** Ça va.
old vieux/vieil (vieille) (1), âgé(e) (4); **be . . . years old** avoir... ans (4); **get older** vieillir; **How old is . . . ?** Quel âge a... ? (4); **oldest** aîné(e)
omelet omelette (f) (8)
on sur (1); **get on** monter dans (5); **on foot** à pied (4); **on Mondays** le lundi (P); **on page . . .** à la page... (P); **on sale** en solde (5); **on . . . Street** dans la rue... (10); **on the corner (of)** au coin (de) (10); **on the courtyard side** côté cour (10); **on the ground/floor** par terre (3); **on the weekend** le week-end (P); **on time** à l'heure (4); **On what floor?** À quel étage? (3); **put on** mettre (5); **try on** essayer (5)
once une fois (6); **all at once** tout d'un coup (6); **once more** encore une fois; **Once upon a time there was . . .** Il était une fois... (6)
one un(e) (P); on (4); **no one** ne... personne; **not one** ne... aucun(e); **one another** se, nous, vous (7)
oneself se (7)
one-way ticket aller simple (m) (9)
onion oignon (m) (8); **onion soup** soupe (f) à l'oignon (8)
online en ligne (1)
only uniquement (6); seul(e) (1), seulement (8), ne... que; **only child** fille unique (f), fils unique (e)
Ontario Ontario (m) (9)
open ouvrir; **Open your book.** Ouvrez votre livre. (P)
opening time l'heure (f) d'ouverture (6)
opera opéra (m) (9)
opinion avis (m); **in your opinion** à votre avis (8)
opportunity: have the opportunity to avoir l'occasion de
opposite contraire (m)
optimistic optimiste (1)
or ou (P)
orange orange (f) (8); **orange juice** jus (m) d'orange (2)
orange orange (3)
Orangina Orangina (m) (2)
orchestra orchestre (m) (4)
order (food and drink) commander (2), ranger (7)
order ordre (m); **in order** en ordre (3); **in order to** pour (1)
orderly bien rangé(e) (3)
organic products produits bio (mpl) (8)
organization organisation (f)
organized organisé(e)
origin origine (f); **of . . . origin** d'origine... (7)
Orleans: New Orleans La Nouvelle-Orléans (4)
other autre (1); **each other** se, nous, vous (7); **on the other hand** par contre; **on the other side (of)** de l'autre côté (de); **sometimes . . . other times** quelquefois... d'autres fois (7)

ought to devoir (6)
our notre (nos) (3)
ourselves nous (7); nous-mêmes
out: dine out dîner au restaurant (2); **go out** sortir (2); **Take out a sheet of paper.** Prenez une feuille de papier. (P); **watch out (for)** faire attention (à) (8)
outdoor de plein air (4)
outdoors en plein air
outgoing extraverti(e) (1)
outing sortie (f) (6)
outside à l'extérieur, dehors, en plein air; **outside of** *hors de
oven four (m); **microwave oven** four (m) à micro-ondes
over (par-)dessus, plus de; **over there** là-bas (1); **start over** recommencer; **this/these . . . over here** ce (cet, cette, ces) ...-ci (3); **that/those . . . over there** ce (cet, cette, ces) ...-là (3)
overcast: The sky is overcast. Le ciel est couvert.
overcoat manteau (m) (5), pardessus (m)
owe devoir (6)
own propre
oyster huître (f) (8)

P

pack your bag faire sa valise (f) (9)
package (of) paquet (de) (m) (8), colis (m)
page page (f) (P)
pain douleur (f)
paint peindre
painter peintre (mf)
painting tableau (m) (3), peinture (f) (1)
pajamas pyjama (m)
pal copain (m), copine (f) (6)
palace palais (m) (6)
pale pâle
panties slip (m); **panty hose** collant (m)
pants pantalon (m) (5)
papa papa (m)
paper papier (m); **sheet of paper** feuille (f) de papier (P)
parade défilé (m)
pardon me pardon (P)
parents parents (mpl) (4)
Parisian Parisien(ne) (mf) (9)
park parc (m) (1)
parking lot parking (m) (1)
part partie (f)
participate (in) participer (à)
particular: in particular en particulier
partner partenaire (mf) (7)
part-time à temps partiel
party (social) fête (f) (1), soirée (f) (6), (political) parti (m)
party faire la fête
pass passer (2), (test) réussir à (8); **pass by the house of . . .** passer chez... (2)
passenger passager(-ère) (mf)
passion passion (f) (7)
Passover la pâque juive (f)
passport passeport (m) (9)
past passé (m); **in the past** dans le passé (6), autrefois
past passé(e) (5); **It's a quarter past two.** Il est deux heures et quart. (P)
pasta pâtes (fpl)
pastime loisir (m) (2)
pastry pâtisserie (f) (8); **bakery-pastry shop** boulangerie-pâtisserie (8)
pâté pâté (m) (8)
patience patience (f) (4); **have patience** avoir de la patience (4)
patient patient(e) (mf)

patient patient(e) (6)
pay (for) payer (2); **pay attention (to)** faire attention (à) (8); **pay the bill** régler la note (10)
peace paix (f)
peaceful tranquille
peach pêche (f) (8)
peanut cacahuète (f)
pear poire (f) (8)
peas petits pois (mpl) (8)
pen stylo (m) (P)
pencil crayon (m) (P)
people gens (mpl) (1), on (4); **poor people** les pauvres (mpl); **some people** certains (mpl) (8); **young people** les jeunes (gens) (mpl)
pepper poivre (m) (8)
per par (3)
percent pour cent
perfect perfectionner
perfect parfait(e) (7)
perfectly parfaitement (7)
performer artiste (mf)
perhaps peut-être (3)
period époque (f) (6), période (f)
permit permettre (de); **permitted** permis(e)
person personne (f) (6)
personal personnel(le) (3); **personal belongings** effets personnels (mpl) (3); **personal service** service personnalisé (m) (8)
personality personnalité (f) (1)
personally personnellement
Peru Pérou (m) (9)
pessimistic pessimiste (1)
pharmacist pharmacien(ne) (mf)
pharmacy pharmacie (f) (10)
philosophy philosophie (f) (1)
phone téléphone (m) (2); **on the phone** au téléphone (2)
phone téléphoner (à) (3); **phone each other** se téléphoner (7)
photo photo (f)
physical appearance aspect physique (m) (7)
physics physique (f) (1)
piano piano (m) (2)
picnic pique-nique (m)
picture tableau (m) (3), photo (f)
pie tarte (f) (8); **apple pie** tarte (f) aux pommes (8)
piece (of) morceau (de) (m) (8); **piece of advice** conseil (m) (8)
pierced percé(e)
pineapple ananas (m)
pink rose (3)
pity pitié (f); **have pity (for / on)** avoir pitié (de) (10); **what a pity** c'est dommage (7)
pizza pizza (f) (8)
place endroit (m) (9), place (f) (3); **at/to/in . . . 's place** chez... (2); **in it's place** à sa place (3); **take place** avoir lieu
place mettre
plaid écossais(e)
plan projet (m) (4); **make plans** faire des projets (4)
plan organiser; **plan on doing** avoir l'intention de faire (4), compter faire (9); **planned** prévu(e)
plane avion (m) (4); **by plane** en avion (4)
plant plante (f) (3)
plastic plastique (m); **plastic bag** sac (m) en plastique
plate assiette (f)
play (theater) pièce (f) (de théâtre) (4)
play (a sport) jouer (à un sport) (2), faire (du sport) (2); **play music** faire de la musique (2); **play the piano** jouer du piano (2)

player: CD / DVD / Blu-ray player lecteur *(m)* CD / DVD / Blu-ray (3); **MP3 player** lecteur *(m)* MP3
plaza place *(f)* (10)
pleasant agréable (1)
please plaire à
please s'il vous plaît *(formal)* (P), s'il te plaît *(familiar)*
pleasure plaisir *(m)*; **With pleasure!** Avec plaisir! (6)
plum prune *(f)*
plumber plombier *(m)*
plus: How much is . . . plus . . . ? Combien font... et... ? (P)
P.M. de l'après-midi, du soir (P)
poem poème *(m)* (9)
point out signaler
police police *(f)*
policeman agent *(m)* de police
polite poli(e)
political politique (1); **political science** sciences politiques *(fpl)* (1)
politics politique *(f)* (7)
poll sondage *(m)*
pollution pollution *(f)*
Polynesia: French Polynesia Polynésie française *(f)* (9)
pool: play pool jouer au billard; **swimming pool** piscine *(f)* (4)
poor pauvre
pop music musique populaire *(f)* (1)
popular populaire (1)
population population *(f)*
pork porc *(m)* (8); **pork chop** côte *(f)* de porc (8); **pork roast** rôti *(m)* de porc
portrait: self-portrait autoportrait *(m)* (P)
Portuguese portugais *(m)*
possibility possibilité *(f)* (4)
possible possible (10); **it is possible that** il est possible que (10)
post office bureau *(m)* de poste (10)
postcard carte postale *(f)* (9)
poster poster *(m)* (3)
potato pomme *(f)* de terre (8)
poultry volaille *(f)* (8)
pound (of) livre (de) *(f)* (8)
poverty pauvreté *(f)*
powerful puissant(e)
practical pratique (3)
preach prêcher
precisely justement (3)
prefer préférer (2), aimer mieux (2); **I prefer . . .** Je préfère... (1)
preferable préférable (10); **it's preferable that** il est préférable que (10)
pregnant enceinte (10)
preparations préparatifs *(mpl)* (9)
prepare préparer (2); **Prepare for the exam.** Préparez l'examen. (P); **prepared dish** plat préparé *(m)* (8)
preschool école maternelle *(f)*
prescription ordonnance *(f)* (10)
present cadeau *(m)* (10)
pretty joli(e) (1), beau/bel (belle) (1); **pretty cool** assez cool (P)
prevent empêcher
price prix *(m)*; **set-price menu** menu à prix fixe (8)
principal principal(e) *(mpl* principaux) (10)
private privé(e) (10)
probable probable
probably sans doute (8); probablement
problem problème *(m)*; **No problem!** Pas de problème! (3)

process: be in the process of doing être en train de faire
product produit *(m)* (8); **organic products** produits bio *(mpl)* (8)
profession profession *(f)* (7), métier *(m)*
professional professionnel(le) (7)
professor professeur *(m)* (1)
program programme *(m)*
programmer programmeur(-euse) *(mf)*
progress progrès *(m)*; **make progress** faire des progrès
promise promettre (de) (6)
pronunciation prononciation *(f)*
protect (oneself) (against) (se) protéger (contre)
proud fier(-ère)
province province *(f)* (3)
prune pruneau *(m)*
psychology psychologie *(f)* (1)
public: public transportation transports en commun *(mpl)* (9)
pullover (sweater) pull *(m)* (5)
punish punir
purple violet(te) (3)
purpose: on purpose exprès
purse sac *(m)* (5)
put (on) mettre (5); **put away** bien rangé(e) (3); **put on make-up** se maquiller (7); **put on weight** prendre du poids; **put up with** supporter (7)

Q
qualify qualifier
quarter quart *(m)* (P); **It's a quarter past two.** Il est deux heures et quart. (P)
question question *(f)* (P); **ask a question** poser une question (3)
quick rapide (8)
quickly vite (7)
quiet tranquille; **be quiet** se taire
quite assez, plutôt; **quite a bit of** pas mal de; **quite simply** tout simplement (10)

R
rabbit lapin *(m)*
radio radio *(f)* (2)
rain pluie *(f)* (5)
rain pleuvoir (5); **It's raining., It rains.** Il pleut. (5)
raincoat imperméable *(m)* (5)
raisin raisin sec *(m)*
Ramadan ramadan *(m)*
rapid rapide (8)
rarely rarement (2)
raspberry framboise *(f)*
rather plutôt (1), assez (1)
raw vegetables crudités *(fpl)* (8)
rayfish raie *(f)* (8)
reach atteindre
react (to) réagir (à)
read lire (2); **Read . . .** Lisez... (P)
ready (to) prêt(e) à (4); **get ready** se préparer; **ready-to-serve dish** plat préparé *(m)* (8)
real réel(le), véritable
realistic réaliste (1)
realize se rendre compte
really vraiment (2)
reason raison *(f)*
reasonable raisonnable
receive recevoir (9)
recent récent(e)
recently récemment (5)
recognize (each other) (se) reconnaître (7)
recommend recommander (10)
record disque *(m)*, *(sports)* record *(m)*

record enregistrer
recorder: video cassette recorder magnétoscope *(m)*
recount raconter (7)
recycle recycler
red rouge (3), *(with hair)* roux (rousse) (4); **red wine** vin rouge *(m)* (2); **turn red** rougir
reflect (on) réfléchir (à) (8)
refrigerator réfrigérateur *(m)*
refuse refuser (de)
region région *(f)* (4)
regional régional(e) *(mpl* régionaux) (4)
register s'inscrire (3)
regret regretter (6)
regularly régulièrement (8)
relationship relation *(f)* (7), rapport *(m)*
relatives parents *(mpl)* (5)
relax se reposer (7), se détendre; **relaxed** décontracté(e)
religion religion *(f)* (7)
religious religieux(-euse)
remain rester
remarried remarié(e)
remember se souvenir (de) (7)
rent loyer *(m)* (3)
rent louer (4)
rental car voiture *(f)* de location (5)
repeat répéter (2); **Please repeat.** Répétez, s'il vous plaît. (P)
replace remplacer
require exiger, demander; **required** requis(e), obligatoire
research recherche *(f)*; **do research** faire des recherches
resemble ressembler à
reservation réservation *(f)* (9); **make a reservation** faire une réservation (9)
reserve: nature reserve parc naturel *(m)*
reserve réserver (9)
residence hall résidence universitaire *(f)* (1)
resources ressources *(fpl)*
respond (to) répondre (à) (6)
rest: the rest (of) le reste (de) (7)
rest se reposer (7); **rested** reposé(e)
restaurant restaurant *(m)* (1); **fast food restaurant** fast-food *(m)* (1); **university restaurant** resto-U *(m)* (6)
restful reposant(e)
restroom toilettes *(fpl)* (3), W.-C. *(mpl)* (10)
retired retraité(e)
return retour *(m)* (9)
return rentrer (2), retourner (5); **return something to someone** rendre quelque chose à quelqu'un (7)
review *(for a test)* réviser (2)
rice riz *(m)* (8)
rich riche (2)
ride: go for a ride faire un tour (4)
right *(direction)* droite *(f)*, (3) *(legal)* droit *(m)*; **to the right (of)** à droite (de) (3)
right correct(e); **be right** avoir raison (4); **right away** tout de suite (6); **right by** tout près (de) (3); **right there** juste là; **right?** n'est-ce pas?, non? (1); **That's right!** C'est ça! (1)
ring bague *(f)*
ring sonner (7)
river fleuve *(m)*, rivière *(f)*
road chemin *(m)*, route *(f)*
roast: pork roast rôti *(m)* de porc; **roast beef** rosbif *(m)* (8)
rock: rock music rock *(m)* (1); **go rock climbing** faire de l'escalade; **hard rock** *hard rock *(m)*
rollerblade faire du roller (6)

rollerblading roller *(m)*; **go rollerblading** faire du roller (6)
romantic romantique; **romantic movie** film *(m)* d'amour (6)
room pièce *(f)* (3), salle *(f)*; **classroom** salle *(f)* de cours (1); **dining room** salle à manger *(f)* (3); **double room** chambre double *(f)* (10); **fitting room** cabine *(f)* d'essayage (5); **living room** salon *(m)* (3); **single room** chambre simple *(f)* (10)
roommate camarade *(mf)* de chambre (P)
round-trip ticket billet aller-retour *(m)* (9)
routine routine *(f)* (7)
row rang *(m)*
rug tapis *(m)* (3)
run courir (9); **run errands** faire des courses (5); **run into (each other)** (se) rencontrer (1)
runny: have a runny nose avoir le nez qui coule
Russia Russie *(f)* (9)
Russian russe *(m)*

S

sack sac *(m)* (5), paquet *(m)* (8)
sad triste
safety sécurité *(f)*
sailing: go sailing faire de la voile
salad salade *(f)* (8)
salami saucisson *(m)* (8)
sale: on sale en solde (5)
salesclerk vendeur(-euse) *(mf)* (5)
salmon saumon *(m)* (8)
salt sel *(m)* (8)
same même (1); **all the same** quand même
sandal sandale *(f)* (5)
sandwich sandwich *(m)* (2); **bread-and-butter sandwich** tartine *(f)* (8); **cheese sandwich** sandwich au fromage *(m)* (2)
Santa Claus le père Noël
satisfied satisfait(e)
Saturday samedi *(m)* (P)
sauce sauce *(f)*
sausage saucisse *(f)* (8)
save sauver (9); **save up money** faire des économies
saxophone saxophone *(m)*
say dire (6); **How do you say . . . in French?** Comment dit-on... en français? (P); **They say that . . .** On dit que... (4)
scallops coquilles St-Jacques *(fpl)*
scarf *(winter)* écharpe *(f)*, *(dressy)* foulard *(m)*
scenery paysage *(m)* (9)
schedule *(classes)* emploi *(m)* du temps, *(train)* horaire *(m)*
school école *(f)* (6); **high school** lycée *(m)* (6)
science science *(f)* (1); **computer science** informatique *(f)* (1); **political science** sciences politiques *(fpl)* (1); **science fiction** science-fiction *(f)*; **social sciences** sciences humaines *(fpl)* (1)
scientist scientifique *(mf)*; **computer scientist** informaticien(ne) *(mf)*
scuba diving plongée sous-marine *(f)*
sculpture sculpture *(f)*
sea mer *(f)* (9)
season saison *(f)* (5)
seat place *(f)*, siège *(m)*
seated assis(e) (9)
second *(in time)* seconde *(f)* (5)
second deuxième (3), second(e); **in second class** en classe économique (9)
secretary secrétaire *(mf)*
section section *(f)*
security sécurité *(f)*

see voir (1); **as you see** comme tu vois (3); **Let's see!** Voyons! (5); **see each other** se voir (7); **See you in a little while.** À tout à l'heure. (P); **See you later!** À plus tard!, À plus! (P); **See you soon.** À bientôt. (P); **See you tomorrow.** À demain. (P)
seem avoir l'air... (4), sembler; **It/That seems nice.** Ça a l'air bien. (3); **It seems to me that . . .** Il me semble que...
self: myself moi-même; **self-portrait** autoportrait *(m)* (P); **self-service restaurant** self-service *(m)* (8)
sell vendre (7); **sell back** revendre (7)
semester semestre *(m)* (P)
send envoyer (2)
Senegal Sénégal *(m)* (9)
sense of humor sens *(m)* de l'humour (7)
sensitive sensible
sentence phrase *(f)* (P); **with a complete sentence** avec une phrase complète (P)
sentimental sentimental(e) *(mpl* sentimentaux) (7)
separate séparer; **separated** séparé(e)
separately séparément
September septembre *(m)* (4)
serious sérieux(-euse), grave
serve servir (4); **served** servi(e) (10)
server serveur *(m)*, serveuse *(f)* (2)
service service *(m)* (8); **service station** station-service *(f)*
set mettre; **set-price menu** menu à prix fixe (8); **set the table** mettre la table
settle (in) s'installer (à/dans) (7)
seven sept (P)
seventeen dix-sept (P)
seventh septième (3)
seventy soixante-dix (2); **seventy-one** soixante et onze (2)
several plusieurs (8)
shall: What shall we do? Qu'est-ce qu'on fait?; **Shall we go . . . ?** On va... ? (2)
shame *honte *(f)*; **It's a shame!** C'est dommage! (7)
shape forme *(f)*; **in shape** en forme (8)
share partager (3); **shared** partagé(e) (3)
shave se raser (7); **have a shaved head** avoir la tête rasée
she elle (1); **she is . . .** c'est..., elle est... (1)
sheet of paper feuille *(f)* de papier (P)
shelf étagère *(f)* (3)
shellfish fruits *(mpl)* de mer (8)
shirt chemise *(f)* (5); **knit shirt** polo *(m)* (5)
shiver frisson *(m)* (10)
shock choquer
shoe chaussure *(f)* (5); **tennis shoes** baskets *(fpl)* (5)
shop magasin *(m)* (4); **bakery-pastry shop** boulangerie-pâtisserie *(f)* (8); **butcher's shop** boucherie *(f)* (8); **fish shop** poissonnerie *(f)* (8); **gift shop** boutique *(f)* de cadeaux (10); **tobacco shop** bureau *(m)* de tabac
shopkeeper marchand(e) *(mf)* (6), commerçant(e) *(mf)* (8)
shopping: go grocery shopping faire les courses; **go shopping** faire du shopping (2); **shopping mall** centre commercial *(m)* (4)
short petit(e) (1), court(e) (4)
shorts short *(m)* (5)
shot piqûre *(f)*; **give a shot** faire une piqûre
should devoir (6); **one shouldn't . . .** il ne faut pas... (10)
shoulder épaule *(f)*; **shoulder-length** *(with hair)* mi-longs (4)
show montrer (3), indiquer (3); **show a movie** passer un film (6)

shower douche *(f)* (7); **take a shower** prendre une douche (7)
showing séance *(f)* (6)
showtime séance *(f)* (6)
shrimp crevette *(f)* (8)
shuttle navette *(f)* (10)
shy timide (1)
sick malade (10); **get sick** tomber malade (10)
side côté *(m)*; **on the courtyard side** côté cour (10); **on the other side (of)** de l'autre côté (de)
sight vue *(f)*; **love at first sight** coup *(m)* de foudre (7)
silver argent *(m)* (2)
similar to semblable à, pareil(le) à
simply simplement (10); **quite simply** tout simplement (10)
since depuis, comme (7), depuis que; **since then** depuis cela
sincere sincere
sing chanter (2)
singer chanteur(-euse) *(mf)*
single célibataire (1), seul(e); **single room** chambre simple *(f)* (10)
sink *(bathroom)* lavabo *(m)* (10), *(kitchen)* évier *(m)*
sir monsieur (M.) (P)
sister sœur *(f)* (1); **sister-in-law** belle-sœur *(f)*
sit (down) s'asseoir; **Sit down!** Asseyez-vous!
site site *(m)* (9)
situation situation *(f)*
six six (P)
sixteen seize (P)
sixth sixième (3)
sixty soixante (2); **sixty-one** soixante et un (2)
size taille *(f)* (4); **medium-sized** de taille moyenne (4)
skate *(fish)* raie *(f)* (8); patin *(m)*
skateboard faire du skateboard (6)
skating patinage *(m)*; **go (ice-)skating** faire du patin (à glace)
skeptical sceptique
ski ski *(m)* (2); **ski jacket** anorak *(m)* (5); **ski lodge** chalet *(m)* à la montagne (10)
ski faire du ski (2); **water-ski** faire du ski nautique (5)
skin peau *(f)*
skinny maigre
skirt jupe *(f)* (5)
sleep dormir (2)
sleepy: be sleepy avoir sommeil (4)
slice (of) tranche *(de)* *(f)*, pavé *(de)* *(m)* (8)
slightly légèrement
slim down maigrir (8)
slip combinaison *(f)*
slow lent(e); **slow motion** ralenti *(m)*
slowly lentement
small petit(e) (1)
smart intelligent(e) (1)
smartphone smartphone *(m)* (3)
smell sentir
smoke fumer (3); **smoked** fumé(e) (8)
smoking section section fumeur *(f)*
snack collation *(f)*
snail escargot *(m)* (8)
sneeze éternuer (10)
snob snob
snorkeling: go snorkeling faire de la plongée avec masque et tuba
snow neige *(f)* (5)
snow neiger (5)
so alors (1), tellement (6), donc (7); **not so much** pas tellement (1); **so many, so much** tant (de); tellement (de); **so-so** comme ci comme ça (P); **so that** afin que

soap savon *(m)*
soccer football *(m)* (1)
social social(e) *(mpl* sociaux*)*; **social sciences** sciences humaines *(fpl)* (1); **social worker** assistant(e) social(e) *(mf)*
society société *(f)*
sociology sociologie *(f)*
sock chaussette *(f)*
sofa canapé *(m)* (3)
soft doux(-ce) (6)
software logiciel *(m)*
sole sole *(f)*
solid-colored uni(e)
solution solution *(f)*
some des (1), du, de la, de l', en (8), quelques (5), certain(e)s (8)
somebody quelqu'un (6)
someone quelqu'un (6)
something quelque chose (2)
sometimes quelquefois (2), parfois (5)
somewhere quelque part
son fils *(m)* (4)
song chanson *(f)*
soon bientôt (P); **as soon as** aussitôt que; **I would just as soon . . .** j'aimerais autant… (10); **See you soon.** À bientôt. (P)
sorry désolé(e) (8); **be sorry that . . .** être désolé(e) que… (10), regretter que… (6)
sort: all sorts of toutes sortes de
sound: How does that sound? Ça te/vous dit? (2)
soup soupe *(f)* (8); **onion soup** soupe *(f)* à l'oignon (8)
south sud *(m)*; **South Africa** Afrique *(f)* du Sud; **South America** Amérique *(f)* du Sud (9)
space espace *(m)*
Spain Espagne *(f)* (9)
Spanish espagnol *(m)* (P)
Spanish espagnol(e)
speak parler (2); **Do you speak . . . ?** Vous parlez…? (P); **I speak . . .** Je parle… (P)
special spécial(e) *(mpl* spéciaux*)* (6); **nothing special** rien de spécial (6)
specialty spécialité *(f)* (4)
speech discours *(m)*
speed vitesse *(f)*
spend *(time)* passer (2), *(money)* dépenser
spider araignée *(f)*
spinach épinards *(mpl)*
spirituality spiritualité *(f)* (7)
spite: in spite of malgré
split partagé(e) (3)
spoiled gâté(e) (6)
spoon cuillère *(f)*
sport sport *(m)* (1); **play sports** faire du sport (2); **sports coat** veste *(f)*; **sports field** terrain *(m)* de sport
spot site *(m)* (9)
sprain one's ankle se fouler la cheville
spring printemps *(m)* (5); **in spring** au printemps (5)
square *(town)* place *(f)* (10)
stadium stade *(m)* (1)
stairs escalier *(m)* (3)
stamp timbre *(m)* (10)
stand: I can't stand . . . Je ne supporte pas… (7), J'ai horreur de…
star étoile *(f)*
start commencer (2); **French class starts . . .** Le cours de français commence… (P)
state État *(m)* (3); **United States** États-Unis (3) *(mpl)*
station: radio station station *(f)* de radio; **service station** station-service *(f)*; **subway station** station *(f)* de métro; **train station** gare *(f)*
stay séjour *(m)* (7); **Enjoy your stay!** Bon séjour! (10)
stay rester (2), *(at a hotel)* descendre (à) (5)
steak bifteck *(m)* (8); **steak and fries** steak-frites *(m)* (8)
steal voler
stepbrother demi-frère *(m)*
stepfather beau-père *(m)* (4)
stepmother belle-mère *(f)* (4)
stepparents beaux-parents *(mpl)*
stepsister demi-sœur *(f)* (6)
stereo chaîne hi-fi *(f)* (3)
still encore (4), toujours
stomach ventre *(m)* (10); estomac
stop: bus stop arrêt *(m)* de bus (3)
stop (s')arrêter (7); **stop by the house of . . .** passer chez… (2); **stopped up** bouché(e)
store magasin *(m)* (4); **bookstore** librairie *(f)* (1)
storm orage *(m)*
story histoire *(f)* (9); conte *(m)* (6)
stove cuisinière *(f)*
straight tout droit (10)
straightened up bien rangé(e) (3)
strange bizarre
strawberry fraise *(f)* (8)
street rue *(f)* (3); **on . . . Street** dans la rue… (10)
strength force *(f)*
stress stress *(m)* (8)
stressed (out) stressé(e)
strict sévère
striped rayé(e)
strong fort(e) (8)
struggle (against) lutter (contre)
stubborn têtu(e)
student étudiant(e) *(mf)* (P); **high school student** lycéen(ne) *(mf)* (6); **student center** centre *(m)* d'étudiants
studies études *(fpl)* (1)
study étudier (1), réviser les cours (2); **I study . . .** J'étudie… (1); **What are you studying?** Qu'est-ce que vous étudiez? (1)
stupid bête (1), stupide
style style *(m)*; **American-style** à l'américaine (8)
stylist: hair stylist coiffeur(-euse) *(mf)*
suburbs banlieue *(f)* (3); **in the suburbs** en banlieue (3)
subway métro *(m)* (4); **by subway** en métro (4)
succeed (in) réussir (à) (8)
such a un(e) tel(le) (7)
sudden: all of a sudden tout à coup (6)
suddenly soudain, tout à coup (6), soudainement
suffer souffrir
sufficiently suffisamment
sugar sucre *(m)* (8)
suggest suggérer (6)
suggestion suggestion *(f)*
suit *(for a man)* costume *(m)* (5), *(for a woman)* tailleur *(m)*; **jogging suit** survêtement *(m)* (5)
suitcase valise *(f)* (9)
summer été *(m)* (5); **in summer** en été (5)
sun soleil *(m)*
sunbathe prendre un bain de soleil (4)
Sunday dimanche *(m)* (P)
sunglasses lunettes *(f)* de soleil (5)
sunny: It's sunny. Il fait (du) soleil. (5)
superior supérieur(e)
supermarket supermarché *(m)* (8)
superstore grande surface *(f)* (8)
supplement supplément *(m)* (10)
supplies provisions *(fpl)*
sure sûr(e), certain(e)
surely sûrement
surf *(Internet)* surfer (2), *(water)* faire du surf; **surf the Net** surfer sur Internet (2)
surprise étonner, surprendre; **be surprised that . . .** être surpris(e) que… (10)
surrounded (by) entouré(e) (de)
swallow avaler
sweater: pullover sweater pull *(m)* (5)
sweatshirt sweat *(m)*
sweatsuit survêtement *(m)* (5)
Sweden Suède *(f)*
sweet doux(-ce) (6)
sweets bonbons *(mpl)*
swim nager (2), se baigner
swimming pool piscine *(f)* (4)
swimsuit maillot *(m)* de bain (5)
Switzerland Suisse *(f)* (9)
swollen enflé(e)
symptom symptôme *(m)* (10)
synagogue synagogue *(f)*
syrup sirop *(m)*
system système *(m)*; **public transporation system** réseau *(m)* de transports en commun (9)

T

table table *(f)* (3)
take prendre (4); **take (along)** *(a thing)* emporter (5); *(a person)* emmener; **take a course** suivre un cours; **take advantage of** profiter de (9); **take a tour** faire un tour (4); **take a trip** faire un voyage (5); **take a walk** faire une promenade (5); **Take out a sheet of paper.** Prenez une feuille de papier. (P); **take place** avoir lieu
tale: fairy tale conte *(m)* de fées (6)
talent talent *(m)*
talented doué(e)
talk parler (2); **talk to each other** se parler (7)
tall grand(e) (1)
tan bronzer (9); **tanned** bronzé(e)
tangerine mandarine *(f)*
tart tartelette *(f)* (8); **strawberry/cherry tart** tartelette aux fraises/aux cerises (8)
taste goûter (9)
taxi taxi *(m)* (4); **by taxi** en taxi (4)
tea (with lemon) thé *(m)* (au citron) (2)
teacher *(elementary school)* instituteur(-trice) *(mf)*; *(secondary school)* professeur *(m)*
team équipe *(f)*
technical technique; **technical courses** technologies *(fpl)* (1)
technician technicien(ne) *(mf)*
technology technologie *(f)* (1)
tee-shirt tee-shirt *(m)* (5)
telephone téléphone *(m)* (2); **talk on the telephone** parler au téléphone (2); **telephone card** carte *(f)* téléphonique (10); **telephone number** numéro *(m)* de téléphone (3)
telephone téléphoner (à) (2); **telephone each other** se téléphoner (7)
television télévision (télé) *(f)* (2)
tell dire (6), raconter
teller: automatic teller machine distributeur de billets *(m)* (10)
temperature température *(f)*
temple temple *(m)*

ten dix (P)
tennis tennis *(m)* (1); **tennis court** court *(m)* de tennis; **tennis shoes** baskets *(fpl)* (5)
tenth dixième (3)
terrace terrasse *(f)* (9)
test examen *(m)* (P), test *(m)* (7), contrôle *(m)*
Texas Texas *(m)* (9)
than: more . . . than plus... que (1)
thank (for) remercier (de) (10); **thank you** merci (bien) (P)
thanks merci (bien) (P)
Thanksgiving jour *(m)* d'Action de Grâce
that ça (P), ce (cet, cette) (…-là) (3), que (1), qui (7), cela (1); **I think that . . .** je pense que... (P); **that is …** c'est... (1); **that/those . . . over there** ce (cet, cette, ces)… là (3)
the le, la, l', les (1)
theater théâtre *(for live performances) (m)* (1); **movie theater** cinéma *(m)* (1)
theft vol *(m)*
their leur(s) (1)
them les (5); **of them** en (8); **to them** leur (9); **with them** avec eux *(m)*, avec elles *(f)* (2)
themselves se (7), eux-mêmes *(mpl)*, elles-mêmes *(fpl)*
then alors (1), ensuite (4), puis, donc (7)
there là (1), y (4); **over there** là-bas (1); **right there** juste là; **that/those . . . over there** ce (cet, cette, ces)… là (3); **there is, there are** il y a (1), voilà (2); **There are . . . of us.** Nous sommes…. (4); **There you are!** Te/Vous voilà!
therefore donc (7)
these ces (…-ci) (3); **these are . . .** ce sont... (1)
they ils, elles, ce (1), on (4)
thick gros(se)
thief voleur *(m)*
thin mince (1); **get thinner** maigrir (8)
thing chose *(f)* (3), truc *(m)* (1); **my things** mes affaires *(fpl)*; **That's not my thing.** Ce n'est pas mon truc. (1)
think (about) penser (à) (2), réfléchir (à) (8); **I think that . . .** Je pense que... (P); **What do you think (about it)?** Qu'en penses-tu?, Qu'en pensez-vous? (5)
third troisième (3); **two-thirds** deux tiers
thirsty: be thirsty avoir soif (4); **I'm thirsty.** J'ai soif. (2)
thirteen treize (P)
thirty trente (P)
this ce (cet, cette) (3); **this . . . over here** ce (cet, cette)… ci; **this evening** ce soir (2); **this is . . .** c'est... (1); **this month** ce mois-ci (4); **this semester** ce semestre (P); **this way** par ici (5)
those ces (…-là) (3); **those are . . .** ce sont... (1); **those (ones)** ceux (celles) (8)
thousand: one thousand mille (3)
three trois (P)
throat gorge *(f)* (10); **have a sore throat** avoir mal à la gorge
through par; **through the window** par la fenêtre
throw jeter; **throw up** vomir (10)
Thursday jeudi *(m)* (P)
thus donc (7)
ticket billet *(m)* (9), ticket *(m)*; **e-ticket** billet électronique; **one-way ticket** aller simple (9); **plane ticket** billet *(m)* d'avion (9); **round-trip ticket** billet aller-retour (9); **ticket window** guichet *(m)*
tie cravate *(f)* (5)
tight étroit(e)
till: a quarter till moins le quart (P)

time *(clock)* heure *(f)* (P), temps *(m)* (2), *(occasion)* fois *(f)* (5); **a long time** longtemps (5); **at that time** à ce moment-là; **At what time?** À quelle heure? (P); **free time** temps libre *(m)* (2); **from time to time** de temps en temps (4); **have a hard time** avoir du mal à (4); **local time** heure locale *(f)* (9); **most of the time** la plupart du temps (7); **official time** heure officielle *(f)* (6); **Once upon a time there was . . .** Il était une fois… (6); **One has a good time.** On s'amuse bien.; **on time** à l'heure (4); **opening time** heure *(f)* d'ouverture (6); **show time** séance *(f)* (6); **sometimes . . . other times** parfois… d'autres fois (7); **the last time** la dernière fois (5); **time period** époque *(f)* (6); **What time is it?** Quelle heure est-il? (P)
timid timide (1)
tip pourboire *(m)*
tired fatigué(e) (6)
tiring fatiguant(e)
title titre *(m)*
to à (P); **from Monday to Friday** *(every week)* du lundi au vendredi (P); **to go to a club** aller en boîte (de nuit) (2); **to . . . 's house/place** chez… (2)
toast pain grillé *(m)* (8)
toasted grillé(e) (8)
tobacco tabac *(m)* (8); **tobacco shop** bureau *(m)* de tabac
today aujourd'hui (P)
toe doigt *(m)* de pied (10)
together ensemble (2)
toilet toilettes *(fpl)* (3), W.-C. *(mpl)* (10)
tolerance tolérance *(f)* (7)
tolerate supporter (7)
tomato tomate *(f)* (8)
tomorrow demain (P); **day after tomorrow** après-demain (4); **tomorrow morning** demain matin (4)
tonight ce soir (2); **See you tonight.** À ce soir. (2)
too aussi (P), trop (3); **That's too bad!** C'est dommage! (7); **too many** trop (de) (8); **too much** trop (de) (6)
tooth dent *(f)* (7)
tour tour *(m)*; **take a tour** faire un tour (4)
tourism tourisme *(m)*
tourist touriste *(mf)*; **tourist office** office *(m)* de tourisme (10)
touristic touristique (9)
toward(s) vers (2)
towel serviette *(f)*
town ville *(f)* (3); **in town** en ville (3)
toy jouet *(m)*
traditional traditionnel(le) (8)
traffic circulation *(f)*
train train *(m)* (4); **by train** en train (4); **train station** gare *(f)*
training: do weight training faire de la muscu(lation) (8); faire des haltères
trait trait *(m)* (7)
translate traduire
translation traduction *(f)*
transportation transport *(m)*; **means of transportation** moyen *(m)* de transport (4); **public transportation** transports *(mpl)* en commun (9)
travel: travel agency agence *(f)* de voyages (9); **travel agent** agent *(m)* de voyages (9)
travel voyager (2)
traveler's check chèque *(m)* de voyage
treatment traitement *(m)*

tree arbre *(m)* (1)
trimester trimestre *(m)*
trip voyage *(m)* (4); **take a trip** faire un voyage (5)
tropical tropical(e) *(mpl* tropicaux) (9)
trouble difficulté *(f)*; **have trouble** avoir des difficultés, avoir du mal (à)
truck camion *(m)*, *(pick-up)* camionnette *(f)*
true vrai(e) (8); **true love** le grand amour (7)
truly vraiment (2)
trumpet trompette *(f)*
truth vérité *(f)*
try (on) essayer (5)
T-shirt tee-shirt *(m)* (5)
Tuesday mardi *(m)* (P)
tuna thon *(m)* (8)
Tunisia Tunisie *(f)*
Turkey Turquie *(f)*
turkey dinde *(f)*
turn (right/left) tourner (à droite/à gauche) (10); **turn in (something to someone)** rendre (quelque chose à quelqu'un) (7); **turn on** mettre; **turn red** rougir
turnover: apple turnover chausson *(m)* aux pommes
TV télé *(f)* (2)
twelve douze (P)
twenty vingt (P)
twin jumeau (jumelle) (1)
two deux (P)
type genre *(m)*
typical typique (2)
typically typiquement

U

ugly laid(e) (1)
umbrella parapluie *(m)* (5)
unbearable insupportable
unbelievable incroyable
uncle oncle *(m)* (4)
under sous (3)
understand comprendre (4); **Do you understand?** Vous comprenez? (P); **I understand.** Je comprends. (P); **No, I don't understand.** Non, je ne comprends pas. (P)
understanding compréhension *(f)*
underwear sous-vêtements *(mpl)*
undressed: get undressed se déshabiller (7)
unfaithfulness infidélité *(f)* (7)
unfortunately malheureusement
unhappy malheureux(-euse)
uniquely uniquement (6)
united uni(e); **United Kingdom** Royaume-Uni *(m)* (9); **United States** États-Unis *(mpl)* (3)
university université *(f)* (P), fac(ulté) *(f)* (2); **university cafeteria** resto-U *(m)* (6)
university universitaire (1)
unless à moins que
unlikely peu probable
unmarried célibataire (1)
unpack défaire sa valise
unpleasant désagréable, antipathique (1)
until jusqu'à (2)
up: get up se lever (7); **go up** monter (5); **straightened up** rangé(e) (3); **up to** jusqu'à (2); **wake up** se réveiller (7); **wash up** faire sa toilette (7)
us nous (9); **with us** avec nous (2)
use utiliser (6), employer
used to habitué(e) à
useful utile (10)
usually d'habitude (2)
utilize utiliser (5)

V

vacation vacances *(fpl)* (4); **on vacation** en vacances (6)
Valentine's Day Saint-Valentin *(f)*
vanilla ice cream glace *(f)* à la vanille (8)
vanity vanité *(f)* (7)
variety variété *(f)*
VCR magnétoscope *(m)*
veal veau *(m)*
vegetable légume *(m)* (8); **raw vegetables** crudités *(fpl)* (8); **vegetable soup** soupe *(f)* de légumes
vegetarian végétarien(ne)
verify vérifier (10)
very très (P); **very near** tout près (de) (3)
vest gilet *(m)*
veterinarian vétérinaire *(mf)*
video vidéo *(f)*; **video cassette** vidéocassette *(f)*; **video cassette recorder** magnétoscope *(m)*; **video game** jeu vidéo *(m)* (2)
Vietnam Viêt Nam *(m)* (9)
view vue *(f)* (3)
vinegar vinaigre *(m)*
violence violence *(f)* (6)
violent violent(e)
violet violet(te) (3)
violin violon *(m)*
virus virus *(m)* (10)
visa visa *(m)*
visit visite *(f)*; **medical visit** consultation *(f)*
visit *(place)* visiter (1), *(someone)* aller voir (4), rendre visite à
vitamin vitamine *(f)* (8)
vocabulary vocabulaire *(m)* (P)
voice voix *(f)*
volleyball volley *(m)* (2)
vomit vomir (10)
vote voter

W

wait (for) attendre (7)
waiter serveur *(m)* (2)
waitress serveuse *(f)* (2)
wake up (se) réveiller (7)
walk promenade *(f)* (5); **take a walk** faire une promenade (5)
walk aller à pied (4), marcher (8); **walk the dog** promener le chien
walking marche *(f)* à pied (5); **go walking** se promener (7), faire de la marche à pied
wall mur *(m)* (3)
wallet portefeuille *(m)* (5)
want vouloir (6), avoir envie de (4)
war guerre *(f)*
warmth chaleur *(f)*
wash (one's face/one's hands) se laver (la figure/les mains) (7); **wash clothes** faire la lessive (5); **wash the dishes** faire la vaisselle (5); **wash up** faire sa toilette (7)
washbasin lavabo *(m)* (10)
waste gaspiller; **waste time** perdre du temps (7)
watch montre *(f)* (5)
watch regarder (2); **watch out (for)** faire attention (à) (8)
water eau *(f)* (2)
watermelon pastèque *(f)*
water-skiing ski nautique *(m)* (5)
way façon *(f)* (6); **show the way** indiquer le chemin (10); **this way** par ici (5)
we nous (1), on (4); **Shall we go . . . ?** On va... ? (2); **What shall we do?** Qu'est-ce qu'on fait?

weak faible
weakness faiblesse *(f)*
wear porter (4); **I wear size . . .** Je fais du.... (5); **What size do you wear?** Quelle taille faites-vous? (5)
weather temps *(m)* (5); **The weather's bad / cold / cool / hot / nice / sunny / windy.** Il fait mauvais / froid / frais / chaud / beau / (du) soleil / du vent. (5); **What's the weather like?** Quel temps fait-il? (5)
Website site *(m)* Web
wedding mariage *(m)*; **wedding anniversary** anniversaire *(m)* de mariage
Wednesday mercredi *(m)* (P)
week semaine *(f)* (P); **in one/two week(s)** dans huit/quinze jours
weekend week-end *(m)* (P); **Have a good weekend!** Bon week-end!; **on weekends** le weekend (P)
weigh peser
weight poids *(m)*; **do weight training** faire de la musculation (8), faire des haltères; **gain weight** prendre du poids; **lose weight** perdre du poids; **put on weight** prendre du poids
welcome bienvenue *(f)*, **You're welcome.** De rien. (P); Je vous en prie., Je t'en prie. (2)
well bien (P); **get well** guérir; **well-behaved** sage (4)
west ouest *(m)*; **West Indies** Antilles *(fpl)* (9)
what qu'est-ce que (1), que (2), comment (P), quel(le) (3), ce que (7), ce qui (7), quoi; **What a mess!** Quel bazar! *(familiar)* (3); **What day is today?** C'est quel jour, aujourd'hui? (P); **What does that mean in English?** Qu'est-ce que ça veut dire en anglais? (P); **What is/are . . . like?** Comment est/sont... ? (1); **What is his/her name?** Comment s'appelle-t-il/elle? (4); **What is your name?** Tu t'appelles comment? *(familiar)* (P); Comment vous appelez-vous? *(formal)* (P); **What luck!** Quelle chance! (5); **What's the weather like?** Quel temps fait-il? (5); **What time is it?** Quelle heure est-il? (P)
when quand (2)
where où (1); **from where** d'où (1)
whereas tandis que
which quel(le) (3); que, qui (7); **about/of which** dont (7); **which one** lequel (laquelle) (6)
while tandis que, pendant que; **See you in a little while.** À tout à l'heure. (P); **while on** au cours de (10)
white blanc(he) (3); **white wine** vin blanc *(m)* (2)
who qui (2)
whole tout (toute) (2); **(loaf of) whole-grain bread** pain complet *(m)* (8); **the whole day** toute la journée (2)
whom qui (2), que (7)
whose dont (7)
why pourquoi (2)
widespread répandu(e)
widow veuve *(f)* (7)
widower veuf *(m)* (7)
wife femme *(f)* (2)
Wi-Fi Wi-Fi *(m)* (1); **Wi-Fi access** accès *(m)* Wi-Fi (10)
win gagner
wind vent *(m)*
windbreaker blouson *(m)*

window fenêtre *(f)* (3); **ticket window** guichet *(m)*
windsurfing: go windsurfing faire de la planche à voile
windy: It's windy. Il fait du vent., Il y a du vent. (5)
wine vin *(m)* (2)
winter hiver *(m)* (5); **in winter** en hiver (5)
wish souhaiter (10)
with avec (P); chez (+ *person*) (7); **coffee with milk** café au lait *(m)* (2)
withdraw money retirer de l'argent (10)
without sans (P); **without doing it** sans le faire
woman femme *(f)* (1); **woman's suit** tailleur *(m)*
wonder se demander
wonderful merveilleux(-euse)
word mot *(m)* (P); **words** *(lyrics)* paroles *(fpl)*
work travail *(m)*
work travailler (2); **Does that work for you?** Ça te/vous convient? (9); **I work . . .** Je travaille... (P)
workbook cahier *(m)* (P)
worker *(manual)* ouvrier(-ère) *(mf)*
world monde *(m)*
world-(wide) mondial(e) *(mpl* mondiaux)
worry (about) (se) préoccuper (de)
worse pire
would: I would like to . . . Je voudrais (bien)... (2); **What would you like to do?** Qu'est-ce que vous voudriez faire... ? (2)
write écrire (2); **How is that written?** Ça s'écrit comment? (P); **Write the answer.** Écrivez la réponse. (P)
writer écrivain *(m)*
wrong: be wrong avoir tort (4); **What's wrong?** Qu'est-ce qui ne va pas? (10)

Y

yard jardin *(m)*
year année *(f)* (4), an *(m)* (4); **be . . . years old** avoir... ans (4); **Happy New Year!** Bonne année!; **New Year's Eve** le réveillon *(m)* du jour de l'An
yellow jaune (3)
yes oui (P), si (*in response to a question or a statement in the negative*) (8)
yesterday hier (5)
yet pourtant (8), déjà (5); **not yet** (ne...) pas encore (5)
yogurt yaourt *(m)* (8)
you tu, vous (P), te (9); **And you?** Et toi?, Et vous? (P); **See you tomorrow!** À demain! (P); **Thank you!** Merci! (P); **There you are!** Te / Vous voilà!; **with you** avec toi, avec vous (7)
young jeune (1)
your ton (ta, tes) (3); votre (vos) (3); **Open your book.** Ouvrez votre livre. (P); **What is your name?** Tu t'appelles comment? *(familiar)* (P), Comment vous appelez-vous? *(formal)* (P); **your friends** tes amis (1)
yourself te, vous (7); toi-même, vous-même(s)
youth jeunesse *(f)* (7); **youth hostel** auberge *(f)* de jeunesse (10)

Z

zero zéro (P), nul(le)
zip code code postal *(m)* (3)
zucchini courgette *(f)*
zydeco music musique *(f)* zydeco (4)

INDEX

A

à,
 contractions with, 152
 with geographical names, 370
 with indirect objects, 360
Accent marks, 22
 spelling-change verbs with, 80, 265, 330, 352
Adjectives,
 agreement, 34–35, 40, 48
 of color, 120
 common irregular, 34–35, 40, 48
 comparative forms of, 38
 demonstrative, 128
 interrogative, 128
 placement, 48
 plural, 34–35, 40
 possessive, 122, 124
Adverbs,
 placement, 76, 184
 time expressions, 158, 192
Agreement,
 adjectives, 34–35, 40, 48
 past participle, 184, 190, 202, 360
 possessive adjectives, 122, 124
aller,
 conditional, 330
 future, 352
 imperative, 154, 408
 passé composé, 190
 present, 152
 subjunctive, 396
 used with infinitives to express the future, 158
Alphabet, 22
appeler, verbs like, 265, 330, 352
Articles,
 definite, 52, 118, 122, 152, 320, 370
 indefinite, 46, 116, 320
 omission, 48
 partitive, 310, 320
avoir,
 conditional, 330
 expressions with, 88, 146
 future, 352
 imperative, 154, 408
 passé composé, 184
 passé composé with, 184
 present, 116
 subjunctive, 396

B

beau, 32, 34, 40, 48
bien, 6, 74, 76, 112, 184
boire,
 imperfect, 324
 passé composé, 184, 324
 present, 324
 subjunctive, 395

C

Cardinal numbers, 10, 90, 110
ce,
 -ci, -là 128
 demonstrative adjective, 128
 vs. il/elle, 34, 48
Cinema, 68, 248–251
Classroom, useful expressions, 20–22
Clothing, vocabulary for, 200–201
Cognates, 36
Colors, vocabulary for, 120
Commands, 154, 408
commencer, verbs like, 80, 232
Comparison of adjectives, 38
Conditional, 330–331
connaître,
 conditional, 364
 future, 364
 imperfect, 364
 passé composé, 364
 present, 364
 subjunctive, 394
 vs. savoir, 364
Consonants, final,
 pronunciation of, 6
Contractions, 118, 122, 152
Countries,
 names of, 368
 prepositions with, 370
Culture
 Africa, 422–425
 America, 106–107, 142–143
 Antilles, 348–349, 376–377, 384–385
 Belgium, 218
 cafés, 88, 96–97
 Canada, 106–107, 134–135
 cinema, 68, 248–251
 clothing sizes, 201
 Côte d'Azur, 64, 66–67
 Côte d'Ivoire, 423
 counting, 10, 90, 110
 Creole culture,
  Louisiana, 142–143
  Antilles, 376–377
 daily life, 16, 262
 départements d'outre-mer, 348–349, 350, 356, 382, 384–385
 eating habits, 96–97, 236, 304–306, 314, 322, 338–339
 education, 20, 32, 38, 44–45, 50, 58–59, 126
 Europe, 216–219
 family, 270, 284
 France, 30–31, 66–67, 180–181, 219, 222–223, 260–261, 302–303, 348–349, 384–385
 francophone music, 412, 414–415
 francophone world, overview, 4–5
 French regions and provinces, 30–31, 219, 222–223, 302–303, 348–349, 384–385
 French West Indies, 348–349, 376–377, 384–385
 friendship, 230
 greetings, 6, 8
 Guadeloupe, 348–349, 350, 356, 376–377, 384–385
 health, 328, 392
 holidays, 160
 hotels, 386
 invitations, 120, 224
 lifestyles, 270
 Louisiana, 142–143, 150, 162, 170–171
 Luxembourg, 216
 Martinique, 348–349, 350, 356, 376–377, 384–385
 metric system, 316
 Monaco, 218
 money, 89, 90
 Montreal, 107, 126
 Morocco, 425
 Nice, 66–67
 Normandy, 302–303
 Paris, 208, 222–223
 pastimes, 68, 74, 182, 210–211
 Quebec, 106–107, 109, 126, 129, 134–135
 relationships, 270, 284, 294–295
 restaurants, 306, 338–339
 Réunion, La, 424
 shopping, 201, 314
 sizes, 201
 Switzerland, 217
 temperatures in centigrade, 194
 twenty-four hour clock, 24–25
 universities in France, 20, 32, 44, 58–59
 vacation, 350, 362

D

Dates, 160–161, 173
Days of the week, 12
de,
 contractions with, 118, 122
 with quantity expressions, 46, 116, 310, 318, 320
 used after a negative, 46, 116, 310, 320
 used to denote possession, 122
Definite articles, 52, 118, 122, 152, 320, 370
Demonstrative adjectives, 128
devoir,
 conditional, 330
 future, 352
 passé composé, 226
 present, 226
 subjunctive, 395
dire,
 conditional, 358
 future, 358
 imperfect, 358
 passé composé, 358
 present, 358
 subjunctive, 394
Direct object pronouns, 202, 360, 366, 408
Directions, 406
dont, 286
dormir,
 passé composé, 184, 234
 present, 234
 subjunctive, 394
 verbs like, 234, 264

E

écrire,
 conditional, 358
 future, 358
 imperfect, 358
 passé composé, 184, 358
 present, 358
 subjunctive, 394
Education, 20, 32, 38, 44–45, 50, 58–59, 126
Elision, 14, 40, 42, 76, 305
Emotion, expressions of, 400, 404
en,
 as a pronoun, 324, 408
 with dates, 160
 with geographical names, 370
 with seasons, 194
ennuyer, verbs like, 265
-er verbs,
 conditional, 330
 future, 352
 imperative, 154, 408
 imperfect, 232
 passé composé, 184, 190
 present, 76
 subjunctive, 394
est-ce que, 42
être,
 after quel, 128
 conditional, 330
 future, 352
 imperative, 154, 408
 imperfect, 232
 passé composé, 184
 passé composé with, 184, 190
 present, 40
 subjunctive, 396

F

faire,
  conditional, 330
  expressions with, 198
  future, 352
  imperfect, 232
  passé composé, 184
  present, 196
  subjunctive, 396
Fairy tales, vocabulary for, 242
Family members, vocabulary for, 144–145
Food, vocabulary for, 88, 304–305, 314–316, 322–323
Francophone world, 4–5
Future,
  formation and use, 352
  expressed using **aller,** 158

G

Gender of nouns, 46
Geographical names,
  prepositions with, 370
  vocabulary for, 368, 370
Greetings, vocabulary for, 6, 8

H

h, aspirate vs. silent, 305
Holidays, 160
Household chores, vocabulary for, 198–199
Housing, vocabulary for, 108–109

I

il/elle, vs. **ce,** 34–35, 48
il faut, 330, 352, 366, 388, 394, 404
il y a,
  meaning *ago,* 192
  meaning *there is / there are,* 46, 158
Immediate future, 158
imparfait,
  formation of, 232
  vs. the **passé composé,** 238, 240, 244, 282
Imperative,
  formation, 154, 408
  with object pronouns, 408
Impersonal expressions, 388, 394
Indefinite article, 46, 116, 320
  omission of, 48
Indirect object pronouns, 360, 366, 408
  after the imperative, 408
Infinitive, 70
  after **savoir,** 364
  vs. the subjunctive, 404
Information questions, 84, 86, 128
Interlude musical, 102–103, 176–177, 256–257, 344–345, 420–421
Interrogative adjective, 128
Interrogative words, 84
Intonation, 42
Introductions, vocabulary for, 6, 8
Inversion, 86
Invitations, 69, 224
-ir verbs,
  conditional, 330
  future, 352
  imperfect, 326
  passé composé, 326
  present, 326
  subjunctive, 394

J

jouer,
  followed by **à** + *sport,* 70
  followed by **de** + *musical instrument,* 70

L

-là, 128
Learning strategies,
  Anticipating a response, 390
  Asking for clarification, 148
  Brainstorming, 133
  Finding the right word, 337
  Guessing meaning from context, 112
  How to learn a language, xvii
  Listening for specific information, 72
  Making intelligent guesses, 94
  Making suggestions, 413
  Noting the important information, 228
  Organizing a paragraph, 293
  Planning and predicting, 312
  Previewing content, 132
  Reading a poem, 336
  Reading for the gist, 36
  Recognizing compound tenses, 354
  Recognizing conversational style, 290
  Revising what you write, 375
  Scanning and previewing a text, 56
  Understanding words with multiple meanings, 374
  Using and combining what you know, 57
  Using cognates and familiar words to read for the gist, 36
  Using logical order and standard phrases, 95
  Using standard formats, 248–249
  Using standard organizing techniques, 209
  Using the sequence of events to make logical guesses, 186
  Using visuals to make guesses, 208
  Using word families and watching out for **faux amis,** 268
  Using word families, 412
  Using your knowledge of the world, 168
  Visualizing your topic, 169
Leisure activities, vocabulary for, 68–69, 74–75, 150, 156, 182, 198
Liaison, 6, 18, 46, 52, 77, 86, 116, 305
lire,
  passé composé, 184, 358
  present, conditional, future, imperfect, 358
  subjunctive, 394

M

manger, verbs like, 80, 232
Meals, vocabulary for, 304–306, 322–323
mettre, 200
  passé composé, 200
Money, 89, 90
Months, vocabulary for, 160
Mood, 394
mourir,
  conditional, 330
  future, 352
  passé composé, 190
Movies, vocabulary for, 225

N

Nasal vowels, 10
Necessity, expressions of, 388, 394
Negation, 40
  ne... jamais, 76
  ne... ni... ni..., 71
  ne... pas, 40
  ne... pas encore, 192
  ne... rien, 196
  with **futur immédiat,** 158
  with imperative, 408
  with indefinite article, 46, 116, 320
  with infinitives, 196
  with pronouns, 152, 202, 264, 324, 360, 408
  with partitive, 310, 320
  with **passé composé,** 184

n'est-ce pas, 42
Nouns,
  gender, 46
  plural, 46, 116
nouveau, 40, 48
Numbers,
  zero to thirty, 10
  thirty to one hundred, 90
  above one hundred, 110
  ordinal, 110

O

Object pronouns,
  with commands, 408
  direct, 202, 360, 366, 408
  indirect, 360, 366, 408
on, 154
Ordinal numbers, 110

P

Participle, past, 184, 190
  agreement of, 190, 202, 280
partir,
  passé composé, 234
  present, 234
  subjunctive, 394
Partitive article, 310, 320
Passé composé,
  formation with **avoir,** 184
  formation with **être,** 190
  of pronominal verbs, 280
  time expressions used with, 192
  vs. the **imparfait,** 238, 240, 244, 282
Past participle, 184, 190
  agreement of, 190, 202, 280
Plural,
  of adjectives, 34, 40
  of nouns, 46, 116
Possessions, vocabulary for, 114, 120
Possessive adjectives, 122, 124
pouvoir,
  conditional, 330
  future, 352
  passé composé, 226
  present, 226
  subjunctive, 396
préférer, verbs like, 80, 330, 352
prendre,
  imperfect, 232
  passé composé, 184
  present, 164
  subjunctive, 395
  verbs like, 164, 184
Prepositions, 114, 118, 152
  contractions with, 118, 122, 152
  pronouns after, 82
  with geographical names, 370
Present subjunctive, formation, use, 394–395, 396, 400, 404
Pronominal verbs,
  immediate future, 272
  imperative, 408
  imperfect, 282
  infinitive, 264, 272
  passé composé, 280
  present, 264–265, 272
  reciprocal, 272
  reflexive, 264–265
Pronouns,
  after prepositions, 82
  direct object, 202, 360, 366, 408
  en, 324, 408
  indirect object, 360, 366, 408
  on, 154
  reflexive, 264–265
  relative, 286
  subject, 40
  y, 152, 408

Pronunciation
  a, au, ai, 152
  adjectives, 35
  avoir, 116, 190
  c vs. **ç,** 80
  conditional, 331
  consonants, final, 6
  de, du, des, 118
  definite articles, 52
  dormir, verbs like, 234
  e, in forms of **ce,** 128
  e, unaccented, 52, 128
  é vs. **è,** 80
  -er verbs, 77
  être, 116, 190
  final consonants, 6
  g, 80
  h, 6, 305
  il vs. **elle,** 35
  imperfect, 232, 238
  indefinite article, 46
  infinitive endings, 70
  inversion, 86
  -ir verbs, 326
  liaison, 6, 18, 46, 52, 77, 86, 116, 305
  nasal vowels, 10
  numbers, 10, 90
  o, 124
  partir, verbs like, 234
  passé composé, 190, 238
  prendre, 164
  qu, 84
  r, 70, 331
  s, 326
  sortir, verbs like, 234
  spelling change verbs, 80
  time, 16
  venir, 164
  vowels, 8, 10, 21

Q
Quantity, expressions of, 46, 116, 310, 318, 320
que,
  in questions, 84, 86, 128
  as a relative pronoun, 286
quel, 128
qu'est-ce que, 84, 128
Questions,
  information, 84, 86, 128
  using **est-ce que,** 42, 84
  using intonation, 42
  using inversion, 86
  using **n'est-ce pas,** 42
  words used in, 84
  yes/no, 42
qui,
  as an interrogative pronoun, 84
  as a relative pronoun, 286

R
Reading selections,
  Ànous2, 428
  Aux trois obus, 94–95
  Avis de l'hôtel, 412–413
  Bébel-Gisler, Dany: *Ma grand-mère m'a appris à ne pas compter sur les yeux des autres pour dormir,* 374–375
  Deux films français, 248–249
  Gentil, Jean: *Deux mots,* 168–169
  Gomez, Lucille: *Le destin d'une lycéenne,* 439
  Ionesco, Eugène: *Conte pour enfants de moins de trois ans,* 290–292
  Je blogue donc je suis, 208–209
  Le beurre de cacahuète, c'est pour les sportifs!, 440
  Lucile Gomez auteur de BD et de blog, 436
  Macrae, Kate: *Les couleurs et leurs effets sur la nature humaine,* 132

Prévert, Jacques: *L'accent grave,* 56–57; *Déjeuner du matin,* 336–337
Tours Guadeloupe Nature, 444
Vivre vert, 432
-re verbs,
  conditional, 330
  future, 352
  passé composé, 276
  present, 276
  subjunctive, 394
Reciprocal verbs, *See* pronominal verbs.
Reflexive verbs, *See* pronominal verbs.
Relationships, vocabulary about, 270, 284
Relative pronouns, 286
Restaurants, vocabulary for, 304–306, 308–309

S
savoir,
  conditional, 364
  future, 364
  imperfect, 364
  passé composé, 364
  present, 364
  subjunctive, 396
  vs. **connaître,** 364
School, vocabulary related to, 20, 22, 44, 50
Seasons, vocabulary for, 194
Sélection musicale, 40, 48, 52, 76, 88, 108, 121, 128, 146, 154, 158, 164, 183, 191, 194, 200, 226, 233, 240, 244, 262, 270, 272, 276, 280, 284, 286, 307, 314, 324, 330, 350, 352, 358, 364, 366, 370, 388, 396, 400, 408
Shopping, vocabulary for, 201, 314–316
sortir,
  passé composé, 190, 234
  present, 234
  subjunctive, 394
Spelling-change verbs, 80, 265, 330, 352
Sports, vocabulary for, 38, 68, 70, 198
Stagiaires, Les, 54–55, 92–93, 130–131, 166–167, 206–207, 246–247, 288–289, 334–335, 372–373, 410–411
Subject pronouns, 40
Subjunctive,
  formation, 394–396
  used after expressions of emotion, 400, 404
  used after impersonal expressions, 394, 404
  with expressions of desire, 400, 404
  with irregular verbs, 395, 396
  vs. the infinitive, 404
Suggestions, making, 154

T
Time,
  expressions, 12, 16–17, 24, 158, 192
  official, 24
  telling, 16–17
Transportation, vocabulary for, 162
tu vs. **vous,** 40

U
University, vocabulary related to, 20, 22, 44–45, 50

V
Vacation, vocabulary related to, 350, 362
venir,
  conditional, 330
  future, 352
  passé composé, 190
  present, 164
  subjunctive, 395
Verbs,
  -er, 76
  -ir, 326
  -re, 276

vieux, 34, 48
Vocabulary
  addresses, 126
  age, expressing, 144, 146
  alphabet, 22
  body, parts of, 392
  café and restaurant, 88, 304–306
  classroom expressions, 20, 22
  clothes, 200–201
  colors, 120
  countries, 368
  courses, 50
  daily activities, 68, 74, 82, 150, 156, 198, 230, 236, 262, 278
  dates, 160
  days of the week, 12
  describing oneself and other people, 14, 32, 34, 38, 40, 144, 146
  directions, 406
  errands, 398
  fairy tales, 242
  family members, 144–145
  food, 88, 304–305, 314–316, 322–323
  French first names, 22
  furnishings, 114, 120
  geography, 368, 370
  greetings, 6, 8
  health, 328, 392
  holidays, 160, 188
  hotel, 386–387
  household chores, 198
  housing, 108–109
  invitations, 68–69, 224
  languages, 14, 50
  leisure activities, 68–69, 74–75, 150, 156, 182, 198
  months, 160
  movies, 225
  neighborhood places, 44–45, 398
  numbers, 10, 90, 110
  pastimes, 68–69, 74–75, 150, 156, 182, 198
  possessions, 114, 120
  quantities, 46, 116, 310, 318, 320
  question words, 84
  school, 20, 22, 44, 50
  seasons, 194
  shopping, 201, 314–316
  sports, 38, 68, 70, 198
  time, expressions of, 12, 16–17, 158
  time, telling, 16–17
  transportation, 162
  travel, 350, 356, 362
  university, 20, 22, 44–45, 50
  vacation, 188, 350, 356, 362
  weather, 194, 196
voir,
  conditional, 330
  future, 352
vouloir,
  conditional, 330
  future, 352
  passé composé, 226
  present, 226
  subjunctive, 396
vous vs. **tu,** 40
Vowel sounds, 8, 10, 21
  bel, nouvel, and **vieil** before, 48
  cet before, 128
  liaison before, 6, 16, 46, 52, 77, 86, 116
  nasal, 10
voyager, verbs like, 80, 232

W
Weather, vocabulary for, 194, 196
Week, days of the, 12

Y
y, 152, 190, 408